Operations Management
STRATEGY AND ANALYSIS

Second Edition

Operations Management
STRATEGY AND ANALYSIS

LEE J. KRAJEWSKI & LARRY P. RITZMAN

The Ohio State University

ADDISON-WESLEY PUBLISHING COMPANY

Reading, Massachusetts ▼ Menlo Park, California ▼ New York
Don Mills, Ontario ▼ Wokingham, England ▼ Amsterdam ▼ Bonn
Sydney ▼ Singapore ▼ Tokyo ▼ Madrid ▼ San Juan

Executive Editor: *Mary Fischer*
Text and Art Development Editor: *Meredith Nightingale*
Production and Art Supervisor: *Peggy J. Flanagan*
Cover and Design Director: *Marshall Henrichs*
Designer and Layout Artist: *Vanessa Piñeiro*
Marketing Manager: *Mac Mendelsohn*
Illustrators: *George Nichols; Boston Graphics, Inc.*
Copy Editor: *Jerrold A. Moore*
Manufacturing Supervisor: *Roy Logan*
Compositor: *Graphic Typesetting Service*
Printer: *Arcata-Halliday Lithograph*

Library of Congress Cataloging-in-Publication Data

Krajewski, Lee J.
    Operations management.

    1. Production management.   I. Ritzman, Larry P.
    II. Title.
    TS155.K788   1990   658.5   89-18172
    ISBN 0-201-50410-3

Dedicated with love
to our families

Judie

Gary, Jeff,
Dan, and Jon

Virginia and Jerry;
Virginia and Larry

Barb

Todd and Karen

Kathryn and Paul;
Mildred and Ray

Cover photo: Skis awaiting the final finish (Courtesy of K2 Corporation). K2 (named for the world's second highest mountain) is the largest domestic manufacturer of skis, selling over 300,000 pairs of skis per year and employing about 400 people worldwide. The company directs its primary marketing thrust at the high end of the market, where model identification and a reputation for quality are particularly important. Toward this end, K2's marketing managers carefully monitor trends in the ski industry, and the research and development department employs product engineers who are highly trained in computer technology, as well as expert skiers.

While most ski manufacturers build skis using a laminate technology, layering various materials as in building a sandwich, K2 is one of a few who utilize a torsion-box construction. Their revolutionary triaxial braiding process (various stages are shown in the part opening photos) creates a tight fiberglass casing around a wood core, producing an extremely strong and durable ski. In an industry characterized by fierce competition, stagnant market size, and numerous technological advances, K2 is an excellent example of a firm that has used operations to gain the competitive edge.

PREFACE

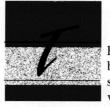he first edition of *Operations Management* reflected our firm belief that, to gain a competitive edge, organizations need a sound operations strategy. The second edition reaffirms that view. Once again, we approach the operations function as a potentially powerful tool for achieving organizational objectives and strategies. Moreover, since many students taking the introductory course will go on to become managers in service or manufacturing organizations, we have made the challenge of managing that function a focus of our text. Our goal is to help students discover the excitement to be found in the dynamic field of operations management. We want students to appreciate what operations managers do and to learn more about the tools they use to solve problems and support key decisions.

The Textbook

The second edition of *Operations Management* contains comprehensive coverage of the basic concepts and issues taught in an introductory operations management course. It also provides comprehensive coverage of the material tested on the American Production and Inventory Control Society certification exams.

Philosophy. This revision reflects our philosophy that OM texts should address both the strategic importance and the analytic tools of operations management. We have woven strategic/managerial issues into the fabric of each chapter in order to emphasize that the decisions managers make in each topical area also relate to a common operations strategy. We present the tools and techniques for solving problems in the context of achieving a firm's overall goals and objectives. This philosophy is reflected in the organization of the text.

Organization.   One of our goals was to write a textbook that offered considerable flexibility in order and depth of coverage, as well as in level (undergraduate or graduate). Thus, instructors will find that our table of contents adapts smoothly to various course syllabi. We chose a chronological organization that moves from positioning decisions to design decisions to operating decisions. However, once Chapters 1 and 2 have been covered, instructors can easily rearrange chapters to suit their individual teaching needs. Those who wish to give more emphasis to applying quantitative methods to operations can assign any of the five supplements (Linear Programming, Queuing Models, and so on) collected at the back of the book. These supplements are linked to earlier chapters through the advanced end-of-chapter problems.

Part 1, Positioning Decisions, consists of two chapters that explore how organizations use the operations function to gain a competitive edge. We discuss strategic issues related to product planning, competitive priorities, and quality management. The chapters in Part 2, Design Decisions, address the trade-offs managers make in creating an operating system that will meet their firms' needs. Issues covered include process design, choice of technology, work measurement, capacity, maintenance, location, and layout. Having determined the appropriate design for their operations, managers must make successful operating decisions. Part 3, Operating Decisions, examines the issues managers face as they coordinate day-to-day activities with an overall operations strategy. The ten chapters in this part explore topics such as forecasting, materials management, independent-demand inventory systems, production and staffing plans, master production scheduling, material requirements planning, just-in-time systems, scheduling, and quality control. Finally, Part 4, Conclusions, summarizes our broad view of operations as a competitive weapon.

Approach.   To drive home the real-world implications of our philosophy, our part introductions describe the experiences of K2 Corporation, a world-class manufacturer of skis, as they relate to key concepts covered within that part. The introduction to Part 4 links the competitive weapon theme to service industries by discussing the issues faced by the management of Waterville Valley Ski Resort.

To ensure that students don't lose sight of the big picture, we emphasize the *practice* of operations management. Our general approach is to paint concepts in broad strokes, then follow up with real-world applications in manufacturing and service industries. A balanced treatment of manufacturing and services is integrated throughout the text. This procedure helps students view the field of operations management as a cohesive whole. We treat manufacturing and services separately when sufficient differences warrant it.

New Coverage. The bottom-line measure of success in the textbook business is acceptance in the marketplace. We were pleased that our first edition was well received. Thus, a challenge of creating a new edition was deciding what to retain and what to change. Naturally, there were new developments in the field to include and outdated material to cull. However, we also wanted to respond directly to our market. As a result, we asked those who use the book, both instructors and students, what improvements they wanted to see. Instructors of the course from various schools across the country offered constructive criticism and thoughtful suggestions, and students provided both written and verbal feedback. We were able to incorporate most of these recommendations into our revision.

To this edition, we added the following new material to enhance our coverage of the ever-changing field of operations management:

- *Time-based competition.* Chapter 2 contains a section addressing the competitive advantages of reducing lead times, illustrated by real company examples.

- *International operations.* Chapter 8 addresses international issues related to location decisions. In addition, examples of international operations are used throughout the text to illustrate the global economy.

- *Total quality control.* We added special sections on this important topic to Chapters 3 and 19. We also summarized the philosophies of numerous leading consultants in the area of quality management.

- *Continuous improvement.* Chapter 16 now addresses the use of just-in-time procedures to gain continuous improvements in operations.

- *Kanban signals.* We added a section to Chapter 16 that discusses the different kinds of kanban signals found in practice, even in the fast-food industry.

    We expanded existing coverage in several areas:

- *Service examples.* We significantly increased examples of service operations, both within the text and in end-of-chapter problems.

- *Quantity discounts.* Chapter 12 contains an expanded discussion of the procedure for determining lot sizes when faced with a schedule of quantity discounts.

- *Just-in-time systems.* We increased our presentation of JIT systems in Chapter 16.

- *MPS and MRP.* We heavily revised the chapters on master production scheduling and material requirements planning to make the material easier for students to understand.

Teaching and Learning Aids

The second edition includes numerous features—some new to this edition—designed to motivate students and make this textbook a better teaching and learning tool. In addition, our goal throughout has been to present concepts as clearly as possible, in simplified language. Some of the teaching and learning aids we have used include the following.

Chapter Outlines and Learning Objectives.   Chapter outlines provide a quick overview of topics covered in each chapter. In addition, we have retained a very popular feature of the first edition: A series of "Key Questions for Managers" opens each chapter, preparing readers for important issues that will be discussed.

Key Terms.   Key terms are boldfaced and defined where they first appear in the text; these terms are also gathered at the end of the chapter and page-referenced for easy review.

Managerial Practices.   Boxed cases, prominently displayed in the text, contain real-world applications of operations management. We replaced most of the cases from the last edition with new ones and added many more in key locations.

Applications.   New to the second edition are in-text applications, designed to help students understand the quantitative material. Whenever we present a new technique, we immediately apply it to a problem and walk the reader through the solution.

Solved Problems and Formula Reviews.   Two other new features, solved problem and formula review sections, appear near the end of appropriate chapters. These special sections review key formulas and work through additional examples of techniques introduced in the chapter. The solved problems serve as models for students working homework problems and reinforce basic concepts.

End-of-Chapter Problems.   We added 50 percent more problems to the end of each chapter and updated 80 percent of the problems from the first edition. In addition, we divided the problems according to level of difficulty to further assist instructors in preparing assignments. Fifty of the over 175 problems that students can solve using the package *Lotus*® *Templates for Production/Operations Management* are identified by a floppy disk logo: ❦

Art and Photo Programs.   The art program was revised with a view to clarifying in-text concepts by using color strategically, not merely decoratively. We also significantly increased the number of photos illustrating real-world applications in both service and manufacturing operations. They are evenly dispersed throughout the text for broad coverage.

Quantitative Supplements. We divided the first edition's appendixes into five separate supplements: Financial Analysis, Linear Programming, Transportation Method, Queuing Models, and Simulation. They are grouped at the end of the text to emphasize their multiple applications and to maximize flexibility of use. The problems associated with these supplements appear at the end of the appropriate chapter in the text, emphasizing the link between technique and problem area.

Ancillary Materials

From an instructor's perspective, having a good textbook to work with is only half the battle. We are committed to creating a total package that will maximize students' learning potential and ease the instructor's burden. To this end, the following ancillary materials are available.

Instructor's Manual. The *Instructor's Manual* includes extensive lecture notes and teaching tips for each chapter. There are also short cases and assignments developed for selected chapters; an annotated bibliography of real-company "war stories"; a listing of useful videos and films and where to find them; and a cross-referencing guide that indicates which problems in the second edition can be solved using various software packages.

Solutions Manual. Solutions are organized in three sections. First, we provide short answers to all numerical problems; we have divided these answers into odd-numbered and even-numbered problems by chapter so that instructors can selectively assign some problems for study and others for grading. Second, we provide complete answers to all discussion questions and problems. Special attention is given to the art to allow easy conversion to transparency masters. Finally, there is a special section of computer solutions to the 50 problems identified by the floppy disk logo in the end-of-chapter problems.

Test Item File and Computerized Test Item File. We have compiled approximately 1200 multiple-choice questions, complete with answers that have been carefully checked for accuracy. The questions are coded according to level of difficulty and include an equal number of conceptual and technique questions. Both a printed version and a computerized version for the IBM PC® and compatibles are available free to adopters. The computerized version, consisting of a program disk and several data disks, enables instructors to custom-design their own quizzes and examinations.

Transparency Masters. Over 500 transparency masters feature key figures, photos, and selected solved problems. Over 250 of these are new visuals that do not appear in the text. Many of the new transparency masters are lists or partial solutions designed to complement the lecture notes in the *Instructor's Manual.*

Study Guide.   Prepared by Mohammad Ala of California State University in Los Angeles, the *Study Guide* contains learning objectives, an overview of each chapter's contents, illustrative cases and solved problems, and unsolved exercises.

Lotus® Templates.   Richard Crandall of Appalachian State University has developed a software package, *Lotus® Templates for Production/Operations Management,* consisting of 34 templates designed with Lotus® 1-2-3®, version 2, with which students can solve over 175 end-of-chapter problems. A floppy disk logo identifies a representative sample of 50 of these problems in the text; solutions appear at the end of the *Solutions Manual.* Although specifically designed to accompany this revision, the templates are flexible enough to solve problems in other OM texts.

Computer Models for Operations Management (CMOM).   CMOM is a user-friendly, stand-alone package developed by Owen P. Hall of Pepperdine University. Basic requirements include an IBM PC® with 256K memory and DOS 2.1 or above. Designed to expand undergraduate and graduate students' learning horizons beyond the problems in the text, the software offers a potpourri of analytical tools for solving many of the quantitative problems encountered in an operations management course.

Acknowledgments

This textbook could not have been revised without the help of a great many people. The entire Addison-Wesley publishing team has been a constant source of support and encouragement. Those most closely involved with the project and for whom we hold the greatest admiration include Mary Fischer, our executive editor, whose experience and editorial judgment helped create a quality product; Meredith Nightingale, our development editor, whose outstanding creativity is superceded only by her good humor; Jerrold A. Moore, whose unequaled skill as a copy editor improved the readability of our drafts; Peggy J. Flanagan, our production supervisor, who studied our text and perfected the art of due-date scheduling and capacity planning; and Loren Hilgenhurst Stevens, the production administrator who so ably coordinated the supplements package.

Reviewers.   We also wish to thank a distinguished group of colleagues who provided extremely helpful guidance for the revision. They include Philip W. Balsmeier, Nicholls State University; Alan Bohl, Temple University; Ronald L. Coccari, Cleveland State University; Chris L. Crute, Kent State University;

Charles Dane, Oregon State University; John Robb Dixon, Boston University; James A. Fitzsimmons, University of Texas at Austin; Barbara B. Flynn, Iowa State University; Timothy Fry, University of South Carolina; Soumen Ghosh, Michigan State University/East Lansing; Gene K. Groff, Georgia State University; J. Donald Phillips, University of Alabama; R. Daniel Reid, University of New Hampshire; Jeffrey L. Rummel, Duke University; Brooke A. Saladin, Wake Forest University; F. B. Simmons, III, University of Akron; Michael Umble, Baylor University; Travis H. Willis, Louisiana Tech University; and Jack Yurkiewicz, Pace University. Special thanks go to Richard J. Penlesky of Marquette University who not only reviewed our drafts but also acted as consultant for many of the ancillary materials.

We also wish to thank our colleagues on the Faculty of Management Sciences, especially W. C. Benton, David Collier, Jim Hutchinson, Keong Leong, David Snyder, and Peter Ward, for their helpful suggestions. Our Ph.D. students, including Linda Katunich, Jay Kim, Neng-Pai Lin, Manoj Malhotra, John McCreery, Peiching Pan, Ram Mohan, and Chwen Sheu, have provided many valuable inputs. Their help has considerably lightened our burden.

Finally, we wish to thank our families for once again putting up with our long periods of enforced solitude. As always, Judie and Barb were wonderfully supportive spouses, even though they must have known that our second elegant dinner at the Peppercorn Duck in only three years was to announce the beginning of the revision process.

Westerville, Ohio   L. J. K.   L. P. R.

BRIEF CONTENTS

CONTENTS

PART

1

POSITIONING DECISIONS

3 QUALITY MANAGEMENT   80

PART

2

DESIGN DECISIONS

4 PROCESS DESIGN 116

5 NEW TECHNOLOGIES 154

6 WORK MEASUREMENT   186

7 CAPACITY AND MAINTENANCE   226

8 LOCATION 258

9 LAYOUT 294

PART

3

OPERATING DECISIONS

10 FORECASTING   342

11 MATERIALS MANAGEMENT   392

12 INDEPENDENT-DEMAND INVENTORY SYSTEMS 432

13 PRODUCTION AND STAFFING PLANS 478

14 MASTER PRODUCTION SCHEDULING   516

15 MATERIAL REQUIREMENTS PLANNING   546

PART

4

CONCLUSIONS

CHAPTER

1

INTRODUCTION

 Chapter Outline

▲ Key Questions for Managers

What are the causes of recent productivity trends and shifts in shares of world markets?

What are the implications of recent employment and productivity trends in the service sector?

How can managers identify and deal with environmental change when formulating corporate strategy?

How does operations strategy relate to corporate strategy?

Should management be concerned only with strategic issues?

What is U.S. industry doing to meet various competitive challenges?

perations management deals with the production of goods and services that we buy and use every day. It is the process that enables organizations to achieve their goals through efficient acquisition and utilization of resources. Every organization, whether public or private, manufacturing or service, has an operations function. The management of that function is the focus of this book. We explore with you the role of operations within the total organization. We explain what operations managers do, as well as some of the latest tools and concepts they use to support key decisions. We show how, by selecting appropriate techniques and strategies, successful operations managers can give their companies a competitive edge. We hope that, as you discover the full impact of operations on our standard of living and way of life, you will agree that operations management is one of the most exciting challenges the modern business world offers.

WHAT IS OPERATIONS MANAGEMENT? ▲

Like other industrial societies, the United States has become a society of organizations, ranging from sports teams, schools, and churches to hospitals, legal institutions, military complexes, and large and small businesses. The purpose of these formal groups is to enable people to produce a vast range of products and services that would be beyond the capabilities of the individual. Operations management is crucial to each type of organization, because only through successful management of people, capital, and materials can an organization meet its goals. Thus every organization has an operations function.

At one time, operations management referred primarily to manufacturing production. However, the emergence of a wide range of nonmanufacturing business activities broadened the scope of the operations management function. Today, the term **operations management** refers to the systematic direction and control of the processes that transform inputs into finished goods and services. This function is essential to systems producing goods and services in both profit and nonprofit organizations.

As Fig. 1.1 illustrates, production and operations management together comprise a system. Inputs include human resources (workers and managers), capital (equipment and facilities), materials, land, energy, and information.

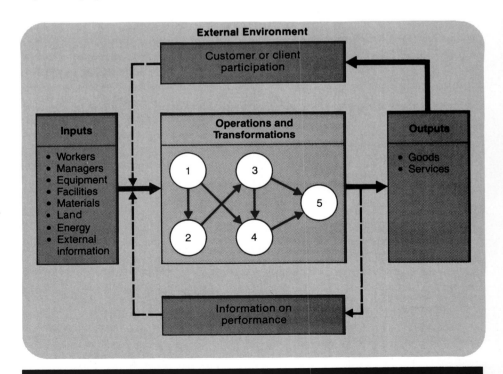

FIGURE 1.1   The Production and Operations Management System

TABLE 1.1 Examples of Inputs and Outputs

Organization	Input	Output
• Jewelry store	Merchandise Store building Sales clerks Registers Jeweler Customers	Customer sales
• Post office	Sorting machines Trucks Postal clerks and carriers Postmaster Mail	Delivered mail
• Hospital	Doctors and nurses Staff Buildings Beds and equipment Power Supplies Patients	Recovered patient
• Manufacturing plant	Machines Plant Raw materials Workers Managers	Consumer goods Materials for purchase by other firms
• University	Faculty and staff Classrooms Library Supplies Students	Graduates Research Public service

The circles represent operations through which products may pass during the transformation process. Because operations encompass a variety of different situations, the types of transformations vary as well. For example, in a factory the transformation would be physical or chemical. At an airline it would be locational. At a school it would be educational. And at a hospital it would be physiological. The operations vary accordingly: a machine center, two or more airport terminals, a classroom, and a hospital room.

The dashed lines in Fig. 1.1 represent two special types of input. The first is participation by customers or clients, which occurs when they not only receive the outputs but also take an active part in the transformation process itself. The second is information from both internal and external sources, such as internal reports on customer service or inventory management, government reports on economic trends, or telephone calls from vendors concerning past-due shipments. Table 1.1 shows specific inputs and outputs for production systems in five different types of organization. The operations manager needs all types of information to manage the production system.

Outputs from manufacturing operations include goods and auxiliary services. Outputs from service operations range from delivered mail (the post office) to a recovered patient (a hospital). Even though inputs and outputs vary among different industries, the underlying transformation process holds true for all production systems.

DIFFERENCES BETWEEN MANUFACTURING AND SERVICES ▲

The differences between manufacturing and service organizations are real, but they also are a matter of degree. For the sake of discussion, we organized these differences into eight categories, as displayed in Table 1.2. Since there are exceptions to every rule, these distinctions actually represent the ends of a continuum.

The first distinction arises from the physical nature of the product. Manufactured goods are *physical, durable* products. Services are *intangible* and *perishable*—often ideas, concepts, or information. The distinction between a goods producer and a service producer is a cloudy one. Service organizations normally provide a package of goods and services. For example, customers expect service as well as food at a restaurant and service as well as quality goods from a retailer.

Durable goods are outputs that can be *inventoried*. They can be stored and transported in anticipation of future demand. Thus with durable goods operations managers can cope with peaks and valleys in demand by creating inven-

TABLE 1.2 Continuum of Characteristics of Goods and Services Producers

More Like a Goods Producer ⟵————————⟶ More Like a Services Producer	
• Physical, durable product	• Intangible, perishable product
• Output can be inventoried	• Output cannot be inventoried
• Low customer contact	• High customer contact
• Long response time	• Short response time
• Regional, national, or international markets	• Local markets
• Large facilities	• Small facilities
• Capital intensive	• Labor intensive
• Quality easily measured	• Quality not easily measured

tories and smoothing output levels. By contrast, services cannot be preproduced. Without inventories as a cushion against erratic customer demand, service organizations are more constrained by time. This constraint doesn't mean that inventories are of no importance to service systems. Hospitals, for example, must maintain an appropriate supply of medications. The difference is that these inventories are inputs, not outputs. As inputs, they must undergo further transformations during provision of the service.

A third distinction is *customer contact*. Most customers for manufactured products have little or no contact with the production system. Primary customer contact is left to distributors and retailers. However, in many service organizations the customers themselves are inputs. For example, at a college, the student studies, attends lectures, takes exams, and finally receives a diploma. Hospitals, jails, and entertainment centers are other places where the customer is present during most of the service operations. Some service operations have low customer contact at one level of the organization and high customer contact at other levels. For example, the branch offices of postal, banking, and insurance organizations deal with customers daily, but their home offices have little direct customer contact. Similarly, the backroom operations of a jewelry store require little customer contact, whereas the sales counter involves a high degree of contact.

A related distinction is *response time* to customer demand. Manufacturers generally offer lead times measured in days or weeks. Many services, on the other hand, must be offered within minutes of customer arrival. The purchaser of a forklift truck may be willing to wait 16 weeks for delivery. By contrast, shoppers at the local supermarket grow impatient if they must wait more than 5 minutes in a checkout line. Since customers usually arrive at a time of their choosing, service operations may have difficulty matching capacity with demand. Furthermore, arrival patterns may fluctuate on a daily or even hourly basis—creating even more short-term demand uncertainty.

Market volume and availability of transportation and distribution facilities all affect the *location* and *size* of an operation. Manufacturing facilities often serve regional, national, or even international markets. This generally means larger facilities, more automation, and greater capital investment than for service facilities. In general, services cannot be shipped to distant locations. Thus service organizations requiring direct customer contact must locate relatively near their customers.

A final distinction is *quality*. As manufacturing systems tend to have tangible products and less customer contact, quality is easier to measure. Service systems, on the other hand, generally produce a mixture of tangibles and intangibles. Moreover, individual preferences affect assessments of quality, making objective measurement difficult. For example, one customer might value a friendly chat with the sales clerk during the purchase. However, another customer might assess quality by the speed and efficiency of the transaction.

SIGNIFICANT PRODUCTIVITY AND
SERVICE SECTOR TRENDS ▲

Two trends—lagging productivity and rapid growth of the service sector—are focusing increasing attention on operations. In this section we look at both trends and their implications for operations managers.

Productivity Trends

Productivity is the value of outputs (goods and services) produced divided by the values of input resources (wages, cost of equipment, and the like) used:

$$\text{Productivity} = \frac{\text{Output}}{\text{Input}}$$

Operations managers play a key role in determining productivity. Their challenge is to increase the value of output relative to the cost of input. If they can generate more output using the same amount of input, productivity increases. If they maintain the same level of output while reducing the expenditure of resources, productivity also increases. In general, productivity has a direct impact on our standard of living. If output per worker goes up, society benefits from increases in per capita income. Conversely, lagging or decreased productivity eventually results in a lower standard of living.

Lagging U.S. Productivity.   Consider the relationship between worker productivity and the U.S. economy. In terms of *total* output, the United States is the most productive nation in the world. With only 5 percent of the world's population, the United States produces 22 percent of the world's goods. At first glance this figure seems impressive. However, the U.S. position relative to other countries has actually declined—from 52 percent in 1950 to 30 percent in 1970 to its current level.

Figure 1.2 shows the percent change in productivity for the business sector of the U.S. economy for the period 1948–1987. Here productivity is measured as the dollar value of output per hour worked.* (The graph excludes farms, which represent less than 5 percent of U.S. output and employment.) For example, in the year 1949–1950 productivity increased by more than 6 percent, in 1951 it increased 3.5 percent, and so on. Evening out the peaks and valleys, you would see that there were fewer large increases in productivity during recent years. Those that did occur had shorter life spans. The dashed line in the graph shows between 1948 and 1973 the average annual increase was 2.5 percent, but between 1974 and 1987 it was less than 1 percent. The overall downward trend is cause for real concern.

---

*A more comprehensive measure, but one that is much more difficult to estimate, would use the dollar value of all inputs as the denominator rather than hours worked.

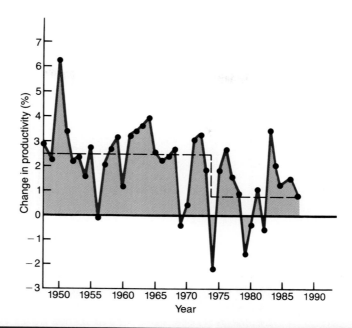

FIGURE 1.2   Percentage Changes in Productivity

Note: The graph shows total output per hour worked in the nonfarm business sector, valued in 1982 dollars.

Source: Economic Report of the President, February 1988, p. 301.

Figure 1.3, which compares annual growth of productivity in manufacturing for seven industrialized countries, presents an even more unsettling picture. Between 1960 and 1986, the United States posted the lowest productivity growth (2.7 percent) of any country shown.* Canada did little better at 3.2 percent growth per year. By contrast, Japan is the leader at 8.2 percent. As a result, U.S. firms are experiencing declining shares of the world market in aircraft, plastics, drugs, agricultural machinery, railway vehicles, and housing fixtures.

Japanese manufacturers have penetrated several U.S. markets. Examples include the automobile, semiconductor, steel, machine tools, consumer electronics, shipbuilding, and telecommunications industries. Fifteen years ago Japan accounted for only 8.5 percent of free-world automobile sales and 0.2 percent of U.S. sales. Its current share of the automobile market is 26 percent of free-world sales and 16.3 percent of U.S. sales. No wonder D. E. Peterson,

---

*The U.S. manufacturing sector has shown signs of revitalization since 1983, posting productivity gains averaging 4.5 percent per year.

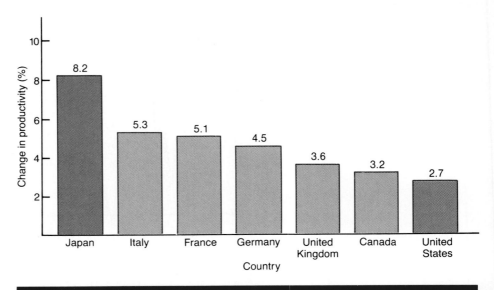

FIGURE 1.3   Annual Percentage Change in Manufacturing Productivity

Note: The graph indicates average output per hour worked, 1960–1986.
Source: Monthly Labor Review, U.S. Department of Labor, Bureau of Labor Statistics, August 1987, p. 105.

president of Ford Motor Company at the time, concluded that "the passwords for the 80s will be productivity and quality."*

Causative Factors.   Analysts have offered many explanations for lagging U.S. productivity. Federal and state government regulations governing occupational safety and health and environmental protection have increased costs, but government statistics don't reflect the impact of safer jobs and cleaner air on the value of output. Also, net investment in new equipment and facilities by U.S. industry over the past decade was only 6.6 percent of total output. No other major industrial country devotes such a small share of total output to new capital investment. (Japan's net investment over the same period was 19.5 percent.) Some experts point to the changing composition of the work force and changing attitudes toward work. Others note spiraling energy costs during the 1970s. Still others argue that, as the level of U.S. productivity is already high, further improvements are difficult to achieve. Moreover, high wages and stringent union contracts are sometimes identified as obstacles to productivity increases. Until the recent devaluation of the dollar, Japan's wage rates averaged just over 50 percent of the U.S. average. Wage rates in Italy, France, and the United Kingdom were only 55–65 percent of U.S. rates. Although the

*From remarks made at the Annual Supplier Dinner, April 28, 1980.

dollar's decline reduced these differentials, there is a cost: The dollar's buying power also is reduced.

Explanations such as these do not tell the full story. For example, Japanese firms operate successfully in the United States—using U.S. workers and paying U.S. costs. Managerial Practice 1.1 on pp. 14–15 describes two Japanese-owned facilities that are achieving higher productivity than their U.S. counterparts. The lesson is clear: Ultimately, the managers and employees of individual organizations are responsible for productivity gains. Thus better operations management is the key to increased productivity and the maintenance of high wages, salaries, and living standards.

Service Sector Trends

Manufacturing firms produce tangible goods, which typically can be stored and transported. Nonmanufacturing firms produce services, which are non-material or less tangible products. The service sector of the economy breaks down roughly into three equal components:

1. Local, state, and federal governments.
2. Wholesale and retail firms.
3. Health, financial service, real estate, insurance, repair service, business service, and personal service firms.

In Fig. 1.4 the top curve shows that between 1940 and 1987 the number of jobs in service-producing industries rose from 50 to 70 percent of total nonfarm jobs. This means that goods-producing industries, of which manufacturing is the major component, currently account for the remaining 30 percent. Although the absolute number of manufacturing jobs has increased, the percentage of manufacturing jobs in the total economy has dropped. This expansion of the service sector has important implications for the field of operations management.

Operations management initially focused on manufacturing organizations and was called *industrial management* or *production management*. Service organization operations were largely ignored and were performed almost at handicraft levels. Times have changed. Today's managers can apply concepts of job design, facility location, capacity, work-force management, inventory, and scheduling to both service organizations and manufacturing firms.

The bottom curve in Fig. 1.4 tells us something about productivity in the service sector. During the 50 years when service jobs rose from 50 percent to 70 percent of the total, consumer expenditures for services rose only from 40 to 49 percent.* Thus the upward trend in expenditures for services (the *output* of a productivity ratio) is not as steep as the upward trend in jobs (the *input*). Apparently, new service workers are not generating a proportional increase

---

*Consumer expenditures do not represent the *total* output of the economy. When all outputs are included, the service sector accounts for almost 70 percent of the gross national product.

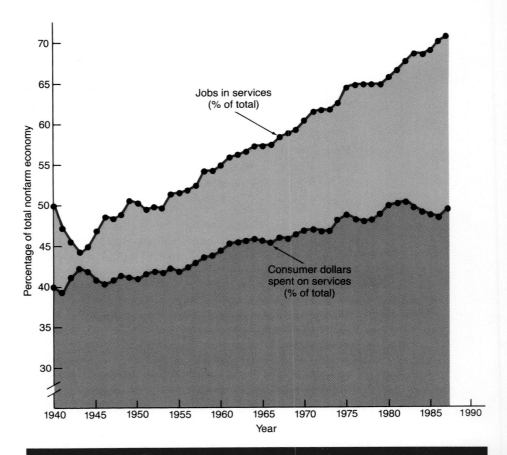

FIGURE 1.4   Employment and Consumer Expenditures in the Service Sector

Note: Transportation and public utilities are not counted here as service producers for employment statistics because of their heavy equipment requirements. If they were counted in the service sector, the number of jobs in services would have been 5 percent larger in 1987, or a total of 76 percent.
Source: Economic Report of the President, February 1988.

in output. One recent study (see Adams and Swaraksa, 1987) projects that over the remainder of the century service sector productivity will rise at a rate of only 0.5 percent per year, well behind the 3.3 percent expected in manufacturing.

Conclusions such as these must be qualified: Statistical data are less reliable for the service sector. The real value (as opposed to cost) of outputs from some parts of the service sector, such as the government, health services, or education, is difficult to quantify. Furthermore, productivity advances vary greatly by industry within the service sector. In software development and telecommunications, for example, U.S. industry is preeminent. Distribution systems, sophisticated health care, and advanced education are other bright spots. There is one indisputable conclusion: A vital service sector is crucial to the U.S. economy, and thus its productivity growth remains an ongoing concern.

You should not conclude that manufacturing is becoming an insignificant part of the U.S. economy. Consumer expenditures and jobs have increased steadily in manufacturing over the years. In real dollars, the value of manufacturing output has risen 257 percent since 1940. Many experts argue convincingly that U.S. firms must keep their mastery over manufacturing, since "you can't control what you can't produce" (see Cohen and Zysman, 1987). However, the service and manufacturing sectors of the economy are complementary. For example, the output of many firms is purchased by other firms as inputs. Over 25 percent of these intermediate outputs are classified as services but go to companies in the nonservice sector. Therefore, our discussion of operations management will span both manufacturing and services.

THREE VIEWS OF OPERATIONS MANAGEMENT ▲

We have mentioned the importance of operations in achieving organizational goals. We have also described how operations management affects productivity, in both the manufacturing and service sectors. In this section we explore operations management from three different perspectives: as a function, as a profession, and as a set of decisions.

As a Function

Figure 1.5 shows that operations is but one of several functions within an organization. Large companies generally assign each function to a separate department, which assumes responsibility for certain activities. However, many of these functions are interrelated. Thus it is essential that top management coordinate them and establish an effective communication network in order

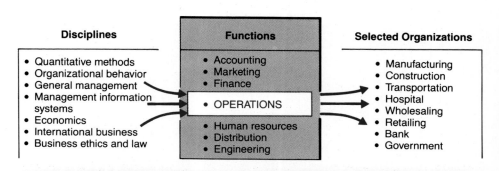

FIGURE 1.5 Operations Management as a Function

to achieve organizational goals. (Owners of small businesses might choose to eliminate separate departments and manage one or more functions, such as marketing or operations, themselves.)

In large organizations an operations or production department is usually responsible for the operations function. *Accounting* collects, summarizes, and interprets financial information. *Marketing* is responsible for generating demand for the company's output. *Finance* secures and invests the company's capital assets. *Human resources* (or personnel) hires and trains employees. *Distribution* transports inputs and outputs. *Engineering* develops product designs and production methods. However, some organizations never need to perform certain functions. For example, the Internal Revenue Service doesn't need a marketing department to stimulate demand. Other organizations find it more economical to contract for a function, such as engineering, when they need it, rather than maintain an in-house department.

MANAGERIAL PRACTICE 1.1

Successful Japanese-Owned Facilities in the United States

Toyota Motor Corporation

In setting up New United Motor Manufacturing, Inc. (NUMMI), Toyota Motor Corporation joined forces with General Motors to revamp a mothballed GM plant in Fremont, California. The NUMMI managers set up a typical Toyota production system with just-in-time delivery and a flexible production line run by teams of workers in charge of their own jobs. Even though NUMMI is operating with the same work force, in the same building, and using much of the same technology as GM had before, productivity has skyrocketed.

The reason is the way Toyota managers organized and operate the plant. In fact, operations have improved so dramatically that outsiders hail the plant as a model of labor–management cooperation. The absentee rate has dropped from 20 percent to 2 percent. Productivity is twice the average level in GM. In fact, NUMMI actually has higher productivity and better quality control than GM's most automated plant, which is operated with the help of more than 300 robots. Production costs are comparable to Toyota's costs in Japan.

Honda of America

Honda of America Manufacturing Company now makes Accords in Marysville, Ohio, at approximately the same cost and almost the same quality as its parent company in Japan. The Marysville plant's productivity is 90 percent of that achieved by its counterpart in Japan. Management's approach to production includes flexible teams, just-in-time delivery, attention to quality, and high employee loyalty. Everybody does several jobs, spreading work more evenly.

Sources: "Japan, U.S.A.," *Business Week,* July 14, 1986; "Productivity: Why It's the No. 1 Underachiever," *Business Week,* April 20, 1987.

Operations managers draw on many disciplines and techniques. Quantitative analysis provides modeling techniques to help solve production problems. Computers and other electronic information systems help manage vast quantities of data. Concepts of organizational behavior aid in designing jobs and managing the work force. Studies of international business methods provide useful ideas about facility location. Thus most operations managers must be generalists. They must also be able to communicate with specialists and be comfortable with a variety of complex concepts and analytic techniques.

As a Profession

Operations has emerged as an excellent career path to upper management positions in many organizations. In 1984, biographies of 237 chief executive officers showed that 36 percent "learned the ropes" in production. This pro-

Site preparation at the idled General Motors plant in Fremont just before the NUMMI startup. The plant, a joint venture with Toyota, has proved to be quite productive since its opening.

portion compares favorably with those for chief executives having backgrounds in finance (22 percent), marketing (21 percent), research (10 percent), and legal (9 percent). The upward mobility of skilled operations managers is closely linked to the current productivity challenge. Promotions tend to go to managers who have successfully met challenging problems.

Figure 1.6 shows a typical organization chart for a manufacturing firm. Each major business function reports to the chief executive officer (CEO). The operations function is further broken down to show the wide range of job

MANAGERIAL PRACTICE 1.2

Want Ads for Operations Managers

Vice-President of Operations

We offer an outstanding and highly visible opportunity for a pragmatic, results-oriented pro to join our headquarters staff. The successful candidate should have significant manufacturing experience with fabricated light metals in a labor-intensive environment. The position reports directly to the Division President.

Director of Operations

Expanding health maintenance organization needs a Director of Operations to function as Chief Operating Officer for a recently established regional component. Individual reports to the Chief Executive officer of the parent organization's health care delivery systems.

Director of Manufacturing

A rapidly growing medium-sized high technology manufacturing concern seeks the expertise of an experienced manufacturing professional. The candidate should have a minimum of five years experience in management, including production planning and control, materials management, MRP, and facilities management.

Operations Manager

Large brokerage firm seeks experienced Back Office Manager. Position involves all daily executing and settlement functions of a self-clearing NYSE member.

Plant Manager

An immediate position is available at our medium-sized manufacturing plant in the Chicago suburbs. Assembly, metal stamping, rubber molding, and flat surface lapping are all part of our process. Specific experience in these operations is not necessary, but a background in Industrial Management is. This is opportunities. In manufacturing, the head of operations usually holds the title Vice-President of Manufacturing (or Production or Operations). The corresponding title in a service organization might be Vice-President (or Director) of Operations. Reporting to the vice-president are the managers of other production departments, such as purchasing, inventory, quality assurance, or supervision. Managerial Practice 1.2 offers a glimpse of the experience required and the accountabilities for these various positions, both in manufacturing and services.

not a desk job. On-the-floor management of work force and total responsibility for the manufacturing facilities will be yours.

Assistant Vice-President, Materials Management

We operate two hospitals, four industrial medicine/urgent care facilities, and a retirement community. The basic function for the Assistant Vice-President is to plan, implement, and control all phases of Pharmacy; Purchasing; Stores; Receiving, Distribution, and Transportation; Central Processing; Laundry; and Printing Services. Bachelor's degree in business preferred, master's degree a plus. Must have 5–10 years in materials management. Hospital experience is a plus.

Production Control Manager

An exciting opportunity for a results-oriented individual with a degree and proven track record. Responsible for controlling work-in-process to achieve on-time delivery and minimum inventory. Demands a self-starter who can coordinate major projects. The ability to interact with all levels of management is essential. A strong appreciation for systems development is needed.

Corporate Director of Purchasing

In this position you will service, select, and interface with a variety of vendors on a national and international basis. You will personally negotiate contracts, providing timely procurement of systems, equipment, materials, and services specified by company managers.

Manager of Quality Control

Local manufacturer needs Quality Control/Quality Assurance professional to direct the total QC/QA function. You must have 10 years experience in the QC/QA field with progressive managerial assignments. Also requires a BS degree. MBA preferred. Proficiency in a second language will be helpful.

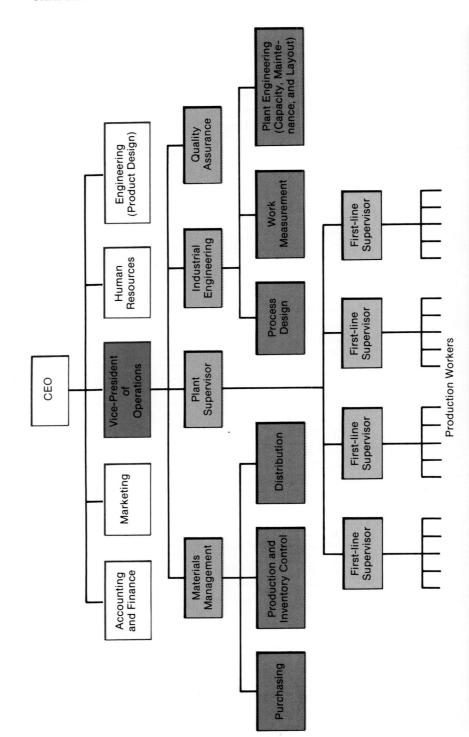

FIGURE 1.6 A Typical Organization Chart

Lower management and entry-level positions in manufacturing carry titles such as inventory control supervisor, first-line supervisor, buyer, scheduler, production control analyst, time standard analyst, and facilities planner. Corresponding titles in the service sector might be department supervisor (insurance), office supervisor (contractor), section head (government), flight scheduler (airlines), operations analyst (bank), and scheduler (trucking).

Professional associations offer operations managers opportunities for professional growth by meeting their counterparts in other organizations and exchanging ideas about problems and their solutions. Key associations are the American Production and Inventory Control Society (APICS), National Association of Purchasing Managers (NAPM), and Operations Management Association (OMA).

As a Set of Decisions

Decision making is an essential aspect of all management activity. Although the specifics of each situation vary, decision making generally involves the same basic steps: (1) recognize and clearly define the problem; (2) collect the information needed to analyze possible alternatives; and (3) choose and implement the most feasible alternative. What sets operations managers apart, however, are the *types* of decisions they participate in with others in top management or actually make themselves. Table 1.3 lists several key decision areas, along with a sample question about each. These questions correspond to major topics covered in other chapters of this book. Therefore they provide a good preview of things to come.

Table 1.3 begins with the *positioning decisions* that affect the future direction of the company. For example, operations managers must help decide which products or services to offer, what the company's competitive priorities will be, what the quality objectives will be, and whether to organize resources around products or processes.

Next are the *design decisions* concerning the production system. Here the operations manager's recommendations and decisions often require long-term commitments. For example, the manager must help determine what the system's capacity should be and then decide what equipment and technologies to purchase, where to locate facilities, and how to organize departments and plan the facility's physical layout.

Operating decisions, sometimes called the operations infrastructure, deal more with operating the facility once it is in place. At this stage, the operations manager decides how to manage inventory, when to release purchase or production orders, which vendors to deal with, how to schedule resources and maintain quality, and how to increase output levels over shorter periods of time.

TABLE 1.3 Decisions in Operations Management	
Decision Area	**Sample Questions**
Positioning Decisions	
Product plans	What products (goods or services) should we offer?
Competitive priorities	Should we excel on the basis of cost, quality, or flexibility?
Positioning strategy	Should we organize resources around products or processes?
Quality management	Should our goal be reliability or top-of-the-line quality?
Design Decisions	
Process design	What processes should we use to make our products?
Work-force management	How should we hire, train, and motivate our employees?
New technologies	Is it time to automate some of our processes?
Capacity	What is the maximum reasonable size for our facility?
Maintenance	How much should we spend to maintain equipment and the facility?
Location	Should we be followers or leaders in picking new store locations?
Layout	How should we physically arrange desks and equipment?
Operating Decisions	
Materials management	Who should be our suppliers? How do we evaluate and support them?
Production and staffing plans	What should be our output rates and staffing levels for this quarter?
Master production scheduling	Should we make-to-stock or make-to-order?
Inventory	How much inventory do we need? How should we control it?
Scheduling	What customers or jobs should we give top priority to?
Quality control	How do we best achieve our quality goals?

CORPORATE AND OPERATIONS STRATEGIES ▲

Business and government leaders increasingly are recognizing the importance of strategic issues for the organization as a whole, as well as for the operations function in particular. During the mid-1980s, President Reagan established a Commission on Industrial Competitiveness to investigate lagging productivity. The commission recommended that the nation's business schools undertake a thoughtful response to the global challenge. Stating that U.S. firms are uncompetitive internationally because they fail to excel in production, the commission concluded that:

> Production courses must deal with strategies of top executives, the translation of production strategies to live decisions of middle managers, and the tactical operation and procedures of lower-level managers.*

Source: "President's Commision Enlists Business-Ed Forum Aid," *Higher Education And National Affairs,* newsletter of the American Council on Education, October 22, 1984, p. 2. Reprinted by permission.

We hope that as you read this book, your appreciation of the strategic issues in operations management will increase. Let's begin by exploring some basic concepts of strategy, starting at the organization level.

Corporate Strategy

Whatever the type of organization, top management is responsible for relating the organization's efforts to its long-term future. Sometimes called long-range planning, setting **corporate strategy** (or organizational strategy) is the process of determining the organization's mission, of monitoring and adjusting to changes in the environment, and of identifying the organization's distinctive competencies.

The Mission.   Determining an organization's mission requires answers to fundamental questions such as:

- What business are we in? Where should we be ten years from now?
- Who are our customers or clients?
- What are our basic concepts and beliefs?
- What are the key performance objectives, such as growth or profits, by which we measure our success?

The Environment.   An organization continually needs to adapt to its changing external environment. Adaptation begins with **environmental scanning**, the process by which managers monitor the environment for potential opportunities or threats. One crucial factor is competition. Competitors may be gaining an edge by broadening product lines, improving quality, or lowering costs. New entrants into the market or product substitutes may threaten continued profitability.

Other important environmental elements include economic trends, technological changes, political conditions, social changes (such as attitudes toward work), and the availability of vital resources. The bargaining power of suppliers and customers can become either a threat or an opportunity. The impact of such changes on current strategies can reveal shortcomings in planning and product development—leading to adjustments in corporate strategy. Over the past decade, many businesses have faced a particularly turbulent environment. Today, some markets grow more slowly, automation is more complicated and expensive, product life cycles seem shorter, and foreign competition is intense. Managerial Practice 1.3 describes environmental scanning both from an individual and a group viewpoint.

Distinctive Competencies.   Environmental impacts cannot be "managed away." Corporate strategies must change to meet them, which means taking into account the organization's unique strengths and weaknesses. An important concept is that few firms succeed by meeting competition head-on, that is, by offering exactly the same products and services as their competitors. Generally, a more successful strategy is to aim for a *niche* in the market, one that takes advantage of what the firm does particularly well.

Distinctive competencies are the unique resources and strengths that management considers when formulating strategy. These competencies include:

1. *An available and competent work force.* Although skilled employees gravitate to good jobs, there is often a significant lag between demand and supply. Having the right employees when you need them is a strength.

2. *An efficient and advantageous location of facilities.* The availability of facilities, such as offices, stores, and plants, is a major advantage because of the long lead time required to build new ones.

3. *The ability to meet and create demand.* An organization that can easily change output levels, attract capital from stock sales, market and distribute its products, or differentiate its products from similar products on the market has a competitive edge.

Strategies versus Tactics.   Distinguishing between strategic and tactical planning is important. All planning is future-oriented. That is, it involves making decisions today about tomorrow. However, there are several differences between strategic and tactical planning. Table 1.4 shows that every planning activity lies somewhere between the two ends of a continuum, with strategy at one end and tactics at the other.

Strategic planning has a relatively longer time horizon than tactical planning. Of course, what is considered a long time depends on the specific operations involved. Because forests take so long to grow, strategic plans in the forest-products industry must look ahead as far as 100 years. A public utility

MANAGERIAL PRACTICE 1.3

Environmental Scanning

"Strategy is trying to understand where you sit in today's world," says GE Chairman John F. Welch, Jr. "Not where you wish you were or where you hoped you would be, but where you are. It's assessing with everything in your head the competitive changes, the market changes that you can capitalize on or ward off. It's assessing the realistic chances of getting from here to there."

Millipore Corp., a maker of high-tech filtration systems, uses environmental scans to keep apace with the increasingly demanding needs and technological advances in the semiconductor industry. "Environmental" task forces of operating managers meet every 18 months to brainstorm what is happening in their markets and where those markets are likely to go in the next 10 years.

Source: "The New Breed of Strategic Planner," *Business Week,* September 17, 1984.

TABLE 1.4 The Planning Continuum	
Strategic Planning ←————————————→ **Tactical Planning**	
• Long time horizon	• Short time horizon
• Less certainty	• More certainty
• Less structured	• More structured
• More ends-oriented	• More means-oriented
• Poorly defined information requirements	• Well-defined information requirements
• Tends to have irreversible impact	• Tends to have reversible impact
• Focuses on the whole	• Focuses on parts

that generates and distributes electric power might plan 30 years ahead. But to a firm competing in a very volatile environment with short lead times for product development and resource acquisition, a long time horizon may be only five years.

Because of their longer time horizons, strategic plans are made with less certainty about what the future holds. Accurately forecasting what will happen far into the future is difficult. Strategic plans also are less structured for two reasons. First, they are more ends-oriented. Strategic planning establishes corporate ends (or performance objectives). By contrast, tactical planning focuses on the means by which these previously established ends can be achieved. Second, strategic planning is less structured because its information requirements are poorly defined. Managers can be less clear about information they need now to make a strategic choice that may not have an impact for five years. Tactical planning, which is more routine and repetitive, requires very specific information. Thus it must be based on more formal, well-defined information systems. These systems are often computerized because of the amount of data involved and the rapid rate at which data changes.

Strategic plans lead to decisions that are major commitments of present and future resources. As a result, they tend to have an irreversible impact. For example, a strategic decision to build a new warehouse has a much greater impact than a tactical choice to order more machine parts this month from a certain supplier. Finally, strategic planning focuses more on the organization as a whole, cutting across functions and departments. This view of strategic planning recognizes that plans and decisions made in one area affect the plans and decisions made in others.

Operations Strategy

Operations strategy specifies how operations can achieve the organization's overall goals, within the framework of corporate strategy. Managers determine operational shortcomings by comparing corporate strategy requirements with the production system's current and projected capabilities. Managers then try

In the forest-products industry, management must create strategic plans that look far ahead. Bunker Hill's "greenhouse," located 3,000 feet underground in a mine in Kellogg, Idaho, provides the company with seedlings to reforest nearby hills.

to overcome any shortcomings by taking advantage of the operation's available resources and distinctive competencies. Or they may change operational strategies regarding automation, facility location, capacity, suppliers, and inventories. If none of these approaches is sufficient, the operations manager must alert top management, so that corporate strategy may be reviewed and, if necessary, revised.

Later in this book we examine the strategic issues of operations management within the context of individual decision areas. For now, we need to emphasize only three points:

1. Operations can be a competitive weapon or a millstone.

2. Managers should link decisions in operations.

3. Although management must first address strategic choices, success also depends on tactical choices based on careful analysis of specific alternatives.

A Competitive Weapon.   Operations concentrates on the resource side of corporate strategy, where the organization usually commits the bulk of its human and financial assets. Twenty years ago, Wickham Skinner suggested that the production system could be either a competitive weapon or a millstone (see Skinner, 1969). He concluded that all too often it has become a millstone, with top management unknowingly abdicating large portions of corporate strategy to operations managers. As a result, many operations policies reflect incorrect assumptions about corporate strategy. This lack of understanding can commit the firm to inappropriate resources for years.

Largely because of foreign competition and the technological explosion, recognition is growing that a firm competes not only with new products, creative marketing, and skillful finance, but also with unique competencies in operations. The organization that can offer superior products and services at lower prices is a formidable competitor.

Linking Decision Areas.   The operations manager must link various decision areas in operations in a way that best complements corporate strategy. Plans, policies, and actions within operations should focus in the same direction and be mutually supportive. Quality, automation, capacity, and inventory decisions must not be made independently. Even though individual choices may make sense on their own, collectively they may not add up to the best result.

Strategy and Analysis.   According to strategic planning, *first-order questions* are the manager's first concern. For example, the manager must decide whether to hold an item in inventory before deciding how low inventory should get before reordering. Similarly, the manager must decide whether to expand on the same site or relocate before deciding how large the new parking lot will be. To help you focus on first-order questions, we introduce each chapter with several key questions for managers. Answers to these questions have a major impact on overall performance.

If you look back at Table 1.3, you'll see more long-range (or strategic) decisions listed at the top. We address them in the first few chapters of this book. The tactical questions covered in later chapters are also important. In fact, tactical decisions have a major cumulative effect. Take, for example, scheduling, shown near the bottom of the table. Scheduling is a decision area requiring detailed analysis and numerous interrelated, cumulative decisions. Just consider the millions of dollars at stake in completing a power plant or a hotel on time.

Much of tactical planning depends on careful analysis. Operations managers have a wide variety of analytic techniques at their disposal. These techniques range from simple lists of pros and cons jotted on a scrap of paper to sophisticated linear programming models, simulation models, and computer-based information systems. Strategy and analysis are both necessary and should complement one another. Although you can view each separately, they are actually part of a whole.

WHAT INDUSTRY IS DOING ▲

To conclude this chapter, we tie together several of the topics we have covered: disappointing productivity trends, a concern for both manufacturing and service organizations, the kinds of decisions operations managers face, and how management can use operations as a competitive weapon. Managerial Practice 1.4 shows what some manufacturing and service companies are doing to improve productivity. The decision areas on which they are focusing—which are covered separately in subsequent chapters—appear in parentheses. These examples offer insight into the role operations managers play in an organization. They also show how an organization can rise to meet the competitive challenge.

Productivity Improvement at Selected Firms

J.C. Penney Company

J.C. Penney plans to modernize 550 of its largest stores. The $1 billion price tag aims at renovating existing stores, rather than opening new ones (*capacity* and *location*). There will be a more stylish look, ranging from potted plants to striking graphics (*layout*). Penney is dropping some lines and expanding others (*product plans*), with an increased emphasis on quality (*competitive priority*). Sales at one of the first renovated stores rose almost 40 percent.

Litton Industry

Litton Industry's industrial automation plant in Flemington, New Jersey, recently installed a computerized materials-handling system (*new technologies*). The system doubled the plant's capacity without adding bricks and mortar (*capacity*). Operations is paying considerable attention to quality, and the number of defect-free units shipped has risen from 87 to 99.5 percent (*quality management*). The number of suppliers has been reduced from 750 to 107 (*materials management*), and the plant works more closely with each on quality and delivery. Statistical process control helps ensure that each step in production is performed correctly (*quality control*). Computerized production planning (*production plans*) and electronic communication with customers (*master production scheduling*) has eliminated the need for big stockpiles of inventory. Combining just-in-time inventory management with faster process time has pared inventories to only a 1.3-month supply, down from a seven-month supply in 1981 (*inventory*). A team approach offers more resource flexibility and job variety (*work-force management*).

Shenandoah Insurance Company

Shenandoah Life installed a new computer system (*new technologies*) to help issue new life-insurance policies to customers who were replacing old ones. The Roanoke, Virginia, company also revamped its procedures so clerks were less specialized (*process design*) and worked in teams (*work-force management*). Over the last three years, the number of transactions processed has risen by 28 percent, while the number of workers handling them has fallen 15 percent.

Ford Motor Company

Ford's Chicago assembly plant turns out 64 Taurus and Sable cars an hour, up from 53 an hour for predecessor LTD and Marquis models. Credit goes to automation (*process design*) and "simultaneous engineering" (*product planning*). Since manufacturing officials became involved in initial planning, cars are being designed to be built efficiently. When internal quality ratings slipped in 1986, the executive vice-president started a series of plant visits as early as 7 A.M. on Saturdays (*quality management*). These visits made a difference in quality, as did the 1986 bonus system, which rewarded a manager's contributions to quality.

Black & Decker

Black & Decker is struggling to meet Japanese competition head-on. It spent $256 million to modernize plants, with strong interest in robots and flexible machining (*process design*). It dropped the chain-saw business, while adding new products such as the hand-held vacuum sweeper (*product plans*). Some plants have been closed (*capacity*), while others have been carefully rearranged to minimize the distance traveled by components through the plant (*layout*). Workers are divided into teams at its Hampstead, Maryland, facility (*work-force management*), hoping to inspire pride and greater quality consciousness (*quality management*). One of the pioneers in introducing material requirements planning in the 1970s (*inventory systems*), the firm is truly international, with operations in 55 different countries (*location*).

Airline Companies

Airlines have made several changes to improve operations. Pan Am took steps to relieve the bottleneck at Kennedy airport, which handled 43 percent of its flights (*capacity* and *location*). Its schedule of connecting flights (*scheduling*), baggage transfer system (*process design* and *layout*), and record of flying on time (*competitive priority*) were concerns. United Airlines has moved from long-haul flights with big jets to traffic hubs and shorter spoke routes with midsized jets (*scheduling* and *capacity*). It cut its work force by 20 percent and is seeking wage concessions from unions (*work-force management*). American Airlines placed firm orders for 156 new planes, with options for another 100. These purchases will give American the youngest fleet in the industry, improve efficiency (*maintenance*), and increase market share (*capacity*) on the airline's busiest routes.

Marriott Corporation

J. Willard Marriott, Jr., CEO of Marriott Corporation, logged 200,000 miles in one year to visit more than 100 of the chain's hotels and resorts. He believes that productivity improvement comes from direct contact with customers and employees (*work-force management*). He even makes spot-checks at all hours (*quality management*) of conditions ranging from dishes to laundry facilities to lobby appearance. This attention to detail communicates the importance he places on each person's role in the organization.

Sources: "Black & Decker Meets Japan's Push Head-On in Power-Tool Market," *Wall Street Journal,* February 18, 1983; "Pan Am Conducts Major Shake-Up to Improve Its Weak Performance," *Wall Street Journal,* April 26, 1984; Upgrading of Factories Replaces the Concept of Total Automation," *Wall Street Journal,* November 30, 1987; "Service Industries Don't Always Raise Productivity," *Wall Street Journal,* April 19, 1988; "U.S. Auto Makers Get Chance to Regain Sales from Foreign Rivals," *Wall Street Journal,* May 16, 1987.

The steps taken by J.C. Penney Company remind us that reducing costs is not the only way to increase productivity. Productivity can be improved when the value of inputs rises, so long as the value of outputs rises even faster. The steps taken by the other companies cited cover almost every decision area in operations management. We see that each decision area in operations management is important and that each plays a vital role in the productivity equation. Organizations have found that there are many roads to success within operations. It would be a mistake to look for a single cure or magic formula.

CHAPTER HIGHLIGHTS

- This book addresses the strategic issues of operations, without sacrificing the analytical side of decision making.

- Production processes transform inputs (workers, managers, equipment, facilities, materials, land, and energy) into outputs (goods and services).

- Service systems, in contrast to manufacturing systems, tend to have intangible products that cannot be inventoried, more direct contact with the customer, shorter response times, local markets, labor-intensive operations, and less measurable quality. Nonetheless, the distinctions are relative. When making decisions, managers of both manufacturing and service organizations must be fully aware of where their organizations are and should be on the continuum between goods producers and service producers.

- Operations management can be viewed as a function, a profession, and a set of decisions; it is concerned with the positioning, design, and operation of production systems.

- Decision areas in which operations managers are involved include product plans, competitive priorities, positioning strategy, quality management, process design, new technologies, workforce management, capacity, maintenance, location, layout, materials management, production and staffing plans, master production scheduling, inventory, scheduling, and quality control. Each succeeding type of decision has a shorter time horizon and is more tactical but has an important cumulative effect on system performance.

- Corporate strategy is the process of determining the organization's mission, monitoring and adjusting to changes in the external environment, and exploiting distinctive competencies.

- Strategic planning, in contrast to tactical planning, has a longer time horizon, less certainty, less structure, an ends orientation, poorly defined information requirements, and a focus on the whole organization.

- Operations strategy is a natural extension of corporate strategy and involves three important concepts: (1) operations can be a formidable competitive weapon; (2) the various decisions in operations must be linked; and (3) first-order decisions are paramount, even though tactical decisions have a major cumulative effect.

- Companies are responding to the competitive challenge by dealing with the full range of decision areas in operations management.

KEY TERMS

corporate strategy   21
distinctive competencies   22
environmental scanning   21
operations management   4
operations strategy   23
productivity   8

STUDY QUESTIONS

1. Identify the inputs and outputs for four of the following types of firms.
   - a. hotel
   - b. public warehouse
   - c. paper mill
   - d. newspaper company
   - e. supermarket
   - f. home office of bank

2. Do the employment shifts to the service sector mean that the demand for goods is declining? Do you expect these employment trends to continue at the same pace? Explain.

3. What are the usual distinctions between goods producers and service producers? Identify at least two types of firms that do not fit the pattern, explaining the reasons for your choices.

4. What does the productivity trend in Fig. 1.2 mean? Do you expect it to continue? Explain.

5. Why is productivity of particular interest to the field of operations management?

6. Which disciplines contribute significantly to the field of operations management? What does this imply about the skills needed by operations managers?

7. What types of jobs are available in operations management?

8. List at least three types of decisions that deal with the design of a production system, along with a sample question for each one. Do the same for three types of decisions that deal with the operation of the production system.

9. What questions does an organizational mission statement answer?

10. How are environmental scanning, adjusting to environmental change, and distinctive competencies related?

11. What are the differences between strategic and tactical planning?

12. How can linking decisions better help make operations a competitive weapon? Can tactical decisions be ignored? Explain.

13. Kathryn Shoemaker established the Grandmother's Chicken Restaurant in Middlesburg five years ago. It features a unique recipe for chicken: "Just like grandmother used to make." The facility is homey, with relaxed and friendly service. Business has been very good during the past two years, both for lunch and dinner. Customers normally must wait about 15 minutes to be served, although complaints about service delays have increased. Kathryn is currently considering whether to expand the current facility or open a similar restaurant in neighboring Uniontown, which has been growing rapidly.

    a. What types of strategic and tactical plans must Kathryn make?

    b. What environmental forces could be at work at Middlesburg and Uniontown that Kathryn should consider?

    c. What are the possible distinctive competencies of Grandmother's?

SELECTED REFERENCES

Adams, F. Gerard, and Subhak Siwaraksa, "A Disaggregated Study of the Service Sector," Discussion Paper 28, The Wharton School, University of Pennsylvania, November 1987.

Berry, Steven, "Practitioner's Views on the Importance of Selected Production Management Topics," *Production and Inventory Management* (Third Quarter 1979), pp. 1–17.

Chase, Richard B., and Nicholas J. Aquilano, *Production and Operations Management: A Life Cycle Approach,* 5th ed. Homewood, Ill.: Richard D. Irwin, 1989.

Cohen, Stephen S., and John Zysman, *Manufacturing Matters: The Myth of the Post-Industrial Economy.* New York: Basic Books, 1987.

Collier, David A., "Managing a Service Firm: A Different Management Game," *National Productivity Review* (Winter 1983–1984), pp. 36–45.

Fitzsimmons, James A., and Robert S. Sullivan, *Service Operations Management.* New York: McGraw-Hill, 1982.

Groff, Gene K., and John R. Muth, *Operations Management: Analysis for Decisions.* Homewood, Ill.: Richard D. Irwin, 1972.

"Hard Times Push B-Schools into Basics," *Business Week* (August 30, 1982), pp. 23–24.

Hax, Arnoldo C., and Nicolas S. Majluf, "The Corporate Strategic Planning Process," *Interfaces,* vol. 14, no. 1 (January–February 1984), pp. 47–60.

Hayes, Robert H., and William J. Abernathy, "Managing Our Way to Economic Decline," *Harvard Business Review* (July–August 1980), pp. 67–77.

Mabert, Vincent A., and Michael J. Showalter, *Cases in Operations Management.* Plano, Texas: Business Publications, 1984.

Porter, Michael E., *Competitive Advantage: Creating and Sustaining Superior Performance.* New York: The Free Press, 1985.

"Schools Again Offer Courses in Production," *Wall Street Journal* (January 26, 1981) p. 23.

Schroeder, Roger G., *Operations Management: Decision Making in the Operations Function,* 3rd ed. New York: McGraw-Hill, 1989.

Skinner, Wickham, "Manufacturing—Missing Link in Corporate Strategy," *Harvard Business Review* (May–June 1969), pp. 136–145.

Skinner, Wickham, *Manufacturing: The Formidable Competitive Weapon.* New York: John Wiley and Sons, 1985.

Stanbeck, Thomas M., Jr., P. J. Bearse, T. J. Noyelle, and R. A. Karasek, *Services: The New Economy.* Totowa, N.J.: Allanheld, Osmun and Co., 1981.

Starr, Martin, "The Performance of Japanese-Owned Firms in America: A Survey Report," Center for Operations, Columbia Business School, 1985.

Steiner, George A., *Top Management Planning.* New York: Macmillan, 1983.

Wheelwright, Steven C., "Manufacturing Strategy: Defining the Missing Link," *Strategic Management Journal,* vol. 5 (1984), pp. 71–91.

Bobbins feed fiberglass threads to be woven into braids.

PART

1

POSITIONING DECISIONS

Every four years at the Olympics, spectators of alpine skiing events witness dramatic examples of international competition—skier competing with skier or racing against the clock. This competitive drive carries over into much of our everyday life. In business, the sport of skiing has spawned a huge competitive industry, from ski resorts to manufacturers of ski equipment. International manufacturers provide the equipment that ski enthusiasts use. With only tenths of a second separating finalists in world-class events, the difference between winning and losing may depend on the quality of a competitor's skis.

Capturing a significant market share depends in part on how a firm uses operations to implement corporate strategy. K2 Corporation, a world-class ski manufacturer, is a firm that uses operations management as a competitive weapon. K2 competes on the basis of high-performance design, consistent quality, and product flexibility. They introduce three new models yearly. Seventy percent of K2's skis are made-to-stock; the rest must meet specific requirements of individual customers. To support this competitive thrust, manufacturing devotes some facilities to high-volume stock items and others to low-volume specials. Operators are responsible for quality at their own work stations. These positioning decisions have placed K2 at the top of the industry.

Like K2, all providers of goods and services strive to achieve a competitive edge. Part 1 examines the decisions operations managers face in aligning operations with their firm's competitive strategy. We explain the link between operations and product design, and why the decision to organize production around a process or product is so critical. We also discuss the importance of good quality and how to achieve it. After studying Part 1, you'll see why operations management is so critical to successful organizations.

CHAPTER 2

PRODUCT PLANNING AND COMPETITIVE PRIORITIES

 Chapter Outline

▲ Key Questions for Managers

What products (goods or services) should we offer?

When should we enter and exit the market during a product's life cycle?

When should we add or drop products?

What should be our competitive priorities?

Should we emphasize price, quality, time, or flexibility?

What is our best positioning strategy?

What impact does this choice have on our other decisions in operations?

hapter 1 explained how corporate strategy defines a firm's mission and answers questions such as: What business are we in? What should it be 10 years from now? Who are our customers? The answers define the products, whether goods or services, that the firm will offer. **Product planning** encompasses all the activities leading up to the introduction, revision, or dropping of products. Although product planning takes place primarily at the corporate strategy level, it is the logical starting point for formulating operations strategy. Knowing product characteristics, the operations manager can effectively design and operate the production system.

Our coverage of product planning begins with a discussion of product life cycles, planning stages, and entrance–exit strategies. We then present competitive priorities, or the ways in which operations must excel to make the offered products competitive. We take you on two plant tours to illustrate the organization of actual operations around those priorities. Finally, we show how an organization's positioning strategy, or choice of either a process focus or a product focus, links decisions throughout the operations function.

PRODUCT PLANNING ▲

Product planning is an ongoing process—it's a job that's never completed. Intense competition, expiration of patents, and rapid technological innovations are all factors that challenge an organization's ability to produce a quality product that meets market demand and to deliver it on time. Corporate strategy is the guide, because product planning must be compatible with a firm's overall goals.

More than $50 billion are spent each year designing new products or improving old ones. In fact, more than half a firm's dollar volume typically comes from products introduced within the last 10 years. Large firms often spend vast sums of money assessing the market, appraising the competition, and designing products. Many small companies, such as the R. L. Drake Company, profiled in Managerial Practice 2.1, start with a limited number of prod-

MANAGERIAL PRACTICE 2.1 ▲

New Products at R. L. Drake Company

R. L. Drake founded a shortwave radio company during World War II. Although the firm remained successful for over 30 years, by 1978 its revenues were dropping rapidly. At the time, ham-radio sales were falling off with little hope for a resurgence. Mr. Drake, the company's chief executive officer, decided to alter his product for use on ships. However, by 1981 Japanese producers began dominating the marine-radio market. Drake's sales were still $7.3 million, but he knew he'd soon be out of business if he couldn't come up with a new product.

A distributor gave Drake the idea of producing satellite-television receivers. No major company was then making receivers for the consumer market, which Drake believed was about to take off. The firm adapted much of its old equipment, including a $250,000 circuit board assembler, to the new product. The gamble paid off. By 1985 Drake's work force numbered 700 employees, and sales had risen to over $600 million.

Then in 1986, the satellite-television industry received a severe blow when HBO began scrambling its signals. Several firms went out of business, leaving R. L. Drake Company the only domestic manufacturer. Management cut the company's work force to less than 300 employees and attempted to deal with excess plant capacity and parts inventory.

By 1988, the company had stabilized its sales and profits, in part by expanding and diversifying its products for the commercial market. Private cable companies are a major source of revenue. Electronic Data Systems (EDS), another important client, buys Drake's products for the installation of a new satellite network designed to link General Motors dealers. Still another sales boost comes from an exploding European market.

Source: "Losing Sales, Radio Company Finds Success in New Product," *Wall Street Journal*, February 27, 1984.

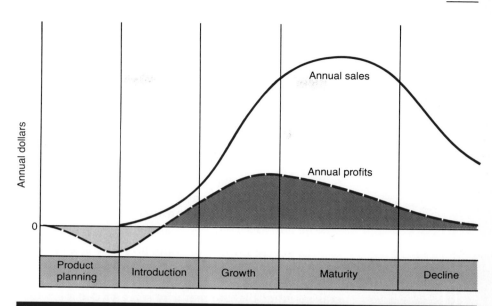

FIGURE 2.1   A Product's Life Cycle

ucts. These products are often based on the founding entrepreneur's own special process or product innovation. As time passes, however, these firms usually must add new products, either to replace those being phased out or to expand their market penetration.

A firm that neglects to introduce new products periodically will eventually decline. Sales and profits from any given product decrease over time, so the pressure is on management to introduce new products before existing ones hit their peak. Let's take a look at the stages of a product's life.

Product Life Cycles

A **product life cycle** consists of five stages through which a product passes: product planning, introduction, growth, maturity, and decline. Figure 2.1 depicts sales and profits associated with each stage.

1. *Product Planning.* During this stage, ideas for new goods or services are generated, screened, and translated into final designs. Profits attributed to a product are negative at this point, as sales have not begun. Although no revenues are coming in, development costs are being incurred.

2. *Introduction.* At this stage, sales begin and profits go from negative to positive. Operations is still refining production efforts, which can best be characterized as fluid and evolving. Marketing efforts may be modest (as when introducing new prescription drugs) or nearing their peak (as with

new textbooks). As sales volumes have not reached their high point, annual profits are small, even though unit profit margins may be large.

3. *Growth*. The product next enters a stage of rapid growth. Early in this stage there is a dramatic jump in sales, and profits rise. The mandate for operations is to somehow keep up with demand; efficiency is less of a concern.

4. *Maturity*. During this stage, sales level off and profits begin to decline. New competitors create pressures to cut costs and slow the squeeze on unit profit margins. Now operations must stress efficiency, although marketing can ease the pressure by intensifying efforts to differentiate the product.

5. *Decline*. At last the product enters a decline stage and ultimately becomes obsolete. Either demand disappears or a better, less expensive product takes its place. Sales and profits decrease to the point where the firm finally drops the product.

A **life-cycle audit** is an evaluation of which stage a product is in, based on how changes in sales and profits compare with those of prior years. For example, when both sales and profits are dropping, Fig. 2.1 suggests that the product is in either the late maturity stage or decline stage. Life-cycle audits spot needs to revitalize or eliminate existing products and to introduce new ones.

APPLICATION 2.1

Management has collected the following data in preparation for a life-cycle audit of one of its products, a packaging material sold to industrial buyers.

Performance Measure	This Year's Performance	Change Over Last Year	Average Annual Change Over Last Four Years
Annual Sales	$30.8 million	+1.0%	+15.8%
Unit Price	1.12/lb.	+2.2	+ 8.5
Unit Profit Margin	0.16/lb.	−0.3	+ 3.2
Total Profits	4.4 million	+1.5	+22.5

In what stage of the life cycle is the product?

Solution

Sales are stabilizing, having grown only one percent over the past year. Average annual growth had been much higher during prior years, at 15.8 percent. Unit-price growth has slowed, and unit profit margins are beginning to shrink. Total profit is also leveling off. All of these signs suggest the *early maturity stage*.

The life cycles vary greatly from product to product. For example, Coleco Industries, a Connecticut toymaker, sought ways to avoid bankruptcy and court protection just three years after riding high on the huge success of its Cabbage Patch Kids line. In the case of R. L. Drake, the demand for shortwave radios lasted for 30 years, whereas the demand for marine radios lasted only three years.

Looking only at the time required for the product planning stage, or the time between when the idea is born and the product is introduced, we find that it took

- Eversharp only eight months to introduce ball-point pens;
- Gerber only one year to introduce strained baby food; and
- Dictaphone Corporation less than two years to introduce the portable recording machine.

By contrast, it took 15 years for

- Xerox to introduce electrostatic copy machines;
- Polaroid to introduce the color-pack camera; and
- Bell Laboratories to introduce transistors.

In the high-tech computer and microchip industry, products can become obsolete in months. Thus companies such as Atari and Intel Corporation generally favor a management style characterized by quick, independent action more than do companies enjoying longer product life cycles.

Entrance–Exit Strategies

The life cycle of a product within a company can be quite different from its cycle within an industry. For example, several competitors of the R. L. Drake Company decided to pull out of the satellite-television receiver market, although the industry will be producing these products for years to come. An **entrance–exit strategy** is a firm's choice of when to enter a market and when to leave it. Choosing one of the three basic strategies shown in Table 2.1 has important implications for the operations function.

TABLE 2.1 Entrance–Exit Strategies

Strategy	Stage to Enter	Stage to Exit	Implications for Operations
A: Enter early and exit late	Introduction	Decline	Transition from low-volume, flexible producer to high-volume, low-cost producer
B: Enter early and exit early	Introduction	Maturity	Low-volume, flexible producer
C: Enter late and exit late	Growth	Decline	High-volume, low-cost producer

Source: Data from Robert H. Hayes and Steven C. Wheelwright, "The Dynamics of Process-Product Life Cycles," *Harvard Business Review* (March–April 1979), pp. 127–136.

Strategy A.   The most natural strategy is for a firm to enter the market when the product is first introduced and stay with it until the end of its life cycle. Polaroid and Xerox are examples of companies that developed a new product and grew with it throughout its life cycle. By entering the market early, the firm gets a head start. This added experience may allow the early entrant to produce a better product at a lower cost than late entrants can produce initially.

Strategy A requires operations to evolve from a low-volume, flexible production system into a high-volume, low-cost system. Such a shift is always a challenge because it means changing over to a whole new way of doing things. Several companies in the personal computer industry, including Apple, Atari, and Commodore International, experienced similar growing pains when they moved from a small, freewheeling venture to a large corporation.

Strategy B.   Small, product-innovative firms often choose to stay in the low-volume, customized business. This strategy requires no painful transition. When the product reaches the maturity stage and profit margins begin to shrink, the firm drops the product and introduces new ones. Throughout the product life cycle, operations management maintains a smaller, flexible production system that can readily be adapted to changing products.

Strategy C.   A firm waits in the wings until other, innovative firms introduce a new product. After it is clear that the product has significant market appeal and will achieve high sales volumes, the firm enters the market with an automated, efficient production facility. Large firms, in particular, may accompany their entry with **preemptive pricing**, that is, setting their prices considerably lower than those of their competitors to ensure the high-volume sales necessary for low unit costs and avoid a transition from low to high volumes. They can exploit their mass-marketing capabilities, establish distribution channels, and gain access to capital markets in order to finance the massive investment needed for top efficiency. A good example is United Parcel Service, the package-delivery giant with annual revenues of $9 billion, which is beginning to muscle into the overnight-express business.

Product Planning Stage

Product planning is most active during the first stage of the product life cycle. As Fig. 2.2 illustrates, it is a four-step process, guided by corporate strategy. An essential part of strategic planning, the firm's mission plays a key role in the conceptualization and design of new goods and services. If its mission is too broad, the firm could enter areas where it has no distinctive competencies. If the mission is too narrow, promising growth opportunities will be missed. Managerial Practice 2.2 shows how three firms, Gould, Inc., General Mills, Inc., and Cummins Engine Company, each either broadened or narrowed its mission in order to establish a more successful product line.

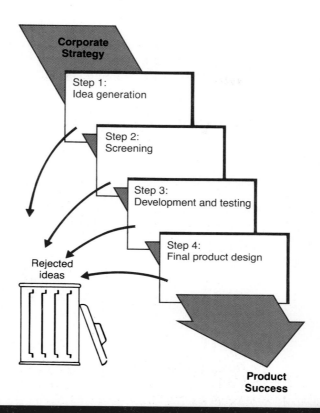

FIGURE 2.2 *Steps in Product Planning*

Step 1: Idea Generation. New product ideas often come from within the firm—from managers, employees, or research and development (R&D) laboratories. They also come from the outside—from distributors, licensers, and inventors. You may be surprised to learn that Du Pont, known for its innovative products, gets two-thirds of its new product ideas from outside sources.

New ideas are either *market-oriented* or *technology-oriented*. The most obvious source of new ideas is marketing, the department responsible for keeping in touch with customer and client needs. Market studies discover better ways to serve established markets, as well as opportunities to enter new ones. Examples of successful market-oriented ideas are dial-a-call services by psychologists, fast-food delivery service to students living in dormitories, and Pizza Hut's five-minute single serving.

Technological advances can affect either the product or the process. Consider the innovations in the electronics and computer industries that are spawning many new products. Other inventions improve the production process, which in turn creates opportunities for more new products. For example, automatic teller machines have allowed banks to offer their customers 24-hour service. Large firms do most of the industrial R&D work, with some 80 percent of R&D being done by firms employing more than 5000 people. Many of the new product ideas are generated by the half a million scientists whose industrial research costs billions of dollars each year. Some successful technology-oriented ideas include lasers for specialized surgery, GM's diesel engine, Reynolds Metals' resealable aluminum cans, low cholesterol eggs, and Tandy's compact disc recorders.

MANAGERIAL PRACTICE 2.2

A Broad or Narrow Mission?

Make It Broader

In order to shed a Rust Bowl image, Gould, Inc., decided to expand its mission. Where once it made only batteries and engine parts, it now offers a wide range of high-tech electronics. When William Ylvisaker took over as chairman in 1967, earnings were only $4.2 million. They have since swelled to $93.6 million. The "new Gould" manufactures minicomputers, semiconductors, factory automation equipment, and test and measurement instruments. Skeptics questioned whether the company could tie together such diversity. However, Gould's product lines are becoming complementary. One example is the minicomputers, which the company also uses in its factory automation line.

Make It Narrower

General Mills, Inc., decided to narrow its mission in order to concentrate on its flagship of food processing and restaurants. The company sold many of its toy and fashion lines, since these higher risk capital-intensive businesses demanded a more entrepreneurial style than the food company's management provided. For example, the Izod sportswear line wasn't keeping up with volatile consumer tastes. Other companies in the food industry narrowed their missions in a similar back-to-basics move, because their diverse products had taken them away from their distinctive competencies.

Cummins Engine Company is betting its future on just one product—diesel engines. It earlier flirted with diversification into products ranging from skis to computer equipment. As a preeminent diesel-engine producer, it has decided to concentrate on what it does best. To fend off foreign competition, Cummins spent over twice its net worth to retool its manufacturing facilities. It also developed new engine models and is moving into the lower horsepower market.

Sources: "Gould Reshapes Itself into High-Tech Outfit Amid Much Turmoil," *Wall Street Journal*, October 3, 1984; "General Mills Inc. Will Spin Off Toy Group and Sell Fashion Units," *Wall Street Journal*, March 27, 1985; "Cummins Decides to Go with Its Strength as It Pins Hopes on Diesel Truck Engines," *Wall Street Journal*, July 3, 1984.

Using the laser beam in Tandy's compact disc recorder is an example of a technology-oriented new product idea.

Step 2: Screening. There is never a dearth of new product ideas. NBC estimates that it wades through 250,000 suggestions or ideas a year. The real question is: Which ideas are worth pursuing? By one estimate, only one in every 60 ideas is actually commercialized, and only eight make it past the screening step. Some ideas do not fit the company's mission. Others fail to meet marketing, operations, or financial criteria.

Marketing criteria help managers measure the potential impact of a new product on the competition and on the firm's existing product line. They include competitiveness, responsiveness to market needs, the idea's patent status, promotional requirements, need for after-market services, and fit with existing distribution channels. *Operations criteria* include the technical feasibility of producing a product and its compatibility with the firm's current processes, work force, equipment, facility locations, and supplier capabilities. *Financial criteria* include the size of the corporation, investment required, degree of risk, predicted annual sales, profit margin per unit, and anticipated length of a product's life cycle. Marketing criteria relate mainly to future revenues, whereas operations criteria relate directly to cost. In a sense, the financial tests bring marketing and operations together.

Step 3: Development and Testing. Next, the firm must test the idea's technical feasibility. In manufacturing industries, engineers may design prototypes for testing and analyzing a product's features. Operations assesses process, facility, and material needs. Finally, marketing conducts tests in limited markets or with customer panels to gauge consumer response to the product's features, packaging, and promotional campaign. The end result of testing should be a product that is technically and economically feasible and that has customer appeal.

The U.K. firm British Aerospace estimates that decisions made during the first 5 percent of Step 3 determine 85 percent of a product's eventual quality, cost, and ease of manufacture. This realization has prompted manufacturing firms to involve operations in development and testing from the outset. Historically, engineering designed the product first and only then would manufacturing get involved. Engineers worked in virtual isolation. Their prototypes were not designed for efficient production and assembly, costly changes and retooling were common, and often the development process was delayed. Today, increased market segmentation and declining product life cycles make short development cycles critical.

Following the precedent established by its Taurus/Sable program, Ford now gives full responsibility for each new product to a program manager. The program manager forms a product team representing every major part of the organization—including manufacturing. Thus each department can express its views while there is still time to alter the product. General Motors is implementing a similar program, called "simultaneous engineering." This process requires design engineers, manufacturing specialists, and marketers to work jointly in designing the product and selecting the manufacturing process. This

MANAGERIAL PRACTICE 2.3

Refining the Service Bundle at Olive Garden Restaurants

General Mills opened the prototype for Olive Garden restaurants at a failed steakhouse in Orlando, Florida, in 1982. Since then the company has spent considerable time and money creating an Italian ambiance and cuisine—they serve some spaghetti but also include other dishes that appeal to the American mass market. General Mills canvassed 1000 restaurants for recipes, interviewed 5000 consumers, and dumped out more than 80 pots of spaghetti sauce before selecting a final service bundle. An important goal of the development-and-testing stage was a tomato sauce that would cling to pasta rather than run to the plate's edge. All new employees watched videotapes instructing them on the details of their jobs. Even the singing waiters' lyrics were carefully crafted. Five years after General Mills opened its prototype's doors, there were 58 Olive Garden restaurants. The firm hopes eventually to operate 500 across the country.

Source: "General Mills Risks Millions Starting Chain of Italian Restaurants," *Wall Street Journal*, September 21, 1987.

concept of working together is a tradition at Honda. Animated discussions among representatives of all departments have earned the nickname "wai-gaya," which loosely translates into "hubbub."

In service industries, firms must define and assess three components of the "service bundle" (see Sasser, et al., 1978): (1) facilitating goods, (2) explicit services, and (3) implicit services. To illustrate, in a restaurant, facilitating goods include food, drink, tables, chairs, and tableware. Explicit services include speed and quality of service, and less tangible characteristics such as taste, aroma, and atmosphere. Implicit services are harder to define because they depend on customer preferences. They could include perceptions of status, comfort, or a general sense of well-being.

Restaurant chains generally begin with a carefully designed prototype. R. David Thomas founded Wendy's Old-Fashioned Hamburgers in 1969. For the first site in Columbus, Ohio, he defined the details of product features such as menu, interior decor, and order processing service. Only after finishing the development-and-testing stage did Wendy's begin to expand and sell franchises. Managerial Practice 2.3 describes a similar process followed by the Olive Garden restaurant chain.

Stage 4: Final Product Design.   During this step, the firm finalizes the details of product characteristics, often by lists of specifications, process formulas, and drawings. For example, engineering drawings for an electric utility boiler would specify types of material and dimensions for each component. This is the stage at which firms commit substantial financial and human resources to the project. Production begins. Marketing starts its promotional program with kick-off sales meetings and presentations at trade exhibits. In services, a super-market would establish maximum customer delay times. Multisite service firms such as Olive Garden restaurants may add a limited number of facilities. If they prove successful, expansion to many new sites may proceed rapidly. In just one decade

- McDonald's went from 738 to 3750 units;
- Holiday Inns grew from 587 to 1750 inns; and
- Manpower, Inc.'s annual revenues grew from $47.3 to $161.2 million.

Managing Product Life Cycles

Product planning is not limited to introducing new products. When a life-cycle audit indicates that a product has reached maturity or entered decline, the firm has several options. It can stay with the product for a few more years, find ways to squeeze costs still more, or revise and rejuvenate the product. Table 2.2 shows how companies in five industries (drugs, major appliances, food, clothing, and minor appliances) ranked various product planning activities. Adding new products ranked first, followed closely by revising existing products.

TABLE 2.2 Importance of Various Product Planning Activities	
Activity	**Importance***
Adding new products	41
Revising existing products	31
Finding new uses of existing products	15
Eliminating products	13

*Average score assigned by firms surveyed, where the highest possible score was 100.

Source: Data from James T. Rothe, "The Product Elimination Decision," *MSU Business Topics,* Michigan State University, Autumn 1970, pp. 45–52.

Revision might mean improving the performance of the product, such as a mix for a faster rising cake. Or it could be an update of an old standby, as with Mattel's revamp of the Barbie doll. Barbie, Mattel's 27-year-old best-seller, had been showing her age. In response to competition from Hasbro's new rock-star doll, Jem, Mattel gave Barbie an after-hours wardrobe of miniskirts, a modern hairdo, and a rock band. This new "story line" helped boost Barbie's sales up to $200 million a year, second only to Hasbro's G.I. Joe.

Product Screening

A critical step in product planning is screening, the stage when most ideas are discarded. However, there is no guarantee that an optimal decision will be made, as the history of the following ill-fated products suggests.

- After painstaking market research, Ford launched the Edsel car with much fanfare. One enthusiastic dealer even unfurled a huge Edsel sign above San Francisco Bay. The company's high expectations were not met, and Ford sold only about 100,000 of the cars.

- IBM poured $40 million into promoting its PCjr. However, because of production delays, the product missed the Christmas season, and customers were dismayed at the high price and limited memory. Despite high initial expectations, the company discontinued production of this model.

- Revlon, Inc., introduced a nail clipper that collected the clippings, but few customers decided that nail clippings were worth saving. The product was withdrawn.

- Extensive taste tests convinced Coca-Cola executives that customers would prefer a new flavor of the world's best-selling soft drink. They were surprised by consumer response, however, so we can now buy "New" Coke and "Classic" Coke.

There are two reasons for such failures. First, a great deal of uncertainty surrounds the choice. Making accurate forecasts of future sales, costs, and competitor reactions is difficult, if not perilous. Historical data for totally new products are nonexistent. Second, multiple criteria cannot be naturally merged into a single measure (such as dollars). Managers are hard pressed to estimate the dollar equivalent of intangibles such as operations compatibility or project risk.

Despite such obstacles, managers must make decisions. Sometimes hard thinking in a quiet room is sufficient. At other times decision makers rely on more formal procedures. We present only two of these formal procedures: a preference matrix and break-even analysis. We discuss two more-advanced techniques, financial analysis and linear programming, in Supplement 1 and Supplement 2, respectively, at the end of this book.

Preference Matrix

A **preference matrix** is a table that allows the manager to rate an alternative according to several performance criteria. The criteria can be scored on any scale, such as from 1 (worst possible) to 10 (best possible), so long as the same scale is applied to all the alternatives being compared. Each score is weighted according to its perceived importance, with the total of these weights typically equaling 100. The total score is the sum of the weighted scores (weight times score) for all the criteria. By rating various alternatives, the manager can compare the scores for new product ideas against each other or against a predetermined threshold.

APPLICATION 2.2

The following table shows the performance criteria, weights, and scores (1 = worst and 10 = best) for a new product, a thermal storage air conditioner. If management wants to introduce just one new product, and the highest total score of any of the other product ideas is 800, should the firm pursue the air-conditioner?

Performance Criterion	Weight (A)	Score (B)	Weighted Score (A × B)
Market potential	30	8	240
Unit profit margin	20	10	200
Operations compatibility	20	6	120
Competitive advantage	15	10	150
Investment requirement	10	2	20
Project risk	5	4	20
		Weighted score =	___

Solution

We calculate the first weighted score in the last column of the table as 30×8 (or 240). Continuing down the column, the results are 200, 120, 150, 20, and 20. Next we sum these weighted scores for a total of 750. This score falls short of the 800 threshold, so we would not pursue the thermal storage air conditioner idea at this time.

Not all managers are comfortable with the preference matrix technique. It requires the manager to state criterion weights before examining the alternatives. However, the proper weights may not be readily apparent. Only after seeing the scores for several alternatives can the manager decide what is important and what is not. The preference matrix also allows a low score on one criterion to be compensated for or overriden by high scores on others, which may or may not be realistic. For example, the investment required for a new manufacturing process might exceed the firm's financial capability. In that case the new product idea must be dropped, no matter how high the scores were for the other criteria.

Break-Even Analysis

When used for product planning, **break-even analysis** is a technique for determining the product volume at which total revenues are equal to total costs. When used to compare production methods, it finds the volume at which two different processes have equal total costs. Here we use it for the first purpose: to evaluate the profit potential of a new product. This technique helps the manager to answer questions such as:

1. Is the product's predicted sales volume sufficient to break even (neither earning a profit nor sustaining a loss)?
2. How low must the variable cost per unit be to break even, based on forecasts of sales and prices?
3. How low must the fixed cost be to break even?
4. How do price levels affect the break-even volume?

Break-even analysis assumes that all costs related to the production of a specific product can be divided into fixed costs and variable costs. Let

$$p = \text{Price charged per unit sold}$$
$$c = \text{Variable cost of each unit produced}$$
$$F = \text{Fixed cost per year}$$
$$Q = \text{Number of units produced and sold per year}$$

The **variable cost,** c, is the portion of the total cost that varies directly with volume of output. This cost includes costs per unit for materials, labor, and usually some variable part of overhead. The **fixed cost,** F, is the portion of the total cost that remains constant regardless of changes in levels of output. This cost represents the annual cost of new equipment and facilities purchased (or rented) for the new product, including depreciation, interest, taxes, and insurance. The fixed cost can also cover salaries, utilities, and portions of the sales or advertising budget. The difference between the price and the variable cost of each unit is often called the unit profit margin ($p - c$), because it contributes both to profits and to meeting fixed costs.

Let's assume that the cost function is linear and consists of the fixed cost plus total variable costs ($F + cQ$). If we set total annual revenues (pQ) equal to the total cost and solve for Q, we get the break-even quantity:

$$pQ = F + cQ$$
$$(p - c)Q = F$$
$$Q = \frac{F}{p - c}$$

We can also find this break-even quantity graphically, as shown in the following application. It is the point where the total revenue line crosses the total cost line.

APPLICATION 2.3

A firm is considering a new product to be sold at $20 per unit. Fixed cost per year would be $100,000, with total variable costs set at $10 per unit. What is the break-even quantity for this product? Use both the algebraic and graphic approaches to get your answer.

Solution

For the firm to break even, the number of units sold (Q) must equal the fixed cost per year (F) divided by the unit profit margin ($p - c$). Thus, using the formula for the break-even quantity, we get

$$Q = \frac{F}{p - c} = \frac{100,000}{20 - 10} = 10,000 \text{ units}$$

The graphic approach requires that we plot two lines—one for costs and one for revenues. We begin by calculating costs and revenues for two different output levels. The following table uses $Q = 0$ and $Q = 20$, although any two reasonably spread out output levels are equally good.

Quantity (thousands of units) (Q)	Total Annual Cost (thousands of $) (100 + 10Q)	Total Annual Revenues (thousands of $) (20Q)
0	$100	$ 0
20	300	400

Since two points define a line, we can now draw the cost line through points (0, 100) and (20, 300). The revenue line goes between (0, 0) and (20, 400). As Fig. 2.3 indicates, these two lines intersect at 10,000 units, the break-even quantity.

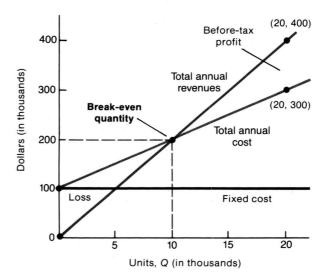

FIGURE 2.3   Graphic Approach to Break-Even Analysis

Break-even analysis cannot tell a manager whether to pursue or drop a new product idea. The technique can only show what is likely to happen for various forecasts of costs and sales volumes. Fortunately, we can go beyond simple break-even analysis and work directly with the underlying cost and revenue equations to evaluate a variety of "what if" questions. This approach is called **sensitivity analysis**, a technique for systematically changing the critical parameters in a model in order to determine their effects. With product planning, we can assess the sensitivity of total profit to different pricing strategies, sales volumes forecasts, or cost estimates.

APPLICATION 2.4

If the most pessimistic sales forecast for the proposed product in Fig. 2.3 were 15,000 units, what would be the product's total profit contribution per year?

Solution

The graph shows that even the pessimistic forecast lies above the break-even volume, which is encouraging. The product's total profit contribution, found by subtracting total costs from total revenues, is

$$pQ - (F + cQ) = 20(15,000) - [100,000 + 10(15,000)]$$
$$= \$50,000$$

COMPETITIVE PRIORITIES ▲

As important as choosing the products themselves is deciding how to excel in producing those products. For example, it is not enough to decide which types of food to offer at a new restaurant. The owner must also determine the restaurant's distinctive competencies. By taking advantage of them, the owner can set the restaurant apart from its competitors. **Competitive priorities** are the dimensions a firm chooses to emphasize in providing its product. There are seven dimensions, which fall into four groups, to choose from:

- *Cost*
    1. Low price
- *Quality*
    2. High-performance design
    3. Consistent quality
- *Time*
    4. Fast delivery time
    5. On-time delivery
- *Flexibility*
    6. Product flexibility
    7. Volume flexibility

A firm gains an advantage by outperforming competitors on one or more of these dimensions. Managerial Practice 2.4 illustrates each competitive priority by referring to the practices of actual firms.

Cost

Lowering prices reduces unit profit margins, an outcome that can be partially offset by the higher volumes that may follow. The firm must also attempt to minimize labor, materials, scrap, and overhead costs. But the ability to lower prices often requires additional investment in more automated facilities and equipment. Lowering prices without jeopardizing quality usually occurs with undifferentiated products in the maturity stage of their life cycles. At that stage output levels tend to be high, equipment is specialized, and efficiency is likely to be at a peak. In the context of break-even analysis, the fixed cost, F, is increased to achieve a sharply reduced variable cost, c.

MANAGERIAL PRACTICE 2.4

Competitive Priorities of Various Firms

Low Price

Earl Scheib, Inc., of Beverly Hills, California, operates 275 shops that offer a "no-frills" face-lift to cars at rock-bottom prices. Unit profit margins are protected by pinching every penny. Sales have increased at an annual rate of 15 percent and earnings are increasing at almost 50 percent per year.

High-Performance Design

C. Hoare & Company, a bank founded in London in 1672, treats clients like royalty but charges a stiff price. Six descendants of the founder still run the family business. At least one is no more than an hour away, day or night. Customers are ushered in by a doorman in a frock coat. Teller counters are rimmed to accommodate umbrellas, with a drip gully carved below in the granite floor. The waiting room is lined with gold-rimmed ledgers in glass cases. Money is no object to the 8000 customers, whom most employees know by sight.

Consistent Quality

McDonald's restaurants are known for uniform design specifications. Eating at McDonald's is definitely a different experience from dining at a five-star restaurant. However, you can count on the same menu and standards of quality from one order to the next and from one restaurant to the next.

Fast Delivery Times

Thomas S. Monaghan was a University of Michigan student in 1960, when he traded a VW for his brother's share of their pizza parlor. He now owns 95

Quality

Two competitive priorities deal with quality. The first one, high-performance design, can mean superior features, close tolerances, and greater durability. It also includes the helpfulness and skill of the work force, whether sales clerks or service station attendants. After-sale support and financing may also be part of the design specifications. For example, IBM now offers installment payment plans, credit cards, and equipment leasing. It leases more than $1.5 billion worth of new equipment, a big boost to sales.

The second competitive priority is consistent quality. It measures the frequency with which the product meets design specifications. A foundry might

percent of Domino's Pizza, which adds an average of two stores daily to its 3700 outlets. His not-so-secret formula: pizza to your doorstep—*pronto*.

On-Time Delivery

Federal Express not only offers fast delivery time (overnight delivery), it also promises that parcels will be "absolutely, positively" delivered on time. Meeting delivery promises comes at a cost. The same relatively inexpensive delivery by the U.S. Postal Service can cost as much as $25 if sent by Federal Express.

Product Flexibility

When hit by an industry-wide slump, National Semiconductor Corporation decided to enter the growing market for custom-designed computer chips. Rather than mass produce the product and sell it through a catalog, the company designs each chip to suit the customer's specific requirements. A custom-made chip can cost as much as $1 million.

Volume Flexibility

Thomas Woods, a 40-year-old contractor in Missouri, made it through the recession of 1979—the worst housing slump since World War II. He took some losses, but feels he learned a great deal about how to control operations during the ups and downs of the housing market.

Sources: "Earl Scheib Is Still King of the No-Frills Paint Job," *Business Week*, May 27, 1985; "Bored with Queues? Some London Banks Let You Skip Them," *Wall Street Journal*, October 26, 1984; "Presto! The Convenience Industry," *Business Week*, April 27, 1987; "National Semiconductor's Custom-Made Chips Are Bucking Company's General Sales Slump," *Wall Street Journal*, February 12, 1985; "Builder Heeds Lessons Learned Surviving Last Housing Slump," *Wall Street Journal*, November 19, 1984.

measure the percent of castings falling within the tolerances allowed for length, diameter, and surface finish. A cereal manufacturer might measure the frequency with which a box's contents match nutritional information on the label.

Time

Two competitive priorities deal with time. The first, fast delivery time, is the elapsed time between receiving a customer's order and filling it. Industrial buyers often call this *lead time*. A good delivery time can be a year for a major customized machine, several weeks for scheduling elective surgery, and minutes for an ambulance. Firms can shorten delivery times by producing to inventory or having slack capacity.

The second time priority reflects variability in delivery time, rather than its average. On-time delivery measures the frequency of meeting delivery-time promises. Manufacturers measure on-time delivery as the percentage of customer orders shipped when promised, with 95 percent often considered the goal. A supermarket might measure on-time delivery as the percentage of customers who must wait in the checkout line for less than three minutes.

Flexibility

Some firms give top priority to one of two types of flexibility. **Product flexibility** is the ability of the firm to accommodate changing product designs or highly customized products. Products are tailored to individual preferences or have very short life cycles. Volumes for any individual product are low, since the firm competes on the basis of its ability to produce difficult, nonstandard products. The extreme case is one-of-a-kind production, where each new order is unique. Product flexibility can also mean the ability to change designs quickly and introduce new products rapidly, as in the high-tech electronics industry.

Volume flexibility, on the other hand, is the ability to quickly accelerate or decelerate the rate of production to handle large fluctuations in demand. The time between peaks can be years, as with the cycles in the home-building industry or political campaigns. It can be months, as with a ski resort. It can even be hours, as with the systematic swings in demand from hour to hour at a major postal facility where mail is sorted and dispatched.

Trade-Offs

Sometimes a firm can improve cost, quality, and flexibility simultaneously. For example, scrap and rework often account for 20–30 percent of a product's cost. By reducing scrap and rework the firm can sharply reduce costs and improve productivity. Improved quality can help stimulate sales to the point where high-volume production is possible. An underlying factor here is **repeatability**, the degree to which the same work can be repeated through job specialization or by producing standardized products and parts. Increased repeatability reduces unit costs, permitting production of a higher quality product at lower prices. Thus improved quality might actually be cost free.

Unfortunately, at some point further improvements on one dimension are accompanied by setbacks on one or more of the others. For example, top-of-the-line specifications, as with Rolls Royce, make premium prices necessary. Higher prices reduce the firm's market share, which in turn cuts repeatability and increases costs. Shorter, more reliable delivery times, increased product flexibility, and customization all may raise prices. The frequently experienced trade-off between product flexibility and cost is illustrated by GM's experience, as presented in Managerial Practice 2.5.

Thus managers must recognize the trade-offs that exist among the seven competitive priority dimensions. Because much depends on the exact situation, managers must judge trade-off outcomes when deciding which dimensions need particular emphasis. For example, it is easy for Earl Scheib, Inc., to emphasize not only low price but also quick (one-day) delivery times. Low product flexibility like that at McDonald's allows a fast, mass-production process. C. Hoare & Company enhances its top-quality image by also having fast delivery times, as by answering loan inquiries the day they are received. Moreover, the resulting increase in the price of the service provided is of little concern to the bank's customers.

MANAGERIAL PRACTICE 2.5

Product Flexibility, Repeatability, and Costs at GM

General Motors Corporation sees simplifying its product lines as a big challenge—and big payoff. GM offers so many models and options that, in theory, it could build cars for 18 months without making an exact duplicate. Since 1986, GM has cut stand-alone options by 40 percent, but that's just the beginning. By 1992 it will eliminate 25 percent of the 175 models offered in 1986.

Maximizing the number of options delights marketing but creates a bottomless pit of manufacturing and bookkeeping costs. Slight variations in basic platform lead to different axles, suspensions, and engines. These variations, in turn, require more planners and analysts.

While streamlining product lines may be a major cost saver, the process isn't risk free. Fewer basic platforms makes it harder to differentiate models, a policy that could perpetuate GM's problem in the early 1980s of look-alike cars. The trick will be to enhance repeatability while creating different-looking models.

Source: "The New-Model GM Will Be More Compact, but More Profitable," *Wall Street Journal,* June 6, 1988.

Setting Competitive Priorities

It is intriguing to see how executives in North America rate the competitive priorities for their businesses. Figure 2.4 shows the average responses to an executive survey. The respondents judged the importance of each competitive priority to their firms over the next three years. The four competitive priorities dealing with quality and time (consistent quality, on-time delivery, high-performance design, and fast delivery time) emerged at the top, well ahead of price and flexibility. Consistent quality has consistently held the number one position in such surveys.

Effective operations strategy begins with periodic reviews of competitive priorities. Managers should assess the firm's current performance in terms of the desired level on all seven dimensions. Performance should also be judged against the industry norm. Finally, the managers set specific, measurable standards. Examples of such standards for each competitive priority are

- Reduce the price to $10 per unit.
- Decrease scrap losses by 10 percent.
- Maintain the current tolerances for product weight.
- Promise deliveries within three weeks after receiving an order.

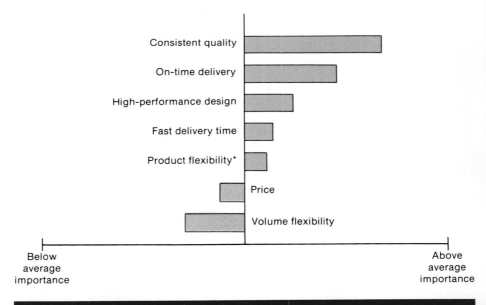

FIGURE 2.4   Competitive Priorities of North American Managers

*Product flexibility is defined as the ability to change designs quickly or introduce new products rapidly.
Source: Jeffrey Miller and Aleda Roth, "Manufacturing Strategies: Executive Summary of the 1988 North American Manufacturing Futures Survey," Boston University, 1988.

- Improve on-time delivery to 95 percent.
- Increase the number of product options by 50 percent.
- Be able to double the production rate in just two months.

TIME-BASED COMPETITION ▲

To be effective in time-based competition, managers must carefully define the steps and time involved in processing customer orders. Next, they must critically analyze each step to see whether production time can be shortened without compromising the quality of the product or service. Significant time reductions in operations can often be achieved simply by changing the way current technologies are used or by turning to automation.

Obviously, companies such as Federal Express and Domino's Pizza give high competitive priority to fast delivery and on-time delivery. But did you know that firms such as Honda and Atlas Door also emphasize time, using it to gain firm footholds in their respective markets (Stalk, 1988)?

More Products in Less Time

In the late 1970s, Honda used time to thwart Yamaha's attempt to replace Honda as the world's largest motorcycle manufacturer. Honda's strategy was to introduce a wide variety of products so quickly that Yamaha would be unable to keep up. In the process, Honda changed its methods for developing, manufacturing, and introducing new products to enable it to speed up execution of new product plans. It also cut prices and advertised heavily. When the contest began, Honda had 60 models of motorcycles. Eighteen months later it had introduced or replaced 113 models, effectively turning over its product line twice. Yamaha also started with 60 models, but could only manage 37 changes to its product line in 18 months. Honda's strategy caused its sales to soar; Yamaha's sales all but dried up. The devastating defeat of Yamaha was a clear warning to Suzuki and Kawasaki not to challenge Honda's leadership. Clearly, Honda had used time to its competitive advantage.

Reducing Response Time

Honda's use of time-based competition was an obvious frontal attack representative of a full-scale product war. However, firms can use time-based competition more subtly with equally devastating results. Atlas Door used time to gain the number one competitive position in an industry previously dominated by large, established firms. Atlas makes industrial doors, a product with limitless options in width, height, and material. Instead of using time reductions to introduce new products (as did Honda), Atlas focused on reducing response time to orders.

Atlas reorganized its factories to allow for a uniform flow of products, thereby reducing the manufacturing time of each product. It also streamlined and automated order-entry, engineering, pricing, and scheduling processes. Today, Atlas can schedule and price 95 percent of telephoned orders while the caller is still on the line. Finally, Atlas developed a system to ensure that all parts necessary for shipment to a construction site would be available at the same time. As a result, Atlas can respond to an order in a few weeks; the industry average is four months. This quicker response time allows Atlas to charge premium prices. Because its time-efficient processes yield lower man-ufacturing costs, it also enjoys big profits. Atlas's competitors did not recognize the thrust of the time-based strategy and still think it will gravitate toward the industry averages as volume increases. However, the enormous lead that Atlas presently enjoys will be very difficult, perhaps impossible, to overcome.

POSITIONING STRATEGIES ▲

For given product plans and competitive priorities, the operations manager must select a **positioning strategy**. This decision determines whether the production system will be organized by grouping resources around the process or around the product. To understand this fundamental choice, look at Fig. 2.5. Each of three products has its own routing pattern (arrow), for a specified sequence of operations (circles).

(a)

(b)

(a) The Bono Tool and Die Company in Elmhurst, Illinois, has a process focus. The photo shows machines grouped together to handle all products requiring this operation. (b) Coca Cola's Atlanta, Georgia, bottling plant uses a product focus to produce 30,000 cases of Coke every day. Here cases are automatically packed with bottles, following a line flow. This operation is one of several sequential operations devoted to the same product.

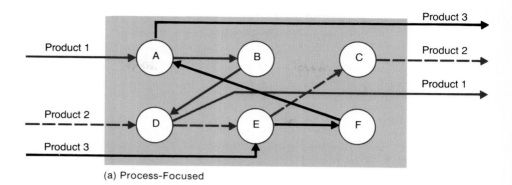

(a) Process-Focused

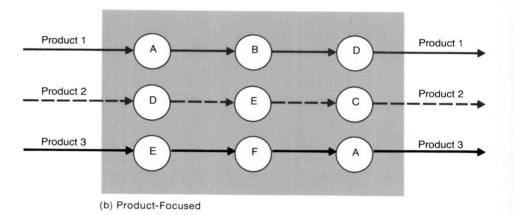

(b) Product-Focused

FIGURE 2.5 Two Different Positioning Strategies

With the **process-focused strategy**, shown in Fig. 2.5(a), the equipment and work force are organized around the process. The operations manager sets aside a single area for each process, and the product must move from one area to another. Thus products 1 and 3 must compete for the same resources at operation A, while products 2 and 3 must do the same at operation E. Note that product 1 follows an A–B–D routing pattern, product 2 follows a D–E–C pattern, and product 3 follows an E–F–A pattern.

In the **product-focused strategy**, shown in Fig. 2.5(b), the equipment and work force are organized around the product. This system creates duplication of operations, but products don't have to compete for limited resources. For example, there are two operations A in the facility, one dedicated to product 1 and one to product 3. The routing pattern for each of the three products is straightforward.

The photographs show actual facilities that are based on entirely different positioning strategies. The tool and die shop in part (a) reflects a process-focused strategy. Different types of machines are grouped together to handle all products requiring a specific function. The bottling operation in part (b) represents a product-focused strategy, in which several sequential operations are devoted to the same product.

A Continuum of Strategies

Actually, numerous positioning strategies exist between these two extremes. This continuum of choices is represented in Figure 2.6 by the diagonal from the process focus to the product focus. This figure also shows how a manager's choice relates to product volume (left to right) and flow pattern (top to bottom). Few firms position themselves too far off the diagonal. Let's find out why this is so.

Process Focus.   A process-focused strategy is appropriate to a firm offering a wide range of customized (made-to-order) products. In such situations product volume tends to be low. If the operations manager were to dedicate resources to individual products, many operations would be duplicated and resources would often be idle. It is far more efficient to organize resources around similar processes. Because each product is unique, routings vary considerably from one order to the next. The resulting flow pattern is jumbled and unpredictable.

A production system with a process focus is often called a **job shop**, as it takes on many different types of small jobs and competes on the basis of resource flexibility. Process-focused businesses in manufacturing include areospace firms and building contractors. In services, they include law firms, architectural firms, and general medical practices.

Intermediate Strategy.   Halfway between a process focus and product focus lies an intermediate strategy. Product volumes are relatively high, and batch operations can handle several customer orders at the same time. If demand is sufficiently predictable, operations can produce some standardized products or components in advance of receiving actual customer orders. The flow pattern is still jumbled, but dominant paths emerge. For example, in some parts of the facility, the manager may dedicate resources to one product or a group of similar parts. Types of businesses that utilize this strategy include heavy equipment manufacturers, garment manufacturers, caterers, automobile repair shops, and small branch offices of service facilities such as brokerage firms and advertising agencies.

Product Focus.   A product-focused strategy fits high-volume production of a few standard products. Packaging and assembly options often make products appear more diverse than they really are. For example, the same soft drink might be packaged in a bottle or a can. Cars on an assembly line might pass through the same basic operations, except for a blackwall or whitewall tire

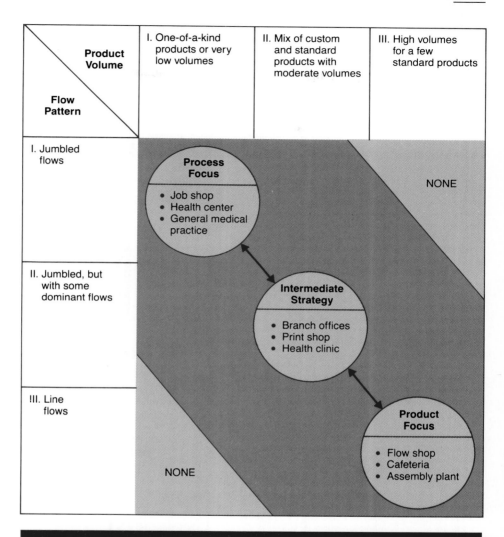

	I. One-of-a-kind products or very low volumes	II. Mix of custom and standard products with moderate volumes	III. High volumes for a few standard products
Product Volume / **Flow Pattern**			
I. Jumbled flows	**Process Focus** • Job shop • Health center • General medical practice		NONE
II. Jumbled, but with some dominant flows		**Intermediate Strategy** • Branch offices • Print shop • Health clinic	
III. Line flows	NONE		**Product Focus** • Flow shop • Cafeteria • Assembly plant

FIGURE 2.6 A Continuum of Positioning Strategies

Source: After Robert H. Hayes and Steven C. Wheelwright, "Link Manufacturing Process and Product Life Cycles," *Harvard Business Review,* January–February 1979, pp. 133–140.

option. This type of production system is often called a **flow shop** because all products follow a linear routing pattern.

High volumes and product standardization allow product-focused operations to be both specialized and efficient. Each task is designed with painstaking detail, and the resulting process moves along at a brisk pace. For example, a fast-food restaurant takes your order, prepares and serves your meal, and

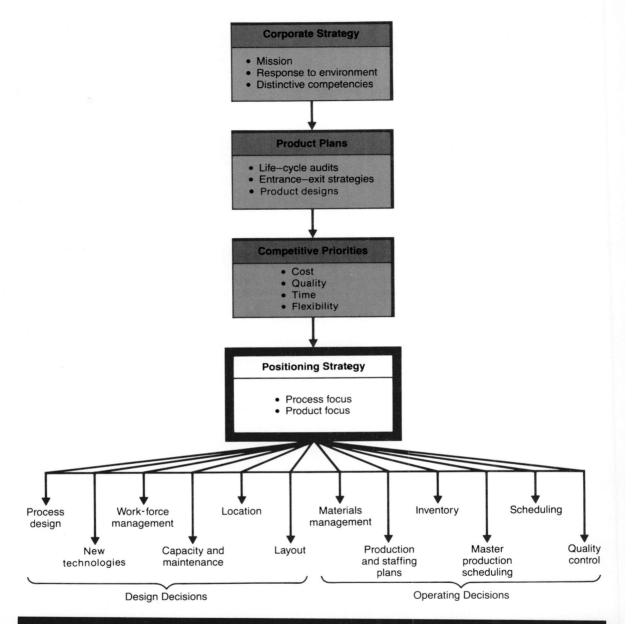

FIGURE 2.7 Positioning Strategy: The Linchpin in Operations Decisions

processes your payment much more quickly than does a large, expensive restaurant. Other product-focused businesses include automobile manufacturers, car washes, and electronic product manufacturers.

Line flows and high volumes lend themselves to highly automated facilities. Such facilities can operate round the clock in order to offset the huge capital investment required. Breweries, food processing plants, oil refineries, and public utilities are only a few of these continuous operations.

Customer Contact. In the service sector, customer contact is another factor for a manager to consider when choosing a positioning strategy. Some service facilities have more face-to-face customer contact than others. When service complexity is high and customer knowledge is low, services must be tailored to each customer's needs. The result is customized, low-volume production, more appropriate to a process-focused strategy. An intermediate strategy fits better when face-to-face contact and back-room work are balanced. For example, in the front office of a bank, customers and employees interact frequently with one another. By contrast, there is little or no customer contact in the back office, where automation and batching of work increases repeatability. Other service facilities, such as home offices, distribution centers, and power plants, involve virtually no face-to-face contact, resulting in standardized services and high volume.

Pulling It All Together

Management must link positioning strategy to product plans and competitive priorities. In process-focused plants, the emphasis is on high-performance design quality, product flexibility (see Sharma, 1987) and volume flexibility. Low price and quick delivery times are less important as competitive priorities. Thus a process focus meshes well with product plans favoring customized products, products with short life cycles, or early exit from the product life cycle. A product focus, on the other hand, is appropriate when product plans call for standard products and long life cycles. Low prices, quick delivery times, and consistent quality are the top competitive priorities. Table 2.3 (p. 62) summarizes these comparisons.

As Fig. 2.7 (opposite) shows, operations managers use positioning strategy to translate product plans and competitive priorities into decisions throughout the operations function. To give you a better idea of how process design, inventory, scheduling, and other operations decisions mesh, let's take a tour of two very different facilities: Longhorn Machine Company and Pinecrest Brewery. Each firm has a different positioning strategy, which has a far-reaching effect on how each facility is designed and operated. As you read, note how decisions are linked at each plant.

TABLE 2.3   Linking Positioning Strategy with Product Plans and Competitive Priorities

	Positioning Strategy	
High-Level Decision	**Process Focus**	**Product Focus**
Product planning	More customized products, with low volumes	More standardized products, with high volumes
	Shorter product life cycles	Longer product life cycles
	Products in earlier stages of life cycle	Products in later stages of life cycle
	An entrance–exit strategy favoring early exit	An entrance–exit strategy favoring late exit
Competitive priorities	High-performance design quality	Consistent quality
	More emphasis on product and volume flexibility	More emphasis on low price
	Long delivery times	Short delivery times

TOURING A PROCESS-FOCUSED PLANT: LONGHORN MACHINE* ▲

David Ream achieved his life-long dream in 1977 by starting his own machine and fabrication shop in San Antonio, Texas. Despite two difficult years, the firm grew steadily. Sales in 1989 exceeded $500,000. Longhorn Machine Company produces a wide variety of small metal parts, which it sells to other manufacturers in the southwest. Some 50 percent of customer orders are one of a kind. The average order is for 35 pieces, but order quantities range from 1 to 500 pieces. Longhorn competes for orders through bidding processes, with the lowest bidders usually winning the jobs. Customer delivery lead times (which Ream calls "cycle times") vary from one to four months, depending on the work involved, materials required, and capacity bottlenecks. Ream sees Longhorn's competitive priorities as producing a wide range of customized jobs, handling peaks and valleys in capacity, and consistently meeting promised due dates. Although volumes are low, unit profit margins are high. The typical order brings in $2100 in revenue. Direct labor and material costs for such an order are approximately equal and total $960. The $1140 difference covers overhead costs, such as employee benefits and equipment depreciation, as well as salaries for Ream, the accountant, and the shop supervisor—and, of course, profit.

Product planning at Longhorn takes the form of bids on new designs. One of Ream's main tasks is to decide how the job will be produced, including the

*A similar case on Norcen Industries can be found in Roger W. Schmenner, *Production/Operations Management: Concepts and Situations*, 2nd ed. Chicago: Science Research Associates, 1984.

operations to be performed and the materials to be purchased. He responds to more than 100 requests per week and wins about 10 percent of the jobs he bids on. Ream relies on two primary sources of information when preparing bids. The first is a blueprint of the detailed design, which the customer provides. If the order is repeat business, the blueprint is already on file. The second is a "routing sheet," listing each operation to be performed, along with time standards and materials costs. If Longhorn has never produced the product before, Ream makes up a new routing sheet based on the blueprint and his estimates of time requirements. He bases these estimates on similar operations performed on other products.

Process Design, Technology, and Work-force Management

Longhorn's estimates reflect actual experience. Whenever a job is released to production, it is accompanied by a blueprint, routing sheet, and a "record card." Each worker posts on the record card the amount of time spent on each operation and the quantity produced. The accountant uses these data to compute the labor cost of each job and to process payrolls. Record cards also serve as a basis for work measurement, providing a frame of reference for revising time standards for use in preparing future bids.

Longhorn uses general-purpose equipment in order to maintain flexibility. Ream estimates the value of the shop's 32 machines at only $350,000. The work force is also flexible. Most workers are trained to operate several different machines. Hourly wages are competitive, starting at $7 per hour and ranging up to $14 per hour for the most highly skilled workers. Incomes are supplemented by frequent overtime (at time-and-a-half) and bonuses. The bonus plan increases pay by about 10 percent, depending on the previous year's profits and worker seniority. Ream ruled out an individual incentive plan because of the variety of jobs and inaccuracy of time standards. Job variety affords workers considerable diversity in work activities. It also necessitates frequent interaction among the workers, shop supervisors, and Ream.

Almost as important to Ream as the bidding process is his search for ways to improve work methods and reduce costs. He and the shop supervisor strive to reduce setup times (the time to change over a machine from one job to the next), improve tooling, make (rather than buy) a component, change routing sequences, or even redesign a product. Such improvements lead to noticeable drops in cost with repeat orders. Most improvements are incremental, with no big technological advances.

Capacity, Location, and Layout

Longhorn Machine operates one full shift of 26 workers, augmented by a second shift of only six workers. Equipment capacity is the main limitation;

work overloads are handled with overtime and increased use of the second shift. Weekly usage per machine varies from 3 to 80 hours, with an average of 45. Because of variations in product mix, even the low-usage machines become bottlenecks from time to time. A **bottleneck operation**, often called a critical resource, is any operation that limits output. Ream describes the workload at most machines as "feast-or-famine." Bottlenecks shift from one machine to another, and anticipating these shifts is difficult. Equipment failures also contribute to bottlenecks. However, they are not critical, since process flexibility permits temporary rerouting to other machines.

Longhorn leases the current 50 × 100-foot building. Space is cramped and Ream is considering relocation options in San Antonio. The current layout groups workers and equipment on a functional basis. For example, there is one area for drill presses, one for welding stations, and one for brake presses. A fair amount of space is needed to store in-process jobs on the shop floor. Because routing patterns vary from job to job and an order goes to an average of 12 different work stations, materials handling paths are complex, with considerable criss-crossing. Machine operators themselves handle the materials.

Materials Management, Production Plans, and Inventory

In order to buffer operations and absorb bottlenecks, Ream quotes reasonably long delivery times to customers. These lead times average two months, even though the typical job takes only 100 work hours for all setup and processing activities. This approach creates considerable work-in-process (WIP) inventory. Most work stations have a queue of three or four jobs waiting to be started, a situation that helps decouple operations and utilize resources more efficiently.

Longhorn Machine has little influence over its suppliers because of its low volumes. Vendor relationships are informal, with no long-term purchasing agreements. Very few purchased items are stocked in inventory. This minimizes inventory levels but lengthens product delivery time. Ream is currently considering stocking some high-usage raw materials and manufactured subassemblies to cut delays. However, owing to the customized nature of the business, products are not stocked in anticipation of future customer demand. Finished goods inventories are almost nonexistent, so the firm needs no warehouses or distribution centers. As soon as an order is finished, it is shipped directly to the customer.

Production planning is informal and doesn't project very far into the future. Ream records the dollar volume of new sales received each week. Using lead-time estimates and orders already booked, he projects total monthly output three months ahead. These projections are not specific to each work station. They influence how aggressively Ream bids on new jobs and when to vary output levels. Overtime or expansion of the second shift relieves excessive backlogs.

Scheduling and Quality Control

Ream uses a manual system to release and follow up on orders. After accepting a bid, he reviews the routing sheet and blueprints. He orders materials from suppliers and tooling from the three tool and die makers in the shop. When all the necessary materials and tooling are ready, he releases the order to the shop. The routing sheet, record card, and blueprint are placed in a folder and sent to the shop supervisor, signaling that production work can begin.

Scheduling work in the shop is time-consuming and chaotic. The supervisor schedules worker assignments for only one or two days in advance. Longer schedules are of little value because of rush orders, rework problems, and bottlenecks. The supervisor paces the work, using four somewhat conflicting decision rules:

1. Try to have only one setup per job at a machine. Setup times range from 15 minutes to 5 hours, averaging 1.5 hours. About 30 percent of the work content of a job is setup, and the rest is processing. This first rule may be broken when a rush job arrives and preempts one already in progress.

2. Maximize utilization of the "automatic" machines. These machines work automatically, requiring a worker only to load and unload them. One worker can operate several such machines simultaneously, cutting costs considerably.

3. Assign jobs to the most proficient workers. Workers are more adept at some jobs than at others. During slack times, the supervisor may violate this rule to train less experienced workers on new tasks. Such cross-training is important in creating a flexible work force.

4. Toward the end of the month, expedite jobs closest to completion regardless of their due date. Ream tries to maximize the number of end-of-the-month shipments, because customers normally pay bills monthly—by the 10th. Although this rule causes what Ream calls the "end-of-month syndrome," it helps Longhorn's cash flow.

Longhorn workers are responsible for the quality of their own work, with spot checks made on outgoing shipments. Scrap and rework are sometimes a problem. In some cases, customers accept shipments deviating from the requested size. In other cases, scrap requires a second shop order to make up for the shortfall.

After an order is completed, the accountant calculates its actual labor and materials cost. When the actual cost deviates too much from standard, the accountant brings this result to Ream's attention. He investigates and often identifies ways to improve the process. In other cases, he adjusts the time standards to make them more realistic for use in preparing future bids.

TOURING A PRODUCT-FOCUSED PLANT: PINECREST BREWERY* ▲

The Pinecrest Brewery in Detroit, Michigan, began production in 1981. It is one of six Pinecrest plants located throughout the country and services an eight-state region in the midwest. The brewery produces five million barrels of beer per year (one barrel is equivalent to 31 gallons). It produces two types of beer (regular and light), which are packaged in cans, bottles, and kegs. Different types of lids, bottle sizes and shapes, and cardboard containers generate more than 80 unique products. Each product is produced in high volume, although packaging can be made to order for large customers. The firm's customers are 105 wholesalers, who in turn sell to retailers in their respective areas. Although the 80 product options permit some product differentiation, the top priorities at Pinecrest are on-time delivery, consistent quality, and competitive prices.

Process Design, Technology, and Work-Force Management

The manufacturing process is capital intensive, with plant and equipment costing $175 million. With a work force of only 370, plant investment is almost $473,000 per employee. More than one third of the work force, including staff and managers, is salaried. Despite the art associated with brewing, automation has increased considerably over the last two decades. Without these advances, the work force at the Detroit plant would be four times as large. Equipment is now highly specialized and technologically advanced. The process flow is linear, following a one-directional routing. The two main production stages are brewing and packaging.

The brewing stage is under the control of the brewmaster. The cycle time to brew a batch is one full month. It begins by producing *wort* from malting barley and other grains. The grains are milled and then placed in huge stainless steel vessels, where brewing water is added. Boiling, separating, cooling, and filtering operations follow, with hops and carbon dioxide added along the way. The end result is beer, which is aged from seven to twelve days before packaging.

The packaging stage is continuous, with no buildup of inventory between successive operations. The process begins by piping beer to the two canning lines, three bottling lines, or single keg line. Equipment on each line fills, caps, and pasteurizes the beer. At the end of the can and bottle lines, the output is boxed into six-packs or cases and then placed on pallets for outbound ship-

---

*A similar case on Jos. Schlitz Brewing Company can be found in Roger W. Schmenner, *Production/Operations Management: Concepts and Situations*, 2nd ed. Chicago: Science Research Associates, 1984.

ment. These are high-speed operations: The can-line rate is almost 100,000 cans per hour.

Most of the work force involved in the brewing and packaging processes play a monitoring role, watching the equipment and instrument panels. Workers tend to do the same job day after day, with little diversity. Even though employees may move from one packaging line to another, depending on the production schedule, the work hardly varies. Workers are paid hourly rates, and as output is equipment-paced, there is no incentive system. Job changes are won on the basis of seniority, and most involve workers moving from the night shift to the day shift. Union relations are satisfactory, with some 40 grievances per year. Owing to the high capital intensity of the brewery, management is particularly sensitive to maintaining good labor–management relations. However, information flows primarily from management to the workers and is provided infrequently. The main information flowing upward concerns equipment maintenance problems. Work measurement is not important at Pinecrest Brewery because output rates are well known and routings are uniform.

Capacity, Location, and Layout

The Detroit plant is located on 156 acres of land and contains more than one million square feet of floor space. The plant operates three shifts per day, five days per week. Approximately 30 percent of the floor space is used for brewing; the remainder is used for the packaging lines and the warehouse. Equipment utilization is a top concern of management. Capacities are well understood and carefully balanced. The line fillers, which are particularly expensive at $500,000 each, are the limiting factor in each line. Machines after the fillers in the lines have somewhat higher output rates, providing some cushion against temporary failure. Equipment maintenance is vital. The maintenance department monitors equipment design and installation and maintains it to minimize unexpected failures. Maintenance personnel respond quickly to equipment failures when they do occur.

Although economies of scale are significant, Pinecrest Brewery also has high enough sales volumes to warrant multiple plants, which are strategically located throughout the country. Having plants in several locations reduces the company's transportation costs and shortens transportation lead times to wholesalers. High volumes and transportation costs encouraged suppliers to build plants close to Pinecrest's Detroit plant. Both inbound and outbound shipments are made by rail and truck. Docks can handle 30 freight cars and 19 trucks at the same time. The plant was designed so that 75 percent of the output could be shipped by either mode. Currently 60 percent of the shipments are made by rail.

The layout at Pinecrest Brewery follows the product flow. Resources in the packaging area are grouped by type of product. Most materials handling is done by automated conveyors.

Materials Management, Production Plans, and Inventory

Production planning varies by manufacturing stage. The brewing operation produces to stock, whereas the packaging lines tend to produce to specific customer orders. Pinecrest promises delivery times of from two to six weeks, but the brewing cycle itself takes four weeks. This forces the brewmaster to produce to forecast rather than booked customer orders. Forecasts are closely monitored, so that enough of each type of beer is available to support the packaging lines without creating excessive work-in-process inventory. One difficulty is seasonal demand; the peak demand in the summer months is double the demand in the winter. In order to smooth production rates and more fully utilize equipment capacity, Pinecrest builds up excess inventory in the slack season and stores this inventory primarily in wholesaler warehouses. This strategy is feasible because pasteurized beer does not spoil.

Pinecrest Brewery prefers to ship packaged beer directly from the line to wholesalers, even though the company has a plant warehouse. Approximately 60 percent of the output is shipped directly. The rest stays at the plant only a short time, and the average finished inventory there represents only two days of supply. Customer relationships are formalized. Each wholesaler orders once a month for delivery four weeks later. Each order specifies the desired product codes, quantities, and due dates. The Detroit plant uses a computer system to monitor the inventory of each wholesaler, to forecast future sales, and even to make suggestions to wholesalers on stocking policies.

Vendor relationships are long-term and formalized. Corporate headquarters negotiates long-term contracts for most major raw materials, although each plant contracts locally for miscellaneous maintenance, repair, and operating (MRO) items. Firm orders are issued to vendors to cover output levels planned for the next month. Tentative orders for two more months are given to suppliers for forward visibility. Avoiding materials shortages is crucial, and raw materials inventories are carefully managed. Much depends on supplier lead times and dependability. Pinecrest Brewery also takes advantage of some quantity discounts. Less than eight hours' supply of bottles and cans is needed. The inventory of bottle labels, on the other hand, averages a five-month's supply because of low holding costs and significant quantity discounts.

At the Detroit plant the same department that handles customer and vendor orders also plans production levels. Production planning goals are to meet customer orders as closely as possible, make full use of capacity, and maintain a stable work force. Monthly plans for exact sizes and sequences for each beer and packaging combination are developed in detail.

Scheduling and Quality Control

Each packaging line is scheduled one full month in advance. The scheduling process begins with the receipt of the next month's orders from wholesalers. Schedulers try to satisfy these orders, while maximizing equipment utilization and avoiding an excessive number of setups. Three decision rules are used:

1. Schedule lines so packaging lines are working with the same type of beer.
2. For a given line, run together customer orders calling for the same packaging sizes and types (such as quart bottles), rather than frequently changing over from one size to another.
3. Run both canning lines at the same time; the number of workers needed on the second line is less than if it were operated when the first line is idle.

Using these rules, schedulers determine the start and finish time for the different runs on each line, while trying to satisfy all wholesaler requests. When the schedule is finalized, wholesaler delivery requests are acknowledged, and delivery times are specified. Some deviation from requested delivery times is inevitable: About 20 percent must be revised, but no deviation involves a shift of more than two weeks. Pinecrest Brewery takes pride in filling over 98 percent of its acknowledged orders on time.

Even though schedules are planned a month in advance, some minor changes are tolerated in order to respond to revised customer requests. Usually, swaps between wholesalers can be arranged. Schedule modifications tend to be infrequent and minor. At no time are changes allowed that affect labor requirements scheduled for less than one week ahead.

Pinecrest Brewery emphasizes quality control and has a quality control staff of 30 people who provide services round the clock. More than 1000 lab tests are performed on each batch brewed. Quality control personnel are authorized to stop production whenever corrective action is needed. For example, tests on the number of yeast cells during fermentation are made every three hours, but samples from the canning line are taken hourly. If a sample from a can fails to meet the standard, all output since the last inspection is systematically checked. All cans failing inspection are discarded. Because of the vigilance of the quality control department, large quantities are rarely lost.

All Pinecrest Brewery plants are evaluated as cost centers rather than profit centers. The reason is that, with its geographical market fixed, a plant has no control over sales. A variety of performance measures are assessed weekly, comparing actual results with goals. These measures include barrels produced per week, cost per barrel, quality losses, worker absenteeism, complaints from wholesalers, a taste test, and on-time delivery.

LINKAGES AT LONGHORN MACHINE AND PINECREST BREWERY ▲

Clearly, Longhorn Machine and Pinecrest Brewery utilize different positioning strategies. Product plans and competitive priorities on which these strategies are based differ as well. Longhorn has a process focus. The firm's product plans are for low-volume, customized products. Pinecrest has a product focus. The product volumes at Pinecrest are huge: 155 million gallons per year. Longhorn's competitive priorities center on flexibility. The average delivery time of two months far exceeds the average work content of 100 hours. The opposite is true at Pinecrest where competitive priorities center on price and delivery.

At Pinecrest the delivery time of two to four weeks compares favorably with a four-week brewing cycle. The sharp contrast between Longhorn and Pinecrest gives a sense of how decisions in operations must mesh.

Congruent Operations Decisions

Table 2.4 contrasts the types of decisions made at Longhorn and Pinecrest.

Technological choices can differ significantly according to the particular positioning strategy. To maintain flexibility, Longhorn selected more general-purpose equipment. We can measure the firm's capital intensity by dividing the value of the equipment ($315,000) by the number of employees (32). This translates into almost $10,000 per worker. The amount is but a fraction of the $473,000 per worker at Pinecrest. In order to be cost competitive, Pinecrest must use automation and technology to the fullest.

Capacity policies at the two companies also are quite different. Equipment utilization is much lower at Longhorn, with the average machine operating only 45 hours per week. Unexpected bottlenecks, rush orders, and rework problems are commonplace. At Pinecrest the average machine operates 120 hours per week (three shifts per day). Bottlenecks and other uncertainties are rare, and thus the firm needs less cushion to guard against them. The process's

TABLE 2.4 Linkages at Longhorn and Pinecrest		
Corporate Decision Area	**Process Focus at Longhorn**	**Product Focus at Pinecrest**
Product plan	Low-volume, customized products	High-volume, standardized products
Competitive priorities	Product and volume flexibility	Low price and fast delivery
Operations Decision Area		
Technology	General-purpose equipment and labor intensive	Specialized equipment and capital intensive
Capacity	Lower utilization and big cushion	Higher utilization and small cushion
Materials management	Informal supplier and customer relationships	Formal supplier and customer relationships
Inventory	Considerable work-in-process (WIP) inventory	Little inventory tolerated
Scheduling	Fluid	Planned far ahead

high capital intensity makes slack capacity very expensive. With each filler line valued at $500,000, high capacity utilization is naturally a top concern of Pinecrest's management.

Materials management at Longhorn is only informally related to suppliers and customers. Longhorn's volumes are too small to give the company much clout. By contrast, Pinecrest negotiates long-term contracts with its suppliers of most major raw materials. The company requires customers (105 whole-salers) to place their orders one month in advance. It may even modify delivery requests somewhat to maximize efficiency.

Inventory decisions also link directly to positioning strategy. To decouple operations and deal with the jumbled flows of a process focus, Longhorn allows large amounts of work-in-process inventory to accumulate on the shop floor. Such excesses are not needed or tolerated with the line flows at Pinecrest. Forecasts are closely monitored to minimize WIP inventory. For the more expensive raw materials, such as bottles and cans, less than eight hour's inventory is held.

The process focus at Longhorn requires more fluid scheduling procedures. Detailed plans are not made for more than a day or two ahead because of the uncertainties involved. This reactive, crisis-oriented scheduling process is not found at Pinecrest. There, the concern for top efficiency and the simplicity of line flows demand elaborate scheduling and day-to-day monitoring of performance. Each packaging line is scheduled one full month in advance.

SOLVED PROBLEMS

1. The owner of a small manufacturing business has patented a new device for washing dishes and cleaning dirty kitchen sinks. Before trying to commercialize the device and add it to her existing product line, she wants reasonable assurance of success. Variable cost is estimated at $7 per unit produced and sold and fixed costs per year at $56,000.

   a. If the selling price is set at $25, how many units must be produced and sold to break even? We use both the algebraic and graphic approaches to get our answer.

   b. Forecasted sales for the first year are 10,000 units, if the price is reduced to $15. What would be the product's total contribution to profits in the first year, with this pricing strategy?

Solution

   a. Beginning with the algebraic approach, we get:

$$Q = \frac{F}{p - c} = \frac{56,000}{25 - 7} = 3111 \text{ units}$$

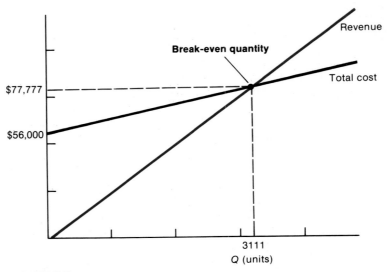

FIGURE 2.8

Using the graphic approach, shown in Fig. 2.8, we first draw two lines:

$$\text{Total Revenue} = 25Q;$$
$$\text{Total Cost} = 56,000 + 7Q$$

The two lines intersect at $Q = 3111$ units, the break-even quantity.

b. Total profit contribution = Total revenue − Total cost

$$= pQ - (F + cQ)$$
$$= 15(10,000) - [56,000 + 7(10,000)]$$
$$= \$24,000$$

2. A company is screening three new product ideas. Resource constraints allow only one of them to be commercialized. Given the performance criteria and ratings in Table 2.5, and assuming equal weights for each performance criterion, which product should management choose?

Solution

Each criterion receives 20 points (arbitrarily).

Product	Calculation	Total Score
A	20(0.3) + 20(0.7) + 20(1.0) + 20(0.4) + 20(0.4)	= 56
B	20(0.9) + 20(0.8) + 20(0.4) + 20(0.7) + 20(0.6)	= 68
C	20(0.2) + 20(0.6) + 20(0.8) + 20(0.6) + 20(0.5)	= 54

The best choice is product B. Products A and C are well behind in terms of total weighted score.

TABLE 2.5

Performance Criterion	Rating		
	Product A	Product B	Product C
1. Demand uncertainty and project risk	0.3	0.9	0.2
2. Similarity to present products	0.7	0.8	0.6
3. Expected return on investment (ROI)	1.0	0.4	0.8
4. Compatibility with current manufacturing process	0.4	0.7	0.6
5. Competitive advantage	0.4	0.6	0.5
	56	*68*	*54*

FORMULA REVIEW

1. Break-even quantity:

$$Q = \frac{F}{p - c}$$

2. Total profit contribution:

$$pQ - (F + cQ)$$

CHAPTER HIGHLIGHTS

- Product planning is an ongoing activity that defines the products (goods or services) to be produced.

- A product's life cycle consists of five stages: product planning, introduction, growth, maturity, and decline.

- There are three strategies for when to enter and exit a product's life cycle. Each places a different demand on the production system. Entering early and exiting late forces a transition from flexibility to low cost.

- The product planning stage involves idea generation, screening, development and testing, and final product design. These steps must fit the firm's mission, which may prove to be too narrow or too broad and have to be modified.

- The preference matrix and break-even analysis, while not limited to product planning, are two techniques used to help screen new product lines.

- Competitive priorities state the dimensions on which the firm should excel. There are seven priorities: low price, high-performance design, consistent quality, fast delivery time, on-time delivery, product flexibility, and volume flexibility. Trade-offs among them are often necessary. Management must judge which trade-offs are best, along with the firm's distinctive competencies, when establishing desired levels for each dimension.

- The positioning strategy that meshes best with product plans and competitive priorities should be selected. The continuum of choices ranges from a process focus to a product focus.
- A process focus organizes resources around the process. This focus fits low volumes and jumbled flow patterns. A product focus organizes resources around specific products, resulting in straightforward flow patterns. It fits high volumes and standardized products.
- The more the customer contact at a service facility, the greater is the tendency toward a process focus.

- Tours of two companies, Longhorn Machine and Pinecrest Brewery, demonstrate how positioning strategy acts as a linchpin in operations decisions. Positioning strategy helps managers to translate corporate decisions into operations decisions.
- A process focus fits with low volumes, high flexibility, general-purpose equipment, labor-intensive technologies, lower capacity utilization, informal relationships with suppliers and customers, large work-in-process inventories, and fluid schedules. The opposite is true of a product focus.

KEY TERMS

bottleneck operation 64	fixed cost 47	preference matrix 45	product-focused strategy 57
break-even analysis 46	flow shop 59	process-focused strategy 57	repeatability 52
competitive priorities 49	job shop 58	product flexibility 52	sensitivity analysis 48
entrance–exit strategy 37	life-cycle audit 36	product life cycle 35	variable cost 47
	positioning strategy 56	product planning 33	volume flexibility 52
	preemptive pricing 38		

STUDY QUESTIONS

1. A sign on the way to an abandoned mine reads: "Choose your ruts carefully; you will be in them for the next 15 miles." How does this caution apply to product planning and choosing competitive priorities?

2. How does the concept of product life cycles illustrate the ongoing need for product planning?

3. How does the decision on when to enter and exit a product's life cycle affect the operations function? With which entrance–exit strategy would a product focus make most sense?

4. The Sealtight Company is a well-diversified manufacturer in the packaging business. It makes a variety of packaging materials and sells them to industrial buyers. Management is currently conducting a life-cycle audit to identify the current stage of each product in its life cycle. The profiles for two products are shown in Table 2.6.
   a. In which stage is product A? Product B? Explain your answers.
   b. For which product would low price be a higher competitive priority? Why?

5. Give an example of each component of the "service bundle" for each of the following products.
   a. An insurance policy   c. Dental work
   b. An airline trip

6. What dimensions of competitive priorities seem to be the most important for each of the following companies?
   a. McDonald's
   b. Toyota
   c. A manufacturer of specialty glues tailored to the needs of industrial buyers in the furniture and mobile-home industries

7. Explain how time-based competition can be used to gain a market niche.

8. What positioning strategy (process focus or product focus) seems best for each of the following types of companies? Briefly defend your choice.
   a. A builder of skyscrapers and bridges
   b. A paper mill
   c. A microwave manufacturer
   d. A manufacturer of a wide variety of men's suits

9. Why do firms offering more customized, low-volume products tend to
   a. compete less on short customer delivery times and low prices?
   b. be less capital intensive?
   c. maintain larger capacity cushions?

TABLE 2.6

Product	Performance Measure	This Year's Performance	Change over Last Year	Average Annual Change over Last Four Years
A	Annual sales	$42.1 million	−3.1%	+1.2%
	Unit price	1.53/lb	+0.0	+0.5
	Unit profit margin	0.22/lb	−2.1	−0.5
	Total profit contribution	6.0 million	−7.4	+0.2
B	Annual sales	5.4 million	+72.1	+35.0
	Unit price	1.30/lb	+7.0	+6.8
	Unit profit margin	0.70/lb	+12.1	+15.1
	Total profit contribution	2.9 million	+80.1	+37.2

10. Why do firms with a product focus tend to
   a. plan production and inventory levels further into the future?
   b. have more formalized supplier relationships?
   c. concentrate inventory less at the work-in-process level?

11. Table 2.4 describes seven ways in which corporate and operations decisions at Longhorn Machine and Pinecrest Brewery link with positioning strategy. State three other ways that decisions within the operations function are linked to positioning strategy. (See Fig. 2.7.) Explain your reasoning.

12. Two forces are at work in the health-care industry. First, there is pressure to make heavy investments in new equipment to keep up with rapid advances in technology. Second, there is pressure for shorter patient stays and more outpatient treatment, thereby helping curb escalating health costs. Use break-even analysis to describe how these forces change fixed costs, break-even inpatient volumes, and the financial position of the typical hospital.

PROBLEMS

Review Problems

1. Mary Williams, owner of Williams Products, is evaluating whether to introduce a new product line. After thinking through the production process and the cost of raw materials and new equipment, Williams estimates the variable cost of each unit produced and sold at $4 and the fixed cost per year at $40,000.
   a. If the selling price is set at $15, how many units must be produced and sold to break even? Use both the graphic and algebraic approaches to get your answer.
   b. Williams forecasts sales of 7000 units for the first year, if the selling price is set at $12. What would be the total contribution to profits from this new product during the first year?
   c. If the selling price is set at $10, Williams forecasts that first-year sales would increase to 10,000 units. Which pricing strategy ($10 or $12) would result in the greatest total contribution to profits?
   d. What other considerations would be crucial to the final decision about making and marketing the new product?

2. A product at the Jennings Company has enjoyed reasonable sales volumes, but its contributions to profits have been disappointing. In 1988, 17,500 units were produced and sold. The selling price is $20 per unit, c is $15, and F is $75,000.
   a. What is the break-even quantity for this product? Use both the graphic and algebraic approaches to get your answer.
   b. Jennings is considering ways to either stimulate sales volumes or decrease variable costs. He feels that it is possible to increase sales by 30 percent or reduce c to 85 percent of

its current level. Which alternative leads to higher contributions to profits, assuming that each is equally costly to implement? *Hint:* Calculate profits for both alternatives and identify the one having the greatest profits.

c. What is the percentage change in the profit margin generated by each alternative in (b)? How does this explain the result you obtained in (b)?

3. The Franklin Electronics Company is a small manufacturer of electronic products. Its executive committee is considering the possibility of introducing a novelty tape recorder. The production department estimates that buying the necessary equipment would increase fixed cost per year by $15,000. The accounting department projects that the product would have to absorb another $20,000 for the additional costs of executive salaries, rent, and taxes. The marketing department believes that the initial advertising budget would have to be $30,000 per year and that its sales budget would increase by another $35,000 per year. The new product would be priced at $30 F.O.B. factory with no quantity discounts. The various operating departments expect the variable cost for labor and materials to be $18 per unit.

a. How many units must be produced and sold for the company to break even?

b. If the advertising budget were increased to $45,000, what would the break-even quantity be?

c. A more automated production process could be used. It would double production's fixed cost, while reducing the total variable cost per unit from $18 to $14. Would this more advanced technology decrease or increase the break-even quantity? Must this always be the case?

4. John Anderson, vice-president of Tri-Arrow Enterprises, has the following estimates of production and sales for the upcoming year for one of Tri-Arrow's products.

$$\text{Expected sales} = 13,000 \text{ units}$$
$$\text{Fixed cost} = \$250,000/\text{yr}$$
$$\text{Variable cost} = \$100/\text{unit}$$
$$\text{Selling price} = \$125/\text{unit}$$

a. What is the expected contribution to profits of this product for the upcoming year?

b. Anderson believes that variable costs may increase because of an increase in raw-material costs. By how much can variable costs increase and still allow this product to positively contribute to profits for the next year?

c. Anderson believes that fixed cost can be reduced by decreasing the projected marketing budget (with no ill effect on expected sales). If variable costs increase by the amount calculated in (b), by how much would fixed cost have to decrease in order to achieve the contribution to profits originally projected?

5. The Forsite Company is screening three new product ideas. Resource constraints allow only one idea to be commercialized at the present time. The following estimates have been made for the five performance criteria that management feels are most important.

Performance Criterion	Rating		
	Product A	Product B	Product C
1. Capital equipment investment required	0.6	0.8	0.3
2. Expected return on investment (ROI)	0.4	0.6	0.9
3. Compatability with current work-force skills	0.5	0.9	0.3
4. Competitive advantage	1.0	0.4	0.6
5. Compatibility with current EPA requirements	0.2	1.0	0.2

a. Calculate a total weighted score for each alternative, using a preference matrix and assuming equal weights for each performance criterion. Which alternative is best? Worst?

b. Suppose that the expected ROI is given twice the weight assigned to each of the remaining criteria? [Sum of weights should remain the same as in (a).] Does this affect the ranking of the three candidate products?

6. You are in charge of analyzing five new product ideas and have been given the information shown in Table 2.7.

TABLE 2.7

Performance Criterion	Rating (1 = worst; 10 = best)				
	Product A	Product B	Product C	Product D	Product E
1. Compatability with current man-ufacturing processes	9	6	3	8	8
2. Project risk	2	10	4	6	7
3. Market potential	6	3	7	5	2
4. Unit project margin	8	4	9	1	6

- Management has decided that criterion 2 and criterion 3 are equally important, criterion 1 is five times as important as criterion 2, and criterion 4 is three times as important as criterion 2.
- Only two new products can be introduced.
- A product can be introduced only if it exceeds 70 percent of the total possible points.
  a. What are the weights on the criteria, if they must sum to 100?
  b. What is the threshold on weighted scores?
  c. Which product ideas do you recommend?

Advanced Problems

Problems 8–11 require reading of Supplement 1, and Problems 12–14 require prior reading of Supplement 2. A computer package is helpful for Problems 8–13, one is mandatory for Problem 14.

7. Melissa Graham has the following data concerning the production of one of her company's best selling products, the Electrotype typewriter.

Year	Total Cost	Units Sold	Selling Price per Unit
1985	$100,000	1000	$115
1986	$140,000	1500	$115
1987	$130,000	1250	$125
1988	$110,000	1200	$125

  a. Determine the break-even quantity using the graphic approach.
  b. Assume that the data from 1985 and 1986 are most representative of the Electrotype operation. What are the annual fixed cost and the variable cost per unit? *Hint:* Solve the following two linear equations for the two unknowns.

$$F + c(1000) = \$100,000$$
$$F + c(1500) = \$140,000$$

8. The following information is available about a product that Highlife Company wishes to introduce.

- The expected product life span is five years. The projected annual demand (in units) for the next five years is 10,000, 12,000, 14,000, 13,000, and 7000, respectively.
- The selling price is $7.50 and the variable cost per unit is $5.00.
- The tax rate is 50 percent.
- The desired rate of return is 12 percent.
- The initial equipment investment for this product is $50,000 and the salvage value of the equipment is $5000.
- Assume straight-line depreciation.
  a. Determine the incremental after-tax cash flows attributable to this product over its life.
  b. Should this product be accepted using the NPV method of analysis?
  c. If management has set a payback period of two years, should the product be accepted?

9. Joan Ruiz designs and makes custom jewelry, which she sells at craft shows on weekends. If Joan purchases a new kiln, she can add ceramic earrings and necklaces to her product line. Based on previous experience, she could produce this line of jewelry for only about four years before she or her customers tire of it. The kiln she wants costs $2400, but Joan estimates that it would be worth $800 in salvage values at the end of four years. If she buys the kiln, she will also have to invest $600 in additional inventory, for a total investment of $3000. At the end of four years, she would liquidate the inventory and get the $600 back. Joan thinks she can sell pairs of earrings or necklaces for $6.00 apiece. She estimates her variable cost at $4.50 per item (a pair of earrings counts as one item). The cost to run the kiln, $300 per year, is her only incremental fixed cost, except for depreciation. Joan believes that she can sell 50 of these items at every craft show. She goes to 20 craft shows every year. Joan wants this investment to earn at least 16 percent. Assume that her tax rate is 50 percent. Calculate the following and make a recommendation concerning her potential investment.

   a. Annual after-tax income
   b. Incremental after-tax cash flows attributable to this expansion of her product line for four years
   c. Net present value of this investment
   d. Payback period

10. Suppose that Joan's jewelry (Problem 9) becomes extremely popular, and she is able to sell 100 items at every craft show for $8.00 apiece. Recalculate your answers in Problem 9. Do these new figures change your recommendation? Explain.

11. The expected product life of Mass Media's new miniature television is 10 years. Annual demand forecasts (units) are as follows:

Year 1	100	Year 6	200
Year 2	100	Year 7	250
Year 3	125	Year 8	200
Year 4	150	Year 9	100
Year 5	175	Year 10	50

- The selling price is expected to be $150.00 for the first three years, $140 for the next three years, and $100 for the remaining four years. The variable cost per unit is $85.00 for all years.
- Mass Media's tax rate is 50 percent.
- Mass Media's desired rate of return is 16 percent.
- The initial capital investment is $20,000, and the salvage value at the end of 10 years is $5000.

- Assume straight-line depreciation.
   a. Determine the after-tax cash flows for this product.
   b. Based on an NPV analysis, should this product be introduced?
   c. If the payback period for Mass Media is five years, should this product be introduced?

12. The Trim-Look Company makes several lines of skirts, dresses, and sport coats for women. Recently it was suggested that the company reevaluate its South Islander line and allocate its resources to those products that would maximize contribution to profits and overhead. Each product must pass through the cutting and sewing departments. In addition, each product in the South Islander line requires the same polyester fabric. The following data were collected for the study.

Product	Processing Time (hr)		Material (yd)
	Cutting	Sewing	
Skirt	1	1	1
Dress	3	4	1
Sport coat	4	6	4

   The cutting department has 100 hours of capacity, sewing has 180 hours, and 60 yards of material are available. Each skirt contributes $5 to profits and overhead; each dress, $17; and each sport coat, $30.

   a. Specify the objective function and constraints for this problem.
   b. Solve the problem using the simplex method.

13. Consider Problem 12 further.
   a. How much would you be willing to pay for
     i. an extra hour of cutting time?
     ii. an extra hour of sewing time?
     iii. an extra yard of material?

     Explain your responses to each question.
   b. Determine the range of right-hand-side values over which the shadow price would be valid for each of the following constraints.
     i. Cutting
     ii. Material

14. The Butterfield Company makes a variety of hunting knives. Each knife is processed on four machines. The following are the processing times required and machine capacities.

| Knife | Processing Time (hr) | | | |
	Machine 1	Machine 2	Machine 3	Machine 4
A	0.05	0.10	0.15	0.05
B	0.15	0.10	0.05	0.05
C	0.20	0.05	0.10	0.20
D	0.15	0.10	0.10	0.10
E	0.05	0.10	0.10	0.05
Capacity (hr)	1500	1400	1600	1500

Each product contains a different amount of two basic raw materials. Raw material 1 costs $0.50 per ounce, and raw material 2 costs $1.50 per ounce. There are 75,000 ounces of raw material 1 and 100,000 ounces of raw material 2 available.

Knife	Raw Material 1 (oz/unit)	Raw Material 2 (oz/unit)
A	4	2
B	6	8
C	1	3
D	2	5
E	6	10

The selling price of each knife is:

Knife	Selling Price (per unit)
A	$15.00
B	25.50
C	14.00
D	19.50
E	27.00

a. If the objective is to maximize profit, specify the objective function and constraints for the problem. Assume that labor costs are negligible.
b. Solve the problem using the simplex method, with a computer package.

SELECTED REFERENCES

Chase, Richard B., and David A. Tansik, "Customer Contact Model for Organization Design," *Management Science,* vol. 29, no. 9 (September 1983), pp. 1037–1050.

Harrigan, Kathryn R., *Strategic Flexibility.* Lexington, Mass.: Lexington Books, 1985.

Hayes, Robert H., and Roger W. Schmenner, "How Should You Organize Manufacturing?" *Harvard Business Review* (January–February 1978), pp. 105–108.

Hayes, Robert H., and Steven C. Wheelwright, "Link Manufacturing Process and Product Life Cycles," *Harvard Business Review* (January–February 1979), pp. 133–140.

Hudson R. G., J. C. Chambers, and R. G. Johnson, "New Product Planning Decisions Under Uncertainty," *Interfaces,* vol. 8, no. 1, part 2 (November 1977), pp. 82–96.

Leavitt, Theodore, "The Industrialization of Service," *Harvard Business Review* (September–October 1976), pp. 63–74.

Miller, Jeffrey G., and Aleda V. Roth, "Manufacturing Strategies: Executive Summary of the 1988 North American Manufacturing Futures Survey," Boston University, 1988.

Powell, Gary N., and George A. Johnson, "An Expectancy-Equity Model of Productive System Performance," *Journal of Operations Management,* vol. 1, no. 1 (August 1980), pp. 47–56.

Roth, Aleda V., and Marjolijn van der Velde, *The Future of Retail Banking Delivery Systems.* Rolling Meadows, Ill.: Bank Administration Institute, 1988.

Sasser, W. Earl, R. Paul Olsen, and D. Daryl Wyckoff, *Management of Service Operations.* Boston: Allyn and Bacon, 1978.

Schmenner, Roger W., *Production/Operations Management: Concepts and Situations,* 2nd ed. Chicago: Science Research Associates, 1984.

Sharma, Deven, "Manufacturing Strategy: An Empirical Analysis." Unpublished dissertation, Ohio State University, 1987.

Skinner, Wickham, *Manufacturing in the Corporate Strategy.* New York: John Wiley and Sons, 1978.

Stalk, George Jr., "Time—The Next Source of Competitive Advantage," *Harvard Business Review* (July–August 1988), pp. 41–51.

Swamidass, Paul M. "Manufacturing Strategy, Environmental Uncertainty and Performance: A Path Analytic Model," *Management Science,* vol. 33, no. 4 (April 1987), pp. 509–524.

Taylor, Sam G., "Are the Process Industries Different?" *23rd Annual Conference Proceedings,* American Production and Inventory Control Society (October 1980), Los Angeles, pp. 94–96.

Wheelwright, Steven C., "Reflecting Corporate Strategy in Manufacturing Decisions," *Business Horizons* (February 1978), pp. 57–65.

Wheelwright, Steven C., and Robert H. Hayes, "Competing Through Manufacturing," *Harvard Business Review* (January–February 1985), pp. 99–109.

CHAPTER 3

QUALITY MANAGEMENT

 Chapter Outline

Key Questions for Managers

How do consumers perceive the quality of our products?

How can we best meet the quality levels dictated by our competitive strategies?

What can we do to reduce the high costs of poor quality?

How can we include employees in the quality improvement process?

What factors in our operations system are causing major quality problems?

uality has become an issue of major concern for operations managers. Recall in Chapter 2 (Fig. 2.4) that North American manufacturers put quality at the top of their priority list for the future. Thus quality has become a competitive weapon. This emphasis on quality doesn't mean that managers can ignore important trade-offs between it and cost, time, and flexibility. The challenge for top managers today therefore is to produce quality products or services efficiently. In essence, managers must decide on the level and reliability (or consistency) of quality to provide. Viewed in this manner, quality management encompasses virtually every topic that we discuss in this book. It puts operations managers squarely in the middle of top-management goal setting and policy making because it is operations—in conjunction with the other functional areas in an organization—that must meet the challenge. In this chapter we explore the competitive implications of quality, focusing on the prevention of quality problems and the costs associated with quality failures. We conclude with some prescriptions for quality excellence provided by respected consultants in the field.

WHAT IS QUALITY? ▲

In Chapter 2 we identified two dimensions of **quality** as competitive priorities: high-performance design and consistent quality. These dimensions are not definitions of quality. Rather, they characterize an organization's competitive thrust. Strategic plans that recognize quality as an essential competitive priority must be based on some operational definition of quality. This task is complicated by the fact that producer and consumer definitions of quality often differ. In this section we briefly discuss these definitions of quality and emphasize the importance of bridging the gap between consumer expectations of quality and operating capabilities.

Producer Definitions of Quality

Within an organization, quality typically means *conformance to specifications*. In manufacturing, for example, a tolerance is specified for the critical dimensions of every part produced. The quality of a part is measured by how close it conforms to these specifications. Parts that fail to meet them are either reworked or scrapped, resulting in consistent quality. Specifications can also define high-performance design. For example, Seagate, a manufacturer of disk drives, emphasizes high-performance design by advertising that its product has a mean time between failure of 30,000 hours. The point is that both consistent quality and high-performance design can be translated into specifications and measured at each step of the manufacturing process. Similarly, in services, quality is maintained by meeting service standards. Holiday Inn, for example, assures the traveler of the same level of comfort and cleanliness at its facilities throughout the world.

Consumer Definitions of Quality

Customers typically define quality as *value*, that is, how well the product or service serves its intended purpose at a price they are willing to pay. Another definition is *fitness for use*, or how well the product performs. These definitions are similar and involve the customer's expectations of the product or service. In assessing value or fitness for use, the customer may consider various aspects of quality, as shown in Table 3.1.

Hardware.   In service industries, hardware quality relates to the interior and exterior aesthetics of the location where a service is provided and to the condition of the equipment used to provide the service. In manufacturing industries, hardware quality refers to product characteristics such as appearance, style, durability, reliability, craftsmanship, and serviceability. Thus both workmanship and product design are judged by the consumer.

TABLE 3.1 Examples of Consumer Perceptions of Quality		
Quality Aspect	**Service**	**Manufacturing**
Hardware	Style and appearance of tableware at a restaurant	Visible appearance of the product
	Age of equipment in a dentist's office	Ease of installation and use of the product
Product or service support	Number of errors in bank statements	Accuracy of billing procedures and ease of correcting errors
	Responsiveness to expressed or implied warranties	Truthfulness in advertising
Psychological impressions	Courtesy of the bellman at a hotel	Knowledge of the salesperson regarding product performance
	Sympathy of the clerk at the customer complaints desk of a retail store	Reputation of the brand name

Support.   Often the product or service support provided by the company is just as important as the quality of the product or service itself. Customers can get very upset with a company if financial statements are incorrect, responses to warranty claims are delayed, or advertising is misleading. Often, good product support can partially offset deficiencies in hardware quality. For example, a customer who just had a brake job understandably would be upset if the brakes began squealing again a week later. A reputable brake shop will give a warranty to redo the work at no additional charge. If it also has a policy of following up with a call to find out whether the customer is satisfied, the company makes very clear its intent to satisfy the customer.

Psychological Impressions.   Not to be overlooked is the psychological aspect of quality. In the provision of services, where the customer is in close contact with the provider, the appearance and actions of the provider are very important. Nicely dressed, courteous, friendly, and sympathetic employees can affect the customer's perception of service quality. For example, rumpled, discourteous, or grumpy bellhops can undermine a hotel's best efforts to provide high-quality service; the guests who encounter them may form lasting negative impressions of the hotel from such encounters.

In manufacturing, product quality is often judged on the basis of contact with salespersons or advertisements. The knowledge and personality of salespersons, as well as the product image presented in advertisements, convey an impression of product quality in customers.

Implications for Producers.   From this discussion of the consumer's definitions of quality, it should be apparent that defining quality is no easy task. To make things worse, consumers change their perceptions of quality. Take automobiles for instance: Consumer preferences shifted from power and styling in 1970 to fuel economy in 1975 to quality of design and performance in the 1980s. Changes in consumer lifestyles and values in response to changing economic conditions during that time drastically changed customer perception of automobile quality. Today, a buyer is more inclined to invest in a long-lasting product, even if it means paying more for it at the outset. By not identifying these trends and responding to them quickly, U.S. automakers lost opportunities to maintain or increase their market shares relative to foreign competition. In general, business success depends on the accuracy of management's perceptions of customer expectations and the degree to which it can bridge the gap between consumer expectations and operating capabilities.

QUALITY AS A COMPETITIVE ADVANTAGE ▲

Managers have good cause to be concerned with quality, because quality is an issue that pervades the entire organization. Managerial Practice 3.1 shows how Corning Glass Company learned that high quality has become a strategic weapon for gaining increased market share. Conversely, poor quality can adversely affect organizational performance. It erodes the firm's ability to compete in the marketplace and increases the costs of producing a product or service. By improving quality, a firm can overcome these negative factors.

Market Implications

In the past, price was considered to be the key factor in gaining market share, but this is no longer true. Consumers are much more quality-minded and in many cases would prefer to spend more for a product if it will last longer. A survey of 2000 business units conducted by the Strategic Planning Institute of Cambridge, Massachusetts, indicated that the degree of product quality affects a firm's chances of increasing its market share. If product quality is stable, a high-quality product stands a much better chance of gaining market share than does a low-quality product. If customers perceive improvements in quality, the chances of increased market share are better, regardless of the level of product quality.

Good quality can also pay off in higher profits. High-quality products can be priced higher than comparable, lower quality products and yield a greater return for the same sales dollar. In addition, as you will see later in this chapter, high quality can reduce costs, which in turn increases profits. Management is more able to compete on price as well as quality.

Cost Implications

In a recent poll by the American Society for Quality Control, executives seemed to underestimate the cost to their companies of poor quality. A majority claimed that poor quality accounted for less than 10 percent of gross sales. Most experts on the costs of poor quality estimated losses in the range of 20 to 30 percent for defective or unsatisfactory products. However, as illustrated in Managerial Practice 3.2, the costs of poor quality often go beyond the obvious cost of scrap or rework.

For many years consultants such as Joseph Juran and W. Edwards Deming have demonstrated the costs of poor quality to managers in Japan and the United States. But only recently have U.S. managers begun to take action. The result is a conscious effort to reduce the level of defective products and services.

MANAGERIAL PRACTICE 3.1

Total Quality Management at Corning Glass Works

During the 1970s and early 1980s, Corning was shocked by the resurgence of Japanese competitors and the firm's subsequent loss of significant market share. James R. Houghton, Corning's chairman, believed that a change in the company's business culture was the key to improving the quality of the firm's products, services, and management decisions. As a result, Houghton launched a long-term effort to upgrade the quality of Corning's management. The heart of the effort was a broad educational program to change the mind-sets of both managers and workers. Between 1983 and 1987, all 28,000 managers and employees, including the chairman, have taken a course on quality awareness, where quality was defined as meeting the customer's requirements. Other courses offered in the second phase of the program included communications, problem solving, and statistics.

Management also encouraged employees to express their ideas for job improvements. The suggestions for improvements rose from 1000 annually to 7800; nearly 5000 of them were accepted. Many suggestions for improvements resulted in large cost savings. For example, the catalytic converter plant reduced its defect rate from six percent to *two tenths of a percent or less*. This feat helped Corning become the supplier of several Japanese automobile manufacturers. In general, Corning has cut scrap rates by 50 percent or more, leading to better quality and lower prices. By 1987, Corning had once again become a leader in the industry.

Source: Gerald J. Barry, "Stay Tuned," *The Quality Review*, Spring 1988, pp 34–39.

Four major categories of cost are associated with quality management and are defined in Table 3.2. **Prevention costs** increase as the quality level (as measured by product or service design) or reliability (as measured by conformance to specifications) increases. That is, improving quality requires the expenditure of time, effort, and money.

Appraisal costs decrease as quality level or quality reliability increases. Quality appraisal helps management to identify quality problems. As preventive measures improve quality, fewer resources are needed for quality inspections and the subsequent search for causes of any problems that are detected.

MANAGERIAL PRACTICE 3.2

The Costs of Poor Quality

First Federal Savings and Loan Association of Rochester

An employee of the First Federal Savings and Loan Association of Rochester accidentally loaded a canister of $20 bills into the slot for $5 bills at one of the branch office's automatic teller machines. Once the error was discovered, a line of eager cardholding customers formed. Although the maximum withdrawal was $200, customers were receiving as much as $800 from the machine. Before it was over, the machine had overpaid a total of $5000.

U.S Sprint

Thousands of U.S. Sprint customers are receiving bills that are months overdue and that contain calls never made. Other customers aren't receiving any bills. During 1987 the company lost hundreds of millions of dollars because of billing problems and the cost of building its fiber-optic communications system. Recently, a former salesman received a $1.7 million payment in settlement of a dispute based on his claim that billing system errors deprived him of commissions dating back to 1985. In 1987, U.S. Sprint lost $1.1 billion on revenues of $3.1 billion.

Vickers Shipbuilding and Engineering

A mistake by employees of the Vickers Shipbuilding and Engineering Company has led to an investigation as to how a 20 by 30 foot section of a British nuclear-powered submarine was welded into position upside down. Apparently, signs indicating which end was up either fell off or went unnoticed. It could cost as much as $1.86 million to correct the mistake.

Sources: "Automatic Teller Users Had Larceny in Their Hearts," *The Columbus Dispatch*, April 27, 1988; "Errors Continue to Plague U.S. Sprint's Billing System," *New York Times*, March 3, 1988; "Oops! Part of a Sub Is Built Upside Down," *The Columbus Dispatch*, April 9, 1988.

	TABLE 3.2 Costs Associated with Quality Management	
Cost Category	**As Quality Increases, Costs**	**Comments**
Prevention	Increase	Costs are associated with preventing defects before they happen. Included are the costs of process design, product design, employee training, and vendor programs.
Appraisal	Decrease	Costs are incurred in assessing the level of quality attained by the operating system. Included are the costs of quality audits and statistical quality control programs.
Internal failure	Decrease	Costs result from yield losses and the need to rework products or services because of defective workmanship.
External failure	Decrease	Costs include those of warranty repairs, loss of market share, and lawsuits arising from injury or property damage from use of the product or service.

The Japanese have the philosophy that no worker should pass a defective unit downstream to the next work station. This is known as *quality at the source* and is a good way to reduce the appraisal costs of quality management.

Internal failure costs decrease as the level or reliability of quality increases. Various preventive measures can be used to reduce the number of rejects and thereby reduce scrap, rework, overtime, machine failure, inventory costs, and a number of other costs. We cover this topic in more detail later in this chapter.

Finally, **external failure costs** also decrease as the level or reliability of quality increases. Not only do warranty repair costs and losses in market share decrease, but also legal liability for injury or damage resulting from use of the product or service will decrease.

The implication of all this is that improving quality by spending more on preventive measures is a good investment for any organization. However, it depends on whether management is talking about quality level or quality reliability. If it is trying to increase the *quality level* by better product and process design, for example, management is actually addressing business objectives and trade-offs among the competitive priorities of price (cost), quality, time, and flexibility in the hope of doing better in the marketplace. In this situation, reductions in other costs of poor quality may not completely offset increased prevention costs. As a result, management may have to raise the price of the product or service, moving closer to a competitive priority of quality rather than price. That is why a Mercedes Benz costs more than a Ford, and a night at a Hilton hotel costs more than a night at a Howard Johnson's motel.

Alternatively, if management is trying to increase *quality reliability* by better conformance to specifications, the added prevention costs may be more than offset by the reduced appraisal, internal failure, and external failure costs. For the same set of product or service specifications, less waste is generated, and savings can be enormous. That is why many firms are spending large sums of money to improve quality. The overwhelming evidence is that improving quality reliability makes the trade-off between prevention costs and other costs of poor quality worthwhile.

In the remainder of this chapter, we discuss prevention, internal failure costs, and external failure costs in more detail. We defer discussion of quality appraisal to Chapter 19.

PREVENTING QUALITY PROBLEMS ▲

Any effort to improve quality requires the support of top management. The reason is that improving quality raises issues for the entire organization, having employee, product and process design, and purchasing implications.

Organizational Issues

One of the ways to improve quality is to demolish the organizational barriers between departmental empires and force managers in different functional areas to work together to design and produce more reliable products or services. Although this is easier said than done, several efforts at moving organizations in this direction are being tried.

Quality Assurance Groups.   Sometimes, organizational barriers between departments encourage the development and testing of products or services in a vacuum without interaction with other departments. This may lead to premature introduction of products or services into the market. One way to increase the likelihood of a rational approach to the design and testing of new products is to have a quality assurance group.

Quality assurance is broader than quality control. **Quality assurance** is any activity concerned with maintaining quality at the desired level. It also deals with the detection of quality problems if they do occur. In such cases, a quality assurance group conducts rigorous tests to make sure that the problems have been corrected. Management thus can be assured that the firm is marketing a high-quality product or service. The quality assurance group should be staffed by people who have the confidence of the various departmental managers. In a manufacturing company, the group determines the cause of actual problems encountered by the consumer, identifies potential problems, and initiates corrective actions. To help the group discover design or workmanship problems, its budget may even include an allotment to buy back products that have been in service a long time or products that have failed prematurely. In service organizations as well as manufacturing companies, the quality assurance group assists management in establishing and updating quality standards, developing information feedback systems, developing quality cost data, and performing quality improvement studies.

Marketing Interface.   Marketing managers must provide information about customers' perceptions of quality, if management is to develop reasonable quality goals. In addition, marketing can help improve product quality by not pressuring for premature release of new products. For example, Gillette, Inc., had advertised its introduction of a new shaving cream. Just before the first shipments were to be made, the firm discovered that the cans averaged slightly less product weight than was printed on the label. Considerable pressure to ship the "slightly defective" product could have developed. Instead, Gillette's top management focused on correcting the defect. The shipments were late, but customers received all they paid for.

Employee Considerations

The field of quality management draws on a wide variety of skills. The following are examples of job titles used by various manufacturing and service organizations.

- Quality Engineer
- Reliability Engineer
- Technician
- Inspector
- Product Specialist
- Tester
- Auditor
- Quality Assurance Manager
- Quality Control Manager
- Lab Technician
- Chemist

Employees such as these are not the only ones who must be concerned about quality. Quality must be the concern of all employees, from the CEO to the hourly worker on the assembly line. The challenge of quality management is to instill an awareness of the importance of good quality in all employees and to motivate employees to improve product quality. Managerial Practice 3.3 depicts two organizations that believe that employees are the key to quality improvements.

Individual Development. On-the-job training programs can help improve quality. Programs aimed at new work methods for experienced workers and short courses in current practices for new employees can increase productivity and reduce the number of product defects. Some companies train workers on related jobs to help them understand how defects in their own work can cause problems for others. They may even be encouraged to propose remedial action when defects occur. Top management can also benefit from training programs. Texas Instruments initiated a quality improvement program in which 300 top executives attended an outside training program on quality management. Later, 20,000 other employees attended a 16-hour, in-house course.

Monetary Incentives. Some of the incentive for improving quality comes from merit pay and bonuses. Companies may tie monetary incentives directly

MANAGERIAL PRACTICE 3.3 ▲

Employees: The Key to Quality Improvements

Internal Revenue Service (IRS)

By April 8, 1988, the IRS had processed 52.7 million tax returns. Unfortunately, the General Accounting Office reported that 20.7 percent contained errors and that the IRS was responsible for about half. Although these error rates were lower than expected due to sweeping changes in the tax law, IRS commissioner Larry Gibbs and senior IRS management initiated a program to make fundamental changes to the organization's culture.

Currently 85 percent of the top 11,000 managers have completed a quality management course taught by J. M. Juran, a well-respected consultant in this area. These managers will, in turn, train others within the 100,000-plus work force scattered throughout the country. The general theme is that quality goes at the front end (customer service) and involves everyone.

Scandinavian Airline System (SAS)

In 1979 SAS was operating in the red as a result of deregulation and rapidly rising fuel prices. Jan Carlzon, president of SAS, decided that SAS should be a customer-driven company, based on service quality. He set out to reshape the corporate culture to influence the norms and values of the people who deliver the service. His most important step was to introduce the concept of the "moment of truth," or the moment when a customer directly encounters

Sources: "Little Improvement Seen in Error Rate of IRS," by Gary Klott, *New York Times*, April 14, 1988; "There Is a Better Way to Stretch the Federal Dollar," by John L. Buckman, *The Quality Review*, Spring 1988, pp. 8–14; "The Moment of Truth," by Osvald M. Bjelland, *The Quality Review*, Spring 1988, pp. 40–41.

to quality improvements. The Marriott Corporation, for example, has a profit-sharing plan whereby employees can elect to contribute at least 5 percent of their earnings, and the company makes a contribution from profits. Presumably, as quality of service increases, profits increase and employees are rewarded. Texas Instruments takes a more direct approach. Top managers are ranked by the quality of the products they produce and receive pay increases and bonuses based on this ranking.

Quality Circles

Another way to promote employee participation and improve quality is to develop quality circles, a concept originated by Kaoru Ishikawa. A **quality circle** is a small group of supervisors and employees who meet to identify,

an SAS representative. SAS carried 12 million passengers in 1986. Each passenger meets an average of five SAS front-line employees. Therefore, customers encountered SAS services on 60 million different occasions in 1986. This concept drove home the importance of the employee in the delivery of quality services. The company went into the black in 1980 and earned a profit margin of about 10 percent by 1986.

Scandinavian Airline System cabin attendants interacting with passengers. According to Jan Carlzon, SAS president, they are experiencing the "moment of truth."

analyze, and solve production and quality problems. The philosophy behind quality circles is that most employees take more pride and interest in their work if they are allowed to help shape it. Typically, participation in a quality circle is voluntary, and the group sometimes meets after normal working hours. Groups are kept small, perhaps 6–10 employees, to let all members interact freely. Consequently, a company may have a large number of quality circles. For example, one IBM facility has 800 quality circles.

One quality circle can generate hundreds of ideas for improvements in a year. Many be minor, and some may not prove feasible. However, management must seriously consider all these ideas if quality circles are to work. Benefits in the form of improved quality, productivity, and cost savings can be

MANAGERIAL PRACTICE 3.4

Quality Circles and Participative Management at GM and GE

General Motors

General Motors is attempting a significant cultural change, although change in an organization the size of GM comes slowly. The firm is encouraging employees to participate in the decision-making process in areas that deeply affect the workplace. The concept is particularly emphasized in the new UAW/ GM Quality Network, a process emphasizing teamwork and continuous quality improvement. One manifestation of this program is the quality audit and review. This is a daily event where groups of managers and production employees at GM assembly plants meet to review the quality of the cars they have built. Quality measurements closely related to customer perceptions of quality are emphasized.

General Electric

Many firms have had success with quality circles, but the experiences of GE over the past 20 years demonstrate how difficult it is to get management to consistently support such programs. GE began experimenting in the late 1960s, and by 1975 had established work teams in 12 plants. Today, only one of the original 12 plants continues the quality circle program. The one original plant still using quality circles was built in 1973. It was designed for a participative management approach in that it has only four job categories, as opposed to 21 at similar GE plants. In 1983, another plant started a program of participative management and within three years boasted a 25 percent increase in productivity. Nonetheless, managers who fear a loss of power, refuse to accept group suggestions, or meddle with the incentives of the quality circles, and unions that do not support participative management have undermined many attempts to start quality circles.

Sources: General Motors Public Interest Report, 1988, pp. 1–12; "The Revolt Against Working Smarter," by Bill Saporite, *Fortune*, July 21, 1986, pp. 58–65.

substantial. Managerial Practice 3.4 highlights the experiences of two large manufacturing companies with quality circles.

Product and Process Design Implications

Preventing quality problems involves more than solving people problems. Proper design of the product and the process used to make it also are very important.

Product Design. Typically, the more design changes there are, the greater the defect rates are. Thus stable product designs can help reduce quality problems. If design changes are called for because of customer considerations, there is no easy answer. If the company tries to minimize such changes it might become less competitive in the marketplace. If changes are a response to the introduction of new products, the firm could imitate Japanese manufacturers by emphasizing reliability engineering and careful shakedowns of new designs.

Often a firm redesigns a product to better conform to the capability of its operations. The trade-off here is higher quality and increased competitiveness in exchange for the added time and cost required to test the product thoroughly before introducing it. Costs associated with inadequate planning and testing are illustrated by Novatel's experience with its new cellular phone. Novatel Communications Limited, the only manufacturer of cellular phones in Canada, has designed a new portable unit that could be disconnected and used outside the car. First, testing delays withheld the new product from the market for five months. Then wiring problems caused the firm to recall its newest car phone in September 1987. The sales Novatel lost as a result of these errors could have been salvaged by more thorough checking during the design and testing stages.

Process Design. The design of the process used to produce the good or service greatly affects its quality. Neglect is one of the biggest culprits. For example, the Zhdanov Vladmir Tractor Works in the USSR had nearly 20 percent of its tractors rejected by state inspectors, causing the plant to miss its 1987 production quota. To improve the quality of its tractors, Zhdanov is undertaking a five-year, $387 million renovation of its 43-year old plant. It is also installing 100 computer workstations to give managers instant access to production schedules, deliveries, and data needed to allow the manufacture of more customized tractors.

Process design is closely related to product quality and quality management. The experience at Zhdanov is common throughout the business world and emphasizes the lack of attention given to quality in the past. The approach taken to quality management depends on the organization's positioning strategy, as described in Chapter 2. Firms with a process focus are more likely to compete on the basis of high-performance design and rely largely on employee involvement to ensure quality. However, firms with a product focus are more likely to compete on the basis of consistent quality, utilize quality specialists,

Semiconductors Require a Clean Environment

Semiconductors, or "chips," are the things that make computers think and are packed with thousands of transistors whose features are measured in microns. One micron is one-hundredth the width of a human hair. A particle one-tenth the size of a semiconductor's smallest feature can destroy it by causing a short circuit or leakage of the tiny charges stored in the chip. With such a requirement for cleanliness, chips are difficult to manufacture. Why? Because the people who make them are filthy. At rest, a person sheds at least 100,000 particles a minute of flaking flesh, saliva, hair spray, dandruff, lint and other things. Head movement causes 500,000 particles, slow walking five million, and exercise, 30 million. Breathing is bad and a sneeze is disastrous. One particle is enough to destroy a chip.

Companies have gone to great lengths to build "clean rooms" with strictly controlled air flows and temperatures. Employees must wear bunny suits, with hoods, breathing apparatus, boots and gloves. Some companies even require an air shower after suiting up. Even with all this, touching a chip is forbidden because a "glove print" can damage the chip. Special suction devices must be used to handle the chips at each step of the process.

Two Bell Laboratories technicians insert silicon wafers into a hexode reactor. The five-inch wafers are automatically mounted on a hexagonal column, which is then enclosed in an atmosphere-tight housing so that ion-etching can take place. The operation requires carefully controlled atmospheric conditions.

Source: "Why You Shouldn't Sing 'La Marseillaise' in Computer Factory," by Erik Larson, *Wall Street Journal*, December 28, 1984.

and have more formal controls. Automated inspection becomes more likely. In some cases, such as at breweries, much of the quality is designed into the process itself, and periodic sampling is used to check quality levels. Managerial Practice 3.5 reveals the lengths to which companies in the semiconductor industry must go to compete in a market where high quality and low price are vital.

The purchase of new machinery can help prevent or overcome quality problems. Suppose that the design specification for the distance between two holes in a metal plate is 3.000 in. ±0.0005 in. Suppose also that too many plates are defective; that is, the space between holes falls outside the design specification. One way to reduce the percentage of defective parts produced by the process would be to purchase new machinery having the capability to produce metal plates with holes 3.000 in. ±0.0003 in. apart. Reducing the percentage of defective parts would increase conformance to the design specifications. The trade-off would be greater process costs.

Linking Product Design to Process Design.   One of the keys to obtaining high quality is to make sure the product or service is designed to fit the firm's capability to produce it. That means getting operations managers and product designers together early in the product stages, as pointed out in Chapter 2. The result is much better quality. For example, in 1984 the instrument console for the Ford Escort had 22 parts. Based on the notion that simpler is better, Ford redesigned the console for 1987 to have only six parts. As a consequence labor costs dropped 83 percent, material costs went down 39 percent, and quality rose 10 percent.

Management should be concerned with linking each aspect of quality prized by the customer to the raw materials, parts, assemblies, and process steps that build a particular attribute into the product. Design drawings show parts and assemblies and how they are to be put together. However, they cannot pinpoint a problem in product design that needs to be corrected in order to satisfy a customer's particular quality concern. One way to identify such problems is to develop a **fishbone diagram**, a method first developed by Kaoru Ishikawa, which relates a product defect to potential contributing factors. The diagram helps management trace customer complaints directly to the operations involved. Production operations having no bearing on a particular defect aren't shown on the fishbone diagram for that defect.

For example, Fig. 3.1 shows a fishbone diagram for one quality problem related to the manufacture of castings: fractured surface of the cast metal (identified as the main arrow of the diagram). Four factors are considered critical: casting temperature, mold coating, composition of molten metal, and mold temperature. These factors are identified as the main connecting arrows of the fishbone. Subfactors are identified by secondary arrows. The relevant subfactors should be checked if a critical factor is suspected of causing the quality problem. Thus if mold coating is suspected, the subfactors checked would be coated volume, fine-coal mixing ratio, and degree of dryness—to

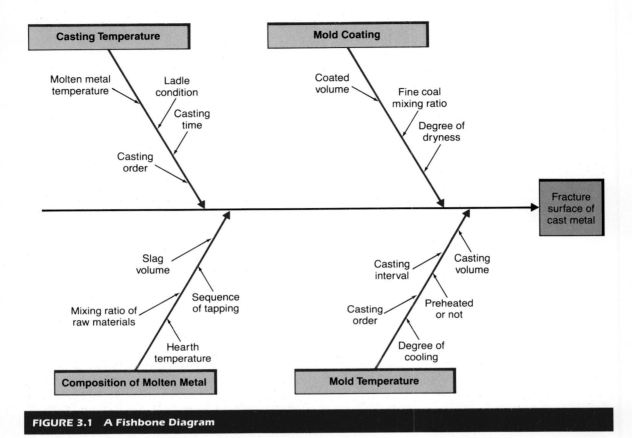

FIGURE 3.1   A Fishbone Diagram

Source: Reprinted with permission of The Free Press, a division of Macmillan, Inc., from *Japanese Manufacturing Techniques: Nine Hidden Lessons in Simplicity* by Richard J. Schonberger, p. 72. Copyright © 1982 by Richard J. Schonberger.

see whether any of these operations is causing the problem. The benefits of fishbone diagrams go beyond identifying potential causes of a problem. The process of constructing a fishbone diagram itself calls to managerial and worker attention the critical factors affecting product quality.

Purchasing Considerations

Since the production of most goods and services requires the input of some raw materials or purchased items, the operations manager must pay attention to the quality of these inputs. Large companies have hundreds and even thousands of suppliers, some of which supply the same parts. Quality assurance for the items they supply is an enormous task. Purchased parts of poor quality can have a devastating effect on a company with a product focus. For example, on September 17, 1984, the Ford Motor Company halted Tempo and Topaz production at its Kansas City, Missouri, and Oakville, Ontario, plants. A faulty engine part purchased from an outside supplier apparently caused some gears in the engine to lose a few teeth during a test run. Approximately 5500 hourly workers were temporarily laid off. In addition, Ford lost about 2000 cars each day that production was stopped.

Regardless of the number of suppliers involved, both the buyer's approach and specification management are keys to controlling supplier quality. The firm's buyer may emphasize positive reports of money saved, orders placed, and on-time delivery performance of suppliers, overriding negative reports on quality performance unless top management places a high priority on quality. In a survey of the air-conditioning industry, companies with the highest quality reported that they placed quality above price when evaluating supplier contracts (see Garvin, 1983). Operating under such a priority, a competent buyer will identify supplier capabilities. The buyer will then concentrate on those suppliers and products that offer an opportunity for quality improvement at a reasonable cost. From a technical standpoint, this is no easy task. However, after such suppliers have been identified, the buyer should work with the supplier to obtain essentially defect-free parts. The buyer can do so by examining and evaluating trade-offs, handling problems of off-specification materials firmly but diplomatically, and participating in corrective actions. Thus patience, understanding, and trust are qualities needed in a buyer.

Specification management is also important. The specifications for purchased parts and materials must be clear and *realistic*. Sometimes, specifications are set arbitrarily to a tight limit to protect the designer in case something goes wrong. In other cases, the specifications make the product uneconomical to produce or service later. Specifications have implications for the buyer, who is trying to identify quality standards for the firm's suppliers and at the same time keep costs down. As a check on specifications, buyers in some companies initiate *process capability studies* for important products. These studies amount to trial runs of small product samples to ensure that all components, including the raw materials and purchased parts, work together to form a product having the desired quality level. Analysis of study results may identify unrealistic specifications and lead to changes.

Top management also has some responsibilities regarding supplier quality. If it wants the purchasing department to identify several low-cost, qualified suppliers, top management must allow purchasing enough time to obtain and analyze the information. An unrealistic deadline can lead to poor selections based on incomplete information about supplier qualifications. In addition, top management can help tear down organizational barriers that hamper communication between purchasing and other departments, such as engineering and quality control. Some of the information needed to assess supplier qualifications requires sampling products and analyzing in detail the supplier's manufacturing process, a task usually performed by quality control personnel and engineers in cooperation with the supplier's technical staff. This effort requires cooperation between purchasing and other departments that have the technical capabilities to do these analyses.

INTERNAL FAILURE COSTS ▲

Internal failure costs result from defects generated during production of a good or service and fall into two major cost categories: *yield losses,* which are incurred if a defective item must be scrapped; and *rework costs.* With rework, the item is rerouted to some previous operation(s) for correcting the defect. In the case of a service, the customer calls or returns in person to have the defect corrected.

Yield Losses

Your first thought about yield losses may be the cost of the material lost. Although that is only a fraction of the total cost involved, it is a good place to start. Suppose that you wanted to determine how many units of a specific raw material you would need to ensure a given number of nondefective product units from the production process. Let

d_i = the average proportion of defective units generated at operation i of the process

n = the number of operations in the production process for the product

M = the desired number of units of finished product

B = the average number of units of the raw material needed at the start of the production process—the decision variable

Then

$$B(1 - d_1)(1 - d_2) \cdots (1 - d_n) = M$$

or

$$B = \frac{M}{(1 - d_1)(1 - d_2) \cdots (1 - d_n)}$$

APPLICATION 3.1

Consider the simple four-operation process depicted in Fig. 3.2. Each operation generates the following average proportion of defects.

Operation	Proportion Defective
1	0.01
2	0.04
3	0.02
4	0.06

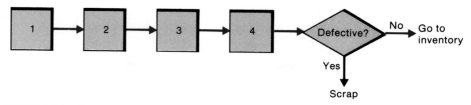

FIGURE 3.2   A Four-Operation Production Process

How many units of the raw material, on the average, are needed at operation 1 to ensure 100 units of nondefective product after operation 4?

Solution

The output of each operation is the input for the next operation. The input for operation 2 is B multiplied by the proportion of nondefective units generated by operation 1, or $B(1 - 0.01)$. The input for operation 3 is $B(1 - 0.01)(1 - 0.04)$, and so on. Consequently,

$$B(1 - 0.01)(1 - 0.04)(1 - 0.02)(1 - 0.06) = 100$$

and

$$B = \frac{100}{0.8755}$$

$$= 114$$

Thus 114 units of the raw material are needed at the start.

In the preceding application, the 14 extra units of the raw material required because of the defectives generated at each operation increase raw-material costs by 14 percent. However, other costs are hidden from the casual view of the unwary manager. Suppose that all 114 units are moved from one operation to the next and finally checked for quality after the last operation, a common practice in many firms. What are the hidden costs? More labor and machine hours are required to produce the same quantity of product than for a defect-free process. For example, each operation must process 114 units per day. If no defectives were generated, each operation would only have to process 100 units per day. Thus the firm must spend 14 percent more for labor and machine costs because of yield losses. The increase in machine hours could also cause failures and increase machine downtime. In addition, since more material has to be processed, to get the required daily quantity, product manufacturing time will increase. The implications for customer service are an increase in the percentage of orders past due and, ultimately, lost future sales. In-process and end-of-production inspections are based on the assumption that inspectors will catch all the defects generated by the process. If the inspectors fail to do so, downstream operations incur additional costs such as those already discussed. Finally, work-in-process costs rise because more material must flow between operations.

Rework Costs

Sometimes, when a defective part or production lot is discovered, it can be sent back to a previous operation to be corrected. Suppose that an operations manager wants to estimate the average daily number of units of a certain product that must be reworked. In this case,

P_j = the probability that a lot (or batch) of product j will be defective and have to be reworked

L_j = lot size of product j

N_j = average number of defective-free lots of product j required per day

Q_j = average number of units of product j produced at the rework operation per day

Then, assuming that all quality problems can be solved by reworking the product (as opposed to scrapping it),

$$Q_j = \frac{L_j N_j}{1 - P_j}$$

APPLICATION 3.2

Let's consider our simple four-operation application again, except that this time there is no scrap. Instead, let's suppose that the product is produced in lots of 10, that an entire lot can be defective, and that 100 defect-free units are still required at the end of the day. Units are inspected after operation 3, and there is a 10 percent chance that operation 3 will produce a defective lot; if it does, the lot must be sent back for rework. This situation is shown in Fig. 3.3. How many units per day of the product can be expected to require reworking because of operation 3?

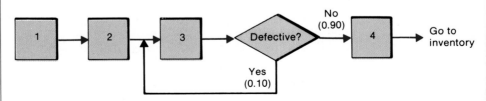

FIGURE 3.3   Inspection and Rework in a Four-Operation Production Process

The Effects of Rework on a Four-Operation Production Process

Operation	Probability of Rework per Lot	Operation to Route to	Average Number of Units Processed per Lot*	Average Number of Units Processed per Day†
1	0	—	10	100
2	0	—	10	100
3	0	—	11.1	111
Inspection	0.10	3	11.1	111
4	0	—	10	100

*The average number of units processed per lot equals $10[1.0 + 0.1 + (0.1)^2 + (0.1)^3 + \cdots]$, or approximately 11.1.

†Since 10 lots per day are required, the average number of units processed per day equals 10 times the average number of units processed per lot.

Solution

The accompanying table shows how this situation affects the operation of the system. Processing 10 lots per day would, on average, result in one lot that needs rework. This means that operation 3 and inspection would be expected to process at least 110 units per day. However, the lot that has to be reworked has a 10 percent chance of being defective again. If the chances of rework are independent of whether the lot has already been reworked, there is a 1 percent chance [or $0.10(0.10) = 0.01$] that the lot will have to be reworked twice. Consequently, the average number of units processed per lot is $10[1.0 + 0.1 + (0.1)^2 + (0.1)^3 + \cdots] = 10/(1 - 0.10)$, or approximately 11.1 units, including the first time every lot must be processed. Thus the expected number of units per day worked by operation 3 and inspection is 111 units [or $10(10)/(1 - 0.10)$] over an extended period of time.

Let's consider each of the costs associated with rework in the preceding application. Obviously, more labor, machine, and inspection hours would be needed at operation 3—in this case, 11 percent more than in the case of no rework. In addition, most situations involving rework involve an increase in the number of setups, even if only a portion of a lot must be reworked. Furthermore, work-in-process inventory levels increase because the units to be reworked stay in a semifinished state longer. The value of that inventory also increases because of the added labor and machine costs needed to produce it correctly. Finally, the manufacturing time for the average production lot increases because of the possibility that it may have to be rerouted for rework. Consequently, promised due dates may not be met, or the lead time for customer delivery may have to be increased to such an extent that the company can no longer compete in the marketplace.

Rework problems are not restricted to manufacturing processes. For example, the service department of an automobile dealer performs many maintenance and repair services for car owners. The customers bring their coughing, choking, wheezing, rattling, smoking, or abnormally smelling cars to the service department for repair. If the mechanic does not correct the problem, or creates a new one, the customer must bring the car back to get the job done right. The costs of shoddy service include the additional labor and diagnostic-machine time and the ill will of the car owner. In other cases, the service system comes to the customer and rework costs involve the added labor and travel time. Such is the case of the TV repairman who must return to a customer's home to correct a problem that should have been taken care of the first time.

Quality at the Source

Rather than trying to "inspect quality into the product," as we have just described, the Japanese approach is to ensure "quality at the source." In other words, an employee does not pass defective units to the next operation.

To demonstrate some of the advantages of this approach, consider Table 3.3. Suppose that each operator passed only nondefective units to the next operation. That is, operator 1 passes only 113 units to operator 2, 108 units to operator 3, and so on. The operations manager still needs capacity for 114 units per day at operation 1, but capacity only for 113 units at operation 2, 108 at operation 3, and 106 at operation 4. Consequently, fewer machine and labor hours (regular and overtime) are required to produce the 100 units needed. Figure 3.4 compares the labor and machine hours required for the same amount of defect-free output using the two approaches to quality assurance.

TABLE 3.3   The Effects of Yield Loss on a Four-Operation Production Process

Operation	Percentage of Units Defective	Units Processed	Number of Defective Units Added by Operation*	Number of Good Units Passed to Next Operation
1	1	114	1	113
2	4	114	5	108
3	2	114	2	106
4	6	114	6	100
Total number of defective units produced			14	

*Rounded to the nearest number of whole units. The number of defective units is equal to the number of nondefective units passed to the operation by the previous operation multiplied by the percentage of defectives generated at the operation. For operation 2, for example, 113(0.04) = 5 defective units.

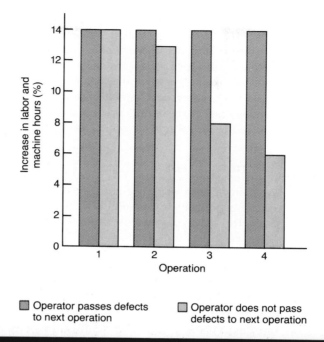

FIGURE 3.4 Implications of Yield Losses in a Four-Operation Production Process

Also, assuming no delays for machine or worker availability, ensuring quality at the source significantly reduces manufacturing lead time because the process times per batch at operations 2, 3, and 4 are less. Moreover, there is less wear and tear on the equipment, which reduces maintenance and downtime costs. Even though the cost of scrap is the same, there is a savings in the work-in-process inventory investment; no value is added to materials made defective at an early operation only to be scrapped at the end of the production line. In total, the savings can be significant. Similar arguments can be made for the case of rework.

Obviously, the ideal solution is to produce no defective units because this quality level can significantly reduce operating costs. Recognizing that this condition may not be practical or economical in many instances, we contend that ensuring quality at the source can result in significant savings, regardless of the percentage of defective units generated at each operation. This approach can also decrease the need for inspectors and thereby reduce appraisal costs.

EXTERNAL FAILURE COSTS ▲

External failure costs arise from product or service failures at the customer level. We differentiate them from internal failure costs because they are incurred to correct defective products or services that somehow escaped internal checks and controls. A customer—as opposed to a firm's production worker or quality inspector—finding a defect has a number of implications for the producer. The most obvious implication is the loss of market share and future profits because bad news travels fast: Dissatisfied customers tell their friends, who in turn tell others; consumer protection groups alert the media. The potential impact on future profits is difficult to assess, but without doubt poor quality erodes market share and profits. These aren't the only external failure costs. There are also warranty service and litigation costs.

Warranty Costs

A warranty is a written guarantee of the integrity of a product or service and of the producer's responsibility to replace or repair defective parts or to reperform the service to the customer's satisfaction. Usually, a warranty is given for some specified time period. For example, television repairs are usually guaranteed for 90 days and new automobiles for five years or 50,000 miles, whichever comes first.

Encountering defects and correcting them after the product is in the customer's hands is costly. As Fig. 3.5 shows, the place to catch the defect is where it occurs: in the production process. The closer a product is to its finished state, the costlier it is to find defects and correct them. When the product has finally been shipped to the customer, the cost to fix a defect skyrockets. It is very expensive to send a customer engineer from IBM to a remote computer installation to find out what is wrong and fix it. Similarly, the cost of sending a team of electrical engineers to India to diagnose and repair a problem with a switch gear in an electric power station is prohibitive.

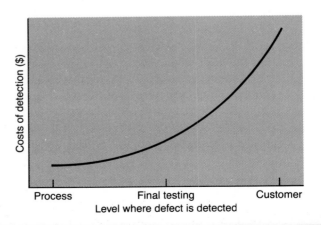

FIGURE 3.5   The Costs of Detection of a Defect

Litigation Costs

Unfortunately, defective products can injure and even kill consumers who purchase them. Such a defect could mean poor product design and/or non-conformance to specifications. An increasing number of states are adopting **strict liability laws** that force companies to pay damages—often large amounts—to injured plantiffs or heirs, even when they have not proved that the manufacturer was negligent in designing the product. All that needs to be shown is that a product was defective and that it caused the injury or death. At present, there is no nationwide, uniform code on product liability. Each state can have its own set of rules, which creates a chaotic situation for companies that sell their products in more than one state.

Chaotic as the situation may be, its one common element is the high cost of litigation. For example, the Ford Motor Company, whose 23 million automatic transmissions manufactured from 1968 to 1980 were alleged to slip from park into reverse if the engine were left running, at one time faced more than 1000 lawsuits exceeding $500 million in claims for injuries and deaths supposedly caused by the transmissions. The Firestone Tire and Rubber Company, whose Firestone 500 tire allegedly had defects in construction causing premature wear, resolved nearly 8000 lawsuits arising from these allegations and spent $180 million, including recalls, to solve the problem.

Litigation is costly not only in terms of legal fees but also in terms of bad publicity. More and more frequently, lawsuits brought on behalf of injured plaintiffs are spotlighted by the news media. Procter & Gamble's Rely tampon, allegedly the cause of toxic shock syndrome, and Merrell-Dow Pharmaceuticals' Bendectin, allegedly the cause of birth defects, are examples of costly litigation and media notoriety. Rely and Bendectin were eventually taken off the market because of bad press. Regardless of whether the company is judged to be at fault in a court of law, the cost of litigation is enormous.

PRESCRIPTIONS FOR EXCELLENCE IN QUALITY ▲

In this chapter we have described companies in both the manufacturing and service sectors that are making significant improvements in the quality of their products and, in so doing, increasing their competitive advantage. Where did they find the keys to their success? Many of them, after having been thrashed in the marketplace by their international competitors, sought the help of one of a small group of respected consultants in the area of quality management. We conclude this chapter with a brief summary of their general philosophies.

W. Edwards Deming: Quality Is Management's Responsibility

Achieving excellence in quality starts with top management, asserts W. Edwards Deming, considered to be the father of quality control in Japan. Deming urges a company to have a definite strategic plan for where it is going and how it will get there. Management should embrace the philosophy that mistakes, defects, and unsuitable materials are no longer acceptable and should be eliminated. The quality of supervision should be improved by allowing more time for supervisors to work with employees and providing them with the tools they need to do the job. Management should also create an environment in which employees will not fear reporting problems or recommending improvements. This fear usually results from imagined retaliation that will affect the reporting worker or fellow workers. For example, a quality assurance inspector may incorrectly report the result of an inspection to avoid exceeding the quota of allowable defectives for the work force. Work standards (see Chapter 6) should not be defined only as numbers or quotas but should include some notion of quality to promote the production of defect-free output. Management also has the responsibility to train (or retrain) employees in new skills to keep pace with changes in the workplace.

Management must develop the proper tools to manage quality. Such tools are not only the machines or hand tools that help to gauge the quality of a produced item, but also statistical methods to control processes or incoming materials and to help identify the sources of quality problems. Statistical methods can even be used to determine whether more worker training is needed. Deming believes that statistical methods are the backbone of management's arsenal of tools for managing quality. We explore some of these methods in Chapter 19.

Joseph M. Juran: A Quality Trilogy

Juran, like Deming, pioneered the education of the Japanese in quality management and significantly affected the unbelievable quality improvement demonstrated by Japanese manufacturers over the past 40 years. He is a well-respected author and consultant, but like Deming, he was not "discovered" by American business until the early 1980s. Juran's experience indicates that over 80 percent of quality defects are caused by factors controllable by management. Consequently, management continually needs to seek improvements through sound quality management, which Juran defines as the trilogy of quality planning, control, and improvement.

Quality planning involves deciding the proper quality level and reliability and linking product and process design to achieve the quality characteristics desired. Quality control compares products to standards and acts to correct discrepancies. This part of the trilogy, treated in detail in Chapter 19, provides the information to identify needed improvements. Juran's prescription for the final part of the trilogy is to get into the habit of making significant annual improvements. Select an area with chronic quality problems, convince others that a breakthrough solution is needed, analyze alternatives to the problem, select an alternative and implement it. Make sure that proper controls are put in place to monitor the results. Juran believes that annual improvement, hands-on management, and training are fundamental to achieving excellence in quality.

Armand V. Feigenbaum: Total Quality Control

Total quality control (TQC) is a concept whereby quality is a responsibility to be shared by all the people in an organization, but especially the workers who actually make the product. Total quality control was first introduced by Armand Feigenbaum, but it was the Japanese who made it work at the level of the individual worker. In Japan, the foreman and the workers, not a quality control department, have primary responsibility for quality reliability. Everyone else is expected to contribute to the overall improvement of quality—from the secretary who avoids typing errors, to the salesperson who presents the product properly, to the engineer who builds automatic error detecting devices, to the manager who approves funding for quality improvement projects. In other words, TQC involves all the functions that relate to a product or service.

In TQC, all personnel share the view that quality control is an end in itself. Errors or defects should be caught and corrected (if possible) at the source. (The cost advantages of quality at the source were apparent in our discussion of internal failure costs.) In TQC, quality at the source becomes a way of life, and workers even have the authority to stop a production line if they see quality problems. At Kawasaki's U.S. plant, lights of different colors strung along the assembly lines indicate the severity of the quality problem detected. Workers activate a yellow light to indicate that a problem has been detected and a red light when the problem is serious enough to stop the production line. If the line is stopped, the problem must be resolved quickly because each lost minute results in less output and costs money. In TQC, quality reliability or consistency has a higher priority than the level of output. We expand on the concept of TQC in Chapter 19.

Kaoru Ishikawa: Total Company Involvement

Admittedly influenced by the thinking of Deming, Juran, and Feigenbaum, Kaoru Ishikawa has made significant contributions of his own to the thought and practice of quality management. He is credited with originating the concept of quality control circles and their use. He also developed the fishbone diagram, which, as you saw earlier, helps to identify causes of quality problems.

Ishikawa concluded that, in the West, quality control is generally relegated to only a few staff specialists—and usually only in response to a serious problem. By contrast, his studies of Japanese managers revealed them to be totally committed to quality, a commitment that lasts the life of the organization. He favors total company involvement relative to inputs for quality improvement and that even nonspecialists in quality improvement should provide suggestions. This view is similar to Feigenbaum's.

Phillip B. Crosby: Quality Is Free

Having been a corporate vice-president and director of quality at ITT for fourteen years, it is no wonder that Phillip B. Crosby gained a lot of attention when he published his book *Quality Is Free* in 1979. Then, the conventional wisdom was that any level of quality had the same price. An 8 percent level of defects cost so much. Reducing that level to 3 percent defects would cost a lot more. Why? Improved machines would have to be purchased or better materials used in the products or more skilled labor hired. Crosby pointed out that what costs money are all the things involved in not doing the job right the first time. He is referring to the hidden costs of poor quality: increased labor and machine hours, increased machine failures and downtime, customer delivery delays and lost future sales, and even increased warranty costs. All these costs are over and above the loss of materials to scrap. The total typically dwarfs the cost of creating an environment that fosters achievement of high quality.

Crosby, now a consultant, advocates a goal of zero defects. To have any other goal is tantamount to declaring a commitment to producing a certain amount of defective material. Continuous improvement should be the means that management uses to achieve zero defects.

Genichi Taguchi: Quality Engineering

The major tenet behind Genichi Taguchi's approach to quality is that of developing high-quality products in a way that reduces costs. He calls it "quality engineering," which involves combining engineering and statistical methods to achieve improvements in cost and quality by optimizing product design and manufacturing processes. In team interaction sessions, employees and managers hypothesize critical factors affecting the quality of a selected product. An experimental design is set up and an experiment conducted to gather data. Statistical techniques are then used to determine the factor(s) contributing most to the product's quality problems and the settings that would optimize their performance. A follow-up experiment is conducted at the optimal settings to verify the results.

Users believe that Taguchi's methods aid communication between functional groups. His methods also permit efficient fine tuning of processes, permitting fewer adjustments with more predictable effects from each adjustment.

At this point you are probably thinking that all these people are saying about the same thing. To a large extent you're right. While each has his own niche, or points of emphasis, they all propose total management commitment to quality. Anything less propagates status-quo behavior which, for most companies today, is not good enough.

SOLVED PROBLEMS

1. The Crampton Electric Company manufactures semiconductors for the electronics industry. Although the company produces many types of semiconductors, one of its products requires only four operations. The raw material is a silicone bar, 3 inches in diameter. The bar is sliced on the first operation, and the slices are processed on three more machines to complete the product. However, each of the four machines generates a certain percentage of defective units.

Operation	Machine	Defectives
1	Saw	2%
2	Scrubber	1
3	Edge grinder	5
4	KOH	3

a. Demand for the product is 1000 slices per day. How many slices must the saw cut in order to ensure 1000 units of acceptable output from KOH?

b. Assume that all defects are discovered after each operation. What is the implication for the quantity of silicone bar needed?

c. What is the percentage of extra capacity required at each machine owing to the defect rates of the machines?

Solution

a. Let d_i be the proportion of yield loss at operation i, and B be the raw-material input in units. To produce 1000 units of defect-free product at the end of the process, the total number of units required is

$$B(1 - d_1)(1 - d_2)(1 - d_3)(1 - d_4) = 1000$$

$$B(0.98)(0.99)(0.95)(0.97) = 1000$$

or

$$B = \frac{1000}{0.8940}$$

$$= 1118.5 \quad \text{or} \quad 1119 \text{ units}$$

The saw, being the first operation, must cut 1119 pieces on the average to ensure that 1000 pieces come from KOH.

b. The operations require 11.9 percent more silicon bar than if there were no yield losses.

c. Each machine must process the following number of slices.

Operation	Defective	Units Processed	Defect-free Output*
Saw	2%	1119	1097
Scrubber	1	1097	1086
Edge grinder	5	1086	1031
KOH	3	1031	1000

*Final answers rounded to the nearest whole number.

Based on these data, the saw requires 11.9 percent more capacity, the scrubber 9.7 percent, the edge grinder 8.6 percent, and KOH 3.1 percent. All are based on the defect-free rate of 1000 slices per day.

2. After the last operation in a three-operation production process, an inspector determines whether an entire lot must be reworked. Historically, 20 percent of the lots have to be reworked. If rework is required, the entire lot is moved back to operation 2, and the lot must also go through operation 3 again. The size of each production lot is 50 units, and the daily requirement is 200 units. Estimate the average extra capacity per day required at operation 2, operation 3, and inspection.

Solution

As the daily requirement is 200 units, there is no need to determine L and N individually. Because the defective units must pass through operations 2 and 3 and inspection every time, only the average number of units processed per day for any one of the operations has to be determined; they will all be the same. Let's use operation 2 and $P_2 = 0.20$. Then,

$$Q_2 = \frac{L_2 N_2}{1 - P_2} = \frac{200}{1 - 0.20} = 250 \text{ units}$$

Operation 2 must process 250 units per day as opposed to the defect-free rate of 200 units per day—a 25 percent increase. Thus operation 3 and the inspection station must also handle 250 units per day.

FORMULA REVIEW

1. Number of units of raw material required at the start of a production process:

$$B = \frac{M}{(1 - d_1)(1 - d_2) \cdots (1 - d_n)}$$

2. Average number of units processed at a rework operation:

$$Q_j = \frac{L_j N_j}{1 - P_j}$$

CHAPTER HIGHLIGHTS

- Quality is a competitive weapon. The challenge for operations managers is how to produce products or services both efficiently and to meet the quality demanded by customers.

- Quality can be defined from the producer's perspective as conformance to specifications and from the consumer's perspective as value or fitness for use. Value, or fitness for use, may be judged on the basis of hardware quality, product or service support, and psychological impressions.

- Quality management is important because of the impact on market share, price and profits, and the costs of poor quality. The four major categories of cost associated with quality management are prevention, appraisal, internal failure, and external failure.

- Prevention costs increase as the quality reliability level increases. Appraisal, internal failure, and external failure costs all decrease as quality is improved through preventive measures.

- Increasing prevention expenditures to increase quality through better product and process design may involve trade-offs among the competitive priorities of price (cost), quality, time, and flexibility. Increasing prevention expenditures to obtain better conformance to specifications may be offset by savings in appraisal, internal failure, and external failure costs. Better quality reliability and a reduction in total costs may be possible.

- The prevention of quality problems can be addressed organizationally by using quality assurance groups and fostering close cooperation between operations and marketing.

- Employee-related strategies for preventing quality problems include employee training, adequate monetary incentives, and quality circles. Quality problems can also be prevented by having product and process designs that are stable and that foster quality reliability. Linking product design to process design can increase quality reliability. One useful analytic technique is the fishbone diagram, which identifies possible causes of a particular quality problem.

- The role of the buyer in identifying supplier capabilities and working with suppliers to achieve higher levels of quality is as important as comparing purchased parts and materials against specifications.

- The costs of internal failure arise from yield losses and rework. In addition to the cost of scrapped material, yield losses and rework increase the costs of labor hours, machine hours, machine failure, and work-in-process inventory. Lead times also increase, which has an impact on future sales.

- The quality-at-the-source approach dramatically reduces yield loss and rework costs.

- External failure costs consist of warranty and litigation costs. These costs can be extremely large but can be significantly reduced with effective quality management.

KEY TERMS

appraisal costs   86
external failure costs   87
fishbone diagram   95
internal failure costs   87
prevention costs   86
quality   82
quality assurance   88
quality circle   91
strict liability laws   105
total quality control (TQC)   107

STUDY QUESTIONS

1. Your company makes Christmas-tree lights. Define *quality* from both the producer's and consumer's perspective by giving examples of conformance to specifications and factors that influence the consumer's perceptions of product quality.

2. You own a small company that provides an income-tax preparation service. Define *quality* from both the producer's and consumer's perspective by giving examples of conformance to specifications and factors that influence the consumer's perceptions of service quality.

3. Suppose that you are the proprietor of an independently owned motel located at the intersection of two interstate highways. Give an example of each of the three aspects of quality (Table 3.1) for your motel service.

4. What are the implications of quality management for the marketing function of an organization?

5. Explain why poor quality can be expensive for companies manufacturing a product or producing a service.

6. What roles does a quality assurance group play in the prevention of quality problems?

7. As a manager, what can you do for your employees to improve the quality of output?

8. What are the implications of *product* design for quality management? Of *process* design?

9. Suppose that you are the purchasing manager of a company that buys raw materials from hundreds of suppliers, some of which supply the same raw materials. You are convinced that the quality of these materials, as measured by conformance to specifications, can be improved. Disregarding sampling plans, what can you do to improve the quality of the raw materials your company needs? Do the engineering group and top management also have some responsibilities? Explain.

10. Why are internal failure costs so expensive?

11. Explain why the costs of detecting quality problems increase dramatically with the distance from the source of the problem.

12. What is the essence of the total quality control concept? Do you think that it can be easily applied in the United States?

PROBLEMS

Review Problems

1. Wyandotte Manufacturing is a manufacturer of women's apparel. One of its products requires five operations. The raw material is a bolt of cloth 60 inches wide. The first operation cuts the bolt of material in 36-inch lengths. Each piece of material is then processed by four more machines in order to produce the final garment. The following data are available concerning this process.

Operation	Machine	Defective
1	Bolt cutter	2%
2	Pattern cutter	4
3	Stitcher 1	3
4	Stitcher 2	2
5	Presser	1

a. Demand is 500 garments per day. How many cuts must the bolt cutter make in order to produce 500 finished units?

b. If all defects are found after each individual operation, what can be said about the amount of material needed?

c. How much extra capacity is required at each machine because of the defect rates?

d. Why is the percentage of extra capacity required more than the defect percentages

at the bolt cutter, the pattern cutter, and the stitchers?

e. Besides extra capacity costs, other costs are higher because of poor quality in this case?

2. The following data apply to a four-operation production process.

Operation	Machine	Defective
1	A	5%
2	C	4
3	G	6
4	F	3

For each unit of raw material, R100, introduced into this process one unit of final product, X123, is produced. There are currently 530 units of R100 available. A customer wishes to place an order for 500 units of X123. Should the order be accepted? Assume that the customer will not accept a partial shipment.

3. A product is made in a four-operation process, with a final inspection at the end of the fourth operation. The inspector determines whether the entire batch must be reworked. If it does, the batch must be reprocessed through operations 3 and 4. Typically, 25 percent of the batches must be reworked. The size of each batch is 100 units, and 10 batches are required each day. Additional information about this process is as follows:

Operation	Capacity (units/day)
1	1100
2	1100
3	1250
4	1200
Inspection	1500

a. Is it possible to meet the requirement of 10 batches per day? If not, how many batches per day can be produced?

b. What effect does the percentage of rework have on cost?

Advanced Problems

A computer package is helpful for Problem 5.

4. Westwood Company produces two different products using four different operations. Prod-

uct A is processed at operations 1, 2, and 4, and then inspected for quality (1−2−4−I). The routing of product B is 1−2−3−4−I. The percentage of defective products at each operation (excluding inspection) is 2 percent. If the inspector determines that rework is necessary, each product is returned to operation 2. Historically, the rework rate has been 15 percent for product A and 20 percent for product B. If after rework, the inspector rejects the product, it is scrapped without further rework. The following information is available about the processing times (min/unit) of each product at each operation.

Operation	Product	
	A	B
1	0.20	0.20
2	0.10	0.08
3	—	0.10
4	0.15	0.20

a. If 1000 units of each product are required each day, how many units of raw material are needed for each product?

b. What is the expected daily load for operation 4 from these two products if 1000 units of each are required?

5. A product goes through five operations and a final inspection during manufacture. If the product is rejected at final inspection after initial processing, it is returned to operation 3 for reprocessing. If it is rejected at final inspection after rework, it is scrapped. Historically, 25 percent of the product has been returned for rework. The following is the rate of defectives produced at each operation.

Operation	Defective
1	8%
2	5
3	6
4	4
5	7

a. If one unit of raw material produces one unit of final product, how many units of defect-free product can be produced by 5000 units of raw material?

b. Suppose that management has the opportunity to reduce the defective rate of operation 3. Illustrate graphically the effect of decreasing d_3 on final output levels.

c. Suppose that management has the opportunity to reduce the rework rate of the entire production process by utilizing more effective final inspection techniques. Graphically illustrate the effect on final output levels of reducing the rework rate.

d. What costs must be considered before management implements either reduction program?

SELECTED REFERENCES

Aubrey, C. A., and L. A. Eldridge, "Banking on High Quality," *Quality Progress,* vol. 14, no. 12 (December 1981), pp. 14−19.

Crosby, Phillip B. *Quality Is Free.* New York: McGraw-Hill, 1979.

Deming, W. Edwards, "Improvement of Quality and Productivity Through Action by Management," *National Productivity Review,* vol. 1, no. 1 (Winter 1981−1982), pp. 12−22.

Deming, W. Edwards, *Out of the Crisis.* Cambridge, Mass.: Massachusetts Institute of Technology Center for Advanced Engineering Study, 1986.

Feigenbaum, A. V., *Total Quality Control: Engineering and Management,* 3rd ed. New York: McGraw-Hill, 1983.

Garvin, David A., "Quality on the Line," *Harvard Business Review* (September−October 1983), pp. 65−75.

Hostage, G. M. "Quality Control in a Service Business," *Harvard Business Review* (July−August 1975), pp. 89−106.

Ishikawa, Kaoru, *Guide to Quality Control.* Tokyo: Asian Productivity Organization, 1972.

Juran, J. M., and Frank Gryna, Jr., *Quality Planning and Analysis.* 2nd ed. New York: McGraw-Hill, 1980.

Reddy, Jack, and Abe Berger, "Three Essentials of Product Quality," *Harvard Business Review* (July−August 1983), pp. 153−159.

Schonberger, Richard J., *Japanese Manufacturing Techniques.* New York: The Free Press, 1982.

Takeuchi, Hirotaka, and John A. Quelch, "Quality Is More than Making a Good Product," *Harvard Business Review* (November−December 1981), pp. 14−19.

A braided tube forms around the ski core.

PART

2

DESIGN DECISIONS

Once a firm has identified its market niche and the competitive priorities that spell success, it must design an operations system to meet its needs. K2 Corporation, for example, chose an intermediate positioning strategy that allowed product flexibility, as well as high-volume production of some products. High-performance design and consistent quality became the top competitive priorities. The next step was designing a manufacturing process that would deliver.

For product flexibility, K2 installed general-purpose machinery that allowed easy changeovers from product to product. For design and quality, they invested in a triaxial braiding process, which gave designers greater control over longitudinal and torsional flexes in the skis. K2's plant has a process layout with five departments: parts, molding, base finishing, graphics, and finishing. Molding has fifty-two general-purpose presses, some dedicated to high-volume products. Within base-finishing and finishing, machines are arranged to take advantage of the common machine sequences that most products require. Machine maintenance is critical because the plant runs at full capacity.

Like K2, successful manufacturing and service firms need operating systems that support their competitive strategies. Part 2 examines the trade-offs managers face in choosing between critical aspects of process design and the tools they use to analyze different designs. We also explore ways to manage cutting-edge technologies. The sections on work measurement and learning curves lead to discussion of capacity determination issues. A firm's geographical location is another critical design decision. Collectively, the issues presented in Part 2 set the stage for execution of the operations strategy.

CHAPTER

4

PROCESS DESIGN

 Chapter Outline

▲ Key Questions for Managers

What processes should we use to produce our goods and services?

How capital intensive should our operations be?

Do we need general-purpose or special-purpose equipment?

How flexible should our work force be?

How much should we vertically integrate?

How much should we involve the customer in the production process?

How do we merge the human element into process design?

Should our jobs be specialized or enlarged?

 ven after management decides on product plans, competitive priorities, positioning strategy, and quality, many questions remain unanswered. One of the essential questions is: *How should we make our products?* The question is easy, but the answer involves many difficult choices in selecting the best mix of human resources, equipment, and materials.

Process design decisions are strategically important. Wrong choices can affect an organization's ability to compete over the long run. Process design directly affects productivity because much of the "input" of the output/input ratio is set during process design. However, process design choices are not made once and for all—it is an ongoing activity. The principles and techniques that we present in this chapter apply to both first-time and redesign choices.

We begin by defining and considering four facets of process design: capital intensity, resource flexibility, vertical integration, and customer involvement. We turn next to some basic techniques for analyzing new and existing processes: process charts, multiple activity charts, and flow diagrams. We conclude the chapter with a discussion of work-force management, which deserves careful consideration in any organization. In Chapter 5 we explore technological advances, another important aspect of process design, and the ever-widening array of choices they present.

WHAT IS PROCESS DESIGN? ▲

Process design is the selection of inputs, operations, work flows, and methods for producing goods and services. Input selection includes choosing the preferred mix of human skills, raw materials, and equipment consistent with an organization's positioning strategy and its ability to obtain these resources. Operations managers must determine which operations will be performed by workers and which by machines. They also determine the transformations (refer back to Fig. 1.1) that will be used to meld human beings and machines into cohesive production processes. Process design or redesign decisions must be made when:

- A new or substantially modified product or service is being offered.
- Competitive priorities have changed.
- Demand volume for a product or service is changing.
- Current performance is inadequate.
- Competitors are gaining a comparative advantage by using a different process, or a new technology is available.
- The cost or availability of inputs has changed.

Not all these situations lead to a change in the current process. Sometimes, the costs of change clearly outweigh the benefits. Whether or not changes are made, process design must take into account other choices concerning product design, product quality, capacity, and layout. Process design decisions also depend on where products are in their life cycle, competitive priorities, and positioning strategy.

A robot hoists a heavy plastic tub at GE's Appliance Park in Louisville, Kentucky. Industrial robots are very much in evidence at this capital-intensive plant.

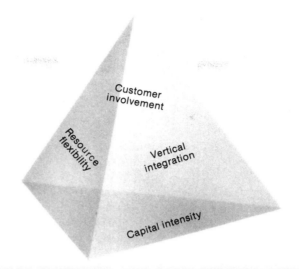

FIGURE 4.1   Facets of Process Design

FACETS OF PROCESS DESIGN ▲

Whether considering processes for offices, service industries, or manufacturers, operations managers must weigh four common facets of process design. **Capital intensity** is the mix of equipment and human skills in a production process; the greater the relative cost of equipment, the greater is the capital intensity. **Resource flexibility** is the ease with which equipment and employees can handle a wide variety of products, output levels, duties, and functions. **Vertical integration** is the degree to which a firm's own production system handles the supply chain from raw materials to final consumer. The more a firm's production system manages the supply chain, the greater is the degree of vertical integration. **Customer involvement** reflects how much and in what ways the customer becomes a part of the production process.

Because the facets of process design are interrelated, a manager's choices concerning one may significantly affect choices concerning the others. Figure 4.1 depicts the four related facets as a three-dimensional pyramid. Think of the edges as the linkages and trade-offs between pairs of facets. Thus sales, as well as production costs, are affected by the manager's choices. For example, automation of GE's dishwasher plant in Louisville, Kentucky, helped increase the firm's market share from 32 to 40 percent.

Capital Intensity

Whether designing a new process or redesigning an existing one, the operations manager must determine which tasks will be performed by humans and which by machines. With the increased sophistication of modern computer hardware and software, process designers face an ever-widening set of choices. These choices range from operations requiring very little automation to operations in which equipment performs specific tasks with very little human intervention.

Although expensive investments, computers can significantly increase productivity. For example, Saga Corporation, the leading operator of college dining halls, is considering a computer system for its back room operations. Waitresses would punch in orders at a dining room terminal. The computer would then print out orders in the kitchen, track their progress, and prepare next-day shopping lists. Such a system would cost $45,000 per restaurant, but would cut ordering time and speed delivery of the dinner check. Management also hopes that by streamlining operations, the business can accommodate overflows, which otherwise might be turned away on busy nights.

More capital intensity is not always best. A case in point is E.T. Wright's shoemaking plant, which a recent survey selected as one of the country's 10 best-managed factories. The company still relies on skilled artisans and hand labor to make its arch-preserver shoes. Competitive priorities call for a unique product of high quality, even if a pair of shoes retails for more than $100. The firm has not been able to achieve these priorities with high capital intensity.

Some types of equipment can be acquired a piece at a time, allowing the user to try it out without making a large and risky initial capital investment. Examples of such equipment are new photocopy machines and stand-alone word processors and printers. However, many technological choices involve large and costly systems—and a great deal more capital and risk.

Resource Flexibility

In Chapter 2 we discussed product flexibility and volume flexibility as competitive priorities. Process design affects the firm's ability to achieve either one. And the choices that management makes concerning employees, facilities, and equipment determine the degree of resource flexibility. For example, when product plans call for short life cycles or high product flexibility, equipment must be general purpose and employees need to perform a broad range of duties.

Until recently, there has been a strong inverse relationship between capital intensity and resource flexibility. Production volumes had to be high before a firm could afford the capital investment required for economical operation. Figure 4.2 illustrates this relationship for two processes. Process 1 calls for inexpensive, general-purpose equipment. It gets the job done, but not at peak

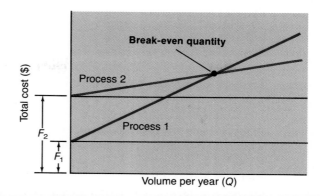

FIGURE 4.2 Relationship Between Capital Intensity and Product Volume

efficiency. In terms of break-even analysis, the fixed cost, F_1, is relatively small, but the variable unit cost (slope of the total-cost line) is large. Process 2 is much more capital intensive, which drives up F_2. Its virtue is greater efficiency and therefore a smaller unit cost. Unfortunately, the firm achieves this efficiency only by dedicating special-purpose equipment to a narrow range of products or tasks. The break-even quantity in Fig. 4.2 is well to the right on the graph. Therefore, unless volumes are high enough (which is less likely with high product flexibility), the cost of process 2 is not warranted.

Exceptions to the inverse relationship between capital intensity and flexibility are beginning to emerge. As you will see in Chapter 5, technologies allowing certain types of flexible automation are now available. They are capital intensive but allow for more resource flexibility than was possible in the past.

Resource flexibility also has important implications for the work force. Operations managers must decide whether to have a **flexible work force**. Members of a flexible work force are capable of doing many tasks, either at their own work stations or as they move from one work station to another. Such flexibility often comes at a cost, requiring greater skills and thus more training and education. Nevertheless, benefits can be large. For example, Westinghouse recently overhauled its Sumter, South Carolina, plant so that employees are now able to perform a variety of tasks. As a result, productivity and capacity have increased. General Motors' new billion-dollar Saturn plant in Spring Hills, Tennessee, is another example. In a bid for Japanese-style efficiency, GM's plant features a revolutionary labor contract having only five job classifications and allowing considerable worker flexibility. Elsewhere in the auto industry, union contracts specify as many as 110 job classifications, severely limiting resource flexibility.

We showed in one study that worker flexibility is one of the best ways to achieve reliable customer service and alleviate capacity bottlenecks (Ritzman, King, and Krajewski, 1984). We found resource flexibility to be particularly crucial to process-focused positioning strategy. Resource flexibility helps absorb the feast-or-famine workloads at individual operations that are caused by low-volume production, jumbled routings, and fluid scheduling.

Administrators of large urban hospitals face worker flexibility issues when making decisions about staffing and degrees of specialization. Many hospitals use all registered nurses (RNs) instead of a mix of RNs, licensed vocational nurses (LVNs), and aides. Registered nurses have a higher education level and earn more than LVNs and aides, but they are more flexible and can perform all nursing tasks. Sometimes hospitals choose the opposite extreme (worker specialization) in an attempt to hold costs down. In the USSR, for example, delicate eye surgery is performed in an "assembly line," consisting of patients on stretchers that move past five work stations. A surgeon at each station has three minutes to complete a specific portion of the operation before the patient moves on to the next surgeon. Obviously, these surgeons are highly specialized. Resource flexibility has been sacrificed, but great speed and economy are attained.

The type of work force required also depends on the need for volume flexibility. When conditions allow for a smooth, steady rate of output, the likely choice is a permanent work force that expects regular full-time employment. If the process is subject to hourly, daily, or seasonal peaks and valleys in demand, the use of part-time or temporary employees to supplement a smaller core of full-time employees may be the best solution. However, this approach may not be practical if knowledge and skill requirements are too high for a temporary worker to grasp quickly.

Vertical Integration

As Managerial Practice 4.1 illustrates, firms may have different strategies for procuring necessary resources. All businesses buy at least some inputs to their processes, such as raw materials, manufactured parts, or professional services, from other producers. Management makes decisions about vertical integration by looking at the entire supply chain—from acquisition of raw materials to delivery of finished product. The more processes in the chain the organization controls, the more vertically integrated it is.

Extensive vertical integration is generally more attractive when volumes are high, and task specialization and high repeatability lead to greater efficiency. For example, Atlantic Foods has the volume to keep a team of six workers busy peeling eggs at the rate of 10,000 per shift, but a local restaurant doesn't. Similarly, a corner grocery store lacks the sales volume and resources to operate its own trout farm, as does Kroger Company.

Once a firm achieves high volumes it is more likely to pursue backward integration. *Backward integration* represents movement toward the sources of raw materials and parts. *Forward integration* means that the firm owns more channels of distribution, such as its own distribution centers (warehouses) and retail stores.

Vertical integration can reduce resource flexibility because a large investment in facilities and equipment may not be easy to reverse. For example, Kroger recently had to do something about the resources it had tied up in idle equipment and facilities. With inflation under control, customers became less enthusiastic about house brands and generic (no brand) products, turning more toward national brands. This shift created excess manufacturing capacity,

MANAGERIAL PRACTICE 4.1

Choosing the Right Amount of Vertical Integration

More Integration

- Kroger Company, the largest food retailer in the United States during 1982, on the basis of domestic sales, has considerable vertical integration. It operates dairies, a trout farm, and plants making peanut butter, crackers, coffee, and many other dry groceries. It sells these products under the Kroger label.

- Some of the largest U.S. corporations, such as Chase Manhattan, IBM, and GE, have joined together to start their own insurance company. The company offers to all of them high-risk coverage that big casualty insurers are reluctant to provide.

Less Integration

- Although it's an old and controversial idea, more government work is being contracted out. Costs are often cut as much as 20 percent, without sacrificing quality. This approach goes beyond providing garbage collection, road repairs, and public transportation. Private industry is now under contract in some cases to staff control towers at small airports, operate prisons, run wastewater treatment plants, trim trees, and demolish buildings.

- Restaurants and food-service operators need hard-boiled eggs for salad bars and sandwiches. Many find it more efficient to buy precooked egg products than to process their own. Some suppliers use machines to peel their eggs, but Atlantic Foods feels that quality is improved by doing it manually. A team of six employees set a record of peeling 10,000 eggs in just one shift.

Sources: "Aggressive a Century, Kroger Is Retrenching to Stem Fall in Profits," *Wall Street Journal*, May 31, 1981; "Wall Street Eyes an Ultimate Junk Bond," *Fortune*, February 3, 1986; "When Public Services Go Private," *Fortune*, May 27, 1985; "Boiled-Egg Peelers Aim for Perfection, and That's No Yolk," *Wall Street Journal*, July 9, 1985.

which Kroger had to find a way to utilize. It is doing so by making ice cream and dough for frozen pizza for its competitors, who in turn sell the products under their own labels. While this may be an ideal solution, excess capacity did limit Kroger's resource flexibility and range of acceptable business opportunities.

Hollow corporations have a strategy opposite to that of Kroger's: gaining flexibility but taking a different risk. A **hollow corporation** is a small central firm that relies on other firms for most of its production—and for many of its other functions—on a contract basis. It is sometimes called a *network company*, because its few employees spend most of their time on the telephone coordinating suppliers. Lewis Galoob Toys, Inc., which features trendy toys, is a good example. Its 115 employees account for $58 million in sales, but the company subcontracts all its engineering and production and most of its marketing and accounting functions. Emerson Radio (consumer electronics) and Liz Claiborne (apparel) are other examples. Hollow corporations can move in and out of markets quickly, riding the waves of fashion and technology. They are vulnerable, however, for they add little value to the product. Their suppliers can integrate forward or their customers can integrate backward. A hollow corporation's risk of losing its business to suppliers or customers increases as product volumes increase and product life cycles lengthen.

Make or Buy.   Backward integration is often referred to as the *make-or-buy decision*. The operations manager must study all the costs and advantages of each approach. Break-even analysis is a good starting point. However, it is applied differently from the way it was done for product planning (see Chapter 2), because the assumption is that the decision doesn't affect revenues. Rather than finding the quantity where total costs equal total revenues, the analyst finds the quantity for which the total costs for two alternatives are equal. For the make-or-buy decision, this is the quantity for which total "make" cost equals the total "buy" cost. The buy option may or may not have a fixed cost. To find the break-even quantity, set the two cost functions $(F + cQ)$ equal to each other and solve for Q. The formula from Chapter 2 does not apply in this case.

APPLICATION 4.1

The manager of a fast-food restaurant featuring hamburgers is adding salads to the menu. There are two options, and the price to the customer will be the same for each one. The "make" option is to install a salad bar stocked with vegetables, fruits, and toppings and let the customer assemble the salad. The salad bar would have to be leased and a part-time employee hired. The manager estimates a fixed cost at $12,000 and variable costs totaling $1.50 per salad. The "buy" option is to have preassembled salads available for sale. They would be purchased from a local supplier, at $2.00 per salad. With preassembled salads it would be necessary to install and operate additional refrigeration, with a fixed cost of $2,400.

The manager expects to sell 25,000 salads per year. What is the break-even quantity?

Solution

Set the fixed cost plus the variable cost $(F + cQ)$ for the buy option equal to the equivalent costs for the make option, and solve for Q:

$$\$2,400 + 2.0Q = \$12,000 + \$1.5Q$$
$$\$0.5Q = \$9,600$$
$$Q = 19,200 \text{ salads}$$

The break-even quantity is 19,200 salads. Since the 25,000-salad sales forecast exceeds this amount, the make option is preferred. The make option has the lower variable cost, so its total cost will be smaller than the buy option beyond the break-even quantity.

Equally important are qualitative factors. The customers of the restaurant in Application 4.1 might be willing to pay more for a salad that they can make to their own tastes (that is, more product flexibility). Or perhaps a preassembled salad doesn't fit the customers' image of the restaurant. Although some "make" decisions require sizable capital investments, they may take better advantage of the firm's human resources, equipment, and space.

Own or Lease. When a firm decides on more vertical integration, it must also decide whether to own or lease the necessary facilities and equipment. The lease option is often favored for items affected by fairly rapid changes in technology, items that require frequent servicing, or items for which industry practices have made leasing the norm, as in the photocopier industry. Leasing is also common when a firm has a short-term need for equipment. For example, in the construction industry projects usually take months or years to complete, so heavy equipment is often leased only as needed.

Many firms lease payroll, security, cleaning, and other types of services, rather than employing personnel and using their own resources to provide these services. Frequently, an organization can hire a firm with the desired expertise and obtain a higher quality of service at a lower cost than it could obtain from a staff of its own.

At Wendy's SuperBar customers assemble their own salads and make selections from Mexican and Italian dishes.

Customer Involvement

The fourth facet of process design is the extent to which customers interact with the process. In many service industries customer contact is crucial. Customers at Wendy's SuperBar are involved in terms of (1) self-service, (2) product selection, and (3) time and location.

Self-Service.   To save money, some customers prefer to do part of the process formerly performed by the manufacturer or dealer. Self-service is the process design choice of many retailers, particularly when price is a competitive priority. Some product-focused manufacturers also use self-service to advantage. Their customers become the final assemblers of toys, bicycles, furniture, and other products. Production, shipping, and inventory costs frequently are lower, as are losses from damage.

Product Selection.   A business that competes on product flexibility frequently allows customers to come up with their own product specifications or even become involved in designing the product. For example, salad bar customers have more control over portions and ingredients. Another good example of customer involvement is in custom designed and built homes. The customer is heavily involved in the design process. During construction, the customer inspects the work-in-process at various times. Furthermore, customer involvement is not likely to end even when the owner occupies the house. Most builders guarantee their work for some extended time period, and most owners find reasons to exercise this warranty.

Time and Location. For industries in which service cannot occur without the customer's presence, time and location issues affect the process design. If the service is delivered to the customer, client, or patient by appointment, decisions involving the location of such meetings become part of process design. Will customers be served only on the supplier's premises, will the supplier's employees go to the customers' premises, or will the service be provided at yet a third location? Operators of emergency ambulance services cannot provide service without a patient. They cannot predict when the next call for service will come in or where the ambulance will have to go, so they must design their response processes accordingly. On the other hand, certified public accountants, in their role as independent auditors, frequently work on their clients' premises, a situation in which both the time and place are likely to be known well in advance.

High customer involvement processes tend to be less capital intensive and to have more resource flexibility than do low customer involvement processes. These conditions are particularly true when there is a need for full service, customized orders, unpredictable demands, and service provided at customer locations. Exceptions, such as telephone exchanges, vending machines, and automatic bank tellers, can be found, mainly because these processes require minimal personalized attention.

Trade-offs Between Facets

We have already identified several trade-offs among the four facets of process design. By using the three fundamental relationships (trade-offs) shown in Fig. 4.3, with capital intensity as a common facet, we can infer trade-offs between all pairs of facets. For example, vertical integration and capital intensity are directly related, but customer involvement and capital intensity are inversely related. Since vertical integration and customer involvement relate to a common factor oppositely, we conclude that they are related inversely. Such relationships are not based on cause and effect. The underlying variable is repeatability, which comes from high product volumes, standardization of parts, task specialization, and low customer involvement. Increasing repeatability opens the door for

1. more automation (and therefore capital intensity);
2. less need for resource flexibility; and
3. more opportunities for vertical integration.

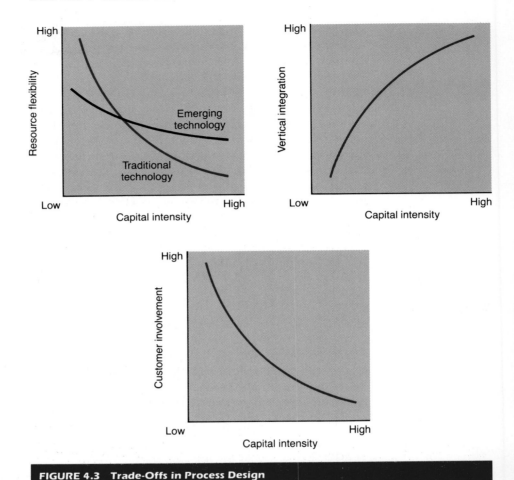

FIGURE 4.3   Trade-Offs in Process Design

Of course, these are general tendencies rather than unbreakable laws. Exceptions can be found, but these relationships provide a way of understanding how process design choices can be linked coherently.

Capital Budgeting

Capital budgeting is a method used to allocate scarce funds among competing investment alternatives. Ideas for improving a process often call for capital investment in facilities and equipment. For example, further vertical integration by a firm invariably requires more equipment and perhaps a new facility. As most of a firm's assets are usually committed to operations, many ideas for capital expenditures and proposals for their inclusion in the firm's capital budget originate there.

Operations managers are constantly looking for ways to encourage innovative ideas for improving productivity. At the same time, they must screen out ideas that don't fit with established operations strategy or generate enough benefits for the investment required. Benefits can be labor savings, materials cost reduction, less scrap, better quality, lower inventory, better customer service, or higher revenues. Benefits can also be more qualitative, such as greater resource flexibility, which expands opportunities for future products. The operations manager must estimate the costs, benefits, and risks involved in the proposed change. These estimates are then analyzed by means of one or more capital budgeting techniques, such as net present value, payback, or internal rate of return. A brief review of these techniques is found in Supplement 1.

The final decisions in capital budgeting are made by top management—or even the board of directors when a major capital investment is proposed. They make sure that very large investments in equipment and facilities are in line with corporate strategies, particularly with respect to product plans and competitive priorities.

PROCESS ANALYSIS ▲

The four facets of process design represent broad, strategic issues. There is another, more tactical side to process design: the careful, detailed analysis of each process. **Process analysis**, sometimes called *methods study* or *work simplification*, is the systematic study of the activities and flows of each process in order to improve it.

In this section we present three basic techniques for analyzing activities and flows within processes: process charts, multiple activity charts, and flow diagrams. These techniques can be used systematically to question the process itself and each detail of the process. The operations manager can highlight tasks that can be simplified or indicate where productivity can otherwise be improved. Managers can use these techniques to design new processes and redesign existing ones and should use them periodically to study all operations. However, the greatest payoff is likely to come from applying them to operations having one or more of the following characteristics.

- The process is a bottleneck. That is, work piles up waiting to go through this process, and people or machines are idle while waiting for the output of the process.
- The process consumes a great amount of time.
- The process results in a lot of waste materials.
- The process involves disagreeable or dangerous working conditions.
- The process requires a great deal of physical movement.

All three analytic techniques involve breaking a process into detailed components. In order to do this, the manager should ask six questions:

1. *What* is being done?

2. *When* is it being done?

3. *Who* is doing it?

4. *Where* is it being done?

5. *How long* does it take?

6. *How* is it being done?

Answers to these questions are challenged by asking still another series of questions: *Why?* Why is the process even being done? Why is it being done where it is being done? Why is it being done when it is being done? Such questioning can often lead to some creative answers that can cause a breakthrough in process design.

These techniques are closely related to techniques presented in Chapter 6 (work measurement), as time estimates are needed for the different tasks in the process. However, time estimates are also needed in many other aspects of operations management, such as for capacity, production planning, staffing, and scheduling decisions.

Process Charts

A **process chart** is an organized way of recording all the activities that are performed by a person, by a machine, at a work station, or on materials. For our purposes we group these activities into five categories: operation, transportation, inspection, delay, and storage. An *operation* is productive work that changes, creates, or adds something. Examples are mixing tar, stone, and sand to get asphalt; drilling a hole; or serving a customer at a store. *Transportation* (sometimes called materials handling) is the movement of the study's subject from one place to another. The subject can be a person, a material, a tool, or a piece of equipment. Examples of transportation are a customer walking from one end of a counter to another, a crane hoisting a steel beam to a location, or a conveyor carrying a partially completed product from one work station to the next. *Inspections* check or verify something, but do not change it. Checking for blemishes on a surface, weighing a product, or taking a temperature reading are examples of inspections. *Delays* occur when the subject is held up awaiting further action. Time spent waiting for materials or equipment, time for clean-up, or time that workers, machines, or work stations are idle because there is nothing for them to do are examples of delays. *Storage* occurs when something is put away until a later time. Supplies being unloaded and placed in a storeroom as inventory, equipment put away after use, or papers put in a file cabinet are examples of storage. Depending on the situation, other activity categories may be used, such as subcontracting/outside services or distinguishing between temporary storage and permanent storage.

In order to complete a process chart for a new process, the analyst must identify each step performed. If the process is an existing one, the analyst can actually observe the steps, categorizing each step according to the subject being studied. Changing the subject (say, from the product being made to the worker) might also change the category to which a step is assigned. The analyst then records the distance traveled and the time* taken to perform each step. After recording all the activities and steps, the analyst obtains total times and distances, summarizes the activities, and estimates the annual cost of the entire process.

Making a Batch of Brownies.   Figure 4.4 shows a process chart for making a batch of brownies at a bakery. The process begins with the baker removing preassembled brownie mix and ends when the large pan of brownies is removed from the oven. Raw materials (the brownie mix, water, and eggs) and equipment and container (bowl mixer, measuring container, and pan) must be assembled. The brownie mix must be prepared, the oven preheated, and the brownies baked. The analyst broke this process into 35 steps, making the baker the subject of the study. A summary of times and distances traveled is shown at the upper-right hand corner of the process chart. The times add up to 74.4 minutes, and the baker travels a total of 550 feet.

It is helpful to know the annual cost of the process charted, which becomes a benchmark against which other methods for performing the process can be evaluated. The annual labor cost can be estimated by finding the product of:

- Time in hours to perform the process each time.
- Variable cost per hour.
- Number of times the process is performed per week.
- Number of weeks per year in which the process is performed.

APPLICATION 4.2

The baker earns $17 per hour (including fringe benefits) and makes 12 batches per week. What is the annual labor cost?

Solution

$$\text{Annual labor cost} = \frac{74.4 \text{ min}}{60 \text{ min/hr}}(\$17/\text{hr})(12/\text{wk})(52 \text{ wk/yr}) = \$13,154$$

Adding in the cost of materials would yield a sizable variable cost, and brownies are but one of many products made at the bakery.

Now comes the creative part of process analysis. Suppose that you are the analyst. You should now ask the what, when, who, where, how long, and how questions, challenging each of the 35 steps. There is always a better way, if you can just think of it. Look at the summary to see which activities take the most time. Time-consuming activities offer the greatest potential for improvement.

---

*See Chapter 6 on the various ways to establish time standards.

								Summary		
Process: making one batch of brownies							Activity	Number of Steps	Time	Distance
Subject charted: baker							Operation ◯	18	22.5	—
Beginning: remove brownie mix from bin							Transport ⇨	13	11.7	550
Ending: remove brownies from oven							Inspect ☐	2	0.2	—
							Delay D	2	40.0	—
							Store ▽	0	—	—

Step No.	Time (min)	Distance (ft)	◯	⇨	☐	D	▽	Step Description
1	1.3		X					Remove preassembled mix from bin
2	0.2		X					Place mix on counter
3	1.2	60		X				Walk to cabinet
4	0.4		X					Remove bowl and mixer
5	1.2	60		X				Return the bowl and mixer to counter
6	0.2		X					Place bowl and mixer on counter
7	1.3		X					Open bag of mix and dump into bowl
8	1.2	60		X				Walk to cabinet
9	0.3		X					Remove pan and measuring container
10	1.2	60		X				Return with them to counter
11	0.2		X					Place them on counter
12	0.6	30		X				Walk to refrigerator
13	0.8		X					Remove eggs from refrigerator
14	0.6	30		X				Walk back to counter
15	0.1		X					Place eggs on counter
16	2.8		X					Break eggs into brownie mix
17	2.2		X					Use mixer to stir eggs and brownie mix
18	0.9	40		X				Pick up measuring container; walk to sink
19	1.4		X					Fill measuring container with water
20	0.8	40		X				Walk back to counter
21	0.3		X					Pour water into brownie mix
22	4.3		X					Use mixer to stir ingredients in bowl
23	0.1				X			Inspect mixture in bowl
24	1.9		X					Pour mixture into pan
25	0.1				X			Inspect mixture in pan
26	0.3		X					Discard egg shells
27	0.9	40		X				Take bowl, mixer, and container to sink
28	4.0		X					Wash and dry them
29	0.6	20		X				Return them to cabinet
30	0.2	10		X				Walk to oven
31	10.0					X		Turn on oven; let oven preheat
32	1.0	50		X				Walk to counter
33	1.3	50		X				Pick up pan; walk to oven; place in oven
34	30.0					X		Wait 30 minutes to bake; turn off oven
35	0.5		X					Open oven; remove pan; close oven

FIGURE 4.4   Process Chart for Making Brownies at a Bakery

APPLICATION 4.3

What improvement can you make in the process? Pay particular attention to the preheating delay and unnecessary activities.

Solution

Your analysis should verify the following three ideas for improvement. You may also be able to come up with others.

1. *Eliminate the preheating delay.*
   The two preheating delays account for 40 minutes, or more than 50 percent of the time needed for the entire process. The first delay is at step 31, when the baker waits 10 minutes for the oven to preheat. If the oven were turned on earlier, he could be doing other things as the oven heated. Turning on the oven during the first trip to the cabinet (step 3) yields an added bonus: Since the oven is located on the way to the cabinet, some travel time is saved.

2. *Combine the trips for equipment.*
   The baker walks to the cabinet twice to get tools. This is inefficient because the tools aren't heavy or large enough to require two trips. Even if they were unwieldly, he could use a cart. Combining steps 3–5 and 8–10 saves time, as the baker gathers all the tools at once and eliminates 120 feet of travel.

3. *Eliminate the first mixing.*
   Steps 16, 17, 21, and 22 can be rearranged to add the eggs and water to the brownie mix before mixing. This cuts out another step and a little time.

This simple example illustrates how to use a process chart to analyze a process. In other manufacturing or service industry environments, the method is the same, even though the processes, materials, and equipment are different. To make a process more efficient, the analyst should question each delay and then analyze the operation, transport, inspection, and storage activities to see whether they can be combined, rearranged, or eliminated. Improvements in productivity can be significant.

Multiple Activity Charts

A process chart describes the work being done by or on just one subject. However, simultaneously tracking multiple subjects may be more revealing. A **multiple activity chart** is a record of the activities performed by or on several subjects over a given time period. Multiple activity charts are useful in helping a manager divide work more equally among employees, reduce time required for certain activities, or rearrange activities to shorten a job's overall time, and decide how to utilize people, work stations, or machines more effectively. Managers frequently use multiple activity charts to find ways to minimize idle time.

The first step is to determine the process to be studied. The analyst divides a sheet of paper into columns, with one for each person, material, or work station. The analyst next observes the process and establishes a time standard for each activity (see Chapter 6). Finally the analyst charts the time required to perform each activity, using vertical bars having lengths that represent these times.

An Orthodontist's Office.   Managerial Practice 4.2 describes an orthodontist's office. Figure 4.5 is a multiple activity chart for this office. It provides columns for the orthodontist, technicians 1 and 2, and the four patient work stations A, B, C, and D. We are interested only in one of the receptionist's activities—seating the patients—so we do not need an extra column for the receptionist.

This multiple activity chart represents what typically happens during one of the busiest morning hours. Technician 1 works on patients in chairs A and

MANAGERIAL PRACTICE 4.2 ▲

Treating Patients in an Orthodontist's Office

Dr. Edward Wilson is an orthodontist with a large, well-established practice. He sees current patients for biweekly adjustment of their braces on three mornings each week, from 7:00 A.M. until noon, and on two afternoons from 2 to 5 P.M. The procedure followed during these routine visits is for the receptionist to seat the patient in one of four chairs; Dr. Wilson then checks the patient. After his check, which takes about one minute, one of two orthodontic technicians adjusts the patient's braces. The adjustment procedure takes the technicians about eight minutes per patient. After the braces are adjusted, Dr. Wilson again checks the patient and makes any necessary final adjustment. This final check takes about two minutes. Dr. Wilson has developed very efficient procedures because many of his patients are students and professional business people who do not want to miss school or work for long periods. His objective is to get them in and out of the chair in 20 minutes or less.

Dr. Wilson currently has four chairs and employs two technicians. The technicians take about one minute between patients to wash their hands, and each technician is allowed to take a five minute break at the end of each hour. At their busiest, Dr. Wilson and the technicians are able to process 12 patients per hour.

MULTIPLE ACTIVITY CHART

LOCATION: Dr. Wilson's Office   DATE: 10-8-86   TIME: UNITS: Minutes

OBSERVER: S. Perry   METHOD: ✓ PRESENT   BEGIN: 7:06 AM

   ____ PROPOSED   END: 8:06 AM

PROCESS: Routine check-up of patients - 4 chairs   TOTAL ELAPSED: 60 Min.

SUMMARY:

ITEM	TIME SPENT: WORKING	IDLE	OTHER*	% UTILIZATION
Dr. Wilson	36	24		36/60 = 60%
Technician 1	53	7		53/60 = 88%
Technician 2	53	7		53/60 = 88%
Chair A	36	20	4	36/60 = 60%
Chair B	36	18	6	36/60 = 60%
Chair C	36	17	7	36/60 = 60%
Chair D	36	15	9	36/60 = 60%

*IDENTIFY OTHER: Chair is occupied, but patient is idle. Treat as idle time.

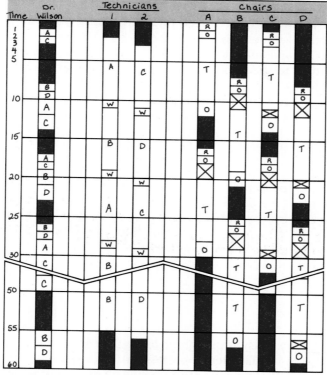

A: Working on patient in chair A

B: Working on patient in chair B

C: Working on patient in chair C

D: Working on patient in chair D

O: Orthodontist working on patient

R: Receptionist seats patient

T: Technician working on patient

W: Washing hands

X: Chair occupied but patient idle

■: Idle time

FIGURE 4.5   Multiple Activity Chart for Orthodontist: Four Chairs

B, and technician 2 works on patients in chairs C and D. At the top of the chart, the summary shows that the technicians were busy for all but 7 minutes of the hour.

Their utilization is a very high 88 percent, or the time they are occupied divided by the period of time being studied. Dr. Wilson's utilization is much lower. He is occupied only 36 minutes of the hour, for a utilization of 36/60 = 60 percent. The chart also indicates the amount of time that each chair is unoccupied or is occupied by a patient waiting for the next step in the process. On the morning of this analysis the patient in chair A had to spend only 4 minutes waiting, but the chair was unoccupied for 20 minutes of the hour (shown as idle time). Patients in chair D had to wait 9 minutes, but the chair was empty for only 15 minutes. As this waiting time was spread over three patients, for three minutes each, it was probably acceptable to them.

APPLICATION 4.4

Many patients are referred to Dr. Wilson, and he would like to expand his practice without devoting more hours to routine brace adjustments. He is thinking of adding two more chairs and hiring two more technicians. He would continue to spend one minute with the patients before the technicians work on them and about two minutes with them after the technicians have finished. How many more patients can he see, and what will be the utilizations and patient wait times, with the expansion?

Solution

The new chart is shown in Fig. 4.6. The orthodontist now has as little unoccupied time as the technicians. All are busy for 53 of the 60 minutes for utilization ratios of 88 percent. Even though almost every patient has to wait before and after seeing the technician, no patient's total time in the chair exceeds 20 minutes, so that goal can be met. It appears that Dr. Wilson can add two chairs and an additional technician to his staff and see 18 patients every hour instead of 12, but he and his technicians would be very busy.

Studies such as these have made dentistry a much different business than it used to be. The dental profession stands out in the health-care industry as a leader in productivity improvement over the past several decades. These substantial gains are being studied carefully by the rest of the health-care industry.

MULTIPLE ACTIVITY CHART

LOCATION: _Dr. Wilson's Office_   DATE: _____   TIME: UNITS: _Minutes_

OBSERVER: _S. Perry_   METHOD: ___ PRESENT   BEGIN: _____

   ✓ PROPOSED   END: _____

PROCESS: _Routine check-up of patients – 6 chairs_   TOTAL ELAPSED: _60 Min._

SUMMARY:	TIME SPENT:			
ITEM	WORKING	IDLE	OTHER*	% UTILIZATION
Dr. Wilson	53	7		53/60 = 88%
Technician 1	53	7		53/60 = 88%
Technician 2	53	7		53/60 = 88%
Technician 3	53	7		53/60 = 88%
Chair A	36	17	7	36/60 = 60%
Chair B	36	16	8	36/60 = 60%
Chair C	36	14	10	36/60 = 60%
Chair D	36	13	11	36/60 = 60%
Chair E	36	11	13	36/60 = 60%
Chair F	36	12	12	36/60 = 60% (includes 1 min. of next hr)

*IDENTIFY OTHER: _Chair is occupied, but patient is idle. Treat as idle time._

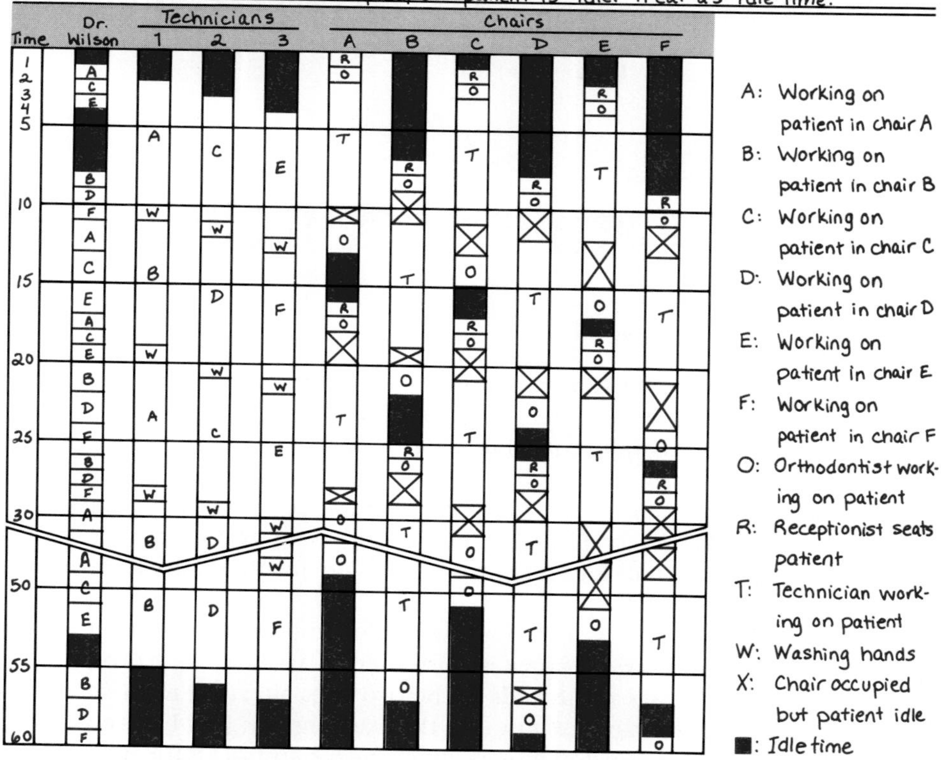

A: Working on patient in chair A
B: Working on patient in chair B
C: Working on patient in chair C
D: Working on patient in chair D
E: Working on patient in chair E
F: Working on patient in chair F
O: Orthodontist working on patient
R: Receptionist seats patient
T: Technician working on patient
W: Washing hands
X: Chair occupied but patient idle
■: Idle time

FIGURE 4.6   **Multiple Activity Chart for Orthodontist: Six Chairs**

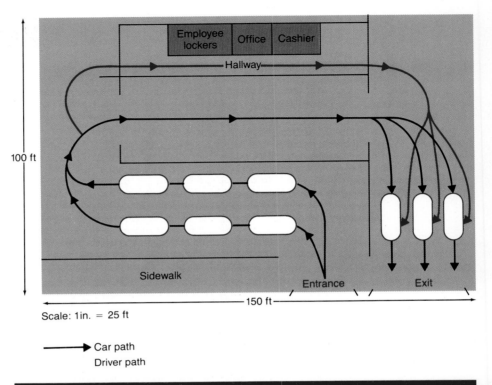

Scale: 1 in. = 25 ft

→ Car path
Driver path

FIGURE 4.7 Flow Diagram for a Car Wash Facility

Flow Diagrams

When an operation involves considerable movement of materials or people, a flow diagram is a useful analytical tool. A **flow diagram** traces the flows of people, equipment, or materials through a process. To make a flow diagram, the analyst first makes a rough sketch of the area in which the process is performed. On a grid (graph paper or other paper marked off in squares), the analyst plots the path followed by the person, material, or equipment. The analyst uses arrows to indicate the direction of movement, that is, the direction of flow.

Figure 4.7 shows a flow diagram for a car wash facility, illustrating the flows of cars and customers. Cars enter one of two lines from the street. The cars at the ends of the two lines alternate in forming a single line that rounds a sharp corner into the washing bay. Just before a car enters the washing bay, the customer gets out of the car and walks through a separate door and hallway to the office and pays for the service. The car proceeds through the washing bay, and the customer exits through the hallway and out a second door to rejoin the car after it is rolled to an open area and wiped down. The customer gets back into the car and drives away. The facility used to have only one waiting line, and, during peak periods, the line of cars would extend back into the street, blocking traffic. The owner used a flow diagram to determine that the second waiting line could be added without changing the flow of the other operations.*

WORK-FORCE MANAGEMENT ▲

Deciding how to make products inevitably leads to evaluating the human element, a fundamental part of process design. One reason is that process design affects the quality of work life and the level of employee satisfaction. Another is that payroll and employee benefits are major costs for most organizations. The many issues to consider in work-force management have no single set of answers because human beings are complex and somewhat unpredictable. Whole books have been written on the issues involved in job design, unions, organizational behavior, motivation, leadership, and resistance to change. Here we take only a brief look at issues related to job design.

Job Design

Job design is the specification of a job's content and the determination of the skills and training an employee needs in order to perform that job.

Scientific Management. Traditional job design got its start over 100 years ago when Frederick Taylor proposed an approach known as scientific management. **Scientific management** is the philosophy that any operation can be improved by breaking it into components, measuring the work content of the components, and finding ways to improve work methods. Process charts, multiple activity charts, and flow diagrams align closely with this philosophy. Taylor believed that managers should study jobs scientifically, using careful analysis and experimentation, to find the most economic way to perform a task. The manager should choose workers and train them in the new method and then install it in operations. Taylor stressed the need for teamwork between management and workers. He believed that management must accept the responsibility for coordinating work so that output is not restricted by poor planning and timing. Taylor also believed that scientific management would work only if the economic benefits of increased output were shared by both management and workers.

---

*Queuing and simulation analysis, described in Supplements 4 and 5 are more extensive methods to study waiting lines.

Taylor's methods dealt primarily with the technical aspects of job design. His "engineering approach" was concerned primarily with ways to best reach, grasp, and move objects; the number of repetitions to be performed before a rest was needed; and the best physical position for the worker. Taylor began his work in the steel industry, but his theories spread throughout many industries and were widely practiced by the early 1900s. Undoubtedly, scientific management techniques practiced by industrial engineers contributed greatly to the rise in U.S. productivity that occurred between 1900 and 1950. Even today, many of Taylor's concepts continue to be the first that managers apply when seeking to increase productivity.

Economic Trade-offs of Specialization.   Whether to define a job in narrow or broad terms is one of the toughest decisions in job design. Engineers, sociologists, psychologists, economists, managers, and workers all have different ideas. The actual choice varies widely. Many U.S. industries have achieved tremendous economic success with narrowly designed jobs for their workers. This result is particularly true for firms with a product focus. Other firms have had great success using teams, with each member being able to perform all parts of the task assigned to the team.

Arguments in Favor of Job Specialization	Arguments against Narrowly Defined Jobs
Workers need less time to learn highly specialized methods and procedures.	The inability to divide tasks perfectly creates an imbalance of work. Consequently, some workers have idle time and others do not.
The work pace is faster, leading to more output in less time.	The need for coordination and materials handling increases.
The education and skill requirements of the work force are much lower, so wages paid workers can be lower.	Highly repetitive work may have adverse behavioral consequences, such as costly employee turnover, low output rates, and poor quality.

Idle time, increased coordination and materials handling, and adverse behavioral consequences all represent *costs* of job specialization. The most puzzling part of finding a reasonable trade-off in costs lies in the behavioral dimension of job design.

Behavioral Considerations.   Taylor considered only economic benefits in his theory of job design, but people also work for other reasons. Social needs (that is, needs to be recognized, to belong to a group, and so on) and individual needs (that is, to feel important, to feel in control, and so on) influence how people perform their jobs. In narrowly designed jobs, workers have fewer opportunities to control the pace of work, receive gratification from the work itself, advance to a better position, show initiative, and communicate with fellow workers.

Sociologists and psychologists contend that highly repetitive jobs lead to monotony, which in turn leads to boredom and sometimes to poor job performance. Some symptoms of poor job performance exhibited by blue-collar workers include high turnover rates, absenteeism, grievances, and intentional disruption of production. White-collar workers may exhibit many of the same behaviors. Other behaviors, such as excessive personal illness and incomplete work assignments, are more subtle and difficult to detect. But the consequences may be even more costly to the organization.

The remedy usually suggested to overcome the boredom of highly specialized jobs is **job enlargement,** which assigns a greater variety of tasks to workers and/or includes more involvement in self-supervision. A job is enlarged *horizontally* when the worker is assigned a greater variety of tasks, say, eight or ten rather than one or two. A job is enlarged *vertically* when the worker gets more involved in planning or inspecting his or her own work. For example, a worker may be given the responsibility for operating several machines, inspecting the output, deciding when machines need maintenance, and even performing some types of maintenance. Job enlargement is closely related to worker flexibility. A worker with an enlarged job knows how to do more tasks and can work in many locations in a facility.

Sometimes, work teams are formed to achieve job enlargement. They give members an opportunity to learn how to perform all the jobs for which the team is responsible. Work teams provide opportunities for communication and for the worker to feel a greater sense of accomplishment. General Motors has successfully used teams at its plants in Fremont, California, and Shreveport, Louisiana. Worker participation and worker flexibility are key words to the plants' team philosophy. Based on the high level of productivity attained at these plants, GM decided to introduce teams into all its 175 plants.

Many studies of the relationships among specialization, boredom, job satisfaction, and productivity have been made in the last 30 years. Unfortunately, the evidence from them is mixed. For example, one recent study showed that job enlargement through work teams increased job satisfaction and improved productivity nearly 70 percent (Fisher, 1980). Other studies reported that enlarged jobs decreased productivity. In a study of bank employees, some jobs were enlarged vertically and some were simplified. The performance of some employees with enlarged jobs improved, but the performance of others did not. It appears that the need for job enlargement depends on the local culture, nature of the work, employee job perceptions, group interactions, and type of supervision given (Hackman, 1978).

Sociotechnical Theory. In the early 1950s, Eric Trist's studies in the coal fields of Great Britain led to a theory of job design that combined technical

MANAGERIAL PRACTICE 4.3

Building Satisfaction and Productivity

- Honda of America Manufacturing, Inc., tries various ways to build employee satisfaction. Among them are a suggestion system, safety awards, and the New Honda Circle in which employees work together to come up with ways the company can be more productive. "I have learned from our associates that without employee satisfaction, we would not enjoy long-term productivity," says Shoichiro Irimajiri, company president.

- GM is setting up a new compensation system to increase productivity of its salaried employees. Annual cost-of-living raises are dropped in favor of "pay-for-performance" merit increases. "A merit increase is something you have to earn," says Mr. Roberts, vice president for corporate personnel. "To treat people fairly you have to treat people differently."

- GM's new Saturn plant is pouring its money into people management. It plans to hire exceptionally motivated workers, put them through intensive training, give them more say in how their jobs get done, and pay them a salary plus a performance bonus—just like Saturn executives.

- At AT&T Technologies' printed circuit board plant in Richmond, Virginia, bonuses are based on productivity. Workers perform trouble-shooting tasks previously left to supervisors. They also make suggestions on how the manufacturing process could be improved, suggestions management listens to.

- The H. J. Heinz Company has a "Profit Improvement Program" (PIP) to institutionalize the constant pressure for higher productivity in a price-competitive industry. Teams of *salaried workers* from different disciplines initiate projects having major cost-saving potential. Examples include new processes for peeling potatoes, reclaiming heat from blanching ovens, reducing the amount of can overfilling, automating tuna processing (even though fish come in different sizes), and taking staggered breaks at British plants (rather than completely shutting down the lines for the breaks). Another program, called "People Excellence Products" (PEP), encourages *hourly workers* to form teams to improve quality and cut costs.

Sources: "Honda Plant Aims at Flexibility," *The Columbus Dispatch*, October 8, 1987; "GM's New Compensation Plan Reflects General Trend Tying Pay to Performance," *Wall Street Journal*, January 26, 1988; "Back to the Future at Saturn," *Fortune*, August 1, 1988; "America's Best Managed Factories," *Fortune*, May 28, 1984; "Heinz Pushes to be the Low Cost Producer," *Fortune*, June 24, 1985.

elements with behavioral considerations. This theory holds that the job designer needs to recognize two dimensions in any production system: the technical subsystem and the social subsystem. If one is emphasized and the other neglected, inefficiency will result. Work organizations are viewed as sociotechnical systems in which people use technology to carry out sets of tasks related to a specified purpose. People and equipment are inputs to the system. The fit of people and equipment determines the level of economic performance and job satisfaction, which are the output (Trist, 1981). Thus the entire work system, rather than its individual tasks, becomes the basic unit for analysis. Similarly, the work group becomes more important than the individual.

Other Dimensions

Managerial Practice 4.3 describes what some firms are doing to build a satisfied and productive work force. Job design is clearly a major concern, as are employee selection, training, and compensation. How line supervisors interact with employees, or "associates" as Honda calls them, can be critical. You will also see behavioral issues in other decisions made by operations managers. Among them are work measurement, layout, production planning, scheduling, and quality control.

SOLVED PROBLEMS

1. Two different manufacturing processes are being considered for making a new product that is to be introduced soon. The first process is less capital intensive, with a fixed cost of only $50,000 per year and a variable cost of $400 per unit. The second process has a fixed cost of $200,000 but would have a variable cost of only $150 per unit. What is the break-even quantity, beyond which the second process becomes more attractive than the first?

Solution

We set fixed cost plus variable cost $(F + cQ)$ for the first process equal to the equivalent costs for the second process and solve for Q:

$$\$50,000 + \$400Q = \$200,000 + \$150Q$$
$$\$250Q = \$150,000$$
$$Q = 600 \text{ units}$$

The break-even quantity is 600 units, beyond which the second process is better.

								Summary			
Process: making one batch of brownies							Activity	Number of Steps	Time	Distance	
Subject charted: baker											
Beginning: remove brownie mix from bin							Operation ◯	15	20.7	—	
Ending: remove brownies from oven							Transport ▷	11	9.6	430	
							Inspect ☐	2	0.2	—	
							Delay D	1	30.0	—	
							Store ▽	0	—	—	

Step No.	Time (min)	Distance (ft)	◯	▷	☐	D	▽	Step Description
1	1.3		X					Remove preassembled mix from bin
2	0.2		X					Place mix on counter
3	1.3	50		X				Walk to oven; turn it on for preheating
4	0.2	10		X				Continue walking on to cabinet
5	0.5		X					Remove bowl, mixer, pan, and measuring container
6	1.2	60		X				Return to counter with equipment
7	0.3		X					Place equipment on counter
8	1.3		X					Open bag of mix and dump into bowl
9	0.6	30		X				Walk to refrigerator
10	0.8		X					Remove eggs from refrigerator
11	0.6	30		X				Walk back to counter
12	0.1		X					Place eggs on counter
13	0.9	40		X				Pick up measuring container; walk to sink
14	1.4		X					Fill measuring container with water
15	0.8	40		X				Walk back to counter
16	0.3		X					Pour water into brownie mix
17	2.8		X					Break eggs into brownie mix
18	5.0		X					Use mixer to stir ingredients in bowl
19	0.1				X			Inspect mixture in bowl
20	1.9		X					Pour mixture into pan
21	0.1				X			Inspect mixture in pan
22	0.3		X					Discard egg shells
23	0.9	40		X				Take bowl, mixer, and container to sink
24	4.0		X					Wash and dry them
25	0.6	20		X				Return them to cabinet
26	1.2	60		X				Walk to counter
27	1.3	50		X				Pick up pan; walk to oven; place in oven
28	30.0					X		Wait 30 minutes to bake; turn off oven
29	0.5		X					Open oven; remove pan; close oven

FIGURE 4.8

2. Consider again the process analysis for baking a batch of brownies.

    a. Prepare a revised process chart that implements the three ideas proposed in Application 4.3. The only new information is:
- The oven is 50 feet from the counter.
- Walking to the oven and turning it on for preheating takes 1.3 minutes.
- The cabinet is 10 feet from the oven. Walking takes 0.2 minutes.
- Removing the bowl, mixer, pan, and measuring container takes 0.5 minutes.
- Placing the equipment on the counter takes 0.3 minutes, up from 0.2 minutes because the measuring container is brought along on the trip.
- The total mixing time (combining both mixings into one) is 5.0 minutes.

    b. What other ideas do you have for improving the process?

Solution

    a. Figure 4.8 shows the revised process chart. We eliminate six steps and about 20 percent of the total time and distance traveled.

    b. The 30-minute delay at step 28 stands out. The baker should start the next job while the brownies bake or make up more preassembled brownie mix for future batches. Another idea is to put step 27 right after step 21, which eliminates step 26 and 1.2 minutes.

CHAPTER HIGHLIGHTS

- Process design deals with *how* to make a product. Many choices must be made concerning capital intensity, resource flexibility, vertical integration, customer involvement, and the human element.

- Process design is of strategic importance and is closely linked to the productivity levels a firm can achieve. It involves the selection of inputs, operations, work flows, and methods used to produce goods and services.

- Process design decisions are made when a new product is to be offered, an existing product modified, demand levels change, current performance is inadequate, new technology is available, costs or availability of inputs change, or competitive priorities change.

- Four facets of process design are: capital intensity, resource flexibility, vertical integration, and customer involvement. *Capital intensity* concerns the mix of capital equipment and human skills in a process. *Resource flexibility* reflects the degree to which equipment is general purpose and individuals can handle a wide variety of work. *Vertical integration* concerns the decisions to make or buy parts and services. Such decisions are made by looking at the entire chain of supply from acquisition of raw materials to delivery of the finished product to the consumer and then determining which processes the firm itself wants to perform. *Customer involvement* is the extent to which customers are allowed to interact with the production process. Self-service, product selection, and the timing and location of the interaction must all be considered.

- Trade-offs among these facets are often necessary. For example, higher capital intensity is usually associated with lower resource flexibility, higher vertical integration, and lower customer involvement. The variable underlying these relationships is repeatability.

- Process design choices often require investment in new facilities or equipment. Operations managers must assess benefits and costs of each investment proposed. After the necessary estimates have been made, break-even analysis or net present value techniques can be applied.

- Three techniques for analyzing process activities and flows are process charts, multiple activity charts, and flow diagrams. All are organized ways of studying the details of a process in order to improve it by designing or redesigning it.

- Scientific management is an engineering approach to job design that is concerned with the most economic way to perform the job.

- Managers must decide whether jobs are to be narrowly or broadly defined. Advantages of narrowly defined jobs are short learning time, fast work pace, and low labor costs. Disadvantages are creation of more idle time for some workers, increased materials handling and coordination, and adverse behavioral consequences.

- Job enlargement, both horizontal and vertical, is usually the remedy suggested to overcome the boredom of highly specialized jobs. Results of studies of links among specialization, boredom, job satisfaction, and performance (productivity) have been mixed. The relationships seem to depend on the specific characteristics of the situation.

- The sociotechnical theory of job design considers both the technical and the social requirements of the job. The focus is on the work group instead of the individual worker.

KEY TERMS

STUDY QUESTIONS

1. When you registered for this course you had to go through a registration process. Think of this process from the standpoint of your university or college. Identify elements of the process for which process design or redesign is needed.

2. Compare the process of preparing and serving your own lunch at home with the process of preparing and serving lunch to others at a local pizza parlor. What inputs in terms of materials, human effort, and equipment are involved in each process? How are these inputs similar? How are they different?

3. Process design choices cannot be isolated from decisions in other areas of operations management. Comment on this statement from the standpoint of a manager of a bookstore. *Hint:* Look over the table of contents to get some ideas.

4. How much capital intensity do you recommend for a business having an extremely unpredictable product demand? How much vertical integration? Explain.

5. The number of mail-order businesses has increased dramatically in the United States in the last ten years. Compare the processes of a business selling ski equipment and clothing by direct mail to the processes of a retail store handling the same items. How do they differ in terms of capital intensity, resource flexibility, vertical integration, and customer involvement? How are they the same?

6. Suppose that you and a friend decide to start a business selling sandwiches and snacks in college dormitories late at night. What decisions must you make regarding vertical integration? How will your customers be involved in your process?

7. Suppose that a grocery store has decided to add an in-store bakery. The next decision to be made is whether to install a drive-in window for the bakery so that customers do not have to enter the store in order to purchase baked goods. The store manager expects that this window would do a high volume of business early in the morning, as people purchase donuts on their way to work. How is this window likely to affect other processes in the store? What processes will have to be performed by the employees in the bakery that they would otherwise not perform? How would customer involvement differ from that in the rest of the grocery operations?

8. Why are human resources crucial to process

design? Does this relationship depend on whether a firm is highly capital intensive?

9. What are the arguments for and against narrowly defined jobs?

10. What is the difference between horizontal and vertical job enlargement? How is the issue of job enlargement related to the arguments for and against narrowly defined jobs?

11. What opportunities do workers lack in some work environments? Compare an assembly-line worker in a highly automated plant and a secretary in a busy law office. Which opportunities are each likely to have? Which are they likely to lack?

12. What is sociotechnical theory? How does it differ from scientific management?

PROBLEMS

Review Problems

1. Goliath Manufacturing must implement a manufacturing process that reduces the amount of toxic by-products. Two processes have been identified that provide the same level of toxic by-product reduction. The first process will incur $150,000 of fixed cost and $750 per unit of variable cost. The second process has a fixed cost of $100,000 and a variable cost of $900 per unit.

   a. What is the break-even quantity beyond which the first process is more attractive?

   b. What is the difference in total cost if the quantity produced is 500 units?

2. Dr. Wilson (see Managerial Practice 4.2) estimates that adding two new chairs will increase fixed cost by $100,000, including the annual equivalent cost of the capital investment and the salary of one more technician. Each new patient is expected to bring in $1875 per year in additional revenue with variable cost estimated at $150 per patient. The two new chairs will allow him to expand his practice by as many as 200 patients annually. How many patients would have to be added for the new process to break even?

3. Hahn Manufacturing has been purchasing a key component of one of its products from a local supplier. The current purchase price is $1750 per unit. Efforts at standardizing parts have succeeded to the point where this same component can now be used in five different products. Annual component usage should increase from 150 to 1000 units. Management is now wonder-

ing whether it is time to make the component in-house, rather than to continue buying it from the supplier. Fixed cost would increase by about $40,000 per year for the new equipment and tooling needed. The cost of raw materials and variable overhead would be about $1250 per unit, while labor cost would go up by another $315 per unit produced.

   a. Should Hahn make rather than buy?

   b. What is the break-even quantity?

   c. What other considerations might be important?

4. Suppose that you are in charge of a large mailing to the alumni of your college, inviting them to contribute to a scholarship fund. The letters and envelopes have been individually addressed (mailing labels were not used). The letters are to be folded and stuffed into the correct envelope, the envelopes are to be sealed, and a large commemorative stamp is to be placed in the upper right-hand corner of each envelope. Make a process chart for this activity. Assume that it is a one-person operation. Estimate how long it will take to stuff, seal, and stamp 1000 envelopes. Assume that the person who is doing this work is paid $7.50 per hour. How much will it cost to process 1000 letters, based on your time estimate? Consider how each of the following changes individually would affect the process.

   • Each letter has the greeting "Dear Alumnus or Alumna," instead of the person's name.

   • Mailing labels are used, and they have to be put on the envelopes.

   • Prestamped envelopes are used.

   • Envelopes are to be stamped by a postage meter.

   • Window envelopes are used.

   • A preaddressed envelope is included for contributions.

   a. Which of these changes would reduce the time and cost of the process?

   b. Would any of these changes be likely to reduce the effectiveness of the mailing? If so, which ones? Why?

   c. Would the changes that increase time and cost be likely to increase the effectiveness of the mailing? Why?

   d. What other factors need to be considered for this project?

5. Prepare a multiple activity chart for a hypothetical worker whose job is to load and unload two dry-cleaning machines (call them machines A and B). Use the following conditions.

- It is the beginning of the day, and all machines are empty.
- The machines are identical.
- Each machine takes two minutes to load and four minutes to unload.

The machines run for 15 minutes each time they are loaded. The worker starts by loading machine A and then machine B. The machines are close enough together that the travel time from one to the other can be ignored. After the initial loading, the worker unloads and reloads each machine as soon as the machine stops running, or as soon as the worker is available. (In other words, the worker does not waste time.)

   a. Complete the multiple activity chart for the two machines and for the worker for one hour. Calculate the utilization (percentage) for each.

   b. Assume that the machines are not turned off until the end of the day. What is the percentage utilization of the machines and the worker for the second hour and every hour thereafter?

6. Suppose that the dry-cleaning worker in Problem 5 is given three machines to tend. Complete a multiple activity chart for three machines and one worker under the same conditions.

   a. What is the percentage utilization of the worker and the machines? Compare your answer to that obtained for two machines.

   b. Is it possible, hypothetically, for a worker to be utilized 100 percent? Is it possible practically? What would you likely observe if you watched a person actually working at 100 percent utilization?

7. Diagrams of two self-service gasoline stations, both located on corners, are shown in Fig. 4.9(a) and (b). Both have two rows of four pumps and a booth in which an attendant receives payment for the gasoline. At neither station is it necessary for the customer to pay in advance. The exits and entrances are marked on the diagrams. Analyze the flows of cars and people through each station.

   a. Which station has the most efficient flows from the standpoint of the customer?

   b. Which station is likely to lose the most sales from potential customers who cannot gain access to the pumps because another car is headed the other direction?

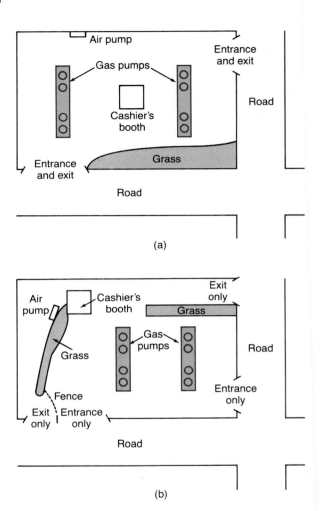

FIGURE 4.9

   c. At which station can a customer pay without getting out of the car?

8. You have been asked by the management of Just Like Home restaurant to analyze some of its processes. One of these processes is making a single-scoop ice cream cone. Cones can be ordered by a server (for table service) or by a customer (for take-out). Figure 4.10 illustrates the process chart for this operation.

- The ice cream counter server earns $10 per hour (including variable fringe benefits).
- The process is performed 10 times per hour (on average).

Process: making one single-scoop ice-cream cone							Summary			
Subject charted: server at counter						Activity	Number of Steps	Time	Distance	
Beginning: walk to cone storage area						Operation ○	6	1.70	—	
						Transport ⇨	6	0.54	31	
Ending: give server or customer the cone						Inspect ☐	1	0.25	—	
						Delay D	1	0.50	—	
						Store ▽	0	—	—	

Step No.	Time (min)	Distance (ft)	○	⇨	☐	D	▽	Step Description
1	0.10	5		X				Walk to cone storage area
2	0.05		X					Remove empty cone
3	0.10	5		X				Walk to counter
4	0.05		X					Place cone in holder
5	0.12	8		X				Walk to sink area
6	0.50					X		Ask dishwasher to wash scoop
7	0.12	8		X				Walk to counter with clean scoop
8	0.05		X					Pick up empty cone
9	0.05	25		X				Walk to flavor ordered
10	0.75		X					Scoop ice cream from container
11	0.75		X					Place ice cream in cone
12	0.25				X			Check for stability
13	0.05	25		X				Walk to order placement area
14	0.05		X					Give server or customer the cone

FIGURE 4.10

- The restaurant is open 363 days a year, 10 hours a day.

a. What is the total labor cost associated with the process?

b. How can this operation be made more efficient? Draw a process chart of the improved process. What are the annual labor savings if this new process is implemented?

Advanced Problems

Problems 10–13 require prior reading of Supplement 1; Problems 14 and 15, Supplement 2; Problems 16–19, Supplement 4; and Problem 20, Supplement 5. A computer package is useful for all problems except 9 and 14; one is mandatory for Problem 15.

9. Make a multiple activity chart for a pizza baker who is assembling pizzas and baking them in two ovens that each hold two pizzas. Assume that demand for the pizzas is so high that all possible output will be used. Use the following conditions.

   - Each pizza takes 5 min to assemble.

   - Pizzas must bake for 17 min and be removed promptly.

- It takes 1 min to put a pizza in the oven and 1 min to take it out. Assume that this does not prolong the baking time for any other pizza in the oven.
- An oven may be opened to put in a pizza or take one out, even if another pizza is baking.
- If a pizza is being assembled, and it is time to take another one out of the oven, the assembly process is interrupted to do so. The baker then continues assembling the first pizza.

Prepare a multiple activity chart for the baker and ovens from 5:00 P.M. until 6:30 P.M. Assume that the ovens are hot but empty at 5 P.M.

a. How many pizzas can the baker turn out in this period of time?

b. How many pizzas are in the oven at 6:30?

c. What is the percentage utilization of each oven shelf?

d. What percentage of the time is each oven being used (with one or two pizzas in it)?

e. What is the percentage utilization of the baker?

Hint: You will probably need a column for each shelf of each oven and one for the baker. Use any symbols that you think are appropriate.

10. A local restaurant is considering adding a salad bar. Managerial Practice S1.1 gives the related data and assumptions. Table S1.1 shows the NPV financial analysis.

Another option (instead of the salad bar) is to assemble, store and sell preassembled salads. In order to do so, an investment outlay of $6000 to remodel the kitchen would be required. The price and variable cost of each salad would drop to $2.25 and $1.50, respectively. Fixed cost (excluding depreciation) would be $900, since there is no longer a need to hire someone to keep the salad bar stocked. The other assumptions about total demand, project life, tax rate, hurdle rate, salvage value, and depreciation method remain unchanged.

a. Based on the NPV method, is the salad bar or preassembled salad option best?

b. What is the payback period for each option?

c. What other factors might influence your decision?

11. Suppose that the demand estimate for salads in Problem 10 is revised upward to 36,000 salads per year.

a. Evaluate both options using the NPV method.

b. Evaluate both options using the payback method.

c. Does the higher demand estimate change any of your conclusions?

12. Dr. Wilson, an orthodontist, is considering the expansion of his office from four to six chairs. Each chair requires an investment of $200,000. He will have to hire one new technician at $18,000 per year. Other additional costs are expected to be negligible. The two new chairs will allow him to expand his practice by 200 patients per year. Each new patient is expected to bring in $1,500 per year in before-tax revenue. Dr. Wilson will depreciate the chairs over a 5-year period, and at the end of that time the chairs are expected to have no value. Assume that Dr. Wilson is in the 50 percent tax bracket and requires a return of 20 percent on an investment. Calculate the following.

a. The incremental after-tax cash flows attributable to the two new chairs.

b. The net present value of the investment.

c. The payback period.

d. The number of new patients Dr. Wilson will have to add in order to break even (before taxes) on an annual basis.

13. A grocer is thinking of adding an in-store bakery, which would require an investment of $35,000. The grocer expects the bakery to generate incremental after-tax cash flows of $12,000 for each of the next six years. What is the present value of the stream of expected cash flows? (Use 18 percent for the hurdle rate.)

a. What is the net present value?

b. What is the payback period?

c. What advice would you give the grocer about the proposed investment?

d. What other issues should the grocer consider?

14. The plant manager of a plastic pipe manufacturer has the opportunity to use two different routings for a particular type of plastic pipe. Routing 1 uses extruder A and routing 2 uses extruder B. Both routings require the same melting process. The following table shows the time requirements and capacities of these processes.

	Hours per 100 ft		
Process	Routing 1	Routing 2	Capacity (hr)
Melting	1	1	45
Extruder A	3	0	90
Extruder B	0	4	160

In addition, each 100 feet of pipe processed on routing 1 uses 5 pounds of raw material, whereas each 100 feet of pipe processed on routing 2 uses only 4 pounds. This difference results from differing scrap rates of the extruding machines. Consequently, the profit per 100 feet of pipe processed on routing 1 is $60 and on routing 2 is $80. A total of 200 pounds of raw material is available.

   a. Write the constraints and objective function for this problem.

   b. Use the graphic method of linear programming to find the optimal solution.

15. Use the simplex method to solve Problem 14, both manually and on the computer.

16. The Kramer Company employs a large number of salespersons. Although many of them are on the road at any one time, they generate an average of 1.5 sales documents per hour. These documents have to be typed and Kramer employs one typist for this sales force who can type and proof them at an average rate of 2 per hour.

   a. What is the average utilization of the typist?

   b. What is the probability that more than three documents are waiting or being typed?

   c. What is the average number of documents waiting to be typed?

   d. What is the average waiting time for documents in queue?

17. The Lone Star Company has a stockroom that utilizes an automatic stock picker. Workers arrive at the stockroom with production orders requiring various purchased parts and raw materials. The clerk feeds the information into a computer and the order is picked by a mechanical device and returned to the clerk. Workers arrive at the stockroom at the rate of 20 per hour. The speed of the automatic stock picker can be adjusted, although actual service times for a given order depend on the nature of the materials being ordered. Setting the machine too fast causes more failures, whereas setting it too slow causes delays on the shop floor. Answer the following questions, assuming that the single-server queuing model applies.

   a. If the time required for the clerk to enter the order is negligible, what average service rate should the stock picker be set at to ensure only a 30 percent chance that 3 or more workers are in queue or being served?

   b. What is the average time a worker spends in the system?

   c. What is the average number of workers waiting to be served?

18. The Hairy Knoll is a discount barbershop where the students from the Kingston Barber School serve their apprenticeship. There are only three barber chairs, each manned by an eager student. An instructor oversees the operation and gives guidance as needed. Patrons are served on a first-come, first-served basis and arrive at the rate of 10 customers per hour according to a Poisson distribution. The time required for a haircut averages 15 minutes according to an exponential distribution.

   a. What is the probability that there will be no customers in the shop?

   b. What is the probability that there will be five or more customers in the shop?

   c. What is the average number of customers waiting in queue?

   d. What is the average waiting time in queue?

19. Consider further the Hairy Knoll barbershop described in Problem 18. Suppose that it is desirable to have idle time for the students so that they can sweep the floor and be given additional instruction in cutting hair. The dean of the Kingston Barber School believes that the added expense of remodeling the Hairy Knoll to have four barber chairs could be offset by slightly increased prices, if the average waiting time in queue per customer is less than five minutes. Assuming that the price change will not affect the rate of customer arrivals, should the Hairy Knoll be remodeled?

20. The Canyon Del Oro Service Station performs maintenance and minor repairs to automobiles. Customers arrive early in the morning and leave their cars for the day, expecting to pick them up after work. There is a risk, however, that the work needed on a given car cannot be completed that day. It depends on the nature of the work to be performed on the other cars brought in the same day, as well as the specific work required for a particular car. Historically, an average of 2.5 cars had to be held over to the next day. The manager of the station is contemplating adding another mechanic to reduce that backlog. A simulation model was developed with the following distribution for customer arrivals per day.

Number	Probability	RN
8	0.10	00 – 09
9	0.25	10 – 34
10	0.30	35 – 64
11	0.25	65 – 89
12	0.10	90 – 99

With the addition of the extra mechanic, the maximum number of cars that could be serviced per day is

Number	Probability	RN
9	0.30	00 – 29
10	0.40	30 – 69
11	0.30	70 – 99

The number of cars that can be repaired varies from day to day because of the nature of the work to be done on the cars. In the simulation for a specific day, the number of cars needing service (NCNS) is determined first. Next, the maximum number of cars repaired (MNCR) is determined. If MNCR ≥ NCNS, all cars are repaired for that day. If MNCR < NCNS, then NCNS − MNCR cars must be held over until the next day. These cars must be added to the number of cars arriving the next day to obtain the NCNS for the next day. The simulation continues in this manner until a specific number of days has been simulated.

Assuming that the service station is empty at the start, simulate 15 days of operation using the following random numbers.

(73,80), (25, 30), (86, 97), (48, 41), (30, 79), (79, 60), (53, 32), (72, 57), (83, 53), (44, 58), (82, 04), (12, 83), (08, 65), (53, 27), (77, 49)

For each pair of random numbers, the first determines the number of arrivals and the second the capacity. What is the average daily number of cars held overnight, based on your simulation?

SELECTED REFERENCES

Abernathy, William J., "Production Process Structure and Technological Change," *Decision Sciences*, vol. 7, no. 4 (October 1976), pp. 607–619.

"And Now, the Post-Industrial Corporation," *Business Week*, March 3, 1986.

Chase, Richard B., "Where Does the Customer Fit in a Service Operation?" *Harvard Business Review* (November–December 1978), pp. 137–142.

Hackman, J. Richard, Jone L. Pearce, and Jane Camins Wolfe, "Effects of Changes in Job Characteristics on Work Attitudes and Behaviors," *Organizational Behavior and Human Performance*, vol. 21 (1978), pp. 289–304.

Harrigan, K.R., *Strategies for Vertical Integration*. Lexington, Mass.: D. C. Heath, 1983.

Hauck, Warren C., *Motivating People to Work: The Key to Improving Productivity*. Atlanta: Industrial Engineering and Management Press, 1984.

Kantrow, Alan M., "The Strategy–Technology Connection," *Harvard Business Review* (July–August 1980), pp. 6–21.

Kilbridge, Maurice, and Leon Wester, "An Economic Model for the Division of Labor," *Management Science*, vol. 12, no. 6 (February 1966), pp. B255–B269.

Knights, David, Hugh Willmott, and David Collison (Eds.), *Job Redesign*. Hants, England: Gower Publishing Company Limited, 1985.

Levitt, Theodore, "The Industrialization of Service," *Harvard Business Review* (September–October 1976), pp. 63–74.

Lovelock, Christopher H., and Robert F. Young, "Look to Consumers to Increase Productivity," *Harvard Business Review* (May–June 1979), pp. 168–178.

Nadler, Gerald, *Work Design*. Homewood, Ill.: Richard D. Irwin, 1970.

Niebel, Benjamin W., *Motion and Time Study*. Homewood, Ill.: Richard D. Irwin, 1976.

Paul, William J., Keith B. Robertson, and Frederick Herzberg, "Job Enrichment Pays Off," *Harvard Business Review* (March–April 1969), pp. 61–78.

Pierce, Jon L., and Randall B. Dunham, "Task Design: A Literature Review," *Academy of Management Review* (October 1976), pp. 83–96.

Ritzman, Larry P., Barry E. King, and Lee J. Krajewski, "Manufacturing Performance—Pulling the Right Levers," *Harvard Business Review* (March–April 1984), pp. 143–152.

Shostak, Arthur B., and William Gomberg, *Blue-Collar World.* Englewood Cliffs, N.J.: Prentice-Hall, 1964.

Skinner, Wickham, "Operations Technology: Blind Spot in Strategic Management," *Interfaces,* vol. 14 (January–February 1984), pp. 116–125.

Steers, Richard M., and Richard T. Mowday, "The Motivational Properties of Tasks," *Academy of Management Review* (October 1977), pp. 645–658.

Swamidass, Paul M., "Manufacturing Flexibility," *OMA Monograph 2*, January 1988.

Trist, Eric L., "The Sociotechnical Perspective," in A. H. Van de Ven and W. F. Joyce (Eds.), *Perspectives on Organization Design.* New York: John Wiley & Sons, 1981.

Walker, Charles R., "The Problem of the Repetitive Job," *Harvard Business Review,* vol. 28 (May 1950), pp. 54–58.

Wheelwright, Steven C., and Robert H. Hayes, "Competing through Manufacturing," *Harvard Business Review* (January–February 1985), pp. 99–109.

CHAPTER 5

NEW TECHNOLOGIES

▲ Chapter Outline

Key Questions for Managers

What new technologies would enhance the productivity of our employees?

Is it time for us to have an electronic data interchange system?

Can an electronic mail system help our office?

How can low-cost automation, group technology, and flexible manufacturing help us achieve the benefits of repeatability?

Should we have fixed or programmable automation?

Can economies of scope give us a competitive edge?

What types of CIM should we use for product design, materials handling, and manufacturing?

How should we justify and implement new automation projects?

 apital intensity, as you learned in Chapter 4, is an important facet of process design. In this chapter, we take a look at some newer, often more capital intensive, technologies. For our purposes, we define **technology** as any manual, automated, or mental process used to transform inputs into goods and services. Each operation has a technology, even if it is manual. Invariably, managers have several technologies from which to choose. For example, look at the options for the simple process of sawing lumber:

1. A worker using a simple hand saw.

2. A worker operating and controlling a portable power saw.

3. A rigidly mounted power saw, which a worker must set up, load, and unload, but which automatically guides the lumber into the blade.

4. A high-speed, continuously running power saw, which automatically feeds and unloads lumber with only infrequent worker intervention.

Note that the options for sawing lumber differ in one important respect: Some are more automated than others. The word *automatic*, which comes from the Greek word for self-acting, has been around for well over 200 years. During the late 1940s, someone in the automobile industry coined the word **automation,** which today means a system, process, or piece of equipment that is self-acting and self-regulating.

Because technology is changing so rapidly, it's more important than ever for operations managers to make intelligent, informed decisions about automation. Many new opportunities are the result of advances in computer technology. Deciding whether to take advantage of such opportunities is closely related to process design. The stakes are high because such choices affect the human as well as the technical aspects of operations. Job satisfaction and positive employee attitudes can be maintained only if technological change is managed well.

We can't possibly cover all new technologies in a single chapter. Therefore we focus on some of the ways manufacturing and service operations commonly use automation. Our discussion covers three basic areas: technology in the service sector, technology in manufacturing (including computer-integrated manufacturing), and managing technological change. We begin with the service sector, since it is such a dominant force in the U.S. economy today.

SERVICE SECTOR TECHNOLOGY ▲

Table 5.1 shows examples of automated processes in several service industries. Although we take many of these processes for granted, some are quite remarkable. In the following sections, we explore a few examples of automation in the service industries.

Electronic Funds Transfer and ATMs

The banking industry began automating during the 1930s when check sorting machines were invented. Since then financial service institutions have improved efficiency in ways that are visible to the customer. Two successful new technologies are electronic funds transfer (EFT) systems and automatic teller machines (ATMs). The EFT systems transfer money automatically between bank accounts. ATMs are computers that allow customers to make withdrawals and deposits and check their account balances electronically—24 hours a day. Banks also benefit because ATM systems are relatively inexpensive to operate. For example, the average operating cost per ATM transaction is $0.66, compared with a teller cost of between $0.90 and $1.20. Citicorp spends $900 million annually on automation in hopes of gaining a competitive edge over its rivals. Its latest innovation is a full-color, touch-screen ATM.

A 1987 survey showed that banks expect to rely even more on ATMs and home banking in the future. During the 1990s, self-service technologies may handle as much as 60 percent of all withdrawals in certain markets, a dramatic increase from the current 13 percent. (See Roth and Van der Velde, 1988.) Forecasters expect automated deposits to grow from 9 to 53 percent and cash advances from 11 to 53 percent.

TABLE 5.1 Automation in Service Industries

Industry	Automated Process
Banking	Electronic funds transfer
	Encoded check processor
	Automatic teller machines
	Trust portfolio analysis
Transportation	Autopilots
	Toll booths
	Ship navigation systems
	Bay Area Rapid Transit System
Communications	Electronic data interchanges
	Electronic mail systems
	On-line databases
	Linked communication and information systems
	Teleconferencing/picture phones
Health care	CAT scanners
	Ambulance electronic dispatching
	Dentists' chair system
	Medical information systems
Education	Personal and home computers
	Speak and spell computer systems
	Electronic library cataloguing
	Language translation computers
Utilities and government	Meter reading
	Optical mail scanners
	One-worker garbage truck
	Airborne warning and control systems
Restaurants and food	Bar codes
	Vending machines
	French fryers
	Rotating service cafeterias
Wholesale and retail trade	Integrated computer order systems
	Dry cleaner's conveyors
	Point-of-sale electronic terminals
	Distribution warehouses
Hotels and motels	Electronic reservation systems
	Elevators
	Automatic sprinklers
	Electronic key and lock systems
Leisure activities	Television games
	Video-disc machines
	Disney World
	Beach surf rake

Source: David A. Collier, Service Management: The Automation of Services, Reston, Va.: Reston Publishing Company, 1985.

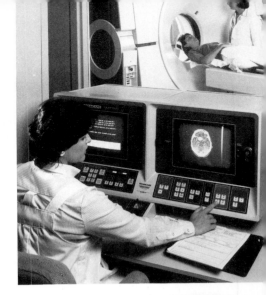
(a)

With automated goods and services emerging at such a rapid rate, it is essential that operations managers make informed decisions about the technology options available to them. Several technological advances within the service sector affecting such everyday concerns as health, transportation, and communication include (a) a technician and a nurse performing a CAT scan on a patient, (b) a commuter preparing to board a Bay Area Rapid Transit (BART) train, which brings a greater level of automation to San Francisco's public transportation, and (c) a multi-position letter-sorting machine at an urban post office that allows each of 12 operators to process 50 to 60 letters per minute.

(b)

(c)

Electronic Data Interchange

Electronic data interchange (EDI) systems are integrated systems in which computers at one organization are linked by phone lines or some other communication channel and exchange data directly with computers at another organization. Special communications software translates documents into and out of a generic form, allowing organizations to exchange information even if they have different hardware and software components. In the transportation industry EDI helps transmit invoices, freight bills, and other shipping related documents. The system minimizes the paperwork involved in most information transactions, improves accuracy, saves time, and can even cut inventory. Managerial Practice 5.1 illustrates two EDI applications—one in services and one in manufacturing.

On-line Databases

A growing number of public computer networks are offering a collection of on-line databases and related computer services to subscribers. Users access information through a special terminal or a personal computer linked to the master computer by a modem. The master computer contains an electronic library, or collection of databases, which the service updates regularly.

A vast quantity of information is available. Some databases are built on numbers: economic indicators, stock market prices, and so forth. Others build collections of key subjects or words: weather data, ski conditions, the status of

MANAGERIAL PRACTICE 5.1 ▲

EDI Payoffs at Super Valu Stores and Navistar

- Super Valu Stores, Inc., figures it's saving $5000 to $6000 a week with EDI because it no longer has to manually process invoices and other documents that arrive by mail or over the phone. The food wholesaler should soon be saving $600,000 a year as a result of cuts in the clerical staff, which checks purchase orders against invoices. It may also be able to reduce inventory.

- Navistar International Corporation, a firm that makes trucks and engines, achieved even more striking results. Navistar was an early EDI user. During the first 18 months following installation of EDI, the firm cut truck inventories by a third, or $167 million. EDI executes transactions instantaneously and thus enables the company to keep better track of inventory.

Source: "Computers Bringing Changes to Basic Business Documents," *Wall Street Journal*, March 6, 1987.

In what is believed to be the first police application of its kind, officers in St. Petersburg, Florida, test a cellular phone by using a personal computer connected to the GTE Mobilnet network to transfer a report from their patrol car directly to precinct headquarters.

bills in Congress, and full texts of several major newspapers and magazines from around the world, to name a few. By 1985, more than 2000 databases were commercially available. Thus computers have given decision makers instant access to vast quantities of data never before so readily available.

Electronic Mail Systems

An **electronic mail system** usually consists of a host mainframe hooked up to numerous microcomputers. Special communications software allows users to contact the central computer to leave or pick up messages. Electronic mail bypasses time-consuming interoffice memos and eliminates the annoying game of "telephone tag." Another advantage is that the message sender can communicate with several people at the same time. For example, if several customer service representatives need information about price changes or product availability, the service manager could send this information to all of them simultaneously.

Linked Communication and Information Systems

Increasingly, companies are linking employees' microcomputers to a central mainframe computer in order to give authorized personnel access to corporate information. These systems provide decision makers at all levels in the organization with timely and accurate information. A good example is Wal-Mart Stores, Inc., which recently spent $20 million on a satellite network linking its 1182 outlets to its Bentonville headquarters. Among other things, the linked system alerts store managers to buying opportunities. Managerial Practice 5.2 shows how linked computer systems increased productivity and improved accuracy at Dayton Power and Light.

Bar Codes

Bar coding has widespread implications for wholesaling, retailing, warehousing, and manufacturing operations. A **bar code** is a pattern of wide and narrow black bands and alternating white spaces that a computer reads with the aid of an optical scanner or wand. The code can be printed directly on the product or on an attached label.

Computerized checkout procedures have helped firms such as K mart and Wal-Mart dramatically increase productivity and manage inventory with greater accuracy and efficiency. As the system scans bar codes, it automatically records both price and item and updates inventory records. The customer receives a precise record of the transaction and quicker, more accurate service. Today, more than half the nation's supermarkets use bar codes. Other users include public libraries, VCR rental stores, retailers, and discount retailers.

In manufacturing, bar codes allow computers to monitor labor distribution, inventory levels, quality losses, tool locations, and employee attendance.

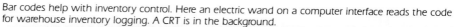

Bar codes help with inventory control. Here an electric wand on a computer interface reads the code for warehouse inventory logging. A CRT is in the background.

Allen-Bradley, a Milwaukee manufacturer of industrial controls, uses bar codes in its fully automated assembly line. The bar codes identify which of several products coming down the line will be assembled next. The computer then instructs each automated station to perform the appropriate operations and to select the correct parts to install from the 200 available.

Integrated Computer Order Systems

Integrated computer order systems currently link many suppliers directly to their customers. The customers place orders electronically and, in some cases, reserve inventory in the supplier's warehouse. For example, airlines place computer terminals in travel agencies to facilitate processing customers' reservations. American Hospital Supply has placed terminals in the purchasing agent's office at many hospitals. The ability to place an order and receive delivery quickly reduces the need to stockpile supplies, thus lowering inventory carrying costs.

MANAGERIAL PRACTICE 5.2

Meter Reading by Computer

Meter readers for Dayton Power and Light Company, an electric and gas utility, collect their daily readings on portable computers. Each evening files from these portables are read into microcomputers at 14 different regional office locations. The microcomputers transfer accumulated data to the central mainframe computer, which uses the new readings to update customer accounts. The entire updating process, which used to take the better part of each night, is now done in minutes.

The new system has greatly reduced data entry duties and chances for human error. Only meter readers key data into the system via their portables at the meter sites. The portables are programmed to check each entry against upper and lower limits, based on the customer's past usage. If an entry falls outside normal bounds, the computer will beep, signaling a possible error.

Currently, Dayton is pursuing an even more advanced technology, by Energy Innovations, that will fully automate the meter reading process. First, microcomputer attachments are fitted to the meters, as indicated in photo (a). (The meter's cover was removed to show the attachments.) The command center shown in photo (b), which can be linked up to 16 meters, collects and stores the data. At prearranged times, it calls the central, or host, computer shown in photo (c), transmits data, and receives instructions for its next transmission. All data are transmitted over existing power and telephone lines.

Source: "Utility-Bill Errors Could Soon Be Thing of Past with New Meter-Reading Devices," *Wall Street Journal,* August 14, 1985.

MANUFACTURING TECHNOLOGY ▲

Advances in technology can dramatically change factory operations as well as service processes. Managerial Practice 5.3 describes how Ford Motor Company uses computer-controlled machines, computer-aided design, welding robots, automated spray machines, and power-and-free conveyors to make the Aerostar minivan. In this section we explore these and other new technologies, as well as criteria managers must consider when deciding when or to what degree to automate.

Repeatability and Automation

When deciding which technologies to use, the operations manager should not assume that the best decision is more automation. Automation requires large outlays for equipment and thus increases fixed costs. Automation can also increase maintenance costs and decrease resource flexibility. On the other

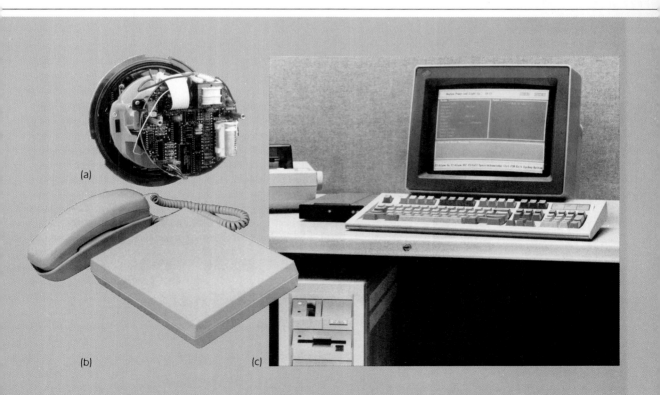

(a)

(b)

(c)

hand, if repeatability is high enough, the benefits of automation will overcome the drawbacks. These benefits can include increased labor productivity, products of consistently higher quality, shorter cycle times, increased capacity, lower inventory, higher sales, and spreading fixed costs over larger product volumes.

The higher volumes that characterize a product focus increase repeatability and make automation an attractive option. With one production line dedicated to a single product, line flows simplify materials handling, setups are eliminated, and labor costs drop. There's less need to decouple one operation from the next, allowing management to cut inventories. The Japanese refer to a product focus as *overlapped operations*, where materials move directly from one operation to the next without waiting in queues.

Unfortunately, volumes are not always high enough to justify dedicating a single line to one product. In such situations, managers may still derive the

MANAGERIAL PRACTICE 5.3

Manufacturing Ford's Aerostar

To produce Aerostar, Ford's most versatile entry in the minivan market, Ford Motor Company uses some of the most sophisticated manufacturing technology in the world. The company has enlarged its St. Louis assembly plant and reequipped it with new facilities and tooling. The new technology includes more than 550 computers linked in a network that continuously monitors the computer-controlled machines. Computers and other innovative manufacturing technologies allow Ford to build vehicles of very consistent quality.

Industrial designers use computer graphics to design Aerostar's roof panel. Electronic data is converted into computer commands that operate numerically controlled mills for machining sheet-metal dies and inspection tools. Computers also compare roof panels stamped from the dies against original design data. By using computer-aided design and manufacturing techniques, production is able to ensure a uniform fit between body panels. The tight fit means less wind and road noise and better protection from the weather.

Aerostar's underbody assembly line uses 40 welding robots, including 24 gantry models—Ford's first overhead-mounted robots. The gantry robots carry up to 200 pounds of tooling and require less floor space than side-mounted models. Robots and other automated equipment perform over 97 percent of Aerostar's 4000 spot welds. They also apply enamel to Aerostar's interior surfaces. The robots and automatic spray machines that apply paint to the exterior produce a defect-free finish of consistent quality. The automated process eliminates repetitive operations that workers have found to be tedious.

Aerostar's chassis and trim department uses a material handling system called *power-and-free-conveyors*. These conveyors eliminate conventional under-

Source: Ford Motor Company, "Second Quarter Report to Stockholders," Summer 1985.

benefits of high repeatability with low-cost automation, group technology, or flexible automation.

Low-Cost Automation

If volumes aren't sufficient to keep several workers busy on one production line, the manager might set up a smaller line that will keep one worker busy. This is the theory behind the **one worker, multiple machines (OWMM)** concept, a process in which a worker operates several different machines simultaneously in order to achieve a line flow. It isn't unusual to have one worker operate several identical machines. For example, in the semiconductor industry one worker operates several saws that cut silicon bars into slices for computer chips. The difference with OWMM is that there are several different machines in the line.

the-line floor pits, which separate workers from their co-workers and make it difficult to reach parts. By contrast, the new conveyors give all employees easier access to the vehicle.

Robots at Ford Motor Company's state-of-the-art Atlanta assembly plant weld front ends for the Mercury Sable and its Ford counterpart, the Taurus.

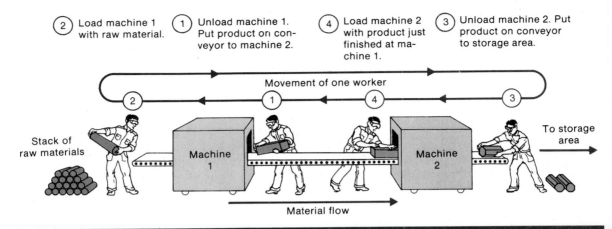

FIGURE 5.1   **One Worker, Multiple Machines (OWMM) Concept**

Figure 5.1 illustrates a two-machine OWMM, although in actual operations four or five machines are more typical. Each machine operates on its own for much of the cycle, and the worker steps in only when necessary. The process reduces inventory as well as labor requirements. The addition of several low-cost automated devices can maximize the number of machines at OWMM sta-

MANAGERIAL PRACTICE 5.4 ▲▲

Leading-Edge Technology Isn't Always Best

- General Motors' most automated plant is a $500 million truck factory in Hamtramck, Michigan. Recently GM discovered that the plant, which operates with the help of 300 robots, has lower productivity and poorer quality control than the organization's labor-intensive plant at Fremont, California. GM runs the Fremont plant in a joint venture with Japan's Toyota.

- CalComp, Inc., a maker of graphic plotters in Anaheim, California, also learned that automation isn't the only way to increase productivity. According to President William P. Conlin, "I knew manufacturing was going to be our downfall or our solution." Manufacturing became the solution after CalComp decided to de-automate, streamline, and simplify. Gone is the assembly line. Workers push materials around in carts. CalComp's plotter now has 50 percent fewer parts, 30 percent lower assembly costs, and a 45 percent smaller price tag. CalComp rakes in a 40 percent margin, not a bad return for a $300,000 investment.

Sources: "Living with Smart Machines," *The Economist,* May 21, 1988; "The Productivity Paradox," *Business Week,* June 6, 1988.

tions: automatic tool changers, loaders and unloaders, start and stop devices, and fail-safe devices that detect defective parts or products.

The OWMM concept is being widely applied in Japan. For example, since 1979 Mitsubishi Electric Company has converted more than 25 percent of its machine operations to OWMM. It is decidedly "low-tech," but as Managerial Practice 5.4 demonstrates, sometimes less automation is best.

Group Technology

A second option for achieving repeatability with low-volume processes is **group technology (GT)**. This manufacturing technique groups parts or products with similar characteristics into *families* and sets aside groups of machines for their production. Families may be based on size, shape, manufacturing or routing requirements, or demand. The goal is to find a set of products with similar processing requirements and minimize machine changeover or setup. For example, all bolts might be assigned to the same part family, because they all require the same basic processing steps regardless of size or shape. Figure 5.2 shows 13 parts belonging to the same family.

The next step is to organize the machine tools needed to perform the basic processes into separate areas called *cells*. Rather than group similar machines, the operations manager arranges the machines for line flows. Thus in each cell the machines require only minor adjustments to accommodate each batch from the same family of parts, greatly simplifying product changeovers. By also simplifying product routings, GT cells reduce the time a job is in the shop. Queues of materials waiting to be worked on are shortened or eliminated.

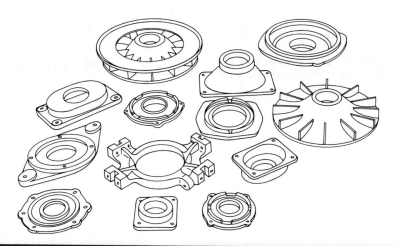

FIGURE 5.2   Thirteen Parts Belonging to the Same Family

Source: Mikell P. Groover, *Automation, Production Systems, and Computer-Aided Manufacturing.* Englewood Cliffs, N.J.: Prentice-Hall, 1980, p. 540. Reprinted by permission.

Frequently, materials handling is automated so that, after loading raw materials into the cell, a worker doesn't handle machined parts until the job is completed. To summarize, GT cells provide the following benefits:

- Less set-up time.
- Lower work-in-process inventory.
- Less materials handling.
- Reduced cycle time.
- Increased opportunities for automation.

Figure 5.3 compares process flows before and after creating GT cells. Part (a) shows a shop floor where machines are grouped according to function: lathing, milling, drilling, grinding, and assembly. Flows of materials are very jumbled. By contrast, the manager of the shop in part (b) has identified three product families that account for a majority of the firm's production. One family always requires two lathing operations followed by one operation at the milling machines. The second family always requires a milling operation followed by a grinding operation. The third family requires the use of a lathe, milling machine, and drill press. For simplicity, Fig. 5.3 shows only the flows of parts assigned to these three families. The remaining parts are produced at machines outside the cells, and still have jumbled routings. However, by creating three GT cells, the manager has definitely created more line flows and simplified routings.

Flexible Automation and Economies of Scope

There are two types of automation: fixed and flexible (or programmable). **Fixed automation** is a process that configures flow lines to produce one type of part or product. Equipment performs simple operations in a fixed sequence. Until the mid-1980s, most U.S. automobile plants were dominated by fixed automation—and some still are. Chemical processing plants and oil refineries also utilize this kind of automation.

Operations managers consider fixed automation when demand volumes are high, product designs are stable, and product life cycles are long. These three conditions compensate for the process's two primary drawbacks: large initial investment cost and relative inflexibility. The investment cost is particularly high when a single, complex machine must be capable of handling many operations. Because the system is designed around a particular product, changing equipment to accommodate new products is difficult and costly. On the plus side, fixed automation maximizes efficiency and yields a rock-bottom variable cost per unit.

Flexible Automation.   Flexible, or programmable automation, is another option for achieving repeatability when volumes are low. **Programmable automation** is an automatic process that can be reprogrammed to handle various products.

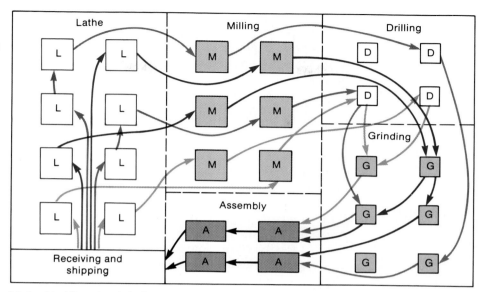

(a) Jumbled flows in a job shop without GT cells

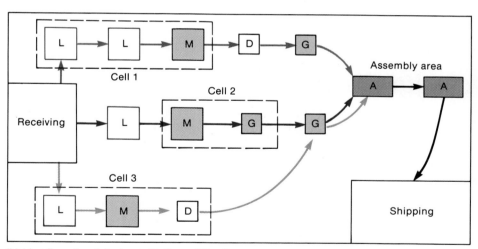

(b) Line flows in a job shop with three GT cells

FIGURE 5.3 Process Flows before and after the Use of GT Cells

Source: Mikell P. Groover, *Automation, Production Systems, and Computer-Aided Manufacturing.* Englewood Cliffs, N.J.: Prentice-Hall, 1980, pp. 540–541. Reprinted by permission.

The ability to reprogram machine instructions is useful in both product-focused and process-focused operations. For example, suppose that a machine has been dedicated to a particular product (product focus) that has reached the end of its life cycle. The machine can simply be reprogrammed with a new sequence of operations for a new product. When a machine makes a variety of products in small batches (process focus), changeovers are simple. There is a program for each product, and an operator simply enters the appropriate instructions to switch the process back and forth.

Economies of Scope.   Programmable automation breaks the traditional inverse relationship between resource flexibility and capital intensity (see Chapter 4). With programmable automation, both high capital intensity and high resource flexibility are possible. The result has been called **economies of scope**, which is the ability to produce multiple products more cheaply in combination than separately. In such situations, two conflicting competitive priorities—high product flexibility and low price—become more compatible.

Opportunities for economies of scope are not without limit. Someone must identify a family of parts or products with enough collective volume to fully utilize equipment, often in multiple shifts. Adding a product to the family results in one-time programming (and sometimes fixture) costs. *Fixtures* are reusable devices that maintain exact tolerances by holding the product firmly in position while it is processed.

COMPUTER-INTEGRATED MANUFACTURING ▲

The popular press often writes about the factory of the future—a fully automated factory that manufactures a wide variety of products without human intervention. While some "peopleless" factories do exist and others will be built, the concept goes beyond displacing people with automation.

Computer-integrated manufacturing (CIM) is an umbrella term for the total integration of product design and engineering, process planning, and manufacturing by means of complex computer systems. Less comprehensive computerized systems for production planning, inventory control, or scheduling are often considered part of CIM. Computerized integration of all phases of manufacturing—from initial customer order to final shipment—is CIM's ultimate goal.

Computer-integrated manufacturing helps many manufacturing firms, even those with high wage rates, remain competitive in the global marketplace. In the following sections, we describe several technologies that make up CIM: computer-aided manufacturing, computer-aided design, numerically controlled machines, robots, automated materials handling, and flexible manufacturing systems. The purpose of using these technologies is to increase productivity, improve quality, and offer more flexibility.

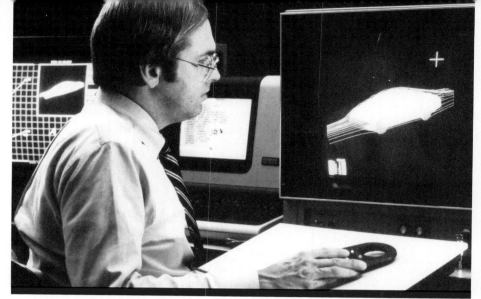

General Motors uses CAD/CAM to study aerodynamics.

Computer-Aided Manufacturing

The component of CIM that deals directly with manufacturing operations is called **computer-aided manufacturing (CAM).** It utilizes computers to design production processes and to control machine tools and materials flow. The various types of programmable automation are a basic part of CAM.

Computer-Aided Design

Computer-aided design (CAD) is a computerized design process for creating new parts or products or altering existing ones. The heart of CAD is a powerful desktop computer and graphics software that allow a designer to manipulate geometric shapes. These electronic design systems, which cost between $25,000 and $125,000, are replacing drafting that traditionally has been done by hand. The designer creates drawings on a display monitor and instructs the computer to show several views of the subject according to specified dimensions. The computer can also simulate the reaction of a part to strength and stress tests. Using the design data stored in the computer's memory, manufacturing engineers and other users can quickly obtain printouts of plans and specifications for a part or product at any time.

Analysts can use CAD to store, retrieve, and classify data about various parts. This information is useful in forming GT cells or creating families that lend themselves to flexible automation. Computer-aided design also helps designers avoid wasting time reinventing the wheel. Designers can quickly access and modify old designs, rather than start from scratch.

A *CAD/CAM system*, which integrates the design and manufacturing function through a computer, is the first step toward a paperless factory. The system translates final design specifications directly into detailed machine instructions for manufacturing the part. Standard Knapp, a small manufacturer of specialized packaging equipment, ventured into CIM by installing a CAD/CAM system. The first product took half the normal time to design and produce. An unexpected benefit was that the parts of the initial prototype fit together— contrary to previous experiences. Still another benefit of CAD/CAM is that it avoids duplication of efforts between engineering and manufacturing.

Numerically Controlled Machines

Numerically controlled (NC) machines are large machine tools programmed to produce small- to medium-sized batches of intricate parts. By following a preprogrammed sequence of instructions, NC machines can drill, turn, bore, or mill many different parts in various sizes and shapes. These machines were first developed in the early 1950s at the Massachusetts Institute of Technology through research sponsored by the U.S. Air Force. The objective was to find more efficient methods of manufacturing jet aircraft.

Numerically controlled machines are currently the most commonly used form of flexible automation. The newer models receive their instructions from a computer, not from a punched tape or card as in the past. **Computerized numerically controlled (CNC) machines** are usually stand-alone pieces of equipment, each controlled by its own microcomputer. Over 40 percent of the

A robot reaching through a truck's front-door window to apply a sealant bead. Safety equipment has been removed to provide a clear view of the robot. Safety equipment must be in place prior to operation.

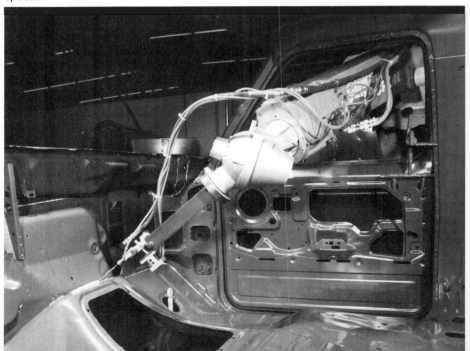

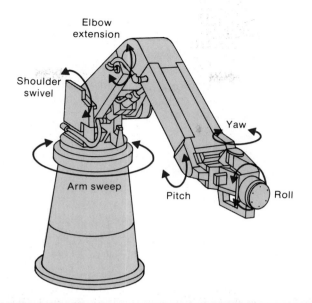

Elbow extension

Shoulder swivel

Yaw

Arm sweep

Pitch

Roll

FIGURE 5.4   Robot and Its Standard Movements

Source: Chris Voss, "Managing New Manufacturing Technologies," *OMA Monograph 1,* September 1986. Reprinted by permission.

world's NC machines are at work in Japan. Since the early 1980s, Japanese industry has spent twice as much as North American or European industry on factory equipment, and more than half this equipment has been CNC machines.

Industrial Robots

Robots are more glamorous than the NC workhorses. The first industrial robot joined the GM production line in 1961. Today there are more than 20,000 "steel-collar" workers in North America, 28,000 in Europe, and 80,000 in Japan. Building robots has become a $1 billion business.

Industrial robots are versatile, computer-controlled machines programmed to perform various tasks. They operate independently of human control. Most are stationary and mounted on the floor, with an arm that can reach into difficult locations. Figure 5.4 shows the six standard movements of a robot's arm. Not all robots have every movement.

The robot's hand, sometimes called an *end effector* or *tool,* actually does the work. The hand (not shown in Fig. 5.4) can be changed to perform different tasks. At present, these tasks commonly include handling materials, spot welding, spray painting, assembly, and inspection and testing. Second generation robots equipped with sensors that simulate touch and sight have opened up new applications. For example, robots can wash windows, pick fruit from trees, mix chemicals in laboratories, and handle radioactive materials.

TABLE 5.2 Robots: Current Practice

Characteristic	Actual Experience
Investment cost	From $20,000 to $100,000, depending on sophistication
Payback period	Typically less than three years
Return on investment	Typically from 12% to 18%, with some as high as 40%
Operating life	From 15,000 to 25,000 work hours
Annual maintenance cost	10% of initial investment cost; major overhaul after 10,000 hours
Best volume levels	More than 50,000 units per year and less than 500,000 units per year
Installation time	One to five days, depending on complexity

Source: Mitchell, Roger H., and Vincent A. Mabert, "Robotics: Myths and Realities for Smaller American Manufacturers," *Business Horizons*, July/August 1986. Reprinted by permission.

The initial cost of a robot depends on its size and function. Other costs include modifications to both product and process to accommodate the robot, preparation of the work site, installing and debugging the robot, and retraining and relocating workers. Benefits from robot installation include less waste materials, more consistent quality, and savings in labor. Robots are the drudges of the work force, performing highly repetitive tasks without tiring, taking a lunch break, or going to the restroom. They accept zero wages and perform hazardous tasks without complaint. Table 5.2 highlights other characteristics of industrial robots.

Automated Materials Handling

In both manufacturing and service industries, how, when, and by whom materials are handled is an important technological choice. **Materials handling** covers the processes of moving, packaging, and storing a product. Each process costs time and money and adds no value to the product. Therefore operations managers are always looking for ways to automate the flow of materials to and from an operation.

The amount of justifiable materials handling automation depends on positioning strategy, as illustrated in the Longhorn and Pinecrest tours in Chapter 2. When operations have a process focus, job paths vary and there is little repeatability in materials handling. In such situations, automation can't be justified. At Longhorn, for example, workers move materials and equipment in open-top containers, carts, or lift trucks. However, when operations have a product focus and repeatability is high, handling can be automated. Pinecrest Brewery has opted for extensive fixed automation, and materials literally flow through pipes from one vat to another.

The managers at Longhorn and Pinecrest made the right decisions for their particular operations. However, other types of flexible automation are now available for firms with positioning strategies that fall between those of Longhorn and Pinecrest. Let's look at two such technologies: AGVs and AS/RS.

AGVs. An **automated guided vehicle (AGV)** is a small, driverless, battery-driven truck that moves materials between operations. Most models follow a cable installed below the floor, but optical paths and free-ranging methods have extended their capabilities. They can go anywhere so long as there is aisle space and a relatively smooth floor. Instructions are issued from either an on-board computer or a centralized computer.

The AGV's ability to route around problems such as production bottlenecks and transportation blockages helps production avoid expensive, unpredictable shutdowns. Furthermore, AGVs give just-in-time delivery of parts, thus reducing stockpiles of expensive inventories throughout the plant. The automotive industry now uses AGVs in some plants as mobile assembly stands, primarily for heavy loads. Workers prefer them to inflexible conveyors, because the AGVs

The electronic assembly system of Northern Telecom in Toronto is a good example of CIM and automated materials handling. Here is just part of the system. A vision cell in the lower left foreground inspects a circuit pack. Possible defects are passed to an operator's graphic display. In the right background, inspected packs are loaded to an IBM robot, which inserts and solders components. The boards next pass through a Freon cleaner in the left background. (Courtesy of David Dilts.)

don't leave until the workers have done the job correctly at their own pace. NCR Corporation installed a $100,000 AGV system at one of its electronics fabrication facilities. Machines run along a 3000-foot guidepath at $1\frac{1}{2}$ miles per hour, ferrying parts between the stockroom, assembly stations, and the AS/RS.

AS/RS.   An **automated storage and retrieval system (AS/RS)** is an automated method of storing and retrieving materials and tools. A computer controls the entire system, which includes racks, bins, and stackers. With support from AGVs, an AS/RS can receive and deliver materials without the aid of human hands. For example, IBM's new distribution center in Mechanicsburg, Pennsylvania, ships out 105,000 spare computer parts and related publications each day—a staggering volume. The new facility has an AS/RS and thirteen AGVs. Computer control assigns newly arrived materials to one of 37,240 storage locations. If optical sensors confirm that the materials will fit, the automated system moves them along to the proper location. Production at this highly automated facility is 20 percent higher and accuracy of filled orders has increased to 99.8 percent.

Flexible Manufacturing Systems

A **flexible manufacturing system (FMS)** is a configuration of computer-controlled, semi-independent work stations where materials are automatically handled and machine loaded. Like NC machines and industrial robots, an FMS is a type of flexible automation and is part of CIM. Such systems require a large initial investment ($5 million to $20 million), but little direct labor to operate. The three key components of an FMS are:

1. several computer-controlled work stations, such as CNC machines or robots, that perform a series of operations;

2. a computer-controlled transport system for moving materials and parts from one machine to another and in and out of the system; and

3. loading and unloading stations.

Workers bring raw materials for a part family to the loading points, where the FMS takes over. Under the direction of the central computer, transporters begin delivering the materials to various work stations. At each station, they pass through a specific sequence of operations unique to each part. The route is determined by the central computer. The goal is to synchronize activities in order to maximize the system's utilization. Since automatic tool interchange capabilities make it possible to switch tools quickly, setup times for machines are short. This flexibility often allows more than one machine to perform an operation. As a result, production continues even when one machine is down for maintenance. Bottlenecks are avoided by routing parts to another machine when one is busy.

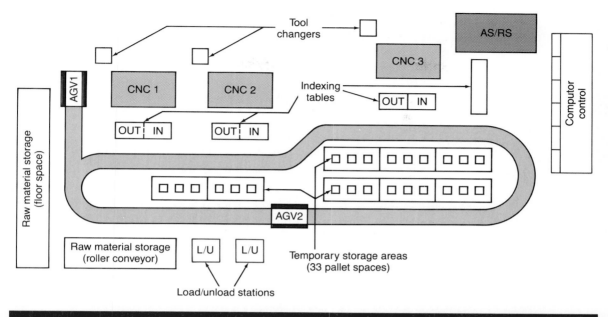

FIGURE 5.5   A Flexible Manufacturing System at Mazak Corporation

Source: Courtesy of Vincent Mabert and Mazak Corporation. Reprinted by permission.

Figure 5.5 shows the layout of an FMS at the Mazak Corporation plant in Kentucky.* The plant produces turning and machining centers. Specific characteristics of this FMS are:

1. The computer control room (right) housing the main computer, which controls the transporter and sequence of operations.

2. Three CNC machines, each with its own microprocessor, which control the details of the machining process.

3. Two AGVs, which travel around a 200-foot-long oval track, moving materials on pallets to and from the CNCs. When the AGVs' batteries run low, the central computer directs them to certain spots on the track for recharging.

4. Indexing tables, which lie between each CNC and the track. Inbound pallets from an AGV are automatically transferred to the right side of the table. Outbound pallets holding finished parts are automatically transferred to the left side for pickup.

---

*We are indebted to Vincent Mabert for much of the information about this FMS, including Fig. 5.5 and the photos of the system.

5. A tool changer located behind each CNC, which loads and unloads tool magazines. Each magazine holds an assortment of tools. A machine automatically selects tools for the next specific operation. Changing from one tool to another takes only two minutes.

6. Two load/unload stations, to which workers are assigned during one of three shifts; loading takes 10 to 20 minutes.

7. An automatic AS/RS (upper right), where finished parts are stored. The AGV transfers parts on its pallet to an indexing table, which then transfers them to the AS/RS. The process is reversed when parts are needed for assembly into finished products elsewhere in the plant.

This particular system typifies the future that many envision for FMSs. It fits with an intermediate positioning strategy involving medium-level variety (5 to 100 parts) and volume (annual production rates of 40 to 2000 units per part). The system can simultaneously handle small batches of many products. In addition, an FMS can be used a second way. At any given time, an FMS can produce low-variety, high-volume products in much the same way that fixed automation does. However, when these products reach the end of their life cycles, the FMS can be reprogrammed to accommodate a different product. This flexibility makes FMS very appealing, even to product-focused firms where life cycles are short.

MANAGING TECHNOLOGICAL CHANGE ▲

Management of both service and manufacturing industries is looking to emerging technologies for improvements in productivity and quality. Selecting the right technologies can give a firm a competitive edge, but its operations managers must make informed decisions with courage and vision. Although they offer no guarantees of success, four useful guidelines for making such decisions have emerged from recent experience.

Initial Planning and Simplification

Before considering automation, a manager should simplify and streamline current operations to eliminate duplication and waste. The "base case" against which to justify new automation should be what the current operation can achieve, *not* what it is achieving. Several showcase CIM plants have not lived up to expectations because automation preceded streamlining.

When the time comes to automate, management should plan well, making sure that operations strategy and competitive priorities match technological choices. Operations managers should state precisely what they expect from automation. They should quantify goals and perform structured analysis, rather than settle for an undefined goal of reduced costs. Managers at successful CIM plants, such as Allen-Bradley, Caterpillar, and Hewlett-Packard, approached automation incrementally, without committing to overly ambitious projects.

(a)

(b)

(c)

(d)

(e)

(f)

Views of Mazak's FMS. (a) End view with CNC 1 on the immediate left. The AGV is coming down the track just left of center. In the center are pallets of stored parts. The computer control room is behind the windows on the second floor. (b) CNC 2 and an AGV that has just received a finished part from CNC 1. (c) Closeup view of a pallet and fixture for positioning a particular part the same way each time. (d) The tooling magazine (right) and the tool changer (left) assigned to each CNC. (e) An AGV at the position marked AGV 1 in Fig. 5.5. (f) View of AS/RS in the background, where finished parts are stored.

Justification

How to justify investment in emerging technologies is a controversial topic. Traditional techniques of financial analysis, such as the net present value method (see Supplement 1), would reject some very successful CIM projects. The problem is not with the technique itself, but how it is applied. Labor savings still justify most automation projects, but labor is a shrinking component of total costs. For example, fixed costs now comprise nearly 70 percent of a flexible manufacturer's total bill. As Managerial Practice 5.5 shows, a narrow focus on labor can foreclose excellent automation projects.

Operations managers must look beyond direct costs to the impact of automation on customer service, delivery times, inventories, and resource flexibility. Although quantifying a firm's ability to move quickly into a new market may be difficult, such intangibles make the difference. The smart operations manager also realizes that the base case of doing nothing is *not* the status quo. A firm that fails to automate—while its competitors do just that—can lose its competitive advantage. The result may be declining revenues and layoffs.

MANAGERIAL PRACTICE 5.5

The New Math at Allen-Bradley and Rockwell International

- Allen-Bradley's new $15 million, 50-machine, flexible-assembly facility produces motor starters in 125 different configurations at a rate of 600 an hour. The company didn't justify automation with a narrow investment-driven focus. Instead, it began with the corporate strategy and then developed a manufacturing plant that would achieve the desired goals. After deciding to compete anywhere on price (corporate strategy), they justified the facility investment (operations strategy) on the basis of quality, cost, market share, competition, and profitability. "If there is a time to ignore conventional return-on-investment calculation, it's when your long-term goals are at stake," says Tracy O'Rourke, Allen-Bradley's CEO.

- At Rockwell International's Collins Defense Communications facility, management decided to create a strategic advantage in manufacturing, rather than relocate in order to chase low labor rates. Its CIM program is an $11 million addition to the existing plant. Labor savings did not justify the investment, since employment in the assembly areas remained constant. Instead, justification came from increased flexibility; the facility now handles both high and low production rates economically. Quality is better and skilled, experienced employees work where their expertise helps the most.

Source: "Automation and the Bottom Line," *Industry Week*, May 26, 1986.

The Human Side

Automation affects jobs at all levels: Some are eliminated, some are upgraded, and some are downgraded. Even when the changes resulting from automation are small, people-related issues may become large. For example, poorly trained and poorly motivated workers can cause enormous damage, as illustrated by the nuclear accidents at Three Mile Island and Chernobyl. The operations manager must anticipate such changes and prepare for them. The transition is easiest when automation is part of capacity expansion or a new facility and thus doesn't threaten existing jobs. In other situations early education and retraining is essential. Before Chrysler opened its CIM plant in Sterling Heights, Michigan, it put its employees collectively through 900,000 labor hours of training.

Another key to successful implementation is involving employees in the design of new systems. When Ford revamped its plant to make the Aerostar (see Managerial Practice 5.3), management reviewed proposed methods with workers who were directly responsible for specific operations. Employees made 434 suggestions, about 60 percent of which were adopted.

Leadership

The operations manager should identify a team to lead and coordinate new automation projects. All departments affected by the automation should be represented on the team. A "project champion" who promotes the project at every opportunity and who has contagious enthusiasm should be in charge. This leader should be respected by all team members and preferably should have had experience dealing with equipment vendors. Top management's ongoing support of the team must be evident throughout the project. Everyone should know that the operations manager is knowledgeable about the project, stands behind it, and will give it the resources it needs to succeed.

CHAPTER HIGHLIGHTS

- In order to achieve better quality and higher productivity, operations managers must pay continuing attention to technological advances.
- Advances in computer technology have significantly broadened technological choices in both service and manufacturing industries.
- EFTs, ATMs, EDIs, on-line databases, electronic mail systems, linked communication and information systems, bar codes, and integrated computer order systems are examples of newer technologies in the service sector.
- Repeatability is one of the keys to increased productivity in manufacturing. Higher product volumes allow for higher resource utilization. Little

time is lost to machine changeovers, and materials handling is minimized.

- If product volumes are too low to justify dedicating a production line to a single product, it may be possible to obtain repeatability with low-cost automation. In such cases the one worker, multiple machines (OWMM) concept or group technology (GT) cells, where machines are arranged to produce families of parts, may be feasible. Flexible automation is a third way to achieve the benefits of repeatability for low volumes.
- Fixed automation maximizes efficiency for high-volume products with long life cycles, but pro-

grammable (flexible) automation provides economies of scope. Flexibility is gained and setups are minimized because the machines can be reprogrammed to follow new instructions. Numerically controlled (NC) machines and robots are examples of programmable automation.

- Computer-integrated manufacturing (CIM) goes beyond labor savings, by totally integrating product design, engineering, process planning, and manufacturing through complex computer systems. Computer-aided manufacturing (CAM) is the part of CIM that deals directly with manufacturing.

- A CAD/CAM system links computerized product design and production. It's the first step toward a paperless factory.

- Managers automate materials handling systems when there is enough repeatability. Two new methods used are the automated guided vehicle (AGV) and the automated storage and retrieval system (AS/RS).

- Programmable automation includes flexible manufacturing systems (FMSs), which consist of several computer-controlled work stations, an interconnecting transport system, and areas for loading and unloading. An FMS is very expensive to acquire but is flexible enough to accommodate new product families.

- Operations managers must make informed choices about investing in new automation and how to implement them. Success is more likely if the manager first simplifies current operations, sets goals, recognizes all costs and benefits, deals with people-related issues, and provides the necessary leadership and support.

KEY TERMS

STUDY QUESTIONS

1. What development over the last 20 years has contributed to greater technological choices in the service and manufacturing sectors?

2. Suppose that an electric utility company contracts to have its meter readers read meters for the local water company in addition to reading its own. What productivity improvements might result if the electric company and the water company were viewed as a single entity? Could meter readers read as many electric meters in a day if they read water meters too? If the electric utility uses an integrated system of computers in meter reading, what additional network links would be required?

3. What are some of the newer technologies that can be used to improve office productivity?

4. In what ways is an automatic teller machine (ATM) more flexible than a human bank teller? In what ways is the human bank teller more flexible? What are the advantages of an ATM system to the bank? What are the advantages to the customer? How does an ATM allow the bank to increase repeatability?

5. How can bar codes improve both service and manufacturing operations?

6. How does repeatability influence technological choices?

7. What is the one worker, multiple machines (OWMM) concept? What is a group technology (GT) cell? What is a flexible manufacturing system (FMS)? What do they all have in common? How do they differ?

8. Explain the difference between fixed and programmable automation. Give examples of each.

9. What is computer-integrated manufacturing (CIM)? Is it a good choice for all manufacturers?

10. What are some of the advantages of computer-aided design (CAD)?

11. What do numerically controlled (NC) machines and robots have in common?

12. What is materials handling? Why is it said that "the best materials handling is no handling at all"? Compare materials handling in two industries: one with a product focus and one with a process focus.

13. In what ways do an AGV and an AS/RS qualify as flexible automation?

14. What are the elements of a flexible manufacturing system (FMS)? Why is this kind of system flexible?

15. Why is the use of traditional techniques of financial analysis as a method of justifying automation projects criticized? Must CIM projects just be accepted as a leap of faith and an act of hope?

PROBLEMS

Advanced Problems

These problems require prior reading of Supplement 1. A computer package is helpful, but not mandatory, for the financial analysis.

1. Valley Memorial Hospital is considering two different computerized information systems to improve nurse productivity. The first alternative is a portable computer system. It will require a one-time investment in computer hardware, computer software, and employee training of $150,000. After-tax cash flows attributable to this investment are expected to be $30,000 per year for the next 10 years. These estimated savings would accrue from increased employee productivity and the value of having timely and accurate information. The second alternative is to install a mainframe computer linked to bedside terminals. This system will require an investment of $350,000 but is expected to generate after-tax cash flows of $45,000 per year for 10 years. The hospital must earn 12 percent on its investments. Assume that both systems will have no salvage value at the end of 10 years.
   a. Calculate the net present value and payback periods for each alternative.
   b. Based on your financial analysis, what do you recommend?
   c. Are there any valid considerations other than financial?

2. Interstate Bank is considering the installation of a new automatic teller machine (ATM). Two locations are available for this ATM: one within a local shopping mall and the other at the branch bank just outside the mall. An initial investment of $50,000 is required for the ATM at either location. The operating costs of the mall ATM would be $25,000 per year. The branch bank ATM would have operating costs of $20,000 per year. The slightly higher costs of the mall ATM are based on the additional cost of leasing mall space and an expected larger number of ATM transactions. The additional revenue (from an increase in new accounts) generated because of the installation of each ATM would also differ, with the mall ATM generating $50,000 per year and the branch bank ATM generating $47,000 per year. Assume a tax rate of 50 percent and desired rate of return of 16 percent on investments. The ATMs have an expected life of 10 years with no salvage value at the end of that time.
   a. Calculate the net present value and payback periods for each alternative.
   b. Based on your analysis, what location do you recommend?
   c. Are there other factors that must be considered when evaluating these alternatives?

3. The manager of A Loaf of Bread, a gourmet supermarket, wants to install a computerized cash register system in the store. The system under consideration consists of electronic cash registers (ECRs) linked to an in-store computer. The ECRs are capable of electronically weighing and pricing produce and tracking sales of other items by using look-up codes. In addition, the system will have scanning equipment. The scanning equipment allows the UPC product symbols to be read at the checkout stands and recorded by the in-store computer, automatically updating of product inventory, as well as recording sales. The installation of the system will require an initial investment of $200,000. The after-tax cash inflows attributable to the installation of this system would be $36,000 for the next seven years. This after-tax cash inflow is based only on the estimated savings due to a reduction in labor costs. Although other costs will increase—for equipment maintenance and rental—less labor will be required to price items, such as changing price stickers, manually. The store must earn 12 percent on its investments. There is no salvage value at the end of 7 years.

a. Based on NPV analysis, should the system be implemented?

b. The increase in checker productivity and the availability of timely, accurate inventory records is estimated to increase after-tax cash inflows by $14,000 per year. Should this system be implemented if these savings are considered?

c. What else does the manager of A Loaf of Bread need to consider before making this decision?

4. National Power and Electric, a supplier of electric power to the north central United States, is considering the purchase of a robot to repair welds in nuclear reactors. Two types of vision system robots are being considered: a "smart" robot, whose actions in the reactor would be controlled by what it "sees," and a different kind of robot, whose actions in the reactor would be controlled by an external operator. The "smart" robot requires an initial investment of $300,000, while the operator-controlled robot requires an initial investment of $240,000. Both robots have an expected life of five years with no salvage value at the end of that time. Welds are currently repaired by a human welder. The job is hazardous, so the welder's annual salary and fringe benefits total $110,000. Buying either robot eliminates the need for the human welder. However, the operator-controlled robot requires an operator whose annual salary (and benefits) would be $40,000. The "smart" robot requires an extra $20,000 in technical support. National Power and Electric seeks at least 18 percent on its investments and its tax rate is 50 percent.

a. Calculate the net present value for each alternative.

b. Based on your financial analysis, what do you recommend?

c. Based on other factors, should either robot be purchased?

SELECTED REFERENCES

Amstead, B. J., P. F. Oswald, and M. L. Bregman, *Manufacturing Processes,* 7th ed. New York: John Wiley & Sons, 1977.

Bylinsky, Gene, "The Race to the Automatic Factory," *Fortune,* February 21, 1983, pp. 52–60.

Collier, David A., *Service Management: The Automation of Services.* Reston, Va.: Reston Publishing Company, 1985.

Collier, David A., "The Service Sector Revolution: The Automation of Services," *Long Range Planning,* vol. 16, no. 6 (December 1983), pp. 11–13.

Doyle, Lawrence E., Carl A. Keyser, James L. Leach, George F. Schrader, and Morse B. Singer, *Manufacturing Processes and Materials for Engineers,* 3rd ed. Englewood Cliffs, N.J.: Prentice-Hall, 1985.

"Flexible Manufacturing Systems," *Modern Materials Handling,* September 7, 1982.

Gaimon, Cheryl, "The Optimal Acquisition of Automation to Enhance the Productivity of Labor," *Management Science,* vol. 31, no. 9 (1985), pp. 1175–1190.

Gerwin, Donald, "Do's and Don'ts of Computerized Manufacturing," *Harvard Business Review* (March–April 1982), pp. 107–116.

Gold, Bela, "CAM Sets New Rules for Production," *Harvard Business Review* (November–December 1982), pp. 88–94.

Goldhar, J. D., and Mariann Jelinek, "Plan for Economies of Scope," *Harvard Business Review,* (November–December 1983), pp. 141–148.

Green, Timothy J., and Randall P. Sadowski, "A Review of Cellular Manufacturing Assumptions, Advantages and Design Techniques," *Journal of Operations Management,* vol. 4, no. 2 (February 1984), pp. 85–97.

Groover, Mikell P., and E. W. Zimmers, Jr., *CAD/CAM: Computer-Aided Design and Manufacturing.* Englewood Cliffs, N.J.: Prentice-Hall, 1984.

Hausman, W. H., L. B. Schwartz, and S. C. Graves, "Optimal Storage Assignment in Automatic Warehousing Systems," *Management Science,* vol. 22, no. 6 (1976), pp. 629–638.

Hyer, Nancy, and Urban Wemmerlov, "Group Technology and Productivity," *Harvard Business Review* (July–August 1984), pp. 140–149.

"IBM's Automated Factory—A Giant Step Forward," *Modern Materials Handling,* March, 1985.

Jaikumar, Ramchandran, "Postindustrial Manufacturing," *Harvard Business Review* (November—December 1986), pp. 69–76.

Jenkins, K. M., and A. R. Raedels, "The Robot Revolution: Strategic Considerations for Managers," *Production and Inventory Management* (Third Quarter 1982), pp. 107–116.

Kaplan, Robert S., "Must CIM Be Justified by Faith Alone?" *Harvard Business Review* (March–April 1986), pp. 87–95.

Levitt, Theodore, "The Industrialization of Service," *Harvard Business Review* (September–October 1976), pp. 63–74.

Mertes, Louis H., "Doing Your Office Over—Electronically," *Harvard Business Review* (March–April 1981), pp. 127–135.

Poppel, Harvey L., "Who Needs the Office of the Future?" *Harvard Business Review* (November–December 1982), pp. 146–155.

Rosenthal, Stephen, "Progress Toward the Factory of the Future," *Journal of Operations Management,* vol. 4, no. 3 (May 1984), pp. 203–229.

Roth, Aleda V., and Marjolijn van der Velde, *The Future of Retail Banking Delivery Systems.* Rolling Meadows, Ill.: Bank Administration Institute, 1988.

Seligman, Daniel, "Life Will Be Different When We're All On-Line," *Fortune,* February 4, 1985, pp. 68–72.

Skinner, Wickham, "Operations Technology: Blind Spot in Strategic Management," *Interfaces,* vol. 14, no. 1 (January–February 1984), pp. 116–125.

Starr, Martin K., and Alan J. Biloski, "The Decision to Adopt New Technology—Effects on Organizational Size," *Omega,* vol. 12, no. 4 (1984), pp. 353–361.

Stecke, Kathryn E., and James J. Solberg, "Loading and Control Policies for a Flexible Manufacturing System," *International Journal of Production Research,* vol. 19, no. 5 (1981), pp. 481–490.

Stone, Philip J., and Robert Luchetti, "Your Office Is Where You Are," *Harvard Business Review* (March–April 1985), pp. 102–117.

Suresh, Nallan C., and Jack R. Meredith, "A Generic Approach to Justifying Flexible Manufacturing Systems," *Proceedings of the First ORSA/TIMS Special Interest Conference,* August 15–17, 1984.

Thomas, Dan R. E., "Strategy Is Different in Service Businesses," *Harvard Business Review* (July–August 1978), pp. 158–165.

White, Robert B., "A Prototype for the Automated Office," *Datamation* (April 1977), pp. 83–90.

CHAPTER 6

WORK MEASUREMENT

 Chapter Outline

▲ Key Questions for Managers

How can we get the time standards we need to compare alternative process designs or project future capacity requirements?

How can we estimate the amount of labor needed for a new product or service?

Which method of work measurement can we use most effectively in a given situation?

How much total production do we need before the cost per unit is low enough to be competitive in a new market?

How will our methods of work measurement change as we introduce more automation?

rederick Taylor inspired the management philosophy called scientific management. As we mentioned in Chapter 4, his main premise was that any operation could be improved by breaking it into components, measuring their work content, and seeking ways to improve work methods. In addition to blazing new trails in the area of work methods improvement, Taylor used a stopwatch to measure the output of manual operations. His pioneering work focused management's attention on the importance of work measurement and finding more efficient ways to improve performance. Work measurement is the basis for estimating an operating system's output, taking into consideration the effects of learning. As you will see, this information is necessary to the design of new systems and the management of existing ones. In this chapter, we first discuss the methods available for determining output standards and then explore the implications of learning for operations strategy and planning.

WORK STANDARDS ▲

A **standard** is a commonly accepted basis for comparison. With respect to work measurement, we usually refer to either labor standards or machine standards. A **labor standard** is the time required for a trained worker to perform a given task following a prescribed method with normal effort and skill. Labor standards are more difficult to develop than are machine standards, because factors such as skill, effort, and stamina vary from one employee to another. By contrast, machines of the same type, such as robots, perform the same repetitive tasks with little variation from unit to unit.

The key to creating a labor standard is defining "normal" performance. Suppose, for example, that you are the manager of a fast-growing company that manufactures frozen pizza. You want to create a standard for pizza assembly. You observe as a worker spreads sauce over the pizza shell, adds pepperoni and cheese, places the pizza in a box, and puts the assembled product on a cart for fast freezing. The entire process takes 20 seconds. You calculate that at this pace a worker could assemble 1440 pizzas in an eight-hour day.

Before settling on 20 seconds as the standard, however, you have to take some tangible factors into consideration. For example, the worker you observed may be an exceptionally energetic and efficient person. If she had considerable experience, her skills might be well above average. Moreover, your estimate of 20 seconds per pizza should also take into account fluctuations in pace and rest periods scheduled during the workday. Generally, you cannot use the time per unit observed over a short period of time for one employee as a standard for an extended period of time for all employees. Creating labor standards requires some modification of observed times, based on the judgment of skilled observers.

Thomas Monaghan (center), president of Domino's Pizza, demonstrates the proper procedure for assembling a pizza.

Areas of Controversy

Work standards is one of the most controversial areas of operations management because of the conflicts that often arise between management and labor. When an organization uses output standards as the basis for pay, unions object if they feel that standards are set "too high," and management objects if they feel that standards are "too low." Of course, setting output standards at either extreme makes it difficult to plan for appropriate capacity levels, increases costs, and reduces profits.

The controversy is not confined to differences between labor and management. Managers often disagree among themselves over the use of engineered work standards. Some believe that the costs of large industrial engineering staffs and the hidden costs of labor–management conflicts outweigh the benefits of elaborate standards. Others believe that using engineered standards for piecework incentives actually defeats their purpose, which is to increase worker productivity. To keep management from raising standards, employees may be secretive about new work methods that they devise to increase output.

Work Standards as a Management Tool

Many companies that develop work standards experience productivity gains. For example, Managerial Practice 6.1 shows how one firm uses work measurement to remain competitive in the package delivery industry.

The controversial nature of work standards points to the need for effective work-force management and the structuring of appropriate incentives. A manager may use standards to define a day's work or to motivate workers to improve their normal performance. For example, under an incentive compensation plan, workers can earn a bonus for output that exceeds the standard. Managers use work standards in a variety of other ways such as:

1. *Comparing alternative process designs*. Time standards are used to compare different routings for an item. The manager can also use time standards to evaluate new work methods and to estimate the advantages of utilizing new equipment.

2. *Scheduling*. Managers need time estimates in order to assign tasks to workers and machines in ways that effectively utilize resources.

3. *Capacity planning*. With the aid of time estimates for tasks, managers can determine current and projected capacity requirements for given demand requirements. Long-term capital investment and work-force staffing decisions also can require these time estimates.

4. *Establishing prices and costs*. Using labor and machine time standards as a base, managers can develop cost standards for current and new products. Cost standards can also be used to develop budgets, determine prices, and reach make-or-buy decisions.

5. *Performance appraisal*. A worker's output can be compared to the standard output over a period of time to determine how well the worker is performing. Work measurement methods can also be used to estimate the proportion of time workers are idle or otherwise unproductive.

Work measurement is used more for some of these purposes than for others. A survey of 1500 firms indicated that the most frequent use of work measurement was for estimating and costing (89 percent of the firms), followed by incentive compensation plans (59 percent), scheduling (51 percent), and performance appraisal (41 percent). Only 2 percent of the firms used work measurement for staffing and capacity planning (Rice, 1977).

METHODS OF WORK MEASUREMENT ▲

Various methods of work measurement are available to the manager, but the choice of which method to use often depends on the purpose for which the data will be used. For example, managers might need a high degree of precision when comparing actual work method results to standards. A stop-watch

MANAGERIAL PRACTICE 6.1

United Parcel Service Remains Competitive

United Parcel Service (UPS), the nation's largest package delivery firm, employs more than 1000 industrial engineers to set standards for myriad closely supervised tasks. The emphasis on efficiency has reached the point where engineers accompany truck drivers on their rounds, timing all activities and looking for ways to improve performance. For example, drivers making a delivery are instructed to beep their horns as they stop at the curb. The noise is intended to alert the customer, who will start for the door before the delivery person actually arrives. Meanwhile, the delivery person walks to the customer's door at the brisk rate of three feet per second, then knocks rather than waste seconds searching for a doorbell. Supervisors ride with the least efficient drivers until they learn to finish on time.

UPS faces a competitive battle with Roadway Services, Inc., a company with a very different approach. Roadway hopes to gain the edge in productivity by eliminating people as much as possible through automation. At Roadway bar coding, laser scanners, computers, and automated sorting equipment help cut delivery time. At UPS legions of workers still sort packages. If the competition intensifies, improving productivity will be the heart of UPS's counterattack. Work measurement will help the firm identify areas for improvement.

Source: "United Parcel Service Gets Deliveries Done by Driving Its Workers," by Daniel Machalba, *Wall Street Journal*, April 22, 1986.

study or predetermined times might be required. Alternatively, estimating the percentage of time that an employee is idle while waiting for materials requires a method such as work sampling. Consequently, a manager may use more than one approach to obtain needed work measurement information. We present and discuss four of the more commonly used methods in this section.

Time Study Method

The method used most often for setting time standards for a task is **time study**. A job is divided into a series of smaller work elements representing the accepted work method for the job. Using a stopwatch, an analyst times a trained worker performing the work elements for a number of work cycles, then calculates the average time for each element. With this information and a performance rating based on judgment, the analyst develops a time standard for the task.

Selecting Work Elements.   Figure 6.1 shows an observation sheet used in a time study of packaging ceramic coffee cups. This particular operation requires only four work elements. Several considerations are involved in selecting the work elements for a time study. First, each work element should have definite starting and stopping points to facilitate taking the stopwatch readings. Second, work elements that take less than three seconds to complete should be avoided because they are difficult to time. For example, work element 2 could have been divided into three detailed elements: (1) pick up liner with left hand; (2) expand liner to open the holes for each cup; and (3) insert liner into carton. As each of these activities is done very quickly, obtaining accurate times for each one would be difficult. Finally, the work elements should correspond to the standard work method that has been running smoothly for a period of time in a standard work environment. Incidental operations not normally involved in the task should be identified and separated from the repetitive work.

Timing the Elements.   After the work elements have been identified, a worker trained in the work method is selected for study. The analyst then times the worker on each element to get an initial set of observations. Figure 6.1 shows the results of the *continuous method* of timing. For each work element, the r row shows the stopwatch reading upon completion of that element, and the watch is not reset until the end of the study. To avoid unnecessary writing, whole numbers are shown only when they change from the last observation. For example, the stopwatch reading for the second observation of the element "put liner into carton" was actually 2.56, but only .56 was written on the form. In order to get the observed time for a work element, the analyst merely records the difference between two successive continuous watch readings in

OPERATION: Coffee Cup Packaging						DATE 1/23		OPERATOR: B. Larson CLOCK NO: 43-6205				
OBSERVER: S. Johnson	START 9:00 (AM) PM					STOP 9:22 (AM) PM		ELAPSED STUDY TIME 21.68	TIME PER PIECE 21.68/10 = 2.168			

ELEMENT DESCRIPTION		OBSERVATIONS										$\bar{t}$	F	RF
		1	2	3	4	5	6	7	8	9	10			
1. Get two cartons*	t	.48		.46		.54		.49		.51		.50	0.5	1.05
	r	.48		.85		9.14		.53		.83				
2. Put liner into carton	t	.11	.13	.09	.10	.11	.13	.08	.12	.10	.09	.11	1.0	.95
	r	.59	.56	.94	.82	.25	.23	.61	.50	.93	.83			
3. Place cups into carton	t	.74	.68	.71	.69	.73	.70	.68	.74	.71	.72	.71	1.0	1.10
	r	1.33	3.24	5.65	7.51	.98	.93	14.29	16.24	18.64	20.55			
4. Seal carton and set aside	t	1.10	1.15	1.07	1.09	1.12	1.11	1.09	1.08	1.10	1.13	1.10	1.0	.90
	r	2.43	4.39	6.72	8.60	11.10	13.04	15.38	17.32	19.74	21.68			

NORMAL TIME FOR CYCLE

ALLOWANCES (% of normal time) ___15%___   STANDARD TIME ___2.45___ Min/piece

FIGURE 6.1   Time Study Observation Sheet

*This element occurs only on every other cycle.

row *t* after completing the timing part of the study. For example, in observation 1, the clock read .48 minutes after element 1 and .59 minutes after element 2. Thus the difference, .11 minutes, appears in the *t* row of element 2. An alternative technique, called the *snap-back method*, involves resetting the watch to zero after each work element has been completed. Although this technique gives work element times directly for each observation, it requires the observer to read and record the times and to reset the watch at the end of each element. Sometimes, two watches are used, one for recording the previous work element and the other for timing the present work element. However, if some work elements are done quickly, noting accurate times may be difficult.

Frequently, a review of the sample data will reveal a single, isolated time recorded for an element that differs greatly from other times recorded for the same element. The cause of such variation should be investigated. If it is an "irregular occurrence," such as dropping a tool or a machine failure, the analyst should not include it in calculating the average time for the work element.

Sometimes, the decision to include an observed time must be made in consultation with the union. The average observed time based only on representative times is called the **select time ($\bar{t}$).**

Determining Sample Size. Figure 6.1 shows that the analyst observed only 10 cycles of the packaging operation. Was this number enough? Typically, those who use the time study to set standards want an average time estimate that is very close to the true long-range average 95 percent of the time. A formula, based on the normal distribution, allows us to determine the sample size, n, required:

$$n = \left[\left(\frac{1.96}{p}\right)\left(\frac{s}{\bar{t}}\right)\right]^2$$

where

n = required sample size

p = precision of the estimate

$\bar{t}$ = select time for a work element

s = sample standard deviation of representative observed times for a work element

The constant 1.96 represents the ± 1.96 standard deviations from the mean that leave a total of 5 percent in the tails of the normal curve. The term $s/\bar{t}$ is called the **sample coefficient of variation**. The precision of the estimate, p, is expressed as a proportion of the true (but unknown) average time for the work element.

APPLICATION 6.1

The manager of a frozen pizza company authorized a time study of the pizza assembly process. The select time for assembling a pizza is 0.60 minutes and the sample standard deviation of its representative observed times is 0.20 minutes, all based on a pilot study of 20 cycles. What is the appropriate sample size if the estimate for the select time is to be within 4 percent of the true average time 95 percent of the time?

Solution

We have $\bar{t} = 0.60$, $s = 0.20$, and $p = 0.04$. The coefficient of variation is

$$\frac{s}{\bar{t}} = \frac{0.20}{0.60} = 0.33 \quad \text{or} \quad 33\%$$

The sample size should be:

$$n = \left[\left(\frac{1.96}{0.04} \right)(0.33) \right]^2 = [16.17]^2 = 261$$

This sample size means that 241 (or 261 − 20) more cycles must be observed.

Setting the Standard.   The final step is to set the standard. In order to do so, the analyst first determines the **normal time (*NT*)** for each work element. Here the pace of the worker being observed is judged. Not only must the analyst assess whether the worker's pace is above or below average, but also *how much* above or below average. The analyst assigns a **performance rating factor (*RF*)** to the worker's performance on each work element. For example, in Fig. 6.1, the performance rating factor for work element 3 is 1.10. A performance rating factor greater than 1.0 means that the worker worked at a faster than average pace (that is, produced more output in a given amount of time). In other instances, the worker worked at a slower than average pace. The rating factor is solely a judgment call by the analyst, based on experience.

The analyst multiplies the select time ($\bar{t}$), the frequency (*F*) of the work element per cycle, and the rating factor (*RF*) to obtain the normal time for a work element; that is,

$$NT = \bar{t}(F)(RF)$$

APPLICATION 6.2

Refer again to the coffee cup packaging data in Fig. 6.1. What are the normal times for each work element and the normal time for the complete cycle?

Solution

All the data needed to determine the normal times are contained in the three columns at the far right of Fig. 6.1. Thus

Element 1: NT = 0.50(0.50)(1.05) = 0.26 min
Element 2: NT = 0.11(1.00)(0.95) = 0.10 min
Element 3: NT = 0.71(1.00)(1.10) = 0.78 min
Element 4: NT = 1.10(1.00)(0.90) = 0.99 min
Total = 2.13 min

Since element 1 only occurs every other cycle, its average time per cycle must be half its average observed time. That's why $F = 0.50$ for that element. All others occur every cycle. The normal time for the complete cycle is 2.13 minutes.

The **normal time for the cycle (*NTC*)** is 2.13 minutes in the preceding application, but we cannot use that time as a standard. It does not account for fatigue, rest periods, or unavoidable delays that occur during an average workday. Consequently, we must add some **allowance time** to the normal time to adjust for these factors. Thus the **standard time (*ST*)** is

$$ST = NTC(1 + A),$$

where A is the proportion of the normal time to be added for allowances.*

APPLICATION 6.3

Suppose that the proportion of the normal time to be added for allowances is 0.15. What is the standard time for the coffee cup packaging operation and how many cartons can be expected per eight-hour day?

Solution

Since $A = 0.15$,

$$ST = 2.13(1 + 0.15) = 2.45 \text{ min/carton}$$

This translates into

$$\frac{480 \text{ min/day}}{2.45 \text{ min/carton}} = 196 \text{ cartons/day}$$

Judgment in Time Study. Several aspects of a time study require the use of judgment by the analyst. First, the analyst must take care when defining the work elements to be included in the study. As we have pointed out, these work elements must not be too short and must have definite starting and stopping points. Also, some work elements may occur infrequently and irregularly. The analyst must be sure to include times for these work elements as well.

Second, the analyst may have to eliminate some observed times because the elements are nonrepresentative of the work. An obvious case would be one where the worker accidentally dropped a tool. However, nonrepresentative elements are not always that obvious. In some cases a chance happening such as a machine malfunction can distort the results. If these nonrepresentative times aren't excluded, the standard will be incorrect. However, the analyst must use judgment in deciding which times, if any, should be excluded.

Another area where judgment plays a role is in the amount of allowance time to be used. Most allowances range from 10 to 20 percent of normal time.

---

*Another formula for the standard time is given by $ST = NTC/(1 + A)$. In this formula, A represents the proportion of the *standard time* to be added for allowances.

They are intended to account for factors such as fatigue or unexpected delays that are difficult to measure. As you will see later in this chapter, work sampling can be used to estimate some of the factors in allowance time.

Finally, the aspect of time study that requires the greatest amount of judgment is that of performance rating. Usually only one worker is observed during a study, and that worker's performance will seldom conform to the notion of normal used in the definition of standard. Thus the analyst has to make an adjustment in the average observed time in order to estimate the time it would take a trained operator to do the task at a normal pace.

Unfortunately, the analyst cannot avoid the use of judgment or the need to arrive at a performance rating by studying all the workers and using their average time as normal. However, if the workers are fast, it would not be fair to set the standard based on their average time, particularly if a wage incentive plan is involved. Conversely, if the workers are slow, basing the standard on their normal time would be unfair to the company. Further, the possibility that workers will slow their pace when they are being observed in a time study is very real. Consequently, the use of judgment in assigning performance rates seems to be a necessary, but often controversial, aspect of conducting a time study.

Overall Assessment of Time Study.   Time study is the most frequently used method for setting time standards. Qualified analysts can typically set reasonable standards using this method, and workers understand the process. However, the method has some limitations. Its use is not appropriate, for example, when setting standards for "thinking" jobs, such as a mathematician solving a problem, a professor preparing a lecture, or an automobile repairman diagnosing the cause of a problem. Nor is it appropriate for nonrepetitive jobs, such as nonroutine maintenance repair, where the nature of the task differs each time. In addition, the use of a stopwatch is an art, and an inexperienced person should not conduct time studies. Obviously, errors in recording information can result in unreasonable standards. Similarly, an inexperienced person may not include all the work elements. Finally, unions may object to time study because of the judgment and subjectivity involved. Nonetheless, time study conducted by an experienced observer is usually a satisfactory, although imperfect, tool for setting equitable time standards.

Elemental Standard Data Approach

If thousands of work standards are needed in a plant, the amount of time and the cost required to use the time study method may be excessive. In such cases analysts often use **elemental standard data** in order to derive standards for various jobs. This approach is based on the notion that a high degree of similarity exists in the work elements of certain jobs. The time standards for work elements that are common to a class of jobs can be stored in a database for future use. A work measurement approach, such as time study, can be used to compile standards for these common elements. Sometimes, the time required for a work element depends on certain variable characteristics of the jobs. In these situations an equation that relates these characteristics to the time required for the work element can also be stored in the database for later use. Once established, the database can provide the data needed to estimate the normal times for jobs requiring these work elements. However, allowances must still be added to arrive at standard times for the jobs.

The elemental standard data approach has the advantage of reducing the number of time studies needed. In addition, the database can be used to develop standards for new work before production begins. This advantage is helpful in product costing and pricing, as well as production planning. Also, when work methods change for an element, the normal time for that element can easily be determined. Then with the time stored in the database, it can be easily and quickly applied to each job requiring that work element.

However, this approach also has some disadvantages. Although the need for time studies is reduced, they probably can't be eliminated. In general, the analyst should develop the normal times for the database using the time study method. Also, companies like to use time studies periodically to check the standards developed by the elemental standard data approach. Another consideration is that specifying all the job variables that affect times for each work element may be difficult. Consequently, the equations attempting to relate these variables to the time for that work element may not be very good.

Predetermined Data Approach

The predetermined data approach carries the elemental standard data approach one step further. The analyst divides each work element into a series of micromotions that are common to a wide variety of tasks. The normal times for these micromotions are stored in a database, along with modifications for job variables, so that the normal time for any task can be developed by accessing the database.

One of the most commonly used predetermined data systems is **methods time measurement (MTM)**. Actually, there are a variety of MTM databases, but we focus on the most accurate, MTM-1. In MTM-1 the basic micromotions are reach, move, disengage, apply pressure, grasp, position, release, and turn. The normal times for these micromotions, modified for job variables, were developed from motion picture studies of a sample of workers in various industrial settings. Trained observers applied performance ratings to the observations. Table 6.1 shows the *move* motion from the MTM-1 data. A time measurement unit (TMU) is 0.0006 minutes. The weight allowances adjust the time estimates for different object weights. There are similar tables for other motions.

TABLE 6.1   MTM Predetermined Data for the *Move* Micromotion

Distance Moved (in)	Time TMU				Wt. Allowance			Case and Description
	A	B	C	Hand In Motion B	Wt. (lb) Up to	Dynamic Factor	Static Constant (TMU)	
¾ or less	2.0	2.0	2.0	1.7				
1	2.5	2.9	3.4	2.3	2.5	1.00	0	A Move object to other hand or against stop.
2	3.6	4.6	5.2	2.9				
3	4.9	5.7	6.7	3.6	7.5	1.06	2.2	
4	6.1	6.9	8.0	4.3				
5	7.3	8.0	9.2	5.0	12.5	1.11	3.9	
6	8.1	8.9	10.3	5.7				
7	8.9	9.7	11.1	6.5	17.5	1.17	5.6	
8	9.7	10.6	11.8	7.2				
9	10.5	11.5	12.7	7.9	22.5	1.22	7.4	B Move object to approximate or indefinite location.
10	11.3	12.2	13.5	8.6				
12	12.9	13.4	15.2	10.0	27.5	1.28	9.1	
14	14.4	14.6	16.9	11.4				
16	16.0	15.8	18.7	12.8	32.5	1.33	10.8	
18	17.6	17.0	20.4	14.2				
20	19.2	18.2	22.1	15.6	37.5	1.39	12.5	
22	20.8	19.4	23.8	17.0				
24	22.4	20.6	25.5	18.4	42.5	1.44	14.3	C Move object to exact location.
26	24.0	21.8	27.3	19.8				
28	25.5	23.1	29.0	21.2	47.5	1.50	16.0	
30	27.1	24.3	30.7	22.7				
Additional	0.8	0.6	0.85		TMU per inch over 30 inches			

Source: Copyright © by the MTM Association for Standards and Research. No reprint permission without written consent from the MTM Association, 16-01 Broadway, Fair Lawn, N.J. 07410.

Setting standards using predetermined data involves several steps. First, each work element must be broken into its basic micromotions. Then, the degree of difficulty of each motion must be rated. Next, the normal times for each motion from the tables are added to get the normal time for the task. Finally the normal time is adjusted for allowances to give the standard time.

The predetermined data approach offers some advantages over the other approaches we have discussed. First, standards can be set for new jobs before production begins, which cannot be done with the time study method. Second, new work methods can be compared without conducting a time study. Third, a greater degree of consistency in the setting of time standards is provided because the sources of error in time studies, such as data recording errors, are reduced. Finally, this approach defuses the objection of biased judgment in performance rating. Performance ratings are no longer needed in the derivation of a standard.

The predetermined data approach also has its drawbacks. Work must be broken down into micromotions, making this method impractical for firms with a process focus and low repeatability. Moreover, the data may not reflect the situation in any specific plant. What is normal for one plant may not be for another plant. The sample of workers used to develop the predetermined data may not be representative of workers in general. Further, performance time variations can result from many factors—too many to publish in tables such as Table 6.1. In some circumstances, the time needed to move an object may depend on the shape of the object, but the MTM-1 charts do not recognize that. Then, the method is based on the assumption that the times associated with the micromotions can simply be added together to get the total time for a task. This assumption disregards the possibility that the actual time may depend on the specific *sequence* of motions. Finally, there is a danger that the approach will be misused because, on the surface, it appears easy to use. Actually, considerable skill is needed to properly identify all the micromotions and accurately judge the difficulty of the motion. Considerable training and experience are required, and an inexperienced person will come up with poor standards.

Work Sampling Method

Work sampling is another method of work measurement. It is a broader approach, not concerned with timing detailed motions but with estimating the proportions of time spent by people and machines on activities such as producing a product or service, doing paperwork, waiting for instructions, waiting for maintenance, or being idle. These estimates are based on a large number of observations. The underlying assumption is that the proportion of time the activity is observed in the sample will be the proportion of time spent on the activity in general. The sample size affects the degree of precision that can be expected from estimates for a given level of statistical confidence. Data from work sampling can also be used to estimate machine or labor utilization percentages and the allowances needed to set standards for use with the other methods we have discussed, to determine job content, and to help assess the cost of jobs or activities.

Work Sampling Procedure.   Conducting a work sampling study involves the following steps:

1. Define the activities.
2. Design the observation form.
3. Determine the length of the study.
4. Determine the pilot sample size.
5. Select random observation times.
6. Determine the observer schedule.
7. Observe the activities and record the data.
8. Check to see whether additional sampling is required.

APPLICATION 6.4

The hospital administrator at a private hospital is considering a proposal for installation of an automated medical records storage and retrieval system. In order to determine the advisability of purchasing such a system, the administrator needs to know the proportion of time spent by registered nurses (RNs) and licensed vocational nurses (LVNs) accessing records. Presently these nurses must either retrieve the records manually or have them copied and sent to their wards. Define the activities for a work sampling study and design the observation form.

Solution

Figure 6.2 shows an observation form for the work sampling study at the hospital. More detailed activities could be shown, but the hospital administrator is mainly interested in the proportion of time that RNs and LVNs spend accessing records. The other data can be useful for planning purposes and are included to provide a representative example of an observation form. Information on RNs and LVNs is recorded separately because they spend different amounts of time with medical records at this hospital. The form should provide enough space to record the observations as they are made. They can be summarized later for analysis.

Activity

	Accessing records	Attending to patients	Other support activities	Idle or break	Total
RN					
LVN					

FIGURE 6.2   Observation Form for a Hospital Work Sampling Study

A work sampling study should be conducted over a representative period of time. Each activity must be given a chance to occur a representative number of times. For example, if an activity occurs only once a week, it wouldn't make sense to conduct a one-day study because there is a good chance that the activity would not be observed. In such a case, the study should probably span several months. In Application 6.4, accessing records occurs continuously throughout the week and from week to week throughout the year. Consequently, the study should cover several weeks.

This initial study is called a pilot study because the analyst may have to make more observations later. By making a reasonable estimate of the proportion of time an activity takes and the degree of precision required, the analyst can use Table 6.2 to determine the sample size for the pilot study.

APPLICATION 6.5

The hospital administrator suspects that accessing records takes about 20 percent of RNs' time and about 5 percent of LVNs' time. A typical ward, staffed by 8 RNs and 4 LVNs, is selected for the study. The administrator wants to have 95 percent confidence that the estimates for each category of nurses fall within ±0.03 of their true proportions. Use Table 6.2 to determine how many trips the observer will have to take through the ward.

Solution

The administrator's original estimate for the proportion of time spent accessing records is 0.20 for RNs and 0.05 for LVNs and the administrator is willing to accept an error of ±0.03 (or 0.20 ± 0.03 for LVNs and 0.05 ± 0.03 for RNs). Table 6.2 indicates that the sample size should be 683 observations for

RNs and 203 for LVNs. However, there are 8 RNs and 4 LVNs that can be observed on each trip. This implies we need 86 (or 683/8) trips for the observations of RNs and only 51 (or 203/4) trips for the LVNs. Thus an observer schedule that provides for 86 trips through the ward will be sufficient for both nurse groups. This number of trips will generate more observations than needed for the LVNs, but as the observer will be going through the ward anyway he or she might as well record the data.

TABLE 6.2   **Sample Size Requirements for Work Sampling Studies for Various Values of p and Allowable Error***

Proportion of Time for Activity or Delay, P	Absolute Error				
	±0.01	±0.02	±0.03	±0.04	±0.05
0.01 or 0.99	380	95	42	24	15
0.02 or 0.98	753	188	84	47	30
0.03 or 0.97	1117	279	124	70	45
0.04 or 0.96	1475	369	164	92	59
0.05 or 0.95	1824	456	203	114	73
0.06 or 0.94	2166	541	241	135	87
0.07 or 0.93	2500	625	278	156	100
0.08 or 0.92	2826	707	314	177	113
0.09 or 0.91	3145	786	349	197	126
0.10 or 0.90	3456	864	384	216	138
0.11 or 0.89	3759	940	418	235	150
0.12 or 0.88	4055	1014	451	253	162
0.13 or 0.87	4343	1086	483	271	174
0.14 or 0.86	4623	1156	514	289	185
0.15 or 0.85	4896	1224	544	306	196
0.16 or 0.84	5161	1290	573	323	206
0.17 or 0.83	5418	1355	602	339	217
0.18 or 0.82	5668	1417	630	354	227
0.19 or 0.81	5910	1477	657	369	236
0.20 or 0.80	6144	1536	683	384	246
0.21 or 0.79	6371	1593	708	398	255
0.22 or 0.78	6589	1647	732	412	264
0.23 or 0.77	6801	1700	756	425	272
0.24 or 0.76	7004	1751	778	438	280
0.25 or 0.75	7200	1800	800	450	288

*These sample sizes yield a 95 percent confidence that the estimate for P is within a specific absolute error of the population average.

The times of day the observer makes the trips to gather data should be selected at random over the length of the study. This approach reduces the amount of bias in the data. For example, if employees know that they will be observed each day at 2:30 P.M., they may alter their behavior from normal patterns. If that happens, the data won't represent actual performance. After the observation times have been determined, a schedule for the observer can be developed.

Proportion of Time for Activity or Delay, P	Absolute Error				
	±0.01	±0.02	±0.03	±0.04	±0.05
0.26 or 0.74	7388	1847	821	462	296
0.27 or 0.73	7569	1892	841	473	303
0.28 or 0.72	7741	1935	860	484	310
0.29 or 0.71	7907	1977	879	494	316
0.30 or 0.70	8064	2016	896	504	323
0.31 or 0.69	8214	2053	913	513	329
0.32 or 0.68	8356	2089	928	522	334
0.33 or 0.67	8490	2123	943	531	340
0.34 or 0.66	8617	2154	957	539	345
0.35 or 0.65	8736	2184	971	546	349
0.36 or 0.64	8847	2212	983	553	354
0.37 or 0.63	8951	2238	995	559	358
0.38 or 0.62	9047	2262	1005	565	362
0.39 or 0.61	9135	2284	1015	571	365
0.40 or 0.60	9216	2304	1024	576	369
0.41 or 0.59	9289	2322	1032	581	372
0.42 or 0.58	9354	2339	1039	585	374
0.43 or 0.57	9412	2353	1046	588	376
0.44 or 0.56	9462	2365	1051	591	378
0.45 or 0.55	9504	2376	1056	594	380
0.46 or 0.54	9539	2385	1060	596	382
0.47 or 0.53	9565	2391	1063	598	383
0.48 or 0.52	9585	2396	1065	599	383
0.49 or 0.51	9596	2399	1066	600	384
0.50	9600	2400	1067	600	384

APPLICATION 6.6

The hospital administrator estimates that the annual amortization cost and expenses for maintaining the new automated medical records storage and retrieval system will be $150,000. The vendor of the new system estimates that the system will reduce the amount of time the nurses spend accessing records by 25 percent. The total annual salary expense for RNs in the hospital is $3,628,000, and for LVNs it is $2,375,000. The hospital administrator is willing to assume that nurses could productively use any time saved by the new system.

The pilot work sampling study resulted in the data shown in Fig. 6.3. Should the administrator purchase the new system?

	Activity				
	Accessing records	Attending to patients	Other support activities	Idle or break	Total
RN	124	258	223	83	688
LVN	28	251	46	19	344

FIGURE 6.3   Results of the Pilot Study

Solution

Let

P_1 = proportion of time spent by RNs with records

P_2 = proportion of time spent by LVNs with records

From Fig. 6.3, $P_1 = 0.18$ (or 124/688) and $P_2 = 0.08$ (or 28/344). Thus the original estimates were off the mark. However, the sample results fall within the allowable error range for each proportion, and the sample sizes were adequate for the values obtained (see Table 6.2 for $P_1 = 0.18$ and $P_2 = 0.08$). If the sample sizes were too small for the proportions found, additional sampling would have to be performed.

Estimated annual net savings from the purchase of the automatic medical records storage and retrieval system are:

$$\text{Net Savings} = 0.25(\$3,628,000P_1 + \$2,375,000P_2) - \$150,000$$
$$= 0.25[\$3,628,000(0.18) + \$2,375,000(0.08)] - \$150,000$$
$$= \$60,760$$

Based on the results of the work sampling study, the new system appears to be a good investment.

Overall Assessment of Work Sampling.   The work sampling method is used frequently in practice because it offers certain advantages over other approaches. No special training is required for the observers, no stopwatches are needed, and several studies can be conducted simultaneously. It is more economical for studying jobs having long cycle times because less observer time is required; observations are made only at random times. Importantly, workers themselves often prefer this method of work measurement to other approaches.

The major disadvantage to work sampling is the large number of observations required. Even though each is short, many observations are needed to provide a reasonable degree of precision for the estimate. This method is usually not as economical for setting standards for repetitive, well-defined jobs as the other approaches we have discussed.

LEARNING CURVES ▲

The work measurement methods presented so far are based on the assumption that the effects of future learning are negligible. The implication is that the workplace is a stable environment where change does not take place. However, that assumption and its implication are rarely true in today's workplace. Change *does* occur, and where there is change, there is also learning. The two major types of learning are individual and organizational.

With instruction and repetition, workers learn to perform their jobs more efficiently and thereby reduce the number of direct labor hours per unit. Such may be the case for the process illustrated in Fig. 6.4. It shows that the process time per unit is continually reduced until the 140th unit is produced. At that point learning is negligible and a standard time for the operation can be developed.

Organizational learning, in general, and management learning in particular, involve gaining experience in product and process design, automation and other capital investments, and changes in administrative methods or personnel to improve the efficiency of operations. The process-time improvement shown in Fig. 6.4 could have resulted from better work methods, tools, product design, or supervision, as well as from individual worker learning. Changes such as these in the workplace create the need for continually reevaluating

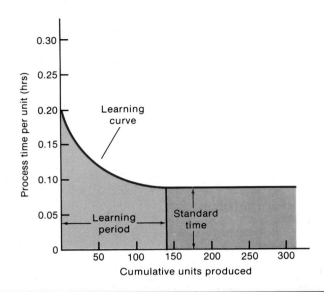

FIGURE 6.4   **Relationship Between Learning Curve and Standard Time per Cycle**

existing standards and setting new ones, as necessary. Managerial Practice 6.2 shows how organizational learning paid off for Florida Power and Light, a large electric utility company.

Projecting the Learning Effect

The learning effect can be represented by a line called a **learning curve**, which displays the relationship between the total direct labor per unit and the cumulative quantity of a product produced. The curve in Fig. 6.4 is an example of a learning curve for one process. The terms *manufacturing progress function* and *experience curve* have also been used to describe this relationship, although the experience curve typically refers to total value-added costs per unit rather than labor hours. The principles underlying these curves are identical to those of the learning curve, however. Here we use the term learning curve to depict reductions in either total direct labor per unit or total value-added costs per unit.

Background.   The learning curve was first developed in the aircraft industry prior to World War II, when it was discovered that the direct labor input per airplane declined with considerable regularity as the cumulative number of planes produced increased. A survey of major airplane manufacturers revealed that a series of learning curves could be developed to represent the average experience for various categories of airframes (fighters, bombers, and so on). The unique aspect of these curves was that although the time required to produce the first unit differed by type of airframe, the rate of learning was surprisingly similar. For example, once production started, the direct labor for the eighth unit was only 80 percent that of the fourth unit, and the twelfth was only 80 percent of the sixth, and so on. In each case, each doubling of quantities reduced production time by 20 percent. Because of the consistency in the rate of improvement, it was concluded that the aircraft industry's rate of learning was 80 percent between doubled quantities of airframes. Of course, for any given product and company, the rate of learning can be different.

Learning Curves and Competitive Strategy. Learning curves enable managers to project the manufacturing cost per unit for a given cumulative production quantity. Firms that choose to emphasize low price in their competitive strategy rely on high volumes to maintain profit margins. These firms strive to move down the learning curve (lower labor hours per unit or lower costs per unit) by increasing volume. This tactic makes entry into a market by competitors difficult. For example, in the electronics component industry, the cost of developing an integrated circuit is so large that the first units produced must be priced high. As cumulative production increases, costs (and prices) fall. The first companies in the market have a big advantage because newcomers, such as Korean firms, must start selling at lower prices and suffer large initial losses.

Projecting learning effects with learning curves or experience curves can be risky. Managers all too easily forget the dynamics of the environment, in which disturbances (such as new products or market changes) can disrupt the

MANAGERIAL PRACTICE 6.2 ▲

Taking Advantage of the Learning Curve

Florida Power and Light has received considerable praise for building its St. Lucie No. 2 nuclear plant in just over six years. The average is 10–12 years. The power company had built three previous plants and industry experts said that the prior experience was critical to St. Lucie No. 2's success. St. Lucie No. 2 is a near clone to the first St. Lucie plant and used two of the same major contractors and much of the same work force. As Bill Derrickson, construction manager for the project, put it, "We aren't virgins in the nuclear business."

Source: "Utility Cuts Red Tape, Builds Nuclear Plant Almost on Schedule," by Ron Winslow, *Wall Street Journal*, February 22, 1984.

Changes to this double assembly line for Boeing 737s in Renton, Washington, will allow more flexibility in changing production rates. Overhead cranes are now used to bring wings from an adjacent assembly area, plus tooling and equipment, to the 737 bay for mating with completed fuselages. Improvements such as these enable Boeing to reduce the time required to produce the 737 mainframe and slide further down the learning curve.

expected benefits of increased production. For example, Douglas Aircraft was forced to merge with McDonnell Company because of financial problems. Douglas assumed that it could reduce the costs of its new jet aircraft following a learning-curve formula and committed to fixed delivery dates and prices with its customers. Continued modification of its planes disrupted the learning curve, and the cost reductions were not realized. Nonetheless, the learning curve has many useful applications. Let's now turn to the problem of formulating a learning curve.

Developing Learning Curves

In the following discussion and applications we focus on direct labor hours per unit, although we could have used costs just as easily. When we develop a learning curve we make the following assumptions.

1. The direct labor required to produce the $n + 1$st unit will always be less than the direct labor required for the nth unit.

2. Direct labor requirements will decrease at a declining rate as cumulative production increases.

3. The reduction in time will follow an exponential curve.

Collectively, these assumptions comprise the basic premise of learning curves: The production time per unit is reduced by a fixed percentage each time production is doubled. Given these assumptions, the labor hours for the first unit produced, and the learning rate, we can draw a learning curve using a logarithmic model. The direct labor required for the nth unit, k_n, is

$$k_n = k_1 n^b$$

where

k_1 = the direct labor hours for the first unit

n = cumulative number of units produced

r = the learning rate

b = log r/log 2

We can also calculate the cumulative average number of hours per unit for the first n units with the help of Table 6.3. It contains conversion factors that, when multiplied by the direct labor hours for the first unit, yield the average time per unit for selected cumulative production quantities.

TABLE 6.3 Conversion Factors for the Cumulative Average Number of Direct Labor Hours per Unit

80 Percent Learning Rate (n = Cumulative production)						90 Percent Learning Rate (n = Cumulative production)					
n		n		n		n		n		n	
1	1.00000	19	0.53178	37	0.43976	1	1.00000	19	0.73545	37	0.67091
2	0.90000	20	0.52425	38	0.43634	2	0.95000	20	0.73039	38	0.66839
3	0.83403	21	0.51715	39	0.43304	3	0.91540	21	0.72559	39	0.66595
4	0.78553	22	0.51045	40	0.42984	4	0.88905	22	0.72102	40	0.66357
5	0.74755	23	0.50410	64	0.37382	5	0.86784	23	0.71666	64	0.62043
6	0.71657	24	0.49808	128	0.30269	6	0.85013	24	0.71251	128	0.56069
7	0.69056	25	0.49234	256	0.24405	7	0.83496	25	0.70853	256	0.50586
8	0.66824	26	0.48688	512	0.19622	8	0.82172	26	0.70472	512	0.45594
9	0.64876	27	0.48167	600	0.18661	9	0.80998	27	0.70106	600	0.44519
10	0.63154	28	0.47668	700	0.17771	10	0.79945	28	0.69754	700	0.43496
11	0.61613	29	0.47191	800	0.17034	11	0.78991	29	0.69416	800	0.42629
12	0.60224	30	0.46733	900	0.16408	12	0.78120	30	0.69090	900	0.41878
13	0.58960	31	0.46293	1000	0.15867	13	0.77320	31	0.68775	1000	0.41217
14	0.57802	32	0.45871	1200	0.14972	14	0.76580	32	0.68471	1200	0.40097
15	0.56737	33	0.45464	1400	0.14254	15	0.75891	33	0.68177	1400	0.39173
16	0.55751	34	0.45072	1600	0.13660	16	0.75249	34	0.67893	1600	0.38390
17	0.54834	35	0.44694	1800	0.13155	17	0.74646	35	0.67617	1800	0.37711
18	0.53979	36	0.44329	2000	0.12720	18	0.74080	36	0.67350	2000	0.37114

APPLICATION 6.7

It takes the manufacturer of diesel locomotives 50,000 hours to produce the first unit and, based on past experience with products of this sort, the rate of learning is 80 percent. Use the logarithmic model to estimate the direct labor required for the fortieth diesel locomotive and the cumulative average number of labor hours per unit for the first 40 units. Draw a learning curve for this situation.

Solution

The estimated number of direct labor hours required to produce the fortieth unit is

$$k_{40} = 50,000(40)^{\log 0.8/\log 2}$$
$$= 50,000(40)^{-0.322}$$
$$= 50,000(0.30488)$$
$$= 15,244 \text{ hr}$$

We calculate the cumulative average number of direct labor hours per unit for the first 40 units with the help of Table 6.3. For a cumulative production of 40 units and an 80 percent learning rate, the factor is 0.42984. The cumulative average direct labor hours per unit is $50,000(0.42984) = 21,492$ hr.

We utilized the logarithmic model to calculate the points for plotting the learning curve in Fig. 6.5, using selected values for the cumulative units produced. We can also calculate the curve by using the basic premise of learning curves. For example, the second unit's labor time is 80 percent of the first; the fourth is 80 percent of the second; and so on.

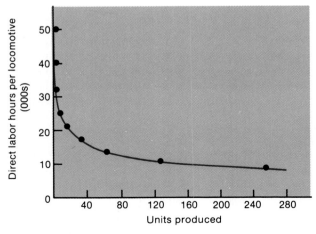

FIGURE 6.5   80 Percent Learning Curve

Estimating the Rate of Learning

If historical data are available, the rate of learning can be estimated with the logarithmic model. In this case, the time required to produce the first unit and the time required to produce the nth unit are known. The solution involves two steps:

1. Estimate the value of b, using the logarithmic model.

$$k_n = k_1 n^b$$

We know k_n, k_1, and n, so we need to solve for b.

$$n^b = \frac{k_n}{k_1}$$

$$b \log n = \log\left(\frac{k_n}{k_1}\right)$$

$$b = \frac{\log(k_n/k_1)}{\log n}$$

2. Use the definition of b to estimate the learning rate, r.

$$\frac{\log r}{\log 2} = b$$

$$\log r = b \log 2$$

$$r = 10^{(b \log 2)}$$

APPLICATION 6.8

A company produces landing-flap assemblies for a large aircraft manufacturer. Suppose that it takes 2500 hours to produce the first assembly and 402 hours to produce the 165th assembly. What is the learning rate for producing a landing-flap assembly?

Solution

$$b = \frac{\log(402/2500)}{\log 165}$$

$$= \frac{-0.7937}{2.2175} = -0.35793$$

$$r = 10^{(-0.35793 \log 2)}$$

$$= 10^{(-0.10775)} = 0.78$$

Consequently, the learning rate is 78 percent. This rate means that when production is doubled, the direct labor per unit is reduced by 22 percent.

Estimates have to be more subjective before production has begun. The analyst can either assume that the learning rate will be the same as that in the past for similar goods produced by the company or that the learning rate will equal that of the industry as a whole for similar applications. In either case actual performance should be monitored, and revisions should be made in the learning rate as data are accumulated.

Blindly accepting the industry learning rate is dangerous because it can be quite different for a specific company. One factor involved is the mix of labor-paced and machine-paced operations. The opportunity to reduce direct labor hours on machine-paced operations is limited because the output rate is controlled by the capability of the machines, not the workers. The greater the ratio of labor-paced to machine-paced operations, the greater is the effect of learning on direct labor requirements.

Another factor affecting the rate of learning is degree of product complexity. The learning rate for simple products is not as pronounced as it is for complex products. Complex products offer more opportunity to improve work methods, materials, and process design over the product's life. Closely associated with this factor is the experience of the organization with similar products. The greater the difference in the product, relative to anything the company has manufactured in the past, the greater is the expected learning rate.

The rate of capital inputs also affects the learning rate. Here we are referring to the overall reduction of direct labor hours by automation or general improvements in plant and equipment. Capital improvements are introduced at specific points in time and typically have a significant effect. Thus they tend to make the actual learning curve uneven in contrast to a theoretical curve, such as the one shown in Fig. 6.5. Consequently, when estimating the learning rate based on previous experience or industry averages, an analyst must consider anticipated capital inputs.

Using Learning Curves

Learning curves can be used in a variety of ways. Let's look briefly at their use in bid preparation, financial planning, and labor requirement estimation.

Bid Preparation. Estimating labor costs is an important part of preparing bids for large jobs. Knowing the learning rate, the number of units to be produced, and wage rates, the estimator can arrive at the cost of labor by using a learning curve. After calculating expected labor and materials costs, the estimator adds the desired profit to obtain the total bid amount.

Financial Planning. Learning curves can also be used in financial planning to help the financial planner determine the amount of cash needed to finance operations. Learning curves provide a basis for comparing prices and costs and can be used to project periods of financial drain, when expenditures exceed receipts. A contract price is determined, in part, by the average direct labor costs per unit for the number of contracted units. In the early stages of production, the direct labor costs will exceed that average, whereas in the later stages of production the reverse will be true. This information enables the financial planner to arrange in advance with customers and banks to finance certain phases of operations.

Estimating Labor Requirements.   Given a production schedule, an analyst can use learning curves to project direct labor requirements. This information can be used to estimate training requirements and develop hiring plans. We will show how such information is used in production and staffing plans in Chapter 13.

APPLICATION 6.9

The manager of a custom manufacturer just received a production schedule for an order of 64 large turbines. Over the next seven months, the company is to produce 2, 3, 5, 8, 12, 20, and 14 turbines, respectively. The first unit took 30,000 direct labor hours, and experience on past projects indicates that a 90 percent learning curve is appropriate. If each employee works 200 hours per month, estimate the total number of full-time employees needed each month for the next seven months.

Solution

The table on p. 214 shows the production schedule and estimates of labor requirements. Using the cumulative units in column 2 and factors from Table 6.3 (shown earlier) the manager calculated the cumulative average times in column 3. The factor for month 6 had to be interpolated from the factors for 40 units and 64 units in Table 6.3 as follows:

$$0.66357 - \left(\frac{50 - 40}{64 - 40}\right)(0.66357 - 0.62043) = 0.64560$$

The cumulative average time per unit after 50 units is $30,000(0.64560) = 19,368$ hr. The manager calculated cumulative total hours by multiplying column 2 by column 3. He obtained the total hours per month, shown in column 5, by subtracting the successive monthly cumulative totals in column 4. (For example, for month 2, $130,175 - 57,000 = 73,175$ hr.) Finally, he calculated column 6 by dividing the number of work hours per month into column 5. This calculation gave the manager the estimated number of full-time production employees needed.

Estimating Labor Requirements Using a 90% Learning Curve

Month	Production Schedule		Estimates of Labor Requirements			
	Units per month (1)	Cumulative units (2)	Cumulative average time (3)	Cumulative total hours (4)	Total hours/month (5)	Total full-time employees/month* (6)
1	2	2	28,500	57,000	57,000	285
2	3	5	26,035	130,175	73,175	366
3	5	10	23,983	239,830	109,655	548
4	8	18	22,224	400,032	160,202	801
5	12	30	20,727	621,810	221,778	1109
6	20	50	19,368	968,400	346,590	1733
7	14	64	18,613	1,191,232	222,832	1114

*Based on an assumed 200 labor hours in each month.

MANAGERIAL CONSIDERATIONS IN WORK MEASUREMENT ▲

Our discussion of work measurement would not be complete without mentioning compensation plans based on work measurement and the ever-growing role of automation and its effect on work measurement in the future.

Compensation Plans

Compensation plans based on work measurement typically involve incentive schemes. Those used most often are piece rate and individual incentive plans.

Piece Rate Plans.   Piece rate is a compensation plan based on the number of units processed during a day or week. Machine operators are often paid on the basis of output: the faster the operator, the higher the pay. Similarly, workers performing a telephone survey may be paid on the basis of the number of positive contacts they make. In order to set the pay rates for piece rate plans such as these, management must specify what constitutes a fair day's work. As we have shown, work measurement methods can be used to determine standard times that can be used to estimate daily output. Pay rates can be based on these estimates.

Individual Incentive Plans.   Sometimes, incentive plans are used to motivate workers. Such plans reward output that exceeds a predetermined base level. The base level can be set after work measurement methods have been used to determine an expected rate of output for an average worker. One plan is the 100 percent premium plan. Suppose that the base level is set at 50 units of output. Under the plan, a worker who produces 60 units would receive an additional 10/50, or 20 percent, of the base pay rate. If the incentive plan is a 50 percent premium plan, the worker would get a bonus equal to 50 percent of 10/50, or 10 percent, of the base pay rate.

Quality and Compensation Plans.   The purpose of incentive pay is to encourage high levels of output from employees. However, a high rate of output may be achieved at the expense of quality. Where is the advantage to a company if a worker produces at 115 percent of standard but has a 20 percent defective rate?

In Chapter 3 we argued that management, not the worker, is primarily to blame for poor quality. Incentive plans that do not recognize and reward quality may not motivate the worker to produce high quality goods.

Two basic approaches are used to recognize quality in incentive plans. The first is the autocratic approach, which docks the worker's pay for defective production or requires the worker to repair all defects at a lower rate of pay. The latter is not popular with workers because in many cases the defects are not repairable, or they were not the fault of the worker in the first place.

The second is the motivational approach, which is based on the concept of extra pay for extra effort. In the following example there are actually two standards: one for daily production and the other for quality. Suppose that the daily production standard for an item is 1000 units. The daily wage rate is $50, but the operator gets an additional $0.30 for each unit produced over 1000 units. A daily production total of 1040 units would net the operator a bonus of $12.00, bringing daily earnings to $62.00. However, there is also a quality standard of 95 percent defect-free production. If the operator does better than that, a bonus of $0.10 is added for each defect-free unit produced beyond the standard. Suppose that the operator produces 1009 acceptable items. The quality bonus is $1009 - 0.95(1040) = 21$ units. This adds a bonus of $2.10, raising the total daily wage to $64.10.

Many variants of the motivational approach of including quality in work measurement are used in practice. The important point is that quality should be clearly recognized when compensation plans are being developed.

Impact of Automation

The automated factories of the future will offer a much greater challenge to the development and application of work measurement methods (Shell, 1982). There will be less need to actually observe an operation and rate performance because machines will increasingly control processing cycles. Many cycle times will be determined by digital control devices and therefore not have to be observed.

Although there will still be a need to determine allowances for fatigue, the nature of fatigue will shift from physical to mental fatigue. Traditional values for allowance factors may no longer be appropriate.

The method of work sampling will be simplified. An automated factory of the future will have the ability to electronically monitor the state of activity of many of the work units.

Predetermined data systems will still be useful. However, the need will be greater for analyzing robotic motions and the activities of knowledge workers than at present. Systems such as robot time and motion (RTM) are useful for evaluating alternative robotic work methods. The emphasis will shift to measuring the work of knowledge workers because they will comprise a greater proportion of the work force.

Standard data will probably be developed for major segments of the automated manufacturing system, as opposed to separate operations in an item's processing cycle. The times required for major manufacturing segments would be put into a database for use in simulating alternative work methods and estimating product costs before production actually starts.

Our discussion of the impact of automation holds equally well for service industries. In manufacturing or services, the major objective of work measurement will remain unchanged. Management then, as well as now, will still be interested in increasing productivity, improving quality, and reducing costs.

SOLVED PROBLEMS

1. A time analyst observed a job for which the work methods have just been changed. The job is divided into four work elements. The element times for first five cycles, recorded on a continuous basis, are shown in the following table with a performance rating (RF) for each element.

Element	Cycle Times (min)					RF
	1	2	3	4	5	
1	0.50	3.30	5.70	8.20	10.85	1.10
2	0.70	3.45	5.95	8.55	11.10	1.20
3	1.45	4.05	6.50	9.25	11.75	1.20
4	2.75	5.25	7.60	10.35	13.00	0.90

a. Calculate the normal time for this job.

b. Calculate the standard time for this job, assuming that the allowance is 20 percent.

c. What is the appropriate sample size for estimating the time for element 2 within ±5 percent of the true mean time with 95 percent confidence?

d. What sample size is needed for a precision of ±10 percent?

Solution

a. To get the normal time for this job we must first determine the observed times for each work element for each cycle. We do so by subtracting successive continuous clock readings. Table 6.4 contains the data needed to compute the normal time per cycle; all times are representative.

b. Standard time = (Normal time per cycle)(1.0 + Allowances)

$$ST = NTC (1.0 + A)$$
$$= 2.711(1.0 + 0.2)$$
$$= 3.25 \text{ min}$$

c. For work element 2, we have:

$$p = 0.05$$
$$s = \sqrt{\Sigma (t_i - 0.24)^2/(n - 1)} = 0.0742$$
$$\bar{t} = 0.24$$

The sample coefficient of variation = $s/\bar{t}$ = 0.3092, so

$$n = \left[\left(\frac{1.96}{p}\right)\left(\frac{s}{\bar{t}}\right)\right]^2 = \left[\left(\frac{1.96}{0.05}\right)(0.3092)\right]^2$$
$$= 146.9 \quad \text{or} \quad 147 \text{ observations}$$

d. For precision of ±10 percent, the appropriate sample size is

$$n = \left[\left(\frac{1.96}{0.10}\right)(0.3092)\right]^2$$
$$= 36.7 \quad \text{or} \quad 37 \text{ observations}$$

Table 6.4

Work Element	Observation 1	2	3	4	5	$\bar{t}$	F	RF	NT
1	0.50	0.55	0.45	0.60	0.50	0.52	1	1.1	0.572
2	0.20	0.15	0.25	0.35	0.25	0.24	1	1.2	0.288
3	0.75	0.60	0.55	0.70	0.65	0.65	1	1.2	0.780
4	1.30	1.20	1.10	1.10	1.25	1.19	1	0.9	1.071

Normal Time per Cycle (NTC) = 2.711 min

2. A library administrator wants to determine the proportion of the time the circulation clerk is idle. The following information was gathered on a random basis using work sampling.

Day	No. Times Clerk Busy	No. Times Clerk Idle	Total No. Observations
Monday	8	2	10
Tuesday	7	1	8
Wednesday	9	3	12
Thursday	7	3	10
Friday	8	2	10
Saturday	6	4	10

If the administrator wants a 95 percent confidence level and a degree of precision of ±0.04, how many more observations are needed?

Solution

The total number of observations made equals 60. The clerk was observed to be idle 15 times. The initial estimate of the proportion is $P = 15/60 = 0.25$. From Table 6.2, the required sample size for a precision of ±0.04 is 450. As 60 observations have already been made, an additional 390 are needed.

3. The Compton Company is manufacturing a new product that requires methods and materials never before used by Compton. The order is for 80 units. The first unit took 46 direct labor hours while the tenth unit took only 24.

   a. What is the rate of learning on this product?
   b. Estimate direct labor hours for the eightieth unit.

Solution

a.
$$b = \frac{\log (24/46)}{\log (10)}$$
$$= -0.2825$$
$$r = 10^{(-0.2825 \log 2)}$$
$$= 10^{(-0.08504)} = 0.82$$

The learning rate is 82 percent for this product.

b.
$$k_{80} = 46(80)^{(-0.2825)}$$
$$= 13.34 \text{ hr}$$

4. You have just been given the following production schedule for a new product. This product is considerably different from any others your company has produced. Historically, the learning rate has been 80 percent on projects such as this.

Month	Units
1	3
2	7
3	10
4	12
5	4
6	2

The first unit took 1000 hours to produce. If your budget only provides for a maximum of 25 direct labor employees in any month and a total of 15,000 direct labor hours for the entire schedule, will your budget be adequate? Assume 200 work hours in each month.

Solution

The first unit took 1000 hours to produce, and there is an 80 percent learning curve. We can use Table 6.3 to get the data we need for Table 6.5.

The schedule is feasible in terms of maximum direct labor required in any month because it never exceeds 22 employees. However, the total cumulative hours is 16,568, which exceeds the budgeted amount by 1568 hours. Therefore the budget will not be adequate.

Table 6.5

Month	Units Scheduled	Cumulative Production	Cumulative Avg. Time[1]	Cumulative Total Hr[2]	Total Hr/month[3]	Employees per Month[4]
1	3	3	834	2,502	2,502	13
2	7	10	632	6,320	3,818	20
3	10	20	524	10,480	4,160	21
4	12	32	459	14,688	4,208	22
5	4	36	443	15,948	1,260	7
6	2	38	436	16,568	620	4

[1]Values from Table 6.3 multiplied by 1000 and rounded to the nearest whole number.
[2]Cumulative production multiplied by cumulative average time per unit.
[3]Difference between successive total cumulative hours. For example, 6,320 − 2,502 = 3,818 for month 2.
[4]Total hours per month divided by 200 and rounded to the next largest integer.

FORMULA REVIEW

1. Required sample size in a time study:

$$n = \left[\left(\frac{1.96}{p} \right) \left(\frac{s}{t} \right) \right]^2$$

2. Normal time:

$$NT = \bar{t}(F)(RF)$$

3. Standard time:

$$ST = NTC(1 + A)$$

4. Direct labor required for the nth unit:

$$k_n = k_1 n^b$$

where

$$b = \frac{\log r}{\log 2}$$

5. Learning rate:

$$r = 10^{(b \, \log \, 2)}$$

where

$$b = \frac{\log (k_n/k_1)}{\log n}$$

CHAPTER HIGHLIGHTS

- Work measurement results are useful for comparing alternative process designs, scheduling, capacity planning, pricing and costing, performance appraisal, and developing incentive plans. Work measurement data are used most often for estimating and costing, followed by incentive plan development, scheduling, and performance appraisal.

- The most commonly used method of setting time standards for a job is time study. The job is divided into a series of smaller work elements. A stopwatch is used to time a trained worker using the prescribed work method for a number of cycles. The worker's pace is rated and allowances are added to arrive at a standard.

- The elemental standard data approach is an attempt to limit the number of standards that must be derived and used. The time standards for work elements that are common to a class of jobs can be stored in a database for future use in compiling time standards for jobs having the same elements.

- The predetermined data approach further divides each work element into a series of micromotions. The normal times for these micromotions are stored in a database. Standards can be developed without a stopwatch by adding the micromotion times for work elements.

- Work sampling is used most often to estimate the proportion of time spent on various broader activities associated with the production of goods or services. A large number of random observations are needed to make the estimates.

- In situations where significant learning takes place as production increases, learning curves can be used to prepare bids, decide whether to make or buy a component, estimate financial requirements over the life of a contract, and estimate the amount of direct labor needed to meet a production schedule. If the learning rate is 90 percent, for example, each doubling of production volume reduces the direct labor required per unit by 10 percent.

- Firms using a low-price strategy strive to move down the learning curve to reduce labor hours and costs per unit by increasing volume. This approach makes entry into a market by competitors very costly.

- Labor standards used for incentive pay plans should include recognition for product quality.

- The advent of automated factories will facilitate the process of work measurement because much of the work done will be machine-paced and monitored by computers. However, allowances will have to be made for mental fatigue in workers, and there will be more of a need to develop predetermined time systems for knowledge workers.

KEY TERMS

allowance time   195
elemental standard data   196
labor standard   188
learning curve   206
methods time measurement (MTM)   197
normal time (NT)   194
normal time for the cycle (NTC)   195
performance rating factor (RF)   194
sample coefficient of variation (s/t)   193
select time (t)   193
standard   188
standard time (ST)   195
time study   191
work sampling   199

STUDY QUESTIONS

1. An instructor for an introductory class in operations management positions all his students on the 50-yard line of the football field. He declares that anyone who does not reach the goal line in 5 seconds will fail the course. Discuss this intriguing way of grading a class from the perspective of the definition of a standard.

2. The Italian Maiden Pizza Company produces pizza for resale in the frozen food section of large supermarkets. Recently, product designs for a new deep-dish product were finalized. Which work measurement technique should be used to develop time standards for this product before production actually begins?

3. What role does the sample coefficient of variation play in work measurement studies? If management introduces new work methods or tools at a work station and in so doing reduces the variance of the time per cycle, what impact will it have on work measurement studies of that operation?

4. A colleague of yours comments that a time study with the use of a standard stopwatch is a precise method for determining work standards. What is your reply?

5. Your company builds concrete patio floors to customer specifications. The activities are (1) consultation with the customer to get the specifications; (2) drawing the plans; (3) digging the foundation; (4) building the forms; and (5) laying the concrete. How would you develop a time standard for installing patio floors?

6. Two of your assistants are arguing over the precision required for a work sampling study. The proportion of time spent by a group of your employees manually filling out forms for customer orders turned out to be 0.28 in a recent pilot study. There is a proposal to bring in a network of microcomputers to speed this process. One assistant believes that the estimate should be within ±0.01 of the true proportion, while the other thinks that a precision of ±0.05 is sufficient. The pilot study had a sample size of 100. What would you consider in choosing a sample size here?

7. In Chapter 2, Fig. 2.6 depicts the continuum of positioning strategies. Relate what Fig. 2.6 shows to the concepts of learning curves and competitive strategy.

8. Which results in a lower number of direct labor hours per unit: an 80 percent learning curve or a 90 percent learning curve? Explain.

9. A friend of yours firmly believes that if the "factory of the future" is ever realized, there will be no need for work measurement. Comment.

10. Recall the Longhorn Products and Pinecrest Brewery tours in Chapter 2. To what extent can learning curves be used in these two operations? Which of the two would most likely have the higher learning rates?

PROBLEMS

Review Problems

1. A worker assembled 10 parts in 40 minutes during a time study. The analyst rated the worker at 115 percent. The allowance for fatigue, personal time, and other contingencies is 15 percent. Calculate:
   a. Normal time for this job.
   b. Standard time for this job.

2. You have just received the data in Table 6.6 involving an assembly operation in your department. The data are expressed in minutes. Allowances typically constitute 20 percent of the normal time. You have also been told that the schedule calls for 1000 units per day for the foreseeable future. If each employee works 450 minutes per day, how many employees will you need?

3. The information shown in Table 6.7 pertains to a particular operation. The data are expressed in minutes. What is the normal time for this operation?

4. A time analyst observed a job for which work methods had just been changed. The job is divided into four work elements. The element times (in minutes) for the first five cycles, recorded on a continuous basis, are shown in Table 6.8.
   a. Calculate the normal time for this job.
   b. Calculate the standard time for the job, assuming that the allowance is 10 percent.
   c. What sample size is appropriate for estimating the time for element 1 within ±5 percent of the true mean time with 95 percent confidence?

Table 6.6

Work Element	Observation 1	2	3	4	RF
1	0.45	0.41	0.50	0.48	1.0
2	0.85	0.81	0.77	0.89	0.9
3	0.31	0.24	0.27	0.26	0.8
4	0.60	0.55	0.59	0.58	1.1

Table 6.7

Work Element	Observation 1	2	3	4	5	6	7	8	9	10	11	12	F	RF
1	0.20	0.22	0.24	0.18	0.20	0.21	0.22	0.19	0.24	0.18	0.19	0.25	1.0	0.8
2	0.64			0.62			0.59			0.63			0.33	0.9
3	0.40	0.38	0.37	0.41	0.41	0.40	0.36	0.37	0.41	0.42	0.39	0.36	1.0	1.2

Table 6.8

Element	Cycle Times 1	2	3	4	5	F	RF
1	0.10	1.67	2.99	4.68	6.04	1.0	1.1
2	0.40		3.30		6.31	0.5	1.2
3	1.30	2.62	4.34	5.70	7.31	1.0	0.9
4	1.55	2.88	4.59	5.94	7.57	1.0	0.8

Table 6.9

	Observation									
Element	1	2	3	4	5	6	7	8	F	RF
1	0.78	0.70	0.75	0.80	0.79	0.82	0.81	0.80	1.0	1.2
2	0.20	0.21	0.16	0.19	0.23	0.25	0.24	0.26	1.0	1.0
3	0.41	0.36	0.45	0.37	0.39	0.40	0.43	0.44	1.0	1.1
4	0.61	0.60	0.55	0.57	0.63	0.61	0.62	0.60	1.0	0.9

5. A pilot time study has been conducted on a new assembly operation. The data shown in Table 6.9 (in minutes) were obtained. How many additional observations are needed if the estimate of time for element 2 is to be within ±3 percent of the true mean time with 95 percent confidence?

6. Consider the recorded observations of 10 cycles of the cup packaging operation shown in Fig. 6.1.

a. Suppose that we want a sample size that gives an average time within ±5 percent of the true average time 95 percent of the time. Did we make enough observations? If not, how many more should we make?

b. Suppose that all we wanted was a precision of ±10 percent. How many additional observations would we need?

7. The information systems department of Evergreen Life Insurance Company wants to determine the proportion of time that the data entry operator is idle. The following information was gathered randomly using work sampling.

Date	No. of Times Clerk Busy	No. of Times Clerk Idle	Total No. of Observations
8/22	9	4	13
8/23	10	5	15
8/24	9	5	14
8/25	9	7	16
8/26	11	3	14
8/27	10	6	16
8/28	4	8	12

If the department wants a 95 percent confidence level and a degree of precision of ±0.03, how many more observations are needed?

8. Mass Balance Company is manufacturing a new digital scale for use by a large chemical company.

The order is for 30 units. The first scale took 70 hours of direct labor while the third unit took only 50.

a. What is the rate of learning on this product?

b. What is the estimated time for the thirtieth unit?

9. Cambridge Instruments is an aircraft instrumentation manufacturer. It has received a contract from the Department of Defense to produce 20 radar units for a military fighter. The first unit took 90 hours to produce. Based on past experience with manufacturing similar units, Cambridge estimates that the learning rate is 93 percent. How long will it take to produce the fifth unit? The tenth? The fifteenth? The final unit?

10. The following production schedule has been developed for a new product.

Week	Units
1	20
2	65
3	100
4	140
5	120

Historically, the learning rate has been 90 percent on such projects. Your budget allows for a maximum of 40 direct labor employees per week and a total of 7000 direct labor hours for the entire schedule. Assume 40 work hours per week. If the first unit took 30 hours to assemble, is this production schedule feasible? If not, how can it be altered? What additional costs would be incurred?

Advanced Problems

A computer package is helpful for Problems 11–14. Problem 14 requires prior reading of Supplement 1.

11. You have been asked by management to explain the method of work sampling at its weekly meeting. A consultant has recommended this approach to determine the proportion of unproductive time on one of the production lines, and management wants an "insider" to fill them in on the method. To prepare your presentation you had an assistant observe one of the typists from the typing pool for an entire week, categorizing activities as filing, typing, coffee breaks, or idle. The actual times spent on these activities during that week are shown in Fig. 6.6.

   You intend to use this chart to simulate work sampling, rather than sampling in real time. In this way a simple schedule normally requiring a week to execute can be simulated in a few minutes. Afterwards, the estimates from the sample can be compared to the actual amount of time spent on each activity.

   a. Use a random number table to select 20 times during the week you will "observe" the typist. Use a random number first to determine the day, and then use another to determine the time of day. Omit the time period 12 to 1 P.M. each day because this is the standard lunch time. Put these 20 times into an observation schedule.

   b. Using your observation schedule, determine what the typist is doing using Fig. 6.6 at these times. Determine the sample proportion of time spent on each activity.

   c. What are the actual proportions of time spent on each activity from Fig. 6.6? How do the estimates compare? Determine the sample size needed to ensure accuracy within ±0.04 with 95 percent confidence. Based on your experiment, what can you tell management about sample sizes and accuracy?

12. The Bovine Products Company recently introduced a new automatic milking system for cows of all shapes and sizes. The company just completed an order for 18 units. The last unit (number 18) required 22 hours of labor, and the learning rate is estimated to be 90 percent on systems such as this. Another customer has just placed an order for the same system. This company, which owns many farms in the midwest, wants 46 units. How many total labor hours will be needed to satisfy this order?

13. Suppose that you are bidding on a project and you need to know how much to charge per unit. Assume that the product has an 80 percent learning rate. The contract calls for 100 units. You estimate that the first unit will cost $3000.

   a. What is the total cost of the contract quantity?

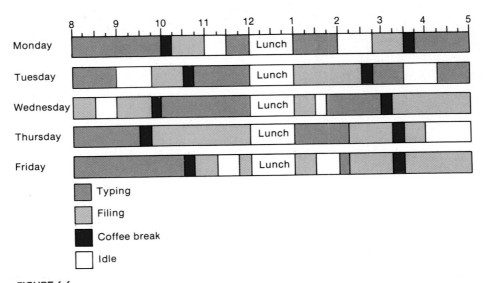

FIGURE 6.6

b. At what point during production will the company begin to make a profit on each unit of the contract if you bid $1000 per unit?

14. As manager of an encoding department in a bank, you are concerned about the amount of time your encoder clerks have to spend cleaning their machines because of malfunctions. You were handed a proposal to modify the design of the machines for a price of $70,000. The modification will reduce the amount of time spent cleaning the machines by 75 percent. You employ 25 encoder clerks at an annual salary of $15,000 each. Any time saved from cleaning the machines can be used to process more checks and reduce the interest charges the bank must pay. To help you decide whether the proposal is worth considering, you had a pilot work sampling study made, which provided the following results.

Activity	Observations
Processing checks	52
Cleaning machine	15
Waiting for checks	25
Breaks	8
Total	100

a. If the life of the modification is 10 years and the bank's tax rate is 50 percent, what is the simple payback period for the proposal based on your sample estimate? (Use straight-line depreciation).

b. Construct a 95 percent confidence interval for your estimate. Would you suggest a larger sample size? Why? *Hint:* Base your confidence interval on the normal approximation to the binomial distribution where the standard error is

$$\sigma_p = \sqrt{\frac{p(1 - p)}{n}}$$

$p \pm Z \times_p$

n = sample size (total)
p = proportion of time spent on item of interest (cleaning machines)

SELECTED REFERENCES

Abernathy, William J., and Kenneth Wayne, "Limits of the Learning Curve," *Harvard Business Review* (September–October 1974), pp. 109–119.

Andress, Frank J., "The Learning Curve as a Production Tool," *Harvard Business Review* (January–February 1954), pp. 1–11.

Barnes, Ralph, *Motion and Time Study: Design and Measurement of Work*, 7th ed. New York: John Wiley & Sons, 1980.

Caruth, Donald L., *Work Measurement in Commercial Banks*. Boston: Bankers Publishing, 1971.

Graves, Clare W., "Deterioration of Work Standards," *Harvard Business Review* (September–October 1966), pp. 118–126.

Moore, Franklin G., *Manufacturing Management*. Homewood, Ill.: Richard D. Irwin, 1969.

Nadler, Gerald, *Work Design*. Homewood, Ill.: Richard D. Irwin, 1970.

Niebel, Richard W., *Motion and Time Study*, 7th ed. Homewood, Ill.: Richard D. Irwin, 1982.

Rice, Robert S., "Survey of Work Measurement and Wage Incentives," *Industrial Engineering*, vol. 9, no. 7 (July 1977), pp. 18–31.

Shell, Richard L., "The Impact of Automation on Work Measurement," *1982 Fall Industrial Engineering Conference Proceedings*, Institute of Industrial Engineers (November 1982), Cincinnati, pp. 348–353.

Sirota, David, "Productivity Management," *Harvard Business Review* (September–October 1966), pp. 111–116.

Yelle, Louis E., "The Learning Curve: Historical Review and Comprehensive Survey," *Decision Sciences*, vol. 10, no. 2 (April 1979), pp. 302–328.

CHAPTER

7

CAPACITY AND MAINTENANCE

 Chapter Outline

CAPACITY PLANNING

MANAGERIAL PRACTICE 7.1 The Agony of Too Much—And Too Little—Capacity

Measuring Capacity

Economies of Scale

MANAGERIAL PRACTICE 7.2 Economies of Scale on Wall Street and in a Paper Mill

Focused Facilities

Capacity Strategy

MANAGERIAL PRACTICE 7.3 Expansion Strategy and Market Share

A Systematic Approach to Capacity Decisions

MAINTENANCE

Varying Maintenance Intensity

MANAGERIAL PRACTICE 7.4 Hi-Tech Maintenance Pays Off

SOLVED PROBLEMS
FORMULA REVIEW
CHAPTER HIGHLIGHTS
KEY TERMS
STUDY QUESTIONS
PROBLEMS
SELECTED REFERENCES

▲ Key Questions for Managers

How should we measure capacity?

What is the maximum reasonable size for our facility?

How much capacity cushion is best for our processes?

Should we follow an expansionist or a wait-and-see strategy?

How should we link capacity to competitive priorities? To other decision areas?

How intense should our maintenance effort be?

After deciding what products should be offered (product planning in Chapter 2) and how they should be made (process design in Chapter 4), managerial attention turns to capacity. **Capacity** is the maximum rate of output for a facility. The facility can be a work station or an entire organization. The operations manager must provide the capacity to meet current and future demand or suffer the consequences of missed opportunities.

Capacity plans are made at two levels. Long-term capacity plans, which we describe in this chapter, deal with investments in new facilities and equipment. These plans look into the future at least two years, but construction lead times alone can force much longer time horizons. Currently, U.S. investment in *new* plant and equipment is more than $400 billion annually. Service industries account for over 62 percent of the total. Such sizable investments require top-management participation and approval, since they are not easily reversed. Short-term capacity plans, which we discuss in later chapters, are constrained by long-term plans. Rather than capital investment decisions, they focus on work-force size, overtime budgets, inventories, and the like.

New equipment and facilities, once purchased, need to be maintained. **Maintenance** is the process of keeping facilities and equipment in good operating condition. Although it is more tactical than capacity strategy, we consider maintenance here because it affects the firm's output rate as surely as adding (or disposing of) equipment. American Airlines is a good example of management linking long-term capacity and maintenance decisions. Recently, the company placed a $2 billion order for 50 Boeing 757-200 jetliners, and took options on an equal number. The added planes will increase capacity on its

Part of the American Airlines fleet at its hub in the Dallas/Fort Worth International Airport. Recent expansion gives American the youngest fleet in the industry and is a key to its strategy of international growth.
Courtesy of American Airlines/Bob Takis, photographer

busiest routes, where seat utilization had reached 70 percent. During the same year, American also spent $6.7 billion on maintenance, or 6 percent of its operating expenses, and averaged 16 mechanics per aircraft. Such capacity and maintenance decisions should increase American's efficiency and market share.

CAPACITY PLANNING ▲

Capacity planning is central to the long-term success of an organization. Too much capacity can be as agonizing as too little capacity, as Managerial Practice 7.1 demonstrates. When choosing a capacity strategy, managers have to consider questions such as: Should we have one large facility or several small facilities? Should we expand capacity before the demand is there, or should we wait until demand is more certain? A systematic approach is needed in order to answer these and similar questions and to develop a capacity strategy appropriate for each situation.

Measuring Capacity

Capacity planning requires a knowledge of current capacity and its utilization. A statistic often used to indicate the degree to which equipment, space, or labor is currently being utilized is the **average utilization rate**, which is calculated as follows:

$$\text{Average utilization rate} = \frac{\text{Average output rate}}{\text{Capacity}}$$

expressed as a percentage. The average output rate and the capacity must be

MANAGERIAL PRACTICE 7.1 ▲

The Agony of Too Much—And Too Little—Capacity

Too Much

- Since government and private reimbursement plans discourage admitting all but the sickest patients, hospital occupancy rates have tumbled. Almost 40 percent of the nation's hospital beds are empty. Nerves are jangled throughout the $500 billion health-care industry. Health maintenance organizations are reeling from a competitive melee. And medicare reimbursements to hospitals lag behind cost increases. Experts predict some hospitals will close and others merge to help cut costs.

- Vacancy rates in the apartment business are in the 7–8 percent range nationally—the highest in 15 years. Owners are offering rent concessions and gifts, such as appliances, to attract tenants. Profit margins are squeezed by attempts to stay competitive, but vacancies are high.

Too Little

- James River Corporation's paper mill in Louisiana faced severe capacity shortages in 1984. The industry was operating at 97 percent utilization, which was not an unalloyed blessing. Customers were frustrated by backlogs and prices went up 25 percent. Some customers placed orders earlier. Others looked overseas for additional supply. Insufficient capacity strained the equipment and management alike.

- About 20 of the nation's big airports operate at levels that seriously strain their capacities. Air travel has surged 60 percent over the last decade. On an average day, La Guardia Airport handles 1000 flights, roughly one every 60 seconds from dawn to midnight. The result is congestion, harried air-traffic controllers, and poor customer service. "Unless we do something to increase capacity," says the director of FAA's eastern region, "the system will collapse on us."

Sources: "The Vital Signs Aren't Very Encouraging," *Business Week*, January 11, 1988; "Apartment Complexes Casting Wider Nets to Lure Tenants," *Wall Street Journal*, September 16, 1987; "When an Industry Is Too Busy," *New York Times*, April 5, 1984; "At La Guardia Airport Passenger Surge Causes Delays and Congestion," *Wall Street Journal*, June 1, 1988.

measured in the same terms, that is, time, customers, or units. As you will see later in this chapter, the utilization rate is an indicator of the need for adding extra capacity. However, in order to plan for proper utilization rates management first needs to measure capacity.

Basic Capacity Measures.   No single capacity measure is applicable to all types of situations. A reasonable capacity measure might be the number of patients that can be treated per day at a hospital, annual sales dollars generated by a retailer, available seat-miles (ASMs) per month of an airline, or number of machines at a job shop. In general, capacity can be expressed in terms of outputs or inputs.

Output measures are the usual choice of product-focused firms. Honda Motors confidently states its capacity to be 1500 cars per day at its Ohio plant. Capacity is well understood as an output rate, since product flexibility is low. Similarly, the managers of Pinecrest Brewery (see Chapter 2 tour) put their capacity at five million barrels per year. For multiple products, however, the capacity measure must recognize the product mix. For example, a restaurant may be able to handle 100 take-out customers *or* 50 sit-down customers per hour. It might also handle 50 take-out *and* 25 sit-down customers or many other combinations of the two types of customer.

Input measures are the usual choice of process-focused firms. For example, Longhorn Machine managers think of capacity as machine hours or number of machines. Just as product mix can complicate output capacity measures, so also can demand complicate input measures. Demand, which invariably is expressed as an output rate, must be converted to an input measure. Only after making the conversion can a manager compare demand requirements and capacity on an equivalent basis.

Defining *Maximum*.   One last complication in measuring capacity lies with the meaning of *maximum*. Capacity often can be expanded temporarily with such options as overtime or subcontracting. While helping with temporary peaks, these options cannot be sustained for long. Employees do not want to work excessive overtime for extended periods. Overtime premiums also drive up costs. Thus measures for both peak and sustained capacity levels are needed. When operating at peak capacity a firm can make minimal profits or even lose money when sales are at a record high. Such was the case at Cummins Engine Company in Columbus, Indiana. In reacting to an unexpected demand surge caused by the weakened dollar, the plant operated three shifts, often seven days a week. Overtime soared and exhausted workers dragged down productivity. So did calling back less skilled workers, laid off during an earlier slump. Cummins reported a quarterly loss of $6.2 million, at the very time when sales stretched capacity.

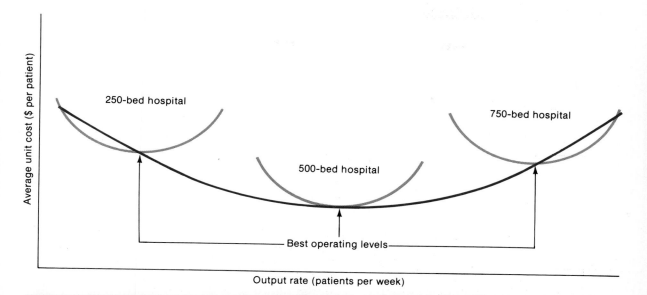

FIGURE 7.1   Economies and Diseconomies of Scale

Economies of Scale

Now that you have an idea of how to measure capacity, let's turn to the issues relating to facility size. Historically, many organizations have subscribed to the concept of **economies of scale**. The concept seems simple: Increasing a facility's size (or scale) decreases the average unit cost. But in reality, it's not at all simple. At some point, a facility becomes so large that **diseconomies of scale** set in. Excessive size can bring complexity, loss of focus, and inefficiencies. In Fig. 7.1, the 500-bed hospital shows economies of scale because the average unit cost at its "best operating level" is less than that of the 250-bed hospital. However, further expansion to a 750-bed hospital leads to higher average unit costs and diseconomies of scale.

Figure 7.1 also shows that there is a second dimension to the concept. Not only is there an optimal size for a facility, but also an optimal operating level for a facility of a given size. Economies (and diseconomies) of scale are represented not just *between* cost curves, but also *within* each one. As the output rate approaches a facility's best operating level, economies of scale are realized. Beyond that level, diseconomies set in.

Although finding the best size and operating level is illusive, managers often set policies regarding the maximum size for any one facility. Employee ceilings of 300 are common for industries such as metal-working or apparel (Schmenner, 1982). The limits are as large as 6000 employees for industries such as transportation equipment or electronics. The real challenge in setting such limits is predicting how costs will change for different output rates and facility sizes. This assessment requires careful attention to the different causes of economies of scale for each situation.

Spreading Fixed Costs.   In the short term, certain costs do not vary with changes in the output rate. These fixed costs include heating costs, debt service, and management salaries (see Chapter 2). Depreciation of plant and equipment already owned is also a fixed cost in the accounting sense. When the output rate—and therefore the facility's utilization rate—increase, the average unit cost drops because fixed costs are spread over more units. Because increments of capacity are often rather large, a firm initially might have to buy more capacity than it needs. However, a fairly wide range of demand increases in subsequent years can then be absorbed without adding fixed costs.

Construction Costs.   A second reason that the 500-bed hospital enjoys greater economies of scale than the 250-bed hospital in Fig. 7.1 is that it costs less to build than twice the cost of the smaller hospital. The 750-bed facility would enjoy similar savings. Its higher average unit costs in Fig. 7.1 can only be explained by diseconomies of scale, which outweigh the savings realized in construction costs.

MANAGERIAL PRACTICE 7.2

Economies of Scale on Wall Street and in a Paper Mill

- In one of the securities industry's boldest maneuvers, Shearson Lehman Brothers Holdings, Inc., bought E. F. Hutton Group, Inc. Shearson's cost-conscious management believes major economies of scale, and eventually big profits, will come by *spreading the fixed costs* of its recently expanded computer capacity to Hutton operations. The high-powered computers track securities inventories and process customer orders and statements.

- Higher volumes give James River Corporation's paper mill in Louisiana some *process advantages*, allowing them to optimize their mix and run lengths. With strong demand, the plant might have orders for 10,000 tons of a certain grade of paper, compared with 5000 tons in less busy times. The mill can set the machine for one long run and not have to halt it so often to adjust for different grades.

Sources: "Shearson's Bold Move to Purchase Hutton Puts It Near Top Spot," *Wall Street Journal*, December 3, 1987; "When an Industry Is Too Busy," *New York Times*, April 5, 1984.

Process Advantages.   Repeatability and high-volume production provide many opportunities for cost reduction. A more efficient process technology may be possible and its capital intensity justified at a higher output rate. The process shifts toward a product-focused strategy, with resources dedicated to individual products. More specialized equipment replaces general-purpose machinery. Dedicating resources to individual products reduces changeovers and setups, as the paper mill in Managerial Practice 7.2 illustrates. Further benefits may include learning curve effects, lower inventory, and a greater ability to improve process and job designs.

Focused Facilities

Prior to 1970, many firms were willing to endure the managerial headaches that went with size. After 1970, however, the nature of competition changed, and economies of scale no longer could guarantee an advantage. Quality and flexibility gained importance. Also, rapid technological change shortened product life cycles, and managers of large facilities found it increasingly difficult to maintain high production volumes. For many companies the time had come to reevaluate the usefulness of large facilities.

The concept of **focused facilities** holds that narrowing the range of demands on a facility will lead to better performance because the operations manager can concentrate on fewer tasks and motivate a work force towards a single goal. First proposed in the early 1970s, this concept persuaded many firms to move

Economies of scale are significant at a paper mill, which is a capital-intensive operation with high fixed costs.
James River Corporation

away from large facilities trying to do everything (Skinner, 1974). For example, one plant attempting to satisfy all target markets may give way to several smaller plants, each serving one market. Or one plant producing all the components and assembling the final product may be split into two plants, one producing the components and one assembling the final product. Thus each can focus on its own individual process technology. Even with a large facility, focus can be gained by having *plants within plants* (PWPs). The competitive priorities, technology, and work force are individualized at each PWP. Boundaries may be established by physically separating subunits, even within the same building. The separation can be less tangible, as by revised organizational relationships.

The focused facilities concept has led some firms to tout the virtues of smallness. The General Electric Aircraft Engine Group once concentrated production in two large complexes but now has eight smaller satellite plants. Hewlett-Packard, S. C. Johnson and Sons, and American Telephone and Telegraph, to name but a few, have also gone to smaller facilities and focused operations. There are fewer layers of management, team approaches to problem solving are easier to use, and lines of communication between departments are shorter. The message is clear: Do not let the facility get too large and make sure that it has enough focus.

Capacity Strategy

Before we look at a systematic approach to capacity decisions, let's consider three dimensions of capacity strategy: (1) capacity cushions; (2) timing and sizing of expansion; and (3) links.

Capacity Cushions.   Average utilization rates should not get too close to 100 percent. When they do it is usually a signal to increase capacity or lose orders or endure declining productivity. The amount by which the average utilization rate falls below 100 percent is called the **capacity cushion**. Specifically,

$$\text{Capacity cushion} = 100 - \text{Average utilization rate}$$

expressed as a percentage. From 1948 to 1982 U.S. manufacturers maintained an average cushion of 18 percent, with a 9 percent low in 1966 and 30 percent high in 1982. The average cushion is now back down to 17 percent. The best-sized cushion varies by industry and firm. In the capital-intensive paper industry machines can cost hundreds of millions of dollars each, so cushions well under 10 percent are preferred. Electrical utilities are also capital intensive, but consider cushions of 15 to 20 percent to be optimal in order to avoid brownouts and loss of service to customers. Clearly, managers must carefully weigh the arguments for both large and small cushions.

We begin with arguments for large cushions. A clerk in the human services department of a state government can handle as many as 50 clients per day. However, demand is not evenly paced. Some days of the week have predictably higher demands than other days. There can even be an hour-to-hour pattern. Such peaks cannot be smoothed out with inventories or by having the customer wait a long time for service. Giving prompt customer service requires a capacity cushion large enough to handle peak demand, particularly in service industries. Customers grow impatient if they have to wait in a supermarket checkout line for more than a few minutes, whereas the buyer of a forklift tractor considers a manufacturer's delivery time of two months to be excellent.

Large cushions are also necessary when future demand is uncertain. One large bank operated its computer for six months at an average 77 percent load on the central processing unit (CPU) during peak demand. Top management felt that the capacity cushion was more than ample and rejected a proposal to expand capacity. During the next six months, the average CPU utilization during peaks surged to 83 percent. Totally unexpected was the dramatic decline in customer service and missed due dates. The capacity cushion proved to be too small to meet the bank's customer service objectives. Another type of demand uncertainty is a changing product mix. Total demand might be stable, but the load can shift unpredictably from one work center to another as the mix changes. Feast-or-famine conditions go along with high product flexibility. An example is a municipal court system, where the capacity (courtroom hours) varies with the nature of the trials and whether a jury is needed. The mix varies from one month to the next.

Other reasons for large capacity cushions lie on the supply (rather than the demand) side. Capacity often comes in large increments, so that expanding even by the minimum amount possible may create a large cushion. Allowances must be made for absenteeism, vacations, holidays, materials delays, work breaks, equipment failures, and scrap losses. Penalty costs for overtime or subcontracting can create the need for further increases in capacity cushions.

The motivation for small cushions is simple: Unused capacity costs money. For capital-intensive firms, minimizing the capacity cushion is vital. The survey results presented in Table 7.1 show that businesses with high capital investment achieve a disappointing 7 percent return on investment (ROI) when the capacity cushion is high. The ROI increases to a more respectable 17 percent when

TABLE 7.1 Return on Investment for Capital-Intensive Businesses

Capacity Cushion	Return on Investment (ROI)*
Low (less than 15%)	17%
Medium (between 15% and 30%)	11
High (above 30%)	7

*ROI measured as pretax income divided by average investment.

Source: Abell, Derek F., and John S. Hammond, *Strategic Market Planning: Problems and Analytical Approaches.* Englewood Cliffs, N.J.: Prentice-Hall, 1979.

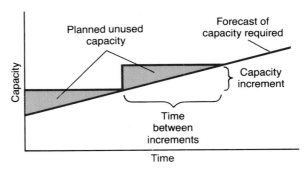

(a) Expansionist Strategy

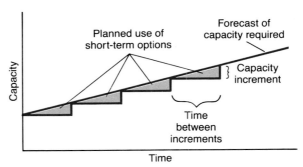

(b) Wait-and-See Strategy

FIGURE 7.2   Two Capacity Strategies

the capacity cushion is low. However, this strong correlation does not exist for labor-intensive firms. The ROI is about the same, regardless of utilization, because the lower investment in equipment makes high utilization less critical.

Timing and Sizing of Expansion. The second dimension of capacity strategy is when to expand and by how much. Figure 7.2 illustrates two extreme strategies: The *expansionist strategy,* which involves large, infrequent jumps in capacity, and the *wait-and-see strategy,* which involves smaller, less frequent jumps. The timing and sizing of expansion are related. That is, when the length of time between increments is increased, the size of the increments must also be increased. The expansionist strategy stays ahead of demand. Even though this approach creates a large capacity cushion, it minimizes the chance that sales will be lost because of insufficient capacity. The wait-and-see strategy lags behind demand, relying on short-term options to fill any shortfalls. Short-term options include authorizing overtime, hiring temporary workers, subcontracting work, postponing preventive maintenance, and allowing stockouts (see Chapter 13). Each such option has its drawbacks. For example, overtime means time-and-a-half wages for nonexempt employees, and maybe lower productivity during overtime hours. And union agreements can limit the amount of allowable overtime. Nonetheless, some mix of short-term options might make the wait-and-see strategy best in certain situations.

Several factors favor the expansion strategy. When economies of scale and learning effects are strong, a firm can reduce its costs and compete more on price. This strategy might increase its market share, as demonstrated by Managerial Practice 7.3. The expansionist strategy becomes a form of preemptive marketing when a firm makes a large capacity expansion, or perhaps just announces that one is imminent. By making it clear that it will do whatever is necessary to compete on cost, the firm is using capacity as a competitive weapon, preempting expansion by others who must sacrifice some of their market share or risk glutting the industry with overcapacity. To be successful, the preempting firm must have credibility that it will carry out its plans and signal them before competition can act.

The wait-and-see strategy is conservative and minimizes risk. When a firm does expand, it might be to renovate existing facilities rather than build new ones. The more a firm invests in any one facility, the more it depends on that facility's success. The wait-and-see strategy reduces the risks of overly optimistic demand forecasts, technological change that would make the facility obsolete, and unpredictable competitive reactions. The wait-and-see strategy has been criticized by some who compare U.S. and Japanese management styles. U.S.

MANAGERIAL PRACTICE 7.3 ▲

Expansion Strategy and Market Share

- With factories operating at 83 percent in 1988, many companies had to expand or lose sales. "When the salesperson tells the boss, 'We're losing sales to others because we can't meet the delivery schedule,' attitudes change," says Paul G. Schloemer, CEO of Parker Hannifin Corporation, a Cleveland-based motion-control equipment concern.

- "Demand is soaring and we want to be there first," says Joseph McHugh, senior executive vice president of Triangle Pacific Corporation. The company is building new plants in Port Gibson, Mississippi, and Beverly, West Virginia.

- "You don't want to repeat past mistakes, but you live with the fear that if you don't expand, somebody else will," says the chief economist of the Chemical Manufacturers Association. Managers are worried about losing market share in the weak-dollar induced boom, even though the chemical industry was burned by early-1980s problems of excess capacity.

Sources: "Manufacturers Are Expanding Capacity," *Wall Street Journal*, June 7, 1988; "Chemical Firms Largely Resist Temptation to Expand," *Wall Street Journal*, January 12, 1988.

managers tend to take fewer risks. They are on the fast track of the corporate advancement, spending only a few years in each succeeding job. They earn promotions by avoiding the big mistake and maximizing short-term profit and ROI. The wait-and-see strategy fits this style but can erode market share over the long run.

Management may choose one of these two strategies or one of the many between these extremes. The choice could even be a *follow-the-leader strategy* of expanding when others do. If others are right, so are you, and nobody gains a competitive advantage. If they make a mistake and overexpand, so have you, but everyone shares in the agony of overcapacity.

Links.   A subsidiary of a large consumer goods manufacturer sold 85 percent of its output to other divisions in the company, with the remaining 15 percent going to outside customers. The capacity of one of its processes was being squeezed. One option was to expand, enabling the subsidiary to attract more outside customers. However, this approach would shift competitive priorities. Rather than being a low-cost supplier to the other divisions, the subsidiary would have to place higher priority on flexibility and quality. Management decided against the expansion, because of poor coupling with other policies.

A recent survey gives us a second example of how managers link capacity with other decisions. Managers were asked which of eight broad categories of processes (such as packaging, changing shapes of metals, and assembling) were performed in their plants. As Fig. 7.3 shows, managers opt for a less focused

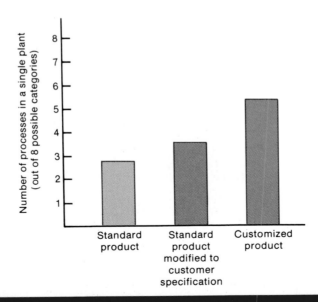

FIGURE 7.3   Product Flexibility Links with Facility Focus

Source: Sharma, Deven, "Manufacturing Strategy: An Empirical Analysis." Unpublished dissertation. Ohio State University, 1987.

TABLE 7.2 Linking Capacity with Other Strategic and Operations Decisions

Decision Area	Change to	Needed Change in Capacity Cushion
Competitive priorities	More emphasis on fast delivery	Larger cushion provides quicker response, even when demand is uneven or uncertain.
Capital intensity	More capital-intensive process design	Smaller cushion increases equipment utilization and achieves acceptable ROI.
Resource flexibility	Less worker flexibility	Larger cushion helps reduce the operation overloads that are more likely to occur with a less flexible work force.
Quality management	Smaller yield losses	Smaller cushion is needed, as there will be fewer unpredictable output losses.
Inventory	Less reliance on inventory to smooth production rate	Larger cushion helps meet increased production during peak periods.
Scheduling	More stable environment	Smaller cushion is needed, as production can be scheduled with more assurance.

facility (more processes in the same facility) when a more customized product (more product flexibility) is being produced.

Finally, Table 7.2 suggests a third link between decisions. When managers change other strategies and operations, they must make corresponding changes in the capacity cushion.

A Systematic Approach to Capacity Decisions

Although each situation is somewhat different, a four-step procedure can, in general, help managers make sound capacity decisions:

1. Estimate future capacity requirements.

2. Identify gaps by comparing requirements with available capacity.

3. Develop alternative plans for filling the gaps.

4. Evaluate each alternative, both quantitatively and qualitatively, and make a final choice.

Step 1: Estimate Capacity Requirements. The beginning point is a demand forecast. Since long-term decisions are involved, forecasts of demand, productivity, competition, and technological changes must extend well into the future. Unfortunately, forecast errors get larger as forecast time horizons become longer. (See Chapter 10 for a more detailed discussion of quantitative and qualitative forecasting methods.)

As we have mentioned, the demand forecast has to be converted to a number that can be compared directly with the capacity measure being used. Suppose that capacity is expressed as the number of available machines at a machining operation. With this particular measure, the analyst must convert the demand rate to the number of machines required. The number of machine hours required per year is

$$R = \sum_{i=1}^{M} D_i \, p_i + \sum_{i=1}^{M} \frac{D_i}{Q_i} s_i$$

where

R = total machine hours required per year

D_i = number of units of product i forecasted per year

p_i = processing time per unit of product i

Q_i = number of units in each lot (or batch) of product i

s_i = standard setup time per lot

M = number of products made at the operation

The number of actual machine hours per year per machine is

$$H = N\left(1 - \frac{C}{100}\right)$$

where

H = hours provided per year by one machine, allowing for capacity cushion

N = number of hours operated on all shifts and all work days in a year

C = capacity cushion (as a percent)

Knowing the total hours required (R) and the amount satisfied per machine (H), the analyst obtains the number of machines required from the ratio

$$M = \frac{R}{H}$$

rounding the answer up to the next integer.

This conversion process isn't limited to machines. The input unit could just as easily be seats in a theater, teller stations in a bank, or any other capacity measure.

APPLICATION 7.1

A work station produces two different products, X and Y. The following table gives the necessary information for each product. The plant operates 250 days per year, with two eight-hour shifts. Management believes that a capacity cushion of 15 percent (beyond the allowance built into the time standard) is best. How many machines are needed at the work station?

Item	Product X	Product Y
Annual demand forecast (units)	2000	6000
Lot size (units)	40	60
Standard processing time (hr/unit)	4	3
Standard setup time (hr/lot)	5	8

Solution

Summing machine hour requirements for both products, we get

$$R = \left[2000(4) + \left(\frac{2000}{40}\right)(5) \right] + \left[6000(3) + \left(\frac{6000}{60}\right)(8) \right]$$

$$= 27{,}050 \text{ hr}$$

The remaining calculations are

$$H = [(250 \text{ days/yr})(2 \text{ shifts/day})(8 \text{ hr/shift})]\left(1.0 - \frac{15}{100}\right)$$

$$= 3400 \text{ hr}$$

$$M = \frac{27{,}050}{3400} = 7.96 \quad \text{or} \quad 8 \text{ machines}$$

Always round up, unless short-term options such as overtime or stockouts are used to cover any shortfalls.

Step 2: Identify Gaps. Any positive difference, or shortfall, between projected demand and current capacity is a capacity gap. However, the correct capacity must be used, and complications arise when multiple operations and several resource inputs are involved. For example, when studying market-share statistics in the early 1970s, many executives concluded that the airlines having the larger share of seats flown attract a larger share of the total passengers. In other words, fly more seats to get more passengers. The response by many airlines was to buy more jumbo jets. It soon became evident that competitors flying smaller planes enjoyed more success. The key factor was the number of departures rather than the number of seats. Thus several airlines had to adjust the capacity imbalance between small and large planes by selling or mothballing jumbo jets. Capacity balance also applies to manufacturing. Expanding the capacity of some operations in a plant may increase overall capacity very little, if other bottleneck operations also are not expanded.

APPLICATION 7.2

Grandmother's Chicken Restaurant is known throughout Middlesburg for its unique chicken recipe and homey atmosphere. Business is booming. Kathryn Shoemaker, the owner, expects total sales for this year (1989) to be $800,000, straining the kitchen's capacity to its limit. Although the kitchen is operating at 100 percent capacity, the dining room can handle a sales volume of up to $1,050,000. Demand is expected to increase $100,000 per year for the next five years. Using annual dollar sales as the capacity measure, what are the capacity gaps through 1994?

Solution

The accompanying table shows the results. For example, demand in 1992 should reach $1,100,000. As the kitchen's capacity is $800,000, there is a $300,000 capacity gap (or $1,100,000 − $800,000). The dining room's 1992 gap is only $50,000 because its current capacity is $1,050,000. For the restaurant as a whole in 1992, the gap is $300,000 because the kitchen is the limiting resource.

Capacity Gaps at Grandmother's Chicken Restaurant

	Annual Estimates ($000)				
Projections	1990	1991	1992	1993	1994
Demand	900	1000	1100	1200	1300
Capacity gaps:					
Kitchen (current capacity, $800,000)	100	200	300	400	500
Dining (current capacity, $1,050,000)	—	—	50	150	250

Step 3: Develop Alternatives.   The next step is to develop alternative plans to cope with projected gaps. One alternative, called the **base case**, is to do nothing and simply lose orders from any demand that exceeds current capacity. Other alternatives include the various short-term options, a number of timing/sizing options for adding new capacity, and expanding at a different location.

Step 4: Evaluate the Alternatives.   In this final step, the manager evaluates each alternative, both quantitatively and qualitatively. Quantitatively, the manager estimates the change in cash flows over the forecast time horizon, compared to the base case. **Cash flow** is the difference between the flow of funds into (inflow) and out of (outflow) an organization over a period of time, including revenues, costs, and changes in assets and liabilities. The manager is concerned here only with calculating the cash flows really attributable to the project. Because these cash flows extend over several years, the net present value technique should be used to reflect the time value of money. (See Supplement 1.)

Qualitatively, the manager has to look at how each alternative fits the overall capacity strategy and other aspects of the business that are not expressed well by financial analysis. Of particular concern might be uncertainties about demand, competitive reaction, technological change, and cost estimates. Some of these factors cannot be quantified and have to be assessed on the basis of judgment and experience. Others can be quantified, and the manager can analyze each alternative, using different assumptions about the future. One set of assumptions could represent a worst case, where demand is less, competition is greater, and construction costs are higher than expected. Another set of assumptions could represent the most optimistic view of the future. This type of "what-if" analysis gives managers an idea of the implications of each alternative before making a final choice.

APPLICATION 7.3

One alternative for Grandmother's Chicken Restaurant is to expand both the kitchen and dining room now, bringing their capacities up to $1,300,000 of sales per year. The initial investment required would be $200,000, made at the end of 1989. Kathryn estimates that her before-tax profit is 20 percent. She arrived at that figure by determining that, for each $100 of sales, $60 are required to cover variable costs and $20 to cover fixed costs (other than depreciation).

What are the before-tax cash flows from this project for the next five years, compared to those of the base case of doing nothing?

Solution

The following table shows the incremental cash inflows and outflows through 1994. The inflows are the profits from added sales made possible by expansion. For example, compared to the base case of losing all sales over $800,000, the expansion adds $300,000 in sales in 1992. To convert added sales into cash inflows, simply multiply added sales by the profit margin (20 percent). The only cash outflow through 1994 is the $200,000 initial investment.

Because we are evaluating an alternative that provides enough capacity to meet all demand through 1994, the added sales are identical to the capacity gaps in Application 7.2. That wouldn't be true if the new capacity were smaller than expected demand in any year. To find the added sales in that case, we

Before-Tax Cash Flows for Expanding to $1,300,000 Capacity

Projections	Annual Estimates ($000)					
	1989	1990	1991	1992	1993	1994
Added sales	—	100	200	300	400	500
Cash inflow	—	20	40	60	80	100
Cash outflow	−200	—	—	—	—	—
Combined cash flow	−200	20	40	60	80	100

subtract the base-case capacity from the new capacity (rather than the demand). The result is smaller than the capacity gap.

MAINTENANCE ▲

Maintaining production capacity, regardless of the degree of capital intensity, is essential to a firm's long-term growth and profitability. The broad view of system maintenance includes, but isn't limited to, machine maintenance. As you will learn later in this section, managers have a number of other options for sustaining a specific output rate. Maintenance also is of paramount importance in many service industries. As recent headlines suggest, maintenance plays a central role in airline operations. The cost of failure is measured in passenger lives lost. Telephone and financial services are other good examples, because their operations are information based and rely on computerized networks that must be virtually 100 percent reliable.

Managers must find ways to ensure adequate output performance, while minimizing the sum of two basic costs: maintenance activity costs and system failure costs. **Maintenance activity costs** are the costs incurred in attempting to maintain the desired output rate. For an automobile, these costs would include oil changes, tune-ups, oil and air filter replacements, brake jobs, and tire balancing, rotation, and replacement. As maintenance intensity increases, so do maintenance activity costs.

System failure costs are the costs incurred when the system fails to perform at the desired output rate. System failures never happen at a "good" time, typically require emergency measures, and can be extremely costly. Hundreds of workers on a production line can be idled, along with expensive equipment, and customer shipments delayed just because one machine fails. Long-term disruption may require a firm to contract out work, rent equipment, hire more skilled workers, or pay overtime premiums. Disrupted or reduced customer services can also be costly in terms of dissatisfied customers, canceled orders, and lost revenue. Even in our automobile example, engine failure resulting in a stalled car on a country road or an accident caused by faulty brakes can be very expensive.

Varying Maintenance Intensity

Managers choose among several ways of intensifying maintenance effort. Managerial Practice 7.4 illustrates two ways: preventive maintenance and equipment design. Table 7.3, on p. 246, lists all the broad options. Some reduce the frequency of breakdowns, others reduce the severity of a breakdown once it occurs, and some do both.

Preventive Maintenance.   Activities that forestall machine breakdowns, including adjustments, replacements, and basic cleanliness, are called **preventive maintenance**. It can be performed after a certain elapsed time or after so many hours of actual machine use. Preventive maintenance can also be triggered by inspections. For example, pilots and ground crews have checklists, which they use to spot problems. Preventive maintenance is an especially attractive option when the time between failures is fairly predictable and when breakdown costs are particularly high. Breakdowns are very costly to high-volume, capital-intensive manufacturers who operate with minimum inventory and work-force buffers. Such manufacturers use preventive maintenance extensively. Toyota operates only two production shifts, leaving a four-hour interval after each shift for preventive maintenance. This practice allows the production shifts to run with a minimum of disruption.

MANAGERIAL PRACTICE 7.4

Hi-Tech Maintenance Pays Off

Preventive Maintenance at GM

General Motors has a new diagnostic system for preventive maintenance. Any shop-floor worker can troubleshoot a machine simply by touching it with a handheld device. Vibration data go into a personal computer and are analyzed using some 1000 "rules" of vibration analysis. The system suggests preventive repair only when needed and avoids fixing parts that aren't ailing.

Equipment Design at Kellogg

Kellogg Company has introduced a steady stream of new products since the early 1980s, some of which depend on new high-tech manufacturing processes. For example, the Raisin Squares cereal has a raisin puree placed inside each nugget. New equipment has proven trouble-free. One reason: Kellogg makes sure the machines are reliable before installing them. The company has an experimental plant in London, Ontario, where it first tests new equipment and production processes.

Sources: "If Your Lathe Is in a Lather, Maybe Charley Can Help," *Business Week*, May 9, 1988; "The Health Craze Has Kellogg Feeling G-r-r-reat," *Business Week*, March 30, 1987.

TABLE 7.3   Ways to Vary Maintenance Intensity

Option	Decreases Breakdown Frequency	Decreases Breakdown Severity
Preventive maintenance	X	
Early replacement	X	
Improved equipment and facility design	X	X
Operator involvement	X	X
Maintenance department capability		X
Redundancy		X
Resource flexibility		X
Inventory		X

Early Replacement.   Replacing parts or entire machines before they fail is actually a form of preventive maintenance. A point is always reached where replacing a machine is more economical than continuing to maintain it. Savings in maintenance and operating costs pay for the investment outlay. The extreme case of replacement is the disposable product, such as the throw-away paper plates and inexpensive telephones now on the market. They are simply discarded for new ones, thereby eliminating the need to clean or repair them.

Improved Equipment and Facility Design.   Facilities and equipment designed for ease of maintenance can be designed and built. Although typically more expensive, they have more reliable components and are engineered to minimize maintenance. They are more trouble-free and easier to repair when trouble does arise. Modular TV designs mean quick repair with economical replacement units. Another example is that of standardizing clearances, connections, and lubricants to simplify repairs when equipment fails. A third example is the practice in the electronics industry to preuse or "burn in" components before final assembly. This minimizes the higher than normal chance for component failure during the first few hours of operation, often called the "infant-mortality period."

Operator Involvement.   Breakdowns are often caused by improper operation of equipment. Firms can increase maintenance intensity by providing better operator training. Operator involvement can also yield other benefits. For example, in some large Japanese manufacturing plants, operators' jobs are expanded to include routine inspection and care of their own equipment. They take pride in keeping their equipment in top shape, rather than leaving it to maintenance specialists. This form of horizontal job enlargement can help foster a committed and well-trained work force. This concept applies as well to workers in retail stores or offices.

Maintenance Department Capability. The capability of a maintenance department to help ensure desired output rates by maintaining plant and equipment adequately is reflected in several ways. Crew size might be much larger than needed *on average* because of breakdown unpredictability. Although this type of capacity cushion is expensive, the response to emergencies is quick. Another way is to include highly trained technicians and state-of-the-art maintenance equipment in the maintenance effort. The department can then meet most contingencies, rather than having to turn to outside contractors. A third way is to emphasize maintenance scheduling. The department may have a sophisticated computer-based system to forecast workloads by skill category and schedule preventive maintenance, while allowing for quick reaction to breakdowns.

Redundancy. A backup capability, coming either from extra machines or from extra components within a machine, to reduce the effects of breakdowns, is called **redundancy.** We have already described how a capacity cushion helps absorb disruptions from equipment failures. Thus backup equipment that provides extra capacity is one form of redundancy.

Redundancy can take another form: Equipment can be designed with extra components so that if one component fails, the other can be activated. This type of design increases equipment **reliability**, which is the probability that a component or system will work at any time. Without redundancy, all components must work for the entire system to work. The reliability of a system with n different components is:

$$r_s = (r_1)(r_2) \ldots (r_j) \ldots (r_n)$$

where

$$r_s = \text{reliability of the system}$$
$$r_j = \text{reliability of the } j\text{th component}$$

When redundancy is provided for one of the components, say the jth component, then r_j must be replaced in the preceding equation by a larger number r_j':

$$r_j' = 1.0 - (1.0 - r_j)^m$$

where

$$r_j' = \text{probability that at least one of the } m$$
$$\text{components of type } j \text{ will work at any time}$$
$$(1.0 - r_j)^m = \text{joint probability that all } m \text{ components}$$
$$\text{of type } j \text{ will fail}$$
$$m = \text{total number of components of type } j$$
$$\text{designed in the equipment}$$

APPLICATION 7.4

A machine has three basic components, with individual reliabilities of 0.78, 0.99, and 0.95, respectively. What is the machine's reliability with no redundancy? What is its reliability with two backups (a total of three units) of the first component?

Solution

The machine's reliability without redundancy is only 0.73, or significantly less than that of the individual components:

$$r_s = (0.78)(0.99)(0.95) = 0.73$$

When two backups are added for the first component, the machine's reliability increases to 0.93:

$$r_s = [1.0 - (1.0 - 0.78)^3](0.99)(0.95) = 0.93$$

Resource Flexibility.   The greater the flexibility of maintenance resources—workers and equipment—the quicker they can respond to service demands. Conversely, specialization results in more capacity bottlenecks. Resource flexibility also applies to the production process itself. If products can be rerouted to alternative operations when equipment at one operation fails, the consequences of a breakdown are less. Cross-trained workers can move to other operations when their own equipment fails, rather than waiting idly until it has been repaired. Of course, too much flexibility can prevent workers from mastering each job. Improper equipment operation can create even more maintenance problems.

Inventory.   Holding spare parts in inventory shortens the time needed to fix a breakdown. This is a particularly good idea for items that have long delivery lead times, have a high rate of usage, and are relatively inexpensive, especially if downtime costs are high. Production inventories can help meet customer demand until production is restored. Air Force policy on jet engines is a good example. In order to have the planes ready when needed, a mix of repaired engines and new components is kept in inventory. Inventories are held both at bases where the aircraft are stationed and at a central depot.

SOLVED PROBLEMS

1. You have been asked to put together a capacity plan for a critical bottleneck operation at the Surefoot Sandal Company. Your capacity measure is number of machines. Three products (men's, women's, and children's sandals) are manufactured. The time standards (processing and setup), lot sizes, and demand forecasts are given in Table 7.4. The firm operates two eight-

TABLE 7.4

Product	Time Standards		Lot Size (pairs/lot)	Demand Forecast (000 pairs/yr)
	Processing (hr/pair)	Setup (hr/lot)		
Men's	0.05	0.5	240	80
Women's	0.10	2.2	180	60
Children's	0.02	3.8	360	120

hour shifts, five days per week, and 50 weeks per year. Experience shows that a capacity cushion of 5 percent will suffice.

(a) How many machines are needed?

(b) If the operation currently has two machines, what is the capacity gap?

Solution

(a) Summing up the machine hour requirements for all three products, we get

$$R = [80{,}000(0.05) + (80{,}000/240)(0.5)]$$
$$+ [60{,}000(0.10) + (60{,}000/180)(2.2)]$$
$$+ [120{,}000(0.02) + (120{,}000/360)(3.8)]$$
$$= 14567$$

The number of hours provided per machine are:

$$H = (2 \text{ shifts/day} \times 8 \text{ hours/shift} \times 250 \text{ days/year})\left(1.0 - \frac{5}{100}\right) = 3800$$

The capacity requirement is 3.8 machines, which rounds up to 4 machines:

$$M = \frac{14567}{3800} = 3.8 \quad \text{or} \quad 4 \text{ machines}$$

(b) The capacity gap is 1.8 machines (or $3.8 - 2$). Two more machines should be purchased, unless management decides on short-term options to help fill the gap.

2. Another capacity alternative for Grandmother's Chicken Restaurant (see Application 7.3) is a two-stage expansion. This alternative expands only the kitchen now, bringing its capacity up to that of the dining area ($1,050,000 of sales per year). If sales in 1990 and 1991 live up to expectations, expand both the kitchen and the dining room at the *end* of 1992 up to the $1,300,000 sales level. The initial investment would be $80,000 at the end of 1990 and an additional investment of $170,000 at the end of 1992. What are the before-tax cash flows for this alternative through 1994, compared with the base case of no expansion?

Solution

Table 7.5 shows the cash inflows and outflows. The 1992 cash flow is unusual in two respects. First, the added sales is only $250,000 (or 1,050,000 − 800,000) instead of $300,000 (or 1,100,000 − 800,000), since the restaurant's capacity falls somewhat short of demand. Second, there is an outflow at the end of 1992, when the second-stage expansion occurs.

TABLE 7.5

Projection	Annual Estimate ($000)					
	1989	1990	1991	1992	1993	1994
Added sales	—	100	200	250	400	500
Cash inflow	—	20	40	50	80	100
Cash outflow	− 80	—	—	− 170	—	—
Combined cash flow	− 80	20	40	− 120	80	100

3. A rocket has two different components that can fail. The reliability of the first component is 0.80, and 0.70 for the second component. What is the reliability of the rocket, if the designer provides redundancy with a backup for each component?

Solution

The reliability of the first component, when enhanced with a backup, becomes

$$r_1' = 1.0 - (1.0 - 0.80)^2 = 0.96$$

$$r_2' = 1.0 - (1.0 - 0.70)^2 = 0.91$$

Therefore the whole rocket's reliability is 0.87, or

$$r_s = (r_1')(r_2') = (0.96)(0.91) = 0.87$$

FORMULA REVIEW

1. Capacity requirements:

$$R = \sum_{i=1}^{M} D_i p_i + \sum_{i=1}^{M} \frac{D_i}{Q_i} s_i$$

$$H = N\left(1 - \frac{C}{100}\right)$$

$$M = \frac{R}{H}$$

2. Reliability:

$$r_s = (r_1)(r_2) \ldots (r_j) \ldots (r_n)$$
$$r_j' = 1.0 - (1.0 - r_j)^m$$

CHAPTER HIGHLIGHTS

- Operations managers must plan for timely acquisition of additional capacity and maintenance of desired output levels. Both of these decision areas are crucial to an organization's long-term success.

- Long-term capacity planning involves investment in new facilities and equipment. Maintenance strives to keep existing facilities and equipment in good operating condition.

- Capacity can be stated in terms of either input or output measures. Complications in measuring capacity arise from changes in product mix and differentiation of peak and sustained capacity levels.

- Economies of scale derive from spreading fixed costs, reduced construction costs, and process advantages. Diseconomies of scale have forced many firms to focus their operations and move to smaller, rather than larger, facilities.

- Capacity cushions can be small or large, depending on the cost of unused capacity, required delivery times, supply uncertainties, and uneven or uncertain demand.

- Three capacity strategies are expansionist, wait-and-see, and follow-the-leader. The expansionist strategy is attractive when there are economies of scale, learning effects, and a chance for preemptive marketing. The wait-and-see strategy minimizes risk by relying more on short-term options. The follow-the-leader strategy maintains the current balance between competitors.

- Capacity choices must be linked to other operations management choices, ranging from competitive priorities to scheduling.

- The four steps in capacity planning are: (1) estimate capacity requirements; (2) identify gaps; (3) develop alternatives; and (4) evaluate the alternatives.

- Managers must balance maintenance activity costs and system failure costs. The intensity of maintenance can be varied in eight major ways: preventive maintenance, early replacement, improved equipment design, operator involvement, maintenance department capability, redundancy, resource flexibility, and inventory.

KEY TERMS

average utilization rate 229
base case 242
capacity 227
capacity cushion 234
cash flow 243
diseconomies of scale 231
economies of scale 231
focused facilities 233
maintenance 227
maintenance activity costs 244
preventive maintenance 245
redundancy 247
reliability 247
system failure costs 244

STUDY QUESTIONS

1. What factors make capacity planning a particular challenge?

2. What are the different ways of responding to capacity gaps?

3. What capacity measure would you recommend for a drive-in window at a bank? For an entire toy manufacturing plant? What complications might you run into when using these measures?

4. What types of estimates and forecasts are needed for capacity planning? For maintenance planning?

5. A young boy has set up a lemonade stand on the corner of Speedway and Park. Temperatures get up to 110° during the summer. The intersection is near a major university and a large construction site. Explain to this young entrepreneur how his business might benefit from economies of scale.

6. Explain to the young entrepreneur in Question 5 the sorts of things that might lead to diseconomies of scale.

7. You are the manager of a small messenger service. Currently your average messenger utilization rate is 96 percent. Adding another messen-

ger would reduce your average utilization rate to 85 percent. What factors would you consider in making a decision about this capacity increase?

8. Application 7.3 describes a one-stage expansion for Grandmother's Chicken Restaurant, whereas Solved Problem 2 describes a two-stage expansion. Which alternative resembles the expansionist strategy? The wait-and-see strategy? Qualitatively, what factors favor the wait-and-see strategy?

9. Table 7.3 lists the eight managerial options for system maintenance. Discuss each of them as they would relate to the operation of a ten-speed bicycle.

10. How does operator involvement relate to maintenance and job design? Worker flexibility?

11. Suppose that your automobile is 10 years old. Discuss the cost trade-offs you would consider for replacing the car now versus waiting another year. Also, do you think that the best preventive maintenance interval would change if you decided to replace your automobile every two years instead of every 10 years? Explain.

PROBLEMS

Review Problems

1. A critical machining center makes three basic components that go into Speakman Manufacturing Company's products. Table 7.6 shows the time standards, lot sizes, and demand forecasts for the components. Because of demand uncertainties, the operations manager obtained three demand forecasts (pessimistic, expected, and optimistic). The machine center operates on two eight-hour shifts, five days per week, 52 weeks per year. The manager believes that a 10-percent capacity cushion is best.

a. What is the minimum number of machines needed? The expected number? The maximum number?

b. If the operation currently has three machines and the manager is willing to expand capacity by 20 percent through short-term options, what is the capacity gap?

2. Up, Up and Away is a producer of kites and windsocks. Relevant data on a bottleneck operation in the shop for the upcoming fiscal year are given in the following table.

Item	Kites	Windsocks
Demand forecast (units/yr)	20,000	9,000
Lot size (units)	25	75
Standard processing time (hr/unit)	0.25	0.75
Standard setup time (hr/lot)	2	3

The shop works two shifts per day, eight hours per shift, 250 days per year. There currently are four machines and a 20-percent capacity cushion is desired. How many machines should be purchased to meet the upcoming year's demand, without resorting to any short-term capacity solutions?

3. Sleep Tight Motel has the opportunity to purchase an adjacent tract of land. Expanding the facility onto this land would increase the motel's capacity from the current 1989 sales level of $515,000 per year to $600,000 per year. Sleep Tight's before-tax profit is 20 percent of sales. Based on the following demand forecasts, what before-tax cash inflows will the expansion produce for the next decade?

TABLE 7.6

Component	Time Standards Processing (hr/unit)	Time Standards Setup (hr/lot)	Lot size (units/lot)	Demand Forecast (000 units/yr) Pessimistic	Demand Forecast (000 units/yr) Expected	Demand Forecast (000 units/yr) Optimistic
A	0.10	1.2	60	18	20	28
B	0.25	5.3	80	13	15	20
C	0.09	9.1	120	20	30	45

Year	Annual Demand ($000)	Year	Annual Demand ($000)
1990	517	1995	570
1991	520	1996	595
1992	525	1997	625
1993	535	1998	660
1994	550	1999	700

4. Amanda Sharp owns a retail store that is experiencing significant growth. She is trying to decide whether to expand its capacity from $800,000 in sales per quarter currently to about the $900,000 level. The before-tax profit from additional sales is 25 percent. Sales are seasonal, with peaks in the spring and summer quarters. Demand forecasts expressed in sales per quarter are

Year	Quarter	Sales per Quarter ($000)
1990	1	720
	2	850
	3	830
	4	700
1991	1	850
	2	940
	3	920
	4	830

Demand in 1992 and beyond is expected to exceed $900,000 per quarter. If Amanda expands toward the end of 1989, the slowest part of the year, how much will her quarterly before-tax cash flow increase through 1991? Beyond 1991?

5. The semiconductor in a machine has three components, each with its own reliability. Component 1 has a reliability of 0.99, component 2, 0.92, and component 3, 0.88.

    a. What is the reliability of the semiconductor?

    b. If one backup is provided for component 2, and two backups for component 3, what is the reliability of the new system?

6. An intricate part for a commercial airliner has a reliability of only 0.75, despite all engineering efforts to increase it. If redundancy is provided with three backups, giving a total of four replicates, would you want to be a passenger on that plane?

Advanced Problems

Problems 7–17 require prior reading of Supplement 1; Problem 12, Supplement 2; Problems 13–15, Supplement 4; and Problems 16 and 17, Supplement 5. A computer package is helpful for problems 7–15.

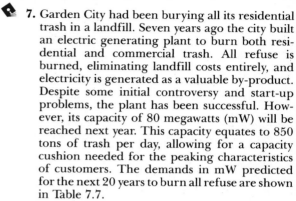

7. Garden City had been burying all its residential trash in a landfill. Seven years ago the city built an electric generating plant to burn both residential and commercial trash. All refuse is burned, eliminating landfill costs entirely, and electricity is generated as a valuable by-product. Despite some initial controversy and start-up problems, the plant has been successful. However, its capacity of 80 megawatts (mW) will be reached next year. This capacity equates to 850 tons of trash per day, allowing for a capacity cushion needed for the peaking characteristics of customers. The demands in mW predicted for the next 20 years to burn all refuse are shown in Table 7.7.

    The mayor is considering three alternatives.

Alternative 1: Expand enough at the end of year 0 to last for 20 years. This means a 50-mW increase (130 − 80).

Alternative 2: Expand at the end of year 0 and at the end of year 10.

Alternative 3: Expand at the end of years 0, 5, 10, and 15.

Each alternative would provide 130 mW of capacity at the end of 20 years. The value of the plant at that time will be the same, regardless of the alternative chosen. There are significant economies of scale in construction costs: A 12.5-mW expansion costs $25 million; a 25-mW expansion costs $36 million; and a 50-mW expansion costs only $54 million. The level of future interest rates is uncertain, leading to uncertainty about the return that can be expected from

TABLE 7.7

Year	Capacity	Year	Capacity	Year	Capacity
0	80	7	97.5	14	115
1	82.5	8	100	15	117.5
2	85	9	102.5	16	120
3	87.5	10	105	17	122.5
4	90	11	107.5	18	125
5	92.5	12	110	19	127.5
6	95	13	112.5	20	130

the expansions. The mayor believes that the necessary return could be as low as 10 percent and as high as 14 percent. (See Supplement 1.)

    a. Compute the cash flows for each alternative, compared to a base case of doing nothing. (*Note:* As a municipal utility, the operation pays no taxes.)

    b. Which of the three alternatives minimizes the present value of construction costs over the next 20 years, if the discount rate is 10 percent? 14 percent?

    c. Since the decision involves public policy and compromise, what political considerations does the mayor face?

8. Complete the financial analysis begun in Problem 4. Amanda estimates construction costs at $200,000 and the investment life at 20 years. She uses straight-line depreciation ($10,000 per year), pays taxes of 40 percent, and expects a return on her investment of at least 16 percent. Salvage value is assumed to be negligible.

    a. How much do 1990 after-tax profits increase if Amanda expands at the end of 1989? Does this benefit exceed the $32,000 opportunity cost [$200,000(0.16)] of investing at that time?

    b. Repeat (a) for an expansion at the end of 1990, calculating the after-tax cash inflow in 1991.

    c. Calculate the net present value of the 1990 expansion, recognizing the cash inflows for 1991 through 2010 (20 years). Should Amanda plan to expand at all? Explain.

9. Calculate the net present value for the single-stage expansion in Application 7.3 and two-stage expansion in Solved Problem 2. Which expansion possibility is best? Assume that federal and state taxes are 50 percent of profits and use a discount rate of 0.16. Other assumptions are shown in Table 7.8.

10. Two new alternatives have come up for expanding Grandmother's Chicken Restaurant. (See Problem 9.) They would involve more automation in the kitchen. Both feature a special cooking process that retains the original recipe taste of the chicken. Although the process is more capital intensive, it also drives down the labor cost, so that the before-tax profit for *all* sales (not just the sales from the capacity added) goes up from 25 to 28 percent. This increases the pretax profit by three percent of each sales dollar through $800,000 and by 28 percent of each sales dollar between $800,000 and the new

TABLE 7.8

Single-Stage Expansion	Two-Stage Expansion
Initial investment of $200,000 at the end of 1989	Initial investment of $80,000 at the end of 1989 and an additional investment of $170,000 at the end of 1992
20-year life	20-year life for initial investment and 17-year life for the additional investment
Depreciation of $10,000 per year with no salvage value	Depreciation of $4000 per year through 1992 and $14,000 (or $4,000 + $10,000) per year thereafter, with no salvage value

capacity limit. Otherwise, the new alternatives are much the same as the original two. The two new alternatives are:

- Expand both the kitchen and dining area now (at the end of 1989, bringing capacity up to $1,300,000 of sales per year. The construction cost, including the new automation, would be $336,000 (rather than the earlier $200,000). Assume a 20-year life, straight-line depreciation of $16,800 per year, and the same tax rate (50 percent).

- Expand only the kitchen now, bringing its capacity up to $1,050,000 of annual sales. At the end of 1992, expand both the kitchen and dining area up to the $1,300,000 volume. Construction and equipment costs would be $424,000, with $220,000 at the end of 1989 and the remainder at the end of 1992. The initial investment has a 20-year life and the subsequent investment has a 17-year life. As with the first new alternative, the contribution margin goes up to 28 percent. Annual depreciation would be $11,000 through 1992 and $23,000 thereafter.

With both new alternatives, the salvage value will be negligible at the end of 2009 (20 years from now).

    a. Calculate the net present value for each alternative, keeping the 16 percent discount rate. Which alternative is best?

    b. Should Grandmother's Chicken Restaurant expand with the new or the old technology?

11. A new diagnostic machine costs $70,000 and has a life of 10 years. Riverside Hospital currently has a machine that is six years old. Annual maintenance and operating costs vary with the age of such a machine. The following information was gathered. The salvage values are after-tax inflows.

Age (yr)	Maintenance and Operating Costs ($000)	Salvage Value ($000)
1	12	63
2	14	56
3	16	49
4	18	42
5	20	35
6	22	28
7	24	21
8	26	14
9	28	7
10	30	0

Management is currently evaluating three policies:

- Keep the current machine for another four years, when its salvage value reaches zero.
- Buy a new machine now and every four years thereafter.
- Buy a new machine now and every two years thereafter.

Under all three policies, a new machine is bought at the end of year 4, so cash flows need to be projected only that far. The salvage value, but not a new investment outlay, should be included in year 4.

Using the first policy as the "base case," an analyst calculated the following cash flows ($000) for the policy of replacing the machine every four years.

Year	Investment	Salvage Value	Annual Cost Savings
0	70	28	—
1			24 − 12 = 12
2			26 − 14 = 12
3			28 − 16 = 12
4		42	30 − 18 = 12

a. What are the cash flows from replacing the machine every two years? Remember that the annual cost savings will be higher in the last two years, as maintenance and operating costs drop back to only $12,000 in the third year with the new machine.

b. Calculate the net present value for replacing the machine every two or four years, compared to the base case. Use straight-line depreciation, a discount rate of 12 percent, and a tax rate of 50 percent. Since the annual depreciation in this example will be the same for all three policies, depreciation does not shield the cost savings from taxes. Should the machine be replaced now? If so, is it better to wait two years or four years until the next replacement?

12. The following is a linear programming model for analyzing the product mix of a company that produces three products.

$$\text{Max } z: \$0.5x_1 + \$6x_2 + \$5x_3$$

Subject to:

$$4x_1 + 6x_2 + 3x_3 \leq 24 \text{ (machine A time)}$$

$$1x_1 + \frac{3}{2}x_2 + 3x_3 \leq 12 \text{ (machine B time)}$$

$$3x_1 + 1x_2 \leq 12 \text{ (machine C time)}$$

$$x_1, x_2, x_3 \geq 0$$

Let s_1, s_2 and s_3 be the slack variables for the machine A, machine B, and machine C constraints, respectively. Table 7.9 is a partially completed optimal tableau for the problem.

Consider each of the following statements independently, state whether it is true or false, and explain each answer.

a. If an added hour of capacity for machine A costs $0.50, we could *add* 20 hours of machine A capacity at an expected increase in contribution to profits and overhead of $5.56.

b. We could *reduce* machine B capacity by 9 hours and reduce the contribution to profits and overhead by $8, exclusive of layoff and other incidental costs.

c. We could *reduce* machine C capacity by 5 hours without any effect on the contribution to profits and overhead, exclusive of layoff and other incidental costs.

Table 7.9

c_j	$0.5	$6	$5	0	0	0	
Solution Variables	x_1	x_2	x_3	s_1	s_2	s_3	Quantity
	2/3	1	0	2/9	−2/9	0	8/3
	0	0	1	−1/9	4/9	0	8/3
	7/3	0	0	−2/9	2/9	1	28/3
z_j							
$c_j - z_j$							

13. The son of a local hamburger magnate is preparing to open a new fast-food restaurant called Hasty Burgers. He is presently designing the drive-in window operation. Based on the arrival rates at his father's outlets, customers are expected to arrive according to a Poisson distribution with a mean of 25 customers per hour. The service rate is flexible, as the work methods are yet to be designed; however, the service times are expected to follow an exponential distribution. The drive-in window is a single-server operation.

a. What service rate is needed to keep the average number of customers in the service system (line plus being served) to 5?

b. For the service rate from (a), what is the probability that more than 5 customers are in line and being served?

c. For the service rate from (a), what is the average waiting time in queue for each customer? Does this seem satisfactory for a fast-food business? Explain.

🖎 14. The manager of the Lucky Lode Casino is concerned about the number of slot machines that are down for repair. Three employees in the maintenance department are responsible for repairing slot machines. A maintenance worker can fix one slot machine per hour on average, with an exponential distribution. A recent study revealed that an average of 2.7 machines failed per hour according to a Poisson distribution. Each machine that is down costs the casino $60 per hour in lost profits. A new maintenance worker would cost $40 per hour, including wage, fringe benefits, and tools. The manager is not sure whether any new personnel should be added. If some should be added, the manager must also determine how many. Since you had written on your résumé that you are familiar with the multiple-server model, the manager has asked you to analyze the situation. What would you recommend to the manager, based on your analysis?

15. The College of Business and Public Administration at Benton University has a copy machine on each floor for use by the faculty. Heavy use of the five copy machines causes them to fail frequently. Maintenance records show that a machine fails every 2.5 days (or $\lambda_0 = 0.40$ failures/day). The college has a maintenance contract with the authorized dealer of the copy machines. Since the copy machines fail so frequently, the dealer has assigned one person to the college to repair them. This person can repair an average of 2.5 machines per day. Answer the following questions using the finite-source model.

a. What is the average utilization of the maintenance person?

b. On average, how many copy machines are being repaired and waiting to be repaired?

c. What is the average time spent by a copy machine in the repair system (queue plus repair)?

16. The Yellowstone Ferry takes cars from Creepy Hollow to Boynton Corners on the other side of Phantom Lake. The ferry has a capacity of five cars and takes exactly one hour to make the round trip from Creepy Hollow to Boynton Corners and back. If more than five cars arrive during the hour, the excess must wait until the next trip. In such an event, the price of the ticket is discounted 20 percent. The arrival distribution at Creepy Hollow is:

Number of Cars per Hour	Probability
3	0.20
4	0.35
5	0.20
6	0.15
7	0.10

a. Suppose that the owner of the ferry charges $5 per car. Disregarding any revenues that might be generated on the trip back from Boynton Corners to Creepy Hollow, estimate the average hourly revenue for the trip from Creepy Hollow to Boynton Corners. Base your estimate on a simulation of 10 hours using the following random numbers.

26, 03, 39, 26, 86, 48, 33, 70, 77, 01

b. What is the average utilization of the ferry from Creepy Hollow to Boynton Corners?

17. The cities of Abalone and Bennington are connected by a series of large lakes. Ships and barges going from the steel mill in Abalone to the manufacturing plants in Bennington must pass through the Bear Canyon locks and canal, which connect two of the larger lakes. A maximum of two ships or barges per day can traverse the locks and canal. However, vessels arrive at the canal according to the following probability distribution.

Vessels Arriving per Day

Number	Probability	RN
1	0.33	00–32
2	0.34	33–66
3	0.33	67–99

If a vessel arrives at the canal but cannot pass through the system the same day, it must wait overnight in the holding area for passage the next day. Use the following random numbers.

47, 76, 09, 54, 87, 82, 17, 52, 17, 19

a. Simulate the arrival and passage of 10 vessels.
b. Determine the maximum number of vessels held overnight in any one day.

SELECTED REFERENCES

"America's Best Managed Factories," *Fortune,* May 28, 1984, pp. 16–24.

"Avoiding Plant Failures Grows More Difficult for Many Industries," *Wall Street Journal,* January 8, 1981.

Bott, Kevin, and Larry P. Ritzman, "Irregular Workloads with MRP Systems," *Journal of Operations Management,* vol. 3, no. 4, 1983, pp. 169–182.

Bowman, Edward H., "Scale of Operations—An Empirical Study," *Operations Research* (June 1958), pp. 320–328.

Buffa, Elwood S., *Meeting the Competitive Challenge: Manufacturing Strategy for U.S. Companies.* Homewood, Ill.: Dow Jones–Irwin, 1984.

Hardy, Stan, and Lee Krajewski, "A Simulation of Interactive Maintenance Decisions," *Decision Sciences,* vol. 6, no. 1 (January 1975), pp. 92–105.

Hayes, Robert H., and Steven C. Wheelwright, *Restoring Our Competitive Edge: Competing Through Manufacturing.* New York: John Wiley & Sons, 1984.

Miller, Jeffrey, and Aleda Roth, *Manufacturing Strategies: Executive Summary of the 1988 North American Manufacturing Futures Survey.* Research report, School of Management, Boston University, 1988.

Sassar, W. Earl, "Match Supply and Demand in Service Industries," *Harvard Business Review* (November–December 1976), pp. 133–140.

Schmenner, Roger W., *Making Business Location Decisions.* Englewood Cliffs, N.J.: Prentice-Hall, 1982.

Skinner, Wickham, "The Focused Factory," *Harvard Business Review* (May–June 1974), pp. 113–121.

"Small Is Beautiful Now in Manufacturing," *Business Week,* October 22, 1984, pp. 152–156.

Wilkinson, John J., "How to Manage Maintenance," *Harvard Business Review* (March–April 1968), pp. 36–47.

CHAPTER

8

LOCATION

▲ Chapter Outline

Key Questions for Managers

Should we open facilities overseas? If so, how should they be managed?

What factors should we consider to be dominant in picking a new location? Secondary?

Should we expand on site, add a new facility, or relocate the existing facility?

Should we locate near suppliers, the work force, or customers?

How does the quality of life enter our location decision?

Should we be leaders or followers in picking locations for new retail outlets?

Should we organize multiple plants by product line, market area, or process? What about flexibility?

 here is an amusing story about how the CEO of a midwest electric supply company made his location decision. The CEO was flying across the southern United States when the jet's fuel supply indicator suddenly plunged to empty. After frantically radioing for help, the pilot landed at a nearby airport in rural Arkansas. The CEO was not only extremely grateful, he found the small town much to his liking. Within a few weeks, he had designated the town as the site for his new manufacturing plant.

Although similar stories abound, you should not conclude that location decisions are based on executive whim. On the contrary, such decisions have a significant impact on other issues such as operating costs, the price at which goods and services can be offered, and a company's ability to compete in the marketplace. Thus location decisions have many strategic implications. For example, have you ever wondered why White Castle restaurants often locate near manufacturing plants? Or why many competing new-car sales showrooms locate near one another? In the first case, White Castle's strategy is to achieve market segmentation by catering to blue-collar workers. As a result they tend to locate near the target population and away from competitors such as Wendy's and McDonald's. By contrast, managers of new-car showrooms deliberately locate near one another because customers prefer to do their comparative shopping in one area. In each case, management's location decision reflects a different strategy.

Recognizing the strategic impact of location decisions, we first examine overall trends in location patterns and then consider factors that influence location choices. Consideration of strategic issues only may not indicate the best location for a facility. Depending on whether management is planning a single facility or multiple facilities, there may be two very different sets of variables to assess. We will discuss both types of situations.

SIGNIFICANT TRENDS ▲

In the United States, manufacturing firms build more than 3000 new plants and expand 7500 others in a typical year. When we also take into account the construction and remodeling of numerous stores, office buildings, warehouses, and other facilities in the service industries, the impact of location decisions becomes readily apparent. Analyzing location patterns to discover the various underlying strategies is fascinating. In the United States, four location trends stand out: (1) geographic diversity, (2) movement to the growing Sunbelt, (3) movement out of declining urban areas, and (4) internationalization of production. Let's look briefly at each trend.

Geographic Diversity

Today the tendency of industries to concentrate in certain geographic regions is lessening. Electric machinery and electronics remain key industries in New England, as do fabricated metals in the Mid-Eastern part of the country. However, these industries are relatively less important in those regions than they were just a decade ago.

The trend toward geographic dispersion has two primary causes. The first is *improved transportation and communication technology*, factors that reduce transportation costs and facilitate supervision and coordination. For example, modern air transportation can move goods quickly from, say, Kansas City to New York or even from Osaka, Japan, to Kansas City. Telecommunications (voice and data) technology allows facilities to service larger market areas. For example, in service industries, home offices centralize more back-room operations and provide support to branches located near the customer.

The second factor behind geographic dispersion is the *narrowing of regional wage differentials*. The Pacific region (California, Oregon, Washington, Alaska, and Hawaii) still enjoys the highest income per capita. However, this lead slipped from 120 percent of the national average in 1960 to only 111 percent in 1980. The South (Maryland south to Florida and west to Texas) has the lowest income per capita, but has moved up from 78 to 89 percent of the national average over the same two decades.

FIGURE 8.1   The Migration to the Sunbelt

Numbers indicate the degree of manufacturing intensity with (1) the most intense and (8) the least intense.

The two factors mentioned have expanded considerably the number of attractive locations. In fact, many industries now find that the exact location of a new facility is not so critical. Nevertheless, managers must avoid "the big mistake." For example, the National Seating and Dimensional Company relocated to West Virginia for low labor rates but went bankrupt trying to achieve the necessary worker skill levels. Other firms, such as most textile firms that decided to remain in New England, went bankrupt for *not* relocating. Clearly, a poor location decision can negate sound decisions that a manager may make in other areas.

The Move to the Sunbelt

The map in Fig. 8.1 divides the United States into the Sunbelt (Southern and Pacific regions, indicated by color) and the Frostbelt (North Central, Great Lakes, Mid-Eastern, and New England regions, shaded gray). The relatively mild climate of the Sunbelt has enticed many individuals and industries away from the Frostbelt. But climate is not the only incentive. The Sunbelt also offers lower labor costs, less unionism, and possibly a stronger work ethic. As a result, many firms formerly entrenched in the industrial heartland of the Great Lakes and Mid-Eastern regions have opened facilities in the Sunbelt. This migration south and west has been accelerated by declining transportation and communication costs.

According to one forecast, by the year 2000 the Sunbelt will account for 55 percent of the U.S. population, up from 48 percent in 1980. Manufacturing industries are following close behind. Currently, the Sunbelt accounts for more than 40 percent of the nation's manufacturing employment, up from 34 percent in 1967. Nevertheless, the Mid-Eastern and Great Lakes regions still lead in *sales density*, which is dollars of retail sales per square mile. Since service organizations need people with purchasing power, these regions will remain strong markets for service industries.

Decline of Urban Areas

Many manufacturing plants have relocated from crowded, older cities to suburban and rural areas. In fact, over the past two decades more than 50 percent of new industrial jobs in the United States went to nonurban regions. A similar shift is taking place in Japan and the industrialized European countries. Moreover, organizations such as IBM and J.C. Penney have recently relocated their corporate offices. Reasons for these movements include the high cost of living, high crime rate, and general decline of the quality of life in many large cities.

Internationalization of Production

Wage-rate differentials, expanding foreign markets, and improved transportation are breaking down barriers of time and space between countries. For years, U.S. firms have built production facilities overseas. That trend is accelerating, and for the first time, foreign businesses are building facilities in this country in a big way. In 1987, for example, Japanese firms invested $4.7 billion in the United States. Britain, Canada, and West Germany collectively invested a similar amount.

By 1990, U.S. manufacturers plan to increase offshore sales from 10 percent to 14 percent of total sales and to increase offshore purchases from 6.5 to 10 percent of total purchases (Miller and Roth, 1988). Robert E. Mercer, chairman of the Goodyear Tire and Rubber Company, concludes that "in order to compete effectively in the industry today, you have to be a global player."*

By locating in a foreign country, a firm can make its product where it is to be sold. This local presence can increase sales or decrease the threat of import quotas. As the accompanying photo shows, like many other service companies, McDonald's has joined the international trend. In 1985, McDonald's

---

*"A Global Fight in the Tire Industry," *The New York Times*, March 10, 1988.

The strategy behind the internationalization of McDonald's is to marry the advantages of large corporate size with the freewheeling style of smaller franchises. McDonald's franchise owners take charge of their own operations and adapt them to local cultures. In Japan Ronald McDonald was renamed Donald McDonald because the name is easier to pronounce. Franchises in France sell wine, franchises in Australia sell mutton pot pie, and franchises in the Philippines sell noodles. This photo shows one of McDonald's busiest franchises worldwide—the unit in the Ginza, one of Tokyo's principal shopping areas.

opened a record 220 restaurants outside the United States, nearly 40 percent of all new McDonald's locations. The result of all this internationalization is a more linked world economy.

Setting up facilities abroad means adapting to the norms and customs of various ethnic communities. Managers often must reevaluate their on-the-job behavior (such as superior–subordinate relationships), worker attitudes, and hiring and promotion practices, to name only a few. Unfortunately, many managers are poorly equipped to handle such differences. For example, few U.S. managers speak a foreign language. There are currently more English teachers in the Soviet Union than students studying Russian in the United States. Several U.S. franchisers, such as Century 21 Real Estate, Levi Strauss, and Quality Inns International, found that the problems of penetrating British markets went beyond language. Although the language is basically the same, the British conduct business differently.

As Managerial Practice 8.1 illustrates, the general economic and political climates of other countries may have long-range consequences for multinational operations. Managers in charge of overseas plants must deal with unfamiliar labor laws, tax laws, and regulatory requirements. A different economic environment can mean that a seemingly sound policy on automation is actually inappropriate because of an unexpected cost mix. Managers must also decide to what degree to transplant their corporation's production methods overseas and how much control the home office should retain. Decisions differ: To manage offshore units, PepsiCo chose to use local talent, whereas Scott Paper Company decided to send American employees abroad.

FACTORS AFFECTING LOCATION DECISIONS ▲

Facility location is the determination of a geographic site on which to locate a firm's operations. Managers must weigh many factors when assessing the desirability of a particular site. In fact, there are comprehensive checklists covering the myriad factors that could be important in any given situation. As Managerial Practice 8.2 (p. 266) suggests, when GM decided on the location of its Saturn facility, it gave particular weight to union attitudes, outbound transportation costs, quality of life, and the availability of utilities. In order to pare the checklist to a reasonable size, we will disregard those factors that do not meet at least one of two conditions:

1. The factor must be sensitive to location. A factor will influence choice only if management is convinced that the degree of factor achievement will vary among the locations under consideration.

2. Management must consider the difference in degree of factor achievement to be significant. Even a 50 percent differential is not important when applied to a minor cost category.

MANAGERIAL PRACTICE 8.1

A Linked World Economy

- AVX Corporation of Great Neck, Long Island, produces specialized electronic components. The firm's plant in Northern Ireland is successfully competing against aggressive Japanese competitors. Financial incentives from the Irish government and a skilled work force were strong incentives for AVX to establish this overseas plant.

- In 1988, American, Japanese, South Korean, and European firms opened 250 new plants along the northern border of Mexico. Called *maquiladoras*, most such plants assemble foreign parts and reexport the finished product to the United States. For example, Ford assembles Mercury Tracers there, and Chrysler plans to assemble the Plymouth Reliant and Dodge Aries models in new *maquiladoras*. The massive devaluation of the peso in 1982 put Mexico's wages in the ballpark with those of newly industrialized Asian countries.

- Four Japanese electronics companies (NEC, Fujitsu, Seiko, and Kyocera) have manufacturing plants in the Portland, Oregon, area. They manufacture products such as personal computer printers and advanced fiber-optics telecommunications equipment.

Sources: "Business in a Nation in Turmoil," *New York Times*, April 18, 1988; "The Magnet of Growth in Mexico's North," *Business Week*, June 6, 1988; "Chrysler Plans to Shift All Production of 'American' K-Cars to Mexican Plant," *Wall Street Journal*, April 25, 1988; "Why Oregon Suddenly Looks Good to High-Tech Companies," *Business Week*, November 5, 1985, pp. 138–140.

Managers can divide location factors into dominant and secondary factors. Dominant factors are derived from competitive priorities and have a particularly strong impact on sales or costs. For example, a labor-intensive plant might require low wage costs in order to remain competitive. Secondary factors are also important, but management may downplay or even ignore some of them if others are relatively more important. Thus for GM's Saturn plant, which makes many parts on site, inbound transportation costs were not a location requirement or even an important secondary factor.

Dominant Factors in Manufacturing

According to interviews and survey data, five groups of factors dominate location decisions for new manufacturing plants (Schmenner, 1982). The percentage shown for each group represents the proportion of respondents who picked it as a "must" when considering a new location.

1. Favorable labor climate (76%)
2. Proximity to markets (55%)

James Sayer, general manager of the AVX Corporation plant in Colerain, Northern Ireland, chatting with workers who package ceramic capacitors at the factory.

3. Quality of life (35%)

4. Proximity to suppliers and resources (31%)

5. Proximity to company's other facilities (25%)

Favorable Labor Climate. For 76 percent of the respondents, a favorable labor climate was a dominant factor in making location decisions. Labor climate is a function of wage rates, training requirements, attitudes toward work, worker productivity, and union strength. Many executives believe that weak unions or a low probability of union organizing efforts is a major advantage. One indicator of this attitude is that, although 50 percent of U.S. industry is unionized, only 20 percent of new plants being opened have unions. Labor-intensive firms that give strong consideration to labor climate include manufacturers of textiles, furniture, and consumer electronics.

Proximity to Markets. After determining where the demand for goods and services is greatest, management must select a location for the facility that will supply that demand. Locating near markets is particularly important when

MANAGERIAL PRACTICE 8.2

GM's Saturn Plant in Tennesseee

General Motors Corporation needed a location for its new Saturn manufacturing complex for small cars. The facility would be the most integrated car operation in the United States, with many parts made by one of several feeder plants located on site. After considering 60 different location factors and over 1000 possible sites in two-dozen states, GM concluded that Spring Hill, Tennessee, offered the "best balance." Saturn Corporation headquarters and the engineering staff would remain in Michigan near Detroit.

Spring Hill is near Nashville, a metropolitan area offering a variety of educational and cultural activities. Major rail and highway routes provide access to most customers within a 500-mile radius. The state offers a stable economic climate, with adequate water and electric power. Although a Michigan site would be closer to existing suppliers, the facility will make most major parts on site.

Although Tennessee historically is an anti-union state, the Saturn facility is operated by a UAW work force. The contract is quite innovative, providing for an unprecedented degree of worker flexibility and more of a "consensus decision-making" structure.

Source: "GM Is Expected to Put Saturn Complex in Tennessee as UAW Board Votes Pact," *Wall Street Journal,* January 29, 1985.

goods are bulky or heavy and outbound transportation rates are high. For example, manufacturers of products that are relatively inexpensive to produce, such as paper, plastic pipe, and heavy metals all emphasize proximity to their markets.

Quality of Life.   Respondents from all but one of the industrial groups gave quality of life a relatively low rating. The lone exception was high-tech executives, who rated it at the top of their lists. For them, attracting and keeping a good engineering staff is more important than labor environment or transportation costs. Quality schools, recreational facilities, and an attractive lifestyle can make the difference in their location decisions.

Proximity to Suppliers and Resources.   Most respondents rated proximity to suppliers and resources of relatively low importance. The exception was industries dependent on bulky or heavy raw materials. In such cases inbound transportation costs become a dominant factor, forcing these firms to locate facilities near suppliers. For example, it is practical to locate paper mills near forests and food processing facilities near farms. Another advantage of locating near suppliers is the ability to maintain lower inventories.

Proximity to the Parent Company's Facilities.   In many companies, plants supply parts to other facilities or rely on other facilities for management and staff support. These ties require frequent coordination and communication, activities that can become more difficult as distance increases.

Other important factors may emerge, depending on the situation. They include the cost of shuffling people and materials between plants, utility costs (telephone, energy, water), local and state taxes, financing incentives offered by local or state governments, and relocation costs. After management narrows the location choice to a specific site, still other factors arise: room for expansion, land and construction costs, accessibility to multiple modes of transportation, insurance, competition from other firms for the work force, local ordinances (such as pollution or noise control), community attitudes, and many others.

Dominant Factors in Services

For service industries, location is a key factor in determining how conveniently customers can carry on business with a firm. For example, few people would patronize a dry cleaner or a supermarket if they had to travel for miles from their homes to a remote location. Thus the influence of location on revenues tends to dominate all other factors. Residential density, traffic volumes, and income levels are all important aspects of estimating sales and revenue.

Warehouse location is another example. As with locating manufacturing plants, low transportation costs are a requirement. The difference is that proximity to markets takes on greater importance for warehousing and distribution operations. With a warehouse close by, many firms can hold inventory closer to the customer, thus reducing delivery time and promoting sales.

One complication in estimating the sales potential at different locations is the impact of competitors. Management must not only consider the current location of competitors, but also try to anticipate their reaction to the firm's new location. Customers often shop at the nearest stores. Therefore it often pays to avoid areas where competitors are already well established. In other cases, locating near competitors is actually more advantageous. This is clearly the case for new-car sales showrooms, as we noted earlier, and for fast-food chains, as described in Managerial Practice 8.3. The strategy is to create a **critical mass**, whereby the total number of customers attracted to several competing firms clustered in one location is greater than the total number who would shop at the same stores at scattered locations. Recognizing this effect, some firms use a follow-the-leader strategy when selecting new sites.

MANAGERIAL PRACTICE 8.3 ▲

Location Factors for a Fast-Food Restaurant Chain

In just a decade a fast-food restaurant chain grew from one to a thousand restaurants in North America and Japan. The exterior style and interior decor of all units are built to company specifications. Twenty percent of the stores are company-owned, with the rest owned by franchisers. In either case, management considers six primary factors when making location decisions:

1. Area employment.
2. Retail activity.
3. Competitor locations.
4. Traffic flow.
5. Residential density.
6. Accessibility and visibility.

Area employment is crucial because the target market is 20- to 45-year-old workers on their lunch breaks. Areas with shopping centers, manufacturing plants, and large offices are ideal, so long as firms allow employees to take lunch breaks off premises. *Retail activity* in the area is important, as shoppers often decide on impulse to go to the restaurant. Being near *competitor locations*

SINGLE-FACILITY LOCATION ▲

We begin by considering locating only one new facility. If it is part of a firm's larger network of facilities, we will assume that there is no interdependence. This assumption holds in the situation described in Managerial Practice 8.3. That is, a decision to open a restaurant in Tampa, Florida, is independent of whether the chain has a restaurant in Austin, Texas.

On-Site Expansion, New Plant, or Relocation

Management must first decide whether to expand on site, build another facility, or relocate to another site. A survey of *Fortune* 500 firms during the 1970s showed that 45 percent of expansions were on site, 43 percent were in new plants at new locations, and only 12 percent were relocations (Schmenner, 1982). On-site expansion has the advantage of keeping management together, reducing construction time and costs, and avoiding splitting up operations. Eventually however, a plant may expand to the point where focus is lost and

is seen as an advantage. Successful food outlets nearby indicate a good market. By observing competitors, management can assess the volume and direction of customer flows throughout the day and compare the volume with national averages. *Traffic flows* are important because most business comes from people in cars, and 40 percent of sales is from the drive-by window. Management considers a traffic flow of 16,000 cars per 24-hour period good. *Residential density* is another important factor. A population of 20,000 residents within a two-mile radius is considered good and ensures nighttime and weekend business. An upper-middle class population is preferred. *Accessibility and visibility* make up the last dominant factor. Management carefully considers possible backups of traffic into and out of the site during the noon rush hour. The volume and direction of traffic by time of day, traffic signals, intersections, and traffic medians are all part of accessibility. Visibility involves distance from the street and the size of nearby buildings and signs.

Data are collected for each site for management's review, including information on all six dominant factors. For example, a manager must fill out an on-site evaluation form covering 16 characteristics. There are competitive analysis forms and a work map showing the location of current stores, competition, retail centers, plants, and the like. Management relies on judgment and past experience to make a decision about each site. The chain is also considering using more analytical methods to assist with more difficult decisions involving potential market saturation.

diseconomies of scale set in. Poor materials handling, employee "job bumping," increasingly complex production control, and simple lack of space all argue for building a new plant or relocating the existing one.

Those advocating building a new plant cite additional reasons, such as not having to rely on production from a single plant, escaping unproductive labor, modernizing with new production technology, and reducing transportation costs. Most firms that choose to relocate are small (less than 10 employees). They tend to be single-plant companies cramped for space and needing to redesign their production processes and layouts. Over 80 percent of all relocations are within 20 miles of the first location, so as to retain the current work force (Schmenner, 1982).

A Systematic Selection Process

The process of selecting a new facility location involves a series of steps. First, the process is triggered by a perception that opening a facility—such as a new retail outlet or warehouse—in a new location will lead to increased profits. Those responsible for making the decision can be a staff team in a large corporation or the individual owner of a small company.

Next, someone must identify the important location factors and break them into dominant and secondary categories. The analyst begins by considering alternative regions, then narrows the choices to alternative communities and finally to specific sites. The analyst may thoroughly evaluate between 5 and 15 sites. During the evaluation stage, the analyst collects data from various sources, including location consultants, state development agencies, city and county planning departments, chambers of commerce, land developers, electric power companies, banks, and on-site visits.

The data are than analyzed, often using various quantitative models. Management may request a projection of cash flows for all quantifiable financial factors. These cash flows may be broken down into separate cost categories (such as inbound and outbound transportation, labor, construction, and utilities) and separate revenue sources (such as stock or bond issues, sales, and interest income). These financial factors can then be converted to a single measure of financial merit, such as present value or payback (see Supplement 1).

Management then evaluates qualitative factors pertaining to each site. Some managers are content with seeing only the expected performance on each factor. Others prefer to calculate a weighted score for each site, much the same way that a preference matrix is calculated for product planning (refer back to Chapter 2).

The end result is a report containing site recommendations, as well as a summary of the data and analyses on which they are based. In large companies, an audio-visual presentation of the key findings may be presented to top management.

APPLICATION 8.1

A new medical facility, Health-Watch, is to be located in a fast-growing portion of a city. The accompanying table shows the location factors, weights, and scores (1 = poor to 5 = excellent) for one potential site. The weights in this case add up to 100 percent. What is the weighted score for this site?

Weighted Location Score for a Medical Facility's Site

Location Factor	Weight (a)	Score (b)	Weighted Score (a × b)
Total patient miles per month	25	4	
Facility utilization	20	3	
Average time per emergency trip	20	3	
Expressway accessibility	15	4	
Land and construction costs	10	1	
Employee preferences	10	5	___
		Weighted Location Score =	___

Solution

We calculated the weighted scores for the last column as 100 (or 25 × 4), 60, 60, 60, 10, and 50. These weighted scores add up to 340, which can be compared with the total scores for other sites being evaluated. The site with the highest weighted score is best. In this technique, management selects the factors and their weights. The factors and weights will differ from application to application. What is important in one situation can be unimportant or less important in another.

Load–Distance Method

Several of the location factors relate directly to distance: proximity to markets, average distance to target customers, proximity to suppliers and resources, and proximity to other company facilities. The **load–distance method** of evaluating locations deals with proximity factors and utilizes a mathematical model. The objective is to minimize the total weighted loads moving into and out of the facility. The loads are weighted by distance, so you can express the distance between two grid coordinates on a map. (You will also use this approach for layout planning in Chapter 9.)

Distance Measures.   Look at Fig. 8.2 and imagine that point A at coordinates (20, 10) represents a possible location for a new warehouse. Point B at coordinates (80, 60) represents one of the plants supplying the new warehouse.

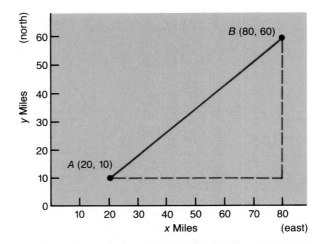

FIGURE 8.2   Distance Between Two Points

What is the distance between the two facilities? The best answer is the actual travel distance. For example, if shipments travel by truck, the distance depends on the highway system and the specific route taken. Calculating this actual travel distance, however, can be time-consuming. For a rough calculation, which is the real purpose of the load–distance method, you can use either a euclidean or rectilinear distance measure.

Euclidean distance is the straight-line distance, or shortest possible path, between two points. In Fig. 8.2, the distance between points A and B is the length of the hypotenuse of a right triangle, or

$$d_{AB} = \sqrt{(x_A - x_B)^2 + (y_A - y_B)^2}$$

where

d_{AB} = distance between points A and B

x_A = x-coordinate of point A

y_A = y-coordinate of point A

x_B = x-coordinate of point B

y_B = y-coordinate of point B

Rectilinear distance assumes that the trip between two points is made with a series of 90° turns, as along city blocks. This distance is essentially the sum of the two dashed lines representing the base and side of the triangle in Fig. 8.2. The distance traveled in the x-direction is the absolute value of the difference in x-coordinates. Adding this result to the absolute value of the difference in the y-coordinates gives us

$$d_{AB} = |x_A - x_B| + |y_A - y_B|$$

APPLICATION 8.2

What is the euclidean distance between points A and B in Fig. 8.2? The rectilinear distance?

Solution

Calculating the euclidean distance, we get

$$d_{AB} = \sqrt{(20 - 80)^2 + (10 - 60)^2} = 78.1$$

The rectilinear distance,

$$d_{AB} = |20 - 80| + |10 - 60| = 110$$

is longer.

Calculating a Load–Distance Score. You can use either of the distance measures* to calculate a load–distance score for any potential location. Simply multiply the loads flowing to and from a facility by the distances traveled. These flows may be shipments from suppliers, between plants, or to customers. They can also represent travel to or from the facility by employees or clients. Adjustments may be necessary, as when an inbound trip is twice as costly per mile as an outbound shipment. Expressed mathematically, the load–distance model is

$$ld = \sum_i l_i d_i$$

where

ld = total load–distance score, summed over all flows

l_i = load (such as tons or number of trips) traveling between the facility being located and location i

d_i = distance (actual, euclidean, or rectilinear) between the facility being located and location i

APPLICATION 8.3

The Health-Watch facility is targeted to serve the seven census tracts shown in Fig. 8.3. The coordinates for the center of each census tract are shown, along with the projected populations. What is the total ld score if the facility is located at (7, 2), using rectilinear distance?

---

*In Application 8.2, the euclidean and rectilinear measures give quite different numbers: 78.1 versus 110. However, our interest is in the *relative* performance of different locations, and we use only one of the distance measures throughout the calculations. When it comes to finding the best location, the distortion caused by using one measure, when the other more closely approximates the actual distance, is relatively small.

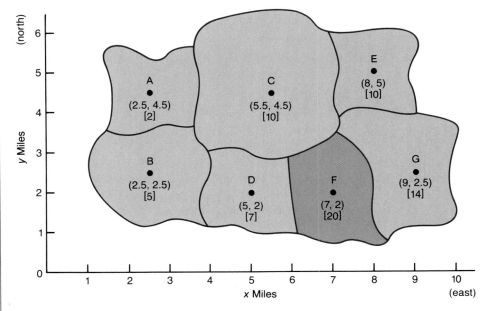

FIGURE 8.3   Census Tracts in a City

Note: Numbers in parentheses are census tract coordinates; the number in the brackets is the population of the census tract in thousands.

Solution

The distance between census tract A at (2.5, 4.5) and the proposed location at (7, 2) is 4.5 miles in the east–west direction, plus 2.5 miles in the north–south direction, or 7 miles. This distance multiplied by the population equals 14, which is the *ld* score for census tract A. The sum of the *ld* scores for all tracts gives us the total *ld* score of 168 for location (7, 2). The results are shown in the following table.

Census Tract	Coordinates x	Coordinates y	Population (000) (*l*)	Rectilinear Distance (*d*)	*l* × *d* (000)
A	2.5	4.5	2	4.5 + 2.5 = 7	14
B	2.5	2.5	5	4.5 + 0.5 = 5	25
C	5.5	4.5	10	1.5 + 2.5 = 4	40
D	5	2	7	2 + 0 = 2	14
E	8	5	10	1 + 3 = 4	40
F	7	2	20	0 + 0 = 0	0
G	9	2.5	14	2 + 0.5 = 2.5	35
				Total *ld* =	168

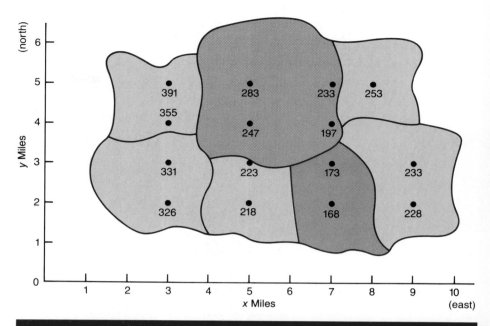

FIGURE 8.4 Load–Distance Scores from Grid Search

It is possible to solve directly for the "optimal" location in Application 8.3.* However, practical considerations rarely allow managers to select this exact location. For example, land may not be available there at a reasonable price, or other location factors may make the site undesirable. Further, the rectilinear distance measure may be unrealistic. For such reasons, the analyst should evaluate an array of location alternatives using the load–distance score method and either a full-grid search or patterned search. Any distance measure can be used with these search procedures.

Full Grid Search. Intuitively, the location that minimizes ld is the one that generates big loads going short distances. Costing out different locations with this model is a relatively simple matter, following some systematic search process. Figure 8.4 shows the results of a full grid search. The total ld scores were calculated for several alternative locations (black dots). Of the points investigated, the (7, 2) location is best because its score of 168 is the lowest of the 15 points investigated. Should an acceptable medical facility site not be available in the immediate area of (7, 2), Fig. 8.4 shows the implications of selecting a

*So long as rectilinear distance is assumed, the optimal site will have an x-coordinate at the median value of l_i ordered in the x-direction and a y-coordinate at the median value of l_i ordered in the y-direction. For more on this *cross-median* technique, see Fitzsimmons and Sullivan, 1982 and Problem 13 at the end of this chapter.

location elsewhere. For example, a two-mile deviation directly north to (7, 4) increases the score to only 197, which is less of a penalty than the same deviation to the east or west.

Patterned Search.   A patterned search is a quicker method. The analyst begins by locating the facility at the center of gravity of the target area. This location is usually not the optimum for the euclidean or rectilinear distance measures, but still is an excellent starting point.† Its coordinates, denoted x^* and y^*, are

$$x^* = \frac{\sum_i l_i x_i}{\sum_i l_i} \quad \text{and} \quad y^* = \frac{\sum_i l_i y_i}{\sum_i l_i}$$

Using the center of gravity as the starting solution, the analyst next evaluates locations in the vicinity, say, one-half mile north, south, east, and west. If one of these locations has a lower load–distance score than the starting solution, the best one becomes the new starting solution. The analyst continues the process by searching in the near vicinity of this new starting solution. Eventually, none of the directional changes uncovers a better solution. The current "starting solution" is then your final solution. Patterned search has the advantage of speed but does not yield the added information that a full grid search does.

APPLICATION 8.4

What is the target area's center of gravity for the Health-Watch medical facility in Application 8.3?

Solution

We begin the patterned search with the following information:

Census Tract	Coordinates x	y	Population (000) *l*	*lx*	*ly*
A	2.5	4.5	2	5	9
B	2.5	2.5	5	12.5	12.5
C	5.5	4.5	10	55	45
D	5	2	7	35	14
E	8	5	10	80	50
F	7	2	20	140	40
G	9	2.5	14	126	35
			$\sum l_i = 68$	$\sum l_i x_i = 453.5$	$\sum l_i y_i = 205.5$

---

†If the distance measure is $[(x_i - x^*)^2 + (y_i - y^*)^2]$, that is, the square of the euclidean measure, the center of gravity location is optimal.

Next we solve for x^* and y^*.

$$x^* = \frac{\sum_i l_i x_i}{\sum_i l_i} = \frac{453.5}{68} = \underline{\underline{6.7}}$$

$$y^* = \frac{\sum_i l_i y_i}{\sum_i l_i} = \frac{205.5}{68} = \underline{\underline{3.0}}$$

The center of gravity is (6.7, 3.0). It is in the general vicinity of location (7, 2), which was found to be best from the grid search in Figure 8.4.

MULTIPLE-FACILITY LOCATIONS ▲

Sometimes a new facility must be located within a network of existing, interdependent facilities. This situation introduces new issues, such as plant charters and how to allocate work to each facility.

Plant Charters

When a company has several plants, management must figure out how best to divide responsibilities among them. At least informally, each has a **plant charter**, which states its responsibilities and focuses its activities. Four types of plant charter are listed below, with the percentage in parentheses indicating frequencies found in actual practice (Schmenner, 1982):

1. Product plant (58%).
2. Market-area plant (31%).
3. Process plant (9%).
4. General-purpose plant (3%).

Product Plant.　A **product plant** is a facility that specializes in a certain product line or family of products. The most popular strategy is for one plant or just a few plants to serve all market areas. Product specialization allows higher volume production than is possible otherwise. This strategy is particularly attractive when (1) production of certain products requires a favorable labor climate or proximity to suppliers and resources, and (2) outbound transportation costs are not excessive. Product plants tend to be nonunion, experience changing product mixes, and are more independent and self-sufficient, having their own staff and engineering capabilities.

Market-Area Plant.　As its name implies, a **market-area plant** is a facility that produces all or most of the products for its assigned market area. Management chooses this strategy when the dominant location factor is proximity to markets. It is practical in situations where heavy or bulky products result in high outbound transportation costs, such as in the paper, plastics, pipe, glass, and oil refining industries. Because producing these commodity-like goods requires little customization, a product-focused strategy and high capital intensity can be used effectively.

Market-area plants also make sense when fast delivery times and customized products (rather than low transportation costs) are crucial. By establishing small beachhead plants for each market area early in the product life cycle, the firm maintains access to specific market areas. Initial costs can be high, but the payoff can be equally high as sales expand.

Process Plant.   A **process plant** specializes in a certain segment of the firm's production. Each plant utilizes only a few technologies. This segregation provides higher volumes for each process, which is important when economies of scale are significant. Some process plants produce components that are sent on to a final assembly plant. However, process plants are utilized more frequently to produce complex products, such as computers. Even if a firm prefers less vertical integration, it may have developed a special technology that gives it a competitive advantage, which is ideal for a process plant. Process plants tend to have the highest capital intensity and are the most dependent on the rest of the corporation.

General-Purpose Plant.   The **general-purpose plant** maximizes product and resource flexibility. Many Department of Defense and NASA suppliers have such plants. Also, thousands of workshops in towns and cities across the country are general-purpose plants. Multiplant firms rarely operate general-purpose plants. Normally, when a firm has grown to the point of having several plants, there is enough repeatability to focus on product, market, or process.

Manual Methods of Location Analysis

When a new facility (such as a branch bank, warehouse, or plant) is to be added to a network of other facilities, location selection becomes more complex. Management must not only decide where to put the new facility, it must also decide how to reallocate work among facilities to take the best advantage of the new operation. Changing work allocations in turn affects the size (or capacity utilization) of the facilities. Thus the multiple-facility location problem has three dimensions—location, allocation, and capacity—which must be solved simultaneously. In many cases, the analyst can identify a workable solution by merely looking for patterns in the data and using trial-and-error calculations.

Manufacturing or Distribution Systems.   In manufacturing or distribution systems, management can choose the sources of demand (plants, warehouses, distributors, retail outlets) that each new facility will serve. One approach is to divide the total market into regions, with a facility located (or to be located) in each region. Dividing the market into regions determines each facility's capacity and work allocation: Each facility serves its region and it must have enough capacity to do so. A goal of management may be to make all facilities similar in size in order to obtain economies of scale. The only remaining decision, then, concerns the specific location for each facility within its region. Single-facility location techniques, such as full grid search or patterned search, can be used for this purpose.

The first division of a market into regions may not be satisfactory. If it isn't, the market should be divided in different ways and the analysis repeated for each alternative. Specifically, the entire process involves the following steps.

1. Divide the total market area into n regions, one for each proposed facility.

2. Based on the demand in its region, calculate the capacity required for each facility.

3. Find the best location for each facility within its region, using a single-facility location technique.

4. Calculate the total load–distance score for the entire market, which is the sum of the load–distance scores for each region.

5. If the solution is acceptable with respect to capacity and the load–distance score, stop. Otherwise, repeat the process for alternative divisions of the market into regions until an acceptable solution is found.

We call this procedure the *allocate-first* method, as the decision on allocating work to facilities comes before the capacity and location decisions. Solved Problem 4 at the end of this chapter illustrates this method.

Service or Retail Systems. In service or retail systems the customers often choose the facility to serve them. This condition requires a different approach to location, allocation, and capacity decisions. Using a simple trial-and-error approach, the analyst would first select some tentative facility locations. Making an assumption about how customers select specific locations, the analyst obtains allocation and capacity estimates for each location. After evaluating the solutions obtained, the analyst can try other reasonable locations in the same manner. Specifically, the entire process involves the following steps.

1. Select n trial locations, one for each proposed facility.

2. Assign estimated customer demand to each facility according to an assumed customer selection process, such as "go to closest facility" or "go to the facility closest to other desired services or stores."

3. Based on the assigned demand calculate the capacity required for each facility.

4. Calculate the total load–distance scores (or some other measure reflecting the ways in which the customers would reach the facilities) for the n facilities.

5. If the solution is acceptable, stop. Otherwise, select new trial locations and repeat the process.

We call this procedure the *locate-first* method because the location decision precedes the allocation and capacity decisions.*

APPLICATION 8.5

Perform one full iteration of the locate-first method for the medical facility analysis begun in Application 8.3. Assume that two facilities, rather than one, are to be built. From the various location factors important to management, the choices have been narrowed to four locations, one each at the centers of gravity of census tracts B, C, D, and G. Work with rectilinear distance.

Solution

Step 1. Let's try locations C and G.

Step 2. We calculate (see accompanying table) the distance from each census tract to each of the candidate locations (C and G). For example, A and C are 3 miles apart (or $|2.5 - 5.5| + |4.5 - 4.5|$). The results show that a facility at C would serve A through E, leaving F and G to be served by a facility at G.

Census Tract	Coordinate x	Coordinate y	Population (000) l	Distance To C	Distance To G	Nearest Facility
A	2.5	4.5	2	3	8.5	C
B	2.5	2.5	5	5	6.5	C
C	5.5	4.5	10	0	5.5	C
D	5	2	7	3	4.5	C
E	8	5	10	3	3.5	C
F	7	2	20	4	2.5	G
G	9	2.5	14	5.5	0	G

Step 3. Measuring capacity as the population served, we calculate C's capacity as 34 (or 2 + 5 + 10 + 7 + 10) and G's capacity as 34 (or 20 + 14).

Step 4. We find the total *ld* score by multiplying the loads by the distances to the nearest facility:

$$ld = 2(3) + 5(5) + 10(0) + 7(3) + 10(3) + 20(2.5) + 14(0) = 132$$

---

*Another approach to retail location problems is a model developed by David Huff (see Fitzsimmons and Sullivan, 1982).

Step 5. The facility capacities are well balanced. Whether the load–distance score of 132 is satisfactory can be assessed only by evaluating several other pairs of locations in the same way (see Problem 10 at the end of this chapter). The results, coupled with other important location factors, lead to the final choice of two locations.

Computer-Assisted Methods of Location Analysis

Many location analysis problems are far more complex than those discussed so far and call for computer assistance. Consider the complexity that a medium-sized manufacturer faces when distributing products through warehouses (often called *distribution centers*) to various demand centers. The problem is to determine the number, size, allocation pattern, and location of the warehouses. There could be thousands of demand centers, hundreds of potential warehouse locations, several plants, and multiple product lines. Transportation rates depend on the direction of shipment, product, quantity, rate breaks, and geographical area.

This kind of complexity requires use of a computer if the analyst is to make a comprehensive evaluation. Three basic types of computer models have been developed for this purpose: heuristic, simulation, and optimization.

Heuristics. Solution guidelines, or rules of thumb, that find feasible—but not necessarily the best—solutions to problems are called **heuristics.** Their advantages include efficiency and an ability to handle general views of a problem. The patterned search procedure described earlier for single-facility location problems and the allocate-first method for multiple-facility location problems are two typical heuristic procedures. One of the first heuristics to be computerized for location problems was proposed more than two decades ago to handle several hundred potential warehouse sites and several thousand demand centers (Kuehn and Hamburger, 1963). Many other heuristic models are available today for analyzing a variety of situations. (See Khumawala and Whybark, 1971.)

Simulation. A modeling technique that reproduces the behavior of a system is called **simulation.** It allows manipulation of certain variables and shows the effect on operating characteristics of interest. (See Supplement 5.) For location problems, simulation models allow the analyst to evaluate different location alternatives by trial and error. It is up to the analyst to seek out the most reasonable alternatives. Simulation handles more realistic views of a problem and involves the analyst in the solution process itself. For each run, the analyst inputs the facilities to be opened, and the simulator typically makes the allocation decisions based on some reasonable assumptions that have been written into the computer program. One of the more sophisticated simulations was used by the Ralston Purina Company to assist in locating warehouses (Markland, 1973). There were 137 demand centers, 5 field warehouses, and 4 plants with their associated warehouses. Random demand at each demand center by product type was simulated over a period of time. Demand was met by the closest warehouse having available inventory. Data were produced by simulating inventory levels, transportation costs, warehouse operating costs, and back orders. The simulation showed that the least-cost alternative would be to consolidate the five field warehouses into only three. Ralston Purina made this change and saved $132,000 per year.

Optimization.   In contrast to heuristics and simulation, **optimization** involves procedures to determine the "best" location. Even though this approach might appear to be preferable, it has two limitations: (1) most optimization procedures utilize more simplified and less realistic views of a problem; and (2) they do not generate a variety of solutions, which is important to do because of the qualitative factors that are being ignored. Undoubtedly, the most sophisticated and realistic optimization techniques have been applied at Hunt-Wesson Foods, Inc. (Geoffrion, 1976). As a result of the analysis, five changes were made in the company's network, reportedly saving millions of dollars.

The *transportation method* was one of the first optimization procedures developed for solving multiple-facility location problems. This technique finds the best allocation patterns for a set of location and capacity choices, assuming that costs increase linearly with the size of the shipments between facilities. The analyst must try several choices, much as with simulation, but is assured that the allocation pattern for each one is optimal. Because of its importance to several areas of operations management, the transportation method is described more fully in Supplement 3. We see next how this technique can be applied to a location problem.

APPLICATION 8.6

The Sunbelt Pool Company has a plant in Phoenix and makes a line of swimming pool accessories that is sold throughout the South. Business is booming and exceeds the plant's 400-unit capacity. The estimated demand at its three major warehouses is 200, 400, and 300 units, respectively. Management is trying to decide whether to build a second 500-unit plant. Atlanta is one location under consideration. Shipping costs per unit from Phoenix to its three warehouses are $5.00, $6.00, and $5.40, respectively. Shipping costs from Atlanta would be $7.00, $4.60, and $6.60, respectively. What is the minimum transportation cost for the entire system if the second plant is built at Atlanta?

Plant	Warehouse			Capacity
	1	2	3	
Phoenix	5.0 / 200	6.0	5.4 / 200	400
Atlanta	7.0	4.6 / 400	6.6 / 100	500
Requirements	200	400	300	900 / 900

FIGURE 8.5 Optimal Transportation Tableau

Solution

Figure 8.5 shows the optimal tableau. Phoenix will ship 200 units to warehouse 1 and 200 units to warehouse 3. Atlanta will fully supply warehouse 2 and 100 units of warehouse 3's demand. The total transportation cost will be 200($5.00) + 200($5.40) + 400($4.60) + 100($6.60) = $4580.

The analysis made in Application 8.6 could be repeated for any other likely plant locations. However, such analyses provide but one input to management's final decision because total transportation costs are not likely to be the only consideration. Thus management might use the preference matrix approach (see Application 8.1) to evaluate each of the locations that is particularly attractive in terms of transportation costs. This final step would account for the full set of location factors.

SOLVED PROBLEMS

1. An electronics manufacturer must expand by building a second facility. The search has been narrowed to four locations, all of which are acceptable to management in terms of dominant factors. The assessment of these sites in terms of seven location factors is shown in Table 8.1. For example, location A has a factor score of 5 (excellent) for labor climate. The weight for this factor (20) is the highest of any.
   Calculate the weighted score for each location. Which location would you recommend?

TABLE 8.1

Location Factor	Factor Weight	Factor Score for Each Location			
		A	B	C	D
1. Labor climate	20	5	4	4	5
2. Quality of life	16	2	3	4	1
3. Transportation system	16	3	4	3	2
4. Proximity to markets	14	5	3	4	4
5. Proximity to materials	12	2	3	3	4
6. Taxes	12	2	5	5	4
7. Utilities	10	5	4	3	3

Scoring key: 5 = Excellent to 1 = Poor.

Solution

Based on the weighted scores in Table 8.2, location C is the preferred site, although location B is a very close second.

TABLE 8.2

Location Factor	Factor Weight	Weighted Score for Each Location			
		A	B	C	D
1. Labor climate	20	100	80	80	100
2. Quality of life	16	32	48	64	16
3. Transportation system	16	48	64	48	32
4. Proximity to markets	14	70	42	56	56
5. Proximity to materials	12	24	36	36	48
6. Taxes	12	24	60	60	48
7. Utilities	10	50	40	30	30
Total		348	370	374	330

2. The operations manager has narrowed the search for a new facility location to three communities. The annual fixed costs (for land, property taxes, insurance, equipment, and buildings) and the variable costs (for labor, materials, transportation and variable overhead) are

Community	Fixed Cost per Year ($000)	Variable Cost per Unit ($000)
A	150	62
B	300	38
C	500	24
D	600	30

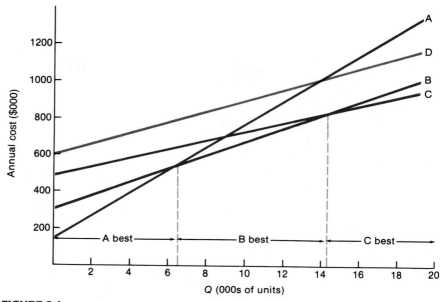

FIGURE 8.6

a. Plot the total cost curves for each community on a single graph. Identify on the graph the approximate range over which each community provides the lowest cost.

b. Using break-even analysis (see Chapters 2 and 4), calculate the break-even quantity between A and B and between B and C.

Solution

a. Figure 8.6 shows that Community A is best for low volumes, B for intermediate volumes, and C for high volumes. Community D is dominated by C, as both its fixed *and* variable costs are higher.

b. The break-even point between A and B is

$$\$150,\!000 + \$62Q = \$300,\!000 + \$38Q$$
$$Q = 6250 \text{ units}$$

The break-even point between B and C is

$$\$300,\!000 + \$38Q = \$500,\!000 + \$24Q$$
$$Q = 14,\!286 \text{ units}$$

3. A supplier to the electric utility industry has a strategy of market-area plants because the product is heavy and transportation costs are high. One market area includes the lower part of the Great Lakes region and the

TABLE 8.3

Customer Locations	Tons Shipped (000)	xy-Coordinates
Three Rivers, Mich.	5	(7, 13)
Fort Wayne, In.	92	(8, 12)
Columbus, Ohio	70	(11, 10)
Ashland, Ky.	35	(11, 7)
Kingsport, Tenn.	9	(12, 4)
Akron, Ohio	227	(13, 11)
Wheeling, W.V.	16	(14, 10)
Roanoke, Va.	153	(15, 5)

upper portion of the Southeastern region. Over 600,000 tons are to be shipped to eight major customer locations, as shown in Table 8.3.

a. Calculate the center of gravity (rounding to the nearest $\frac{1}{10}$ unit of distance).

b. Calculate the load–distance score for this location, using rectilinear distance.

Solution

a. The center of gravity is (12.4, 9.2).

$$\Sigma \, l_i \,=\, 5 + 92 + 70 + 35 + 9 + 227 + 16 + 153 = 607$$

$$\Sigma \, l_i x_i \,=\, 5(7) + 92(8) + 70(11) + 35(11) + 9(12) + 227(13)$$
$$+\; 16(14) + 153(15) = 7504$$

$$x^* \,=\, \frac{7504}{607} = 12.4$$

$$\Sigma \, l_i y_i \,=\, 5(13) + 92(12) + 70(10) + 35(7) + 9(4) + 227(11)$$
$$+\; 16(10) + 153(5) = 5572$$

$$y^* \,=\, \frac{5572}{607} = 9.2$$

b. The load–distance score is

$$ld \,=\, 5(5.4 + 3.8) + 92(4.4 + 2.8) + 70(1.4 + 0.8)$$
$$+\; 35(1.4 + 2.2) + 9(0.4 + 5.2) + 227(0.6 + 1.8)$$
$$+\; 16(1.6 + 0.8) + 153(2.6 + 4.2)$$
$$=\; 2662.4$$

4. Apply the allocate-first method to the medical facility analysis introduced in Application 8.3. Assume that two facilities, rather than one, are to be built. For step 1, divide the service into eastern and western regions. Use the center of gravity in step 3 and rectilinear distance in step 4.

Solution

Step 1. Let facility 1 serve the western region (census tracts A, B, C, and D) and facility 2 the eastern region (census tracts E, F, and G).

Step 2. Measuring capacity as the population served, we calculate facility 1's capacity as 24 (or 2 + 5 + 10 + 7). Facility 2's capacity is much larger at 44 (or 10 + 20 + 14).

Step 3. The centers of gravity are (4.5, 3.4) for facility 1 and (7.9, 2.8) for facility 2, after rounding to the nearest $\frac{1}{10}$ unit of distance.

Facility 1:
$$x^* = \frac{2(2.5) + 5(2.5) + 10(5.5) + 7(5.0)}{2 + 5 + 10 + 7} = 4.5$$

$$y^* = \frac{2(4.5) + 5(2.5) + 10(4.5) + 7(2.0)}{2 + 5 + 10 + 7} = 3.4$$

Facility 2:
$$x^* = \frac{10(8.0) + 20(7.0) + 14(9.0)}{10 + 20 + 14} = 7.9$$

$$y^* = \frac{10(5.0) + 20(2.0) + 14(2.5)}{10 + 20 + 14} = 2.8$$

Step 4. The load–distance score for the two facilities is 131.6.

$$ld = [2(2.0 + 1.1) + 5(2.0 + 0.9) + 10(1.0 + 1.1) + 7(0.5 + 1.4)]$$
$$+ [10(0.1 + 2.2) + 20(0.9 + 0.8) + 14(1.1 + 0.3)]$$
$$= 131.6$$

Step 5. The capacities of the two facilities are quite different. If this imbalance is of particular concern, we can redivide the market and repeat the process until we obtain an acceptable solution.

FORMULA REVIEW

1. Euclidean distance:
$$d_{AB} = \sqrt{(x_A - x_B)^2 + (y_A - y_B)^2}$$

2. Rectilinear distance:
$$d_{AB} = |x_A - x_B| + |y_A - y_B|$$

3. Load–distance score:
$$ld = \sum_i l_i d_i$$

4. Center of gravity:
$$x^* = \frac{\sum_i l_i x_i}{\sum_i l_i} \quad \text{and} \quad y^* = \frac{\sum_i l_i y_i}{\sum_i l_i}$$

CHAPTER HIGHLIGHTS

- Four trends affecting business location patterns are geographic diversity, the growing Sunbelt, the decline of urban areas, and the internationalization of production.

- Despite the advantages of international production, differences in language, politics, and culture introduce new problems.

- Location decisions depend on many factors. For a given situation some factors can be disregarded entirely; the remainder can be divided into dominant and secondary factors.

- Five groups of factors dominate most plant location decisions: favorable labor climate, proximity to markets, quality of life, proximity to suppliers and resources, and proximity to other company facilities. Which ones are "musts" depends on the type of business.

- Proximity to markets, clients, or customers is particularly dominant in service industries. A complicating factor in estimating the sales potential of a location is competition. Having competitor facilities nearby can be an asset or a liability, depending on the type of business.

- Most facility expansions occur on the same site; they are less disruptive and quicker. A point is reached, however, when focus is lost by not adding another facility or relocating the existing one. These alternatives have additional advantages, such as opportunities to modernize processes and reduce transportation costs. Relocation is chosen primarily by smaller firms, which typically move only short distances.

- One way of considering qualitative factors is to calculate a weighted score for each alternative location, using the preference matrix approach.

- The load–distance model brings together concerns of proximity (to markets, suppliers, resources, and other company facilities) during the early stages of location analysis. Either the euclidean or the rectilinear distance measure can be used to determine distances to reasonable locations. These alternatives can be assessed by making a full grid or patterned search. The center of gravity of an area is a good starting point for making a patterned search.

- Firms can choose among four multiplant strategies. Product plants are favored when labor climate or proximity to suppliers (or resources) is crucial. Market-area plants seek to (1) minimize outbound transportation costs; or (2) provide a quick, customized response to customers. With process plants, each plant performs a different segment of the production process. The plants tend to be more capital intensive, with larger economies of scale. General-purpose plants are rare in multiple-plant operations. They maximize flexibility without focusing on the product, market, or process.

- Multiple-facility problems have three dimensions: location, allocation, and capacity. Trial-and-error methods can begin with a proposed allocation and capacity plan and then determine the preferred locations using single-facility techniques. If customers pick the facility serving them, the process must be reversed by using the locate-first method.

- Location analysis for multiple facilities can be extremely complex. A variety of computerized heuristic, simulation, and optimization models have been developed over the last two decades to help analysts deal with this complexity. The transportation method is a basic tool for finding allocation patterns.

KEY TERMS

critical mass   268
euclidean distance   272
facility location   264
general-purpose plant   278
heuristics   281
load–distance method   271
market-area plant   277
optimization   282
plant charter   277
process plant   278
product plant   277
rectilinear distance   272
simulation   281

STUDY QUESTIONS

1. What factors have expanded the range of possible locations?

2. What are the attractions of the Sunbelt for manufacturing plants? What can make foreign locations attractive?

3. Why does an overseas location confront a manager with a different set of problems?

4. Describe briefly the five dominant factors in plant location. For each one, identify a business for which it would be crucial.

5. Which location factor is particularly important to service industries? How is it related to competitor locations?

6. Under what conditions does a firm usually choose to relocate rather than expand on site?

7. What are the advantages of building another plant versus on-site expansion?

8. What process can a firm use to pick a new facility location?

9. Financial analysis, such as net present value or payback, can assist in making a location decision. Explain why it normally is insufficient as the sole basis for making the decision.

10. "Euclidean and rectilinear distances differ. Furthermore, neither is correct in terms of actual distance. Therefore neither should be used for location analysis." Comment on this statement.

11. A full grid search is less efficient than a patterned search, but may be preferable. Why?

12. Under what conditions would each of the four multiplant strategies likely be adopted?

13. At what point does a multiple-facility location problem break down into several single-facility location problems?

14. Why does the manual method for a multiple-facility problem depend on who decides how work is allocated?

15. What are the advantages and disadvantages of heuristic, simulation, and optimization computer models for multiple-facility location analysis?

PROBLEMS

Review Problems

1. Would your recommendation change in Solved Problem 1, if factors 2, 4, and 6 were ignored (that is, given weights of 0)?

2. An analyst collected the following information on where to locate an office complex.

Location Factors	Factor Weight	Factor Score A	B	C
Construction	20	7	8	4
Taxes	10	6	7	6
Business services	10	5	4	5
Real estate cost	20	8	7	3
Cost of living	20	5	7	9
Transportation	10	7	8	6
Community services	10	6	5	6

Scoring key: 1 = Poor to 10 = Excellent

a. Which location should be chosen on the basis of the total weighted score: A, B, or C?
b. If the analyst weights the factors equally, does the choice change?

3. An operations manager narrowed down her choice for a new plant to three locations. Fixed and variable costs are

Location	Fixed Cost per Year ($000)	Variable Cost per Unit ($000)
A	420,000	940
B	1,680,000	210
C	1,050,000	530

a. Plot the total cost curves for each community on a single graph (see Solved Problem 2). Identify on the graph the range in volume over which each location would be best.
b. What break-even quantities define each range?

4. Two location alternatives are under consideration for a new plant: Montgomery, Alabama, and Raleigh, North Carolina. The Montgomery location is superior in terms of costs. However, the owners believe that sales volume would decline because this location is farther from the market, and the firm's customers prefer local suppliers. The selling price of the product is $1.50 per unit in either case. Using the following information, determine which location yields the highest total profit contribution per year.

Location	Fixed Cost per Year	Variable Cost per Unit	Expected Annual Demand (Units)
Montgomery	$1,100,000	$45	20,000
Raleigh	1,600,000	60	25,000

5. The following three points are the locations of important facilities in a transportation network: (20, 30), (40, 60), and (70, 0). The coordinates are in miles.
   a. Calculate the euclidean distances (in miles) between each of the three pairs of facilities.
   b. Calculate these distances using rectilinear distances.

6. The best location found so far in Fig. 8.4 was (7, 2), with a load–distance score of 168. Search in the neighborhood of this point for a better solution, trying (6.5, 2), (7, 2.5), and (7.5, 2). Continue using rectilinear distances.

7. Mailmanna, Georgia, is considering the relocation of its main post office. The current facility has been outgrown and needs modernizing. Besides, a lot of money is unnecessarily being spent transporting mail to and from the facility. Growing suburbs have shifted the population density from where it was 40 years ago, when the current facility was built. In addition, last year a new airport was built much farther from the main post office. Ralph U. Reddie, the current postmaster, asked his assistants to draw a grid map showing the new airport and ten aggregated mail-source points. These aggregated mail-source points are the result of grouping 40 substations in Mailmanna into 10 larger ones. They represent points where mail is picked up and delivered. Two major-highway entry points into the city for mail from surrounding areas were also included. The coordinates and trips per day to and from the 10 aggregated mail-source points, the two entry points (E1 and E2), the airport (A), and the current main post office (M) are shown in the following table. In effect, M acts as a mail-source point even after relocation.
   a. Calculate the center of gravity as a possible location for the new facility (round to the nearest whole number).
   b. Compare the load–distance scores for the location in (a) and the current location, using rectilinear distance.

Mail-Source Point	Round Trips per Day (l)	xy-Coordinates (miles)
1	7	(3, 12)
2	6	(2, 8)
3	3	(3, 3)
4	3	(6, 1)
5	3	(8, 5)
6	2	(13, 5)
7	3	(13, 3)
8	3	(14, 6)
9	2	(15, 10)
10	6	(10, 10)
E1	5	(18, 1)
E2	10	(2, 5)
A	15	(6, 14)
M	3	(10, 3)

8. Reconsider Solved Problem 3 and evaluate the four points that are 0.5 unit of distance north, east, south, and west of the center of gravity. For example, the point north is location (12.4, 9.7). Use rectilinear distances. Does this limited pattern search yield a better solution?

9. A manufacturer is investigating which location would best position its new plant relative to two suppliers (located in cities A and B) and two market areas (represented by cities C and D). Management has limited the search for this plant to those four locations. The following information has been collected.

Location	xy-Coordinates (miles)	Tons per Year (000)	Freight Rate ($/ton-mile)
A	(200, 300)	5	4
B	(500, 200)	4	2
C	(100, 100)	5	2
D	(400, 400)	3	3

   a. Which of the four locations gives the lowest total cost, assuming euclidean distances? *Hint:* The cost of inbound shipments from supplier B is $8000 per mile (4000 × $2) between location B and the new plant.
   b. Which location is best, assuming rectilinear distances?
   c. What is the center of gravity (coordinates)?

10. Reconsider the two-facility problem in Application 8.5. Find, by trial and error, a better solution than opening medical facilities at locations C and G. Limit your search to locations B, C, D, and G, staying with rectilinear distance.

   a. What is the total load–distance score of your improved solution?

   b. How much capacity is needed at each medical facility in your solution?

11. Management wants to locate two facilities to serve two groups of demand points. The following data were collected.

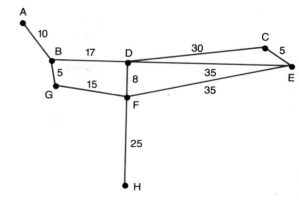

FIGURE 8.7

Demand Point	xy-Coordinates (Miles)	Trips per Day (l)
A	(0, 10)	15
B	(15, 30)	5
C	(20, 15)	10
D	(10, 0)	25
E	(30, 30)	20
F	(40, 45)	30
G	(45, 30)	15

   a. Draw a grid map showing the locations of the demand points.

   b. Use the allocate-first method and divide the points into two groups on a north–south basis. The north facility will serve B, E, F, and G, while the south facility will serve A, C, and D. Let the facility locations be the centers of gravity of the two areas, rounding to the nearest whole numbers. What is the total load–distance score for the entire system, assuming euclidean distance?

   c. Repeat (b) for an east–west division. The west facility will serve A, B, C, and D, while

the east facility will serve E, F, and G. Is this solution better or worse than the one in (b)?

12. A firm plans to open two new facilities that maximize proximity to population centers. It is assumed that customers will go to the nearest available facility. A map of the area is shown in Fig. 8.7. The numbers are the actual distances between centers. Locations B and F are highway intersections, rather than population centers. Population densities and distances between each pair of points are given in Table 8.4. For example, the shortest distance from A to E (and vice versa) is 62.

   a. Management wants to limit the locations to these eight points and is giving particular attention to a plan for locating facilities at C and H. Calculate the total load–distance score for this plan.

   b. Try at least one other plan that you think might improve on this score.

TABLE 8.4

From	To								Population Density
	A	B	C	D	E	F	G	H	
A	0	10	57	27	62	30	15	55	5
B	10	0	47	17	52	20	5	45	0
C	57	47	0	30	5	38	52	63	10
D	27	17	30	0	35	8	22	33	20
E	62	52	5	35	0	35	50	60	20
F	30	20	38	8	35	0	15	25	0
G	15	5	52	22	50	15	0	40	4
H	55	45	63	33	60	25	40	0	20

Advanced Problems

Problems 14–18 require prior reading of Supplement 3, and a computer package is useful for solving Problems 13–18.

13. Continuing to assume rectilinear distance, use the cross-median technique (see earlier footnote) to find the optimal location for the problem in Application 8.3.

   a. First calculate the median value, which is one half the sum of the loads to all facilities.
   b. Order the facilities on the basis of their x-coordinates, starting with the facility having the smallest and ending with the one having the largest. Maintaining this order, add the facility loads until the total reaches or exceeds the median value calculated in (a). Identify the facility that corresponds to the last load that entered the sum. Its x-coordinate is optimal for the new facility.
   c. Repeat (b), except order the facilities on the basis of their y-coordinates, from smallest to largest. The y-coordinate of facility corresponding to the last load entering the sum is optimal for the new facility.
   d. How does the optimal solution compare with the best location shown in Fig. 8.4, in terms of the load–distance score?

14. The Acme Company has four factories that ship products to five warehouses. The shipping costs, requirements, and capacities are shown in the following tables. Use the transportation method to find the shipping schedule that minimizes shipping cost.

	Shipping Cost (S/case) to				
From	W1	W2	W3	W4	W5
F1	1	3	4	5	6
F2	2	2	1	4	5
F3	1	5	1	3	1
F4	5	2	4	5	4

Requirement (000)	Capacity (000)
W1: 60	F1: 80
W2: 70	F2: 60
W3: 50	F3: 60
W4: 30	F4: 50
W5: 40	

15. Consider further the Acme Company situation described in Problem 14. Suppose that the company is contemplating closing F4 because of high operating costs. If this were done, 50,000 units of capacity would be added to F3. The logistics manager is worried about the effect of this move on transportation costs. Presently, F4 is shipping 50,000 cases to W2 at a cost of $2 per case. As the shipping cost is $5 per case from F3 to W2, the manager estimated that closing F4 would increase transportation costs by $150,000.

   a. What is the potential flaw in the logistics manager's thinking?
   b. Make a better estimate of the expected change in transportation cost. Assume that current distribution costs total $410,000.

16. Consider the facility location problem at the Giant Farmer Company described in Managerial Practice S3.1. Find the minimum-cost shipping plan if the new plant were located in Atlanta.

17. The Pelican Company has four distribution centers (A, B, C, and D) that require 50,000, 40,000, 60,000, and 40,000 gallons of diesel fuel, respectively, per month for their long-haul trucks. Three fuel wholesalers (1, 2, and 3) have indicated their willingness to supply up to 80,000, 100,000, and 50,000 gallons of fuel, respectively. The total cost (shipping plus price) of delivering 1000 gallons of fuel from each wholesaler to each distribution center is shown in the following table.

	Distribution Center			
Wholesaler	A	B	C	D
1	1.70	1.60	1.60	1.60
2	1.50	1.80	1.60	1.70
3	1.80	1.50	1.80	1.60

Currently, wholesaler 1 is supplying 40,000 gallons to distribution center B and 10,000 gallons to C. Wholesaler 2 is shipping 50,000 gallons to A and 50,000 gallons to C. Wholesaler 3 is shipping 40,000 gallons to D. Does the present delivery arrangement minimize the cost to the Pelican Company? If not, find a plan that minimizes total costs.

18. The Kramer Corporation produces and markets a certain product, which it stocks in various warehouses throughout the country. Recently, its market research group compiled a forecast

indicating that a significant increase in demand will occur in the near future, after which demand will level off for the foreseeable future. The company has decided to satisfy this demand by constructing new plant capacity. The company already has plants in Boston and Chicago and has no desire to relocate those facilities. Each plant is capable of producing 800,000 units per year.

After a thorough search, the company has developed two alternative sites and three capacity alternatives. Alternative 1 is to build an 800,000-unit plant in Denver. Alternative 2 is to build an 800,000-unit plant in Houston. Alternative 3 is to build a 400,000-unit plant in Denver and a 400,000-unit plant in Houston.

The company has four warehouses that distribute the product to retailers. The market research study provided the following data.

Warehouse	Expected Future Annual Demand (units)
Cleveland (CL)	400,000
Los Angeles (LA)	900,000
San Francisco (SF)	500,000
St. Louis (St. L)	600,000

The logistics department compiled the following cost table that specified the cost per unit to ship the product from each plant to each warehouse in the most economical manner, subject to the reliability of the various carriers involved.

Plant	Warehouse			
	CL	LA	SF	St. L
Boston	$0.12	$0.52	$0.58	$0.20
Chicago	0.08	0.48	0.50	0.07
Denver	0.25	0.33	0.40	0.20
Houston	0.30	0.39	0.42	0.18

As one part of the location/capacity decision, management would like to estimate the total distribution cost for each alternative. Use the transportation method to calculate these estimates.

SELECTED REFERENCES

Chaiken, Jan M., and Richard C. Larson, "Methods for Allocating Urban Emergency Units: A Survey," *Management Science*, vol. 19, no. 4, part 2 (December 1972), pp. 627–636.

Fitzsimmons, James A., "A Methodology for Emergency Ambulance Development," *Management Science*, vol. 19, no. 6 (February 1973), pp. 627–636.

Fitzsimmons, James A., and Robert S. Sullivan, *Service Operations Management*. New York: McGraw-Hill, 1982.

Fulton, Maurice, "New Factors in Plant Location," *Harvard Business Review* (May–June 1971), pp. 4–17, 166–168.

Geoffrion, Arthur M., "Better Distribution Planning with Computer Models," *Harvard Business Review* (July–August 1976), pp. 92–99.

Hamel, Gary, and C. K. Prahalad, "Do You Really Have a Global Strategy?," *Harvard Business Review* (July–August 1985), pp. 139–148.

Harms, Craig S., "A Comparison of Facility Location Techniques." Unpublished doctoral dissertation, The Ohio State University, 1984.

Hayes, Robert H., and Steven C. Wheelwright, *Restoring Our Competitive Edge: Competing Through Manufacturing*. New York: John Wiley & Sons, 1984.

Khumawala, Basheer M., and D. Clay Whybark, "A Comparison of Some Recent Warehouse Location Techniques," *The Logistics Review*, vol. 7, no. 3 (Spring 1971).

Kolesar, P., and W. E. Walker, "An Algorithm for the Dynamic Relocation of Fire Companies," *Operations Research*, vol. 22, no. 2 (March–April 1974), pp. 249–274.

Kuehn, Alfred A., and Michael J. Hamburger, "A Heuristic Program for Locating Warehouses," *Management Science*, vol. 9, no. 4 (July 1963), pp. 643–666.

Markland, Robert E., "Analyzing Geographical Discrete Warehousing Networks by Computer Simulation," *Decision Sciences*, vol. 4, no. 2 (April 1973), pp. 216–236.

Miller, Jeffrey G., and Aleda V. Roth, "Manufacturing Strategies: Executive Summary of the 1988 North American Manufacturing Futures Survey," Boston University, 1988.

Schilling, David A., "Dynamic Location Modeling for Public-Sector Facilities: A Multi-Criteria Approach," *Decision Sciences*, vol. 11, no. 4 (October 1980), pp. 714–724.

Schmenner, Roger W., *Making Business Location Decisions*. Englewood Cliffs, New Jersey: Prentice-Hall, 1982.

Schmenner, Roger W., "Multiple Manufacturing Strategies among the *Fortune* 500," *Journal of Operations Management*, vol. 2, no. 2 (February 1982), pp. 77–86.

Skinner, Wickham, *Manufacturing in the Corporate Strategy*. New York: John Wiley & Sons, 1978.

CHAPTER 9

LAYOUT

▲ Chapter Outline

▲ Key Questions for Managers

Should we have a process, product, hybrid, or fixed layout?

What performance criteria do we need to emphasize?

What centers should we work into the layout?

What type of layout pattern makes sense for our warehouse?

What is the best trade-off between proximity and privacy for our office layout?

Should we have a paced or unpaced line?

What is the desired output rate for our line?

Should we consider a mixed-model line?

What should we do to humanize product layouts?

 e've already considered what products to offer, what positioning strategy to use, what types of work to perform, what types of employees and technology to employ, how much plant and equipment capacity to provide, and where to locate facilities. Facility layout decisions also deal with questions concerning what, how much, and where, translating the broader decisions into actual physical arrangements of people, equipment, and space for the purpose of producing goods and services. In this chapter we examine layout in a variety of settings, along with techniques of layout analysis.

WHAT IS LAYOUT PLANNING? ▲

Layout planning involves decisions about the physical arrangement of economic activity centers within a facility. The goal is to allow workers and equipment to operate at peak effectiveness and efficiency. An **economic activity center** can be anything that consumes space: a person or group of people, a machine, a workbench or work station, a department, a stairway or an aisle, a timecard rack, a cafeteria or storage room, and so on. The term *physical arrangement* raises four questions for the manager:

1. *What centers should the layout include?* Centers should reflect the process design and maximize productivity. For example, a central storage area for tools is most efficient for certain processes, but keeping tools at individual work stations makes more sense for others.

2. *How much space and capacity does each center need?* Inadequate space can reduce productivity, deprive employees of privacy, and even create health and safety hazards. However, excessive space is wasteful, can also reduce productivity, and can isolate employees unnecessarily.

3. *How should each center's space be configured?* The amount of space, its shape, and the elements in it are all interrelated. For example, placement of a desk and chair relative to the other furniture in an office is determined by the size and shape of the office, as well as the activities performed there.

4. *Where should each center be located?* Location, whether in the middle of the facility or in a back room, can have a significant effect on productivity.

The fourth question has two dimensions: relative location and absolute location. Managers must consider both when modifying existing layouts in order to increase productivity. Look at the plan on the left in Fig. 9.1. It shows the location of five departments (A–E) on a floor, where department E has been allocated twice the space of the others. The location of A relative to B is the same as the relative location of C to D, so the distance between A and B is equal to the distance between C and D. Relative location is normally the crucial issue in both materials handling cost and communication effectiveness.

Now look at the plan on the right. Although the relative locations are the same, absolute locations have changed. This modified layout might prove unworkable. For example, the cost of moving department C to the northwest corner could be excessive. Or C could be a dock that must abut a railroad spur, which currently comes in on the northeast side of the building; the cost of extending the spur could also be prohibitive.

FIGURE 9.1   Identical Relative Locations and Different Absolute Locations

STRATEGIC ISSUES ▲

Operations managers must tie layout choices to higher level managerial decisions, as Managerial Practice 9.1 illustrates. For example if a retailer shifts its product plans and competitive priorities, it must communicate this shift through the "spatial language" of facility layout. If the retailer plans to sell higher quality, higher priced merchandise, the store layout should convey exclusiveness and luxury.

Layout has many practical and strategic implications. Proper layout facilitates the flow of materials and more efficient utilization of labor and equipment. Layout can also reduce hazards to workers, improve employee morale, and aid communication between workers or between supervisors and subordinates. Of course, the type of operation will determine layout requirements. Several fundamental layout choices facing managers are: whether to plan for current or future (and less predictable) needs, whether to select a single-story or multiple-story design, whether to open up the planning process to employee suggestions, what type of layout to choose, and what performance criteria to emphasize. Because of their strategic importance, we focus on the last two issues.

Choosing a Layout Type

The choice of layout type depends largely on the firm's positioning strategy. There are four basic types of layout: process, product, hybrid, and fixed.

Process Layout. When positioning strategy calls for low-volume, high-variety production, the operations manager must organize resources (employees and equipment) around the process. (See Fig. 2.5 in Chapter 2.) A **process layout**, which groups work stations or departments according to function, accomplishes this purpose. For example, all drilling equipment is located in one area of a machine shop, or all budget apparel is displayed in one area of a department store. The process layout is most common when the same operation must intermittently produce many different products or serve many different customers. Demand levels are too low or unpredictable for management to set aside human and capital resources exclusively for a particular product line or type of customer. Resources are relatively general purpose, flexible, and less capital intensive. Because the process layout is less vulnerable to changes in product mix or new marketing strategies, it is more flexible. Equipment utilization is high because the requirements for all products can be pooled. In addition, employee supervision can be more specialized, an important factor when job content requires a good deal of technical knowledge.

As you saw in Chapter 2, a process focus (and the accompanying process layout) also has its disadvantages. Processing rates tend to be slower, and productive time is lost in changing from one product to another. More space and capital is tied up in inventory, which is needed to decouple work stations from variations in output rates. The time lags between when jobs are started and finished are relatively long. Materials handling tends to be costly. Variable path devices, such as carts rather than conveyors, must be used because of the diversity in routings and the jumbled flows. A major challenge in designing a process layout is to locate centers so that they bring some order to the apparent chaos of the process-focused operation.

MANAGERIAL PRACTICE 9.1 ▲

Matching Layouts to Strategies

Three large retailers—Sears, Roebuck & Company, K mart Corporation, and J.C. Penney—plan to retain their separate identities while changing their strategies. All three plan to offer better quality merchandise in more attractive stores. They will still offer bottom-of-the-line quality, but the overall price mix will rise.

The focus of the new strategies is layout. These new layouts employ striking graphics and use "racetrack" aisles to guide customers past more of the store's merchandise. Sears will spend $1.7 billion on 622 stores, while K mart is spending $2.25 billion to remodel many of its 1024 full-sized stores. J.C. Penney plans to spend about $1 billion on its 550 largest stores. For example, the

(a)

Product Layout.   When a facility's positioning strategy calls for repetitive or continuous production, the operations manager dedicates resources to individual products. This strategy is achieved by a **product layout**, which arranges work stations or departments in a linear path. Output is balanced to move the product along in a smooth, continuous flow. Operations arranges resources

company spent $3.2 million on its Glenbrook Mall store in Fort Wayne. Planners eliminated some departments, such as paint, hardware, and major appliances, and expanded others, such as apparel, jewelry, luggage, and housewares. As the accompanying photographs illustrate, Penney upgraded its image with better quality carpeting, new mannequins, softer lighting, and more attractive displays of merchandise. Sales have increased 40 percent at the Fort Wayne store.

Source: "Large Retailers Are Changing Strategy and Image by Remodeling Stores, Upgrading Product Lines," *Wall Street Journal*, July 10, 1984.

J.C. Penny upgraded its image and increased its sales by redesigning merchandise displays in many departments. These photos show (a) before, and (b) after, layouts of the men's clothing departments.

(b)

around the product's route, rather than share them across many products.*
An automated car wash is a good example. Product layouts often follow a
straight line, but this arrangement is not always best or possible. In such cases,
managers may opt for L, O, S, or U shapes. A product layout is often called a
production, or *assembly, line.* The difference is that an assembly line is limited to
assembly processes.

Product layouts rely heavily on specialized, capital-intensive resources.
Therefore they are riskier for products with short or uncertain product lives.
Their advantages are the mirror image of the disadvantages of process layouts.
Faster processing rates, lower inventories, and less unproductive time lost to
changeovers and materials handling are examples of these advantages.

One of the mysteries in process layouts—where to locate centers—is trivial
for product layouts. Obviously, if a product's routing is A–B–C, A should be
placed next to B and B next to C in the layout. This arrangement, which simply
follows the product's routing, ensures that all interacting pairs of centers are
as close together as possible (have a common boundary). The challenge of
product layouts is to group activities into work stations and achieve the desired
output rate with the least resources. The composition and number of work
stations are crucial decisions.

Hybrid Layout.　　More often than not, a positioning strategy combines elements of both a product and process focus. This intermediate strategy calls
for a **hybrid layout**, which arranges some portions of the facility as a process
layout and others as a product layout. Operations managers often create a
hybrid layout when introducing group technology (GT) cells, one worker-
multiple machine (OWMM) stations, or flexible manufacturing systems (FMS).
Each of those technologies helps to achieve repeatability, even when product
volumes are too low to justify dedicating a single line to one product. They
become "islands of automation," representing miniature product layouts, as all
resources needed to make the family of parts are brought together as one
center. The rest of the facility represents a process layout. Hybrid layouts also
occur in facilities having both fabrication and assembly operations. Fabrication
operations, where components are made from raw materials, tend to have a
process focus. Assembly operations tend to have a product focus.

A retail store is an example of a hybrid layout in a nonmanufacturing
setting. The manager may group similar merchandise, enabling customers to
find desired items easily (a process layout). At the same time the layout often
leads customers along predetermined paths, such as up and down the "racetrack" aisles mentioned in Managerial Practice 9.1 (a product layout). The
intent is to maximize exposure to the full array of goods, thereby stimulating
sales.

---

*We demonstrate later that some product layouts, called mixed-model lines, can handle several
products so long as their processing requirements are similar.

Fixed-Position Layout. The fourth basic type of layout is the **fixed-position layout**. In this arrangement, the product is fixed in place; workers, along with their tools and equipment, come to the product to work on it. This type of layout makes sense when the product is particularly massive or difficult to move, as in shipbuilding, assembling locomotives, making huge pressure vessels, building dams, or repairing home furnaces. A fixed-position layout minimizes the number of times that the product must be moved and often is the only feasible solution.

Performance Criteria

Another fundamental choice to be made in layout planning is that of performance criteria. The operations manager must use personal judgment in deciding what factors to emphasize in different situations. Table 9.1 shows the performance criteria that get the most attention in four different settings.

Capital Investment. Floor space, equipment needs, and inventory levels depend in part on whether management selects a process or product layout. When volumes are low, higher resource utilization is possible with a process focus. This focus reduces equipment and space needs, although management must also consider the possible disadvantage of more space and investment in inventory. Capital investment is an important criterion in all settings. If the objective is to increase privacy by adding partitions, the amount of investment required rises. If an existing layout is to be revised, renovation costs can be significant. The remodeling plans at Penney, Sears, and K mart stores (see Managerial Practice 9.1) have a total price tag of almost $5 billion.

TABLE 9.1 Performance Criteria for Four Different Settings

Manufacturing Plant	Office	Warehouse	Retail Store
Capital investment	Capital investment	Capital investment	Capital investment
Materials handling	Communication	Stockpicking	Customer convenience
Flexibility	Flexibility	Flexibility	Flexibility
Work environment	Atmosphere	Work environment	Atmosphere
Maintenance	Organizational structure	Shelf life	Sales
Employee attitudes	Employee attitudes		
Labor productivity			

Modular furniture and moveable partitions make it easy to rearrange this office when work requirements change.

Materials Handling.   Relative locations of centers should allow large flows to go short distances. Frequent trips or interactions between work centers should be recognized by locating these centers close to each other. In a manufacturing plant, this approach minimizes materials handling costs. In a warehouse, stock-picking costs are reduced by storing items typically needed for the same order next to each other. In a retail store, customer convenience is improved if items are grouped predictably to minimize customer search and travel time. In an office, communication and cooperation often can be improved by putting people or departments who must interact frequently near each other. Telephone calls and memos can be poor substitutes for face-to-face communication.

Flexibility.   A *flexible* layout is best for many situations. Layout flexibility may mean that a layout remains desirable even after significant changes occur in the mix of customers served by a store, goods made at a plant, item space requirements in a warehouse, or organizational structure in an office. Making a layout flexible in this sense depends in part on management's ability to forecast well. Layout flexibility may also mean that the layout is designed to minimize the cost of changing it later to meet new conditions. Having modular furniture and partitions, rather than permanent load-bearing walls, is one way to minimize the cost of office layout changes. So can having wide bays (fewer columns), heavy duty floors, and extra electrical connections in a plant.

Other Criteria.   Table 9.1 shows other criteria that can also be important. Labor productivity can be affected if certain work stations can be operated by common personnel in some layouts but not in others. Downtime spent waiting for materials can be caused by materials handling difficulties resulting from poor layout. Equipment maintenance can be made difficult by inadequate space or poor access. The work environment, including temperature, noise level, and safety, can be layout-related; its counterpart in an office or store is the atmosphere created by the layout. Office layouts can reinforce the organizational structure by putting all members of the same department in the same area. Encouraging sales is an important criterion for a store layout. Some warehouse layouts make it easier to pick stock on a FIFO (first-in, first-out) basis, minimizing loss from spoilage or limited shelf life. Finally, employee attitudes may depend on whether the layout allows workers to socialize, reflects equitably the employee's level of responsibility, or puts the worker under the watchful eyes of the supervisor.

PROCESS LAYOUTS: A THREE-STEP PROCEDURE ▲

The approach to designing a layout differs, depending on whether a process layout or product layout has been chosen. We do not consider fixed-position or hybrid layouts any further. When management decides on a fixed-position format, the layout problem is basically solved. As for the hybrid layout, part of it is designed using process-layout principles and part is designed using product-layout principles.

Let's begin with an approach to process layout. Three basic steps are involved, whether the design is for a new layout or for revising an existing layout: (1) gather information; (2) develop a block plan; and (3) design a detailed layout.

Gather Information (Step 1)

Figure 9.2 illustrates the type of information needed to begin designing a revised layout for Longhorn Machine. If necessary, refer back to the company tour you took in Chapter 2.

Space Requirements by Center. As Fig. 9.2 shows, Longhorn has grouped its processes into six different departments, or centers. For example, department 1 is the burr and grind area, and department 6 is the inspection area. The exact space requirements of each department, in square feet, are listed in Fig. 9.2(a). When calculating space requirements, the layout designer must tie them to capacity plans. First the designer itemizes the specific equipment and space needs for each center, then adds enough "circulation" space to provide for aisles and the like. Circulation space may consume at least 25 percent of the center's total space.

Available Space. Figure 9.2(b) shows the current block plan of Longhorn's plant. A **block plan** is a rough space allocation for each department and indicates its placement. When describing a new facility layout, rather than a modification of an existing one, the plan need only provide the facility's dimensions

Department	Square feet
1. Burr and grind	1000
2. NC equipment	950
3. Shipping and receiving	750
4. Lathes and drills	1200
5. Tool crib	800
6. Inspection	700
Total	5400

(a) Space Requirements by Center

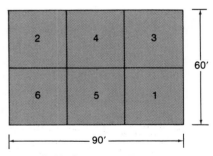

(b) Available Space and Current Block Plan

From–To Matrix (trips/day)

From \ To	1	2	3	4	5	6
1. Burr and grind		20		20		80
2. NC equipment			10		75	
3. Shipping and receiving				15		90
4. Lathes and drills					70	
5. Tool crib						
6. Inspection						

(c) Closeness Ratings

1. Shipping and receiving (department 3) should remain where it is, since it is next to the dock.

2. Keep lathes and drills (department 4) at its current location because relocation costs are prohibitive.

(d) Other Considerations

FIGURE 9.2   Layout information for Longhorn Machine

and space allocations. According to the Longhorn plan, the available space is 90 feet by 60 feet, or 5400 square feet. The designer could begin the design by dividing the total amount of space into six equal blocks (900 square feet each), one for each department. Actually, inspection needs only 700 square feet, and lathes and drills needs 1200 square feet. However, the equal-space approximation is good enough until the designer reaches the last step—detailed layout.*

Closeness Ratings.   The layout designer must also know which centers need to be located close to each other. Either a From–To matrix or a REL chart provides the needed information.

Figure 9.2(c) shows a **From–To matrix** for Longhorn. This matrix gives the number of trips (or some other measure of materials movement) between

---

*If this approximation is too rough, a finer grid can be used, say, with four rows and six columns. A larger department (such as lathes and drills) could then be assigned more block spaces than the smaller departments.

each pair of departments. The designer estimates the number of trips from routings and ordering frequencies for typical items made at the plant, statistical sampling, or polling supervisors and materials handlers. The right-hand portion of the matrix shows the number of trips in *both* directions.* The largest number of trips is between departments 3 and 6 (at 90 trips), with 1 and 6 close behind at 80 trips. Thus the designer should locate department 6 near both 1 and 3, which is not the arrangement in the current layout.

A **REL chart** (REL is short for *relationships*) displays closeness ratings as letters, rather than numbers, and thus reflects the qualitative judgments of managers and employees. An A rating could represent the judgment that it is absolutely necessary to locate two departments close to each other, E for especially important, I for important, O for ordinary closeness, U for unimportant, and X for undesirable. The A rating is higher than the E, but as the assessment is qualitative, the designer doesn't know by how much.

Other Considerations.   Figure 9.2(d) shows the last information gathered for Longhorn. Some performance criteria depend on the absolute location of a department. For example, moving a department might be unwise because of relocation costs, noise, or management preference. A REL chart cannot reflect these criteria. Similarly, a From–To matrix tends to focus only on materials handling. The layout designer must handle other considerations, such as those shown in Table 9.1, qualitatively and list them separately.

Develop a Block Plan (Step 2)

The second step in layout design is to develop a block plan that satisfies performance criteria and area requirements insofar as possible. The most elementary way to do this is by trial and error, which depends on the designer's ability to spot patterns in the data. There is no guarantee that the designer will identify the best or even a nearly best solution. However, one study showed that such an approach, at least when supplemented by the use of a computer to evaluate solutions, often compares quite favorably with more sophisticated techniques (Scriabin and Vergin, 1975).

APPLICATION 9.1

Find an acceptable block plan for Longhorn using trial and error.

Solution

A good place to start is with the largest closeness ratings in Fig. 9.2(c) (say, 70 and above). A reasonable block plan would locate departments as follows:

---

*This approach assumes that materials handling costs do not depend on the direction of flow. If this is not true, the numbers would have to be weighted differently.

1. departments 3 and 6 close together;
2. departments 1 and 6 close together;
3. departments 2 and 5 close together;
4. departments 4 and 5 close together; and
5. departments 3 and 4 at their current locations because of the other considerations.

If after several attempts you cannot meet all five requirements, drop one or more and try again. If you can meet all five easily, add more requirements (such as for interactions below 70).

The block plan in Fig. 9.3 was worked out by trial and error and satisfies all five requirements. Start by keeping departments 3 and 4 in their original locations. As the first requirement is to locate departments 3 and 6 close to each other, put 6 in the southeast corner of the layout. The second requirement is to have departments 1 and 6 close to each other, so place 1 in the space just to the left of 6, and so on.

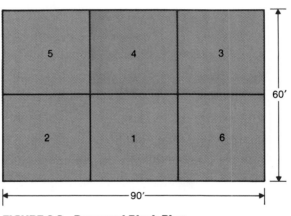

FIGURE 9.3 Proposed Block Plan

Having a total desirability score is helpful in at least some respects for comparing alternative block plans. The designer could easily adapt the load–distance method for location problems (see Chapter 8) to this purpose when *relative* locations are a primary concern (such as for materials handling, stockpicking, and communication effectiveness). In terms of materials handling costs,

$$ld = \sum_{j=i}^{n} \sum_{i=1}^{n} l_{ij} d_{ij}$$

where

ld = total load–distance score measuring the materials handling difficulties of the block plan*

l_{ij} = load, measured as the number of trips between departments i and j in both directions[†]

d_{ij} = units of distance (actual, euclidean, or rectilinear) between departments i and j, where $d_{jj} = 0$ (see Chapter 8 for distance computations)

n = total number of departments

APPLICATION 9.2

How much better, in terms of the ld score, is the proposed block plan? Use the rectilinear distance measure.

Solution

The accompanying table applies the formula to both plans. To fill in the first two columns, return to the From–To matrix in Fig. 9.2 and list each pair of departments that have a nonzero load. For the third column, calculate the

Load–Distance Scores: Current and Proposed

Department Pair (ij)	Closeness Rating (l_{ij})	Current Plan		Proposed Plan	
		Distance (d_{ij})	$l_{ij}d_{ij}$	Distance (d_{ij})	$l_{ij}d_{ij}$
1, 2	20	3	60	1	20
1, 4	20	2	40	1	20
1, 6	80	2	160	1	80
2, 3	10	2	20	3	30
2, 5	75	2	150	1	75
3, 4	15	1	15	1	15
3, 6	90	3	270	1	90
4, 5	70	1	70	1	70
			$ld = \overline{785}$		$ld = \overline{400}$

*A more elaborate treatment of l_{ij} is to multiply the number of trips by the cost to move one load for one unit of distance. The cost depends on the materials handling methods used for transfers between departments, as well as the type of materials to be moved.

[†]Since l_{ij} represents the merged flow between department pairs in both directions, j needs to be summed only from i (rather than 1) to n.

rectilinear distances between the departments in the current layout. For example, in Fig. 9.2(b), departments 1 and 2 are in the southeast and northwest blocks of the plant. The distance between the centers of these blocks is three units of distance (two horizontally and one vertically), and each unit measures 30 feet. For the fourth column, multiply the loads by the distances and add the results for a total *ld* score of 785 for the current plan. Similar calculations for the proposed plan produce an *ld* score of only 400.

Although the *ld* score for the proposed layout in Application 9.2 represents an almost 50 percent improvement, the designer may be able to do better. However, the designer must first determine whether the revised layout is worth the cost of relocating four of the six departments (all but 3 and 4). If relocation costs are too high, a less expensive proposal must be found. The calculations made for the current plan offer some clues. Much of the 785 score comes from trips between departments 3 and 6 (270) and between departments 1 and 6 (160). One option is to switch the locations of departments 5 and 6, putting department 6 closer to both 1 and 3. Additional calculations show that the *ld* score for this plan drops to 610, and only two departments have to be relocated. Perhaps this is the best compromise.

Design a Detailed Layout (Step 3)

After finding a satisfactory block plan, the layout designer translates it into a detailed representation, showing the exact size and shape of each center, the arrangement of elements (such as desks, machines, or storage areas), and the location of aisles, stairways, and other service space. These visual representations can be two-dimensional drawings, three-dimensional models, or even computer-aided graphics. This last step in the layout design process is important because it helps decision makers grasp the essence of the proposal and even spot problems that might otherwise be overlooked. If others in the company are to be involved in layout decisions, the detailed layout becomes the focus of the discussion with them. Figure 9.4 is a good example of a detailed layout.

AIDS FOR PROCESS LAYOUT DECISIONS ▲

Finding an acceptable block plan is a complex process in real-life situations. A 20-department problem has 20! possible layouts, which means 2.43×10^{18} possibilities. If a computer evaluated one possibility each microsecond, 8 hours a day, it would take the computer 250,000 years to arrive at the final solution. Fortunately, several computationally feasible aids are now available for helping managers make process layout decisions.

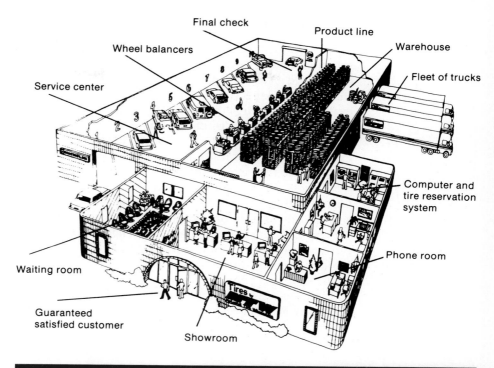

Final check

Product line

Wheel balancers

Warehouse

Service center

Fleet of trucks

Computer and tire reservation system

Phone room

Waiting room

Guaranteed satisfied customer

Showroom

FIGURE 9.4   Detailed Layout of National Tire Wholesale

Source: National Tire Wholesale.

Automated Layout Design Program

Automated layout design program (ALDEP) is a computerized heuristic that uses REL chart information to construct a good layout. Being a heuristic method, it generally provides good—but not necessarily the best—solutions. The program constructs a layout from scratch, adding one department at a time. The program picks the first department randomly. The second department must have a strong REL rating with the first (say, A or E), the third must have a strong rating with the second, and so on. When no department has a strong rating with a department just added, the system again randomly selects the next department. The program computes a score for each solution generated and prints out the layouts with higher scores for the manager's consideration. The score is computed differently from the *ld* score used earlier. First, the letter ratings are converted into numerical equivalents, say, 6 for A, 5 for E, 4 for I, 3 for O, 2 for U, and 0 for X.* Second, these numerical equivalents are added to the total score whenever they belong to departments that touch somewhere along their borders.

---

*These numerical equivalents are arbitrary, and others could be used. After numerical equivalents have been established, it is also possible to compute *ld* scores as we did earlier.

Computerized Relative Allocation of Facilities Technique

Another powerful computer software package is **computerized relative allocation of facilities technique (CRAFT),** a heuristic method that uses a From–To matrix and a series of paired exchanges of departments to find an acceptable solution. Working from an initial block plan (or starting solution), CRAFT evaluates all possible paired exchanges of departments. The exchange that helps the most (that is, causes the greatest reduction in the total *ld* score) is made, creating a new starting solution. This process continues until no other exchanges can be found to reduce the *ld* score. The starting solution at this point is also the final solution, which is printed out, along with the *ld* score.

Other models have been developed to handle multiple floors and relocation costs (see Cinar, 1975, and Hicks and Cowan, 1976). Goal programming, a special form of linear programming, has been used to optimize a solution with several criteria simultaneously (see Ritzman et al., 1979). One particularly intriguing development is a method that better integrates the last two steps of layout planning (the block plan and detailed layout). A detailed configuration (called a *design unit*) is preassigned to each center and must be maintained throughout the solution process. This constraint prevents unusual shapes from occurring and helps the manager better visualize the final layout (see Jacobs, 1987).

PROCESS LAYOUTS: TWO SPECIAL CASES ▲

We conclude the discussion of process layouts with two special cases: warehouses and offices, both of which are of great importance. A typical manufacturer spends 6 percent to 8 percent of income from sales for warehousing, and the 60 million Americans working in offices are paid over $1 trillion. Much of the preceding discussion still applies, but each of these two special cases has unique aspects.

Warehouse Layouts

Warehouses are similar to manufacturing plants in that materials are moved between activity centers. At the centers, transformation is one of storage, rather than a physical or chemical change. Figure 9.5(a) illustrates the simplest type of warehousing situation. A-1 Distribution Systems receives items at the dock and moves them to a storage area. At a later date, stockpickers withdraw inventory to fill individual customer orders. For example, according to the table in Fig. 9.5(b), 280 trips per week are made between the dock and the storage area for toasters.

A Simpler Method.   We can find a layout solution by the method used in Applications 9.1 and 9.2. Or we can use an even simpler method, which is

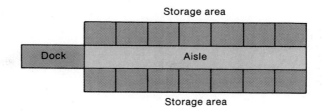

(a) Dock and Storage Space

Department	Trips to and from dock	Area needed (blocks)
1. Toasters	280	1
2. Room air-conditioners	160	2
3. Microwaves	360	1
4. Stereos	375	3
5. TV s	800	4
6. Radios	150	1
7. Bulk storage	100	2

(b) Trips and Space Requirements

FIGURE 9.5   Layout Information for A-1 Distribution Systems

guaranteed to minimize the *ld* score. This shortcut is possible because all travel takes place between the dock and individual departments; there is no travel between departments. The decision rule is as follows:

1. *Equal areas.* If all departments require the same space, simply place the one generating the most trips closest to the dock, the one generating the next largest number of trips next closest to the dock, and so on.

2. *Unequal areas.* If some departments need more space than others, give the location closest to the dock to the department with the largest ratio of trip frequency to block space. The department with the second highest ratio gets the next closest location, and so on.

APPLICATION 9.3

Find a layout for A-1 that minimizes the *ld* score.

Solution

Since the departments at A-1 have different area requirements, we must first obtain the ratio of trips to block spaces. Department 3 (microwaves) has the highest ratio. Although only 360 trips per week are involved, the department

3	5	5	6	4	2	7
Dock	**Aisle**					
1	5	5	4	4	2	7

FIGURE 9.6   Best Block Plan for A-1 Distribution Systems

occupies only one block of prime space. Ranking the remaining departments by their ratios (shown in parentheses), we get: 1 (280), 5 (200), 6 (150), 4 (125), 2 (80), and 7 (50). Figure 9.6 shows the layout derived from this ranking. Department 3 had first choice and could have been placed in either of the two locations nearest the dock. We chose the top one arbitrarily and assigned the bottom one to department 1.

Some Qualifications.   Our proposed layout might not be the best warehouse design for three reasons. First, demand for different items is often seasonal. Thus an efficient layout might place radios close to the dock for Christmas but move air conditioners near the dock during the summer.

Second, if better space utilization is crucial, other aspects of the layout come into play. For example, an 82,000-square-foot, 32-foot-high, racked warehouse can handle the same volume as a 107,000-square-foot, low-ceiling warehouse. Productivity gains of as much as 50 percent in order picking have been reported, which can help offset the added rack and equipment costs of such high-density designs. Another space-saving possibility is to assign all incoming materials to the nearest available space, rather than to a predetermined area where all like items are clustered. The location of each item is recorded in a computer. When it's time to retrieve an item, the system prints its location on the shipping bill. When more than one item is on the bill, the computer identifies the shortest route for the order picker. Canadiana Outdoor Products in Brampton, Ontario, introduced a computer system with terminals mounted on the lift-trucks. This arrangement allowed drivers to track the exact location and contents of each storage bin in the warehouse. With this new system, Canadiana can handle quadrupled sales with less storage space.

The third reason that our proposed layout might not be best is that another layout *pattern* might be better. At A-1 it is an out-and-back selection pattern, where one item is picked at a time, but there are other options. On a route collection trip, the order picker selects a variety of items to be shipped to a given customer. When batch picking, the order picker gathers the quantity of an item required to satisfy a group of customer orders to be shipped in the same truck or rail car. Finally, in the zone system, each picker is assigned to a zone. The picker gathers all needed items from the zone and places them on a powered conveyor line. Figure 9.7 illustrates the zone concept for a warehouse serving several toy supermarkets (such as Children's Palace). The conveyor line consists of five feeder lines and one trunk line. When the merchandise arrives at the control station, an operator directs it to the correct tractor trailer for outbound shipment. The advantage of the zone system is that pickers do not need to travel throughout the warehouse to fill orders; they are responsible only for their assigned zones.

Office Layouts

Over 40 percent of the U.S. work force is employed in offices. The layout of offices can affect both productivity and the quality of work life. In a recent survey three fourths of the 1400 employees polled said productivity could be raised by improvements in their work environments.

Proximity. Accessibility to co-workers and supervisors can enhance communication and develop mutual interest. Conversations tend to be more formal when people are located farther away from each other. The famous Hawthorne

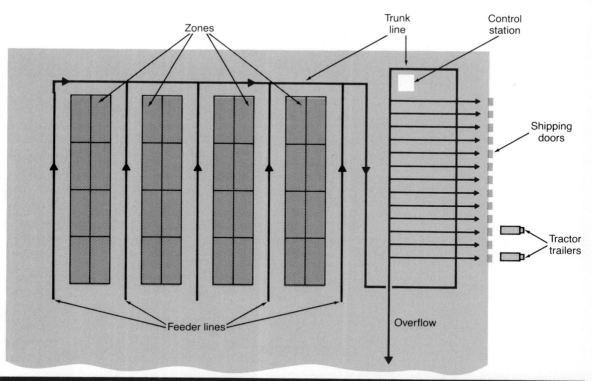

FIGURE 9.7   Zone System for a Warehouse

study in 1939 showed that the physical work setting influences group formation (Homans, 1950). Management used spatial language to tell the workers in the experimental group that they were important. Management changed both the absolute and relative locations of the workers by moving them to a separate room and away from the watchful eyes of a supervisor. The revised layout facilitated contact between workers and the setting of group norms. More recent studies confirm that proximity to others can be beneficial in helping clarify what is expected of an employee on the job and in other ways.

Most formal procedures for designing office layouts try to maximize the proximity of workers whose jobs require frequent interaction. Data collected on the frequency and importance of interactions can be used in a REL chart or a From–To matrix. Certain procedures can be used to help identify natural clusters of workers who can then be treated as a center in a block plan (see Jacobs et al., 1980). The goal of such approaches is to design layouts around work flows and communication patterns.

The headquarters of Johnson Wax has a grand, spacious layout designed by Frank Lloyd Wright. However, some people would feel too exposed in such an open office setting.

Privacy.   Another key factor in office design—and one that is somewhat culturally dependent—is privacy. Outside disruptions, crowding, and feeling lost in the crowd can hurt a worker's performance. Employee reaction to open offices at Sperry Rand's and McDonald's world headquarters were favorable. However, when a newspaper publishing company tried to increase worker proximity by going from private work spaces to an open-plan office, the results were disappointing (see Oldham and Brass, 1979). Employees felt like they were in a fishbowl and that they had little control over their environment. Studies at several state government departments (see Schuler et al., 1981) revealed a strong link between privacy and satisfaction with the supervisor and the job.

Some Options.   Providing both proximity and privacy for employees poses a dilemma for management. Proximity is gained by opening up the work area. Privacy is gained by more liberal space standards, baffled ceilings, doors, partitions, and thick carpeting that absorbs noise. However, these features can be expensive and reduce layout flexibility. Thus management must generally arrive at a compromise between proximity and privacy. Four different approaches are available: traditional layouts, office landscaping, activity settings, and electronic cottages. The choice requires an understanding of work requirements, the work force itself, and top management's philosophy of work.

Traditional layouts call for closed offices for some employees and open areas (or bullpens) for all others. The closed offices, with their solid doors and floor-to-ceiling walls, go to management and those employees whose work requires privacy. The resulting layout may be characterized by long hallways lined with closed doors, producing considerable isolation. Open areas are filled uniformly with rows of desks. In traditional layouts each person has a designated place. Its location, size, and furnishing signify the person's status in the organization.

An approach developed in Germany during the late 1950s puts everyone (including top management) in an open area (see Managerial Practice 9.2). Desks and equipment are arranged in smoothly flowing patterns. An extension to this concept is called office landscaping: Attractive plants, screens, and portable partitions increase privacy and cluster or separate groups. Movable work stations and accessories help maintain flexibility. Because the work stations (or cubicles) are only semiprivate, employees may have trouble concentrating or feel uncomfortable trying to hold sensitive discussions. Construction costs are as much as 40 percent less than for traditional layouts, and rearrangement costs are less still.

Activity settings represent a relatively new concept for achieving both proximity and privacy (Stone and Luchetti, 1985). Multiple work places cover the full range of work needs, including a library, teleconferencing facility, reception area, conference room, special graphics area, and shared terminals. Employees move from one activity setting to the next as their work changes during the day. Each person also gets a small, personal office as a home base.

Offices Without Walls

- Hewlett-Packard's Waltham, Massachusetts plant is designed with open offices. A big bullpen with shoulder-high dividers splits up the space. The idea is to achieve closer cooperation among employees at *all* levels. The plant manager's office is on the shop floor. "We don't go for the peacock alleys of executive offices with secretaries guarding the boss's door," says manager Ron Rankin. However, the corporate nurse still keeps earplugs in inventory for employees bothered by noise.

- When Japan's Sumitomo Rubber Industries Ltd. bought out a Dunlop tire plant in Birmingham, England, it embraced the Japanese practice of removing conspicuous signs of employee status. Sumitomo encouraged all executives to spend time on the shop floor, removed the executive parking lot, and provided "team" jackets that all employees had to wear. Many expected job barriers to blur, but some managers saw the changes as a step backward.

Sources: "America's Best-Managed Factories," *Fortune*, May 28, 1984; "Britain's 'Intransigent' Rubber Workers Bow to Japanese Management Practices," *Wall Street Journal*, March 29, 1988; "The Difference Japanese Management Makes," *Business Week*, July 14, 1986.

Former Honda of America President Irimajiri worked in an open office with little privacy and few status symbols.

Some futurists expect more and more employees to work at home, connected to the office through the computer. Called telecommuting or electronic cottages, this approach represents a modern-day version of the cottage industries that existed prior to the Industrial Revolution. The privacy of the home may be ideal for certain kinds of routine work. However, Hartford Insurance Group had difficulty with telecommuting. Some managers complained that they couldn't supervise—much less get to know—employees they couldn't see. Unreliable telephone lines linking home terminals to the company's computer also caused difficulty.

PRODUCT LAYOUTS ▲

Product layouts raise entirely different management issues from those of process layouts. Often called a production line or assembly line, a product layout arranges work stations in sequence. The product moves from one station to the next until it is finished at the end of the line. Typically, one worker operates each station, performing repetitive tasks. There is little inventory to decouple stations, so the line's output is only as fast as the slowest work station. The key is work stations with well-balanced workloads. We begin with this line-balancing problem, and then conclude by discussing the broader issues.

Line Balancing

Line balancing is the process of assigning work to stations in a line so as to achieve the desired output rate with the smallest number of work stations. The analyst begins by breaking the work to be done on the line into **work elements**, the smallest units of work that can be performed independently. The analyst then obtains the labor standard (see Chapter 6) for each element and identifies the work elements (called *immediate predecessors*) that must be done before the next can begin. Managerial Practice 9.3 provides the necessary information for Green Grass, Inc.

Precedence Diagram.   Most lines must satisfy some technological precedence requirements but also allow for some latitude and more than one sequence of operations. To help you visualize immediate predecessors better, let's run through construction of a **precedence diagram**.* We denote the work elements by circles, with the time required to perform the work shown below each circle. Arrows lead from the immediate predecessor requirements to the next work element.

---

*Precedence relationships and precedence diagrams are important in the entirely different context of project scheduling, as discussed in Chapter 18.

Line Balancing at Green Grass, Inc.

Green Grass, Inc., is expanding its product line to include a new fertilizer spreader called the Big Broadcaster. This spreader cuts fertilizer application time to 30 percent of that required with traditional methods. Operations plans to make the Big Broadcaster on a new assembly line in one of the Green Grass plants. The firm will purchase most parts from outside suppliers. Management decided against further vertical integration until customer response to the new spreader is better known. Karen Annay, the plant manager, obtained the following information concerning work elements, labor standards, and immediate predecessors for the Big Broadcaster.

Work Element	Description	Time (sec)	Immediate Predecessor(s)
Attach leg frame			
1	Bolt leg frame to hopper	51	None
2	Insert impeller shaft into hopper	7	1
3	Attach agitator to shaft	24	2
4	Secure with cotter pin	10	3
Attach axle			
5	Insert bearings into housings	25	1
6	Slip axle through first bearing and shaft	40	5
7	Slip axle through second bearing	20	4, 6
Attach drive wheel			
8	Slip on drive wheel	35	7
9	Place washer over axle	6	8
10	Secure with cotter pin	15	9
11	Push on hub cap	9	10
Attach free wheel			
12	Slip on free wheel	30	7
13	Place washer over axle	6	12
14	Secure with cotter pin	15	13
15	Push on hub cap	9	14
Mount lower post			
16	Bolt lower handle post to hopper	27	7
17	Seat post in square hole	13	16
18	Secure leg to support strap	60	17
Attach controls			
19	Insert control wire	28	11, 15, 18
20	Guide wire through slot	12	19
21	Slip T handle over lower post	21	20
22	Attach on-off control	26	21
23	Attach level	58	22
24	Mount name plate	29	18
Total		576	

APPLICATION 9.4

Construct a precedence diagram for the Big Broadcaster.

Solution

Figure 9.8 shows the complete diagram. Begin with work element 1, which has no immediate predecessors. Next add elements 2 and 5, for which element 1 is the only immediate predecessor. After entering labor standards and arrows showing precedence, add elements 3 or 6, and so on.

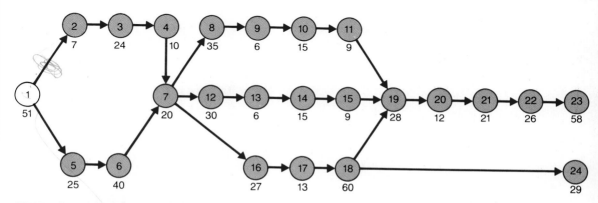

FIGURE 9.8   Precedence Diagram for Assembling the Big Broadcaster

Desired Output Rate.   Closely related to demand forecasts, the output rate also depends on rebalancing frequency, capacity utilization, and job specialization. All else being equal, production rates should match demand rates as closely as possible. Matching ensures on-time delivery and prevents the buildup of unwanted inventory. The disadvantage is that it increases rebalancing frequency. Each time a line is rebalanced, the jobs of many workers on the line must be redesigned. If the line is speeded up, a worker is given fewer work elements. If the line is slowed down, a worker is given more work elements. Time spent relearning jobs temporarily hurts productivity. The changeover may even require a new detailed layout for some stations. A good example of avoiding frequent changes is the automobile assembly plant. When demand falls and inventory becomes excessive, management lays off a whole shift, rather than gradually scaling back the output rate.

Capacity utilization is another factor that has to be considered. Multiple shifts increase equipment utilization, which is crucial for capital-intensive facilities. However, higher pay rates or low demand may make multiple shifts undesirable or unnecessary. A third policy area related to the desired output rate is job specialization. As the desired output rate from a line increases, fewer work elements can be assigned to a station and jobs become more specialized. (See Chapter 4.) Recently, General Motors added a second shift to its Orion Township plant in Michigan. The line is designed to build 67 Cadillac and Oldsmobile cars an hour, an output rate that implies considerable job specialization.

Cycle Time.   After determining the desired output rate for a line, the analyst can calculate the line's cycle time. A line's **cycle time** is the maximum time allowed for work on a unit at each station.* If the time required for work elements at a station exceeds the line's cycle time, the station will be a bottleneck, preventing the line from reaching its desired output rate. The target cycle time is the reciprocal of the desired hourly output rate, or

$$c = \left(\frac{1}{r}\right)(3600 \text{ sec/hr})$$

where

$$c = \text{cycle time in sec/unit}$$
$$r = \text{desired output rate in units/hr}$$

Theoretical Minimum.   In order to achieve the desired output rate, the line balancing problem is to assign every work element to a station, satisfy all precedence requirements, and minimize the number of stations (n) formed. If each station is operated by a different worker, minimizing n also maximizes productivity. The ultimate in balance is when the sum of the work-element times at each station equals c. The workload at each station then is perfectly balanced, and no station has any idle time. Normally, this goal is a practical impossiblity, owing to the unevenness of work-element times and the loss of flexibility caused by precedence requirements. However, assuming perfect balance provides a benchmark: the smallest number of stations possible, called the **theoretical minimum (TM)** number of stations. Rounding up for fractional values, as fractional stations are impossible,

$$TM = \frac{t}{c}$$

where t is the total amount of productive time required to assemble each unit, or the sum of all work-element times.

---

*Except in the context of line balancing, *cycle time* is the elapsed time between starting and completing a job. Some researchers and practitioners prefer the term *lead time*.

APPLICATION 9.5

Green Grass's plant manager has just received marketing's latest forecasts of Big Broadcaster sales for the next year. She wants the line to be designed to make 2400 spreaders per week for at least the next three months. The plant will operate five days per week, one shift per day, and eight hours per shift. A few utility workers are used in the plant to relieve others for breaks, cover for absenteeism, and help at temporary bottlenecks. Since equipment failures will be negligible, the line should be operating 40 hours per week.

What should be the line's cycle time? What is the smallest number of work stations that the plant manager could hope for in designing the line for this cycle time?

Solution

The plant manager begins with the cycle time, first converting the desired output rate (2400 units per week) to an hourly rate. Dividing by 40 hours per week (one eight-hour shift, five days per week), she gets 60 units per hour, so

$$c = \left(\frac{1}{r}\right)(3600 \text{ sec/hr})$$

$$= \left(\frac{1}{60}\right)(3600)$$

$$= 60 \text{ sec/unit}$$

The plant manager now calculates the theoretical minimum number of stations. The previously estimated total amount of productive work to be done is 576 seconds per spreader. (See table in Managerial Practice 9.3.) Dividing by the cycle time, assuming perfect balance, she gets

$$TM = \frac{t}{c} = \frac{576}{60} = 9.6 \quad \text{or} \quad 10 \text{ stations}$$

Three Related Goals. Minimizing n ensures automatically that we (1) minimize idle time, (2) maximize efficiency, and (3) minimize balance delay. These goals are used interchangeably in line balancing, so you need to be familiar with each one:

$$\text{Idle time} = nc - t$$

$$\text{Efficiency (\%)} = \left(\frac{t}{nc}\right)(100)$$

$$\text{Balance delay (\%)} = 100 - \text{Efficiency}$$

Idle time is the total unproductive time for all stations in the assembly of each unit. Each of the n stations spends c seconds per unit, which means that nc is the total time (productive time and idle time) spent per unit. Subtracting the total productive time t gives us the idle time. Efficiency is the ratio of productive time to total time, expressed as a percent. **Balance delay** is the amount by which efficiency falls short of 100 percent. So long as c is fixed, we can optimize all three goals by minimizing n.

APPLICATION 9.6

Suppose that we can find a solution for Green Grass with only 10 stations, the theoretical minimum (or $n = TM = 10$). What would be the line's efficiency?

Solution

$$\text{Efficiency} = \left(\frac{t}{nc}\right)(100)$$

$$= \frac{576}{(10)(60)}(100)$$

$$= 96\%$$

Thus if we find a solution that achieves TM, the efficiency (sometimes called the *theoretical maximum efficiency*) will only be 96 percent.

Finding a Solution.   An overwhelming number of assembly line solutions are possible, even for Green Grass's rather simple problem. The number of possibilities expands as quickly as for process layouts. Once again, computer assistance is available. One software package, for example, considers every feasible combination of work elements that do not violate precedence or cycle time requirements when forming a new station. The combination that minimizes the station's idle time is selected (see Hoffman, 1963). If any work elements remain unassigned, a second station is formed, and so on.

The approach that we use here is even simpler. At each iteration, a work element is selected from a list of candidates and assigned to a station. This process is repeated until all stations have been formed. Two commonly used decision rules for selecting from the candidate list are:

Rule 1. Pick the candidate with the *longest work-element time*. This rule tends to assign the work elements most difficult to fit into a station as quickly as possible. Work elements having shorter times should be saved for fine tuning the solution.

Rule 2. Pick the candidate having the *largest number of followers.* Figure 9.8 shows, for example, that work element 18 has six followers and 21 has two followers. This rule helps to keep options open for forming subsequent stations. Otherwise, precedence requirements may leave only a few possible sequences of work elements, all requiring an unnecessary amount of idle time as a result.

Let's now develop solutions manually using these rules. Our overall solution procedure is much like the logic that would be used in computer programs:

Step 1. Let $k = 1$, where k is a counter for the station being formed.

Step 2. Make a list of candidates. Each work element included in the list must satisfy three conditions:

- it has not yet been assigned to this or any previous station;
- all its predecessors have been assigned to this or a previous station; and
- its time cannot exceed the station's idle time, which accounts for all work elements already assigned. If none has been assigned, the station's idle time equals the cycle time.

If no such candidates can be found, go to step 5.

Step 3. Pick a candidate using one of the two decision rules. Assign it to station k.

Step 4. Calculate the cumulative time of all tasks assigned so far to station k. Subtract this total from the cycle time to find the station's idle time. Go to step 2.

Step 5. If some work elements are still unassigned, but none is a candidate for station k, a new station must be started. Begin the new station by incrementing k by 1 and go to step 2. Otherwise, you have a complete solution. Stop.

APPLICATION 9.7

Find a line-balancing solution using the manual solution procedure and largest work-element time rule to pick candidates (see step 3).

Solution

The worksheet in Fig. 9.9(a) shows how to proceed, and the first few iterations reveal the pattern. Beginning with the first station S1 ($k = 1$), the precedence diagram shows that only element 1 can be a candidate. It is the only one with all immediate predecessors (none, in this case) already assigned. With element 1 assigned, station S1 has an idle time of 9 seconds. For the second iteration,

Station (Steps 1 and 5)	Candidates (Step 2)	Choice (Step 3)	Cumulative time (sec) (Step 4)	Idle time ($c = 60$ sec) (Step 4)
S1	1	1	51	9
	2	2	58	2
S2	3, 5	5	25	35
	3	3	49	11
	4	4	53	7
S3	6	6	40	20
	7	7	20	0
S4	8, 12, 16	8	35	25
	9	9	41	19
	10	10	56	4
S5	11, 12, 16	12	30	30
	11, 13, 16	16	57	3
S6	11, 13, 17	17	13	47
	11, 13	11	22	38
	13	13	28	32
	14	14	43	17
	15	15	52	8
S7	18	18	60	0
S8	19, 24	24	29	31
	19	19	53	3
S9	20	20	12	48
	21	21	33	27
	22	22	59	1
S10	23	23	58	2

(a) Worksheet

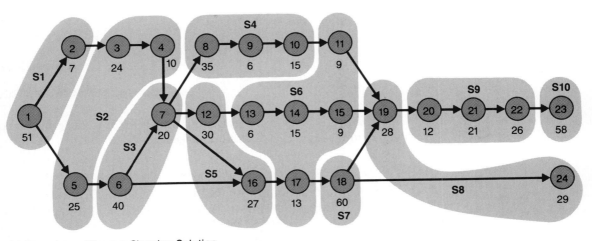

(b) Precedence Diagram Showing Solution

FIGURE 9.9   Big Broadcaster Solution Using Longest Work-Element Time Rule

only element 2 is a candidate. Element 5 cannot be a candidate because its time exceeds 9 seconds. With station S1 now consisting of elements 1 and 2, its idle time drops to only 2 seconds. No candidates remain, as adding either 3 or 5 brings the work content of S1 over the cycle time. We therefore move on to the second station S2 ($k = 2$). The candidates are 3 and 5, with 5 picked because its time is longer (25 versus 24). This is the first instance of a real choice because each previous iteration had only one candidate. Continuing on, we find that the final solution calls for only 10 stations. The corresponding precedence diagram is shown in Fig. 9.9(b). The efficiency is 96 percent and the balance delay only 4 percent. Since $n = TM = 10$, we can do no better than this with a 60-second cycle time.

Such a happy ending does not always occur, and sometimes another procedure would do better. Computer-based techniques tend to give acceptable, though not necessarily optimal, results. Human judgment and pattern recognition often allow us to improve on computer generated solutions. In fact, manual methods are still the more prevalent in practice.

A Larger View

Management options go far beyond that of balancing a line for a given cycle time. Let's consider four of these options.

Pacing. Managers must decide whether to use inventory to decouple workstations. Paced lines have no buffer inventory, making them particularly susceptible to capacity losses and variability in work-element times. Capacity losses, alignment problems, or missing components mean slowing down the entire line or pulling unfinished work off the line to be completed later. With unpaced lines, inventory storage areas are placed between stations. These storage areas make unexpected downtime at one station less likely to delay work downstream, but do increase space and inventory costs.

Behavioral Options. The most controversial aspect of product layouts is behavioral response. Absenteeism, turnover, and grievance statistics point to lines as likely generators of personnel problems. High specialization (say, cycle times less than 2 minutes) and paced production are frequently identified as reasons for low job satisfaction. Many companies are exploring job enlargement and rotation to increase job variety. Such efforts are not always successful because workers may react unfavorably to enlarged jobs. Workers generally favor inventory buffers as a means of avoiding mechanical pacing. One study even showed that productivity increased on unpaced lines.

Another option for humanizing assembly lines is that of involving worker groups more in decisions about who is assigned to each station, when jobs are rotated, which specific work elements are assigned to a station, and even how these tasks are performed. In Sweden, Volvo allows considerable group control. Management identifies for each group the type of work to be done, specifies the desired daily output rate, and provides the necessary resources. Each group decides the rest. The quality circles pioneered in Japanese industry, which are now becoming more widespread in the United States, are another example of employee involvement.

Other behavioral options include arranging station layouts to facilitate social interaction, creating stations where two or more people work together, and giving particular attention to personnel selection. Some workers, such as those from rural communities, are less likely to enjoy line work. Others actually prefer routine work.

Mixed-Model Lines.   A **mixed-model line** produces several items belonging to the same family, such as the Cadillac de Ville and Oldsmobile 98 models. Although it has important advantages, such as having both high-volume production *and* product flexibility, mixed-model production can seriously complicate scheduling. Information must be communicated for each unit about the specific parts to be produced at each station. Care must be taken to alternate from one model to another, so as not to overload some stations for too long. Despite these difficulties, the mixed-model line is often the only reasonable choice. When product plans call for many customer options, volumes may not be high enough to justify a separate line for each model.

Modify Cycle Times.   A line's cycle time depends on the desired output rate (or sometimes on the maximum number of work stations allowed). In turn, the maximum efficiency possible from the line varies considerably with the cycle time selected. Thus exploring a range of cycle times makes sense. A manager might go with a particularly efficient solution even if it doesn't match the output rate. The manager can compensate for the mismatch by varying the number of hours the line operates, that is, by varying the amount of overtime, extending shifts, or adding extra shifts. Multiple lines might be the answer instead.

Another possibility is to let finished-goods inventory build up for some time and then rebalance the line at a lower output rate to deplete the excess. Management's policy on the frequency of rebalancing applies here. Japanese automobile manufacturing strategy calls for rebalancing lines about 12 times a year. In the United States, the overall average is only about 3 times per year. The Japanese strategy minimizes inventories and balance delay. The major disadvantage of the Japanese approach is that it disrupts production during changeover from one line configuration to another. Greater work flexibility, cross-training, and job rotation, which are additional elements of the Japanese approach (see Chapter 16), can help to minimize this disruption.

SOLVED PROBLEMS

1. A manager wants to know whether the plant's current process layout is adequate. Figure 9.10 shows the current layout and a From–To matrix for it. Safety and EPA regulations require departments E and F to remain at their current locations.

   a. Use trial and error to find a better layout.

   b. How much better is your layout over the current one, in terms of the *ld* score? Use rectilinear distance.

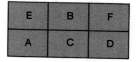

(a) Current Block Plan

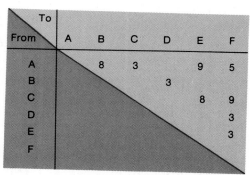

(b) From–To Matrix

FIGURE 9.10

Solution

   a. In addition to keeping departments E and F at their current locations, a good plan would locate the following department pairs close to each other: A and E, C and F, A and B, and C and E. Figure 9.11 was worked out by trial and error and satisfies all these requirements. Start by placing E and F at their current locations. Then because C must be as close as possible to both E and F, put C between them. The rest of the layout falls into place.

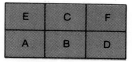

FIGURE 9.11

TABLE 9.2

Department Pair	Closeness Rating (l_{ij})	Current Plan			Proposed Plan	
		Distance (d_{ij})	$l_{ij}d_{ij}$		Distance (d_{ij})	$l_{ij}d_{ij}$
A, B	8	2	16		1	8
A, C	3	1	3		2	6
A, E	9	1	9		1	9
A, F	5	3	15		3	15
B, D	3	2	6		1	3
C, E	8	2	16		1	8
C, F	9	2	18		1	9
D, F	3	1	3		1	3
E, F	3	2	6		2	6
			$ld = \underline{\underline{92}}$			$ld = \underline{\underline{67}}$

    b. Table 9.2 reveals that the *ld* score drops from 92 for the current plan to 67 for the revised plan, a 27 percent reduction.

2. Develop a layout for the warehouse docking area shown in Fig. 9.12, using rectilinear distances. Each of seven departments (A–G) requires one block space—except C, which needs two spaces. The daily trips to and from the dock are 390 for A, 180 for B, 220 for C, 250 for D, 160 for E, 120 for F, and 220 for G.

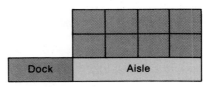

FIGURE 9.12

Solution

Sequencing departments by the ratio of trips per block space, we get: A, D, G, B, E, F, and C. Giving preference to those higher in the sequence produces the layout shown in Fig. 9.13. There are other optimal solutions because some locations are equidistant from the dock.

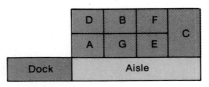

FIGURE 9.13

TABLE 9.3

Work Element	Time (sec)	Immediate Predecessor(s)
1	40	None
2	30	1
3	50	1
4	40	2
5	6	2
6	25	3
7	15	3
8	20	4, 5
9	18	6, 7
10	30	8, 9
	Total = 274	

3. A company is setting up an assembly line to produce 60 units per hour. Table 9.3 identifies the work elements, times, and immediate predecessors.

   a. What is the desired cycle time?

   b. What is the theoretical minimum number of stations?

   c. Work out a solution using the largest work-element time rule, showing your solution on a precedence diagram.

   d. What are the efficiency and balance delay of the solution found?

Solution

   a. Substituting in the cycle-time formula, we get

$$c = \left(\frac{1}{r}\right)(3600 \text{ sec/hr})$$

$$= \left(\frac{1}{60}\right)(3600 \text{ sec/hr})$$

$$= 60 \text{ sec/unit}$$

   b. The sum of the work-element times is 274 seconds, so

$$TM = \frac{t}{c}$$

$$= \frac{274}{60}$$

$$= 4.6 \quad \text{or} \quad 5 \text{ stations}$$

which may not be achievable.

Station	Candidate	Choice	Cumulative time (sec)	Idle time ($c = 60$ sec)
S1	1	1	40	20
S2	2, 3	3	50	10
S3	2, 6, 7	2	30	30
	5, 6, 7	6	55	5
S4	4, 5, 7	4	40	20
	5, 7	7	55	5
S5	5, 9	9	18	42
	5	5	24	36
	8	8	44	16
S6	10	10	30	30

(a) Worksheet

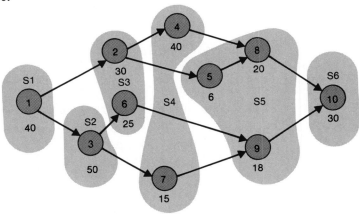

(b) Precedence Diagram Showing Solution

FIGURE 9.14

c. The worksheet and precedence diagram for the solution are shown in Fig. 9.14.

d. Calculating the efficiency, we get

$$\text{Efficiency} = \frac{t}{nc}(100)$$

$$= \frac{274}{(6)(60)}$$

$$= 76\%$$

so the balance delay is 24% (or 100% − 76%).

FORMULA REVIEW

1. Load-distance score—process layouts:

$$ld = \sum_{j=i}^{n} \sum_{i=1}^{n} l_{ij} d_{ij}$$

2. Cycle time (in seconds):

$$c = \left(\frac{1}{r}\right)(3600 \text{ sec/hr})$$

3. Theoretical minimum number of work stations:

$$TM = \frac{t}{c}$$

4. Idle time (in seconds) $= nc - t$.

5. Efficiency (%) $= \left(\dfrac{t}{nc}\right)(100)$.

6. Balance Delay (%) $= 100 - $ Efficiency.

CHAPTER HIGHLIGHTS

- Layout decisions go beyond placement of economic activity centers. Equally important are which centers to include, how much space they need, and how to configure their space.

- There are four layout types: process, product, hybrid, and fixed. Management's choice must be coupled with its positioning strategy. A process focus requires a process layout, whereas a product focus calls for a product layout. Hybrid layouts, such as OWMM, group technology cells, and FMS, reflect an intermediate positioning strategy.

- Capital investment, materials handling cost, and flexibility are important criteria in judging most manufacturing and warehouse layouts. Entirely different criteria, such as sales or communication, might be emphasized for stores or offices.

- Designing a process layout involves gathering the necessary information, developing an acceptable block plan, and translating the block plan into a detailed layout. Information needed for process layouts includes space requirements by center, available space (including the block plan for an existing layout), closeness ratings, and other considerations. Closeness ratings can be tabulated on either a From–To matrix or a REL chart. A manual approach to finding a block plan begins with listing key requirements, based on large closeness ratings or other considerations. Trial and error is then used to find a block plan that satisfies most of the requirements. A load–distance score helps evaluate the plan for relative location concerns.

- Several computer-based models, such as ALDEP and CRAFT, are now available to aid layout decision making.

- The simplest warehouse situation is the out-and-back selection pattern. Departmental proximity to the dock depends on the ratio of trip frequency to space needs. Other patterns are the route collection trip, batch picking, and the zone system.

- The effect of a layout on people is particularly apparent in offices. Layout affects productivity and the quality of work life. Four approaches to proximity–privacy trade-offs are traditional layouts, office landscaping, activity settings, and electronic cottages.

- The line-balancing problem is to assign tasks to stations so as to satisfy all precedence and cycle-time constraints, while minimizing the number of stations required. This in turn minimizes idle time, maximizes efficiency, and minimizes balance delay. The desired output rate from a line depends not only on demand forecasts, but also on frequency of rebalancing, capacity utilization, and job specialization. One approach to line balancing is to create one station at a time. A work element selected from a list of candidates is added to a station at each iteration. Two commonly used decision rules for making this choice are the longest work-element time and largest number of followers rules.

- Management must look beyond the narrow view of line balancing. Line pacing, behavioral options, single or mixed-model lines, and modifying the cycle time are options that are available to ensure the success of a product layout.

KEY TERMS

automated layout design
  program (ALDEP)   309
balance delay   322
block plan   303
computerized relative allocation of facilities technique (CRAFT)   310
cycle time   320
economic activity
  center   296
fixed-position layout   301
From–To matrix   304

hybrid layout   300
layout planning   296
line balancing   317
mixed-model line   326
precedence diagram
  317
process layout   297
product layout   299
REL chart   305
theoretical minimum
  (*TM*)   320
work elements   317

STUDY QUESTIONS

1. What are the types of choices that must be made in designing a layout? Which ones are the most strategic?
2. How does a process layout differ from a product layout? Illustrate each with an example that you have encountered at work or where you live.
3. With which other decision areas is layout strongly connected? Explain.
4. Identify the types of layout performance criteria that might be most important in the following settings.
   a. Bank   c. Law firm
   b. Parking lot   d. Small metal fabricator
5. An office of 120 employees must be revised to accommodate 30 new employees. While changing the layout, it makes sense to review it to be sure that it is as effective as possible. You want to improve communication, find space for everyone, create a good work environment, and

minimize adverse reactions to space reductions and relocations.
   a. What information would you gather? How?
   b. How would you analyze this information?
   c. How much employee involvement would you recommend? Why?
6. Consider the layout of a retail store you recently visited as a customer. What criteria seemed most important to those who designed it? Why?
7. Think of a small- to medium-sized class that you have taken where there was no assigned seating. Did you tend to sit in the same seat each time? Which criterion discussed for office layouts were you implicitly satisfying?
8. Layouts are often designed to fit current work activities and interaction patterns. These, in turn, are partially shaped by the existing layout. Comment on this apparent circularity.
9. What information is needed before you can solve a line-balancing problem?
10. Suppose that a line's desired output rate is 20 units per hour. Why might management consider cycle times other than 180 seconds?
11. Why might employee dissatisfaction be higher on assembly lines? What steps might help to alleviate this problem? Will these steps always lead to higher satisfaction and productivity? Explain.

PROBLEMS

Review Problems

1. The Foghorn Tool and Machine Company is a job shop specializing in precision parts for aerospace markets. Figure 9.15 shows the From–To matrix and the current block plan for the key manufacturing centers of the 75,000-square-foot facility. Using rectilinear distance (the current distance from inspection to shipping and receiving is 3 units of distance), calculate the change in the load–distance (*ld*) score if Foghorn exchanges the locations of the tool crib and inspection.
2. Use trial and error to find a particularly good block plan for Foghorn (see Problem 1). Because of excessive relocation costs, shipping and receiving (department 3) must remain at its current location. How good is your new layout, once again assuming rectilinear distance?
3. The Department of Philosophy at a large western university must assign six new faculty mem-

From \ To	1	2	3	4	5	6
1. Burr and grind		20		30		90
2. NC equipment					85	
3. Shipping and receiving				50		95
4. Lathes and drills					70	40
5. Tool crib						
6. Inspection						

(a) From–To Matrix (trips/day)

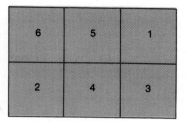

(b) Current Block Plan

FIGURE 9.15

bers to offices. The From–To matrix in Fig. 9.16(a) shows the expected frequency of contact between professors. The block plan in Fig. 9.16(b) shows the available office locations (1–6) for the six faculty members (A–F). Assume equal-sized offices and rectilinear distance. Owing to their academic positions, Professor A must be assigned to location 1 and Professor D to location 6. What are the best locations for the other four professors? What is the *ld* score for your layout?

4. As director of the Office of Budget Management for Michigan's state government, Todd Paul manages a department of 120 employees assigned to eight different sections. Workloads have expanded to the point that 30 new employees must be hired and placed somewhere within the existing layout. While changing the layout, Paul wishes to improve communication and create a good work environment. One special consideration is that the State Controlling Board (section 2) should occupy the upper-right location of the block plan. A From–To matrix was developed from questionnaires sent to each of the 120 current employees (Fig. 9.17). It contains section names and area requirements and represents the closeness ratings between each of the sections.

From \ To	A	B	C	D	E	F
Professor A			6			
Professor B				12		10
Professor C				2	7	
Professor D						4
Professor E						
Professor F						

(a) From–To Matrix (contacts/day)

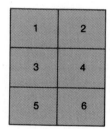

(b) Sketch of Available Space

FIGURE 9.16

From \ To	1	2	3	4	5	6	7	8	Area needed (blocks)
1. Administration		11		8		6	10	17	2
2. State Controlling Board					3		4		1
3. Program clearing house				1		3	2		3
4. Social services					12		2		2
5. Institutions						5	15	10	2
6. Accounting							4		1
7. Education								1	1
8. Internal audit									4

FIGURE 9.17

a. Develop a square block plan (4 rows and 4 columns) for Paul. Calculate a score for your plan as you would do using ALDEP. In other words, add the closeness rating (6 for A, 5 for E, and so on) between two sections to the total score only if the sections share at least some of the same boundary (merely touching the corner doesn't count).

b. What behavioral issues does Paul need to address when revising the layout?

5. The layout configuration for a warehouse docking area is shown in Fig. 9.18, along with the travel frequencies and area requirements of the seven departments (A–G). An out-and-back selection pattern is used. What is the best layout?

TABLE 9.4

Part Category	Trips per Day	Number of Sections Needed
A	90	1
B	70	2
C	320	2
D	210	3
E	45	1
F	65	1
G	120	2

TABLE 9.5

Section	Distance to Assembly Line	Section	Distance to Assembly Line
1	70	7	190
2	80	8	200
3	90	9	220
4	120	10	290
5	140	11	300
6	145	12	320

Department	Trips to and from dock	Area needed (blocks)
A	260	2
B	180	1
C	381	3
D	250	4
E	80	1
F	190	2
G	220	1

(a) Required Information

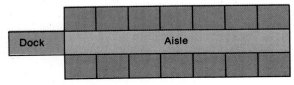

(b) Layout Configuration
FIGURE 9.18

6. Big Reaper plans to produce several new and larger truck models on an assembly line at its Barbville manufacturing facility. Four major warehousing areas in the plant, divided into 12 equal sections, will be used to store the parts and components needed for the new models. Based on current inventory and output plans, the average number of trips per day between storage and the assembly line have been estimated for each of seven basic part categories. The number of storage sections needed for each one (Table 9.4) and the distance from each section to the assembly line (Table 9.5) have also been calculated. Assign each part category to one or more storage sections, so as to provide the right amount of space for each. Find the assignment that minimizes travel from storage to the assembly line. Owing to size restrictions, part category G cannot be assigned to section 1 or 2.

7. Table 9.6 has been partially completed from the information in Managerial Practice 9.3 and Fig. 9.8 for the Big Broadcaster.

a. Complete Table 9.6 by filling in the last column.

b. Find a line-balancing solution using the largest number of followers rule. Break ties using the largest work-element time rule. If a tie remains, pick the work element with the highest numerical label.

c. Calculate the efficiency and balance delay of your solution.

8. Klondike, Inc., has developed a new camera that even a child can operate with minimal instruction. Beautiful shots are possible simply by pressing a button. Management wants to establish two assembly lines to make the camera. Each line includes 11 work elements and must pro-

TABLE 9.6

Work Element	Number of Followers	Work Element	Number of Followers
1	23	13	
2	20	14	
3	19	15	
4	18	16	
5	19	17	
6	18	18	
7	17	19	
8	8	20	
9	7	21	
10	6	22	
11	5	23	
12	8	24	

duce 45 cameras per hour. The following table gives the standard times and immediate predecessors for each work element to be performed.

Work Element	Work-Element Time (sec)	Immediate Predecessor
1	55	—
2	8	1
3	50	—
4	15	—
5	33	3, 4
6	63	2, 5
7	12	—
8	42	—
9	31	7, 8
10	46	9
11	16	6, 10

a. Construct a precedence diagram.
b. What cycle time (in seconds) corresponds to 45 cameras per hour?
c. What is the theoretical minimum number of stations for each line?
d. Use the longest work-element time rule to balance the line.
e. What is the efficiency of your line? How does it compare with theoretical maximum efficiency?
f. Can you find a way to improve the line's efficiency?

9. The *trim line* at Universal Engines is a small subassembly line that, along with other such lines, feeds into the final chasis line. The entire assembly line is to make Universal's new E cars and will be composed of more than 900 work stations. The trim line itself involves only 13 work elements and must handle 20 cars per hour. In addition to the usual precedence constraints, there are two *zoning constraints*. First, work elements 11 and 12 should, preferably, be assigned to the same station; both use a common component and assigning them to the same station conserves storage space. Second, work elements 8 and 10 cannot be performed at the same station. Work-element data are:

Work Element	Work-Element Time (min)	Immediate Predecessor
1	1.8	—
2	0.4	—
3	1.6	—
4	1.5	1
5	0.7	1
6	0.5	5
7	0.8	2
8	1.4	3
9	1.4	4
10	1.4	6, 7
11	0.5	8
12	1.0	10
13	0.8	9, 11, 12

a. Draw a precedence diagram.
b. What cycle time (in *minutes*) results in the desired output rate?
c. What is the theoretical minimum number of stations?
d. Using trial and error, balance the line as best you can.
e. What is the efficiency of your solution?

10. An assembly line must produce 40 bathroom scales per hour. The following table gives the necessary information.

Work Element	Work-Element Time (sec)	Immediate Predecessor
1	20	—
2	55	1
3	25	2
4	40	2
5	5	2
6	35	1
7	14	4, 5
8	40	3, 6, 7

a. Draw a precedence diagram.
b. What cycle time (in seconds) ensures the desired output rate?
c. What is the theoretical minimum number of stations? The theoretical maximum efficiency?
d. Design the line, using the longest work-element rule. What is its efficiency?
e. Can you find any way to improve the line's balance? If so, explain how.

Advanced Problems

A computer package is recommended for Problem 15(b).

11. Eastern Electronics makes various products for the communications industry. One of its manufacturing plants makes a device for sensing when telephone calls are placed. A From–To matrix and the current layout are shown in Fig. 9.19. Management is reasonably satisfied with the current layout, although it has heard some complaints about the placement of departments D, G, K, and L. Find a revised block plan for moving only these four departments, using trial and error. Show that the load–distance score is improved, assuming rectilinear distance.

12. A paced assembly line has been devised to make electric can openers, as shown in the table:

Station	Work-Element Assigned	Work-Element Time (min)
S1	1	2.8
S2	3, 4	1.5, 1.4
S3	2, 5, 6	0.5, 1.5, 0.7
S4	7	2.3
S5	8	2.5
S6	9, 10, 11	1.7, 0.8, 0.3
S7	12, 13	1.2, 1.8

a. What is the maximum hourly output rate from this line? (*Hint:* The line can go only as fast as the slowest work station.)
b. What cycle time corresponds to this maximum output rate?
c. If there is a worker at each station and the line operates at this maximum output rate, how much idle time is lost during each eight-hour shift?
d. What is the line's efficiency?

13. Sanders Manufacturing seeks a better layout for its plant. Figure 9.20(a) shows the departments to be located on the first floor of the plant. Fig-

From \ To	A	B	C	D	E	F	G	H	I	J	K	L
A. Network lead forming									50	70		80
B. Wire forming and subassembly						120			50	70		
C. Final assembly					40	120					90	
D. Coil and terminal eyeletting				80				120				
E. Presoldering									40	50		
F. Final testing			30						40	80		
G. Inventory storage												
H. Coil winding											60	
I. Coil assembly			70		40							
J. Network preparation	90											
K. Soldering			80									
L. Network insertion			60									

(a) From–To Matrix (trips/day)

(b) Current Block Plan

FIGURE 9.19

Department		Square feet
1	Materials storage	1,300
2	Forming	500
3	Machining	1,000
4	Painting	600
5	Assembly	1,400
6	Stamping	1,200
7	Saw	800
8	Inspection	700
82	Elevator	100
83	Stairs	200
84	Office	800
99	Aisle	2,200
	Total	10,800

(a) Space Requirements by Center

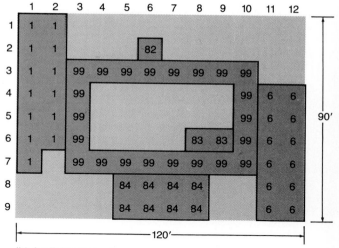

(b) Available Space *

*Productive space lost to elevator, stairs, office, and aisle is shown, along with required locations for departments 1 and 6.

Department		2	3	4	5	6	7	8
1	Materials storage	O (1)	O (1)	U	E (1)	U	O (1)	E (1)
2	Forming		E (1)	U	A (2,3)	U	I (1)	O (1)
3	Machining			I (1)	O (1)	U (1)	I (1)	U
4	Painting				E (2,3)	O	U (1)	E (4)
5	Assembly					X (5,6)	I (1)	I (1)
6	Stamping						I (1)	O (1)
7	Saw							I (1)
8	Inspection							

Closeness ratings		Explanation codes	
Rating	Definition	Code	Meaning
A	Absolutely necessary	1	Materials handling
E	Especially important	2	Shared personnel
I	Important	3	Ease of supervision
O	Ordinary closeness	4	Space utilization
U	Unimportant	5	Noise
X	Undesirable	6	Employee attitudes

(c) Closeness Ratings (REL Chart)

1. Owing to noise factors and the need for special foundations, the stamping department should be put in the southeast corner.
2. Materials storage should be on the northwest side, since this is where the shipping and receiving dock will be placed.

(d) Other Considerations

FIGURE 9.20

ure 9.20(b) divides the available space into 9 rows and 12 columns. Each block represents 100 square feet, which means that 13 blocks should be allocated to materials storage, 5 blocks to forming, and so on. Productive space is lost to the elevator, stairs, office, and aisle. Their positions, plus those for departments 1 and 6, must remain fixed. Figure 9.20(c) gives a REL chart. The letters indicate the closeness score, whereas the numbers in parentheses explain the reason for the rating. For example, it's necessary (rating = A) for the forming department and the assembly department to be close to each other because personnel are shared and supervision is easier.

a. Develop an acceptable layout for Sanders, working the remaining departments around the pre-positioned departments.

b. Calculate a score for your plan, as you would do using ALDEP (see Problem 4). Consider spaces separated only by the aisle to be adjacent.

14. Bradford Assemblies, Inc., manufactures customized wire harnesses for kitchen appliances, snowmobiles, farm machinery, and motorcycles. Figure 9.21(a) shows the From–To matrix, and

From \ To	1	2	3	4	5	6	7	8	9	10	11	12	13	14	15	16	99	Area needed (blocks)
1. Terminal storage		1		8	4		4											6
2. Shipping and receiving			1								2							6
3. Wire storage				8		5												6
4. Finished goods					11	16		1										6
5. Terminating						18	5			6			3	5	5			6
6. Cutting I							2											3
7. Cutting II								2		6			1	1	1			2
8. Painting										3								3
9. Processing																		3
10. Work-in-process													3	2	3			10
11. Rest rooms																		1
12. Supplies													2	2	1			4
13. Assembly I														2	2			4
14. Assembly II															1			4
15. Custom assembly																		3
16. Offices																		3
99. Dead space																		20

(a) From–To Matrix

	1	2	3	4	5	6
1	4	4	2	2	99	99
2	4	4	2	2	3	3
3	4	4	2	2	3	3
4	5	1	1	1	3	3
5	5	1	1	1	10	10
6	5	6	6	6	10	10
7	5	7	7	11	10	10
8	5	9	9	9	10	10
9	5	8	8	8	10	10
10	12	12	12	99	99	99
11	13	14	12	99	99	99
12	13	14	15	99	99	99
13	13	14	15	99	99	99
14	13	14	15	99	99	99
15	16	16	16	99	99	99

(b) Current Layout

FIGURE 9.21

Fig. 9.21(b) shows the current layout of the plant.

   a. Find a better layout, but keep departments 2, 16, and 99 (dead space) at their current positions.
   b. Calculate scores for both plans, as you would do using ALDEP (see Problem 4). How much better is your plan?

15. Green Grass's plant manager (see Managerial Practice 9.3) is willing to consider a line balance with an output rate of less than 60 units per hour, if the gain in efficiency is sufficient. Operating the line longer (either with a second shift or overtime) or setting up two lines are ways to compensate.

   a. Calculate the theoretical maximum efficiency for output rates of 30, 35, 40, 45, 50, 55, and 60. Is there any possible gain in efficiency if the output rate is reduced to as low as 30?
   b. Use the longest work-element time rule to explore solutions over the range of output rates where efficiency gains might be achieved.

SELECTED REFERENCES

Ackerman, K. B., and B. J. LaLonde, "Making Warehousing More Efficient," *Harvard Business Review* (March–April 1980), pp. 94–102.

Arcus, A. L., "COMSOAL: A Computer Method of Sequencing Operations for Assembly Lines," *International Journal of Production Research*, vol. 4, no. 4 (1966).

Buffa, Elwood S., G. C. Armour, and Thomas E. Vollmann, "Allocating Facilities with CRAFT," *Harvard Business Review* (March–April 1964), pp. 136–158.

Chase, Richard B., "Survey of Paced Assembly Lines," *Industrial Engineering*, vol. 6, no. 2 (February 1974), pp. 14–18.

Cinar, U. "Facilities Planning: A Systems Analysis and Space Allocation Approach." In C. M. Eastman (Ed.), *Spatial Synthesis in Computer-Aided Building Design.* New York: John Wiley & Sons, 1975.

Eastman, C. M., *Spatial Synthesis in Computer-Aided Building Design.* New York: John Wiley & Sons, 1975.

El-Rayah, J., "The Efficiency of Balanced and Unbalanced Production Lines," *International Journal of Production Research*, vol. 17, no. 1 (1979), pp. 61–75.

Ghosh, Soumen, and Roger Gagnon, "A Comprehensive Literature Review and Hierarchical Taxonomy for the Design and Balancing of Assembly Lines." Working Paper Series, College of Administrative Science, Ohio State University (January 1986).

Hicks, P. E., and T. E. Cowan, "CRAFT-M for Layout Rearrangement," *Industrial Engineering*, May 1976.

Hoffman, T. R., "Assembly Line Balancing with a Precedence Matrix," *Management Science*, vol. 9, no. 4 (July 1963), pp. 551–562.

Homans, G. C., *The Human Group.* New York: Harcourt Brace, 1950.

Jacobs, F. Robert, "A Layout Planning System with Multiple Criteria and a Variable Domain Representation," *Management Science*, vol. 33, no. 8 (August 1987), pp. 1020–1034.

Jacobs, F. Robert, John W. Bradford, and Larry P. Ritzman, "Computerized Layout: An Integrated Approach to Spatial Planning and Communication Requirements," *Industrial Engineering*, vol. 12, no. 7 (July 1980), pp. 56–61.

Kilbridge, M. D., and L. Wester, "A Heuristic Method of Assembly Line Balancing," *Journal of Industrial Engineering*, vol. 12, no. 4 (July–August 1961), pp. 292–298.

Kottas, J. F., and H. Lau, "Some Problems with Transient Phenomena When Simulating Unpaced Lines," *Journal of Operations Management*, vol. 1, no. 3 (February 1981), pp. 155–164.

Liggett, R. S., and W. J. Mitchell, "Interactive Graphic Floor Plan Layout Method," *Computer Aided Design*, vol. 13, no. 5 (September 1981), pp. 289–298.

Muther, Richard, *Practical Plant Layout.* New York: McGraw-Hill, 1955.

Oldham, G. R., and D. J. Brass, "Employee Reactions to an Open-Plan Office: A Naturally Occurring Quasi-Experiment," *Administrative Science Quarterly*, vol. 24 (1979), pp. 267–294.

Pinto, Peter D., David Dannenbring, and Basheer Khumawala, "Assembly Line Balancing with Processing Alternatives," *Management Science*, vol. 29, no. 7 (July 1983), pp. 817–830.

Ritzman, Larry P., John W. Bradford, and F. Robert Jacobs, "A Multiple Objective Approach to Space Planning for Academic Facilities," *Management Science*, vol. 25, no. 9 (September 1979), pp. 895–906.

Schuler, Randall S., Larry P. Ritzman, and Vicki L. Davis, "Merging Prescriptive and Behavioral Approaches for Office Layout," *Journal of Operations Management*, vol. 1, no. 3 (February 1981), pp. 131–142.

Scriabin, M., and R. C. Vergin, "Comparison of Computer Algorithms and Visual Based Methods for Plant Layout," *Management Science*, vol. 22, no. 2 (October 1975), pp. 172–181.

Seehof, J. M., and W. O. Evans, "Automated Layout Design Program," *Journal of Industrial Engineering*, vol. 18, no. 12 (December 1967), pp. 690–695.

Steel, F. I., *Physical Settings and Organization Development.* Reading, Mass.: Addison-Wesley, 1973.

Stone, Philip J., and Robert Luchetti, "Your Office Is Where You Are," *Harvard Business Review* (March–April 1985), pp. 102–117.

A wooden ski core enters the triaxial braiding process

PART

3

OPERATING DECISIONS

With the operating system designed, the manager must coordinate daily activities with the firm's overall operations strategy. For example, in K2's market—the ski industry—sales are seasonal, with peak selling periods occurring from June to September and November to December. There are also machine capacity restrictions to consider, such as K2's molding presses, which have lengthy setup times. Operating decisions are critical, because they often determine the degree to which a firm achieves its competitive priorities.

K2 prepares for heavy seasonal sales with a production plan that calls for building finished goods inventories from January to May. Seasonal employees cover vacation times in order to maintain a complement of 350 employees year round. K2 uses overtime and subcontracting sparingly. The firm also develops a master schedule for specific products that takes into account molding press capacities. The press schedule drives material flows throughout the plant. In addition, K2 reduced the average manufacturing time from five weeks to five days by implementing a just-in-time (JIT) production system. To improve productivity further, K2 trains operators to monitor critical quality measures throughout the manufacturing process.

K2 illustrates how a firm should link operating decisions to product plans and competitive priorities. Part 3 begins with forecasting and materials management, functions tied to most operating decisions. We discuss selecting an inventory management system and distinctions between independent and dependent demands—critical for understanding reorder point, material requirements planning, and JIT systems. We also look at approaches to production/staffing plans and master production schedules—both important inputs to workforce, operations, and project schedules. We conclude with quality control, which affects the outgoing quality of the system.

CHAPTER

10

FORECASTING

 Chapter Outline

Key Questions for Managers

Why is forecasting important to us?

When can we best use time series models and when can we best use causal or qualitative models?

What sort of controls do we need to impose on the forecasting system?

How can we design the best forecasting system for a given situation?

Is it always true that the most sophisticated forecasting system is the best for our use?

any managers wonder how they can predict with certainty what will happen in the future. The answer is simple: They can't. Instead, managers must work with probabilities, or the likelihood that certain events will occur. In their planning processes, managers use forecasts and accept the fact that forecasting involves errors. A **forecast** is a prediction of future events. Such predictions are rarely perfect, regardless of the quantity of historical data and the extent of the manager's experience. Fortunately, forecasting methods have been improved to the point where they provide useful estimates for planning purposes.

Both forecasting successes and failures are common. For example, in 1983 a management team at the Sunbeam Appliance Corporation developed new forecasting procedures. The process involved obtaining sales estimates from 200 top customers, projecting sales ahead for one year, and updating the forecast each month. The firm used these improved sales forecasts to develop more accurate manufacturing schedules. The result was a 45 percent reduction in inventories.

Recently, however, Intel grossly overstated the demand for its new 80386 chip, which is used in millions of high-performance PCs. Wary of potential shortages, customers had ordered more chips than they needed for the near future, distorting the true magnitude of demand. By the time Intel's plants caught up with actual demand, the company faced an unexpected glut. Each chip is worth $200 on the market, and experts estimated that Intel may have overproduced by 800,000 chips in 1988.

In operations management, planning often requires forecasts of customer demand for goods or services. Examples such as Sunbeam and Intel only emphasize the importance of accurate forecasts. Thus operations managers should take pains to learn about the advantages and limitations of the various forecasting methods available to them.

DEMAND CHARACTERISTICS ▲

Why does forecasting customer demand pose a challenge? The answer is that demand for goods and services can vary greatly. Demand for letter sorting at a metropolitan post office peaks just before Christmas and again just before Easter. But demand for haircuts at a local barbershop may be quite stable from week to week. The forecaster often must act like a detective to uncover the underlying pattern of demand in a given situation, using whatever information is available. In this section, we first discuss the factors that affect demand in a particular situation and then address the basic components of demand.

Factors Affecting Demand

What causes the demand pattern for a particular product? If we knew the answer to that question, forecasting would be much easier. Unfortunately, many factors affect demand at any given time. Table 10.1 shows two major categories of factors: external and internal.

External Factors.   Management cannot directly control external factors, particularly the general state of the economy. Although a booming economy may positively influence demand, the effect may not be the same for all products. Furthermore, certain economic activities affect some goods and services, but not others. Local, state, and national governments affect demand by passing legislation regarding taxes, interest rates, or environmental regulations. For example, limiting the sulphur content of coal used in steam-powered electric generating plants reduces the demand for high-sulphur coal.

Table 10.2 shows some common demand indicators and corresponding sources of information. **Leading indicators** are time series with turning points that typically precede the peaks and troughs of the general business cycle. For example, an upswing in residential building permits may precede an increase

---

TABLE 10.1   Factors Affecting Demand for Goods and Services

External Factors	Internal Factors
General state of the economy	Product design
Government actions	Price and advertising promotions
Consumer tastes	Packaging design
Public image of product	Salesperson quotas or incentives
Competitor actions	Expansion or contraction of geographical market target areas
Availability and cost of complementary products	Product mix
	Backlog policy

TABLE 10.2 Demand Indicators	
Leading Indicators	**Data Source**
New corporations	Dun & Bradstreet
Business failures	Dun & Bradstreet
Residential building contracts	F. W. Dodge Corporation
Commercial/industrial building contracts	F. W. Dodge Corporation
Common-stock prices—industrial	Dow Jones
Wholesale commodity price index	Bureau of Labor Statistics
Average hours worked per week— manufacturing	Bureau of Labor Statistics
New orders for manufacturing durable goods	Department of Commerce
Coincident Indicators	**Data Source**
Gross national product (GNP)	Department of Commerce
Corporate profits	Department of Commerce
Unemployment	Bureau of Labor Statistics
Nonagricultural employment	Bureau of Labor Statistics
Nonfood wholesale prices	Bureau of Labor Statistics
Index of industrial production	Federal Reserve Board
Bank debits	Federal Reserve Board
Freight carloadings	Association of American Railroads
Lagging Indicators	**Data Source**
Personal income	Department of Commerce
Retail sales	Department of Commerce
Manufacturers' inventories	Department of Commerce
Consumer installment debt	Federal Reserve Board
Bank rates on business loans	Federal Reserve Board

in the demand for plywood by several weeks and homeowner's insurance by several months. **Coincident indicators** are time series with turning points that generally match those of the general business cycle. **Lagging indicators** follow those turning points, typically by several weeks or months. Knowing that a series is a lagging indicator can be useful. For example, a firm interested in expanding and needing a business loan should realize that interest rates will drop to a low point several weeks after the business cycle reaches its trough.

Returning to Table 10.1, let's look briefly at other external factors that affect demand. Consumer tastes can change quickly, as they often do in clothing fashions. The consumer's image of a product can be another big factor. In the late 1970s and early 1980s, for example, foreign-car sales increased dra-

In 1983 Coleco grossly underestimated the demand for their Cabbage Patch Kids doll during the Christmas season. The customers outside this toy store arrived at 11:30 P.M. to wait for the store to open the next morning. The store received a shipment of 24 dolls, which were sold within ten minutes.

matically as a percentage of total car sales in the United States. Why? Because consumers believed that foreign cars were more fuel efficient and of superior quality.

In addition, competitors' actions regarding prices, advertising promotions, and new products also affect sales. For example, the Miller Lite commercials where former athletes argue whether the product "tastes right" or is "less filling" affects consumer demand for competitors' beer products. Finally, the success of complementary products affects demand. The location of Honda's Marysville, Ohio, plant stimulated the sales of many automobile parts and components in that area. Future demand for products from their suppliers depends on the overall success of Honda in that location.

Internal Factors.   Internal decisions can affect the demand for products. Recognition by management that these decisions can be controlled encourages management to respond actively, rather than passively, to demand. The term **demand management** describes the process of influencing the timing and volume of demand or adapting to the undesirable effects of unchangeable demand patterns. The lower part of Table 10.1 shows some of the ways in which management can affect demand.

Factors such as product design, price and advertising promotions, packaging design, salesperson quotas or incentives, and expansion or contraction of geographical market target areas can all contribute to changes in demand volume. For example, Managerial Practice 10.1 shows how rebates can boost car sales. However, the purpose of demand management goes beyond merely increasing customer demand. Management must also consider the timing of demand, an extremely important factor in efficiently utilizing resources and production capacity.

Trying to produce for peak customer demand during the peak demand period can be very costly. To avoid this situation, firms often use price incentives or advertising promotions to encourage customers to make purchases before or after traditional times of peak demand. For example, telephone companies encourage customers to make long distance calls after normal business hours by offering lower evening and weekend rates. This practice reduces the amount of resources needed to handle peak demand. Another tactic is to introduce a product that has a different heavy seasonal demand period. Firms with the technology to produce tractor lawn mowers might also produce snowmobiles to even out resource and production requirements over the year. In this way costly changes in work-force level and inventory can be minimized.

Finally, some companies use backlogs to stabilize resource requirements over time. When an inquiry or order is received, the producer specifies a delivery date, which depends on the current workload and capacity. Doctors, dentists, and other professionals use this approach by asking patients to make appointments for their services. Manufacturers of custom-built products also work to backlogs of demand.

Components of Demand

The five basic components of most business demand series are the average, trend, seasonal influence, cyclical movement, and random error. The first four of these components combine in varying degrees to define the underlying time pattern of demand and are affected by both external and internal factors.

MANAGERIAL PRACTICE 10.1 ▲

Demand Management at GM

In the first quarter of 1988, General Motors Corporation reported that financial incentives to car buyers helped it to regain some of its lost share of the car and truck market. The company's share of the car market improved to 37.5 percent, from 33.4 percent in the final period of 1987. Rebates on the purchase of new cars were largely responsible for the upswing in retail sales. The increased sales reduced dealer stocks but the rebate program caused a drop in the company's earnings.

Source: "Market Share Higher, Profits Lower at GM," by John Holusha, *New York Times*, April 22, 1988.

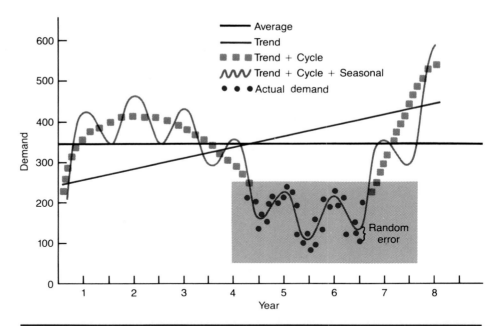

FIGURE 10.1   The Components of a Demand Series over Time

Figure 10.1 shows the demand series for a particular product. The trend, seasonal influence, and cyclical movement components have a significant impact on the demand pattern for this product. Preparing useful forecasts for this product depends on the forecaster's ability to estimate accurately the effects of these components in the future. As you will see later in this chapter, estimating the average, trend, and seasonal influence isn't too difficult. Estimating cyclical movement is much more difficult. Forecasters often do not know the duration of the cycle because they cannot predict the events that cause it. National and international events, such as a presidential election, war in the Middle East, or an embargo on foreign-built machine tools, can affect demand. The ability to make intelligent long-range forecasts depends on accurate estimates of cyclical movement.

The fifth component, random error, is the remaining demand after all known causes of demand (such as the average, trend, seasonal influence, and cyclical movement) have been identified. Random error is the component of demand that makes every forecast wrong. Random error is caused by chance variation and, by definition, chance variation cannot be predicted. The insert in Fig. 10.1 shows the relationship of random error to actual demand.*

---

*If we make an error in estimating the trend, seasonal, or cyclical components, the error terms may be highly correlated with each other and consequently not a result of chance variation. In such cases we say that there is *autocorrelation* in the error terms.

FORECASTING AND OPERATIONS MANAGEMENT ▲

Because demand exhibits many different characteristics, several different types of forecasting methods are needed. The forecaster's objective is to develop a useful forecast from the information at hand. In order to achieve this objective, the forecaster must select the appropriate technique. This choice sometimes involves a trade-off between forecast accuracy and cost. Three general types of forecasting techniques are used for demand forecasting: **time series* analysis, causal methods**, and **qualitative techniques**. Time series analysis is a statistical approach that relies heavily on historical data to project the future size of demand, but recognizes trends and seasonal patterns. Causal methods mathematically express the relationship between the factor to be forecast and related factors, such as promotional campaigns, economic conditions, and competitors' actions. Qualitative techniques translate managerial judgment, expert opinion, and/or survey results into quantitative estimates. We describe each technique in more detail later in this chapter. First, however, let's consider the conditions under which these techniques are likely to be applied. Table 10.3 contains examples of demand forecasting applications and the typical planning horizon for each.

TABLE 10.3 Demand Forecast Applications

Application	Time Horizon		
	Short Term (0–3 Months)	Medium Term (3 Months–2 Years)	Long Term (More than 2 Years)
Forecast quantity	Individual products	Total sales Groups or families of products	Total sales
Decision area	Inventory management Final assembly scheduling Work-force scheduling Master production scheduling	Staff planning Production planning Master production scheduling Purchasing Distribution	Facility location Capacity planning Process design
Forecasting technique	Time series Causal Qualitative	Causal Qualitative	Causal Qualitative

---

*A time series is a list of repeated observations of a phenomenon, such as demand, arranged in the order in which they actually occurred.

Short Term

In the short term (here, 0–3 months in the future) managers are typically interested in forecasts of unit demand for individual products. There is little time to satisfy demand, so forecasts need to be as accurate as possible for planning purposes. Time series analysis is the method most often used for short-term forecasting. It is a relatively inexpensive way to generate the large number of forecasts required. In the short term, the quality of these forecasts can be very good.

Causal models are not used extensively for this purpose. They are much more costly than time series analysis and require more time to develop. In the short term, operations managers rarely can wait for development of causal models, even though they may be more accurate than time series models. Finally, managers use qualitative techniques for short-term forecasts when historical data are not available for a specific item, such as the introduction of a new product. However, these forecast methods are also more expensive than forecasts generated from time series analysis.

Medium Term

The time horizon for the medium term is between three months and two years. For planning purposes the level of forecast detail required is not so great as for the short term. Managers typically forecast total sales demand in dollars or in the number of units of an aggregation of goods or services into groups or families of similar products. The need for medium-term forecasts arises from planning problems related to issues of capacity, such as those shown in Table 10.3. Causal models are commonly used for medium-term forecasts. These models typically do a good job of identifying periods when the growth rate of demand will change, as when slow sales growth will turn into rapid decline. Determination of these *turning points* is very important for the operations manager, particularly in the medium and long term.

Some qualitative methods of forecasting are also helpful in identifying turning points. However, as we mentioned earlier, they are most often used in situations where no historical data exist. Time series analysis typically does not yield accurate results in the medium or long term, primarily because it assumes that existing patterns will continue in the future. This assumption may be valid for the short term, but is less accurate over longer time horizons.

Long Term

For time horizons exceeding two years, forecasts are usually developed for total sales demand in dollars or some other common unit of measurement, such as barrels, pounds, or kilowatts. Accurate long-term forecasts of demand for individual products not only are very difficult to make, but they also are too detailed for long-range planning purposes. Table 10.3 shows that three decision areas—facility location, capacity planning, and process design—require market demand estimates for an extended period into the future. Causal models and qualitative methods are the primary techniques used for long-term forecasting. However, even mathematically derived causal model forecasts have to be tempered by managerial experience and judgment because of the time horizon involved and the potential consequences of decisions based on them.

TIME SERIES ANALYSIS ▲

In the simplest form of time series analysis, the only information used is the historical record of demand. The analyst isn't concerned with changes in the external and internal factors listed in Table 10.1 and assumes that what has occurred in the past will continue to occur in the future. Methods of time series analysis focus on the average, trend, and seasonal influence characteristics of time series. The analyst's task is to try to replicate these characteristics when projecting future demand.

Forecasting the Average

Consider Fig. 10.2, which shows patient arrivals at a medical clinic over the past 28 weeks. This graph is useful because it enables the analyst to hypothesize the nature of and reasons for this demand pattern. For purposes of discussion

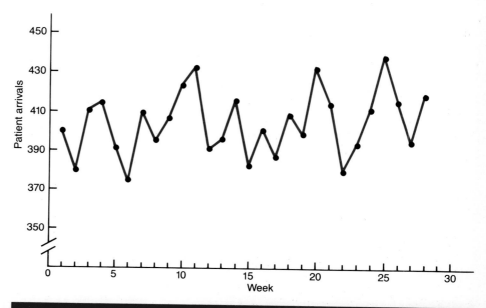

FIGURE 10.2 Weekly Patient Arrivals at a Medical Clinic

let's assume that you are the analyst. Let's further assume that this series has only an average and random errors. The simple moving average and exponential smoothing models are useful for forecasting the average of a time series.

Simple Moving Average.   You can use the simple **moving average method** to estimate the average of a demand time series and remove the effects of random fluctuation. This method is most useful when demand does not have a pronounced trend or any seasonal influences. To use a moving average model you simply calculate the average demand for the N most recent time periods and use it as the forecast for the next time period.* Specifically, the calculation involves

$$\text{Average:} \qquad A_t = \frac{D_t + D_{t-1} + D_{t-2} + \cdots + D_{t-N+1}}{N}$$

Forecast: $F_{t+1} = A_t$

Where: D_t = actual demand in period t

N = total number of periods in the average

A_t = average computed for period t

F_{t+1} = forecast for period $t + 1$

You update the forecast for each new period by averaging the same number of past demands. You keep the same value of N by replacing the oldest demand from the previous average with the most recent demand.

APPLICATION 10.1

Compute a three-week moving average forecast for the arrival of medical clinic patients in week 4, using the actual number of patient arrivals in weeks 1 through 3.

Week	Patient Arrivals
1	401
2	380
3	411

If the actual number of patient arrivals is 415 in week 4, what is the forecast for week 5?

---

*In this section our calculations for the series average are carried to one decimal place. If the time series is expressed in discrete units, such as patient arrivals, the *forecast* should be rounded to the nearest integer in practice.

Solution

The moving average at the end of week 3 is

$$A_3 = \frac{411 + 380 + 401}{3} = 397.3$$

Thus the forecast for week 4 is 397 patients.

The forecast for week 5 requires the actual arrivals from weeks 2–4, the three most recent weeks of data.

$$A_4 = \frac{415 + 411 + 380}{3} = 402.0$$

The forecast for week 5 is 402 patients. Continuing—by finding the average of each week—you can obtain the forecast for succeeding weeks.

For purposes of comparison we calculated a three-week and a six-week moving average forecast for the medical clinic data. Figure 10.3 shows this comparison, along with actual patient arrivals. This information provides clues regarding the choice of an N value. Note that the three-week moving average

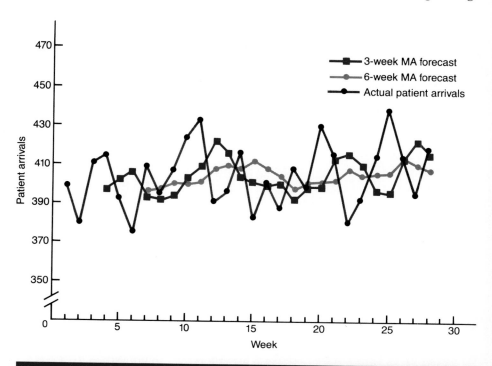

FIGURE 10.3 Comparison of Three-Week and Six-Week Moving Average Forecasts

forecast varies more and reacts more quickly to large swings in demand. This sensitivity can be an advantage if, for example, the underlying average of the series is changing over time because of an unsuspected trend in the data. Conversely, the six-week moving average forecast is more stable because large swings in demand tend to cancel each other.

Including more historical data in the average results in a forecast that is less susceptible to random variations. However, if the underlying average in the series is changing, the forecasts will tend to lag behind the changes for a longer period of time because it takes longer to get all the old data out of the forecast. Generally, you should use large values for N for demand series that are stable and small values for N for those that are susceptible to changes in the underlying average. We address other considerations for the choice of N when we discuss choosing the best method of forecasting.

Weighted Moving Average.   In the simple moving average method each demand has the same weight in the average, namely, $1/N$. In the **weighted moving average method**, each historical demand in the average can have its own weight, so

$$\text{Average:} \quad A_t = W_1 D_t + W_2 D_{t-1} + \cdots + W_N D_{t-N+1}$$

$$\text{Forecast:} \quad F_{t+1} = A_t$$

$$\text{Where:} \quad \sum_{i=1}^{N} W_i = 1$$

The weighted moving average method allows you to emphasize recent demand over earlier demand. The forecast will be more responsive to changes in the underlying average of the demand series. Alternatively, it allows you to emphasize the levels of demand from several periods ago that have an impact on current demand. In this way "time-lag" effects can also be recognized.

APPLICATION 10.2

The analyst for the medical clinic has assigned weights of 70 percent to the most recent demand, 20 percent to the demand one week ago, and 10 percent to the demand two weeks ago. Using the data for the first three weeks from Application 10.1, calculate the weighted moving average forecast for week 4.

Solution

The average demand in week 3 is

$$A_3 = 0.70(411) + 0.20(380) + 0.10(401) = 403.8$$

The forecast for week 4 therefore is 404 patients.

Now suppose that the actual demand for week 4 is 415 patients. The new average and the forecast for week 5 would be

$$A_4 = 0.70(415) + 0.20(411) + 0.10(380) = 410.7$$
$$F_5 = 411 \text{ patients}$$

The weighted moving average method has the same shortcomings as the simple moving average method: You must retain data for N periods of demand in order to calculate the average for each period. Keeping this amount of data isn't a great burden in simple situations, such as our three-week and six-week examples. However, some time series are quite stable, and moving average calculations for 200 or more periods are not uncommon. Thus for a company that has to forecast many different demands, data storage and update costs can be high.

Single Exponential Smoothing. Perhaps the most frequently used forecasting method is **single exponential smoothing** because of its simplicity and the small amount of data needed to support it. It is called *single* because only the average of the series is estimated. The basic premise of exponential smoothing is that recent demands should have more weight than earlier ones in computing the average for forecasting purposes. However, unlike the weighted moving average method, single exponential smoothing requires only three items of data: the average for the last period; the demand for this period; and a smoothing parameter, alpha (α). As before, you calculate an average of past demands at the end of the current period and use it as a forecast for the next period. You do not need much data in order to make the forecast. You can also adjust the amount of emphasis given to the most recent demand levels by simply adjusting the smoothing parameter.

The equations for the average of a demand series and the forecast using exponential smoothing are

Average: $A_t = \alpha D_t + (1 - \alpha)(A_{t-1})$

Forecast: $F_{t+1} = A_t$

Where: α = smoothing parameter with a value between 0 and 1

Larger α values emphasize recent demand and result in forecasts that are more responsive to changes in the underlying average. Smaller α values treat past demand more uniformly and result in more stable forecasts.* Exponential smoothing gets its name from the nature of the weights placed on each successive historical demand used to calculate the average. Table 10.4 shows the general expressions for the weights to be placed on the 10 most recent levels of demand in a series and the corresponding numerical weights for three

---

*A_t can also be calculated using the forecast for period t: $A_t = \alpha D_t + (1 - \alpha)(F_t)$.

TABLE 10.4   *Single Exponential Smoothing Weights*

Demand	Weight	Numerical Weights for $\alpha = 0.1$	$\alpha = 0.2$	$\alpha = 0.8$
D_t	α	0.1000	0.2000	0.8000
D_{t-1}	$\alpha(1 - \alpha)^1$	0.0900	0.1600	0.1600
D_{t-2}	$\alpha(1 - \alpha)^2$	0.0810	0.1280	0.0320
D_{t-3}	$\alpha(1 - \alpha)^3$	0.0729	0.1024	0.0064
D_{t-4}	$\alpha(1 - \alpha)^4$	0.0656	0.0819	0.0013
D_{t-5}	$\alpha(1 - \alpha)^5$	0.0590	0.0655	0.0003
D_{t-6}	$\alpha(1 - \alpha)^6$	0.0531	0.0524	0.0001
D_{t-7}	$\alpha(1 - \alpha)^7$	0.0478	0.0419	0.0000
D_{t-8}	$\alpha(1 - \alpha)^8$	0.0430	0.0336	0.0000
D_{t-9}	$\alpha(1 - \alpha)^9$	0.0387	0.0268	0.0000

assumed values of α. As with the weighted moving average method, the sum of the weights must equal 1, which is implicit in the single exponential smoothing equation. The derivation of the general expressions for the first three weights in the series is as follows:

1. Let $t = 2$.

$$A_2 = \alpha D_2 + (1 - \alpha)A_1$$
$$A_1 = \alpha D_1 + (1 - \alpha)A_0$$

2. Substitute the expression for A_1 into the equation for A_2.

$$A_2 = \alpha D_2 + \alpha(1 - \alpha)D_1 + (1 - \alpha)^2 A_0$$

3. Let $t = 3$.

$$
\begin{aligned}
A_3 &= \alpha D_3 + (1 - \alpha)A_2 \\
&= \alpha D_3 + (1 - \alpha)[\alpha D_2 + \alpha(1 - \alpha)D_1 + (1 - \alpha)^2 A_0] \\
&= \alpha D_3 + \alpha(1 - \alpha)D_2 + \alpha(1 - \alpha)^2 D_1 + (1 - \alpha)^3 A_0
\end{aligned}
$$

APPLICATION 10.3

Again consider the patient arrival data in Application 10.1. Calculate the single exponential smoothing forecast for week 4 using $\alpha = 0.10$.

Solution

The single exponential smoothing method requires an initial value for the average. Suppose that you take the demand data for several recent weeks and average them, arriving at a value of 400 as an estimate of the past average. To obtain the forecast for week 4, using single exponential smoothing with an assumed $\alpha = 0.10$, you can calculate the average at the end of week 3 as follows:

$$A_3 = 0.10(411) + 0.90(400) = 401.1$$

Thus the forecast for week 4 would be 401 patients. If the actual demand for week 4 turned out to be 415, the new average would be

$$A_4 = 0.10(415) + 0.90(401.1) = 402.5$$

and the forecast for week 5 would be 403 patients.

Single exponential smoothing has the advantages of simplicity and minimal data requirements. It is inexpensive to use and therefore very attractive to firms that make thousands of forecasts for each time period. However, its simplicity is also a disadvantage when the underlying average is changing, as in the case of a demand series with a trend. Like any method geared solely to the assumption of a stable average, single exponential smoothing results will lag behind changes in the underlying average of demand. Higher α values may help to reduce forecast errors; however, the lags will still be there to some degree. Typically, if large α values (greater than 0.50, for example) are required for a single exponential smoothing application, chances are good that a more sophisticated model is needed because of a significant trend and/or seasonal influence in the demand series. We address the issue of choosing the best α value later.

Including a Trend

Let's now consider a demand time series that has a trend. Although a number of forecasting methods that recognize a trend are available, we focus on exponential smoothing here because it is so widely used in practice. When a trend is present, the average of the series is systematically increasing or decreasing over time. This means that single exponential smoothing approaches must be modified; otherwise, the forecasts will always be below or above the actual demand. An estimate of the current trend in a time series is the difference between the simple average of the series for the current period and the average for the last period. To obtain a better estimate of a long-term trend, you can reduce the effects of random causes by averaging the current estimates. The method for arriving at the estimate of the trend is similar to the method used to get the estimate of the average with single exponential smoothing.

The method for incorporating a trend in an exponentially smoothed forecast is called **double exponential smoothing** because the estimate for the average, as well as the estimate for the trend, is smoothed. For each period you calculate the

Average:

$$A_t = \alpha D_t + (1 - \alpha)(A_{t-1} + T_{t-1})$$

Current estimate of trend:

$$CT_t = A_t - A_{t-1}$$

Average trend:

$$T_t = \beta CT_t + (1 - \beta)T_{t-1}$$

Forecast:

$$F_{t+1} = A_t + T_t$$

Where:

A_t = exponentially smoothed average of the series in period t

CT_t = current estimate of the trend in period t

T_t = exponentially smoothed average of the trend in period t

F_{t+1} = forecast for next period

α = smoothing parameter for the average with a value between 0 and 1

β = smoothing parameter for the trend with a value between 0 and 1

You need an initial estimate for the average and the trend in order to get started. You can derive these estimates from past data or simply make an educated guess based on past experience.

APPLICATION 10.4

Medanalysis, Inc., provides medical laboratory service to patients of Health Providers, a group of 10 family-practice doctors associated with a new health maintenance program. We are interested in forecasting the number of patients requesting blood analysis per week. Recent publicity about the damaging effects of cholesterol on the heart has caused a national increase in the requests for standard blood tests. Our best guess for the past weekly average is 28 and for the trend is 3 per week. This week's demand was 27 blood tests—below the historical average but reasonably in line with past performance. We use alpha (α) = 0.2 and Beta (β) = 0.2 to calculate the forecast for next week.

Solution

Our calculations for the forecast for week 2 (next week) are as follows:

$$A_1 = 0.2(27) + 0.8(28 + 3) = 30.2$$
$$CT_1 = 30.2 - 28 = 2.2$$
$$T_1 = 0.2(2.2) + 0.8(3) = 2.8$$
$$F_2 = 30.2 + 2.8 = 33.0 \text{ tests}$$

If the actual number of blood tests requested in week 2 turned out to be 44, the updated forecast for week 3 would be

$$A_2 = 0.2(44) + 0.8(30.2 + 2.8) = 35.2$$
$$CT_2 = 35.2 - 30.2 = 5.0$$
$$T_2 = 0.2(5.0) + 0.8(2.8) = 3.2$$
$$F_3 = 35.2 + 3.2 = 38.4 \quad \text{or} \quad 38 \text{ tests}$$

For illustrative purposes, we plotted the trend-adjusted forecast for Medanalysis for a period of 15 weeks in Fig. 10.4. At the end of each week we calculated a forecast for the next week, using the number of blood tests for the current week.

Several comments are in order at this point. First, we did not look very closely at possible α and β values, so we may be able to come up with a better forecast by using different values. (We discuss how to choose the best values after covering forecast errors and their measurement.) Second, we can make forecasts for periods beyond next period by simply multiplying the trend estimate by the number of additional periods that we want in the forecast and add the result to the current average. For example, if we are in week 2 and want

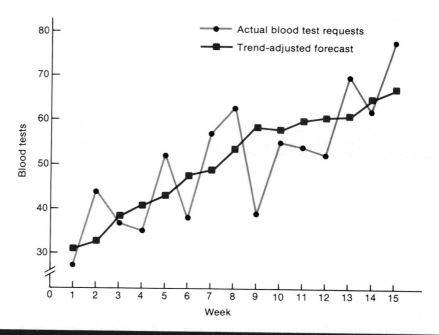

FIGURE 10.4   Trend-Adjusted Forecast for Medanalysis

to estimate the demand for blood tests in week 6, the forecast would be

$$F_6 = 35.2 + 4(3.2) = 48 \text{ tests}$$

However, the farther we project our trend estimate the more tenuous our forecast becomes. In general, the use of time series methods should be restricted to the short term.

Seasonal Influences

Many organizations experience seasonal demand for their goods or services. The volume of letters processed by the U.S. Postal Service increases dramatically during the Christmas holiday period. Demands for products such as lawn and garden supplies, snow shovels, automobile tires, clothing, and construction supplies are subjected to seasonal influences. Even the demand for telephone service is seasonal, as anyone trying to call relatives during holiday periods is well aware. A number of methods are available for forecasting time series with seasonal influences. We present only the **multiplicative seasonal method** here because, although it is simple, it introduces the notion of seasonal factors.

This procedure makes use of simple averages of past demands even though more sophisticated methods for calculating averages, such as moving averages or exponential smoothing, could also be used. First, we need to define the variables encountered in using the procedure:

$D_{y,t}$ = demand in period t in year y

$\overline{D}_y$ = average demand per year in year y

$\tilde{D}_y$ = projected average demand per period for some future year y

$f_{y,t}$ = seasonal factor for period t in year y

$\overline{f}_t$ = average seasonal factor for period t

$F_{y,t}$ = forecast for period t in some future year y

m = number of years of past data

n = number of demand periods each year

The procedure for calculating seasonal factors consists of three steps:

1. Calculate the average demand per period for each year of past data.

$$\overline{D}_y = \frac{\sum\limits_{t=1}^{n} D_{y,t}}{n}$$

2. Divide the actual demand for each period by the average demand per period to get a seasonal factor for each period. Repeat for each year of data.

$$f_{y,t} = \frac{D_{y,t}}{\overline{D}_y}$$

3. Calculate the average seasonal factor for each period.

$$\overline{f}_t = \frac{\sum\limits_{y=1}^{m} f_{y,t}}{m}$$

To forecast a given period t in a future year y, we simply estimate the average demand per period for that year, $\widetilde{D}_y$, and multiply it by the appropriate seasonal factor, or

$$F_{y,t} = \widetilde{D}_y \overline{f}_t$$

APPLICATION 10.5

The manager of the Stanley Steamer carpet cleaning company in Westerville needs a quarterly forecast of the number of customers she will have in 1990. Her carpet cleaning business is seasonal, with a peak in the third quarter and a trough in the first quarter. She gives us the following quarterly demand data from 1986 through 1989.

Quarter	1986	1987	1988	1989
1	45	70	100	100
2	335	370	585	725
3	520	590	830	1160
4	100	170	285	215
Total	1000	1200	1800	2200

We are to forecast customer demand for each quarter of 1990 based on the manager's estimate of total 1990 demand of 2600 customers.

Solution

We begin with 1986 to demonstrate the computation of the seasonal factors for a given year. Note that

$$\sum_{t=1}^{4} D_{1986,t} = 1000$$

Consequently, the average demand per quarter, $\overline{D}_{1986}$, is 250 (or 1000/4) customers. The seasonal factors for 1986 are

$$f_{1986, 1} = \frac{45}{250} = 0.18$$

$$f_{1986, 2} = \frac{335}{250} = 1.34$$

$$f_{1986, 3} = \frac{520}{250} = 2.08$$

$$f_{1986, 4} = \frac{100}{250} = 0.40$$

The table below shows the seasonal factors for the remaining years and, in the last column, the average seasonal factor for each quarter. For example, $\bar{f}_1 = (0.18 + 0.23 + 0.22 + 0.18)/4 = 0.20$.

The projected demand for 1990 is 2600 units. Therefore the average projected demand per quarter, $\widetilde{D}_{1990}$, is 650 (or 2600/4) customers. We make the quarterly forecasts by simply multiplying the seasonal factor for each quarter by $\widetilde{D}_{1990}$, or

$$F_{1990, 1} = 650(0.20) = \quad 130$$

$$F_{1990, 2} = 650(1.30) = \quad 845$$

$$F_{1990, 3} = 650(2.00) = 1300$$

$$F_{1990, 4} = 650(0.50) = \quad 325$$

Calculation of Seasonal Factors

| | 1986 | | 1987 | | 1988 | | 1989 | | Average |
| | Demand | Seasonal Factor* | Demand | Seasonal Factor* | Demand | Seasonal Factor* | Demand | Seasonal Factor* | Seasonal Factor† |
Quarter (t)	$(D_{1986, t})$	$(f_{1986, t})$	$(D_{1987, t})$	$(f_{1987, t})$	$(D_{1988, t})$	$(f_{1988, t})$	$(D_{1989, t})$	$(f_{1989, t})$	$(\bar{f}_t)$
1	45	0.18	70	0.23	100	0.22	100	0.18	0.20
2	335	1.34	370	1.23	585	1.30	725	1.32	1.30
3	520	2.08	590	1.97	830	1.84	1160	2.11	2.00
4	100	0.40	170	0.57	285	0.63	215	0.39	0.50
Total	1000		1200		1800		2200		
Quarterly average demand $(\overline{D}_y)$	250		300		450		550		

*Actual demand in a quarter divided by the average demand per quarter; subject to minor roundoff error.
†Average of the quarterly seasonal factors.

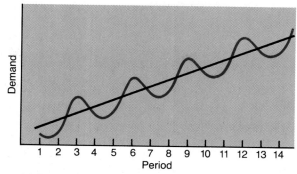

(a) Comparison of Additive Influences

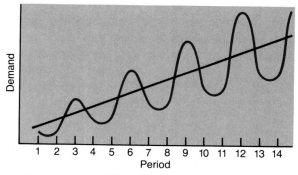

(b) Comparison of Multiplicative Influences

FIGURE 10.5 Comparison of Influences

At the end of each year, you can update the average seasonal factor for each quarter by calculating the average of all historical seasonal factors for that quarter, or by calculating a moving average or single exponentially smoothed average if you want some control over the relevance of past demand patterns.

The multiplicative seasonal method gets its name from the way seasonal factors are calculated and used. Multiplying the seasonal factor by an estimate of the average period demand implies that the seasonal influence depends on the level of demand. The peaks and valleys are more extreme when the average demand level is high, a situation faced most often by firms that produce goods and services having a seasonal demand. An alternative to the multiplicative seasonal method is the *additive seasonal method*, which implies a constant seasonal influence, regardless of the average level of demand. For purposes of comparison, Fig. 10.5(a) shows the pattern of additive seasonal influences, and Fig. 10.5(b) shows that of multiplicative seasonal influences.

Focus Forecasting

Does a more sophisticated forecasting model always produce a better forecast? Is there one best forecasting technique for all goods or services? The answer to both questions is *no*. In 1978, Bernard Smith, an inventory manager at American Hardware Supply, recognized these realities of forecasting and developed what he called **focus forecasting**.

Smith was responsible for an inventory of 100,000 different items purchased by the company's 21 buyers. Originally, the company used a basic exponential smoothing system with a curve-fitting method for projecting seasonal influences. It used these forecasts to determine purchase quantities. However, the buyers were changing 53 percent of the suggested purchase quantities. One of the major reasons was that the buyers did not understand exponential smoothing and, consequently, did not trust the system. Their constant changes resulted in excessive purchases and levels of inventory.

Smith decided to survey the buyers to find out how they arrived at their own forecasts. One buyer computed the percentage increase in demand experienced during the last period and used it to project the increase in demand for the next period. Another buyer simply used the demand from the last period as the forecast for the next period. Other buyers used similar, simple methods for forecasting demand. Each buyer was responsible for a different group of items, and Smith had no reason to believe that any one of the methods would work for all items.

Using the suggested methods from the buyers and adding some statistical methods, including exponential smoothing, Smith selected seven forecast methods as the basis for his focus forecasting technique. Every month the computer uses all seven methods to make forecasts for each item. Historical data are used as the starting point for each method, and forecasts are made for recent demand. The method that produces the best forecast for recent data is used to make the current demand forecast for an item. The following month, the "best" forecasting method for an item may be different from the one chosen for the current month.

Each month the computer prints the forecast for each of the 100,000 items. Buyers may still override the computer forecast. However, Smith claims that his system provides excellent short-term forecasts for American Hardware Supply. The system is used for expensive as well as inexpensive items and has much more credibility with the buyers than the previous system.

Forecast Error

There is a Chinese proverb that says, "To prophesy is extremely difficult, especially with respect to the future." And so it is with forecasting—forecasts will always contain errors. Forecast errors sometimes result from an inability to accurately assess the underlying components of demand and sometimes from random causes outside a firm's control.

Measures of Forecast Error. Before they can think about minimizing forecast error, managers must first have some means of measuring it. **Forecast error** is simply the difference between the forecast and actual demand for a given period. Specifically,

$$E_t = D_t - F_t$$

where

$$E_t = \text{forecast error for period } t$$
$$D_t = \text{actual demand for period } t$$
$$F_t = \text{forecast for period } t$$

However, managers are usually more interested in measuring forecast error over a relatively long period of time. Some commonly used methods are

Cumulative sum of forecast errors: $$CFE = \sum_{t=1}^{n} E_t$$

Standard deviation of forecast errors: $$\sigma = \sqrt{\frac{\sum_{t=1}^{n} E_t^2}{n - 1}}$$

Mean absolute deviation of forecast errors: $$MAD = \frac{\sum_{t=1}^{n} |E_t|}{n}$$

Mean absolute percent error: $$MAPE = \frac{\sum_{t=1}^{n} \frac{|E_t|}{D_t} (100)}{n}$$ (expressed as a percentage)

where n is the total number of periods. Recall that | | is the mathematical symbol used to indicate absolute value, or to disregard positive and negative signs.

The **cumulative sum of forecast errors (*CFE*)** is useful in measuring the *bias* in a forecast. Bias refers to the tendency of a forecast to always be too high or too low. For example, if a forecast is always lower than actual demand, the value of *CFE* will gradually get larger and larger. This increasingly large error indicates that there is some systematic deficiency in the forecasting approach. Perhaps the analyst omitted a trend element or a cyclical influence, or perhaps the seasonality of the demand changed from its historical pattern. We explain later how to use *CFE* to develop a tracking signal to indicate when you should be concerned about forecast performance.

The **standard deviation (σ)** and the **mean absolute deviation (*MAD*)** measure the dispersion of forecast errors. If σ or *MAD* is small, the forecast is typically close to actual demand, whereas if one or the other is large, there is the possibility of a large forecast error.* In practice, *MAD* is a popular measure of forecast error because managers can easily understand it; it is merely the average error for each forecast. This measurement is also used in tracking signals and inventory control. You will see in Chapter 12 that *MAD* or σ can be used to determine safety stocks for inventory items. The greater that *MAD* or σ is, the larger the safety stock required, placing a premium on forecasting methods that result in small forecast errors.

If forecast errors are normally distributed with a mean of zero, which is the usual case if we properly specify the forecast model, there is a simple relationship between σ and *MAD:*

$$\sigma = \sqrt{\frac{\pi}{2}}MAD \simeq 1.25MAD$$

or

$$MAD = 0.7978\sigma \simeq 0.8\sigma$$

where $\pi = 3.1416$. This relationship enables us to use the normal probability tables with *MAD,* which we discuss later.

The **mean absolute percent error (*MAPE*)** relates the forecast error to the level of demand and is useful for putting forecast performance in the proper perspective. For example, an absolute forecast error of 100 when the demand is 200 units results in a larger percentage error than if the same error occurred when the demand was 10,000 units. Application 10.6 shows how these measures of forecast error are calculated.

APPLICATION 10.6

The table on the facing page shows the actual sales of a product and the forecasts made for each of the last eight months. Calculate the common measures of forecast error for this product.

Solution

The table also shows the first set of calculations required to obtain the common measures of forecast error. Using those results and the formulas for the mea-

---

*The standard deviation (σ) is a poor measure of forecast error variability if the forecasts are biased. For example, if all the forecast errors were +10, the standard deviation of forecast errors *should* be 0 (no variation), but the formula for σ would yield a value of greater than zero.

sures, we get

$$\text{Cumulative forecast error } (CFE) = -15$$

$$\text{Standard deviation } (\sigma) = \sqrt{\frac{5275}{7}} = 27.5$$

$$\text{Mean absolute deviation } (MAD) = \frac{195}{8} = 24.4$$

$$\text{Mean absolute percent error } (MAPE) = \frac{81.3\%}{8} = 10.2\%$$

Calculations for Forecast Error Measures

Month (t)	Demand (D_t)	Forecast (F_t)	Error (E_t)	Error Squared (E_t^2)	Absolute Error $(|E_t|)$	Absolute Percent Error $(|E_t|/D_t)100$
1	200	225	−25	625	25	12.5%
2	240	220	20	400	20	8.3
3	300	285	15	225	15	5.0
4	270	290	−20	400	20	7.4
5	230	250	−20	400	20	8.7
6	260	240	20	400	20	7.7
7	210	250	−40	1600	40	19.0
8	275	240	35	1225	35	12.7
Total			−15	5275	195	81.3%

For a *CFE* of −15, we can say that the forecast has a slight bias on the high side. The σ and *MAD* statistics give us measures of forecast error variability. A *MAPE* of 10.2% implies that, on average, the error was about 10 percent of the actual demand. Of course, these measures become more reliable as the number of periods of data increase.

Tracking Signals. A **tracking signal** is a measure that indicates whether a method of forecasting has any built-in biases over a period of time. If a correct forecasting system is being used, *CFE* tends to be zero. However, at any time, random errors can cause *CFE* to be nonzero. The tracking signal formula is

$$\text{Tracking signal} = \frac{CFE}{MAD}$$

Each period, *CFE* is updated to reflect current error. The mean absolute deviation can be calculated in one of two ways: the simple average of all absolute errors (as we demonstrated in Application 10.6), or as a weighted average using the single exponential smoothing method; that is

$$MAD_t = \alpha|E_t| + (1 - \alpha)MAD_{t-1}$$

The latter approach has certain advantages: Less historical data have to be retained for each estimate, and recent forecast performance can be emphasized more than past performance.

The tracking signal measures the number of *MADs* represented by the cumulative sum of forecast errors. You can specify limits based on the normal probability tables, assuming that $MAD = 0.8\sigma$. If the tracking signal falls outside those limits, you should check the forecast model that you're using because it no longer is tracking demand adequately. This approach is useful in computerized forecasting systems because it alerts you to forecasts that need attention. Table 10.5 shows the area of the normal probability distribution within the control limits of 1 to 4 *MADs*.

Choosing the limits for the tracking signal involves a trade-off between the cost of poor forecasts and the cost of checking for a problem when none exists. For example, suppose that $CFE = 180$ and $MAD = 100$; the tracking signal would be $+1.8$. If we had set the control limits of the tracking signal at ± 1.5, we would check our forecasting method to see whether changes in the demand pattern indicate a needed change (1) in the model form (such as adding a trend estimate), or (2) in the values of the smoothing parameters. However, there is a chance that the value of $+1.8$ results from random variation only. In fact, with a limit of ± 1.5, there is a probability of 0.115 (one half the area outside the control limits) that we could get a value of the tracking signal greater than $+1.5$ as a result of random variation.

TABLE 10.5　Percentage of the Area of the Normal Probability Distribution within the Control Limits of the Tracking Signal

Number of *MADs*	Number of σ's*	Percentage of Area within Control Limits[†]
±1.0	±0.80	57.62
±1.5	±1.20	76.98
±2.0	±1.60	89.04
±2.5	±2.00	95.44
±3.0	±2.40	98.36
±3.5	±2.80	99.48
±4.0	±3.20	99.86

*The equivalent number of standard deviations is found by using the approximation of MAD ≃ 0.8.
[†]The area of the normal curve included within the control limits is found in Appendix 5. For example, the cumulative area from $-\infty$ to 0.80 is 0.7881. The area between 0 and $+0.80\sigma$ is $0.7881 - 0.5000 = 0.2881$. Since the normal curve is symmetric, the area between -0.80σ and 0 is also 0.2881. Therefore the area between $\pm 0.80\sigma$ is $0.2881 + 0.2881 = 0.5762$.

TABLE 10.6	Forecast Error Performance of Various Forecasting Methods for a Medical Clinic		
Method	**Cumulative Sum of Forecast Errors (CFE—Bias)**	**Mean Absolute Deviation (MAD)**	**Tracking Signal* (CFE/MAD)**
Simple moving average			
Three-week	23.1	17.1	1.35
Six-week	69.8	15.5	4.50
Weighted moving average			
0.70, 0.20, 0.10	14.0	18.4	0.76
Single exponential smoothing			
$\alpha = 0.1$	65.6	14.8	4.43
$\alpha = 0.2$	41.0	15.3	2.68

*The tracking signal was calculated at the end of week 28, using *MAD* as a simple average of absolute deviations. An exponentially smoothed *MAD* could also have been used.

Choosing a Time Series Method

Another use of forecast error measures is to provide input to the choice of the best forecasting method for a given product. For purposes of illustration, let's return to the medical clinic example in Applications 10.1–10.3 and the methods we used to forecast weekly patient arrivals. For purposes of the following discussion, we add another single exponential smoothing method with $\alpha = 0.2$. We also focus on *MAD* as a measure of forecast error dispersion but could just as well have used the standard deviation.

Criteria for Selection. Table 10.6 shows the forecast error performance of the methods used for the medical clinic if all 28 periods of data are utilized. The criteria to use in making choices of this sort include (1) minimizing bias, (2) minimizing *MAD,* and (3) meeting managerial expectations of changes in the components of demand. The first two criteria are statistical measures based on historical performance; the third reflects expectations of the future that may not be rooted in the past. The tracking signal is useful *after* you have selected a method—to identify when you should closely examine the method to see if it should be changed.

Using Statistical Criteria. Let's begin by selecting the best value of *N* for moving average methods based on *MAD* and bias considerations.* Regardless of the method, we would like to have forecasts with zero bias and zero *MAD.* As this result is impossible, we face a trade-off between bias and *MAD,* as demonstrated in Table 10.6. A value of $N = 3$ weeks gives us a lower bias but

---

*No attempt was made to find the "best" methods in Table 10.6. The results and our discussion should be viewed as illustrative of the uses of forecast measures in the selection of a method.

a greater *MAD* than does a value of $N = 6$ weeks. Normally, preference is given to lower values of *MAD*. However, in this example, the two values of *MAD* are not that much different, whereas the measures of bias are very different. A positive value for *CFE* indicates that, on balance, the forecasts have been too low. This result can be detrimental to clinic operations, particularly if purchasing procedures and staffing schedules are based on the raw forecasts. If the difference in *MAD* is not significant, $N = 3$ seems like a good choice for the simple moving average.

Similar considerations are involved in choosing α for single exponential smoothing. Again, the differences in *MAD* are insignificant, but the differences in bias are significant. Larger α values seem to result in less bias than do smaller values in this example. Consequently, if we were to use single exponential smoothing, $\alpha = 0.2$ would be best.

Which method should we choose, based on the statistical measures of forecast error in Table 10.6? The differences between *MAD*s in our example are managerially insignificant. Consequently, we focus on the bias measure and make our choice from the moving average method with $N = 3$, the weighted moving average method, or the exponential smoothing method with $\alpha = 0.2$. Note that these three methods all give greater weight to the most recent levels of demand and less weight to earlier levels. This weighting is evidence of a trend or seasonal component of demand in the time series. We assumed that the only components of demand were its historical average and random error. If another component were present, we typically would see low N values or high α values. The weighted moving average method provided an acceptable forecast. The weights were nearly equivalent to $\alpha = 0.70$ in the exponential smoothing method.

The tracking signal in Table 10.6 also tells us that something may be wrong. Suppose that we had set the limit at ± 2.5, which means that there is approximately a 2 percent probability that a tracking signal value will exceed 2.5 when nothing is wrong. Then if we had chosen a six-week moving average or any of the exponential smoothing methods, the tracking signal would have indicated a problem with our assumptions. Consequently, for the methods that we have to choose from, the three-week moving average or the weighted moving average look best. However, we would be well advised to explore other methods—particularly one including trends—before making a final selection.

Using Managerial Expectations.   In Table 10.1 we identified several external and internal factors that can affect demand. These factors can lead to changes in the nature of the components of demand, such as a change in the average level, the rate of a trend, or the timing and size of peaks in a seasonal demand series. Such changes can cause historical customer demand data to lose their relevance for projecting future demand. In some cases, managers might use the parameters of a time series model as policy variables, depicting expectations of changes in the underlying components of demand. Managers can use two general guidelines in this regard:

1. For projections of stable demand patterns, low α and β values or large N values give the best results and emphasize historical experience.

2. For projections of changing demand patterns, high α and β values or small N values give the best results. When the historical components of demand are changing, recent history should be emphasized.

Regardless of the basis for choosing these parameters originally, managers should monitor forecast error and modify the parameters as needed. In this way, managers can detect a poor choice and correct it.

CAUSAL METHODS ▲

Causal methods provide the most sophisticated forecasting tools. They are used when historical data are available and the relationship between the factor to be forecasted and other external or internal factors (such as those in Table 10.1) can be identified. These relationships are expressed in mathematical terms and can be very complex. Causal methods are by far the best for predicting turning points in demand and preparing long-range forecasts. A number of sophisticated causal methods are used, but we focus on linear regression because it is one of the most commonly used.

Linear Regression

Linear regression is one of the best known causal methods of forecasting. In this approach one variable, called a **dependent variable**, is related to one or more **independent variables** by a linear equation. The dependent variable, such as demand or cost, is the variable that the manager wants to forecast. The independent variables are assumed to have affected the dependent variable and thereby "caused" the results observed in the past. Also, time could be used as an independent variable as a surrogate representing an unspecified group of variables contributing to trends or seasonal patterns in the data.

To illustrate the use of linear regression we use the simplest of models, in which the dependent variable is a function of only one independent variable.

The linear regression method requires that we first hypothesize a relationship between the dependent variable and the independent variable. In the simplest case, we hypothesize that the relationship would be a straight line:

$$Y_i = \alpha + \beta X_i + u_i$$

where

$$Y_i = \text{the dependent variable value for observation } i$$

$$X_i = \text{the independent variable value for observation } i$$

$$\alpha = \text{the } Y \text{ intercept of the line}$$

$$\beta = \text{the slope of the line}$$

$$u_i = \text{random error}$$

We do not know the α and β values, so we must estimate them from a sample of data. These data are used to calculate a, the estimate of α, and b, the estimate of β, using a technique called *least squares*. The objective is to find values of a and b that minimize the sum of the squared deviations of the *actual* Y_i values from the *estimated* values, or

$$\text{Minimize} \quad \sum_{i=1}^{n} [Y_i - (a + bX_i)]^2$$

where n is the number of data points in the sample.

The process of finding the values of a and b that minimize the sum of squared deviations is complex, so we'll merely state the equations here:

$$a = \overline{Y} - b\overline{X} \quad \text{and} \quad b = \frac{\Sigma XY - n\overline{X}\,\overline{Y}}{\Sigma X^2 - n\overline{X}^2}$$

where

$$a = \text{the estimate of the } Y \text{ intercept}$$
$$b = \text{the estimate of the slope of the line}$$
$$\overline{Y} = \text{the average of the } Y \text{ values}$$
$$\overline{X} = \text{the average of the } X \text{ values}$$

It should be noted that the values of a and b also minimize the cumulative sum of forecast errors, the average error (bias), and the standard deviation of forecast errors. However, they do not minimize mean absolute deviation.

APPLICATION 10.7

You are in charge of inventory for your company. As part of your job, you must obtain forecasts of demand for the products stocked in inventory. During a luncheon meeting with the marketing manager you learned that there was a special advertising budget for a particular product. Sales and advertising data are:

Month	Sales (000 units)	Advertising ($000)
1	264	2.5
2	116	1.3
3	165	1.4
4	101	1.0
5	209	2.0

The marketing manager said that next month the company will spend $1750 on advertising for the product. Use linear regression to develop an equation and a forecast for this product.

Solution

Month	Sales (Y)	Advertising (X)	(XY)	X²
1	264	2.5	660.0	6.25
2	116	1.3	150.8	1.69
3	165	1.4	231.0	1.96
4	101	1.0	101.0	1.00
5	209	2.0	418.0	4.00
Total	855	8.2	1560.8	14.90

$$\overline{X} = \frac{8.2}{5} = 1.64 \quad \text{and} \quad \overline{Y} = \frac{855}{5} = 171.00$$

$$b = \frac{\Sigma XY - n\overline{X}\,\overline{Y}}{\Sigma X^2 - n\overline{X}^2} = \frac{1560.8 - 5(1.64)(171)}{14.9 - 5(1.64)^2}$$

$$= \frac{158.60}{1.452} = 109.229$$

$$a = \overline{Y} - b\overline{X} = 171.00 - 109.229(1.64)$$

$$= -8.136$$

The regression equation is

$$\hat{Y} = -8.136 + 109.229X$$

The forecast for month 6 is

$$\hat{Y} = -8.136 + 109.229(1.75)$$
$$= 183.015 \quad \text{or} \quad 183{,}015 \text{ units}$$

Regression analysis can provide useful guidance for important operations management decisions. However, this approach is relatively costly because of the large amounts of data needed in order to obtain useful linear regression relationships. In Application 10.7 we started with an assumption of a linear relationship between variables. However, we could have made other assumptions, some of which may have been better than the one we chose. In addition, independent variables other than advertising expenditures may also be important. Considerable analysis may be required before an acceptable model is developed. Nonetheless, linear regression models are useful for predicting turning points and can be useful tools for solving many planning problems.

QUALITATIVE METHODS ▲

The time series and causal methods of forecasting require a considerable amount of historical data. As we have shown, these techniques can produce reasonably accurate forecasts. However, adequate historical data is often lacking. Such is the case with the introduction of a new product or the need to forecast long-term technological change. Designed for these situations, qualitative techniques rely on managerial judgment and experience and other forms of qualitative information to generate forecasts. In this section we discuss two of the more successful qualitative techniques currently in use: market research and the Delphi method.

Market Research

Suppose that you are planning a new business that would allow consumers to shop for groceries by using a personal computer in their homes. One way to determine consumer interest is to do market research. **Market research** is a systematic approach to creating and testing hypotheses about the market. Data usually are gathered by survey methods.

Designing and conducting a market research study would include the following activities. First, you would need to design a questionnaire that would

The personal interview is one form of administering a questionnaire. Here an interviewer asks a customer about brand preferences.

request the needed economic and demographic information from each person interviewed. As part of the questionnaire, you would also ask whether the person being interviewed would be interested in using your service. Second, in conjunction with the design of the questionnaire, you would need to decide how to administer it. You have three choices: telephone polling, mailings, or personal interviews.

Third, you would need to select a representative sample of households to survey. The sample should include a random selection within the market area of your proposed service. Finally, after collecting the data, you must analyze it. When doing so, you must exercise a considerable amount of judgment in interpreting the responses, determining their adequacy, and making allowance for economic or competition factors not included in the questionnaire. Also, the response rate on mailed questionnaires is typically poor (30 percent is often considered high), and you must weigh the possibility that the respondents are an atypical group who no longer represent a random sample of your potential market.

Market research can be used to forecast demand for the short, medium, and long terms. Accuracy is excellent for the short term, good for the medium term, and only fair for the long term. Although market research yields many benefits, it has many shortcomings. Among them are lengthy findings that contain numerous qualifications and delays caused by long survey instruments and their subsequent analysis.

Delphi Method

The **Delphi method** is a process of gaining consensus from a group of experts while maintaining their anonymity. This form of forecasting is useful when there are no historical data from which to develop statistical models—when judgment or opinion, based on experience and study of the market, industry, or scientific developments, are the only bases for making informed projections. The process involves a coordinator who sends questions to each member of the group, who may not even know who else is participating. The experts respond to the questions and argue in support of their response. The coordinator pools the responses and prepares a report consisting of a statistical summary of the responses to the questions, as well as a summary of arguments for particular responses to the questions. The coordinator sends the report to the same group for another round. The participants can repeat or modify their previous responses. Some form of consensus is usually obtained in two to four rounds. About two months are required to implement the process. The Delphi method can be used to develop long-range forecasts of product demand and new product sales projections; it is fair to good in identifying turning points in demand.

One of the more useful applications for the Delphi method is that of **technological forecasting**. The rate of technological change is increasing much more rapidly than ever before. Medical science and computer science are just two fields that are experiencing explosive technological change. Replacing a human heart with a mechanical heart has become an accepted medical procedure. Computers become obsolete soon after they are produced. In addition, an almost completely automated factory is possible. What's next? Trying to answer that question is the focus of technological forecasting. The Delphi method can be used to obtain a consensus answer from a panel of experts. The panel members may be asked to specify the scientific advances that they envision, as well as changes in environmental and social forces such as quality of life, governmental regulations, and competitor actions. The questions are typically directed toward specific organizations or industries. The results of such a process can provide direction for a firm's research and development staff.

DESIGNING THE FORECASTING SYSTEM ▲

We have discussed a number of forecasting methods in this chapter. It would seem that all a manager needs to do is choose one, make the forecasts, and proceed to the next stage—analyzing operations management problems. Unfortunately, it isn't that simple. The choice of method is certainly an important aspect of designing a forecasting system, but there are some other important considerations. When designing a demand forecasting system, the manager must determine (1) what to forecast, (2) what software package to use (for a computerized system), and (3) how the system can assist managerial decision making.

Deciding What to Forecast

It is not uncommon to hear operations managers say that forecasts of demand should be made for all goods or services produced by their companies. Although some sort of demand estimate is needed for all items, it may be easier to forecast some aggregation of the products and then derive individual product forecasts. Also, selecting the correct unit of measurement for the forecasts can be as important as choosing the best method.

Level of Aggregation. Very few companies have errors of more than 5 percent in their forecasts of total demand for all products. However, errors in forecasts for individual items range from -100 percent to $+300$ percent, or more (Plossl, 1972). Thus the greater the aggregation is, the more accurate are the forecasts. Many companies employ a two-tier forecasting system in which forecasts are first made for **product families**, a group of goods or services that have similar demand requirements and common processing, labor, and materials requirements. Forecasts for individual items are derived in such a way that their sum equals the total forecast for the family. This approach maintains consistency between planning for the final stages of manufacturing (which requires the unit forecasts) and longer term planning for sales, profit, and capacity (which requires the product family forecasts).

Units of Measurement.   Forecasts that serve as input to planning and the analysis of operations problems are most useful if they are based on product units, rather than dollars. Forecasts of sales revenue are not very helpful because prices can and often do fluctuate. Thus even though total sales in dollars might be the same from month to month, the actual number of units of demand could vary widely. Forecasting the number of units of demand and then translating them to sales revenue estimates by multiplying them by the price is often the better method.

Forecasting the number of units of demand for a product may not be possible. Companies producing goods or services to customer order face this problem. In such situations it is better to forecast the standard labor or machine *hours* required of each of the critical resources, based on historical patterns. For such companies, estimates of labor or machine hours are important to scheduling and capacity planning.

Selecting a Software Package (Computerized Systems)

Many forecasting software packages are available for all sizes of computers. These packages offer a wide variety of forecasting capabilities and report formats. Packages such as General Electric's *Time Series Forecasting System* and IBM's *Consumer Goods System* (COGS) and *Inventory Management Program and Control Technique* (IMPACT) contain forecasting modules used by many firms that have large computer facilities. Since the introduction of microcomputers, scores of software packages have been developed for virtually all of the popular personal computers. The applications range from simple to very sophisticated programs. These microcomputer packages are priced to make them attractive alternatives to traditional mainframe packages.

Some techniques are more cost effective for short time horizons, whereas others are more appropriate for long time horizons. Thus selecting a forecasting software package is usually a decision made jointly by marketing and operations. Typically, an implementation team consisting of marketing and operations staff is charged with selecting a package from the wide variety available. The team may ask their departments for a "wish list" and then categorize the wishes as "musts" and "wants." Their final selection of the package will be based on (1) how well the package satisfies the musts and wants, (2) the cost of buying or leasing the package, (3) the level of clerical support required, and (4) the amount of programmer maintenance required.

Managerial Use of the System

Two aspects of managerial use of a computerized forecasting system deserve special mention. First, single-number forecasts are rarely useful because forecasts are almost always wrong. Consequently, managers know that if they get a single number for forecasted product demand, actual demand will be anything but that figure. A far more useful approach is to provide the manager with a forecasted value and an error range, which can be done by using *MAD*. For example, suppose that the forecasted value for a product is 100 units, with a *MAD* of 10 units. Using Table 10.5, an analyst could say that there is about a 95 percent chance that actual demand will fall within ±2.5 *MAD*s of the forecast. The analyst could tell the manager that the forecast is for 100 units with a 95 percent confidence level that actual demand will fall in the range of 75 to 125 units. This information gives the manager a better feel for the uncertainty in the forecast and allows the manager to better plan inventories, staffing levels, and the like.

The second aspect of managerial use worth noting is the expected amount of managerial interface with the system. Tracking signals should be computed for each forecast, and messages should be generated when the signals exceed the range selected. Managers should have the authority to override a computer-generated forecast with a forecast of their own or modify the methods used when changes in the demand pattern dictate. The GAF Corporation, for example, generates a product-group forecast report that shows both the mathematical forecast and the forecast generated by the market staff based on experience and other nonquantifiable factors. Managers are free to use either forecast, which helps them to gain confidence in the forecasting system.

SOLVED PROBLEMS

In Problems 1, 2, and 3 we have calculated the average to one decimal place and rounded the forecast to the closest integer.

1. The Polish General's Pizza Parlor is a small restaurant catering to patrons with a taste for European pizza. One of its specialties is Polish Prize pizza. The manager must forecast weekly demand for these special pizzas so that he can order pizza shells weekly. Recently, demand has been:

Week of	Number of Polish Prize Pizzas
June 2	50
June 9	65
June 16	52
June 23	56
June 30	55
July 7	60

a. Forecast the demand for Polish Prize pizza for June 23–July 7, using the three-period moving average method.

b. Repeat (a), using the weighted moving average method. The weights are 0.50, 0.30, and 0.20, and 0.50 refers to the most recent demand.

c. Calculate the *MAD* for each method.

Solution

a. $A_t = \dfrac{D_t + D_{t-1} + D_{t-2}}{3}$ and $F_{t+1} = A_t$

Week Forecast Calculated	A_t		Forecast for Following Week (F_{t+1})
June 16	(52 + 65 + 50)/3	=	55.7, or 56
June 23	(56 + 52 + 65)/3	=	57.7, or 58
June 30	(55 + 56 + 52)/3	=	54.3, or 54

b. $A_t = 0.50D_t + 0.30D_{t-1} + 0.20D_{t-2}$

Week Forecast Calculated	A_t		Forecast for Following Week (F_{t+1})
June 16	0.50(52) + 0.30(65) + 0.20(50)	=	55.5, or 56
June 23	0.50(56) + 0.30(52) + 0.20(65)	=	56.6, or 57
June 30	0.50(55) + 0.30(56) + 0.20(52)	=	54.7, or 55

c.

Week (t)	Actual Demand (D_t)	3-Week Moving Average Forecast (F_t)	Absolute Error $(\|E_t\|)$	Weighted Moving Average Forecast (F_t)	Absolute Error $(\|E_t\|)$
June 23	56	56	0	56	0
June 30	55	58	3	57	2
July 7	60	54	6	55	5
Total			9		7
MAD			9/3 = 3.0		7/3 = 2.3

For this limited set of data, the weighted moving average method resulted in a slightly lower mean absolute deviation. However, final conclusions can only be made after analysis of much more data.

2. The monthly demand for units manufactured by the Acme Rocket company has been

Month	Units
May	100
June	80
July	110
August	115
September	105
October	110
November	125
December	120

a. Use the single exponential smoothing method to forecast the number of units for June through December. The initial forecast for May was 105 units; $\alpha = 0.2$.

b. Calculate the absolute percentage error for each month from June through December and the *MAD* and *MAPE* of forecast error as of the end of December.

c. Calculate the tracking signal as of the end of December. What can you say about the performance of your forecasting method?

Solution

a. $A_t = 0.2D_t + 0.8A_{t-1}$ and $F_{t+1} = A_t$

Month Forecast Calculated	A_t		Forecast for Following Month (F_{t+1})
May	$0.2(100) + 0.8(105)$	$=$	104.0, or 104
June	$0.2(80) \ + 0.8(104)$	$=$	99.2, or 99
July	$0.2(110) + 0.8(99.2)$	$=$	101.4, or 101
August	$0.2(115) + 0.8(101.4)$	$=$	104.1, or 104
September	$0.2(105) + 0.8(104.1)$	$=$	104.3, or 104
October	$0.2(110) + 0.8(104.3)$	$=$	105.4, or 105
November	$0.2(125) + 0.8(105.4)$	$=$	109.3, or 109

b.

Month (t)	Actual Demand (D_t)	Forecast (F_t)	Error (E_t)	Absolute Error $(\|E_t\|)$	Absolute Percentage Error
June	80	104	−24	24	30.0%
July	110	99	11	11	10.0
August	115	101	14	14	12.2
September	105	104	1	1	0.9
October	110	104	6	6	5.4
November	125	105	20	20	16.0
December	120	109	11	11	9.2
Total			39	87	83.7%

$$MAD = \frac{87}{7} = 12.4$$

$$MAPE = \frac{83.7\%}{7} = 11.9\%$$

c. As of the end of December, the cumulative sum of forecast errors (*CFE*) is 39. Using the mean absolute deviation calculated in (b), we calculate the tracking signal as follows:

$$\text{Tracking signal} = \frac{CFE}{MAD}$$

$$= \frac{39}{12.4}$$

$$= 3.14$$

The value of the tracking signal indicates a very small probability that a value of 3.14 could be generated completely by chance. Consequently, we should revise our approach. The long string of forecasts lower than actual demand suggests use of a trends method.

3. The demand for Krispee Crunchies, a favorite breakfast cereal for people born in the 1940s, is experiencing a decline in demand. The company wants to closely monitor demand for this product as it nears the end of its life cycle. The double exponential smoothing method is used with $\alpha = 0.1$ and $\beta = 0.2$. At the end of December, the January estimate for the average number of cases sold per month was 900,000 and the trend was −50,000 per month. The following is the actual sales history for January, February, and March. Generate forecasts for February, March, and April.

Month	Sales
January	890,000
February	800,000
March	825,000

Solution

We are given the initial condition as of the end of December and actual demand for January, February, and March. The forecast method must now be updated and a forecast prepared for April. All data are expressed in thousands of cases. Our equations for use with double exponential smoothing are

$$A_t = 0.1D_t + 0.9(A_{t-1} + T_{t-1})$$
$$CT_t = A_t - A_{t-1}$$
$$T_t = 0.2CT_t + 0.8T_{t-1}$$
$$F_{t+1} = A_t + T_t$$

January:

$$A_{Jan} = 0.1(890) + 0.9(900 - 50) = 854.0$$
$$CT_{Jan} = 854.0 - 900.0 = -46.0$$
$$T_{Jan} = 0.2(-46.0) + 0.8(-50.0) = -49.2$$

Forecast for February = 854.0 − 49.2 = 804.8, or 804,800 cases.

February:

$$A_{Feb} = 0.1(800) + 0.9(854.0 - 49.2) = 804.3$$
$$CT_{Feb} = 804.3 - 854.0 = -49.7$$
$$T_{Feb} = 0.2(-49.7) + 0.8(-49.2) = -49.3$$

Forecast for March = 804.3 − 49.3 = 755.0, or 755,000 cases.

March:

$$A_{Mar} = 0.1(825) + 0.9(804.3 - 49.3) = 762.0$$
$$CT_{Mar} = 762.0 - 804.3 = -42.3$$
$$T_{Mar} = 0.2(-42.3) + 0.8(-49.3) = -47.9$$

Forecast for April = 762.0 − 47.9 = 714.1, or 714,100 cases.

4. The Northville Post Office experiences a "seasonal" pattern of daily mail volume every week. The following data for two representative weeks is expressed in thousands of pieces of mail.

Day	Week 1	Week 2
Monday	20	15
Tuesday	30	32
Wednesday	35	30
Thursday	50	48
Friday	70	72
Saturday	15	10
Sunday	5	8
Total	225	215

a. Calculate seasonal factors for each day of the week.

b. If the postmaster estimates that there will be 230,000 pieces of mail to sort next week, forecast the volume for each day of the week.

Solution

a. We calculate the average daily mail volume and divide the actual mail volume for each day by this value to get the seasonal factor. We then average the seasonal factors to get the final factor to use in the forecast.

Day	Week 1 Mail Volume	Seasonal Factor	Week 2 Mail Volume	Seasonal Factor	Average Seasonal Factor
Monday	20	0.622	15	0.488	0.555
Tuesday	30	0.933	32	1.042	0.9875
Wednesday	35	1.089	30	0.977	1.033
Thursday	50	1.555	48	1.563	1.559
Friday	70	2.178	72	2.344	2.261
Saturday	15	0.467	10	0.326	0.3965
Sunday	5	0.156	8	0.260	0.208
Total	225		215		
Average	32.143		30.714		

b. The average daily mail volume is expected to be 32,857 (or 230,000/7) pieces of mail. Using the average seasonal factors calculated in (a), we obtain the following forecasts.

Day	Calculation		Forecast
Monday	0.555(32,857)	=	18,236
Tuesday	0.9875(32,857)	=	32,446
Wednesday	1.033(32,857)	=	33,941
Thursday	1.559(32,857)	=	51,224
Friday	2.261(32,857)	=	74,290
Saturday	0.3965(32,857)	=	13,028
Sunday	0.208(32,857)	=	6,834

FORMULA REVIEW

1. Simple moving average:

$$A_t = \frac{D_t + D_{t-1} + D_{t-2} + \cdots + D_{t-N+1}}{N}$$

2. Weighted moving average:

$$A_t = W_1 D_t + W_2 D_{t-1} + \cdots + W_N D_{t-N+1}$$

3. Single exponential smoothing:

$$A_t = \alpha D_t + (1 - \alpha)(A_{t-1})$$

4. Double exponential smoothing:

$$A_t = \alpha D_t + (1 - \alpha)(A_{t-1} + T_{t-1})$$
$$CT_t = A_t - A_{t-1}$$
$$T_t = \beta CT_t + (1 - \beta)T_{t-1}$$
$$F_{t+1} = A_t + T_t$$

5. Seasonal factors:

$$\overline{D}_y = \frac{\sum_{t=1}^{n} D_{y,t}}{n}$$

$$f_{y,t} = \frac{D_{y,t}}{\overline{D}_y}$$

$$\overline{f}_t = \frac{\sum_{y=1}^{m} f_{y,t}}{m}$$

$$F_{y,t} = \widetilde{D}_y \overline{f}_t$$

6. Forecast error measures:

$$CFE = \sum_{t=1}^{n} E_t$$

$$\sigma = \sqrt{\frac{\sum_{t=1}^{n} E_t^2}{n - 1}}$$

$$MAD = \frac{\sum_{t=1}^{n} |E_t|}{n}$$

$$MAPE = \frac{\sum_{t=1}^{n} \frac{|E_t|}{D_t} (100)}{n} \quad \text{(expressed as a percentage)}$$

$$\text{Tracking Signal} = \frac{CFE}{MAD}$$

7. Linear regression:

$$a = \overline{Y} - b\overline{X}$$

$$b = \frac{\Sigma XY - n\overline{X}\,\overline{Y}}{\Sigma X^2 - n\overline{X}^2}$$

CHAPTER HIGHLIGHTS

- Three general types of demand forecasting are used: time series analysis, causal methods, and qualitative techniques. All three are useful for short-term forecasting, whereas causal methods and qualitative techniques are more appropriate for medium- and long-term forecasting.

- The five basic components of demand are the average, trend, seasonal influence, cyclical movement, and random error. An understanding of the external factors (beyond management's control) and the internal factors (within management's control) that affect the components of demand is essential for making accurate forecasts.

- Simple moving averages, weighted moving averages, and single exponential smoothing are techniques used to forecast the average of a time series. The single exponential smoothing technique has the advantage of requiring a minimal

amount of data to be kept for use in updating the forecast.

- Double exponential smoothing is a method for including a trend estimate in exponentially smoothed forecasts. Estimates for the series average and the trend are smoothed to provide the forecast.

- Although many techniques allow for seasonal influences, a simple approach is the multiplicative method, which is based on the assumption that the seasonal influence is proportional to the level of average demand.

- The cumulative sum of forecast errors (*CFE*), the standard deviation of forecast errors (σ), the mean absolute deviation (*MAD*), and the mean absolute percent error (*MAPE*) are all measures of forecast error used in practice. *CFE* and *MAD* are used to develop a tracking signal that determines when a forecasting method no longer is yielding acceptable forecasts. Forecast error measures can also be used to select the best forecast methods from available alternatives.

- Causal forecasting methods are more sophisticated than time series methods and hypothesize a functional relationship between the factor to be forecasted and other internal or external factors. Linear regression is one of the more popular causal methods used in forecasting.

- Qualitative techniques of forecasting are useful in situations where relevant historical data is lacking. These techniques are based on the judgment, experience, and expertise of those who do the forecasts. Market research and the Delphi method are two examples of qualitative techniques. The Delphi method has been used to make forecasts of technological change.

- Designing a forecasting system involves determining what to forecast, what forecasting method and software package (in computerized systems) to use, and how the system can assist managerial decision making. Deciding what to forecast requires consideration of the level of aggregation required and the units of measure.

KEY TERMS

STUDY QUESTIONS

1. You have thousands of items in your product line and must forecast demand for each one on a weekly basis. Which of the three approaches (time series, causal, or qualitative) would you use? Why?

2. You are the owner–manager of a new movie theater in town. The problem you face is that you get an overflow crowd of teenagers for your Friday and Saturday night showings of the horror movie "Bad Dreams on Mohican Way—Part 16" and very little attendance for other movies shown during the rest of the week. Discuss several ways in which you could use demand management to smooth the load on your facilities over the week and during the day on Saturday.

3. If you had to choose among simple moving averages, weighted moving averages, and single exponential smoothing to forecast demand for a product having no trend or seasonal components, which method would you choose? Why?

4. For what type of demand pattern is the single exponential smoothing method with a low α value most appropriate? Explain.

5. You have just spent eight months developing a method to forecast hourly check volumes to be processed by the encoding department of a large bank. Based on historical data, your method's forecasts resulted in a *MAD* of 500 checks. The first week you used the new method, the actual *MAD* was 1000 checks. Should you be concerned? Explain.

6. How can you use simple linear regression in conjunction with the seasonal factors approach to seasonal forecasting?

7. As a consultant, you have been asked to look into the forecasting problems of a certain company. The company has been plotting the cumulative forecast error for each of its forecasts and using the results to judge the adequacy of its forecasting system. What are your reactions to this approach? What would you recommend?

8. As part of its product planning program, your company is interested in determining when the

gasoline engine will be replaced by some other source of power for the automobile. How would you go about preparing such a forecast?

9. What are the trade-offs you must make in selecting a forecast method on the basis of forecast error?

10. You have received two forecasts for a certain product. The first says that demand next month will be 500 units. The other says that demand next month will be between 400 and 600 units. Which of the two forecasts would you prefer? Why?

PROBLEMS

Review Problems

1. The manager of a hardware store rents rug cleaning machines to customers who prefer to clean their carpets themselves. He is interested in arriving at a forecast of rentals for next week so that he can order sufficient support products, such as defoamer and shampoo. Data for the last ten weeks are:

Week	1	2	3	4	5
Rentals	10	20	12	15	24

Week	6	7	8	9	10
Rentals	11	7	21	12	14

a. Prepare a forecast for weeks 6–10 using a five-week moving average. What is the forecast for week 11?

b. Compute the mean absolute deviation as of the end of week 10.

2. The Plushee Carpet Company sells and installs carpeting for all purposes, both indoor and outdoor. The manager is interested in forecasting the number of requests for carpet installation estimates, so that she can better plan for the number of estimators required. The number of monthly requests for estimates during the past nine months were:

Month	Requests for Estimates
January	39
February	52
March	30
April	35
May	52
June	61
July	46
August	49
September	52

a. Using a four-month moving average, forecast the number of July, August, and September requests.

b. Using a six-month moving average, forecast the number of July, August, and September requests.

c. Compare the performance of the two methods with a simple calculation of forecast error. Explain the relative performances of the two methods.

3. Ted's TV sells and repairs television sets. The manager needs weekly forecasts of repair-service calls in order to schedule repair personnel. The forecast for the week of October 3 was 33 calls. The manager uses single exponential smoothing with $\alpha = 0.2$. Forecast the number of calls for the week of November 7, which is next week.

Week of	Actual Repair Calls
October 3	40
October 10	28
October 17	38
October 24	32
October 31	35
November 7	?

4. The Oracle Mile Bicycle Shop sells bike accessories and replacement parts for most bikes. To maintain good customer service, the manager must forecast demand for the items he sells. One item, the 26×1.75 tire is a popular item. Recent demand for this item has been:

Week	Number of Tires Sold
1	30
2	22
3	25
4	32
5	24
6	27

a. Forecast tire demand for weeks 4−6 using a weighted moving average. The weights are 0.4, 0.3, and 0.3, where 0.4 refers to the most recent demand.
b. Repeat (a), using single exponential smoothing with α = 0.10. Assume that the average at the end of week 2 was 26 tires.
c. What is the forecast for week 7 using each method? Based on these limited data, which method do you have more confidence in? Discuss.

5. Sunnyvale Bank in Yuma, Arizona, recently installed a new automatic teller machine in its downtown branch. The new machine not only performs the standard banking services but also handles loan applications and certain limited investment transactions. The new machine is slightly more complicated to use than the standard one, so management is interested in tracking its past use and projecting its future use. Additional machines may be needed if the projected use is high enough.

   At the end of March the average monthly use was 600 customers, and the trend was +60 per month. The actual use figures for April, May, and June are 680, 710, and 790, respectively. Use double exponential smoothing with α = 0.3 and β = 0.1 to forecast usage for May, June, and July.

6. Consider the following data for the sales of a particular product over the past four weeks.

Week	Sales (Units)
1	19
2	25
3	22
4	30

a. Use single exponential smoothing with α = 0.7 to forecast sales for weeks 2−5. Assume that the average of the time series was 20 units just before week 1.
b. Use double exponential smoothing with α = 0.1 and β = 0.1 to forecast sales for weeks 2−5. Assume that the average of the series was 20 units and that the average trend was 3 units per week just before week 1.
c. Compare the performance of these two methods using appropriate measures of forecast error. Which method seems to fit the data better?

7. The manager of Pickwick Paint Parlor must make her annual purchasing plans for paints, adhesives, and other home maintenance items. One of the items she stocks is Black Cap, a black tar-like preparation for asphalt driveways. The sales of this item are seasonal, with peaks in the spring, summer, and fall months. Quarterly data for the last two years, expressed in gallons, are:

Quarterly	1988	1989
1	40	60
2	200	190
3	500	560
4	100	90
Total	840	900

If the expected sales for Black Cap is 960 gallons for 1990, prepare a forecast for each quarter of the year.

8. The International Can Company supplies containers for many popular brands of soft drinks and beer. The logistics manager needs to plan for monthly shipments of cans via rail to various locations in North America. The key to good customer service is having enough rail cars available. Rail cars are rented and must be scheduled in advance. The number of carloads of cans shipped the past two years is given in Table 10.7 on the facing page.

   Forecast the number of cars needed for each month of 1990, if the total number of carloads is estimated to be 1860.

Table 10.7

Month	1988	1989
January	15	18
February	30	31
March	53	58
April	98	110
May	90	89
June	255	271
July	375	380
August	278	268
September	225	240
October	203	200
November	38	40
December	68	95
Total	1728	1800

9. Demand for a particular service has been:

Month	Number of Customers
June	60
July	48
August	66
September	69
October	63
November	66
December	75
January	72

    a. Use simple linear regression analysis to develop a forecasting model for monthly demand. In this application, the dependent variable (Y) is monthly demand and the independent variable (X) is the month. For June, let $X = 1$; for July, $X = 2$; and so on.

    b. Use the model to forecast demand for February, March, and April. Here $X = 9$, 10, and 11, respectively.

10. The elemental standard data approach (see Chapter 6) makes use of linear regression to derive relationships between the normal time for an activity and some characteristics of the job. For example, the normal time to produce a *core* is a function of the core area. A core is made of packed sand and is used to make the inner portion of a mold for a part; the core displaces the molten metal to form a cavity. Seven work elements are involved in making a core. The normal time for one of the work elements, striking off the sand, and the core area for the last five jobs were:

Job Number	Strike off Sand (min.)	Core Area (in²)
2438	0.120	50
2562	0.101	15
3210	0.145	83
3784	0.117	25
4210	0.130	61

The next job is to have a core area of 70 square inches. How long will it take to strike off the sand?

Advanced Problems

These problems involve considerable computations. We recommend that you use a computer program to solve them.

11. The manager of a public warehouse must schedule employees and plan for additional capacity as needed to ensure proper customer service. One of the important inputs to her plans is the forecast of inbound shipments per month. These shipments determine labor requirements and also affect the need for warehouse space. Data on the inbound shipments for the past three years are:

Month	Inbound Shipments		
	1987	1988	1989
January	2664	1882	1983
February	2365	1922	2291
March	1891	1928	2162
April	1731	1594	1969
May	2441	2020	1845
June	1478	2445	1868
July	2215	2054	2205
August	1373	2662	2122
September	2460	2200	2667
October	2088	2150	2432
November	2467	2635	2419
December	2321	2564	2669

The manager needs a time series method for forecasting inbound shipments. Find the best simple moving average solution you can. You must decide what is meant by "best" and justify your decision.

12. Repeat Problem 11, except this time find the best single exponential smoothing solution you can. Justify your choice.

13. Repeat Problem 11, except this time find the best double exponential smoothing solution you can. Compare the performance of this method with that of the best moving average and the single exponential smoothing methods. Which of the three would you choose?

14. The Central Building Supply Company serves a large building industry in the Midwest region. Many items are stocked, and close inventory control is necessary to assure customers of efficient service. Recently, business has been increasing and management is concerned about

stockouts. A forecasting method that will estimate requirements several months in advance is needed, so that adequate replenishment quantities can be purchased. An example of the sales growth experienced over the last 50 months is the demand for item J785, a common door hinge, shown in Table 10.8.

a. Develop an exponential smoothing solution for forecasting demand for this item. Select the method, find the "best" parameter(s) for it, and justify your choices. Forecast demand for months 51–55.

b. A consultant to Central's management suggested that new residential building contracts would be a good leading indicator for company sales. He quoted a recent university study finding that residential building contracts preceded construction supply sales by five months. He supplied the data shown in Table 10.9.

Table 10.8

Month	J785 Sales	Month	J785 Sales
1	80	26	1296
2	132	27	1199
3	143	28	1267
4	180	29	1300
5	200	30	1370
6	168	31	1489
7	212	32	1499
8	254	33	1669
9	397	34	1716
10	385	35	1603
11	472	36	1812
12	397	37	1817
13	476	38	1798
14	699	39	1873
15	545	40	1923
16	837	41	2028
17	743	42	2049
18	722	43	2084
19	735	44	2083
20	838	45	2121
21	1057	46	2072
22	930	47	2262
23	1085	48	2371
24	1090	49	2309
25	1218	50	2422

Table 10.9

Month	Contracts	Month	Contracts
1	32	26	281
2	29	27	298
3	32	28	314
4	54	29	323
5	53	30	309
6	89	31	343
7	74	32	357
8	93	33	353
9	120	34	360
10	113	35	370
11	147	36	386
12	126	37	389
13	138	38	399
14	145	39	409
15	160	40	410
16	196	41	413
17	180	42	439
18	197	43	454
19	203	44	441
20	223	45	470
21	247	46	469
22	242	47	490
23	234	48	496
24	254	49	509
25	271	50	522

Based on the study findings, contracts in month 1 affected sales in month 6; contracts in month 2 affected sales in month 7; and so on. Use linear regression to develop a forecasting model for sales, with contracts as the independent variable. Forecast sales for months 51–55.

c. Which of the two models do you feel will provide the best forecasts? Explain. Your instructor has the actual data for months 51–55 and will compare them to the forecast you supply.

SELECTED REFERENCES

Adam, Everett E., "Individual Item Forecasting Model Evaluation," *Decision Sciences,* vol. 4, no. 4 (1973).

Box, George E. P., and Gwilym M. Jenkins, *Time Series Analysis: Forecasting and Control.* San Francisco: Holden-Day, 1970.

Brown, R. G., *Statistical Forecasting for Inventory Control.* New York: McGraw-Hill, 1959.

Chambers, John C., Satinder K. Mullick, and Donald D. Smith, "How to Choose the Right Forecasting Technique," *Harvard Business Review* (July–August 1971), pp. 45–74.

Eilon, Samuel, and Joseph Elmaleh, "Adaptive Limits in Inventory Control," *Management Science,* vol. 16, no. 8 (April 1970), pp. B533–B548.

Flowers, A. D., "A Simulation Study of Smoothing Constant Limits for an Adaptive Forecasting System," *Journal of Operations Management,* vol. 2 (1980), pp. 84–94.

Gardner, Everette S., "The Strange Case of the Lagging Forecasts," *Interfaces,* vol. 14, no. 3 (May–June 1984), pp. 47–50.

Gardner, Everette S., and David G. Dannenbring, "Forecasting with Exponential Smoothing: Some Guidelines for Model Selection," *Decision Sciences,* vol. 11, no. 2 (April 1980), pp. 370–383.

Huang, D. S., *Regression and Econometric Methods.* New York: John Wiley & Sons, 1970.

Mabert, Vincent A., "Forecast Modification Based on Residual Analysis: A Case Study of Check Volume Estimation," *Decision Sciences,* vol. 9, no. 2 (April 1978), pp. 285–296.

Makridakis, Spyros, Steven C. Wheelwright, and Victor E. McGee, *Forecasting: Methods and Applications,* 2nd ed. New York: John Wiley & Sons, 1983.

Plossl, George W., "Getting the Most from Forecasts." Paper presented at the APICS 1972 International Conference and reprinted in *Forecasting.* Falls Church, Va.: American Production and Inventory Control Society, 2nd ed., 1979.

Shiskin, Julius, Allan H. Young, and John Musgrave, "The X-11 Variant of the Census II Seasonal Adjustment Program," U.S. Bureau of the Census, Technical Paper no. 15, February 1967.

Smith, Bernard, *Focus Forecasting: Computer Techniques for Inventory Control.* Boston: CBI Publishing, 1978.

Stratton, William B., "How to Design a Viable Forecasting System," *Production and Inventory Management,* vol. 20, no. 1 (First Quarter 1979), pp. 17–27.

Trigg, D. W., and A. G. Leach, "Exponential Smoothing with an Adaptive Response Rate," *Operational Research Quarterly,* vol. 18, no. 1 (March 1967), pp. 53–59.

Whybark, D. Clay, "A Comparison of Adaptive Forecasting Techniques," *The Logistics and Transportation Review,* vol. 8, no. 3 (1972), pp. 13–26.

Wood, Steve D., "Forecasting Patient Census: Commonalities in Time Series Models," *Health Services Research,* vol. 11, no. 2 (1976), p. 158.

CHAPTER

11

MATERIALS MANAGEMENT

▲ Chapter Outline

Should we move to a more integrated organizational structure?

How should we select, evaluate, and support suppliers?

Should we do more centralized buying? Should we use long-term contracts?

Should we add distribution centers and position inventory closer to customers?

Should we place inventory toward end items, purchased items, or somewhere between?

Are our inventories and other cushions too high or too low?

What are our best options for reducing inventory wisely?

How should we link materials management to competitive priorities?

hort-range decisions about supplies, inventories, production levels, staffing patterns, schedules, and distribution are the concern of **materials management.** Decisions in these areas affect the management of materials either directly or indirectly. We begin by examining the role of materials and inventory in the U.S. economy. We then describe materials management tasks, focusing on purchasing and distribution. We conclude by presenting several important inventory concepts, some of which you'll need for subsequent chapters.

IMPORTANCE OF MATERIALS MANAGEMENT ▲

As materials management decisions have short time horizons, they are by definition more tactical than strategic. (See Chapter 1.) However, they have a major cumulative effect and therefore attract considerable managerial attention. There are two reasons for tactical decisions about materials to be considered so important: (1) the central role of materials in production; and (2) the impact of inventories on company profitability.

Central Role of Materials

Managing materials is common to organizations in every segment of the economy. Materials are necessary inputs to churches, governments, manufacturers, wholesalers, retailers, and universities. Manufacturers make products from materials purchased from outside suppliers. Service industries use materials in the form of physical items (facilitating goods) purchased from suppliers—one of the three components of a service bundle (see Chapter 2). The cost of purchased materials is substantial and growing. The typical U.S. manufacturer spent 40 percent of its total income from sales on purchased materials and services in 1945. The proportion rose to 50 percent in 1960 and stands at 60 percent today. Top executives expect it to climb still more (Miller and Roth, 1988).

Only about 15–20 percent of income from sales is now spent on labor (wages, salaries, and benefits), with the remainder contributed to net income, depreciation, taxes, and retained earnings. The proportion spent on purchased materials varies from industry to industry. At one extreme, the petroleum refining industry spends over 80 percent of its income from sales on materials; the pharmaceutical industry is at the other extreme, at only 25 percent. There is also some variation by country. Owing to the lack of natural resources, Japanese firms must spend, on average, 7 percent more of their income from sales on materials than firms in North America and Europe. Despite such variations, one conclusion is clear: Most firms fall within the 45–65 percent range, giving materials great profit-making potential.

APPLICATION 11.1

A company's sales this year will be $100 million. Cost of materials represents 60 percent of income from sales, and 15 percent goes for salaries, wages, and benefits. A 10 percent gross profit (before taxes) is expected. Management wants to increase gross profits by $1 million next year, from $10 million to $11 million. Three options are being considered: increase sales, reduce labor costs (through increased productivity), or reduce materials costs. Which option requires the least percentage change?

Solution

The following calculations show that the company could increase sales by *10 percent* or reduce labor costs by almost *7 percent*. Reducing materials costs requires less than a *2 percent* change to achieve the same increase in profits. Since smaller percentage changes normally are easier (cost less) to achieve, materials have a high profit-making potential.

Alternative	Percent Change
1. Increase sales by $10 million (10% of which yields $1 million in gross profits).	$\left(\dfrac{\$10 \text{ million}}{\$100 \text{ million}}\right)(100) = \underline{10\%}$
2. Reduce labor costs by $1 million.	$\left(\dfrac{\$1 \text{ million}}{\$15 \text{ million}}\right)(100) = \underline{7\%}$
3. Reduce materials costs by $1 million.	$\left(\dfrac{\$1 \text{ million}}{\$60 \text{ million}}\right)(100) = \underline{2\%}$

Impact of Inventory

Materials also are important because of the investment tied up in them. In 1987, $945.2 billion in inventory were held in the U.S. economy. This inventory total is almost three times larger than the economy's monthly sales to final consumers. In effect, the economy holds 3 months' sales volume in inventory.

Consider a second ratio: Inventory investment in the U.S. economy is more than double all business investment (by both the manufacturing and service sectors) in new plants and equipment each year. Each dollar tied up in inventory is a dollar unavailable for investment in new products, technological improvements, or capacity increases.

Figure 11.1, on the following page, shows that most inventory is held by manufacturers, wholesalers, and retailers. Because only 37 percent is held by manufacturers, materials management is of concern throughout the entire economy.

FUNCTION OF MATERIALS MANAGEMENT ▲

Ideally, one person in a firm should make all materials management decisions because they are so interrelated. However, the sheer magnitude of this task makes that impossible. It isn't unusual for a business unit to be responsible for thousands of employees and product items, hundreds of work centers, and several plants and to have hundreds of suppliers. One person trying to develop weekly plans even three months into the future for purchasing, inventory, output rates, work-force levels, and shipping schedules is mind boggling.

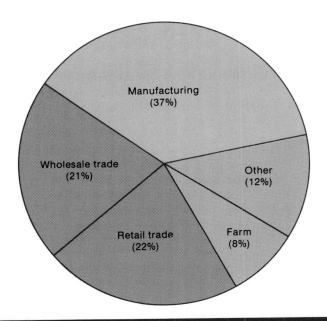

FIGURE 11.1 **Where Inventories Are Held**

Source: Economic Report of the President, 1988.

In practice, several departments in an organization typically specialize in certain aspects of materials management. Table 11.1 shows where manufacturing firms usually assign tasks in materials management. Many of these same tasks are performed in service industries, but "manufacturing" might be called "operations," and "production control" wouldn't even exist. Tasks such as staff planning, work-force scheduling, and operations scheduling (the equivalent of production control in service industries) are usually decentralized. For example, branch managers at retail stores or banks develop schedules for the activities and employees in their own units.

Each task in Table 11.1 is assigned to one of five departments. For example, managers assign vendor selection most often to the purchasing department. Table 11.1 shows not only the most likely assignments but also the level at which the tasks are performed: mainly at the plant level (local) or at the divisional or corporate level (global).

Since the early 1960s, there has been growing sentiment for (1) grouping most materials management tasks under one roof, and (2) elevating the manager of this new group to a higher position in the company. This new department is typically called materials management, although the name logistics management is used sometimes. At one organizational extreme is the *segmented structure*, which is the arrangement traditionally used. Of particular concern is the placement of three departments: (1) purchasing, (2) production control, and (3) distribution. In a segmented organization the manager of each of these departments reports to a different person. At the other organizational extreme is the *integrated structure*, which creates a materials management department headed by a key executive. This structure not only elevates the function, but recognizes that the various materials management tasks are all part of the same broad activity. It brings together all tasks related to flows of materials, beginning with the purchase of raw materials and ending with the distribution of the finished product or service.

TABLE 11.1   Materials Management Task Assignments

Department	Task Assignment	Organizational Level*
Purchasing	Vendor selection	G
	Issuing purchase releases	L
	Inbound transportation	L
Manufacturing	Manufacturing/distribution systems development	G
	Receiving	L
	Factory stockroom operation	L
	Finished goods warehousing at the plant	L
Production control	Assigning delivery due dates to orders	G
	Finished goods inventory control (plant)	G
	Master production scheduling	G
	WIP inventory control	L
	Raw materials inventory control	L
	Detailed production scheduling	L
Distribution	Finished goods inventory control (DCs)	G
	Outbound transportation: DCs to customer	G
	Shipping	L
	Outbound transportation: Plant to DCs	L
Marketing	Forecasting	G
	Processing incoming customer orders	G

*L = tasks done locally, at plant level.
 G = tasks done globally, at divisional or corporate level.

Source: Jeffrey G. Miller, Peter Gilmour, and Roland Van Dierdonck, "Organizing for Materials Management." Working Paper HBS 80-23, Graduate School of Business Administration, Harvard University, 1980.

In one survey, only 10 percent of the firms responding still used a segmented structure. Another 40 percent grouped the three key departments into an integrated structure. The remaining 50 percent used hybrid structures, with only two of the three departments reporting to the same executive. The department most likely to be left out was distribution, which usually continued reporting to marketing.

PURCHASING AND DISTRIBUTION ▲

Although subsequent chapters deal with most of the materials management tasks, they do not include a discussion of certain aspects of purchasing and distribution. Entire books have been written about each of these functions, so we must settle for a brief introduction to them.

Purchasing

Purchasing is the management of the acquisition process, which includes deciding which vendors to use, negotiating contracts, and deciding whether to buy locally or centrally. Purchasing is the starting point of the materials management cycle of acquisition, storage, conversion, storage, and distribution. Acquisition means placing purchase orders with selected vendors in response to requests (called *purchase requisitions*) from others in the firm and then tracking the orders until they are received. Tracking includes following up with the supplier on late orders by writing, telex, or telephone. At a manufacturing firm, the purchasing department normally gets authority to buy from the production control department. For a retailer, deciding what to buy is the same as deciding what merchandise to sell; marketing and purchasing decisions are intermixed.

However, purchasing's role isn't limited to placing and tracking orders. Purchasing is of strategic importance and must satisfy the firm's long-term supply needs, supporting the firm's production capabilities. This task is crucial for any organization, whether retailer, service provider, or manufacturer. We therefore need to look at certain decision areas beyond placing and tracking orders. Let's begin with vendor selection.

Vendor Selection.   Purchasing is the eyes and ears of the organization in the supplier marketplace, continuously seeking better buys. This process begins with the vendor selection decision. Purchasing agents for some companies establish formal rating procedures to help them select new suppliers or periodically review the performance of current suppliers. Three of the many criteria considered in a selection decision almost always are price, quality, and delivery. Beginning with *price*, recall that a typical firm is now spending some 60 percent of its total income from sales on purchased items. Thus finding suppliers who charge lower prices is a key to healthy profit margins.

As important as it is, price is not the only consideration. The *quality* of a supplier's materials can be very important. The hidden costs of poor quality can be high (see Chapter 3), particularly if the defects are not detected until after considerable value has been added by subsequent manufacturing operations. The hidden costs of poor quality are not limited to manufacturers. For a retailer, poor quality can mean loss of goodwill and future sales.

The third of these criteria is *delivery*. Shorter lead times and on-time delivery help the buying firm to maintain acceptable customer service with less inventory. Maimonides Medical Center, a 700-bed hospital in Brooklyn, buys much of its supplies from one vendor. The vendor offers very short lead times from a nearby warehouse, which allowed Maimonides to pare its inventory from about $1200 to only $150 per bed. The benefits of fast and on-time deliveries also apply to the manufacturing sector. Many manufacturing firms seek just-in-time (JIT) delivery from their suppliers in order to minimize inventory levels (see Chapter 16). This constraint means that vendors must have nearby plants or warehouses. For example, Kasle Steel Corporation built a steel-processing plant adjacent to GM's Buick facility in Flint, Michigan, even though it already had two plants only 70 miles away. This new plant is part of a complex (called "Buick City") where all parts are supplied to the GM facility by nearby plants. These clustered suppliers ship very small quantities frequently, to minimize the assembly plant's inventory. There is a 20-minute window during which a quantity of a particular part must be delivered; otherwise, the production line may be shut down.

Vendor Relations. A second purchasing issue of strategic importance is the type of relations maintained with vendors. A firm can relate to a supplier either competitively or cooperatively. The competitive orientation is particularly prevalent in North America. Negotiations between buyer and seller are viewed as a zero-sum game: Whatever is lost by one side is gained by the other. Short-term advantages are prized over long-term commitments. The buyer may try to beat the supplier's price down to the lowest survival level, or push demand to high levels during boom times and order almost nothing during recessions. The supplier, on the other hand, presses for higher prices for specific levels of quality, customer service, and volume flexibility. Which party wins depends largely on who has the most *clout*, as we see in Managerial Practice 11.1. The buyer has the upper hand when

1. the buyer represents a significant share of the supplier's sales;
2. the purchased item is standardized, with substitutes offered by other suppliers;
3. the buyer could integrate backward into the supplier's business;
4. the supplier could not integrate forward into the buyer's business; and
5. switching to a new vendor is not costly.

Conversely, the supplier is more powerful if these situations are reversed.

The cooperative orientation to supplier relations is attracting more attention, particularly because of the success certain Japanese firms have had with it. The buyer and seller are seen as partners, with each helping the other as much as possible. One important variable is the number of suppliers. A cooperative orientation favors few suppliers of a particular item, with just one or two suppliers being the ideal number. One big advantage is increased volumes. The supplier gains repeatability, which helps movement toward the product-focused strategy of a high-volume, low-cost producer. (See Chapter 2.) When contracts are large, the supplier may even have to build a new facility and hire a new work force. Being assured of a long-term relationship may make the difference in whether the supplier builds a new facility, particularly if it is to be located close to the buyer's plant. Fewer suppliers may also help the buyer; they become almost an extension of the buyer.

A cooperative orientation means more than reducing the number of suppliers: It means sharing more information on future buying intentions. This forward visibility allows suppliers to make better forecasts of future demand, making them more efficient and reliable. The buyer visits vendors' plants, cultivates cooperative attitudes, and jealously guards the relationships. The buyer may even suggest ways to improve the supplier's operations. Trust in the supplier may mean that the buyer does not even inspect incoming materials. It can also mean looser specifications on purchase orders, involving the supplier more in designing parts, implementing cost-reduction ideas, and sharing in cost savings.

MANAGERIAL PRACTICE 11.1 ▲

Clout and K mart's Pencil

About 30 K mart buyers take an annual trip in the late fall to a dozen Asian nations. They sign contracts for hundreds of millions of dollars, looking for bargains and new sources of supply. One of the buyers, Joseph Antonini, wouldn't have rated more than a glance on a factory tour back home in New Jersey. However, over at the Hanil Synthetic Fiber Industrial Company plant in South Korea, he gets a different reception. Security guards straighten, workers spring to open his door, dozens applaud, and someone hands him a large floral display. He and his buyers fly first-class and stay only in luxury hotels.

The reason for his royal treatment is that he carries "the pencil"—the buyer's term for authority to order merchandise. "It can go to your head," notes Mr. Antonini, a 20-year K mart veteran. However, the real benefit is K mart's ability to negotiate low prices or extra quality concessions. Its immense orders keep Hanil's knitting machines running longer and more efficiently.

Source: "K mart Apparel Buyers Hopscotch the Orient to Find Quality Goods," *Wall Street Journal*, March 19, 1985.

Neither orientation is always best. The Air Force recently used a *competitive* orientation by dividing a huge jet-engine contract between General Electric and the former exclusive contract-holder, Pratt & Whitney. The Air Force expects competition to save cost. GM is pursuing a *cooperative* orientation by paring down the number of major suppliers (4000, versus only 300 at Toyota), leaving only the most efficient ones. Suppliers who meet GM's tougher requirements will get long-term contracts. This benefit gives suppliers enough volume to recoup investments in cost-saving equipment and new capacity.

Contracting.   Purchasing must decide how to contract for each of the thousands of items that most firms buy. The procedure selected depends a great deal on volume and usage rates. When there is low demand, as with customized items not held in inventory, a buyer has three options: (1) competitive bidding; (2) sole source contracting; and (3) vendor catalogues.

Competitive bidding means that several suppliers are asked to submit formal quotations. The lowest *and* best (most capable) bidder receives the contract. This method is not mandatory in the private sector but is prudent when the expenditure to be made is great, as with heavy equipment or a computer system. If the dollar value of the purchase is low or time is of the essence, sole source contracting or vendor catalogues may be best. With sole source contracting, a company negotiates a contract with a single supplier. This approach reduces purchasing lead time but doesn't guarantee the best buy, particularly if the buyer is unaware of comparative prices. Using vendor catalogues, the buyer simply looks through several and makes a selection. The cost of any further search outweighs the benefits.

Contracting procedures can be quite different with high demand, as with standardized items for which there is continuous demand. There are two options: (1) preselected vendors; and (2) long-term contracts. With the first option, competitive bidding is not used for each order placed. When requisitions are received from production control, purchasing immediately sends to the preselected vendor a purchase order specifying the product, quantity, and delivery due date. Delays caused by vendor selection procedures are avoided.

If demands are high enough, the second option may be used. Actually, it is a special case of using preselected vendors. Long-term contracts covering one or more years are negotiated, with delivery dates, quantities, and often prices left open. The buying firm commits to a supplier for the agreed-on period of time and sends periodic estimates of future needs to the supplier. When a new order is placed, purchasing does not even need to write a purchase order. Most long-term contracts are either *blanket* or *open-ended* contracts. A blanket contract covers a variety of items, whereas an open-ended contract allows items to be added or the contract period extended. Long-term contracts save paperwork and reserve supplier capacity. As annual volumes are large, price concessions are possible. Vendors prefer long-term contracts because they make future demand more certain. Long-term contracts are consistent with the cooperative orientation to supplier relations.

Centralized Buying.   When an organization has several facilities (such as stores, hospitals, or plants), management must decide whether to buy locally or centrally. In deciding which strategy is best for a particular item, management must weigh the advantages and disadvantages of each.

Centralized buying can increase purchasing clout. Savings can be significant, often on the order of 10 percent or more. Increased buying power can mean getting better service, ensuring long-term supply availability, or developing new supplier capability. Two trends favor more centralization: (1) growth of multinational operations, which makes specialized knowledge and skills desirable when buying from foreign sources; and (2) growth of computer-based information systems, which gives specialists at headquarters access to data previously available only at the local level.

Despite these advantages, centralized buying for all items would be a mistake. Items unique to a particular facility should be purchased locally whenever possible. The same holds for purchases that must be closely meshed with production schedules. Centralized purchasing often means longer lead times, with another level in the firm's hierarchy involved. Probably the biggest disadvantage of centralized buying is loss of control at the local level. Plants or divisions may be evaluated as profit or cost centers, even though they may not control a major cost item. Such divisions of authority may dampen the essential entrepreneurial spirit at the local level. Perhaps the best solution is a compromise strategy, whereby local autonomy and centralized buying are both possible. For example, the corporate purchasing group at IBM negotiates contracts on a centralized basis only at the request of local plants. Then, management at one of the facilities monitors the contract for all the participants.

Distribution

Distribution is the management of the flow of materials from manufacturers to customers, involving the storage and transportation of products. While purchasing deals with inbound materials, distribution deals with outbound flows. Distribution broadens the marketplace for a firm, adding time and place value to its products. Transportation costs contribute substantially to an item's price. Some 10 percent of the entire U.S. labor force is engaged in transportation or transportation-related industries. Here we briefly consider three issues faced by distribution managers.

Finished Goods Inventory Placement.   A fundamental choice is where to stock inventory of finished goods. Forward placement means locating stock closer to customers at a warehouse (now usually called a *distribution center*, or DC), or with a wholesaler or retailer. Backward placement means holding the inventory at the manufacturing plant or maintaining no inventory. Forward placement can have two advantages: (1) fast delivery times; and (2) reduced transportation costs. Dubbed the "warm puppy effect," proximity to a stocking point can give customers a more comfortable feeling which, in turn, can stimulate sales.

Forward placement might also help avoid the premium rates of less-than-carload (LCL) shipments. Shipments out of the plant can be concentrated on a few routes (to the DCs), rather than fragmented for scattered customer locations. Even outbound shipments from DCs to customer destinations may now be large enough to achieve full carload (CL) rates more frequently, particularly if several plants are providing a variety of products to the DCs. For example, General Foods mixes products received from various plants at its distribution centers and reships to customers at full CL rates.

Forward placement is not always possible or advisable. If competitive priorities call for product flexibility and customized products, it doesn't make sense even to have finished goods inventory. The risk of creating unwanted products is too great. A second argument against forward placement is the *pooling effect*. The demand in a region may be unpredictably high one month and low the next. If demand in several such regions were pooled, as would be the case with less forward placement, the highs in some regions would tend to cancel the lows in others. Demand is less erratic and more predictable when inventory is placed at a centralized point, rather than at a DC for each small region. Inventories for the whole system can be lower, and costly reshipments from one DC to another can be minimized.

Ethan Allan provides a good example of the pooling effect. Originally, each of the 40 retailers of Ethan Allen products in the New York metropolitan area maintained its own inventory. The aggregate inventory value averaged $3 million, and customer service was poor. The probability that all items in a customer's order were on hand was only 0.25. Ethan Allen solved this dilemma by creating one large field warehouse to serve all 40 retailers. The retailers no longer need to carry separate inventories, except for display purposes. Inventory dropped to $700,000, and the probability of filling a customer's order from DC inventory increased to 0.80.

Selection of Transportation Mode.   The five basic modes of transportation are highway, rail, water, pipeline, and air. Each has its own advantages and limitations.

Highway transportation provides the flexibility of shipping to almost any location in the United States. No rehandling is needed for pickup and delivery. Transit times are good and rates are usually less than rail rates for small quantities and short hauls. Truckers haul 40 percent of U.S. freight, whereas railroads move 30 percent (down from 50 percent in 1947). Rail transportation can move large quantities very cheaply, but transit times are long and variable. This mode is usually best for shipping raw materials, rather than finished goods. Rail shipments often require pickup and delivery rehandling. Water transportation provides high capacity at low unit cost, but transit times are slow and large areas are inaccessible to waterborne carriers. Pipeline transportation is highly specialized, with limited geographical flexibility. It is limited to liquids, gases, or solids in slurry form. No packaging is needed, and operating costs per mile are low. While most pipelines move petroleum, some companies use them to transport fish and coal. Air transportation is the fastest and most expensive mode. Although volumes are increasing geometrically, they still represent only 1 percent of all freight moved. Air transportation is limited by the availability of airport facilities and requires pickup and delivery rehandling.

In addition to these primary modes, special service modes and hybrids, such as parcel post, air express, bus service, freight forwarder, and piggyback, are available. Transportation companies are organized under different forms of ownership and management. A firm may be a *private carrier*, owning and operating its own fleet. It may select a *contract carrier*, negotiating with the carrier for a specified amount, type, and frequency of shipment. A contract carrier does not provide service to the general public, instead serving specific customers. Or the firm may select a *common carrier*, which by law must serve all customers without discrimination. This option gives the firm the least control over carrier availability but makes sense for low-volume producers with geographically dispersed markets.

Scheduling, Routing, and Carrier Selection.   Several activities are involved in the day-to-day control of freight movement. The shipping schedule must mesh with purchasing and production control schedules. It also reflects the trade-off between transportation costs and customer response times. By delaying a shipment for another two days, it may be possible to achieve full carload (CL) rates for a rail shipment or full truckload (TL) rates for truck shipments. Routing choices must also be made. A central post office, operating its own fleet to collect mail from outlying areas, must determine the route to each pickup point. A manufacturer may select a routing that combines shipments to multiple customers and gains lower freight rates. The firm may even negotiate lower rates if it develops routings where large volumes can be shipped on a regular basis. These choices are complex. Even before deregulation, the U.S. freight rate structure seemed chaotic to the uninitiated. Now rates and services vary markedly, depending on the specific mode and carrier chosen.

INVENTORY CONCEPTS ▲

Clearly, materials management exerts great influence on company success, requiring coordination among several decision areas and departments. An essential part of materials management is inventory control. **Inventory** is a stock of materials held to satisfy some eventual demand. Inventory is created when the rate of receipts exceeds the rate of disbursements. It is depleted when disbursements exceed receipts.

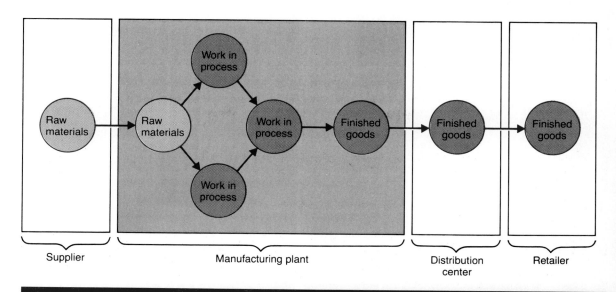

FIGURE 11.2 A Materials Flow System

Accounting Categories

Inventory can be held in various forms and locations, or stocking points, as shown in Fig. 11.2. Inventory for a manufacturing plant exists in three forms, or accounting categories: raw materials, work-in-process, and finished goods. In the system shown in Fig. 11.2, raw materials are kept at two stocking points: the supplier's facility and the plant. The raw materials at the plant pass through one or more processes, which transform them into various levels of work-in-process (WIP) inventory. When this inventory is processed at the final operation, it becomes finished goods inventory. Finished goods can be held at the plant, a DC, and retail locations. Materials flow systems can be more or less complex than that shown. A small retailer must manage only store inventories, a relatively simple system. A large retailer, such as Kroger, often integrates backward to include distribution centers and even manufacturing plants, which creates a more complex system. A process-focused manufacturer such as Longhorn (Chapter 2) ships directly to the customer, creating a simple system with no intervening DCs or retail stocking points. A product-focused manufacturer may integrate backward to the point where it has its own feeder plants, which in turn supply its assembly plants. A multiplant operation is particularly challenging, since inventories must be coordinated at more stocking points.

Bill of Materials

Manufacturing operations abound with inventory terms: parent, component, bill of materials, usage quantity, end item, intermediate item, subassembly, purchased item, routing, and part commonality. One frequent distinction made

(a)

(b)

(a) Raw materials and work-in-progress inventory at Anheuser-Busch: The small containers in the foreground hold the raw materials—blends of hops that are added to the wort. The WIP inventory is the mixture being boiled in the huge brew kettles, which have a capacity of approximately 650 barrels of beer. (b) Finished goods inventory comes off Anheuser-Busch's canning line, which operates 24 hours a day, 365 days a year.

in manufacturing is whether an item is a parent or a component. A **parent** is an item manufactured from one or more component items. The chair in which you are sitting is a parent, made from legs, arms, a seat, and fasteners. A **component** is an item, possibly one of several, that goes through one or more operations to be transformed into a parent.

A **bill of materials (BOM)** is a diagram or record that shows all the components of an item, the parent–component relationships, and usage quantities. The BOM in Fig. 11.3 shows that item A is made from items B and C. Item B, in turn, is made from D and E, and E is made from F. Items A, B, and E are parents, since they are made from other items by passing them through one or more operations. All items except A are also components because they are needed to make a parent. The BOM also provides another type of information. A **usage quantity** is the number of units of a component needed to make one unit of its parent. Figure 11.3 shows usage quantities in parentheses, one for each parent–component relationship. Note that one unit of A is made from two units of B and one unit of C. All other usage quantities are one unit, except for the three units of F needed to make one unit of E.

A BOM introduces another useful set of terms: end items, intermediate items, subassemblies, and purchased items. An **end item** is typically the final product sold to the customer; it is a parent but not a component. Item A in Fig. 11.3 qualifies as an end item. Inventory for end items is classified in accounting statements as either work-in-process (WIP) or finished goods. If work remains to be done on the end item, it is WIP. An **intermediate item** is one that has at least one parent and at least one component. Both items B and E in Fig. 11.3 qualify as intermediate items. Some products have several levels of intermediate items, where the parent of one intermediate item is also an intermediate item. Inventory of intermediate items—whether completed or still on the shop floor—is classified as WIP. A **subassembly** is a special case of an intermediate item: It is *assembled* (as opposed to other types of transformation) from *more* than one component. A **purchased item** is one that has no components because it comes from a supplier, but it has one or more parents. Examples are items C, D, and F in Fig. 11.3. Inventory of purchased items is treated as raw materials in accounting statements.

Another concept related to the notion of parents and components is part commonality, sometimes called *standardization of parts*. **Part commonality** is the

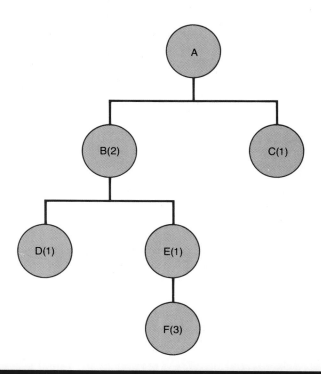

FIGURE 11.3   A Bill of Materials for Item A

degree to which a part (component) has more than one parent. A giant step toward part commonality took place in the early 1800s, when Eli Whitney introduced interchangeable parts for manufacturing firearms. Working toward more standardized parts continues to this day, as Managerial Practice 11.2 shows. Part commonality increases repeatability—which has several advantages for process design (see Chapters 4 and 5)—and helps minimize inventory. Today, almost 90 percent of manufacturing firms have at least some part commonality, with 44 percent reporting that it is extensive (Sharma, 1987).

A companion document to the BOM is a routing. Taken together, they communicate the process design choices that have been made, telling how a particular item is to be manufactured. A **routing** lists the sequence of operations to be performed on an item, the standard times, and the operations at which each component is needed. Each manufactured item has a routing. Figure 11.4 shows the BOM and routing for an item made from three purchased items. Ten operations are performed in making item G from three components (C, D, and K).

Types of Demand

Another important inventory concept is the type of demand, which can be either independent or dependent. The **independent demand** for an item is influenced by market conditions and not related to production decisions for any other item held in stock. In manufacturing, only end items have exclusively independent demand. Components at the WIP level can experience independent demand only when customers ask for spare-part replacements. In the service industry, such as selling merchandise at a single site, parent–

MANAGERIAL PRACTICE 11.2 ▲

Part Commonality at HP

In 1985, Hewlett-Packard Company's computer-terminal business was nearly extinct. Cheaper, Asian-made terminals and personal computers were siphoning market share away. Plant manager Larry Mitchell did something about it. Teaming up with engineering and marketing people, he redesigned the product to have 40 percent fewer parts. The result was a radically new terminal designed for low-cost, high-volume production. The new models saved 55 percent on materials and 75 percent on labor. HP suddenly became the trendsetter on prices, and sales were 150 percent of previous HP levels.

Source: "How HP Built a Better Terminal," *Business Week*, March 7, 1988.

Operation		Standard times (hours)		
Sequence no.	Description	Processing	Setup	Component
1	Shear	0.10	0.40	Raw material C
2	Blank	0.08	0.50	
3	First inspection	0.06	—	
4	Saw	0.33	1.40	Raw material D
5	Heat treat	—	10.00	
6	Subassemble C and D	1.30	—	
7	Sand blast	0.28	0.25	
8	Clean	0.16	—	
9	Impregnate with K	0.45	0.10	Raw material K
10	Final inspection	0.10	—	

(a)

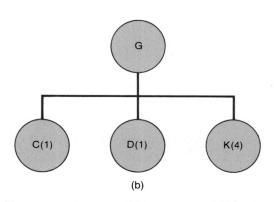

(b)

FIGURE 11.4   Item G: (a) Routing; (b) Bill of Materials

component relationships do not exist. There are no parents and the merchandise experiences only independent demand.

Dependent demand for an item derives from the production decisions for its parents. Suppose that the arm for a stereo turntable, component B, has only one parent, turntable model A, and that the usage quantity is 1. If operations plans to release a production order of 100 model A turntables three weeks from now, the operations manager can expect the demand for B to be zero during the next two weeks but 100 units by the end of the third week. By contrast, the operations manager can only *forecast* independent demand. Entirely different production and inventory control systems will be utilized, depending on whether demand is dependent (being derived) or independent (being forecast).*

---

*Chapter 12 deals more with independent-demand systems, and Chapters 15 and 16 cover dependent-demand systems.

Inventory Placement

Just as distribution managers decide where to place finished goods inventory, manufacturing managers make similar decisions for raw materials and WIP within the plant. Inventory held toward the end-item level means short delivery times—but a higher dollar investment in inventory. Inventory placement at Shamrock Chemicals, as described in Managerial Practice 11.3, illustrates this trade-off. Holding inventory lower in the BOM reduces the cost of carrying inventory, and part commonality might allow more repeatability—but at the cost of longer customer response times.

Managers make inventory placement decisions, in general, by designating an item as either a special or a standard. A **special** is an item made to order. If it is purchased, it is bought to order. Just enough are ordered to cover the latest customer request. Production of a special's parent must be delayed by the special's lead time. A **standard** is an item made to stock and normally is available when needed. Overlaying lead times on the BOM allows the manager to calculate customer response times for different placement strategies. Making an item a standard in effect cuts its lead time to zero, except for shipping time. The customer response time is the total lead time along the longest path down to a standard or the bottom of the BOM, whichever comes first.

APPLICATION 11.2

A manager is evaluating six strategies of inventory placement for item A in Fig. 11.5. Strategy 1 has no standards, 2 makes D a standard, 3 makes C and D standards, 4 makes B a standard, 5 makes B and E standards, and 6 makes A a standard. What are the customer response times for each strategy?

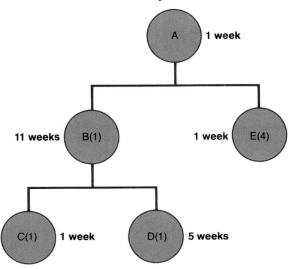

FIGURE 11.5   BOM with Lead Times

Solution

Strategy 1 means that the customer waits 17 weeks after placing the order before it is shipped. The longest path is D–B–A. Once an order is received, it takes 5 weeks to get D, another 11 weeks to make B, and still another week to assemble B and E to make A. Item E is not on the longest path; it can be bought in just one week, whereas B won't be ready for 16 weeks. Similar computations for the other strategies are shown in the following table.

Strategy	Standard Items	Longest Path	Customer Response Time (weeks)
1	None	D–B–A	17 (5 + 11 + 1)
2	D	C–B–A	13 (1 + 11 + 1)
3	C and D	B–A	12 (11 + 1)
4	B	E–A	2 (1 + 1)
5	B and E	A	1
6	A	—	0

Measuring Inventory

Suppose that it costs a firm 35 percent of the dollars tied up in a certain inventory to maintain it for a year. If the inventory level averages 30 percent of sales, the cost to hold inventory is 10.5 percent [or 0.35 (0.30)] of total sales. This cost is sizable in terms of gross profit margins, which often are less than 10 percent. For this reason, managers closely monitor inventories to keep them at acceptably low levels. Inventories are reported to them in three basic ways: (1) average aggregate inventory value; (2) weeks of supply; and (3) inventory turnover.

MANAGERIAL PRACTICE 11.3

Inventory Placement at Shamrock Chemicals

Shamrock Chemicals Corporation is a Newark, N.J., maker of wax compounds used in printing inks. It enjoys sales of more than $15 million because it can ship any compound the same day a customer orders it. End items are treated as standards rather than specials, but Shamrock must maintain a hefty inventory. "We can't be lean and mean in our inventory policy because we can't afford to not have the stuff to ship," says William B. Neuberg, president and owner.

Source: "New Inventory-Expense Rules Increase Costs at Many Firms," *Wall Street Journal,* June 29, 1987.

All methods of measuring inventory begin with a physical count of units, volume, or weight. However, one unit of item A may be worth only pennies, whereas one unit of item B may be valued in the thousands of dollars. The **average aggregate inventory value** is the total value of all items held in inventory on the average, over some time period. It is found by multiplying the number of units of each item on hand by its per unit value to obtain the value of each item and then adding the values of all the items. This total value tells managers how much of a firm's assets are tied up in inventory. Manufacturing firms typically have about 25 percent of their total assets in inventory, whereas wholesalers and retailers average about 75 percent. To some extent managers can evaluate aggregate inventory value by historical or industry comparison, or by managerial judgment. However, they cannot do so realistically without taking demand into account. Managers can include demand rates by using the measures weeks of supply and inventory turnover. **Weeks of supply** is an inventory measure found by dividing the average aggregate inventory value by the sales per week at cost.* Although the numerator includes the value of all items (raw materials, WIP, and finished goods), the denominator represents only the cost of the finished goods sold. **Inventory turnover** (or *turns*) is an inventory measure found by dividing annual sales at cost by the average aggregate inventory value maintained during the year.

To summarize:

$$\text{Weeks of supply} = \frac{\text{Average aggregate inventory value}}{\text{Weekly sales}}$$

$$\text{Inventory turnover} = \frac{\text{Annual sales}}{\text{Average aggregate inventory value}}$$

The "best" inventory level, even when expressed as turnover, cannot be easily determined. Although 6 or 7 turns per year is typical, high-tech firms settle for only about 3 turns. At the other extreme, some Japanese automobile firms report 40 turns per year.

APPLICATION 11.3

A company averaged $2 million in inventory last year, and the cost of goods sold was $10 million. If the company has 52 business weeks per year, how many weeks of supply were held in inventory? What was the inventory turnover?

Solution

The average aggregate inventory value of $2 million translates into 10.4 weeks of supply and 5 turns per year:

---

*In some low-inventory operations, days or even hours are a better unit of time for measuring inventory.

$$\text{Weeks of supply} = \frac{\$2 \text{ million}}{\$10 \text{ million}/52 \text{ wk}} = 10.4 \text{ wk}$$

and

$$\text{Inventory turnover} = \frac{\$10 \text{ million}}{\$2 \text{ million}} = 5 \text{ turns/yr}$$

Inventory Costs

Table 11.2 indicates why the best turnover rate varies so much. Conflicting costs and pressures argue for both low and high inventories. A manager must assess each one before reaching any conclusions about appropriate inventory levels. Let's examine each of these costs, beginning with holding costs.

Holding (Carrying) Cost. The primary reason for keeping inventories low is that inventory represents money invested temporarily in goods for which a firm must pay (rather than receive) interest on the investment. **Inventory holding** (or carrying) **cost** is the cost of keeping items on hand, including interest, storage and handling, taxes, insurance, and shrinkage. Companies usually state an item's holding cost per period of time as a percentage of its value. The annual cost to maintain one unit in inventory during the year typically ranges from 25 to 40 percent of its value.

Table 11.2 shows the components of holding cost. Interest or opportunity cost, whichever is greater, usually is the largest component. To finance inventory, a company may obtain a loan or forgo the opportunity of an investment promising an attractive return. These factors alone can peg holding cost as high as 20 percent.

Then there are storage and handling costs. Inventory takes up space and must be moved into and out of storage. Several years ago, managers at Ford Motor Company were amazed at the small size of certain Japanese plants. Toyota's Kamego engine plant occupies only 300,000 square feet, but achieves the same output rate as the 900,000-square-foot Ford plant recently built in Europe. The essential difference is that Toyota found ways to get by with much less inventory.

TABLE 11.2   Conflicting Pressures on Inventory Levels

Pressures for Small Inventories	Pressures for Large Inventories
Interest or opportunity cost	Customer service
Storage and handling cost	Ordering or setup cost
Property taxes	Labor and facility utilization
Insurance premiums	Transportation cost
Shrinkage costs: Pilferage, obsolescence, and deterioration	Cost of purchased items

Deterioration and limited shelf life of fresh produce mean close inventory control at the Mohican Market in Kingston, New York. Here tomatoes are being unloaded from a truck-greengrocer.

Determining how much to increase holding costs to account for storage and materials handling is not a clear-cut procedure. Managers are tempted to calculate an *allocated cost* for space and materials handling, but that would overstate their costs. In the short run, in fact, a manager may be able to increase inventory well beyond its current level without incurring any new *out-of-pocket* costs for either storage space or materials handling. In order to arrive at a true cost, the manager should follow one guiding principle: Include only those costs that actually change because of the decision being made. If the decision is to store short-term inventories in public warehouses, where the charge is based on the amount of space used, the storage cost is relevant. However, if the decision is to store short-term inventories in the firm's facilities, there is no real storage cost when space is abundant and has no other short-term value.

The final components of holding cost are taxes, insurance, and shrinkage (pilferage, obsolescence, and deterioration). Taxes and insurance are self-explanatory, but the three forms of shrinkage need further explanation. Pilferage is theft of inventory by customers or employees and is a significant percentage of sales for some businesses. Obsolescence occurs when inventory cannot be used or sold at full value, owing to model changes, engineering modifications, or unexpectedly low demand. Deterioration through physical spoilage or damage results in lost value. Food and beverages, for example, lose value and may even have to be discarded when their shelf life is reached. When the rate of deterioration is high, build up of large inventories may be unwise.

If these components of holding cost were the only measures affecting inventory choices, holding inventory would not be rational. The fact that inventory held in the U.S. economy is approaching the $1 trillion mark suggests that other performance measures are also important. The pressures for large inventories listed in Table 11.2 indicate why inventory exists despite its expense. Let's look briefly at each, beginning with customer service.

Customer Service.   Creating inventory, particularly with forward placement, can speed up delivery and improve on-time delivery. Inventory reduces the chance of a stockout or the need for a back order, which are key measures for wholesalers and retailers. A **stockout** is not having a standard item on hand in order to satisfy demand for the item the moment it occurs, resulting in loss of the sales. A **back order** is not having a customer order ready when promised or demanded, but filling the order later. Inventory also increases the percentage of on-time deliveries, a key measure for manufacturers. Translating such measures into a dollar cost, as for holding cost, can be difficult if not impossible. However, this inability does not diminish the importance of customer service and managers must carefully watch all aspects of it.

Ordering Cost.   Placing a new order involves a cost. **Ordering cost** is the cost of preparing a purchase order for a supplier or a production order for the shop. For the same item, the cost is the same, regardless of the order size. For a purchased item, someone has to take the time to decide how much to order, select a vendor, and negotiate terms. Time is also spent on paperwork, follow-up, and receiving. Most of the same activities are involved in placing a production order for a manufactured item, but the type of paperwork changes. In this case, a blueprint and routing must often accompany the shop order.

Setup Cost.   Setup (or changeover) **cost** is the cost involved in changing over a machine to produce a different component or item. This cost also is independent of order size. Labor and equipment time is lost. Different tooling or fixtures may be needed, and the machine may have to be cleaned. Scrap or rework may be substantially higher at the start of the run, making scrap a function of setup frequency.

Labor and Equipment Utilization.   Management can increase work-force productivity and facility utilization in three ways by creating more inventory. First, setup time is unproductive because it does not add value to a product. Setup-time losses can be reduced by placing larger production orders less frequently. Although inventories increase, downtime for setups decreases. Second, productivity drops when a parent order must be rescheduled for lack of components. Many actions may be taken to cope with component unavailability, but each has a cost. The third way that inventories can improve resource utilization is in helping to stabilize a manufacturer's output rate, even when demand is cyclical or seasonal. Inventory built during slack periods can handle the extra demand in peak seasons. Varying the work force through extra shifts, hiring, layoffs, and overtime can be minimized. Equipment capacities can also be less, since capacity does not need to match peak demand.

Transportation Cost. Sometimes, outbound transportation cost can be reduced by increasing inventory levels. Large inventory allows more time to help ensure carload shipments and minimizes the need for expedited shipments by more expensive modes of transportation. As we have already noted, forward placement of inventory can reduce outbound transportation cost, even though the pooling effect is lessened and more inventory is necessary. Inbound transportation cost may also be reduced by creating more inventory. Sometimes, several items are ordered from the same supplier. Combining these orders and placing them at the same time may lead to CL rather than LCL rates.

Cost of Purchased Items. A firm can often reduce total payments to suppliers if it can tolerate higher inventory levels. Suppose that a firm learns that a key supplier is about to increase prices. It might be cheaper for the firm to order a larger quantity than usual—in effect delaying the price increase—even though inventory increases temporarily. Similarly, a firm can take advantage of quantity discounts. A **quantity discount** is an incentive to order larger quantities, where the price per unit drops when the order is sufficiently large.

Types of Inventory

Inventory can be viewed as a necessary evil. Although it costs money to hold, inventory helps maintain customer service, improves resource utilization, and reduces ordering, setup, transportation, and purchased materials costs. Another perspective on inventory is to classify it by purpose. In this context, there are four types of inventory: cycle, safety, anticipation, and pipeline.

Cycle Inventory. One purpose of inventory is to order on a less frequent cycle, saving in several cost categories on the right-hand side of Table 11.2. Determining how frequently to order, and in what quantity, is called **lot sizing**. Two principles apply:

1. The lot size (Q) varies in direct proportion to the elapsed time (or cycle) between orders. If a lot is ordered every five weeks, the average Q must equal five weeks' demand. Large lot cycles go with infrequent orders.

2. The longer the time between orders, the greater the cycle inventory. **Cycle inventory** is the portion of total inventory that varies directly with lot size. More specifically,

$$\text{Cycle inventory} = \frac{Q}{2}*$$

---

*This formula is exact only when the demand rate is constant and uniform. Our research shows that the formula provides a reasonably good estimate for dependent demand, where demand rates are not constant. Factors other than the demand rate, such as scrap losses, can also cause estimating errors when this simple formula is used.

APPLICATION 11.4

The lot size of an item is 100 units and the ordering frequency averages two months. What is the item's annual demand and cycle inventory?

Solution

The first principle tells us that 100 units is a 2-month supply, so a 12-month supply must be six times as large, or 600 units.

The second principle and formula tell us that the average cycle inventory is 50. At the beginning of the interval, cycle inventory is at its maximum, as the lot of 100 has just arrived. At the end of the interval, just before a new lot arrives, cycle inventory drops to its minimum, or 0. Assuming that the demand rate is constant, the average of 100 and 0 is 50, or $Q/2$.

Now consider the advantages of large cycle inventory: better customer service, less frequent orders and setups, and reduced transportation and purchasing costs. Increasing Q (and therefore cycle inventory) normally improves customer service because (1) the possibility of a stockout exists only at the end of a cycle, and (2) there are fewer cycles per year when Q is larger.* Thus a higher Q means fewer risks of stockout. Following similar reasoning, increasing Q also reduces the annual cost of orders and setups, since fewer are made per year. Larger lot sizes also might make CL rates or quantity discount prices possible, thereby decreasing the costs of transportation and raw materials.

Safety Stock Inventory.   Another purpose of inventory is to avoid customer service problems and the hidden costs of unavailable components. **Safety stock inventory** is inventory used to protect against uncertainties in demand, lead time, and supply. An unreliable vendor who deviates frequently from the requested lot size or promised delivery time makes maintaining safety stock desirable. Moreover, if a manufactured item is subject to significant and frequent amounts of scrap or rework, safety stock is needed.

There is a simple way to create safety stock: Place an order for delivery earlier than when the item is typically needed.[†] The replenishment order therefore arrives ahead of time, giving a cushion against uncertainty. For example, suppose that the average lead time from a supplier is three weeks, but a firm orders five weeks in advance just to be safe. This policy creates a safety stock equal to two (or 5 − 3) weeks of supply.

---

*We found exceptions to this relationship between Q and customer service in manufacturing. Larger lot sizes can create more feast-or-famine capacity requirements, which hurt a manufacturer's ability to ship on time. In such cases, larger lot sizes hurt on-time delivery performance.

[†]When orders are placed at fixed intervals, there is a second way: Place an order for more than is typically needed through the next delivery date. (See Chapter 12.)

Anticipation Inventory.   **Anticipation inventory** is inventory used to absorb uneven rates of demand or supply, which business often faces. Manufacturers of air conditioners, for example, can experience 90 percent of their annual demand during just three months of a year. Such uneven demand may lead a manufacturer to stockpile inventory during periods of low demand, so that output levels do not have to be increased much when demand rates hit their peak. Smoothing output rates with inventory can increase productivity because varying output rates and work-force size can be costly. Anticipation inventory also can help when supply, rather than demand, is uneven. A company may stock up on a certain purchased item if its suppliers are threatened with a strike or severe capacity limitations.

Pipeline (Transit) Inventory.   **Pipeline inventory** is inventory in transit, that is, moving from point to point in the materials flow system. Materials move from vendors to the plant, from one operation to the next in the plant, from a plant to a DC or customer, and from a DC to a retailer. Because this movement takes time, pipeline inventory is necessary. Pipeline inventory is the sum of all **scheduled receipts** (sometimes called **open orders**), which are orders that have been placed but not yet received. Pipeline inventory exists in three stages: inbound, within the plant, and outbound. The inbound stage includes scheduled receipts of raw materials that have been paid for but are not yet available for use. Within the plant, the pipeline includes all scheduled receipts for production orders sent to the shop. Thus pipeline inventory in the plant represents WIP inventory. Inventory in the outbound stage consists of finished goods that have been shipped but not yet paid for by the customer.

Pipeline inventory between two points can be measured as the average *demand during lead time*, or

$$\text{Pipeline inventory} = \overline{D}_L = dL$$

where

$$d = \text{average demand for the item per period}$$
$$L = \text{the number of periods in the item's lead time to move between two points; either for transportation or production}$$
$$\overline{D}_L = \text{average demand during the lead time}$$

Note that the lot size does not directly affect the average level of the pipeline inventory.* Increasing Q does inflate the size of a scheduled receipt, but this increase is canceled by a proportionate decrease in the number of orders placed per year.

---

*There can be an indirect effect, however. If the lead time gets longer with larger lot sizes, then $\overline{D}_L$ (and therefore pipeline inventory) will increase.

APPLICATION 11.5

A plant makes monthly shipments to a wholesaler of a particular item in average lot sizes of 280 units. The average demand experienced by the wholesaler is 70 units per week, and the lead time from the plant is three weeks. On average, how much cycle inventory and pipeline inventory does the wholesaler carry?

Solution

$$\text{Cycle inventory} = \frac{Q}{2} = \frac{280}{2}$$

$$= 140 \text{ units}$$

$$\text{Pipeline inventory} = \overline{D}_L = dL = (70 \text{ units/wk})(3 \text{ wk})$$

$$= 210 \text{ units}$$

Reducing Inventory

Particularly during periods of high interest rates, managers are eager to find cost-effective ways to reduce inventory. (We examine various ways for finding optimal lot sizes in Chapter 12.) Several basic tactics—which we call *levers*—can be used to reduce inventory. Table 11.3 shows levers for each type of

TABLE 11.3   Levers for Reducing Inventory

Type of Inventory	Primary Lever	Secondary Lever
Cycle	Reduce Q	Reduce ordering and setup cost Increase repeatability
Safety stock	Place orders closer to the time when they must be received	Improve forecasting Reduce lead time Reduce supply uncertainties Increase equipment and labor buffers
Anticipation	Vary the production rate to follow the demand rate	Level out demand rates
Pipeline	Cut production–distribution lead time	Forward positioning Selection of suppliers and carriers Reduce Q

inventory. A primary lever is one that must be activated if inventory is to be reduced. A secondary lever decreases the penalty cost of applying the primary lever and reduces the need for having inventory in the first place.

Cycle Inventory.   Since the cycle inventory level is approximately equal to $Q/2$, the primary lever is simply to reduce the lot size Q. Several Japanese firms have reduced Q to the point where it is only a fraction of a shift's supply. These lots are extremely small, when compared to traditional lot sizes equaling several weeks' (or even months') supply. However, making such reductions in Q without making any other changes can be devastating. For example, setup costs can skyrocket, which leads to use of the two secondary levers. Managers and the work force should find ways to streamline methods for placing orders and making setups. Such improvements can reduce ordering and setup costs, which then allows Q to be reduced.

Increased repeatability can also help to reduce cycle inventory. Devoting resources exclusively to a single product eliminates the need for changeovers. Or, at least, the increased volumes may justify new setup methods. Other possibilities are the one worker-multiple machine concept, group technology, or flexible automation. (See Chapter 5.) Part commonality might increase volumes to the point where transportation costs and quantity discounts no longer stand in the way of small lot sizes. Another way to increase repeatability and volume is to centralize buying.

Safety Stock Inventory.   Recall that safety stock inventory can be created by releasing orders well before materials or parts are needed. Table 11.3 shows that the primary lever for reducing this type of inventory is to place orders closer to the time when they must be received. However, this approach can lead to unacceptable customer service—unless demand, supply, and delivery uncertainties can be minimized.

Four secondary levers can be used. First, do a better job forecasting demand, so that there are fewer surprises from customers. Perhaps customers can even be encouraged to order items before they need them. A second possibility is to find ways to cut lead times. Cutting lead times reduces demand uncertainty during lead time. For example, local suppliers could be selected whenever possible. A third option is to reduce supply uncertainties. Vendors may be more reliable if production plans are shared with them, permitting them to make more realistic forecasts. Surprises from unexpected scrap or rework can be reduced by improving manufacturing processes. Preventive maintenance can minimize unexpected downtime caused by equipment failure. A fourth secondary lever for reducing safety stock is to rely more on equipment and labor buffers, such as capacity cushions and cross-trained workers. In fact, these are the only buffers available to businesses in the service sector, since they cannot inventory their services.

Anticipation Inventory. Table 11.3 shows that the primary lever to reduce anticipation inventory is simply to match demand rate with production rate. This strategy can be more successful if customer demand can be leveled out by adding new products with different demand cycles, promotional campaigns, or seasonal pricing plans.

Pipeline Inventory. An operations manager has direct control over lead time but not demand rate. Since pipeline inventory is a function of the demand during lead time, it can be cut only by reducing lead time. Various secondary levers can help managers cut lead times. First, we have already established that forward placement of inventory cuts lead time. Second, a firm might find more responsive suppliers, select new carriers for shipments between stocking locations, or improve materials handling within the plant. Introducing a computer system could overcome information delays between a DC and retailer. Third, decreasing Q may help, at least in those cases where lead time depends on lot size. Smaller jobs generally require less time to complete.

MATERIALS MANAGEMENT AND OPERATIONS STRATEGY ▲

Having covered the basic concepts of materials management, we conclude this chapter with a discussion of its links with operations strategy. Compared to a process-focused firm, a product-focused firm (see Chapter 2) tends to have

1. less tolerance for "cushions";
2. less pressure for an integrated organizational structure;
3. longer planning horizons;
4. more formalized vendor and customer relationships; and
5. information systems oriented to forecasts and inventory records.

Cushions. One strategy for capacity planning (see Chapter 7) favors large capacity cushions that require extra equipment and result in lower utilization rates. Two other cushions are extra workers and high inventories. All firms use these cushions, but in varying degrees. A firm with a product focus has less tolerance for cushions for three basic reasons. First, there is less need for a buffer because operations are less complex. For example, an operation with a product focus is characterized by (1) high repeatability, (2) low product and volume flexibility, and (3) streamlined routings.

Second, there is less need to buffer against uncertainty. On the demand side, the higher volumes of a product focus make it easier to forecast customer demand. Low product flexibility means fewer last-minute design changes from customers or engineers. On the supply side, higher volumes give a company more clout in finding reliable suppliers. The high volumes within the firm's

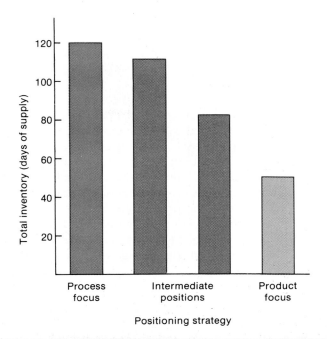

═══
FIGURE 11.6   Positioning Strategy and WIP Inventory
═══

Source: Deven Sharma, ''Manufacturing Strategy: An Empirical Analysis.'' Unpublished dissertation, Ohio State University, 1987.

own plant reduce the uncertainty in both lead times and production quantities caused by capacity bottlenecks, rework, and scrap. Short lead times mean small WIP inventories. Figure 11.6, based on a survey of 110 companies, clearly shows that product-focused firms carry less WIP inventory.

Third, a firm with a product focus is likely to emphasize low price as a competitive priority. Minimal cushions are critical to higher productivity and lower costs. Large safety stock inventories and extra workers are too costly a luxury.

Integrated Organizational Structure.   We have previously mentioned the trend toward an integrated organizational structure, in which three key departments (purchasing, production control, and distribution) report to the same executive. Integration requires a high degree of coordination and cooperation among these departments, as well as with manufacturing and marketing. Although integration seems a good idea, the number of firms that have an integrated structure and the number that don't are fairly even.

Integration comes at a cost and should be pursued only when benefits exceed costs. Benefits are greatest in the uncertain environment of a process focus. Demand and supply uncertainties mean unexpected changes and updates, which in turn call for more coordination. When uncertainty is low, an organization can afford to be more compartmentalized and fragmented. Turning from benefits to costs, some aspects of the distribution function are simplified with a process focus, as there is little finished goods inventory and few, if any, DCs to manage. Making the distribution department part of an integrated structure therefore doesn't add much complexity in a process-focused firm. Finally, the greater ability to create finished goods inventory with a product focus uncouples operations from distribution. Distribution is more likely to be housed with marketing and separated from purchasing and production planning.

Planning Horizons.   Production plans and schedules project farther into the future for a product focus for two reasons. First, forward scheduling is feasible. Increased demand and supply certainty means that schedules can be developed with greater assurance. Recall that Pinecrest Brewery allowed few of the last-minute disruptions that were commonplace at Longhorn (see Chapter 2). Therefore Pinecrest could schedule the packaging line a month in advance, whereas the supervisor at Longhorn could schedule worker assignments only one or two days ahead. Second, a product focus creates a strong incentive to plan ahead. Maximizing facility and equipment utilization has top priority because the facility is so capital intensive. High utilization rates depend on forward scheduling.

Vendor and Customer Relationships.   Both vendor and customer relationships are more formal and extensive with a product focus. Firms negotiate annual supply contracts with key suppliers, rather than using the full purchasing cycle for each new purchase. Contract terms tend to be more attractive than terms for individual purchases. With high volumes, a firm can exert more control over suppliers, and, conversely, suppliers naturally cater to larger customers. Distribution channels also are more formal because markets are more scattered, requiring a network of regional DCs. With a process focus and its high product flexibility, positioning inventory at DCs close to the customer is impossible. Typically, shipments are made directly from the plant to the customer.

Information Systems.   Information requirements for a product focus are oriented to demand forecasts and current inventory levels. Items tend to be standards rather than specials. This situation differs from that of process-focused firms, where information is oriented to the bidding process and specific customer orders. Here, output plans are communicated by releasing jobs with detailed routing information.

SOLVED PROBLEMS

1. Item A has 6 components: B, C, D, E, F, and G. You have the following information about them.

- Items D and E are purchased items. They both have a single parent: item B.

- Items F and G are also purchased items. They both have a single parent: item C.

- Items B and C are intermediate items. They both have a single parent: item A.

  a. Draw the bill of materials for item A. Assume that all usage quantities are one-for-one.

  b. Specify the customer response time in each of the situations (i)–(iii) for the following lead times.

A: 1 week	E: 6 weeks
B: 2 weeks	F: 4 weeks
C: 3 weeks	G: 3 weeks
D: 3 weeks	

    i. All items are specials.

    ii. Only item E is a standard.

    iii. Only items E and F are standard.

Solution

  a.

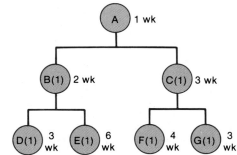

  b. The response time is determined by finding the longest time path from the end item to the bottom of the bill of materials or a standard item, assuming that standard items are immediately available.

   i. All items are specials: The longest path is E–B–A at 9 weeks.

   ii. Only item E is a standard: The longest path now is F–C–A at 8 weeks.

   iii. Only items E and F are standard: The longest path now is G–C–A at 7 weeks.

2. A DC experiences an average weekly demand of 50 units for one of its items. The product is valued at $650 per unit. Average inbound shipments from the factory warehouse average 350 units. Average lead time (including ordering delays and transit time) is two weeks. The DC operates 52 weeks per year and carries a one week supply of inventory as safety stock and no anticipation inventory.

   a. What is the average aggregate inventory value being held by the DC?

   b. How many weeks of supply are held? What are annual sales? What is the inventory turnover?

   c. What type of inventory (cycle, safety stock, or pipeline) is the biggest target for inventory reduction? What is the primary lever?

Solution

   a.

Type of Inventory	Calculation		Inventory Value
Cycle	(350 units/2)($650/unit)	=	$113,750
Safety	(1 wk)(50 units/wk)($650/unit)	=	32,500
Anticipation	0		0
Pipeline	(50 units/wk)(2 wk)($650/unit)	=	65,000
Average aggregate inventory value		=	$211,250

   b.

$$\text{Weeks of supply} = \frac{\$211,250}{(50)(650)} = 6.5 \text{ wk}$$

$$\text{Annual sales} = (50 \text{ units/wk})(52 \text{ wk/yr})(\$650/\text{unit}) = \$1,690,000$$

$$\text{Turnover} = \frac{\$1,690,000/\text{yr}}{\$211,250} = 8 \text{ turns/yr}$$

   c. Cycle inventory, valued at $113,750, is the largest component of the average aggregate inventory value. The primary lever is to reduce the lot size ($Q = 350$).

FORMULA REVIEW

1. Weeks of supply $= \dfrac{\text{Average aggregate inventory value}}{\text{Weekly sales}}$

2. Inventory turnover $= \dfrac{\text{Annual sales}}{\text{Average aggregate inventory value}}$

3. Cycle inventory $= \dfrac{Q}{2}$

4. Pipeline inventory $= \overline{D}_L = dL$

CHAPTER HIGHLIGHTS

- Materials management deals with purchasing, inventories, production plans, staffing plans, schedules, and distribution. Managing materials is a common organizational function in every segment of the economy.

- Purchased materials now represent about 60 percent of the total income from sales for a typical manufacturer. The ratio of inventory to final sales per month averages 3:1 for the U.S. economy. Inventory investment is more than double annual investment in new equipment and facilities. These three statistics are strong motivators for managing materials better.

- Decisions in materials management by necessity involve several departments specializing in certain aspects of materials management. There is growing sentiment for more integrated organizational structures, bringing purchasing, production control, and distribution into a single department headed by a key executive.

- In addition to order placing and tracking, purchasing is responsible for vendor selection, vendor relations, and contracting.

- Distribution is responsible for finished goods inventory placement, transportation mode selection, and shipping schedule, route, and carrier selection.

- Forward placement of inventory at DCs can cut delivery times and transportation costs, although the pooling effect is less and can result in higher inventory levels. Forward placement is not advisable if product flexibility is high.

- Inventory falls into three accounting categories: raw materials, work-in-process, finished goods.

- A bill of materials introduces the concepts of parents, components, usage quantities, end items, intermediate items, purchased items, and subassemblies. Taken together, the BOM and routing (sequence of operations) tell how an item is to be manufactured.

- Whether an item is subject to independent or dependent demand is a key to how its inventory is managed. Dependent demand can be derived from production plans of parent items, but independent demand must be forecast.

- Inventory placement decisions at the plant level are made according to whether an item is a standard or a special. Managers must balance customer response time and inventory costs.

- Inventory can be measured by average aggregate inventory value, weeks of supply, or inventory turnover. Inventory holding costs have several components: interest (or opportunity cost), storage and handling, taxes, insurance, and shrinkage.

- Pressures working against minimal inventory are customer service, ordering cost, setup cost, labor and equipment utilization, transportation cost, and purchased materials cost.

- The four types of inventory are cycle, safety stock, anticipation, and pipeline. Levers can be used to reduce each type of inventory. Secondary levers have to be used in conjunction with the primary levers.

- Materials management must fit operations strategy. When competitive priorities favor a product focus, the tendencies are for (1) less tolerance for cushions, (2) less pressure for an integrated organizational structure, (3) longer planning horizons, (4) more formalized vendor and customer relationships, and (5) information systems oriented to forecasts and inventory records.

KEY TERMS

STUDY QUESTIONS

1. Some people call inventory the "root of all evil." Tying money up in inventory lessens opportunities to improve productivity. The reasons that make inventory attractive are the same ones that stand in the way of substantial improvements in efficiency. Do you agree or disagree with this position? Why?

2. Since organizations in the service sector do not manufacture products from raw materials, materials management concepts do not apply to them. Do you agree or disagree? Why?

3. It has been said that "if not controlled, work will flow to the competent people until they are submerged." What does this imply for centralizing all materials management functions under one key executive?

4. Suppose that you are a buyer charged with selecting one or more suppliers of an expensive, high-volume part going into a new product line. How would you proceed?

5. What steps would you take to make vendor relations more cooperative? Is a cooperative orientation always best?

6. When would you favor
   a. long-term purchase contracts?
   b. centralized buying?

7. Ethan Allen *reduced* inventory by creating more DCs. Wouldn't forward placement of inventory at DCs *increase* inventory, since there is less of a pooling effect? Explain.

8. With the help of Fig. 11.5 you found that making the end item a standard item provides the best customer response time. What are the cost implications of such a move?

9. You have been asked to review the policies of a company for which the dollar value of inventory now exceeds 40 percent of total sales. How would you go about identifying opportunities for inventory reduction? To what extent can some of your ideas help improve delivery times and reduce transportation costs?

10. The purpose of safety stock inventory is to protect against uncertainty in demand, lead time, and supply. What is the purpose of cycle inventory?

11. What can be done to reduce the cost of buying and holding materials purchased from suppliers?

12. Give three examples of how competitive priorities can affect choices made in materials management.

PROBLEMS

Review Problems

1. A company enjoys $400 million sales and a 12 percent gross profit margin (before taxes). Cost of materials is 60 percent of income from sales.

The materials manager believes that $18 million can be saved through improved purchasing policies.

   a. What would be the percentage change in cost of materials?

   b. What percentage change in sales would be necessary to achieve the same result in gross profits?

2. Joan Pontius, the materials manager at Money Enterprises, is beginning to look for ways to reduce inventories. A recent accounting statement shows inventories at the following levels.

Raw materials	$2,345,000
Work-in-process	$5,670,000
Finished goods	$2,161,930

This year's cost of goods sold should be about $29.4 million. Assuming 52 business weeks per year, express total inventory as

   a. weeks of supply.

   b. inventory turns.

3. One product line is experiencing 7 turns per year, and its annual sales volume (at cost) is $750,200. How much inventory is being held, on the average?

4. Consider the bill of materials in Fig. 11.7.

   a. How many immediate parents (one level above) does item I have? How many immediate parents does item E have?

   b. How many unique components does item A have at all levels?

   c. How many purchased items does item A have at all levels?

   d. How many intermediate items does item A have at all levels?

   e. The items have the following lead times.

A: 2 weeks		F: 3 weeks
B: 1 week		G: 5 weeks
C: 3 weeks		H: 3 weeks
D: 2 weeks		I: 2 weeks
E: 4 weeks		

What is the customer response time if

   i. all items are specials?

   ii. only items E and I are standard?

   iii. only items E, F, G, H, and I are standard?

5. Item A is made from components B, C, and D. Item B, in turn, is made from C. Item D is also an intermediate item, made from B. Usage quantities are all one, except that two units of item C are needed to make one unit of B. Draw the bill of materials for item A.

6. What is the customer response time (in weeks) for item A, based on the following information and the BOM shown in Fig. 11.8?

Item	Lead Time (weeks)	Type of Item
A	2	Special
B	8	Standard
C	3	Special
D	4	Special
E	2	Special
F	15	Standard

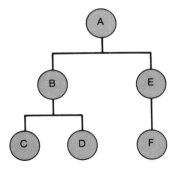

FIGURE 11.8

7. Consider the BOM in Fig. 11.9, on which lead times are overlaid.

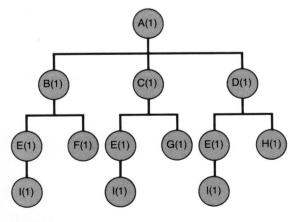

FIGURE 11.7

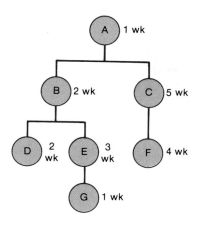

FIGURE 11.9

a. What would be the customer response time if every item is a special?
b. What would be the customer response time if items D and F are made standards?

8. A subassembly is produced in lots of 450 units. It is assembled from two components worth $50. The value added (for labor and variable overhead) in manufacturing one unit from its two components is $40, bringing the total cost per completed unit to $90. The typical lead time for the item is 5 weeks and its annual demand is 1872 units. There are 52 business weeks per year.

a. How many units of cycle inventory are held, on average, for the subassembly? What is the dollar value of this cycle inventory?
b. How many units of pipeline inventory are held, on average, for the subassembly? What is the dollar value of this inventory? *Hint:*

Assume that the typical job in pipeline inventory is 50 percent completed. Thus one-half the labor and variable overhead costs has been added, bringing the unit cost to $70 (or $50 + $40/2).

9. The Foresite Company periodically evaluates its vendors to spot problem areas. One of its essential raw materials is supplied by three vendors. Purchases currently are equally distributed among the vendors. Ratings (high values mean good performance) based on six weighted performance criteria are shown in Table 11.4 for the vendors.

a. Calculate a total weighted score for each vendor using a preference matrix. (See Chapter 2.)
b. What changes, if any, do you recommend in the company's purchasing policy?

Advanced Problems

A computer package is helpful for all of these problems.

10. Suppose that a product has an annual demand of 390 units. The lot size is 130 units, and the lead time is four weeks. The firm has 52 business weeks per year.

a. If 390 units must be ordered over the course of a year, at a rate of 130 units per order, how many orders will be placed?
b. Multiply your answer in (a) by both the lot size and lead time. This number is the *unit-weeks* of pipeline inventory held at one time or another during the year.
c. Divide your answer in (b) by 52 to get the average pipeline inventory (in units) per week.

TABLE 11.4

Performance Criterion		Rating		
		Vendor A	Vendor B	Vendor C
1. Price	0.2	0.4	0.8	0.5
2. Quality	0.3	0.3	0.5	0.8
3. Delivery	0.2	0.4	0.5	0.7
4. Production facilities and capacity	0.1	0.6	0.7	0.7
5. Warranties and claims policies	0.1	0.7	0.9	0.8
6. Financial position	0.1	0.8	0.8	0.9

TABLE 11.5

Item	Lead Time (wk)	Inventory Policies (Weeks of Supply)		
		Lot Size	Safety Stock	Anticipation
A	1	1	1	0
B	11	4	0	1
C	1	4	1	0
D	5	8	0	0
E	2	4	2	0

d. Now set up a mathematical expression for pipeline inventory, using D for annual demand, Q for lot size, and L for lead time. How does your final expression, simplified, relate to the notion that pipeline inventory is approximated by $\overline{D}_L$?

11. End item A is assembled from 1 unit of B and 4 units of purchased item E. Item B is manufactured from 1 unit of purchased item C and 1 unit of purchased item D. The weekly demand for item A averages 10 units. Because there is no part commonality, the demand for items B, C, D, and E can be derived from demand for A. The per unit purchase price is $30 for C, $40 for D, and $25 for E. The added cost to manufacture B from C and D is $70 per unit, bringing the value of one finished unit of B to $140 (or $30 + $40 + $70). The value of one unit of B is only $105 (or $30 + $40 + $70/2) if it is in the pipeline as WIP, assuming that it is half finished on the shop floor. Similar reasoning applies to item A, which costs $20 (value added only) to manufacture from B and E. Table 11.5 gives lead times and management's current policies on lot sizes, safety stock, and anticipation inventory. For example, the lot size of item D is 80 units [or (8

wk)(10 units/wk)]. No anticipation inventory is held, except an average of 10 units per week for item B.

a. Draw the bill of materials for item A.
b. What is the value of one unit of A upon completion? While it is being manufactured from B and E (i.e., still WIP)?
c. Calculate the average number of units held in inventory for each item, broken down as cycle, safety stock, anticipation, and pipeline inventory. Then convert your answer to dollar equivalents.
d. How much inventory is being held in total, summed across all five items. How many weeks of supply is being held, as only item A is sold to the customer? What is the inventory turnover?
e. Which item and type of inventory is the best target for improvement? Which primary lever should be applied?

12. The bill of materials from item A shows that it is made from two units of B. Item B, in turn, is made from two units of purchased item C. The per unit purchase price of item C is $10. Table 11.6 gives additional information. No anticipation inventory is held.

TABLE 11.6

Item	Demand (units/wk)	Value Added ($/unit)	Lot Size (units)	Safety Stock (units)	Lead Time (wk)
A	40	50	80	20	1
B	80	20	160	0	2
C	160	—	400	100	1

a. What is the dollar value of inventory held, on average, for each item, broken down by cycle, safety stock, and pipeline inventory?
b. How many weeks of supply are held to support the demand for item A?
c. Where is the greatest opportunity for inventory reduction?

SELECTED REFERENCES

Ammer, Dean S., *Materials Management.* Homewood, Ill.: Richard D. Irwin, 1962.

Banerjee, Avijit, "An Integrated Inventory Model for a Purchaser and a Vendor," *Proceedings of the 1985 Annual Meeting,* American Institute for Decision Sciences (November 1985), pp. 746–748.

Buffa, Elwood S., *Meeting the Competitive Challenge.* Homewood, Ill.: Dow Jones-Irwin, 1984.

Burt, D., *Proactive Purchasing.* Englewood Cliffs, N.J.: Prentice-Hall, 1984.

Clark, James T., "Inventory Flow Models: Preparing for Zero Inventory," Fall Seminar on Zero Inventory Philosophy and Practices, St. Louis, Missouri, American Production and Inventory Control Society, (October 1984).

Corey, E. Raymond, "Should Companies Centralize Procurement?" *Harvard Business Review* (November–December 1978), pp. 102–110.

Dobler, Donald W., Lamar Lee, Jr., and David N. Burt, *Purchasing and Materials Management.* New York: McGraw-Hill, 1984.

McLeavey, Dennis W., and S. L. Narasimhan, *Production Planning and Inventory Control.* Newton, Mass.: Allyn and Bacon, 1985.

Miller, Jeffrey G., and P. Gilmour, "Materials Managers: Who Needs Them?" *Harvard Business Review* (July–August 1979), pp. 143–153.

Miller, Jeffrey G., and Aleda V. Roth, "Manufacturing Strategies: Executive Summary of the 1988 North American Manufacturing Futures Survey," Research Report, Boston University, 1988.

Narasimhan, Ram, "An Analytical Approach to Supplier Selection," *Journal of Purchasing and Materials Management* (Winter 1983), pp. 27–32.

Pittiglio, Rabin, Todd, and McGrath, "Assessing High Tech Inventory Management," *P&IM Review and APICS News* (July 1984), pp. 52–55.

Schonberger, R., and J. Gilbert, "Just-In-Time Purchasing: A Challenge for U.S. Industry," *California Management Review,* vol. 26, no. 1 (Fall 1983), pp. 54–68.

Sharma, Deven, "Manufacturing Strategy: An Empirical Analysis." Unpublished dissertation, Ohio State University, 1987.

Van Dierdonck, Roland, and Jeffrey G. Miller, "Designing Production Planning and Control Systems," *Journal of Operations Management,* vol. 1, no. 1 (August 1980), pp. 37–46.

Vollmann, Thomas E., William L. Berry, and D. Clay Whybark, *Manufacturing Planning and Control Systems.* Homewood, Ill.: Richard D. Irwin, 1988.

CHAPTER

12

INDEPENDENT-DEMAND INVENTORY SYSTEMS

▲ Chapter Outline

▲ Key Questions for Managers

How large should our cycle and safety stock inventories be?

What type of system—a Q system, a P system, or some hybrid—should we use to control inventories?

Should we use a manual or computerized system?

Which items demand our closest attention and control?

How much effort must we spend to maintain accurate inventory records?

How often should we update our lot sizes, safety stocks, and lead times?

How do we handle quantity discounts and should we hedge against price increases?

hapter 11 explained that an important key to managing inventory is whether an item is subject to dependent or independent demand. The operations manager employs very different production and inventory control systems in these two situations. For example, if a guitar manufacturer knows he will produce 500 guitars next month, there is a way (see Chapter 15) to calculate the number of component items—such as strings and sound boxes—that must be in stock at a given time. However, the owner of a bookstore may not be sure how many copies of the latest best-seller customers will purchase during the coming month. As a result, she may decide to stock extra copies as a safeguard.

This chapter covers the case of independent demand, which is the type of demand the bookstore owner faces. Independent-demand inventory includes:

1. wholesale and retail merchandise, amounting to 43 percent of the U.S. economy's inventory;

2. service-industry inventory, such as medical supplies for hospitals, stamps and mailing labels for post offices, and office supplies for law firms;

3. end-item and replacement-part inventories at manufacturing firms; and

4. maintenance, repair, and operating supplies (MRO) at manufacturing companies, that is, items that do not become part of the final product, such as employee uniforms, fuel, paint, and machine repair parts.

We begin with key features of independent-demand items, including typical problems that a manager faces. We then discuss a fundamental question: the size and frequency of new orders. Given this foundation on economic lot sizes, we consider three common inventory control systems—continuous review, periodic review, and hybrid systems. We conclude with practical issues.

433

KEY FEATURES OF INDEPENDENT DEMAND ▲

Figure 12.1 shows how market conditions influence independent demand (first defined in Chapter 11). Demand from any one customer can be "lumpy." However, since low demand from some customers is often offset by high demand from others, total demand can be fairly constant. Thus total demand may follow a relatively smooth pattern, with some random fluctuations. Dependent-demand items exhibit a very different pattern. Demand for those items occurs only when operations releases an order for one of the parents. Such orders can be relatively infrequent, unless the item has many parents and they are ordered frequently. The result is a lumpy, on-again, off-again pattern. Managerial Practice 12.1 illustrates a typical situation facing a manager of independent-demand inventories.

Even though independent demand is fairly smooth, choosing the best lot sizes is not that straightforward. For example, the manager in Managerial Practice 12.1 orders only every five months. This policy keeps ordering costs low, but helps cause the low inventory turnover.

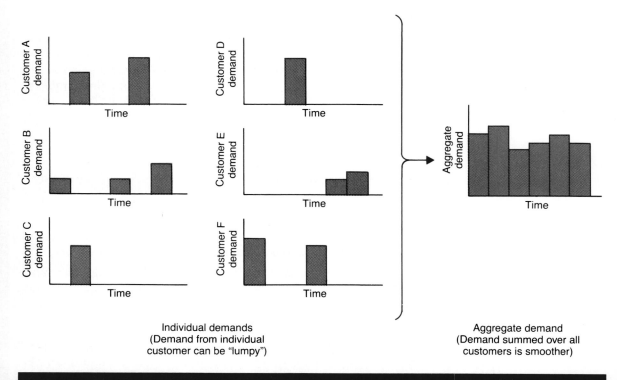

Individual demands
(Demand from individual
customer can be "lumpy")

Aggregate demand
(Demand summed over all
customers is smoother)

FIGURE 12.1   Independent Demand Is Smoother

Inventory control is important in retail settings. Here the owner of a retail store discusses inventory records of clothing stock with her manager.

MANAGERIAL PRACTICE 12.1

Inventory Management for a Retailer

A museum of natural history opened a gift shop two years ago. The shop's product plan calls for ten general groups of merchandise: containers, art works, Eskimo crafts, Indian goods, geological items, paper goods, books, jewelry, scientific instruments (such as binoculars and barometers), and seasonal goods. Each group in turn breaks down into more specific categories. For example, the containers group consists of ceramic, glass, wood, metal, bookend, basket, and birdfeeder items.

Annual sales now exceed $230,000 and are still climbing. However, managing inventories has become a problem.

- *High Inventories:* Inventory turnover is much too low, which squeezes profit margins and causes cash-flow problems. High inventories are caused by overestimating future sales for some items and by the current strategy of reviewing most items only every five months. Presently, there is no way to spot slow-moving or obsolete items, let alone monitor pilferage.

- *Stockouts:* Despite the high aggregate inventory, many items are sold out before replenishment orders arrive. Sales clerks report several stockouts each week, and lost sales are significant.

- *Seasonal Sales:* Perhaps the most puzzling inventory problem of all is with the seasonal goods group, which includes men's clothes, women's clothes, Christmas gifts, and toys. These are "one-time" inventory decisions, since any merchandise not sold during the season is sold later at a loss or held for a whole year until the next season.

435

Melanie Cameron

ECONOMIC ORDER QUANTITY ▲

A good starting point for finding reasonable lot sizes is the **economic order quantity (EOQ),** which is the lot size that minimizes total annual inventory holding and ordering costs. It is based on the following assumptions.

1. The demand rate for the item is constant (for example, always 10 units per day).

2. The item is produced or purchased in lots. An order for the item is received all at one time, rather than piecemeal. There are no constraints on the size of each lot, such as truck capacity or materials handling limitations.

3. There are only two relevant costs. The first is inventory holding cost, which is found by multiplying the average inventory level (in units) by the cost to hold one unit for a specific period of time. The second is the fixed cost per lot for ordering or setup. Quantity discounts for large lot sizes and price increases expected in the near future are not considered.

4. Decisions for one item can be made independently of decisions made for other items. For example, there is no advantage in combining several orders going to the same supplier, or in coordinating the orders for a group of items to level out capacity requirements in the shop.

5. There is no uncertainty in demand, lead time, or supply. The demand rate is not only constant (see first assumption), but also is known. The lead time is also constant and known (for example, always 14 days). Finally, there is no uncertainty in supply. The amount received is exactly what was ordered. This assumption rules out short shipments from a vendor or scrap losses in the shop. Given complete certainty, no stockouts arise because the planner can determine exactly when to order to avoid them.

Total Inventory Cost

Based on the *EOQ* assumptions, on-hand inventory behaves as shown in Fig. 12.2. The straight-line depletion of inventory during the period results in an

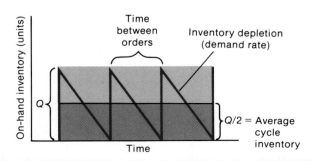

FIGURE 12.2   Cycle-Inventory Levels

average cycle inventory (see Chapter 11) equal to one-half the lot size Q. Consequently, the total cost* of ordering Q units each time a planner or buyer places an order is

Total cost = Annual holding cost + Annual ordering or setup cost

or

$$C = \frac{Q}{2}(H) + \frac{D}{Q}(S)$$

where

C = total cost per year

D = annual demand, in units per year

H = cost of holding one unit in inventory for a year

S = cost of ordering or setting up one lot, in dollars per lot

Q = lot size, in units

The annual holding cost is the average inventory over the course of a year multiplied by the cost of holding one unit for a year. This cost increases linearly as Q increases. The second term on the right-hand side of the equation is the number of lots ordered per year multiplied by the cost to place each order. The average number of orders per year is annual demand divided by Q. For example, if 1200 units must be ordered each year and the average lot size is 100 units, then 12 orders would be placed during the year. The annual ordering or setup cost decreases as Q increases because fewer orders are placed.

APPLICATION 12.1

One of the top-selling items in the container group at the museum's gift shop is a birdfeeder. Sales are 18 units per week and the supplier charges $60 per unit. The cost of placing an order with the supplier is $45. Annual holding costs are 25 percent of a feeder's value, and the museum operates 52 weeks per year. What is the annual cost of the current policy of using a 390-unit lot size?

---

*It usually is convenient (though not necessary) to express the total cost on an annual basis. Any time horizon can be selected, so long as D and H cover the same period of time. If the total cost is calculated on a monthly basis, D must be monthly demand and H must be the cost of holding a unit for a month.

Solution

We begin by computing the annual demand and holding cost as

$$D = (18 \text{ units/wk})(52 \text{ wk/yr})$$
$$= 936 \text{ units}$$
$$H = 0.25(\$60/\text{unit})$$
$$= \$15$$

Thus the annual cost is

$$C = \frac{Q}{2}(H) + \frac{D}{Q}(S)$$
$$= \frac{390}{2}(\$15) + \frac{936}{390}(\$45)$$
$$= \$2925 + \$108$$
$$= \$3033$$

Calculating the Economic Order Quantity

An economic order quantity can be obtained using a trial-and-error process: Various Q values are tried, and the one giving the lowest cost is picked. Figure 12.3 shows the results of the trial-and-error approach to the birdfeeder in Application 12.1. Eight different lot sizes were evaluated in addition to the

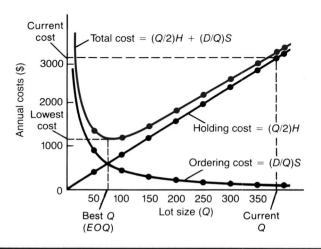

FIGURE 12.3   Total Inventory Cost Function for Birdfeeder

current one. Both holding and ordering costs were plotted, but their sum—the total cost curve—is the important feature. The graph shows that the best lot size, or *EOQ*, is the lowest point on the total cost curve, or between 50 and 100 units. Obviously, reducing the current lot size policy ($Q = 390$) can result in significant savings.

A more efficient approach is to use the *EOQ* formula:

$$EOQ = \sqrt{\frac{2DS}{H}}$$

For those of you who have had calculus, this formula is obtained by taking the first derivative of the total cost function with respect to Q, setting it equal to zero, and solving for Q. Coincidentally, as you can see in Fig. 12.3, the *EOQ* is the order quantity where annual holding costs equal annual ordering costs. The *EOQ* formula has been around a long time, being developed by F. W. Harris more than 70 years ago.

APPLICATION 12.2

For the birdfeeders in Application 12.1, calculate the *EOQ* and its total annual cost. How frequently should orders be placed?

Solution

The *EOQ* is 75 units and the cost $1124. This cost is much less than the $3033 cost of the current policy of placing an order every 5 months.

$$EOQ = \sqrt{\frac{2DS}{H}} = \sqrt{\frac{2(936)(45)}{15}}$$

$$= 74.94 \quad \text{or} \quad 75$$

$$C = \left(\frac{75}{2}\right)(\$15) + \left(\frac{936}{75}\right)(\$45)$$

$$= \$562 + \$562$$

$$= \$1124$$

The *time between orders* (*TBO*), expressed in months, is

$$TBO = \frac{EOQ}{D} \; (12 \text{ mo/yr}) = \frac{75}{936} \; (12)$$

$$= 0.96 \quad \text{or} \quad 1 \text{ mo}$$

Sensitivity Analysis

Subjecting the *EOQ* formula to sensitivity analysis can yield valuable insights into the management of inventories. Different values are systematically substituted into the numerator or denominator of the formula and the results are noted. Sensitivity analysis can be used to help answer questions such as:

1. *What should happen to cycle inventory if the demand rate increases?* Since *D* is in the numerator, the *EOQ* (and therefore the best cycle inventory level) increases in proportion to the square root of the annual demand. Therefore lot size should be increased when demand rises, but at a slower rate than actual demand. This is one reason why higher repeatability, such as that gained from more part commonality or less product flexibility, helps reduce costs.

2. *What happens to lot sizes if setup costs decrease?* Reducing *S* reduces the *EOQ* and, consequently, reduces the average cycle inventory. Smaller lot sizes can now be economically produced, which is why manufacturers are so concerned about cutting setup time and costs. When setups become trivial, a major impediment to small-lot production is removed.

3. *What happens if interest rates drop?* Interest, or the cost of capital, is one component of the holding cost (see Chapter 11). Since *H* is in the denominator, the *EOQ* increases when *H* decreases. Larger lot sizes are justified by lower holding costs. The cycle inventory varies inversely with the square root of *H*.

4. *How critical are errors in estimating D, H, and S?* As the *EOQ* is a function of the square root of these variables, it is rather insensitive to estimating errors.

Limitations

The economic order quantity is optimal only when the five assumptions presented earlier are satisfied. This constraint would seem to invalidate use of the *EOQ* because very few situations are so simple and well-behaved. In fact, different lot-sizing approaches *are* needed to reflect quantity discounts, uneven demand rates, or interactions between items, some of which we introduce briefly later in this chapter. However, the *EOQ* is often a reasonable first approximation of average lot sizes, even when several of the assumptions do not quite apply.

CONTINUOUS REVIEW SYSTEM ▲

One of the best-known inventory control systems is the **continuous review system**, in which the remaining quantity of an item is reviewed each time a withdrawal is made from inventory, to determine whether it is time to reorder. In practice, these reviews may be done only frequently, rather than continuously, such as on a daily basis rather than upon each withdrawal. At each review, a decision is made about an item's inventory position, which, if judged too low, triggers a new order. The **inventory position (*IP*)** measures the item's ability to satisfy future demand, relying only on scheduled receipts (see Chapter 11) and on-hand inventory. More specifically, it is

$$IP = OH + SR - BO$$

where
IP = inventory position of the item (in units)
OH = number of units in on-hand inventory
SR = scheduled receipts (open orders)
BO = number of units either back ordered or allocated

Recall that a back order is an unfilled customer order or commitment. It is an immediate (or past due) demand for an item that is out of stock. Shortages are filled later to avoid lost sales. Allocated inventory is on-hand inventory set aside or earmarked to meet past demand. For example, some of a component's on-hand inventory may be allocated for a parent's order even though inventory has yet to be physically removed from the storeroom.

The continuous review system, sometimes called a **reorder point system (*ROP*),** Q system, or fixed order quantity system, can be described as follows:

Place an order for Q units whenever a withdrawal brings the inventory position to the reorder point R, that is, the minimum level allowed.*

The Q system has just two parameters: Q and R. Each new order is of the same size: Q units. But Q can be based on the EOQ, a price-break quantity, a container size, or some other quantity selected by management.

APPLICATION 12.3

On-hand inventory of an item is only 10 units and the reorder point R is 100. There are no back orders, but one open order for 200 units. Should a new order be placed?

Solution

$$IP = OH + SR - BO$$
$$= 10 + 200 - 0$$
$$= 210$$

As *IP* exceeds R (210 versus 100), don't reorder.

---

*We describe the reorder point more completely in the next section.

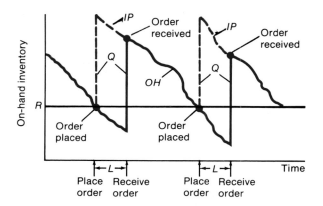

FIGURE 12.4   Illustration of a Q System

Figure 12.4 shows how the system operates. The downward sloping line represents the on-hand inventory, which is being depleted at a fairly steady rate. When it reaches the reorder point R, the horizontal line, a new order for Q units is placed. The on-hand inventory continues to drop throughout lead time L, until the order is received. At that time, which marks the end of the lead time, on-hand inventory jumps vertically by Q units.

The inventory position IP is also shown in Fig. 12.4. It corresponds to the on-hand inventory, except during the lead time. Just after a new order is placed, marking the start of the lead time, IP increases by Q, the size of the new scheduled receipt (dashed line). IP exceeds OH by this same margin throughout the lead time.[†] At the end of the lead time, when the scheduled receipts convert to on-hand inventory, $IP = OH$ once again. The key point here is simple: Compare IP, not OH, with R in deciding whether to reorder. A common error is to ignore scheduled receipts or back orders, which causes erratic inventory behavior.

Selecting the Reorder Point

Recall the assumption made for calculating the EOQ: There is no uncertainty in demand, lead time, or supply. For the museum gift shop application, suppose that the demand for feeders is always 18 per week, the lead time is always two weeks, and the supplier always ships the exact amount ordered on time. In this ideal world, the museum's buyer could wait until the inventory position drops to 36 units [or (18 units/wk)(2 wk)] to place a new order. Thus the reorder point R equals the *demand during lead time*, with no allowance for safety stock; a new order arrives at the moment that inventory drops to zero.

[†]A possible exception is the unlikely situation of long lead times and small lot sizes, when more than one scheduled receipt is open at the same time.

In the real world, behavior isn't nearly so predictable. Demand is a random variable. At best, the museum's buyer knows that *average* demand is 18 feeders per week, which means variable demand during lead time. Suppose that she set R at 46 units, thereby placing orders in advance of when they are typically needed. This approach would create a safety stock of 10 units (or $46 - 36$) to buffer against uncertain demand.*

More formally, the reorder point is

$$R = \overline{D}_L + B$$

where

$$R = \text{reorder point}$$
$$\overline{D}_L = \text{average demand during lead time } L$$
$$B = \text{safety stock or buffer}$$

Since $\overline{D}_L$ is externally determined, the real decision to be made when selecting R concerns the safety stock level B. Deciding on a small or large B is a trade-off between customer service and inventory holding costs. Cost minimization models can be used to find the best B, but they require an estimate of stockout or back-order costs. This task is difficult and is not usually done. The usual approach is for management—based on judgment—to set a reasonable service level policy and then determine the safety stock level that satisfies this policy. Managers express service levels in various ways, such as:

1. The desired probability of not running out of stock in any one inventory cycle, often called the **cycle-service level**.
2. The preferred proportion of annual demand (in units, customer orders, or dollars) instantaneously filled from stock, commonly called the **fill rate.**
3. The number of stockouts tolerated per year.
4. The preferred proportion of days in the year when an item is not out of stock.

For brevity, we will consider only the first measure.

Choosing an Appropriate Service Level Policy

Establishing a policy based on the cycle-service level is natural, as a stockout can occur only at the end of an inventory cycle (sometime during the lead time). Even if a large withdrawal greater than R suddenly depletes inventory, causing a stockout or back order, it happens at the beginning of the lead time; a replenishment order would be placed immediately.

---

*In this discussion we assume that demand is the only source of uncertainty. If lead time were also a random variable, the variability in demand during lead time would be even higher. If there were supply uncertainty, *IP* would also become a random variable because the number of units actually received from scheduled receipts would be uncertain. These additional uncertainties would mandate higher safety stock levels.

Discrete Probability Distribution.   A discrete probability distribution lists each possible demand during the lead time, along with its probability. For simplicity, assume that the demands listed are the only ones that can occur (nothing in between). Set R so that the probabilities of demand at or below its level total the desired cycle-service level. To identify the amount of safety stock B that will be carried with the reorder point selected, subtract $\overline{D}_L$ from R.

APPLICATION 12.4

Based on past records and judgment, the following probability distribution has been estimated for D_L, the demand during lead time of birdfeeders.

D_L(units)	Probability
10	0.10
20	0.15
30	0.20
40	0.25
50	0.20
60	0.10
	1.00

The lead time is two weeks and the average weekly demand is 18 feeders. Museum management selected a 90 percent cycle-service level (9 out of 10 cycles). What reorder point should be used? What is the safety stock?

Solution

The reorder point R should be 50. The probability that this quantity is enough to avoid a stockout during the lead time is 0.90 (or $0.10 + 0.15 + 0.20 + 0.25 + 0.20$). Stated differently, the only time that this quantity is *not* enough is when $D_L = 60$, which happens only 10 percent of the time.

The expected value of the distribution, $\overline{D}_L$, is calculated as

$$\overline{D}_L = 10(0.10) + 20(0.15) + \cdots + 60(0.10)$$

$$= 36 \text{ units}$$

We can now calculate the value of B for $R = 50$ units:

$$R = \overline{D}_L + B$$

$$50 = 36 + B$$

$$B = 14 \text{ units}$$

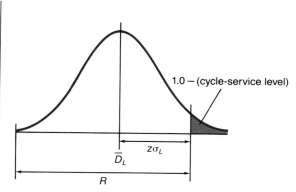

FIGURE 12.5 Normal D_L Probability Distribution

Normal Distribution. We can use the same general approach with other probability distributions, such as the normal distribution shown in Fig. 12.5.

The first step is to obtain estimates of $\overline{D}_L$ and the standard deviation σ_L, either from past history or based on judgment. The next step is to compute the safety stock:

$$B = z\sigma_L$$

where

z = number of standard deviations from the mean needed to implement the cycle-service level

σ_L = standard deviation of D_L probability distribution*

The higher the value of z, the higher will be B and the cycle-service level. If z is 0, there is no safety stock and stockouts will occur during 50 percent of the cycles. Note also the implications for forecasting (see Chapter 10). The better the job of forecasting demand and lead times, the smaller will be the values of σ_L and B. Lower safety stocks are one reward for accurate forecasts.

APPLICATION 12.5

Returning to the birdfeeders, suppose that demand during lead time is normally distributed with $\overline{D}_L$ at 36 units and $\sigma_L = 15$. What safety stock should be carried for a 90 percent cycle-service level? What is R?

---

*Some inventory planners prefer to work with the mean absolute deviation (*MAD*), rather than the standard deviation, because it's easier to calculate. Recall from Chapter 10 that to convert *MAD* to the standard deviation, you simply multiply the *MAD* value by 1.25. Then proceed as usual to calculate B.

Solution

The first step is to find z, the number of standard deviations to the right of $\overline{D}_L$ in Fig. 12.5 that places 90 percent of the area under the curve to the left of that point. Consult the normal table in Appendix 3 and look for 0.90 in the body of the table. The closest number is 0.8997, which corresponds to 1.2 in the row heading and 0.08 in the column heading. Adding these values gives us a z of 1.28. With this information, we can now calculate B as 19 and R as 55.

$$B = z\sigma_L = 1.28(15)$$
$$= 19.2 \quad \text{or} \quad 19$$
$$R = \overline{D}_L + B = 36 + 19$$
$$= 55$$

Calculating Standard Deviation of Demand During Lead Time

Sometimes the standard deviation of demand is known, but over a time interval different from the lead time. For example, records may report only daily demand. The standard deviation of daily demand can be readily calculated, but the lead time may be several days. Fortunately, the following conversion is possible:

$$\sigma_L = \sigma_t \sqrt{\frac{L}{t}}$$

where

$$\sigma_t = \text{known standard deviation of demand over some time interval } t$$

$$\sigma_L = \text{standard deviation of demand during lead time (which must be calculated in order to find the safety stock)}$$

When using this formula, make sure that both L and t are expressed in the same time measure. If t is in weeks, so must be L. After applying the conversion formula, you use the resulting σ_L as before to find the safety stock B.

APPLICATION 12.6

The standard deviation in demand per week is estimated from past records to be 50 units, but the lead time is four weeks. What is the standard deviation of demand during the four-week lead time?

Solution

In this case, $t = 1$ and $L = 4$, so σ_L is 100 units.*

$$\sigma_L = 50 \sqrt{\frac{4}{1}} = 50(2)$$

$$= 100$$

PERIODIC REVIEW SYSTEM ▲

Another popular inventory control system is the **periodic review system**, in which an item's inventory position is reviewed periodically rather than continuously. A new order is placed at the end of each review, and the number of periods (P) between orders is fixed. Demand is a random variable, so the total demand between reviews varies, and the lot size Q changes from one order to the next. Note the differences between this system and the Q system, in which Q is fixed and the time between orders varies. An example of the periodic review system is a soft-drink supplier who makes weekly rounds of grocery stores. Each week, store inventory positions are reviewed and restocked, supposedly with enough items to meet demand until the next week.

In this section, we carry forward unchanged the first four assumptions for deriving the EOQ, but relax the fifth one to allow for demand uncertainty. The periodic review system, also called the P system, periodic order system, fixed interval reorder system, or periodic reorder system, works as follows:

Review the item's inventory position IP every P time periods. Place an order equal to $(T - IP)$ where T is the target inventory, that is, the desired inventory position just after a new order has been placed.

Figure 12.6 illustrates how a P system operates. The downward sloping line again represents on-hand inventory. When the predetermined time P has elapsed since the last review, an order is placed to bring the inventory position (shown as a dashed line) up to the horizontal line that represents T. The lot size for the first review is Q_1, the difference between IP_1 and T. As with the continuous review system, IP and OH differ only during the lead time. When the open order arrives, at the end of the lead time, OH and IP are once again

---

*This formula comes from basic statistics. The standard deviation of the sum of two or more identically distributed independent random variables is the square root of the sum of their variances. Here, the demand for each week in the lead time is an independent random variable. Therefore

$$\sigma_L = \sqrt{50^2 + 50^2 + 50^2 + 50^2}$$

which simplifies to $50 \sqrt{4} = 100$.

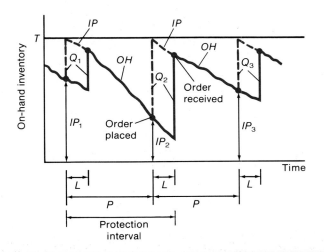

FIGURE 12.6   Illustration of the *P* System

identical. Figure 12.6 shows that lot sizes vary from one cycle to the next. Note that Q_2 is larger than Q_1. The reason is that the inventory position is lower at the second review, meaning that a greater quantity is needed to "order up to" T.

APPLICATION 12.7

There is a back order of 5 units of an item having no on-hand inventory. Now is the time to review. How much should be reordered if T is 400 and there are no scheduled receipts?

Solution

$$IP = OH + SR - BO$$
$$= 0 + 0 - 5$$
$$= -5 \text{ units}$$
$$T - IP = 400 - (-5)$$
$$= 405 \text{ units}$$

That is, 405 units must be ordered to bring the inventory position up to T units.

Selecting the Reorder Interval

The P system also has just two parameters: P and T. Let's first consider P. It can be any convenient interval, such as each Friday or every other Friday. Another option is to base P on the cost trade-offs of the EOQ. For example, if P is expressed in weeks and there are 52 work weeks in a year,

$$P = \frac{EOQ}{D}(52)$$

Dividing the EOQ by D gives us the fraction of a year between orders. Multiplying by 52 converts this fraction into weeks.

Selecting the Target Inventory Level

Now let's consider how to calculate the target inventory T. If you look closely at Fig. 12.6, you will discover that an order must be large enough to make the inventory position IP last beyond the next review, or P periods away. Scheduled receipts do not arrive from the next order until $P + L$ time periods have elapsed. This observation identifies a fundamental difference between the Q system and P system. A Q system needs stockout protection only during the lead time, as orders can be placed at any time and will be received shortly (L periods) thereafter. However, a P system needs stockout protection for $P + L$ periods, shown as the *protection interval* in Fig. 12.6.

Therefore T must at least equal the expected demand during the protection interval $P + L$. This level does not allow for any safety stock. When B is added, it should be enough to protect against demand uncertainty over the entire protection interval. Thus

$$T = \overline{D}_{P+L} + B = \overline{D}_{P+L} + z\sigma_{P+L}$$

where

$\overline{D}_{P+L}$ = average demand until the next review in P periods plus the average demand during one lead time of L periods

σ_{P+L} = standard deviation of demand during $P + L$ time periods

z = number of desired standard deviations to implement the cycle-service level (same as for a Q system)

Because a P system requires safety stock to cover demand uncertainty over a longer time period than for a Q system, a P system requires more safety stock (σ_{P+L} exceeds σ_L).

APPLICATION 12.8

An item's demand is normally distributed with a mean of 40 units per week and a standard deviation of *weekly* demand of 15 units. Lead time is three weeks and the business operates 52 weeks per year. A P system is used. What P approximates the cost trade-offs of a 400-unit EOQ? What T is needed for an 80 percent cycle-service level?

Solution

First, we find D and then P:

$$D = (40 \text{ units/wk})(52 \text{ wk/yr})$$
$$= 2080 \text{ units}$$
$$P = \frac{EOQ}{D}(52) = \frac{400}{2080}(52)$$
$$= 10 \text{ wk}$$

We now find the standard deviation of demand over the protection interval $(P + L = 13)$:

$$\sigma_{P+L} = \sigma_t \sqrt{\frac{P + L}{t}} = 15 \sqrt{\frac{13}{1}}$$
$$= 54 \text{ units}$$

We find the z value for an 80 percent cycle-service level in Appendix 3 ($z = 0.84$). Now solve for T.

$$T = \overline{D}_{P+L} + z\sigma_{P+L}$$
$$= (40 \text{ units/wk})(13 \text{ wk}) + (0.84)(54 \text{ units})$$
$$= 565 \text{ units}$$

We therefore would review the item every 10 weeks and order up to 565 units each time.

Comparative Advantages of the Q and P Systems

Neither the Q nor P system is best in all situations, as shown in Table 12.1. It lists three P-system advantages, which must be balanced against three Q-system advantages. The advantages of one system are implicitly disadvantages of the other one.

P-System Advantages.   The first advantage of P systems is that replenishments can be made at fixed time intervals. This procedure can be administra-

TABLE 12.1 Comparison of *Q* and *P* Systems	
Advantages of *P* System	**Advantages of *Q* System**
Fixed replenishment intervals	Can individualize the replenishment intervals
Can combine orders to same supplier	More suited for quantity discounts or capacity limitations
Perpetual inventory system not mandatory	Less safety stock

tively convenient, particularly if inventory control is but one of several duties of an employee. Some employees prefer to set aside a day or part of a day on a regular basis to concentrate on this particular task. Fixed replenishment intervals are also better for certain transportation systems, where the time of pickups (or deliveries) is fixed on a daily, weekly, or even monthly basis. For example, bread is usually delivered to particular grocery stores on a fixed schedule, which allows the route between stores to be standardized.

The second advantage of *P* systems is that orders for multiple items can be combined.* Similar items being ordered at the same time from the same supplier can be combined into a single purchase order. This approach may result in a "family contract" that can lead to a price break. But even without a price break, combining orders can save the buyer some paperwork and reduce ordering cost. This procedure also makes follow-up of open orders easier. When buyers call suppliers to check on the status of one item, they can also ask about the others listed on the family contracts. Suppliers may also prefer combined orders. For example, all items in the order might be shipped at the same time, reducing transportation costs and increasing vehicle utilization.

The third advantage of *P* systems is that the inventory position *IP* needs to be known only when a review is made. This differs from a *Q* system, where some means must be available on a continuous basis to determine when to reorder. When inventory records are always up-to-date, the system is called a **perpetual inventory system**.

As the next replenishment decision can be required at any time in a *Q* system, management cannot afford the luxury of infrequently updated records. Not needing a perpetual inventory system can be an advantage for small, manual applications. When a decision is made to computerize record keeping, with a transaction report for each receipt or withdrawal, this *P* system advantage disappears.

---

*Combining orders is also possible with a modified *Q* system. Each item is assigned a reorder point *R* as well as a higher *can-order* point. Whenever the first item in the group reaches *R*, it is ordered along with all other items that have reached their can-order points.

Q-System Advantages. The first advantage of Q systems is that the review frequency of each item can be individualized. In a typical P system, administrative convenience or ease in combining orders means the periods between orders are the same for a large number of (if not all) items. Instead, by tailoring the review frequency to each item, the total ordering and holding cost can be reduced.

A second advantage of Q systems is that fixed lot sizes are sometimes desirable or even mandatory, as in the case of quantity discounts for purchases that exceed a certain size. Physical limitations may also require a fixed lot size. Truckload capacities, materials handling methods, and furnace capacities are three examples.

The final advantage of Q systems, lower safety stocks, was addressed earlier. They must guard against demand uncertainty for just the lead time L. For a P system, demand uncertainty must be covered for a $P + L$ elapsed time. This extended coverage forces safety stock to be increased.

In conclusion, the choice between Q and P systems is not clear-cut. Which one is best depends on the relative importance of its advantages (Table 12.1) in various situations. Management must carefully weigh each alternative in selecting the best system.

HYBRID SYSTEMS ▲

Various hybrid inventory control systems are also used. They include some but not all the features of the P and Q systems. We briefly examine three such systems: optional replenishment, base-stock, and visual.

The optional replenishment system, sometimes called the optional review, min–max, or s,S system, is much like the P system. The **optional replenishment system** is a system in which the inventory position is reviewed at fixed time intervals and, if the position has dropped to (or below) a predetermined level, a variable-sized order is placed to cover expected needs. When a new order is placed, it is large enough to bring the inventory position up to a target inventory, similar to T for the P system. However, orders are not placed after a review unless the inventory position has dropped to a minimum level. The minimum level acts as the reorder point R does in a Q system. Its effect is to ensure that a reasonable order quantity is placed. If the target is 100 and the minimum level is 60, the minimum order size is 40 (or $100 - 60$). As the optional review system also avoids continuous reviews, it is particularly attractive when review and ordering costs are both significant.

A **base-stock system** (in its simplest form) is an inventory system in which a replenishment order is issued each time a withdrawal is made. The order quantity Q is equal to the amount of the withdrawal. That is, if 10 units are removed from inventory to fill an order, a 10-unit replenishment order is placed. This one-for-one replacement policy maintains the inventory position at a base-stock level equal to the expected demand during the lead time plus safety stock. The base-stock level therefore is equivalent to the reorder point in a Q system. However, order quantities now vary to keep the inventory position at R at all times. Because this is the lowest IP possible to maintain a specified service level, the base-stock system can be seen as a way to minimize cycle inventory. More orders are placed but each is smaller, which is appropriate for very expensive items, such as replacement engines for jet airplanes. No more inventory is held than the maximum demand expected until a replacement order can be received.

In actual practice, the base-stock system is often modified in one of two ways. First, replenishment orders may be accumulated, so that orders can be made at fixed time intervals, as with the P system. For example, a distribution center may receive weekly shipments from a manufacturing plant, with the quantity shipped equaling the total withdrawals at the DC since the prior week's shipment. Second, replenishment orders may be accumulated to achieve a fixed order quantity, as with a Q system. This second modification to the base-stock system has come about recently with the introduction of the Kanban system by Toyota in Japan. (See Chapter 16.) Small-lot production in standard lot sizes is achieved, leading to minimal inventory levels.

Visual systems are a third hybrid. They are easy to administer because records on the current inventory position are not kept. The historical usage rate can simply be reconstructed from past purchase orders. Visual systems are intended for use with low-valued items that have a steady demand, such as nuts and bolts. Overstocking is common, but the extra inventory holding cost is minimal because the items have such little value. The two basic approaches used are the single-bin system and the two-bin system.

In the **single-bin system,** a maximum level is marked on the storage shelf or bin or on a measuring rod. The inventory level is brought up to the mark periodically, say, once a week. Examples include gasoline storage tanks at service stations and storage bins for small parts at manufacturing plants. This method is essentially a P system, with the target inventory T and current IP established visually.

In the **two-bin system,** an item's inventory is stored at two different locations. The first bin is the place where inventory is first withdrawn. If it is empty, the second bin provides backup to cover demand until a replenishment order arrives. An empty first bin signals the need to place a new order. Premade order forms may be placed near the bins, so that workers can send one to purchasing or even directly to the supplier. When the new order arrives, the second bin is restored to its normal level and the rest is put in the first bin. The two-bin system is really a Q system, with the normal level in the second bin being the reorder point R. The system can also be implemented with just one bin by putting a mark at the reorder point level. Sometimes the reorder point is even built into the product by the supplier. A desk calendar is a good example, with a notice inserted toward the end to remind us to reorder for the new year.

ONE-TIME DECISIONS ▲

One of the dilemmas facing many retailers, as Managerial Practice 12.2 shows, is how to handle seasonal goods. These items are in demand during only one season of the year. To make matters worse, some of these items are stylish or high-fashion goods and probably cannot be sold at full markup next year. Furthermore, the lead time can be longer than the selling season, allowing no second chance to rush through another order to cover unexpectedly high demand. This type of situation is often called the "newsboy problem." If the newspaper seller does not buy enough papers to resell on the street corner, sales opportunities are lost. If the seller buys too many, the overage cannot be sold because nobody wants yesterday's newspaper.

A straightforward way to analyze such problems and decide on the best order quantity is with a payoff matrix. A **payoff matrix** is a table showing the profits for each purchase quantity at each assumed demand level. Each row in the matrix represents a different order quantity and each column represents a different demand level. For each cell in the matrix,

$$\text{Payoff} = \begin{cases} pQ, & \text{if } Q \le D \\ pD - l(Q - D), & \text{if } Q > D \end{cases}$$

MANAGERIAL PRACTICE 12.2 ▲

One-Time Decisions and Inventory Gluts

Linda Koslow is the general manager of a Marshall Field's department store in an affluent suburb of Chicago. Her biggest responsibility is to keep expenses and inventories in line with sales trends. In essence, much of her success depends on her ability to predict shoppers' whims.

The year 1987 was particularly difficult for Marshall Field's. First the October 19 stock-market crash made forecasts for Christmas sales highly uncertain. In addition, an Election Day coat sale on November 3 flopped, partly because of warm weather, which generally depressed sales of winter goods. Koslow knew the five-week Christmas season would be crucial, since that period accounts for a quarter of the store's $90 million in sales and an even larger share of profits. Because of the tough sales climate, she decided to discount many items more aggressively and earlier than originally intended.

Other retailers also found themselves overstocked with inventory, particularly stores specializing in women's clothes. "Part of it stems from overbuying, and the other part stems from fashion confusion over skirt lengths," said Jay Meltzer, analyst for Goldman, Sachs, and Company.

Sources: "Christmas Sales' Lack of Momentum Tests Store Manager's Mettle," *Wall Street Journal*, December 16, 1987; "Business Bulletin," *Wall Street Journal*, November 5, 1987.

where

p = profit per unit sold during the season

l = loss per unit disposed of after the season

Q = purchase quantity

D = demand level

After calculating the payoff matrix, we can obtain the best order quantity Q. A reasonable approach is to pick the Q with the highest *expected* payoff, which takes demand probabilities into account. Using this strategy for all such items over many selling seasons would maximize profits. The expected value is simply an arithmetic mean. We calculate it for a specific Q by (1) multiplying each payoff in the row by the demand probability associated with the payoff, and (2) adding these products.

APPLICATION 12.9

One item sold at a museum of natural history is Christmas ornaments carved from wood. The gift shop makes a $10 profit per unit sold during the season, but takes a $5 loss per unit after the season is over. The following discrete probability distribution for the season's demand has been identified. The levels, along with probability estimates, are

Demand (D)	Demand Probability
10	0.2
20	0.3
30	0.3
40	0.1
50	0.1

How many ornaments should the museum's buyer order?

Solution

Each demand level is a candidate for best order quantity, so the payoff matrix should have five rows. The resulting matrix is

Q \ D	10	20	30	40	50
10	$100	$100	$100	$100	$100
20	50	200	200	200	200
30	0	150	300	300	300
40	−50	100	250	400	400
50	−100	50	200	350	500

sell   +10

old   −5

For example, the payoff when $Q = 40$ and $D = 50$ is

$$pQ = (\$10)(40)$$
$$= \$400$$

whereas when $Q = 40$ and $D = 30$ the payoff is only

$$pD - l(Q - D) = (\$10)(30) - (\$5)(40 - 30)$$
$$= \$250$$

Now we calculate the expected payoff for each Q. For example, the expected payoff for $Q = 30$ is

$$0.2(\$0) + 0.3(\$150) + 0.3(\$300) + 0.1(\$300) + 0.1(\$300) = \$195$$

Making these calculations for each row in the payoff matrix, we get

Order Quantity (Q)	Expected Payoff
10	$100
20	170
30	195
40	175
50	140

Since $Q = 30$ has the highest payoff, at $195, it is the best order quantity.

The need for one-time inventory decisions also can arise in manufacturing plants when (1) customized items (specials) are made (or purchased) to order, *and* (2) scrap quantities are high. A special item is never intentionally held in stock because the demand for it is too unpredictable. In fact, it may never be ordered again. This means that a manufacturer would like to make just the amount requested by the customer—no more, no less. The manufacturer also would like to satisfy an order in just one run to avoid an extra setup and to prevent a delay in delivering goods ordered. These two goals may conflict. Suppose that a customer places an order for 20 units. If the manager orders 20 units from the shop (supplier, if it is a purchased item), one or two units may have to be scrapped. This shortage forces the manager to place a second (or even third) order to replace the defective units. Replacement can be costly if setup time is high and can also delay shipment to the customer. To avoid such problems, the manager could order more than 20 units the first time. If some units are left over, the customer may be willing to buy the extras, or the manager may find an internal use for them. For example, some manufacturing companies set up a special account for obsolete materials. These materials can be "bought" by departments within the company at less than their normal cost, as an incentive to use them.

TABLE 12.2 A Quantity Discount Schedule	
Order Quantity	Price per Unit
0 – 99	$4.00
100 – 199	3.50
200 and over	3.00

QUANTITY DISCOUNTS ▲

In Chapter 11, you learned that quantity discounts, which are price incentives to purchase large quantities, are one of the pressures for higher inventory. Table 12.2 shows one discount schedule from a supplier. The item's price is no longer fixed, as assumed in the *EOQ* derivation. A new approach is needed to find the best lot size.

We begin by recognizing that the total cost now must include cost of materials. For a given price level P, the total cost is

$$C = \frac{Q}{2}(H) + \frac{D}{Q}(S) + PD$$

All other parameters are the same as before, except that H now varies with price level because it is usually expressed as a percentage of unit price.

The total cost equation yields U-shaped total cost curves—one for each price level—as shown in Figure 12.7. No single curve is relevant to all purchase quantities. The relevant or *feasible* total cost begins with the top curve, then drops down, curve by curve, at the price breaks. A **price break** is the minimum quantity needed to get a discount. In Fig. 12.7, there are two price breaks: at $Q = 100$ and $Q = 200$. The result is a single total cost curve, with discontinuities at the price breaks.

Figure 12.7 also reveals something else. The minimum points on the curves, found with the *EOQ* formula at each price level, are not always feasible. For example, the minimum point for the $4.00 curve appears to be about 125 units. However, the quantity discount schedule in Table 12.2 shows that this purchase quantity qualifies for the $3.50 unit price. You must therefore pay attention only to price–quantity combinations, shown as solid lines in Fig. 12.7, as you search for the best lot size.

The three-step procedure for finding the best lot size is:

Step 1. Beginning with the *lowest* price, calculate the *EOQ*s for each price level. Continue until you find the first *feasible EOQ* that lies in the range corresponding to its price.

Step 2. If the *EOQ* for the *lowest* price is feasible, this is the best lot size. Otherwise, go to step 3.

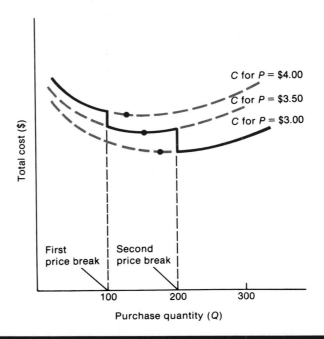

FIGURE 12.7   Total Cost Curves with Quantity Discounts

Step 3. Calculate the total cost of the first feasible *EOQ*. Do the same for each price break greater than the *EOQ*. The quantity with the lowest total cost is the best lot size.

APPLICATION 12.10

The birdfeeder supplier has introduced quantity discounts to encourage larger order quantities. The price schedule is

Order Quantity	Price per Unit
0–299	$60.00
300–499	58.80
500 or more	57.00

The museum's annual demand remains at 936 units, ordering cost at $45 per order, and annual holding cost at 25 percent of the birdfeeder's per unit price. What is the best purchase quantity?

Solution

Step 1. Find the first feasible *EOQ*, starting with the lowest price level:

$$EOQ_{57.00} = \sqrt{\frac{2DS}{H}} = \sqrt{\frac{2(936)(45)}{(0.25)(57.00)}} = 77 \text{ units}$$

As a 77-unit order actually costs $60 per unit, instead of $57 per unit, this *EOQ* is infeasible. We now try the $58.80 level:

$$EOQ_{58.80} = \sqrt{\frac{2(936)(45)}{(0.25)(58.80)}} = 76 \text{ units}$$

This quantity is also infeasible, so we move to the highest price level:

$$EOQ_{60.00} = \sqrt{\frac{2(936)(45)}{(0.25)(60.00)}} = 75 \text{ units}$$

This quantity is feasible.

Step 2. The *EOQ* for the *lowest* price ($P = \$57.00$) is not feasible, so we go to step 3.

Step 3. Calculate the total cost of the first feasible *EOQ* (75 units) and each price-break quantity greater than 75 units (300 units and 500 units).

$$C = \frac{Q}{2}(H) + \frac{D}{Q}(S) + PD$$

$$C_{75} = \frac{75}{2}(0.25 \times 60.00) + \frac{936}{75}(45) + (60.00)(936)$$

$$= \$57,284$$

$$C_{300} = \frac{300}{2}(0.25 \times 58.80) + \frac{936}{300}(45) + (58.80)(936)$$

$$= \$57,382$$

$$C_{500} = \frac{500}{2}(0.25 \times 57.00) + \frac{936}{500}(45) + (57.00)(936)$$

$$= \$56,999$$

The best purchase quantity is 500 units.

PRACTICAL ISSUES ▲

Operating an actual inventory system involves additional issues, such as (1) which items deserve management's tightest control, (2) how to maintain accurate records, and (3) what types of computer support might be advisable. Let's consider each of these issues, beginning with control.

ABC Analysis

Thousands of items are held in inventory by a typical organization, but only a small percentage of them deserve management's closest attention and tightest control. The management-by-exception principle, when applied to inventory, is called **ABC analysis**, which is the process of dividing items into three classes according to their dollar usage. Class A items represent only about 20 percent of the items but account for 80 percent of the dollar usage. Class B accounts for another 30 percent of the items, which represent only 15 percent of the dollar usage. Finally, 50 percent of the items fall in Class C and represent a mere 5 percent of the dollar usage.

An ABC analysis is a two-step process. The first step is to assign each item to a class. The analyst begins by calculating the dollar usage for each item. An item's dollar usage is simply its annual demand rate multiplied by the dollar value (cost) of one unit. After ranking the items on the basis of dollar usage, the analyst assigns approximately the top 20 percent of the items to class A, the next 30 percent to class B, and the bottom 50 percent to class C. These dividing lines between classes are inexact, but class A items normally account for the bulk of the dollar usage.

The second step is for management to tightly control the inventory levels of class A items. Recall the levers for reducing inventory discussed in Chapter 11. If a P system is being used, a manager should carefully check forecasts of D_{P+L} when setting T for class A items; accurate forecasts minimize the safety stock required. A manager can direct that class A items be reviewed frequently to reduce the average lot size. A manager can also demand precise inventory records. If the records show an on-hand balance of 100 units, but the actual balance is 200 units, costly inventory is being carried needlessly. If a class A item is bought outside the firm, purchasing may be able to reduce its cost through centralized buying, switching vendors, or more effective contract negotiation.

For class C items, much looser control is appropriate. A stockout of a class C item can be as critical as for a class A item, but the inventory holding cost of class C items tends to be low. These features suggest that higher inventory levels should be tolerated and that more safety stock, larger lot sizes, and perhaps even a visual system may suffice for class C items.

Inventory Records

Information on the amount of on-hand inventory and scheduled receipts is needed for both inventory management and accounting purposes. Sometimes, only periodic checks are made, as when a facility is shut down once a year for several days to count all inventory. At the other extreme are perpetual inventory records, in which a transaction report is made for each withdrawal and receipt. In manual systems, this information is posted to some type of written record.* In computerized systems, this information is maintained on disk or tape. In either case, on-hand and scheduled receipt balances are updated the same way. Suppose that a scheduled receipt of 300 units is received, but the supplier actually shipped only 295 units, owing to scrap losses. The buyer decides to accept the order as is, rather than requesting a second shipment of 5 units. The buyer will simply release the next order a few days earlier than usual. For this transaction, the correct adjustments would be to (1) increase on-hand inventory by 295 units, and (2) delete the 300-unit scheduled receipt from the records.

Managers must insist on accurate inventory records. One method of keeping track of inventory is to assign responsibility to specific employees for issuing and receiving materials and faithfully reporting each transaction. Inventory accuracy becomes their responsibility, and they are held accountable for it. A second method is to have closed stores, whereby the inventory is actually secured behind locked doors or gates to prevent unauthorized or unreported withdrawals. This method also guards against storing new receipts in the wrong locations, where they can be lost for months. **Cycle counting** is a third method, whereby storeroom personnel physically count a small percentage of the total number of items each day, correcting errors they find. Class A items are counted most frequently. A final method, for computer systems, is to make logic error checks on each transaction reported and fully investigate discrepancies. Examples of discrepancies are (1) actual receipts when there is no record of scheduled receipts, (2) disbursements that exceed the current on-hand balance, and (3) receipts with a nonexistent part number.

These four methods can keep inventory record accuracy within acceptable bounds. Accuracy pays off mainly through better customer service, although some inventory reductions can be achieved by improving accuracy. A side benefit is that auditors may not require end-of-year counts if records prove to be sufficiently accurate.

Computer Support

As you have discovered by now, managing inventories requires many calculations. Since computers excel at massive data manipulation, it isn't surprising

---

*Forms of manual record keeping include Kardex, visirecord, rotary wheel files, books, and logs.

that many companies are computerizing at least parts of their inventory systems. Several inventory system software packages are generally available, in addition to the in-house systems developed by individual companies. Five of the most common uses of such packages are for updating records, providing management reports, automatic reordering, generating exception reports, and recomputing decision parameters. Managerial Practice 12.3 illustrates even more uses.

Updating Records. At the time of each transaction, the computer updates on-hand inventory and scheduled receipt balances. Other information also may be updated and displayed on request, such as recent demand rates, yield losses, price changes, lead times, and vendor performance.

MANAGERIAL PRACTICE 12.3

Computerized Inventory Control for a Competitive Advantage

- At Nissenbaum's auto junkyard in Somerville, Mass., someone on the phone wants an engine for a 1979 Buick. Nissenbaum's, which seems to have everything, doesn't have one of those. So salesman David Butland turns to a nearby personal computer, types a brief message, and patches his request by satellite to 600 yards across the country. Within minutes, he is offered engines from Texas, California, and Maine. He buys the one from Maine for $550, and sells it to the customer for $700. "We probably boosted our looking-for-parts business by 75 percent since we got this," says Mr. Butland, patting the keyboard.

- Philip Cavavetta buys merchandise for his Boston-area drugstore from two wholesalers. One of them, McKesson, is getting more of his business these days because "their computer system is so good," he explains. A clerk in his store walks down the aisles once a week with a McKesson-supplied computer in his palm. If the store is low on an item, the clerk waves his scanner over a label stuck on the shelf. The computer takes note, and when the clerk is finished, transmits the order to McKesson.

- Walgreens, founded in 1901, has become one of the largest and most sophisticated retail operations in the United States. Computer processing and automatic identification of its inventory has been implemented at all five of its DCs. All Walgreens stores are linked into the DC network, so store personnel can place replenishment orders directly from the actual shelf locations.

Source: "Computer Finds a Role in Buying and Selling, Reshaping Businesses," *Wall Street Journal*, March 18, 1987.

One of the major uses of the computer in industry is for inventory control. This inventory analyst is monitoring warehouse stock.

Providing Management Reports. Management can get reports on inventory investment that show measures such as dollar value of inventory, weeks of supply, and turns. These data are often compared to measures from prior periods and can be broken into various categories. For example, individual departments in a department store usually act as autonomous profit centers, and periodic inventory reports for each one help top management assess performance. Other information important to management includes customer service measures (such as the number of stockouts) and the costs of operating the inventory system itself.

Automatic Reordering. The decision rules already described for the Q and P systems can easily be programmed to generate purchase orders, shop orders, or action notices automatically. In some cases, as with class A items, an inventory analyst reviews computer-generated action notices before authorizing a new order or following up on an order when scheduled receipts are late. The computer saves considerable time because it brings only certain types of items and actions to the analyst's attention. After the analyst makes a decision, the computer can also be programmed to generate the paperwork for a purchase order or shop order.

Generating Exception Reports. An **exception report** is a computer-generated report pointing out some unusual situation needing management's attention. For example, actual lead times or demand rates may be deviating considerably from those forecast. Or a transaction report may show an impossibly large withdrawal, based on the current on-hand record. Such exceptions to normal conditions can be displayed on a computer screen or printed out as hard copy for the analyst to assess.

Recomputing Decision Parameters.   A computer can be programmed to periodically recompute parameters such as Q and R for a Q system or P and T for a P system. Costs, lead times, or demands may have changed. Demand forecasts can be revised to recognize new trends. Lead times can be updated, based on recent experience. Current and proposed parameters (such as Q and R) can be simulated, with projections of summary statistics on inventory and customer service levels displayed on a customer screen or printed out.

SOLVED PROBLEMS

1. Suppose that we incorrectly estimate inventory holding cost to be double its true value when computing the *EOQ*.

   a. What is the percentage change in lot size?

   b. What is the new lot size if $D = 936$ units, $S = \$45$, and $H = \$15$? (As in Application 12.1.)

   c. What is the change in total cost?

Solution

   a. Using double the true value of H gives us

   $$Q = \sqrt{\frac{2DS}{2H}} = \sqrt{\frac{DS}{H}}$$

   where the real *EOQ* is

   $$EOQ = \sqrt{\frac{2DS}{H}}$$

   Dividing the first equation by the second and simplifying, we get the square root of ½, or 0.707. Thus the 100 percent error deflates the *EOQ* to 70.7 percent of its true value, a 29.3 percent change.

   b. The correct *EOQ* is

   $$EOQ = \sqrt{\frac{2DS}{H}} = \sqrt{\frac{2(936)(45)}{15}} = 75 \text{ units}$$

Multiplying by 0.707 reduces the *EOQ* to 53 units, which we can verify by using $H = \$30$ in the *EOQ* formula:

$$EOQ = \sqrt{\frac{2(936)(45)}{30}} = 53 \text{ units}$$

c.

$$C = \frac{Q}{2}(H) + \frac{D}{Q}(S)$$

$$C_{75} = \frac{75}{2}(15) + \frac{936}{75}(45) = \$1124$$

$$C_{53} = \frac{53}{2}(15) + \frac{936}{53}(45) = \$1192$$

The estimation error increases total cost from $1124 to $1192, a 6 percent change. This is a relatively small penalty for a 100 percent error in estimating holding cost.

2. A regional warehouse purchases hand tools from various suppliers and then distributes them on demand to retailers in the region. The warehouse operates 5 days per week, 52 weeks per year. Only when it is open can demand be experienced or orders received. The following data are estimated for ⅜″ hand drills with double insulation and variable speeds.

Average daily demand = 100 drills
Standard deviation of daily demand (σ_t) = 30 drills
Lead time (L) = 3 days
Holding cost (H) = $9.30 per unit per year
Ordering cost (S) = $35 per order
Cycle-service level = 92%

The warehouse uses a continuous review system.

a. What Q and R should be used?

b. If on-hand inventory is 40 units and there is one open order for 442 drills and no back orders, should a new order be placed?

Solution

a. D = (100 drills/day)(5 days/wk)(52 wk/yr)
   = 26,000 drills

$$EOQ = \sqrt{\frac{2DS}{H}} = \sqrt{\frac{2(26000)(35)}{9.30}}$$

= 442 drills

Appendix 3 shows that a 92 percent cycle-service level corresponds to $z = 1.40$. Therefore

$$B = z\sigma_L = z\sigma_t \sqrt{\frac{L}{t}} = 1.40(30) \sqrt{\frac{3}{1}}$$

$$= 72.75 \quad \text{or} \quad 73 \text{ drills}$$

We add this value of B to the average demand during lead time to obtain

$$R = \overline{D}_L + B = 100(3) + 73$$

$$= 373 \text{ drills}$$

With a continuous review system, $Q = 442$ and $R = 373$.

b. $IP = OH + SR - BO = 40 + 442 - 0 = 482$ drills
Since IP (482) exceeds R(373), do not place a new order.

3. Suppose that the warehouse uses a periodic review system (P system), but otherwise the data are the same as in Solved Problem 2.

a. Calculate the P in work days that gives approximately the same number of orders per year as the EOQ. Round your answer to the nearest day.

b. What is the value of T?

c. It is time to review the item. On-hand inventory is 412 units; there are no scheduled receipts and no back orders. How much should be reordered?

Solution

a. $P = \dfrac{EOQ}{D}(260 \text{ days/yr}) = \dfrac{442}{26000}(260)$

$\quad = 4.42 \quad \text{or} \quad 4 \text{ days}$

b. $B = z\sigma_{P+L} = 1.40(30) \sqrt{\dfrac{(4 + 3)}{1}}$

$\quad = 111.12 \quad \text{or} \quad 111 \text{ drills}$

$\quad T = \overline{D}_{P+L} + B = 100(4 + 3) + 111$

$\quad = 811 \text{ drills}$

c. $IP = OH + SR - BO = 412 + 0 - 0$

$\quad = 412 \text{ drills}$

$\quad Q = T - IP = 811 - 412$

$\quad = 399 \text{ drills}$

4. The following discrete probability distribution has been estimated for demand during lead time.

D_L (units)	Probability
0	0.15
50	0.30
100	0.20
150	0.10
200	0.10
250	0.10
300	0.05
	1.00

a. With a continuous review system and a 75 percent cycle-service level, what should be the reorder point?

b. What is the safety stock with this R?

Solution

a. R should be 150 because the probabilities of demand being less than or equal to it sum to 0.75 (or 0.15 + 0.30 + 0.20 + 0.10).

b. $\overline{D}_L = 0(0.15) + 50(0.30) + 100(0.20) + 150(0.10)$

$+ 200(0.10) + 250(0.10) + 300(0.05)$

$= 100$

$R = \overline{D}_L + B$

$150 = 110 + B$

$B = 40$ units

5. A hospital uses disposable surgical packages. The supplier's price schedule is

Order Quantity	Price per Unit
0–99	$50
100 or more	45

Ordering cost is $16 per order and annual holding cost is 20 percent of the per unit purchase price. Annual demand is 1800 packages. What is the best purchase quantity?

Solution

Step 1. We first calculate

$$EOQ_{45.00} = \sqrt{\frac{2DS}{H}} = \sqrt{\frac{2(1800)(16)}{(0.2)(45)}}$$

$$= 80 \text{ units}$$

Since it is infeasible, we calculate

$$EOQ_{50.00} = \sqrt{\frac{2(1800)(16)}{(0.2)(50)}}$$

$$= 76 \text{ units, a feasible lot}$$

Step 2. The *EOQ* for the lowest price is infeasible, so we go to step 3.

Step 3.
$$C = \frac{Q}{2}(H) + \frac{D}{Q}(S) + PD$$

$$C_{76} = \frac{76}{2}(10) + \frac{1800}{76}(16) + 50(1800)$$

$$= \$90,759$$

$$C_{100} = \frac{100}{2}(9) + \frac{1800}{100}(16) + 45(1800)$$

$$= \$81,738$$

The **best purchase quantity is the price-break quantity, or 100 units.**

FORMULA REVIEW

1. Total relevant cost:

$$C = \frac{Q}{2}(H) + \frac{D}{Q}(S) \qquad \text{(No quantity discounts)}$$

$$C = \frac{Q}{2}(H) + \frac{D}{Q}(S) + PD \quad \text{(With quantity discounts)}$$

2. Economic order quantity:

$$EOQ = \sqrt{\frac{2DS}{H}}$$

3. Inventory position:

$$IP = OH + SR - BO$$

4. Reorder point:

$$R = \overline{D}_L + B$$

5. Safety stock:

$$B = z\sigma_L \qquad \text{(Continuous review system)}$$

$$B = z\sigma_{P+L} \qquad \text{(Periodic review system)}$$

6. Standard deviation of demand:

$$\sigma_L = \sigma_t\sqrt{\frac{L}{t}} \qquad \text{(Continuous review system)}$$

$$\sigma_{P+L} = \sigma_t\sqrt{\frac{P+L}{t}} \qquad \text{(Periodic review system)}$$

7. Reorder interval (with 52 wk/yr):

$$P = \frac{EOQ}{D}(52)$$

8. Inventory target:

$$T = \overline{D}_{P+L} + z\sigma_{P+L}$$

9. Payoff matrix:

$$\text{Payoff} = \begin{cases} pQ, & \text{if } Q \le D \\ pD - l(Q - D), & \text{if } Q > D \end{cases}$$

CHAPTER HIGHLIGHTS

- Inventory management methods depend on the nature of demand. The two broad categories of demand are: independent and dependent. Independent demand is generated directly by the customer, and total demand for independent-demand items is often more uniform than for dependent-demand items. All types of organizations maintain independent-demand inventories. In the service sector, wholesale and retail merchandise alone accounts for 43 percent of the inventory in the U.S. economy.

- A basic question in inventory management is whether to order infrequently in large quantities or frequently in small quantities. Calculation of the EOQ helps with this choice by providing the lot size Q that minimizes the sum of holding and ordering (or setup) costs. Basic EOQ assumptions include constant demand, receipts in full lots, only two relevant costs, single-item decisions, and no uncertainty.

- In the continuous review system (or Q system), the buyer places orders of a fixed lot size Q whenever the inventory position IP drops to the reorder point R. The reorder point answers the second basic question in inventory management: when to place the next order. The reorder point equals the expected average demand during the lead time D_L and safety stock B to handle demand uncertainties. The size of the safety stock depends on the desired customer service level. The inventory position IP is equal to on-hand inventory plus scheduled receipts minus any back ordered or allocated demand.

- In the periodic review system (or P system), the buyer places orders every P fixed time intervals. The order quantity is the difference between the target inventory T and the current inventory position and can vary from order to order. T is established to cover expected demand and safety stock B over $P + L$ time periods.

- The choice between P and Q systems is not clear-cut. Fixed replenishment intervals, combined orders, type of record keeping, individual replenishment intervals, quantity discounts, and safety stocks all have to be considered.

- Various hybrid inventory systems, including optional replenishment, base-stock, and visual systems, are used in practice. The base-stock system minimizes cycle inventory by maintaining the inventory position at the base-stock level. Visual systems, such as single-bin and two-bin systems, are adaptations of the P and Q systems that eliminate the need for records.

- Retailers, as well as manufacturers of specials, often face one-time inventory decisions. Demand uncertainty can lead to ordering too much or too little, which can result in cost or customer service penalties. The most straightforward approach to one-time inventory decisions is to calculate the expected payoff over a range of reasonable alternatives and choose the one with the best expected payoff.

- When quantity discounts are available, the total relevant cost includes annual holding, ordering, and materials costs. Purchasing larger quantities to achieve price discounts is not always the best strategy.

- ABC analysis helps managers to focus on the few significant items that account for the bulk of inventory dollar usage. Class A items deserve the most attention, with less attention justified for class B and class C items.

- At a minimum, inventory levels must be measured annually. Records are likely to be maintained for on-hand inventory and scheduled receipts balances. Clearly assigned responsibility, closed stores, cycle counting, and logic error checks are methods used to maintain accurate records.

- Computer software packages are available to assist in updating records, providing management reports, expediting automatic reordering, generating exception reports, and recomputing decision parameters.

KEY TERMS

ABC analysis   460
base-stock system   452
continuous review system   440
cycle counting   461
cycle-service level   443
economic order quantity (EOQ)   436

STUDY QUESTIONS

1. What recommendations would you make for managing inventory better at the museum of natural history in Managerial Practice 12.1?

2. When can the cost of materials paid to the supplier no longer be ignored in finding a reasonable lot size?

3. What is the relationship between an item's lot size and the frequency of placing orders for it?

4. How are the best lot size Q and reorder point R affected by
   a. increases in demand?
   b. decreases in setup costs?
   c. increases in interest rates?
   d. forecast errors in D, H, or S?

5. "Its assumptions are so unrealistic that the *EOQ* provides little guidance in managing inventories." Comment.

6. What should be considered in setting a service level policy?

7. Blood is collected for medical purposes at various sites (such as at mobile units), tested, separated into components, and shipped to a hospital blood bank. Each bank holds the components in inventory and issues them as needed to satisfy transfusion requests. There are eight major types of blood and each type has many components (such as red cells, white cells, and plasma). Each component has a different medical purpose and a different lifetime. For example, the lifetime for white cells is only 6 hours, but the lifetime for red cells is now 35 days. What type of management issues are involved in this particular type of inventory control? Does perishability require different records than for other situations? How?

8. What two basic questions are answered by Q and R of the Q system? P and T of the P system?

9. Under what conditions would you prefer to use a Q system? P system? Base-stock system? Visual system?

10. When do one-time inventory decisions arise? What information should be gathered in making a final choice?

11. Suppose that you are a buyer of an important raw material. Rumor has it that a sizable price increase will take place in the near future. How might you decide whether to hedge against the price increase by buying more than usual with the next order?

12. What is the meaning and purpose of ABC analysis?

13. What are the rewards and costs of having accurate inventory records? How can accuracy be increased?

PROBLEMS

Review Problems

1. A discount appliance store sells combination radio and tape cassette players for only $60 per unit. These hand-held units have exceptional sound quality and are in great demand. For these units:
   • Demand = 80 units/wk.
   • Order cost = $70/order.
   • Annual holding cost = 25% of selling price.
   • Desired cycle-service level = 75%.
   • Lead time = 2 wk (12 working days).
   • Standard deviation of weekly demand = 20 units.
   • Current on-hand inventory is 183 units, with no open orders or back orders.

   The store operates 52 weeks per year, 6 days per week. It has a continuous inventory review system.

   a. What is the *EOQ*? What would be the average time between orders (in weeks), using the *EOQ*?

b. What should R be?

c. An inventory withdrawal for 10 units was just made. Is it time to reorder?

d. The store currently uses a lot size of 500 units (that is, $Q = 500$). What is the annual holding cost of this policy? Annual ordering cost? Without obtaining the EOQ, how can you conclude from these two calculations that the current lot size is too large?

e. What is the annual cost saved by shifting from the 500-unit lot size to the EOQ?

2. Consider again the data in Problem 1.

a. Suppose that the weekly demand forecast of 80 units is incorrect, and that it will actually be only 40 units per week. How much higher will total costs be, owing to the distorted EOQ caused by this forecast error?

b. Suppose that actual demand of 80 units is correct but that ordering costs are cut to only $10 under a blanket order arrangement. (See Chapter 11.) However, the buyer does not tell anyone, and the EOQ is not adjusted to reflect this reduction in S. How much higher will total costs be, compared to what they could be if the EOQ were adjusted?

3. Suppose that the discount appliance store (see Problem 1) uses a P system instead of a Q system.

a. What P (in work days) and T should be used to approximate the economics of the EOQ?

b. How much more safety stock (than with a Q system) is needed?

c. It is time for the periodic review. How much should be ordered?

4. Your firm uses a continuous review system (Q system), where the inventory position of each item is updated after every transaction. The firm operates 52 weeks per year. One of the items has the following characteristics.

- Demand (D) = 20,800 units/yr.
- Ordering cost (S) = $40/order.
- Holding cost (H) = $2/unit/yr.
- Lead time (L) = 2 wk.
- Standard deviation of *weekly* demand = 150 units.
- Cycle-service level = 90%.

- Current on-hand inventory is 880 units, with no scheduled receipts and no back orders.

a. Calculate the item's EOQ. What is the average time, in weeks, between orders?

b. Find the safety stock B and reorder point R that provide a 90 percent cycle-service level.

c. For these policies, what are the annual costs of
   i. holding the cycle inventory?
   ii. placing orders?

d. A withdrawal of 15 units just occurred. Is it time to reorder? If so, how much should be ordered?

5. Suppose instead that your firm uses a periodic review system (P system), but otherwise the data are the same as in Problem 4.

a. Calculate the P that gives approximately the same number of orders per year as the EOQ. Round your answer to the nearest week.

b. Find the safety stock B and the target inventory T that provide a 90 percent cycle-service level.

c. How much larger is the safety stock than with a Q system?

6. Suppose that you are a recent graduate who majored in operations management. Your boss has just asked you to review the company's current policies for its continuous review system (Q system). You begin by checking out the current policies for a sample of items. The characteristics of one item are:

- Demand (D) = 12 units/wk. (Assume 52 weeks per year.)
- Ordering and setup cost (S) = $45/order.
- Holding cost (H) = $10/unit/yr.
- Lead time (L) = 3 wk.
- Standard deviation of *weekly* demand = 8 units.
- Cycle-service level = 70%.

a. What is the EOQ for this item?

b. What is the desired safety stock B?

c. What is the desired reorder point R?

d. Suppose that the current policy is $Q = 100$ and $R = 150$. If this item were typical, what would you recommend to your boss?

7. Using the same information as in Problem 6, develop the best policies for a periodic review system (*P* system).

   a. What value of *P* gives the same approximate number of orders per year as the *EOQ*? Round to the nearest week.
   b. What safety stock *B* and target inventory *T* provide a 70 percent cycle-service level?

8. Wood County Hospital consumes 400 boxes of bandages per week. The price of bandages is $80 per box, and the hospital operates 52 weeks per year. The cost of processing an order is $64, and the cost of holding one box for a year is 20 percent of the value of the material.

   a. The hospital orders bandages in lot sizes of 1000 boxes. What *extra cost* does the hospital incur, which it could have saved by applying the EOQ concept?
   b. Demand is normally distributed, with the standard deviation of weekly demand being 100 boxes. The lead time is one-half week. What safety stock is necessary if the hospital uses a continuous review system, and a 99 percent cycle-service level is desired? What should be the reorder point?
   c. If the hospital uses a periodic review system, with *P* = 2 weeks, what should be the target inventory level *T*?

9. A firm operates 50 weeks per year and is trying to determine an inventory policy for one of its products that has the following characteristics.

   • Demand (*D*) = 2400 units/yr and is normally distributed.
   • Standard deviation of *weekly* demand = 8 units.
   • Ordering cost = $45/order.
   • Annual holding cost (*H*) = $4 per unit.
   • Desired cycle-service level = 85%.
   • Lead time (*L*) = 3 wk.

   a. If the company uses a periodic review system, based on the cost trade-offs captured by the *EOQ*, what should be *P* and *T*? Round *P* to the nearest week.
   b. If the company uses a continuous review system, what should *R* be?

10. Management estimates the demand during lead time for an important product to be distributed as follows:

D_L (units)	Probability
50	0.25
100	0.40
150	0.20
200	0.10
250	0.05
	1.00

   a. If a continuous review system is used, what reorder point provides an 85 percent cycle-service level?
   b. What would be the safety stock?

11. Suppose that the demand during lead time distribution for a product is estimated to be

D_L (units)	Probability
0	0.20
50	0.20
100	0.20
150	0.20
200	0.10
250	0.10
	1.00

   a. What reorder point *R* would result in a 90 percent cycle-service level?
   b. How much safety stock *B* is provided with this policy?

12. Matt Herron is the chief buyer at Investment Clothiers, a retail store known for excellence in apparel. It is time to order merchandise for the Christmas season. During a recent trip to Hong Kong, Matt spotted a particular men's shirt that should sell quite well. Based on past experience, Matt expects the demand for such a shirt to range from 100 to 400. He estimates the probability distribution as

Season's Demand	Probability
100	0.20
200	0.30
300	0.30
400	0.20
	1.00

The total cost to Investment Clothiers would be $20 per shirt, and the retail price would be set at $50. Any shirts left over after Christmas would be sold at $15 each. How many shirts should Matt buy if he wants to maximize expected profits?

13. Kay's Pastries are freshly baked and sold at several specialty shops throughout New York. When they are a day old, they must be sold at reduced prices. Daily demand is distributed as

App 12.9

Demand (D)	Probability
1000	0.20
2000	0.50
3000	0.20
4000	0.10
	1.00

Each pastry sells for $0.79 and costs $0.59. Each one not sold at the end of the day can be sold the next day at $0.20 as day-old merchandise. How many pastries should be baked each day?

14. A plumbing supply company received the following price schedule for a popular valve from its supplier.

Order quantity	Price per valve
0–299	$2.40
300–599	2.20
600 or more	2.00

Annual demand is estimated at 8000 valves, and ordering cost at $15 per order. If annual holding cost is 30 percent of the per unit purchase price, what is the best purchase quantity?

15. As inventory manager you must decide on the order quantity for an item that has an annual demand of 3500 units. It costs you $40 each time you place an order. Your holding cost, expressed as a percentage of average inventory value, is 40 percent. Your supplier has provided the following price schedule.

Price per Unit	Minimum Order Quantity
$5.00	1
$4.90	350
$4.75	600
$4.50	2000

What ordering policy do you recommend?

16. McKenzie Industries is considering using ABC analysis to focus attention on its most critical inventory items. A random sample of 20 items has been taken, and the dollar usages have already been calculated as shown in the following table.

Item	Dollar Usage	Item	Dollar Usage
1	$ 9,200	11	$ 300
2	400	12	10,400
3	33,400	13	70,800
4	8,100	14	6,800
5	1,100	15	57,900
6	600	16	3,900
7	44,000	17	700
8	900	18	4,800
9	100	19	19,000
10	700	20	15,500

Rank the items and assign them to an A, B, or C class. On the basis of this sample, does it appear that ABC analysis will help management identify the significant few items?

Advanced Problems

Problems 17 through 20 require prior reading of Supplement 5. A computer package is useful for solving all of these problems.

17. The Georgia Lighting Center stocks more than 3000 lighting fixtures, including chandeliers, swags, wall lamps, and track lights. The store sells at retail, operates six days per week, and advertises itself as the "brightest spot in town." One expensive fixture is selling at an average rate of 5 units per day. The reorder policy is $Q = 40$ and $R = 15$. The lead time is two full days, and new orders are placed at the end of the day. Thus a new order is available for use at the beginning of the third day after an order is placed.

   Simulate the performance of this Q system for the next three weeks (18 work days). Any stockouts result in lost sales (rather than back orders). The beginning inventory is 19 units, and there are no scheduled receipts. Demand is random and is shown for each of the next 18 days in Table 12.3. Fill in the rest of the table.

   a. What is the average daily ending inventory over the 18 days?
   b. How many stockouts occurred?

18. Simulate Problem 17 again, but this time use a P system with $P = 8$ and $T = 55$. Let the next review period be day 1. As before, the beginning inventory is 19 units and there are no scheduled receipts.

   a. What is the average daily ending inventory over the 18 days?
   b. How many stockouts occurred?

 19. In Solved Problem 2, a Q system for hand drills was devised, with $Q = 442$ and $R = 373$. Simulate this system for a 21-day period, using the format of Table 12.4. The daily demand is drawn from a normal distribution with a mean of 100 and standard deviation of 30. The on-hand

TABLE 12.3

Work Day	Beginning Inventory	Orders Received	Daily Demand	Ending Inventory	Inventory Position	Amount Ordered
1	19	—	5			
2		—	3			
3		—	4			
4			1			
5			10			
6			9			
7			7			
8			4			
9			2			
10			7			
11			3			
12			6			
13			10			
14			0			
15			5			
16			10			
17			4			
18			7			

TABLE 12.4

Work Day	Beginning Inventory	Orders Received	Daily Demand	Ending Inventory	Inventory Position	Amount Ordered
1	113	442	143			
2		—	82			
3		—	103			
4		—	127			
5			85			
6			60			
7			94			
8			87			
9			102			
10			42			
11			123			
12			148			
13			85			
14			67			
15			83			
16			123			
17			108			
18			88			
19			120			
20			138			
21			74			

inventory at the start of day 1 is 113 units and one scheduled receipt for 442 units is to arrive on this first day. The lead time for new orders is three full days. Thus if a new order is placed at the *end* of the second work day, it would be available at the *beginning* of the sixth work day.

 a. What is the average daily ending inventory over the 21 days?

 b. How many new orders are placed?

20. In Solved Problem 3, a P system for hand drills was devised, with $P = 4$ days and $T = 811$. Simulate this system for a 21-day period, using the random demand shown in Table 12.4.

 a. What is the average ending inventory over the 21 days?

 b. How many new orders are placed?

21. The fill rate for a certain safety stock level is

$$F = 1 - \frac{n_s}{Q}$$

where

 F = fill rate, expressed as a proportion

 n_s = expected number of units short per cycle for the safety stock level provided

 Q = order quantity

 a. For the probability distribution in Application 12.4, determine the safety stock, cycle-service level, and expected number of units short per cycle for three different reorder points: 40 units, 50 units, and 60 units.

b. For each of the three reorder points, determine the number of orders placed per year and the fill rate for $Q = 36$, $Q = 78$, and $Q = 234$. What conclusions can you draw from your results about the effect of lot size on customer service?

SELECTED REFERENCES

Bragg, Daniel Jay, "The Impact of Inventory Record Inaccuracy on Material Requirements Planning Systems." Unpublished dissertation, Ohio State University, 1984.

Buffa, Elwood S., and Jeffrey G. Miller, *Production-Inventory Systems: Planning and Control*, 3rd ed. Homewood, Ill.: Richard D. Irwin, 1979.

Fogerty, Donald W., and Thomas R. Hoffman, *Production and Inventory Management*. Cincinnati: South-Western, 1983.

Greene, James H., *Production and Inventory Control Handbook*. New York: McGraw-Hill, 1970.

International Business Machines Corporation, *Basic Principles of Wholesale IMPACT*, Publication E20-8105-1.

Johnson, Lynwood A., and Douglas C. Montgomery, *Operations Research in Production Planning, Scheduling and Inventory Control*. New York: John Wiley & Sons, 1979.

Love, Stephen F., *Inventory Control*. New York: McGraw-Hill, 1979.

Ronen, David, "Inventory Service Measures—A Comparison of Measures," *International Journal of Operations and Production Management*, vol. 3, no. 2 (1983), pp. 37–45.

Silver, Edward A. "Operations Research in Inventory Management: A Review and Critique," *Operations Research*, vol. 9, no. 4 (July–August 1981).

Silver, Edward A., and Rein Peterson, *Decision Systems for Inventory Management and Production Planning*. New York: John Wiley & Sons, 1984.

Starr, Martin K., and David W. Miller, *Inventory Control: Theory and Practice*. Englewood Cliffs, N.J.: Prentice-Hall, 1962.

Tersine, Richard J., *Principles of Inventory and Materials Management*, 2nd ed. New York: North Holland, 1982.

CHAPTER 13

PRODUCTION AND STAFFING PLANS

▲ Chapter Outline

Key Questions for Managers

What is the relationship between our positioning strategy and production plan?

How can we adjust the demand pattern to reduce operating costs?

Should we use a level work-force strategy or some variable work-force strategy?

Should we use subcontracting to achieve short-term capacity increases or some combination of overtime and seasonal hiring?

he overall strategy of an organization must somehow be translated into detailed operating plans. The methods that management normally uses are the production plan and the staffing plan. For manufacturing organizations, the production plan links strategic goals and objectives with the master production schedule. For service organizations, the staffing plan links strategic goals with the detailed work-force schedule. In this chapter we focus on production and staffing plans and their relationship to the hierarchy of plans in manufacturing and service organizations.

THE NATURE OF PRODUCTION AND STAFFING PLANS ▲

Managerial Practice 13.1 illustrates the need for production and staffing plans and how they can be used to adapt to changing conditions. A **production plan** is a managerial statement of time-phased production rates, work-force levels, and inventory investment, which takes into consideration customer requirements and capacity limitations. The plan balances the typically conflicting objectives of maximizing customer service, minimizing inventory investment, maintaining a stable work force, minimizing production cost, and maximizing profit. It also provides valuable information for the master production schedule and the material requirements plan, which we cover in later chapters.

A **staffing plan** is to service organizations what the production plan is to manufacturing organizations. It is a managerial statement of time-phased staff sizes and labor-related capacities, which takes into consideration customer requirements and machine-limited capacities. The plan also must balance conflicting objectives involving customer service, work-force stability, cost, and profit. It is useful for developing the specific work-force schedule, which assigns workers to shifts and daily schedules. Table 13.1 shows several types of employees that have to be included in staffing plans for various services.

TABLE 13.1   Types of Employees Typically Included in a Staffing Plan

Service	Employee Type
Airline	Flight attendants
	Pilots
Airport operations	Baggage handlers
	Skycaps
Banking	Tellers
	Encoding clerks
Defense	New enlistees
Emergency	Police officers
	Firemen
Health care	Nurses
Municipal sanitation	Refuse collectors
	Truck drivers
Municipal transportation	Bus mechanics
	Bus drivers
Telephone	Installers
	Linemen
	Operators

MANAGERIAL PRACTICE 13.1 ▲

Typical Production and Staffing Problems

Chrysler Corporation

In response to a change in market demands in the fall of 1987, the Chrysler Corporation announced adjustments to its production plans for the first quarter of 1988. The revised plan included:

- adding a second shift of full car output in Belevedere, Ill., increasing the work force there by 1300 employees;
- increasing output of Jeep, Eagle and minivans by 12–15 percent; and
- temporarily closing plants in Detroit, Newark (Delaware), St. Louis, and Windsor (Ontario), affecting 10,100 hourly workers.

Pacific Bell

Pacific Bell, a subsidiary of Pacific Telesis, was faced with the possibility of using big layoffs to offset the effects of deregulation after the AT&T breakup and a costly union contract in 1986. Rather than order layoffs, the company worked out a deal with the Communications Workers of America that trades off cost reductions for job security. Now, as new technology comes on board or demands for certain services decrease, workers are retrained and assigned to other jobs. In exchange, workers share in the profits if the company meets or exceeds its profit and performance goals and are offered employment security. The company believes that stable staff sizes help to cut costs and boost productivity over the long run.

Sources: "Chrysler Plans Output Rises at 4 Plants, Cuts at 4 Others During First Quarter," by Melinda Grenier Guiles, *Wall Street Journal*, November 24, 1987; "Cutting Costs Without Cutting People," by Bill Saporito, *Fortune*, May 25, 1987, pp. 26–32.

Pacific Bell provides pretraining or job skills enhancement programs for their employees. This employee is participating in a digital electronics program offered in cooperation with a local community college.

Aggregation

Both the production plan and the staffing plan are useful because they are general. The planner can devise a course of action, consistent with strategic goals and objectives, without having to deal with a lot of detail. For example, having to schedule each of the thousands of products and employees at Chrysler Corporation just to find out whether the plan would satisfy budget guidelines, would be a hopeless task. Even if a planner could prepare such a plan, the time and effort required to update its details would make it virtually worthless. For this reason, production and staffing plans are based on aggregated quantities. The aggregations most often used are products, labor, and time.

Product Families.   A group of goods or services that have similar demand requirements and common processing, labor, and material requirements is called a product family (see Chapter 10). Sometimes, product families relate to market groupings or, in the case of production plans, to specific manufacturing processes. A firm's goods or services can be aggregated into a set of relatively broad product families, avoiding too much detail at this stage of the planning process. Common and relevant measurements, such as units, dollars, standard hours, gallons, or pounds, should be used.

Labor.   Labor can be aggregated in various ways, depending on work-force flexibility. For example, if the entire work force is used in the production of every product family, the work force can be considered a single aggregate group for planning purposes. Alternatively, the work force can be aggregated by product family if different parts of the work force are used in the production of different product families. An automobile manufacturer such as Chrysler would find the second approach useful because, under the concept of focused facilities, groups of production lines and even entire plants are devoted to a given product family. (See Chapter 7.) However, economic conditions and changes in consumer demand may cause production cutbacks in one product family and production increases in another. Such was the case in the late 1970s when the price of gasoline rose substantially and consumer preference shifted from full-sized cars to smaller, fuel-efficient cars. Often, labor is not interchangeable because of the scattered locations of the plants processing different product families. In this case, planning for changes in work-force levels and the use of overtime is more useful on a product family basis.

Time.   A **planning horizon** is the length of time covered by a production or staffing plan. Typically, the planning horizon is one year, although it can differ in various situations. Decisions must be made about production rates for each product family, labor levels for each work-force group, and other factors. But how often should these decisions be made during the planning horizon? Daily is too frequent because of the expense and disruptive effect on production rates and the work force. Once a year is not frequent enough to allow for adjustments to reflect seasonal demand or updated forecasts. Thus such decisions are usually made monthly or quarterly. Some companies use monthly planning periods for the near portion of the planning horizon and quarterly periods for the later portion. In practice, planning periods reflect a balance between the needs for (1) a limited number of decision points to reduce planning complexity, and (2) flexibility to adjust production rates and work-force levels when demand forecasts exhibit seasonal variations.

Relationship to Other Plans

Top management needs a financial assessment of the organization's near future, that is, for one or two years ahead. This assessment is called either a business plan (in manufacturing) or an annual plan (in nonprofit services). A **business plan** is a projected statement of income, costs, and profits. It is usually accompanied by budgets, a projected (pro forma) balance sheet, and a projected cash flow statement, showing sources and allocations of funds. The business plan brings together into one coherent package the plans and expectations of a firm's operations, finance, and marketing managers. A for-profit service organization, such as a hospital, retail store, or firm of attorneys, also prepares such a plan. A nonprofit service organization, such as the United Way or a municipal government, prepares a different type of plan, which we call an **annual plan**. This term is not used universally, others commonly used are the *financial plan* or *budget*.

Figure 13.1 illustrates the relationships among the production (or staffing) plan, the business (or annual) plan, and more detailed plans. In the manufacturing sector top management sets the company's strategic objectives for at least the next year in the business plan. It provides the overall framework of demand projections, functional area inputs, and capital budget from which the production plan and the master production schedule (MPS) are developed. The production plan specifies corresponding product family production rates, inventory levels, and work-force levels. The master production schedule, in turn, specifies the timing and size of production quantities for each product in the product families (Chapter 14). Thus the production plan plays a key role in translating the strategies of the business plan into an operational plan for the manufacturing process.

In the service sector, top management sets the organization's direction and objectives in the business plan (for-profit organization) or annual plan (nonprofit organization). In either case, the plan provides the framework for the staffing plan and work-force schedule. The staffing plan presents the number and types of employees needed to meet the objectives of the business or annual plan. The **work-force schedule,** in turn, details the specific work schedule for each category of employee. For example, a staffing plan might allocate 10 police officers for the day shift in a particular district; the work-force schedule might assign 5 of them to work Monday through Friday and the other 5 to work Wednesday through Sunday to meet the varying daily needs for police protection in that district. Thus the work-force schedule implements the staff-

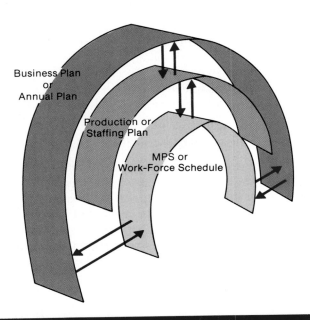

Business Plan
or
Annual Plan

Production or
Staffing Plan

MPS or
Work-Force Schedule

FIGURE 13.1   Relationship of Production and Staffing Plans to Other Plans

ing plan in much the same way that the master production schedule implements the production plan. (A more complete discussion of work-force scheduling is presented in Chapter 17.)

Besides this top-down (broad to detailed) planning process, information flows from lower level to higher level planning (detailed to broad). If a production plan cannot be developed to satisfy the objectives of the business plan, the business plan may have to be adjusted. Similarly, if a feasible master production schedule cannot be developed, the production plan or the business plan may have to be adjusted. A similar situation exists for the business or annual plan, staffing plan, and work-force schedule. The planning process is dynamic, and plans—in particular the production and staffing plans—are based on two-way information flows. We present the details of these information flows in the remainder of this chapter and the following chapters.

MANAGERIAL IMPORTANCE OF PRODUCTION AND STAFFING PLANS ▲

Production and staffing plans play an important role in achieving organizational objectives. In this section we concentrate on the managerial inputs, objectives, alternatives, and strategies associated with production and staffing plans.

Managerial Inputs

Table 13.2 shows the various functional areas that supply managerial inputs to production or staffing plans. Because of the importance of the plan, a high-ranking manager in each area should provide the inputs. One way of ensuring this participation is to create a committee of functional-area representatives. For example, the Bendix Corporation has such a committee, chaired by the general manager, who has the overall responsibility to see that company policies are followed, conflicts are resolved, and a final plan is approved. Each representative furnishes information essential to the development of the plan.

Typical Objectives

The many and varied inputs from the functional areas in an organization make the production or staffing plan an organization plan, not a functional-area plan. Typically, however, the various functional areas have conflicting objectives for the use of the organization's resources.

Table 13.3 shows six objectives commonly considered during development of a production or staffing plan. A little reflection on these six objectives reveals their conflicting nature. For example, maximizing customer service with fast delivery times and on-time delivery can be improved by increasing, not minimizing, the stock of finished goods. A staffing plan at the Internal Revenue Service, which has a seasonal demand for its services, that minimizes costs may

---

TABLE 13.2 Managerial Inputs to Production and Staffing Plans

Area	Typical Inputs
Engineering	New product development
	Major product changes and their impact on resources
	Labor and machine standards
Finance	Cost data
	Financial condition of firm
Human Resources	Labor market conditions
	Capacity of training programs
Manufacturing (or operations)	Current machine capacities
	Work-force productivities
	Current work-force staff levels
	New equipment plans
Marketing	Forecasts
	Economic conditions
	Competitor behavior
Materials	Raw materials availability
	Current inventory levels
	Subcontractor capabilities
	Storage capacities

TABLE 13.3 Typical Objectives in Production and Staffing Plans	
Objective	Comments
Minimize costs/maximize profits	If customer demand is not affected by the plan, minimizing costs will also maximize profits. Many service organizations are nonprofit and seek to minimize costs.
Maximize customer service	As discussed in Chapter 2, delivery time and on-time delivery are two dimensions of time as a competitive priority. Improving these dimensions requires additional work-force, machine capacity, or inventory resources.
Minimize inventory investment	Large accumulations in inventory are expensive because the money could be used for more productive investments.
Minimize changes in production rates	Frequent changes in production rates can cause difficulties in coordinating the supplying of materials and require production line rebalances.
Minimize changes in work-force levels	Fluctuating work-force levels may cause lower productivity because the new employees typically need time to become fully productive.
Maximize utilization of plant and equipment	Firms with a product focus require uniformly high utilization of plant and equipment.

not minimize changes in work-force levels or maximize customer service. Also, a manufacturing firm that uses a stable production rate will necessarily build inventories of finished goods in the face of seasonal demand for its products.

These objectives actually are cost minimization objectives, assuming the level of demand volume is given. However, the weight given to each one in the plan involves cost trade-offs and consideration of nonquantifiable factors. Balancing these various objectives in order to arrive at an acceptable production or staffing plan involves consideration of various decision alternatives. The two basic types of decision alternatives are reactive and aggressive.

Reactive Alternatives

Reactive alternatives are actions that can be taken to cope with demand requirements. That is, the manager accepts forecasted demand as a given and modifies staffing and inventory levels.

Adjust Work-Force Levels. Management can adjust work-force levels by hiring or laying off employees. The use of this alternative can be attractive if the work force is largely unskilled or semiskilled and the labor pool is large. However, for a particular company, the size of the qualified labor pool may limit the number of new employees that can be hired at any one time. Also, new employees must be trained, and the training facilities themselves may limit the number of new hires at any one time.

Overtime and Undertime. An alternative to work-force adjustment is the use of overtime and undertime. Overtime can be used to satisfy production requirements that cannot be completed on regular time. However, overtime is expensive (typically 150 percent of the regular-time pay rate), and in many cases workers do not want to work a lot of overtime for an extended period of time.

Undertime is used when labor capacity exceeds demand requirements. Workers are kept on the payroll, rather than being laid off. This option is often used by companies, such as firms with a process focus, that have highly skilled employees who are hard to replace.

Vacation Schedules. A firm can shut down during an annual lull in sales, leaving a skeleton crew to cover operations and perform maintenance. Depending on the duration of the shutdown, employees would take all, or part, of their allowed vacation time during this period. Automakers, such as General Motors, use this alternative during the Christmas holiday period, not only to do maintenance or install equipment, but also to reduce inventory. Use of this alternative depends on the extent that the employer can mandate the vacation schedules of its employees. If this authority is limited (say, by union contract) and if part-time or seasonal labor can be substituted for full-time personnel, employees could be encouraged to take vacations during periods when these sources of labor are most abundant.

Anticipation Inventory. In Chapter 11, we pointed out that a plant facing seasonal demand can stock anticipation inventory during light demand periods and use it during heavy demand periods. This approach stabilizes production rates and work-force levels but may be very costly. As we have also noted, stocking finished goods is the most expensive form of inventory investment because the value of the product is greatest in its finished state. Plans to stock components and subassemblies that can be assembled quickly when customer orders come in might be preferable to stocking finished goods.

Recall also that providers of services generally cannot use anticipation inventory because services cannot be stocked. However, in some instances services can be performed prior to actual need. For example, telephone company workers usually lay cables for service to a new subdivision before housing construction begins. They can do this work during a period when the workload for scheduled services is low.

Subcontractors.   A short-term capacity source that can be used to overcome capacity shortages is subcontracting. Subcontractors can supply services and build components, assemblies, or even an entire product in some cases. Arrangements with subcontractors can be more permanent if the subcontractor can supply the components or assemblies cheaper than the company can produce them itself. Such is the case with the major automakers, who typically subcontract for underbody frames, steering linkage components, and other items. (See the discussion on vertical integration in Chapter 4.)

Backlogs, Back Orders, and Stockouts.   Another way to cope with a given demand forecast is to plan for order backlogs. A **backlog** is an accumulation of customer orders that have been promised for delivery at some future date. Delivery lead times typically increase during seasonal peaks in demand. Firms with a process focus often use this method. The customer places an order for a customized product or service and it is promised for delivery later. Job shops, TV repair shops, and automobile repair shops work to varying degrees to backlogs.

Back orders and stockouts are used by firms with a product focus. Recall that a back order is a customer order that is not ready for the customer when promised or demanded, and a stockout is simply a matter of not satisfying the demand for a stock item when it occurs. In the former case, the customer has not canceled the order, so the net effect is to push demand requirements to later periods. However, in the latter case, the customer may go to a competitor, resulting in a lost sale. Planned stockouts would only be used when the expected loss in sales and customer good will is less than the cost of adding the capacity needed to satisfy demand.

In conclusion, it is clear that the reactive alternatives collectively define the production rate. Once decisions have been made regarding how to use each of these methods for each period of the planning horizon, the production rate for each period has been specified. In other words, the production rate is a function of the production factors addressed by these alternatives.

Aggressive Alternatives

Attempting to cope with seasonal or volatile demand patterns using reactive alternatives can be costly. Another approach is to attempt to adjust the demand pattern in order to achieve efficiency and reduce costs. **Aggressive alternatives** are actions that attempt to modify demand and, consequently, resource requirements.

Complementary Products.   One way to even out the load on resources is to produce **complementary products** or services having similar resource requirements but different demand cycles. For example, a company producing garden tractors can also produce snowmobiles, making requirements for major components, such as engines, reasonably uniform year round. In the service sector, city parks and recreation departments can counterbalance seasonal staffing requirements for summer activities by offering indoor activities during the winter. The key is to find goods and services that can be produced with existing resources and can level off the need for resources over the year.

Promotional Campaigns.   Advertising can be used to modify seasonal demand patterns by generating customer demand in other than traditional peak periods. For example, producers of matzoh for the Jewish Passover holiday are in a seasonal business.* The Horowitz Margareten factory is at peak production in the fall, producing 1250 sheets of matzoh a minute. However in 1984 the company was not willing to settle for a seasonal business and took steps to level the demand. It started a radio campaign to interest other ethnic groups in traditionally Jewish products, such as matzoh. The intent was to increase demand in the traditional slack periods to smooth demand for its automated production process.

Creative Pricing.   Closely allied to the promotional campaign is creative pricing. Discounts can be offered to customers if they buy products outside traditional peak sales periods. Automobile rebate programs, price reductions for winter clothing in the late summer months, reduced rates for long distance calls after 5 P.M., and "two for the price of one" automobile tire sales—all are examples of creative pricing alternatives.

Planning Strategies

The alternatives that we have discussed are combined in various ways to arrive at an acceptable production or staffing plan. For the remainder of this chapter, let's assume that the expected results of the aggressive alternatives have already been incorporated into the demand forecasts of product families or services. This assumption allows us to focus on the reactive alternatives that serve to define production rates and work-force levels. In this regard a planning strategy amounts to selecting the particular alternatives to be used. There are two pure strategies: the chase strategy and the level strategy. Managerial Practice 13.2 contains examples of these two strategies.

A **chase strategy** adjusts production rates or staff levels to match the demand requirements over the planning horizon. There are many ways in which this can be accomplished. For example, workers can be hired or laid off, or overtime and subcontracting can be used during peak periods. The key point is that anticipation inventory or undertime is not used. Thus the chase strategy has the advantage of low inventory investment and backlogs but at the expense of adjusting production rates or staff levels for every period of the planning horizon.

---

*"New Matzoh Markets Sought," *New York Times*, April 9, 1984.

A **level strategy** maintains a constant production rate or work-force level over the planning horizon. In manufacturing firms a constant production rate is often accomplished by maintaining a stable work force and building anticipation inventory to satisfy peak seasonal demands. Hiring, overtime, or subcontracting can be used if the work force is subject to attrition, but the production rate remains constant. In service firms a level strategy usually involves maintaining a stable work force and using undertime, overtime, and backlogs. The distinguishing feature of a level strategy is that anticipation inventory or undertime is used to help maintain constant output. The advantages are level production rates and a stable work force at the expense of increased inventory investment, undertime, overtime, and backlogs.

Obviously, a range of strategies lies between the chase strategy at one extreme and the level strategy at the other. The best strategy for a company may be a *mixed strategy* of anticipation inventory buildup during slack periods,

MANAGERIAL PRACTICE 13.2 ▲

Chase and Level Strategies in Practice

Grumman Corporation

The loss of a $4 billion Navy contract for a new attack aircraft, a general tightening of the federal military budget, and uncertainty of the future of the A-16 Intruder product prompted Grumman to pursue a chase strategy regarding its work force. In March, 1988, the Grumman Corporation announced it was reducing its work force by eight percent. Layoffs, normal attrition, and reductions in part-time and temporary workers will be used to reduce the work force.

Deere and Company

After negotiating a job-security pact with the union guaranteeing 90 percent of the jobs in each plant, Deere executives have learned to find alternatives to costly worker layoffs and recalls, that is, to follow a level strategy. Instead of hiring more workers, the farm-equipment manufacturer held production of cotton-related equipment 10 to 15 percent below the projected peak demand in the near future. Management felt that even though the company may lose some sales during that period, the stable production levels would help keep factory inventories low and would reduce the expense of hiring and firing workers with each fluctuation in demand.

Sources: "Grumman to Cut 2,600 Jobs, About 8% of Its Work Force," by Philip Gutes, *New York Times,* March 10, 1988; "Firms Alter Production Strategies to Cope with Sweeping Job Pledges in Contracts," by Alex Kotlowitz, *Wall Street Journal,* September 21, 1987.

only a few work-force level changes, and overtime. Regardless of whether a company chooses a pure strategy or some mix, that strategy must reflect its planning objectives. The production plan or staffing plan not only is a product of managerial inputs from the various functional areas, but it also has an impact on the activities of these people and the operations of the functional areas they represent. Thus production and staffing plans affect the direction of the firm over the near and intermediate future and are significant managerial tools.

THE PLANNING PROCESS ▲

Figure 13.2 shows the planning process for production and staffing plans. The overall process is dynamic and continuing; aspects of the plan are updated periodically as new information becomes available and new opportunities emerge.

Demand Requirements

The first step in the planning process is to determine the demand requirements for each period of the planning horizon. The planner can estimate these requirements in various ways (many of which we have already discussed). For staffing plans, the planner bases forecasts of staff requirements for each work-force group on historical demands or managerial judgment and existing backlogs for services. For example, a director of nursing in a hospital can develop a direct-care index for a nursing staff and translate a projection of the patient census into an equivalent total amount of time—and thus number of nurses—required (Wolfe and Young, 1965). Also, a formula developed for police patrol staffing accounts for such factors as the number of calls for service by type, the number of street miles patrolled, and the number of businesses in the community to determine workload and thus the number of police officers or vehicles required (Chaiken and Larson, 1972).

For production plans, however, the requirements could represent the demand for finished goods, as well as external demand for components or parts. The planner can derive future requirements for finished goods from backlogs (for a process focus) or from forecasts for product families made to stock (for a product focus). Sometimes, distributors or dealers indicate their requirements for finished goods in advance of actual orders. These commitments to purchase various quantities of goods in the future provide a reliable forecast of requirements from those sources.

Alternatives, Constraints, and Costs

We presented the alternatives used in production or staffing plans when we discussed the managerial importance of these plans. We now focus on the basic relationships, constraints, and costs.

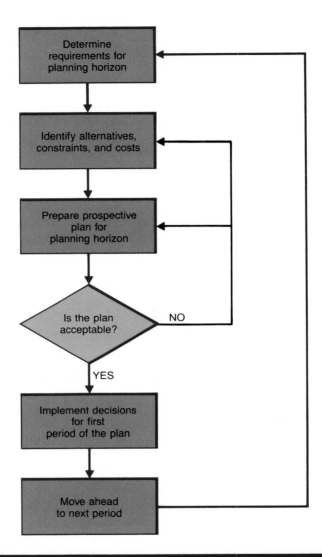

FIGURE 13.2   The Planning Process for Production and Staffing Plans

Basic Relationships.   Two relationships are basic to evaluating and comparing prospective plans: (1) the equation for the number of workers in production or staffing plans; and (2) the equation for the inventory level in production plans. The equation for the number of workers is

Workers in current period	=	Workers at end of last period	+	Hires at start of current period	−	Layoffs at start of current period

Any decisions made about hiring or laying off employees during the current period will affect the number of workers on hand. For example, if the director of a post office has 10 part-time clerks at the end of the third period and decides to hire 5 new part-time employees at the start of the fourth period, the total number of part-time employees for the fourth period would be 15 clerks. In general, an equation such as this is needed for each work-force group in the production or staffing plan.

The equation for the inventory level is

$$
\begin{matrix}
\text{Inventory} \\
\text{at end of} \\
\text{current period}
\end{matrix}
=
\begin{matrix}
\text{Inventory} \\
\text{at end of} \\
\text{last period}
\end{matrix}
+
\begin{matrix}
\text{Production} \\
\text{in current} \\
\text{period}
\end{matrix}
-
\begin{matrix}
\text{Demand} \\
\text{requirements in} \\
\text{current period}
\end{matrix}
$$

The production decision for the current period affects the inventory level at the end of the current period. For example, suppose that a paint manufacturer has an inventory level of 600,000 gallons of paint at the end of January, has a forecasted demand for 100,000 gallons in February, and has decided to produce 250,000 gallons in February. The expected inventory at the end of February would be $600,000 + 250,000 - 100,000 = 750,000$ gallons. As with the equation for the work force, an inventory equation is needed for each product family in the production plan.

Physical and Policy Constraints. Constraints can represent physical limitations or managerial policies associated with the production or staffing plan. For example, a company's training center may be capable of handling only so many new hires at a time, machine capacities may limit maximum output, or inventory storage space may be inadequate. Policy constraints might include limitations on the amount of back ordering, the use of subcontracting or overtime, and the minimum inventory levels to achieve desired safety stocks.

Physical and policy constraints must be satisfied before a production plan or staffing plan can be considered acceptable. Unfortunately, merely choosing alternatives that satisfy the constraints does not ensure that the *best* plan will result. Typically, many plans can satisfy a specific set of constraints.

Costs. In addition to identifying reasonable alternatives and relevant constraints, the planner must gather data on applicable costs. The planner usually considers several types of costs when preparing production or staffing plans:

1. *Regular-time costs.* These costs include regular-time wages paid to employees plus fringe-benefit contributions. Fringe benefits typically include health insurance (hospital, surgical, eye care, dental care); Social Security and retirement funds; and paid vacations, holidays, and certain other types of absence.

2. *Overtime costs.* Overtime wages are typically 150 percent of regular-time wages, exclusive of fringe benefits. Some companies offer a 200 percent rate for working overtime on Sundays or holidays.

3. *Hiring and layoff costs.* Hiring costs include the costs of advertising jobs, interviews, training programs for new employees, and initial paperwork. Layoff costs include the costs of exit interviews and severance pay. In some companies when the work force is reduced, senior employees whose jobs have been eliminated have the right to "bump" less senior employees from their jobs. In the process, a considerable number of employees may change jobs, with the least senior people actually getting laid off. In this case, layoff costs should also include all costs of training and lost productivity caused by bumping.

4. *Inventory holding costs.* Inventory holding costs include the costs of capital tied up in inventory, variable storage and warehousing costs, pilferage and obsolescence costs, insurance costs, and taxes. Only costs that vary with the *level* of inventory investment should be included.

5. *Back-order and stockout costs.* The cost of not satisfying customer demand is difficult to assess. In the case of a back order, costs are incurred for expediting the past-due order, and there is the potential cost of losing the customer's sales to competitors in the future (sometimes called loss of good will). In some cases, orders are not allowed. In other words, the customer is not identified with a specific order that is past due. In these situations, the stockout cost is essentially a lost sales cost consisting of lost profit from the sales plus the loss of good will.

An Acceptable Plan

Developing an acceptable plan is an iterative process (refer back to Fig. 13.2). First, a prospective, or tentative, plan is developed. A production plan with monthly periods must specify monthly production rates, inventory and backlog accumulations, subcontracted production, and monthly work-force levels (including hires, layoffs, and overtime). The plan is prospective at this point because it has not yet been checked against constraints or evaluated in terms of strategic objectives. If the prospective plan is not acceptable for either of those reasons, a new prospective plan must be developed. It may include new alternatives or proposed changes in physical or policy constraints. When management judges the plan acceptable, implementation can begin.

Implementation and Updating

Implementation of production and staffing plans requires the commitment of top management. This commitment begins with the creation of a planning committee, as we suggested earlier, which makes inputs into and reviews the prospective plan. The committee may recommend changes to better balance conflicting objectives. Acceptance of the plan does not necessarily mean that everyone is in total agreement, but it does imply that everyone will work toward achieving it.

PREPARING STAFFING AND PRODUCTION PLANS ▲

In some situations the best planning strategies are fairly obvious. Table 13.4 shows how certain strategies can be fitted to an organization's environment. These strategies are reasonable in a broad sense, even though the extent of their application in any specific situation must still be analyzed. In general, firms that have a process focus can adapt to volume flexibility rather easily and tend to meet variable demand with overtime, subcontracting, or work-force level changes, unless highly skilled, hard-to-find labor is involved. However, firms that have a product focus find volume flexibility difficult to handle and tend to meet fluctuating demand with anticipation inventory, scheduled vacations, or plant shutdowns. In the remainder of this section we develop two staffing plans using trial and error and a production plan using an optimizing method.

TABLE 13.4 Examples of Fitting Strategy to Environment

Organization	Environment	Possible Strategy
City street repair	Labor intensive Unskilled workers Seasonal requirements Ample labor supply	Variable work-force levels Low overtime No subcontracting
Outboard motor company	Costly equipment Skilled labor Costly inventory	Complementary products Off-season promotions Level production rate Limited hires/layoffs Low inventory investment
TV repair service	Steady, increasing demand Skilled employees Tight labor market	Overtime Gradual hires Increase backlog for short-term demand surges
Men's shoe manufacturer	Labor in short supply Low inventory holding cost	Level work force Build up anticipation inventories Low overtime Subcontracting

Staffing Plans

In Application 13.1, we demonstrate the development of two staffing plans, one based on a level strategy and the other on a chase strategy. We term the approach used trial-and-error, because it first requires stating a strategy, then developing a plan, comparing the developed plan to other plans, and finally modifying the plan and/or strategy as necessary. We continue this process until we are satisfied with the results. Table 13.5 contains data that is relevant to the problem.

TABLE 13.5   Data for the Clearwater Post Office Staffing Problem

Requirements

Work-force requirements are shown as the number of part-time employees required for each accounting period. The fiscal year begins on July 1 and ends on June 30. For example, in accounting period 6, it is estimated that 20 part-time employees will be needed to help the full-time work force during the Christmas holiday season.

	Accounting Period													
	1	2	3	4	5	6	7	8	9	10	11	12	13	Total
Requirement	5	6	8	15	17	20	15	15	10	16	14	14	12	167

Ten part-time clerks are currently employed. They have not been subtracted from the requirements shown.

Constraints

1. *Physical:*
   No more than 10 new hires in any period because of limited training facilities.
2. *Policy:*
   No backlogs of mail; demand must be met each period.
   Overtime cannot exceed 25 percent of the regular-time capacity in any period.

Costs

Regular-time wages	$500 per accounting period
Overtime wages	150% of the regular-time rate
Hires	$600 per person
Layoffs	$100 per person

APPLICATION 13.1

The director of the Clearwater Post Office needs a staffing plan for his part-time work force. Part-time employees fill in for absent full-time clerks and help move mail from sorting station to sorting station. The director must determine how many part-time clerks to maintain on the payroll for each of the 13 accounting periods next year. He wants us to develop staffing plans consistent with two alternative strategies:

1. *Level Strategy.* Determine a stable work-force level without using backlogs or subcontractors, but minimize the amount of undertime. Overtime can be used to the maximum in peak periods. The resultant plan is called Plan 1.

2. *Chase Strategy.* Adjust work-force levels as needed to achieve requirements. Do not use overtime, undertime, or subcontractors. The resultant plan is called Plan 2.

Solution

1. *Level Strategy.* We cannot use backlogs or subcontractors, so we must satisfy demand as it occurs in each period. One way to satisfy work-force requirements is to find the work-force level that, when utilized on overtime to the maximum allowed, meets the peak requirement. The most overtime that we can use is 25 percent of the regular-time capacity (w), so we have

$$1.25w = 20 \text{ employees}$$
$$w = \frac{20}{1.25} = 16 \text{ employees}$$

This staff size minimizes the resulting amount of undertime. As there already are 10 part-time employees, the director should immediately hire 6 more.* Plan 1 shows the resulting hires and overtime.

Plan 1: Level Strategy for the Clearwater Post Office Staffing Problem

	Accounting Period													
	1	2	3	4	5	6	7	8	9	10	11	12	13	Total
Requirement	5	6	8	15	17	20	15	15	10	16	14	14	12	167
Staff level	16	16	16	16	16	16	16	16	16	16	16	16	16	208
Hires	6	—	—	—	—	—	—	—	—	—	—	—	—	6
Layoffs	—	—	—	—	—	—	—	—	—	—	—	—	—	0
Overtime	—	—	—	—	1	4	—	—	—	—	—	—	—	5

*An even better plan would be to wait until period 4 to hire employees. However, this approach would not be consistent with a level strategy.

2. *Chase Strategy.* This strategy simply involves adjusting the work force as needed to meet demand. The director should plan to lay off 5 part-time employees immediately, then steadily build the work force to 20 by period 6. After that, we find that the work force can be reduced except for the secondary peak in period 10, when the director should hire 6 more employees. Plan 2 shows the staff level along with the hires and layoffs.

Plan 2: Chase Strategy for the Clearwater Post Office Staffing Problem

	Accounting Period													
	1	2	3	4	5	6	7	8	9	10	11	12	13	Total
Requirement	5	6	8	15	17	20	15	15	10	16	14	14	12	167
Staff level	5	6	8	15	17	20	15	15	10	16	14	14	12	167
Hires	—	1	2	7	2	3	—	—	—	6	—	—	—	21
Layoffs	5	—	—	—	—	—	5	—	5	—	2	—	2	19
Overtime	—	—	—	—	—	—	—	—	—	—	—	—	—	0

Table 13.6 compares the costs of each plan in Application 13.1. You shouldn't be surprised to see that Plan 2—the chase strategy—is less expensive for this situation. Plan 1—the level strategy—calls for a lot of undertime and, unless the director can find productive work for these people during slack periods, it is too costly to have them on the payroll. Intuitively, use of the chase strategy in this situation makes sense—and the economics of the case verify it.

Production Plans

The trial-and-error approach also is useful in production planning. Although the major advantage of the approach is its simplicity, the key to using it lies in the ingenuity of the planner. For production plans, even if a work-force plan has been prepared, the planner still must make many choices for each period of the planning horizon. These decisions relate to the amount of anticipation inventory to produce, the amount of overtime to use, the number of units to subcontract, and other factors.

In this section we present and demonstrate the **tableau method** of production planning.* The method is based on the assumptions that the planner has a capacity plan specifying the maximum capacities of regular time, overtime, and subcontractor production each period; a demand forecast for each period; and the constraint that back orders are not allowed. Given these

---

*This procedure is based on one by E. H. Bowman (1956).

TABLE 13.6	Cost Comparisons for the Clearwater Post Office Staffing Plans	
Cost	**Plan 1: Level Strategy**	**Plan 2: Chase Strategy**
Regular time	208 Worker periods @ $500 = $104,000	167 Worker periods @ $500 = $83,500
Overtime	5 Worker periods @ $750 = 3,750	0 Worker periods @ $750 = 0
Hire	6 Workers @ $600 = 3,600	21 Workers @ $600 = 12,600
Layoff	0 Workers @ $100 = 0	19 Workers @ $100 = 1,900
Total	$111,350	$98,000

assumptions, the tableau method yields the optimal mixed strategy production plan over the planning horizon.

Tableau Method of Production Planning. We begin with a tabulation—called a tableau—of capacity plan and demand forecast quantities, beginning inventory level, and costs for each period of the planning horizon. Figure 13.3 shows such a tableau for a four-period production plan where

$$h = \text{holding cost per unit per period}$$

$$r = \text{cost per unit to produce on regular time}$$

$$c = \text{cost per unit to produce on overtime}$$

$$s = \text{cost per unit to subcontract}$$

$$I_0 = \text{beginning inventory level}$$

$$I_4 = \text{desired inventory level at the end of period 4}$$

$$R_t = \text{regular time capacity in period } t$$

$$OT_t = \text{overtime capacity in period } t$$

$$S_t = \text{subcontracting capacity in period } t$$

$$D_t = \text{forecasted demand for period } t$$

Some elements of the tableau need explanation. First, costs are shown in the upper right-hand corner of each cell. They reflect the cost of producing a unit in one period and carrying the unit in inventory for sale in a future period. For example, in period 1, the regular-time cost to produce one unit is r (column 1). To produce the unit in period 1 for sale in period 2, the cost is $r + h$ (column 2) because we must hold the unit in inventory for one period. Satisfying a unit of demand in period 3 by producing in period 1 on regular

		Period 1	Period 2	Period 3	Period 4	Unused capacity	Total capacity
Period 1	Beginning inventory	0	h	$2h$	$3h$		I_0
	Regular time	r	$r+h$	$r+2h$	$r+3h$		R_1
	Overtime	c	$c+h$	$c+2h$	$c+3h$		OT_1
	Subcontract	s	$s+h$	$s+2h$	$s+3h$		S_1
2	Regular time	✕	r	$r+h$	$r+2h$		R_2
	Overtime	✕	c	$c+h$	$c+2h$		OT_2
	Subcontract	✕	s	$s+h$	$s+2h$		S_2
3	Regular time	✕	✕	r	$r+h$		R_3
	Overtime	✕	✕	c	$c+h$		OT_3
	Subcontract	✕	✕	s	$s+h$		S_3
4	Regular time	✕	✕	✕	r		R_4
	Overtime	✕	✕	✕	c		OT_4
	Subcontract	✕	✕	✕	s		S_4
Requirements		D_1	D_2	D_3	$D_4 + I_4$		

FIGURE 13.3   Production Planning Tableau

time and carrying the unit for two periods costs $r + 2h$ (column 3), and so on. The large Xs indicate that back orders (or producing in a period to satisfy demand in a past period) are not allowed.

Second, it is obvious that the cheapest alternatives are those where the output is produced and sold in the same period. However, we may not always be able to use those alternatives exclusively because of capacity restrictions. Finally, the per unit holding cost for the beginning inventory in period 1 is 0 because it is a function of previous production planning decisions. Similarly, the target inventory at the end of the planning horizon is added to the forecasted demand for the last period. No holding cost is charged because we have already decided to have a specified ending inventory; in this regard it is a sunk cost.*

The method for finding the optimal solution is as follows:

1. Put all capacities from the total capacity column into the unused capacity column.

2. In column 1 (period 1) find the cell with the lowest cost.

3. Allocate as much production as you can to that cell but do not exceed the unused capacity in that row or the demand in that column.

4. Subtract your allocation from the unused capacity for that row. This quantity must never be negative.† If there is still some demand left, repeat steps 2–4 until the demand is satisfied.

5. Repeat steps 2 through 4 for periods 2 and beyond. Take each column separately before proceeding to the next. Be sure to check all cells with unused capacity (but without Xs) for the cell with the lowest cost in a column.

There is one guiding principle to keep in mind while using this method: At the end of the procedure, the sum of all entries in a row must equal the total capacity for that row, and the sum of all entries in a column must equal the requirements for that column. Following this principle ensures that capacities are not exceeded and all demands are met.

In Application 13.2, we demonstrate the development of a production plan using the tableau method. The Tru-Rainbow Company produces a wide variety of paint products for both commercial and private use. The demand for paint is highly seasonal, peaking in the third quarter. The manufacturing manager needs a prospective production plan for the next budget meeting. Table 13.7 contains the relevant data.

---

*If we were analyzing the implications of different ending inventory levels, the holding cost of the ending inventory would have to be added to the costs because ending inventory level would be a decision variable.

†If negative unused capacities cannot be avoided, the solution is infeasible for that capacity plan. More capacity is needed.

TABLE 13.7 Data for the Tru-Rainbow Paint Company Production Problem

Requirements

Demand is expressed in thousands of gallons of paint.

	Quarter				
	1	2	3	4	Total
Demand	300	850	1500	350	3000

Current inventory is 250,000 gallons. The desired ending inventory is 300,000 gallons.

Constraints

The maximum allowable overtime in any quarter is 20 percent of the regular-time capacity in that quarter.

Costs

Regular-time cost per unit	$1.00
Overtime cost per unit	$1.50
Subcontracting cost per unit	$1.90
Inventory holding cost	$0.30 per gallon per quarter

APPLICATION 13.2

Tru-Rainbow's manufacturing manager wants to determine the best production plan using the following capacity plan (expressed in thousands of gallons):

	Quarter			
Capacity Factor	1	2	3	4
Regular Time	450	450	750	450
Overtime	90	90	150	90
Subcontracting	200	200	200	200

The subcontractor can supply a maximum of 200 thousand gallons in any quarter. Production can be subcontracted in one period and the excess held in inventory for a future period if that will avoid a stockout. No back orders or stockouts are permitted.

Solution

Figure 13.4 contains the tableau solution to the problem. In quarter 1 the least expensive alternative is to use the beginning inventory. That leaves a demand of 50,000 gallons to satisfy, so we allocate 50 thousand gallons from quarter 1 regular time production to demand in quarter 1 and reduce the unused capacity by 50. In quarter 2, the least expensive option is to allocate all the regular-time production in quarter 2 to the demand in that quarter. As we are still short 400 thousand gallons, the next option we choose is to allocate 400 thousand gallons from quarter 1 regular-time production. We now have no more regular-time capacity left to allocate in quarters 1 and 2.

The allocations in quarter 3 require capacities from quarters 1 and 2, as well as quarter 3. In other words, we must produce anticipation inventories in quarters 1 and 2 in order to satisfy the peak demand in quarter 3. We simply allocate as much as we can to the low-cost cells, each time making sure that there is some unused capacity to allocate, until the demand is satisfied. Then we update the unused capacities to account for the new allocation. We do the same for quarter 4. A quick check indicates that we have a feasible plan: No unused capacities are negative, the sum of the allocations in each row (including the unused capacity) equals the total capacity for that row, and the sum of the allocations for each quarter equals the demand for that quarter.

The total cost of this prospective production plan is equal to the sum of the allocation in each cell multiplied by the cost per unit in that cell, or $4,010,000. The plan itself must be reconstructed from the tableau. Based on Fig. 13.4, the plan (expressed in thousands of gallons) is:

Quarter	Regular-Time Production	Overtime Production	Subcontracting	Anticipation Inventory
1	450	90	20	510
2	450	90	200	400
3	750	150	200	0
4	450	90	110	300

Whenever production plus subcontracting exceeds quarterly demand, anticipation inventories are being accumulated. In quarter 1, 400,000 gallons are produced on regular time for sale in quarter 2, 90,000 gallons are produced on overtime for sale in quarter 3, and 20,000 gallons are purchased from subcontractors for sale in quarter 3. In total, 510,000 gallons are produced in excess of demand in quarter 1 (see Fig. 13.4). Similarly, when production plus subcontracting is less than quarterly demand, anticipation inventories are being consumed. That is the case in quarter 2, when production plus subcontracting is only 740,000 gallons, but demand is 850,000 gallons. Notice that anticipation inventory goes from 510,000 gallons in quarter 1 to 400,000 gallons in quarter 2. The plan is shown graphically in Fig. 13.5.

labor cost/unit ↗

		Quarter 1	Quarter 2	Quarter 3	Quarter 4	Unused capacity	Total capacity
Quarter	Beginning inventory	0.00 — 250	0.30	0.60	0.90	~~250~~ 0	250
1	Regular time	1.00 — 50	1.30 — 400	1.60	1.90	~~450~~ ~~400~~ 0	450
1	Overtime	1.50	1.80 — 90	2.10	2.40	~~90~~ 0	90
1	Subcontract	1.90	2.20 — 20	2.50	2.80	~~200~~ 180	200
2	Regular time		1.00 — 450	1.30	1.60	~~450~~ 0	450
2	Overtime		1.50 — 90	1.80	2.10	~~90~~ 0	90
2	Subcontract		1.90	2.20 — 200	2.50	~~200~~ 0	200
3	Regular time			1.00 — 750	1.30	~~750~~ 0	750
3	Overtime			1.50 — 150	1.80	~~150~~ 0	150
3	Subcontract			1.90 — 200	2.20	~~200~~ 0	200
4	Regular time				1.00 — 450	~~450~~ 0	450
4	Overtime				1.50 — 90	~~90~~ 0	90
4	Subcontract				1.90 — 110	~~200~~ 90	200
Requirements (demand)		300	850	1500	650	270	3570

FIGURE 13.4   The Tableau Solution for the Tru-Rainbow Problem

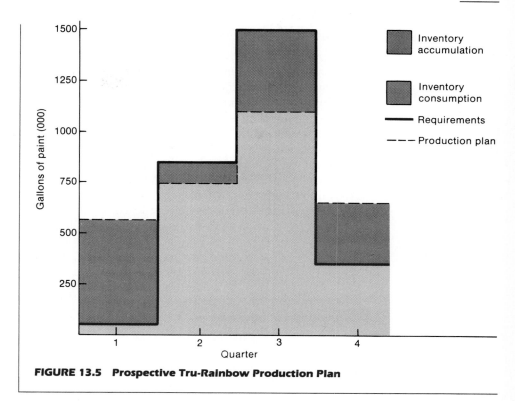

FIGURE 13.5 Prospective Tru-Rainbow Production Plan

Additional Uses of the Tableau Method. The plan we offered to the manufacturing manager in Application 13.2 used a lot of overtime and subcontracting. A better capacity plan—with increases in the work force to boost regular-time production capacity—might result in lower production costs, perhaps even low enough to offset the added capacity costs. A series of capacity plans can be tried and compared to find the best plan. Even though this process in itself involves trial and error, the tableau method finds the best mix of regular time, overtime, and subcontracting for each capacity plan.

Back orders can also be considered. For example, in Application 13.2, regular-time production in quarter 3 could be used to satisfy demand from quarter 2 by replacing the X in the quarter 2 cell for regular-time production in quarter 3 with some appropriate penalty cost. In effect, the Xs in the Tru-Rainbow tableau represent very large costs—large enough that we would not consider back orders. The tableau method can still be used to solve a problem involving back orders, however the solution may not be optimal. In general, using a computer with a routine for the transportation method (see Supplement S3), though, might be easier for large problems or problems involving trial-and-error analysis of the capacity plan or demand forecasts. Also, the solution will be optimal.

Managerial Considerations

Although trial-and-error approaches or mathematical techniques can be useful in evaluating production and staffing plan alternatives, they are only aids to the planning process. You have seen in this chapter that the planning process is dynamic and often complicated by conflicting objectives. Analytic techniques can help managers evaluate plans and resolve conflicting objectives, but managers—not techniques—make the decisions.

After arriving at an acceptable production plan, management must implement it. However, the production plan is stated in aggregate terms. The first step in implementation therefore is to decompose the plan to specific products, work centers, and dates by master production scheduling, the topic of Chapter 14. Staffing plans must also be decomposed to work-force schedules for implementation. We discuss work-force scheduling in Chapter 17.

SOLVED PROBLEMS

1. The Cranston Telephone Company employs workers who lay telephone cables and perform a number of other construction tasks. The company prides itself on good service and strives to meet all commitments on time. Company policy is to complete all service orders within the quarter during which they are placed. Each worker puts in 600 hours per quarter regular time and can work an additional 100 hours overtime. The operations department has estimated that the following work-force requirements for such services will be needed next year.

Quarter	1	2	3	4
Hours	12,000	24,000	30,000	6,000

Wages are $6000 per quarter, with an overtime pay rate of $15 per hour. It costs $8000 to hire, train, and outfit a new employee. Layoff costs are $2000 per employee. Currently, 40 employees work for Cranston in this capacity.

a. Find a level work-force plan that allows for no delay in service and minimizes undertime. What is the total cost of the plan? How many hours in undertime does your plan call for?

b. Use a chase strategy without overtime. What is the total cost of this plan?

c. Propose a mixed-strategy plan and evaluate its total cost.

Solution

a. The peak demand is 30,000 hours in quarter 3. As each employee can work 700 hours per quarter (600 on regular time and 100 on overtime), the level work force that minimizes undertime is 30,000/700 = 42.86, or 43, employees.

Cost		Amount
Regular wages	($6000 per quarter)(43)(4 quarters)	$1,032,000
Overtime wages*	(4200 hrs in Quarter 3)($15 per hour)	63,000
Hire costs	($8000 per hire)(3 hires)	24,000
Total		$1,119,000

*The 43 employees can produce (43)(600) = 25,800 hours of regular time in any quarter. The 30,000-hour requirement in Quarter 3 exceeds this amount by 4200 hours.

b. The chase strategy:

Quarter	Demand (hr)	Work Force*	Hires	Layoffs
1	12,000	20	—	20
2	24,000	40	20	—
3	30,000	50	10	—
4	6,000	10	—	40
Total		120	30	60

*Work force is calculated by dividing the demand for each quarter by 600 hours, or the amount one employee can produce in one quarter.

Cost		Amount
Regular wages	($6000 per quarter)(120)	$ 720,000
Hire costs	($8000 per hire)(30 hires)	240,000
Layoff costs	($2000 per layoff)(60 layoffs)	120,000
Total		$1,080,000

c. The following mixed-strategy plan uses hires and layoffs along with overtime to cut costs from the plans in (a) and (b). This plan was developed by trial and error.

Quarter	Demand (hr)	Work Force	Hires	Layoffs	Overtime (hr)
1	12,000	20	—	20	—
2	24,000	40	20	—	—
3	30,000	43	3	—	4,200
4	6,000	10	—	33	—
Total		113	23	53	4,200

Cost		Amount
Regular wages	($6000 per quarter)(113)	$ 678,000
Hire costs	($8000 per hire)(23 hires)	184,000
Layoff costs	($2000 per layoff)(53 layoffs)	106,000
Overtime	($15 per hour)(4200 hours)	63,000
Total		$1,031,000

2. The Arctic Air Co. produces residential air conditioners. The manufacturing manager would like to develop a production plan for the next year based on the following demand and capacity data (in hundreds of units).

	Period					
	Jan–Feb (1)	Mar–Apr (2)	May–Jun (3)	Jul–Aug (4)	Sep–Oct (5)	Nov–Dec (6)
Demand (D)	50	60	90	120	70	40
Regular time (R)	65	65	65	80	80	65
Overtime (OT)	13	13	13	16	16	13
Subcontractor (S)	10	10	10	10	10	10

Producing a unit on regular time costs $1000, including $300 for labor. Producing a unit on overtime costs $1150. A subcontractor can produce a unit to Arctic Air specifications for $1250. Holding an air conditioner in stock for one two-month period costs $60, and 200 air conditioners are currently in stock. The plan calls for 400 units in stock in period 6. No back orders are allowed.

Find a plan that minimizes costs.

Solution

Figure 13.6 contains the production plan obtained by the tableau method. It can be summarized as follows:

Period	Regular-time Production	Overtime Production	Subcontracting	Anticipation Inventory
1	6500	0	0	1700
2	6500	400	0	2600
3	6500	1300	0	1400
4	8000	1600	1000	0
5	7000	0	0	0
6	4400	0	0	400

The cost of this plan is $44,287,000, assuming that workers are not paid for unused capacity in regular-time production or are productively put to work elsewhere in the organization.

	Period	1	2	3	4	5	6	Unused capacity	Total capacity
	I_0	0 — 2	60	120	180	240	300	~~2~~ 0	2
1	R_1	1000 — 48	1060	1120 — 17	1180	1240	1300	65 ~~17~~ 0	65
	OT_1	1150	1210	1270	1330	1390	1450	13	13
	S_1	1250	1310	1370	1430	1490	1550	10	10
2	R_2	✕	1000 — 60	1060 — 5	1120	1180	1240	65 ~~5~~ 0	65
	OT_2	✕	1150	1210	1270 — 4	1330	1390	~~13~~ 9	13
	S_2	✕	1250	1310	1370	1430	1490	10	10
3	R_3	✕	✕	1000 — 65	1060	1120	1180	~~65~~ 0	65
	OT_3	✕	✕	1150 — 3	1210 — 10	1270	1330	~~13~~ ~~10~~ 0	13
	S_3	✕	✕	1250	1310	1370	1430	10	10
4	R_4	✕	✕	✕	1000 — 80	1060	1120	~~80~~ 0	80
	OT_3	✕	✕	✕	1150 — 16	1210	1270	~~16~~ 0	16
	S_4	✕	✕	✕	1250 — 10	1310	1370	~~10~~ 0	10
5	R_5	✕	✕	✕	✕	1000 — 70	1060	~~80~~ 10	80
	OT_5	✕	✕	✕	✕	1150	1210	16	16
	S_5	✕	✕	✕	✕	1250	1310	10	10
6	R_6	✕	✕	✕	✕	✕	1000 — 44	~~65~~ 21	65
	OT_6	✕	✕	✕	✕	✕	1150	13	13
	S_6	✕	✕	✕	✕	✕	1250	10	10
	D	50	60	90	120	70	44	132	566

FIGURE 13.6

FORMULA REVIEW

1. Number of workers in the work force:

Workers in current period	=	Workers at end of last period	+	Hires at start of current period	−	Layoffs at start of current period

2. Inventory level:

Inventory at end of current period	=	Inventory at end of last period	+	Production in current period	−	Demand requirements in current period

CHAPTER HIGHLIGHTS

- In manufacturing organizations, the production plan links the business plan and the master production schedule. In service organizations, the staffing plan links the annual plan and the workforce schedule.

- Production and staffing plans are managerial statements of time-phased production or service rates, labor requirements, and, in manufacturing, inventory investment that considers customer demand and physical capacity limitations.

- Goods or services, labor, and time are aggregated to reduce the level of detail in the planning process.

- Managerial inputs are required from the various functional areas in the organization. This approach typically raises conflicting objectives, which must be reconciled in the plan. One of the typical manufacturing objectives not considered in a service organization is to minimize investment in finished goods inventory.

- The two basic types of decision alternatives are reactive and aggressive. Reactive alternatives take customer demand as a given quantity. Aggressive alternatives attempt to change customer demand to achieve efficiency in providing goods or services.

- Two pure planning strategies are the level strategy, which maintains a constant work-force size or production rate, and the chase strategy, which allows work-force levels and production rates to vary according to customer demand.

- Developing production and staffing plans is an iterative process of determining requirements;

identifying relevant constraints, alternatives, and costs; preparing a prospective plan; checking for acceptability to top management; and implementing the plan.

- Managers must remember that trial-and-error approaches and mathematical techniques are only aids to the planning process. Managers, not techniques, make the decisions.

KEY TERMS

aggressive alternatives   488
annual plan   483
backlog   488
business plan   483
chase strategy   489
complementary products   488
level strategy   490
planning horizon   482
production plan   480
reactive alternatives   486
staffing plan   480
tableau method   498
work-force schedule   483

STUDY QUESTIONS

1. What is a production plan? Why must quantities be aggregated?

2. How do the production plan and staffing plan relate to other organizational plans?

3. Consider the statement: "Production planning is the responsibility of our manufacturing personnel because it deals with the resources they are responsible for." Comment on that statement in light of the strategic importance of production planning.

4. Give reasons why executives representing the following areas should be interested in production planning.

   a. Marketing   d. Finance
   b. Manufacturing   e. Human resources
   c. Materials   f. Engineering

5. What are the typical objectives to be considered in production and staff planning? Comment on the conflicting nature of these objectives.

6. What is the difference between *reactive* and *aggressive* alternatives in production and staff planning? Provide several examples of each.

7. The *chase* strategy and the *level* strategy represent two extremes in production or staff planning. Define each one and describe the type of environment in which each would work best.

8. Briefly describe the planning process and explain how inputs from functional areas in the organization are solicited and incorporated into production and staffing plans.

9. Compare and contrast the staffing plan in a service organization with a production plan in a manufacturing organization. In what ways are the objectives, alternatives, and planning processes different?

10. The Hometown Bank currently employs eight tellers to staff lobby stations for customer transactions. Customer demand for banking services is variable, with peaks coinciding with the end of the week, end of the month, and holiday seasons. Because of this variability the tellers are idle much of the time; however, during rush periods customers experience lengthy delays. Suppose that you are the operations manager of this bank.

   a. What staffing plan alternatives would you consider?
   b. What data would you need?
   c. What objectives would you consider?

PROBLEMS

Review Problems

1. The Crop-Chemical Company produces chemical fertilizers. The projected manufacturing requirements (in thousands of gallons) for the next four quarters are 60, 30, 120, and 150. Stockouts and back orders are to be avoided. A level production strategy is desired.

   a. Determine the quarterly production rate required to meet total demand for the year. Beginning inventory is zero.
   b. Specify the anticipation inventories that will be produced.
   c. Suppose that the requirements for the next four quarters are 30, 120, 150, and 60. Total demand is the same, but would the production rate in (a) have to be changed? If so, what rate would be needed now?

2. The Barberton Municipal Division of Road Maintenance is charged with road repair in the city of Barberton and surrounding area. Cindy Kramer, road maintenance director, must submit a staffing plan for the next year based on a set schedule for repairs and city budget. Roads cannot be repaired ahead of schedule because funds will not be available to pay the workers. Delaying the repair of roads is equally infeasible because the state will not match city funds if repairs fall behind schedule.

   Kramer estimates that the labor hours required for the next four quarters are 4000, 13,000, 20,000, and 7000 respectively. Each of the 10 workers on the work force can contribute 520 hours per quarter. It costs $6240 in regular-time wages per worker for a quarter and $18 for each hour worked on overtime. Overtime is limited to 20 percent of the regular-time capacity in any quarter. Workers can be hired for $3000 and fired for $2000. Subcontracting is not considered because of the poor reputation of local subcontractors.

   a. Find a level work-force plan that allows no delay in road repair and minimizes undertime. Overtime can be used to its limits in any quarter. What is the total cost of the plan and how many undertime hours does it call for?
   b. Use a chase strategy without overtime. What is the total cost of this plan?
   c. Propose a plan of your own. Compare your plan with those in (a) and (b) and discuss its comparative merits.

3. The Little Shoe Company makes sandals for children. Management has just prepared a forecast of sales (in pairs of sandals) for next year and now must prepare a production plan. The

company has traditionally maintained a level work-force strategy. Currently there are 6 workers who have been with the company for a number of years. Each employee can produce 25 pairs of sandals in a two-month period, the planning period used by Little Shoe. Every year management authorizes overtime in periods 1, 5, and 6, up to a maximum of 20 percent of regular-time capacity. Management wants to avoid stockouts and back orders and will not accept any plan that calls for such shortages. At present there are 120 pairs of sandals in finished goods inventory. The demand forecast is

Period	1	2	3	4	5	6
Sales	240	130	60	180	300	270

a. Is the level work-force strategy with the current work force feasible, assuming that overtime is used in periods 1, 5, and 6? Explain.

b. Find two alternative plans that would satisfy management's concern over stockouts and back orders, disregarding costs. What are the trade-offs between these two plans that must be considered?

4. The Bull Grin Company produces a feed supplement for animal foods produced by a number of companies. Sales are seasonal, but Bull Grin's customers refuse to stockpile the supplement during slack sales periods. In other words, the customers want to minimize their inventory investments, insist on shipments according to their schedules, and won't accept back orders.

Bull Grin employs manual, unskilled labor, who require little or no training. Producing 1000 pounds of supplement costs $810 on regular time and $900 on overtime. These figures include materials, which account for 80 percent of the cost. Overtime is limited to production of a total of 30,000 pounds per quarter. In addition, subcontractors can be hired at $1100 per thousand pounds, but only 10,000 pounds per quarter can be produced this way.

The current level of inventory is 40,000 pounds, and management wants to end the year at that level. Holding 1000 pounds of feed supplement in inventory per quarter costs $110. The

latest annual forecast is

Quarter	Demand (lb)
1	100,000
2	410,000
3	770,000
4	440,000
Total	1,720,000

The following regular-time capacity plan has been proposed:

Quarter	Production Capacity (lb)
1	360,000
2	390,000
3	460,000
4	360,000

Find the optimal production plan and calculate its cost.

5. Consider the Bull Grin Company described in Problem 4. Suppose that the regular-time capacity plan were

Quarter	Production Capacity (lb)
1	430,000
2	430,000
3	430,000
4	430,000

a. Find the optimal production plan and calculate its cost.

b. Compare the plan you developed in Problem 4 with this plan. How are the strategies different? What are the cost implications, considering hirings and layoffs? Use the following information:

- Hiring 1000 pounds of regular-time capacity costs $500.
- Laying off 1000 pounds of regular-time capacity costs $300.
- Currently, there are 360,000 pounds of regular-time capacity. At the end of quarter 4

(or start of quarter 5), management wants to have 360,000 pounds of regular-time capacity again.

- Idle workers representing regular-time capacity can be sent home without pay. Therefore, there is no cost for these under-utilized resources.

Consider again the Bull Grin Company described in Problem 4. Suppose that management is willing to negotiate some price concessions with customers, which would give them an incentive to stockpile feed supplement prior to actual need in their production schedules. Bull Grin management estimates that demand for feed supplement resulting from this new arrangement would be

Quarter	Demand (lb)
1	200,000
2	540,000
3	540,000
4	440,000
Total	1,720,000

a. Find the optimal production plan using the regular-time capacity plan in Problem 4.
b. Find the optimal production plan using the regular-time capacity plan in Problem 5.
c. Which of the two plans is more economic? Use the same hiring and layoff cost information as in Problem 5(b).
d. Using the best plan in (c) and the best plan in Problem 5(b), how much can Bull Grin afford to reduce annual revenues to get the new demand schedule?

Advanced Problems

Problems 7 and 8 require prior reading of Supplement 2, and Problem 10 requires prior reading of Supplement 3. A computer package is required for Problems 7, 8, and 10.

7. Consider the Bull Grin Company in Problem 4. Find the *best* regular-time capacity plan using the same restrictions on overtime and subcontracting. Assume that

- The firm has 180 workers now and management wants to have the same number in quarter 4. Each worker can produce 2000 pounds per quarter.
- Regular time production costs $1620 per worker and idle workers must be paid at that same rate.
- Hiring one worker costs $1000 and laying off a worker costs $600.
- All the other costs and conditions are the same as presented in Problem 4.

You could use a trial-and-error approach on a computer to evaluate various capacity plans until you find the best one. Alternatively, you could use Supplement 2 and build a linear programming model to find the optimal solution.

8. Repeat Problem 7, this time using the demand schedule from Problem 6. Discuss the differences between the solution in Problem 7 and this solution. How has the strategy changed? What do the differences say in general about production planning and demand management?

9. The manager of Gretchen's Hamburger Paradise must prepare an annual staffing plan. The Hamburger Paradise shop is a fast-food shop located in an ideal spot near the local high school. The only products the shop sells are hamburgers, chili, soft drinks, shakes, and french fries. A sample of 1000 customers taken at random revealed that they purchased 2100 hamburgers, 200 pints of chili, 1000 soft drinks and shakes, and 1000 bags of french fries. Thus for purposes of estimating staffing requirements, the manager assumes that each customer purchases 2.1 hamburgers, 0.2 pints of chili, 1 soft drink or shake, and 1 bag of french fries. Each hamburger requires 4 minutes of labor. A pint of chili requires 3 minutes, while a soft drink/shake and a bag of fries each take 2 minutes of labor.

Gretchen's Hamburger Paradise currently has 10 employees who work 80 hours a month. They are high school students who work part-time on staggered shifts. Wages are $400 per month for regular time and $7.50 per hour for overtime. It costs $250 to hire and train a new employee and $50 to fire an employee.

The manager realizes that building up seasonal inventories of hamburgers (or any of the products) would not be wise because of customer taste preferences. Also, any demand not satisfied is a lost sale and must be avoided. Three strategies have come to mind.

- Level work force and use of up to 20 percent of regular-time capacity on overtime in any month.
- Maintain a base of 10 employees, hiring and firing, as necessary, to avoid any overtime.
- Chase strategy, hiring and firing employees as demand changes to avoid overtime.

When performing her calculations the manager always rounds to the next highest integer for the number of employees. She also follows a policy of not using an employee more than 80 hours per month, except when overtime is needed. The projected demand by month (number of customers) for next year is

Jan	Feb	Mar	Apr	May	Jun
3000	2800	3200	3500	3800	4500

Jul	Aug	Sep	Oct	Nov	Dec
4800	4200	3800	3600	3500	3000

a. Develop the schedule of service requirements for the next year.
b. Which of the three strategies is most effective?
c. Suppose that an arrangement with the high school enables the manager to identify good prospective employees without having to advertise in the local newspaper. This reduces the hiring cost to $50, which is mainly the cost of charred hamburgers during training. Will this change the manager's strategy on a cost basis? *Should* the manager change strategies, considering other objectives that may be appropriate?

10. The Vac-Toy division of Innovative Toys Corporation is enjoying a resounding success in its new product. The division produces two models of Vac-Toy, a vacuum cleaner designed to sweep up toys left around the house. One model is deluxe, the other plain, but both require the same technology and resources and can be considered jointly when developing production plans.

The demand for Vac-Toys is high volume and seasonal in nature. It is highest during the winter months when children are indoors.

Demand falls off during the summer because children spend more time outside. The forecasted demand for next year, in thousands of units, is

Jul	Aug	Sep	Oct	Nov	Dec
2	3	4	8	12	20

Jan	Feb	Mar	Apr	May	Jun
16	10	7	4	3	1

Because of the newness of the product and its immediate success, Vac-Toy management has allowed the use of back orders as a means of leveling the load in the factory. Customers are willing to wait many months, if necessary, to get the Vac-Toy they want. Consequently, Hector Krueger, production manager, has proposed a capacity plan that he feels will keep costs down while allowing for some back orders. His plan is

	Capacity (000s of units)		
Months	Regular Time	Overtime	Subcon-tracting
1–4	4	1	1
5–8	9	3	1
9–12	4	1	1

Producing one unit costs $100 on regular time and $120 on overtime. One unit can be subcontracted for $150. Inventory holding costs are $8 per unit per month. Finished-goods inventory is 1000 units, and Krueger wants to have 1000 units in inventory at the end of June.

The best estimate for back-order costs is $30 per unit per month. For example, one unit of production on regular time in month 5, to satisfy demand in month 4, would cost $130 (or $100 + $30). A unit used to satisfy demand in month 3 would cost $160 [or $100 + 2($30)]. Krueger opposes using any subcontracted production for satisfying back-ordered demand. Consequently, only regular-time and overtime production can be used for back orders.

a. Using Krueger's capacity plan, find the production plan that minimizes costs. Specify the monthly quantities of beginning inventory, regular-time production, overtime, subcontracting, ending inventory, and back orders. Determine total cost.

b. Again using his capacity plan, find the production plan that minimizes back orders. What is the total cost of that plan?

c. Provide some suggestions for improving the plan so as to reduce back orders and other costly production alternatives.

SELECTED REFERENCES

Bowman, E. H., "Production Planning by the Transportation Method of Linear Programming," *Journal of the Operations Research Society,* vol. 4 (February 1956), pp. 100–103.

Chaiken, J. M., and R. C. Larson, "Methods for Allocating Urban Emergency Units: A Survey," *Management Science,* vol. 19, no. 4 (December, Part 2, 1972), pp. 110–130.

Hanssman, F., and S. W. Hess, "A Linear Programming Approach to Production and Employment Scheduling," *Management Technology,* vol. 1 (January 1960), pp. 46–51.

Holt, C., C. F. Modigliani, and H. Simon, "A Linear Decision Rule for Production and Employment Scheduling," *Management Science,* vol. 2, no. 2 (October 1955), pp. 1–30.

Jones, C. H., "Parametric Production Planning," *Management Science,* vol. 15, no. 11 (July 1967), pp. 843–866.

Kinsey, John W., "Master Production Planning—The Key to Successful Master Scheduling," *Proceedings of the 24th Annual APICS Conference,* Boston (October 1981), pp. 81–85.

Krajewski, L., and H. Thompson, "Efficient Employment Planning in Public Utilities," *The Bell Journal of Economics and Management Science,* vol. 6, no. 1 (Spring 1975), pp. 314–326.

Lee, S. M., and L. J. Moore, "A Practice Approach to Production Scheduling," *Production and Inventory Management* (1st Quarter 1974), pp. 79–92.

Lee, W. B., and B. M. Khumawala, "Simulation Testing of Aggregate Production Planning Models in an Implementation Methodology," *Management Science,* vol. 20, no. 6 (February 1974), pp. 903–911.

McClain, J. D., and L. J. Thomas, "Horizon Effects in Aggregate Production Planning with Seasonal Demand," *Management Science,* vol. 23, no. 7 (March 1977), pp. 728–736.

Mellichamp, J., and R. Love, "Production Heuristics for the Aggregate Planning Problem," *Management Science,* vol. 24, no. 12 (August 1978), pp. 1242–1251.

Silver, E. A., "A Tutorial on Production Smoothing and Workforce Balancing," *Operations Research* (November–December 1967), pp. 985–1010.

Smith, Linda M., "Marketing's Role in a Manufacturing Environment," *Proceedings of the 23rd Annual APICS Conference,* Los Angeles (October 1980), pp. 248–251.

Taubert, W. H., "A Search Decision Rule for the Aggregate Scheduling Problem," *Management Science,* vol. 14, no. 6 (February 1968), pp. 343–359.

Vollmann, Thomas E., "Capacity Planning: The Missing Link," *Production and Inventory Management* (First Quarter 1973), pp. 61–73.

Wolfe, H., and J. P. Young, "Staffing the Nursing Unit—Part 1: Controlled Variable Staffing," *Nursing Research,* vol. 14, no. 3 (Summer 1965), pp. 236–243.

CHAPTER 14

MASTER PRODUCTION SCHEDULING

▲ Chapter Outline

Key Questions for Managers

How do our competitive priorities affect our approach to master production scheduling?

How can we provide accurate shipping dates to our customers?

How can we get better estimates of cash flows and capacity requirements?

How should our master production schedule relate to our production plan?

roduction planning commits resources to various production needs over an extended period of time, as we demonstrated in Chapter 13. Firms simplify the planning process by aggregating products, work forces, and time periods. Ultimately, however, a firm must produce specific products to satisfy specific customer demands. In this chapter we show how a more detailed plan, the master production schedule, disaggregates the production plan into specific product schedules. We also discuss ways that competitive strategies affect a firm's approach to master production scheduling.

THE MASTER PRODUCTION
SCHEDULING PROCESS ▲

The master production scheduling process begins where we left off in Chapter 13. Using the authorized production plan as a basis, operations develops a prospective master production schedule. A **master production schedule (MPS)** is a detailed plan that states how many end items will be produced within specified periods of time. End items are either finished products or the highest level assemblies from which shippable products are built (see Chapter 11). Time periods are usually measured in weeks, although they may be measured in hours, days, or even months.

Figure 14.1 shows the master production scheduling process. Think of the prospective MPS as a trial that tests whether operations can meet the schedule with the machine capacities, labor, overtime, subcontractors, and other resources estimated in the production plan. Operations revises the MPS until it either finds a schedule that satisfies all resource limitations or determines that no

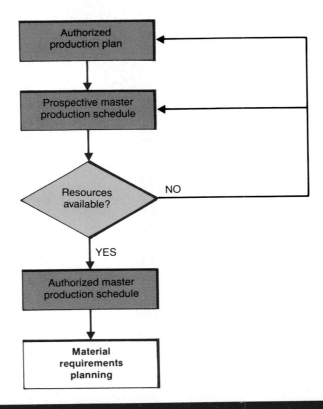

FIGURE 14.1   Master Production Scheduling Process

TABLE 14.1   Typical Responsibilities of a Master Production Scheduler

- Specify delivery promise dates on incoming orders and match actual requirements with the master production schedule.
- Evaluate the impact of "top-down" inputs, such as the introduction of new products in less than the normal lead time.
- Evaluate the impact of "bottom-up" inputs, such as anticipated shortage reports from manufacturing or purchasing, indicating that certain components will not be available as scheduled, or that planned production rates are not being attained.
- Revise the master production schedule when necessary for lack of materials or capacity.
- Bring basic conflicts to the attention of management for resolution.

Source: Oliver Wight, *Production and Inventory Management in the Computer Age.* Boston: Cahners Books, 1974, p. 69.

feasible schedule can be found. In the latter event, the production plan must be revised to adjust production requirements or increase authorized resources. Ultimately, an acceptable prospective MPS emerges and is presented to plant management for authorization. Operations then uses the authorized MPS as input to material requirements planning, which, as you will see in Chapter 15, determines specific schedules for part, component, and assembly production.

In many manufacturing firms, a master production scheduler is responsible for developing an MPS that satisfies the intent of the production plan. Other responsibilities typically include those in Table 14.1. The MPS process may differ from company to company, depending on whether the firm has a process or product focus. Thus the specific procedures and record formats presented later in this chapter illustrate *types of procedures* and may not apply to specific firms. In summary, as Fig. 14.1 illustrates, the MPS process is linked to the authorized production plan and therefore requires feedback from the functional areas that were involved in production planning. In this way, the master production schedule sets in motion the operations that will achieve the production plan's objectives.

The Master Production Schedule

To give you a clearer idea of master production scheduling, let's consider the MPS of a bicycle manufacturer. The company doesn't accept orders for custom designed bicycles; rather, it produces to stock. For production planning purposes, the firm has grouped its entire line of products into several families, based on wheel diameter. One family of bicycles, based on a 20-inch wheel, includes three different styles. Alpha, which comes with training wheels, is designed for children just learning to ride. Dirty Dan is a dirt bike with racing decals and rugged tires. Roadster has hand-caliper brakes, polished aluminum

Product	January				February				March			
	Week				Week				Week			
	1	2	3	4	5	6	7	8	9	10	11	12
Alpha	—	160	—	160	—	240	—	240	—	320	—	320
Dirty Dan	150	150	150	150	225	225	225	225	300	300	300	300
Roadster	40	—	40	—	60	—	60	—	80	—	80	—
Monthly total	1000				1500				2000			

FIGURE 14.2 **Weekly Master Production Schedule**

fenders, and a rearview mirror. All three styles are basically the same bicycle, with minor variations in color and accessories.

The production plan for the 20-inch family calls for 1000 units in January, 1500 units in February, and 2000 units in March. One possible MPS for this family is shown in Fig. 14.2. A basic purpose of the MPS is to set due dates for production orders. For example, Fig. 14.2 shows that in the month of January production is scheduled to complete 40 units of *Roadster* in week 1 and another set of 40 units in week 3.

Another purpose of the MPS is to provide an accurate picture of the resources and materials needed to support the production plan. Recall that the production plan estimates resource requirements, but states resource quantities in aggregate terms. Because it contains more detail, the MPS provides a more accurate picture of resource needs. Also, by specifying the number of end items to be produced during each time period, the MPS determines requirements for all intermediate and purchased items as well. This is the point at which the bill of materials (see Chapter 11) is important. For example, Fig. 14.2 shows 160 units of Alpha scheduled for completion in week 2. This means that by week 2, operations must produce 160 Alpha main frames, 320 20-inch wheels, 160 sets of training wheels, and specific quantities of other parts in order to complete the 160 bicycles on schedule. Thus a good MPS enables a company to make efficient use of its most valuable resources—labor, capital, capacity, and materials. As Managerial Practice 14.1 shows, good master production scheduling *can* make a difference.

Typical Constraints

A master production schedule must satisfy several constraints. First, the sum of the quantities in the MPS must equal those in the production plan. Figure 14.2 demonstrates two aspects of this constraint. Note that each month the total quantities for all three styles equals the total quantity of bicycles specified in the production plan. If the production plan specified quantities in dollars or labor hours, the scheduler would have to convert the MPS quantities to the same unit of measure. However, master production schedules should specify units of *product* for inventory control purposes.

The second aspect of the constraint is that total requirements for a product, as determined in the production plan, must be allocated over time in an efficient manner. For example, in January the plan calls for operations to produce 320 units of Alpha, 600 units of Dirty Dan, and 80 units of Roadster, or a total of 1000 units. The specific mix is based on historical demand and marketing and promotional considerations. The bicycle company's MPS states production quantities in weekly time periods, although they could be days or months. The scheduler for the 20-inch bicycle family must select weekly lot sizes for each product, taking into account economic factors such as production setup costs and inventory carrying costs.

The decision that determines lot size and timing is subject to a second constraint: capacity limitations. Typically several key resources limit production volume. These resources might be certain work stations that are usually short on capacity, storage space for components and finished products, or working capital. The scheduler must acknowledge these limitations and recognize that some products require more critical resources than others.

MANAGERIAL PRACTICE 14.1 ▲

Master Production Scheduling at Nissan

The Nissan Motor Company's automobile assembly plant in Murayama, Japan, has 6600 employees and produces 30,000 cars and 1600 lift trucks per month. The challenge of managing this operation is made simpler by an excellent master production scheduling system, executed in five stages.

Stage 1 specifies a monthly schedule for each model type over a three-month period. Stage 2 specifies the daily production of drive trains during the first month. The third stage defines specific vehicle options for the first ten days of the month. The fourth stage refines the first five days of production and helps synchronize supplier shipments. The last stage is a final assembly schedule, which specifies the exact configuration and build sequence of each vehicle. This process results in a master production schedule performance that is 99 percent on time, as measured every hour.

Source: Roger B. Brooke, "MRP II Nissan Style," *The Oliver Wright Companies Newsletter*, January 1986.

DEVELOPING A PROSPECTIVE MASTER PRODUCTION SCHEDULE ▲

In this section we show how a firm that produces to stock develops a master production schedule. This process includes calculating the projected on-hand inventory, determining the timing and size of MPS quantities, and calculating available-to-promise quantities. Our discussion introduces some basic terminology of master production scheduling and illustrates the trial-and-error aspect of actual scheduling. For simplicity, we assume that our imaginary firm doesn't utilize safety stocks for end items, even though real firms usually do. (Later, in Chapter 15 we address the mechanics of incorporating safety stocks in material requirements planning.) The section concludes with a discussion of linking the production plan and the MPS. You can find details of how eight specific firms develop MPSs in Berry, Vollmann, and Whybark (1979).

Calculating Projected On-Hand Inventories

The **projected on-hand inventory** is an estimate of the amount of inventory available each week after demand has been satisfied. It equals the on-hand balance for the previous week, plus the MPS quantity for the current week, minus the forecast *or* actual orders booked for the current week—whichever quantity is greater. Mathematically, we express this relationship as:

$$I_t = I_{t-1} + MPS_t - \max(F_t \text{ or } CO_t)$$

where

$$I_t = \text{projected on-hand inventory balance} \atop \text{at the end of week } t$$

$$MPS_t = \text{MPS quantity due in week } t$$

$$F_t = \text{forecast of orders for week } t$$

$$CO_t = \text{customer orders booked for shipment} \atop \text{in week } t$$

MPS_t indicates a quantity that management expects to be completed and ready to ship in week t. The scheduler subtracts the greater quantity, F_t or CO_t, recognizing that the forecast is subject to error. If actual booked orders exceed the forecast, the projection will be more accurate if the scheduler uses CO_t. Conversely, if the forecast exceeds booked orders, F_t will provide the best estimate of requirements for week t.

Let's consider a valve manufacturer that produces a limited range of products: valves of varying types and sizes, all made to stock. Management needs to develop a master production schedule for its 3-inch gate valve. Marketing has forecast a demand of 80 units for April and 160 units for May. The MPS

Item: 3-in gate valve
Quantity on hand:

Order policy: 80 units

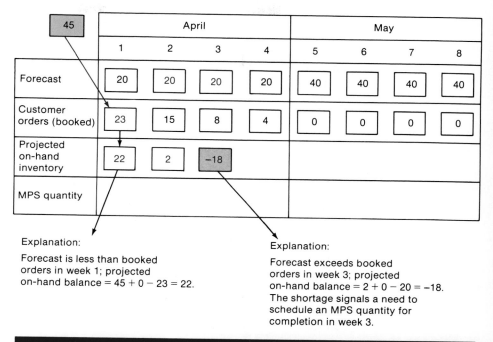

	45	April				May			
		1	2	3	4	5	6	7	8
Forecast		20	20	20	20	40	40	40	40
Customer orders (booked)		23	15	8	4	0	0	0	0
Projected on-hand inventory		22	2	−18					
MPS quantity									

Explanation:

Forecast is less than booked
orders in week 1; projected
on-hand balance = 45 + 0 − 23 = 22.

Explanation:

Forecast exceeds booked
orders in week 3; projected
on-hand balance = 2 + 0 − 20 = −18.
The shortage signals a need to
schedule an MPS quantity for
completion in week 3.

FIGURE 14.3   Projected On-Hand Inventory for 3-inch Gate Valve

should be expressed in weekly time periods to enable operations to closely
control production of components.

Figure 14.3 shows a partial MPS record, to which we'll later add one row.
The forecast row shows marketing's forecast of total sales allocated evenly over
the eight weeks in April and May. Keep in mind that these forecasts may not
reflect *actual* sales. The customer orders row shows the number of actual customer orders promised for shipment each week. Note that customer orders
for 23 valves exceed the forecast of 20 valves for week 1. However, total booked
orders (50) for April are still within that month's forecast (80). The projected
on-hand inventory row shows a stockout in week 3. The shortage signals a
need for more valves in that week. At this stage, the MPS row is still blank.

Determining the Timing and Size of MPS Quantities

The goal to keep in mind when developing a master production schedule is to
maintain a nonnegative projected on-hand inventory balance. As the scheduler

projects shortages in inventory, MPS quantities are scheduled to cover them. The following is a simplified procedure for developing a prospective MPS. Schedule completion of the first MPS quantity for the first week when you expect inventory of the product to run out. You can determine this week by calculating the projected on-hand inventory for each week until a shortage (a negative balance, such as −18 in Fig. 14.3) occurs. The addition of the newly scheduled MPS quantity will keep the projected on-hand inventory balance positive or zero. Continue calculating the projected on-hand inventory until you reach the next period when a shortage occurs. This shortage signals a need for a second MPS quantity. Repeat the process until you reach the end of the planning horizon. In this way, you proceed column by column through the MPS record, filling in the MPS quantities needed to avoid shortages.

APPLICATION 14.1

Determine a prospective MPS for the 3-inch gate valve for a lot size of 80 units. (We present other lot-sizing techniques in Chapter 15.)

Solution

Calculations for 3-Inch Valve Prospective MPS

Week	Beginning Inventory	Require-ments	Shortage?		MPS Quantity		Ending Inventory
1	45	− 23	No	+	0	=	22
2	22	− 20	No	+	0	=	2
3	2	− 20	Yes	+	80	=	62
4	62	− 20	No	+	0	=	42
5	42	− 40	No	+	0	=	2
6	2	− 40	Yes	+	80	=	42
7	42	− 40	No	+	0	=	2
8	2	− 40	Yes	+	80	=	42

The first shortage appears in week 3 (see Fig. 14.3). The firm will be 18 units short unless it schedules an MPS quantity for that period. With 80 units scheduled for completion in week 3, the ending inventory is projected to be 62 units. Those same 80 units will last until week 6, when another 80-unit lot must be scheduled. The second lot lasts until week 8, when a third lot must be scheduled. Figure 14.4 shows the prospective MPS.

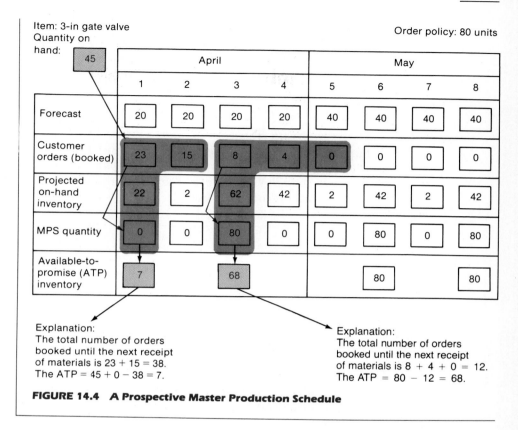

FIGURE 14.4   A Prospective Master Production Schedule

Calculating Available-to-Promise Quantities

The master production schedule shows **available-to-promise (ATP) inventory**, that is, the quantities of end items that marketing can promise to deliver on specified dates. Marketing can also use this information to set shipping dates for new customer orders. The general rule for calculating available-to-promise information is slightly different for the first (current) week of the schedule than for other weeks.

- *The first week:* The ATP inventory for the first week equals current on-hand inventory *plus* the MPS for the first week, *minus* the cumulative total of booked orders, up to (but not including) the week in which the next MPS quantity arrives.

- *Subsequent weeks:* For each week in which an MPS quantity is scheduled for completion, the ATP inventory equals that week's MPS quantity *minus* the cumulative total of booked orders from that week up to (but not including) the week in which the next MPS quantity arrives. Projected on-hand inventory isn't used in this calculation because on-hand inventory was used to calculate the first week's ATP inventory.

APPLICATION 14.2

Suppose that you have received the following orders for the 3-inch gate valve (shown in order of arrival). As they arrive you must make a decision to accept or reject them. Which can you accept for shipment and what would your updated MPS record look like?

Order	Amount (Units)	Week Requested
1	5	2
2	38	5
3	24	3
4	15	4

Solution

First, you must determine the ATP inventories for the 3-inch gate valve. Return to the data in Fig. 14.4. The ATP in the first week is 45 (current on-hand inventory) + 0 (MPS quantity) − [23 (booked orders) + 15 (booked orders)], or 7 units. The on-hand inventory of 45 units can satisfy all booked orders until week 3, when the first MPS quantity arrives. This leaves 7 extra units for new orders to be shipped in weeks 1 and 2 and beyond. The ATP inventory in week 3 is 80 − (8 + 4 + 0) = 68 units. These 68 units can be promised for shipment in weeks 3, 4, and 5. As there are no booked orders in May, ATP inventories for weeks 6 and 8 equal 80, the respective MPS quantities. Thus 80 units are available for new orders in weeks 6, 7, and 8.

You can now take action on the orders as follows:

Order	Action	Reason
1	Accept	The amount requested (5) is less than the ATP (7) for weeks 1 and 2. The adjusted ATP inventory for week 1 is 2 units.
2	Accept	The new ATP inventory for week 3 would be 68 − 38 = 30 units.
3	Accept	The new ATP for week 3 is 30 − 24 = 6 units.
4	Reject	The ATP for weeks 1 and 3 total only 8 (or 2 + 6) units, which is less than the quantity requested. Try to reschedule shipment for week 6 or later.

Figure 14.5 shows the updated MPS record.

Item: 3-in gate valve

Order policy: 80 units

Quantity on hand: 45

	April				May			
	1	2	3	4	5	6	7	8
Forecast	20	20	20	20	40	40	40	40
Customer orders (booked)	23	20	32	4	38	0	0	0
Projected on-hand inventory	22	2	50	30	−10	30	−10	30
MPS quantity	0	0	80	0	0	80	0	80
Available-to-promise (ATP) inventory	2		6			80		80

FIGURE 14.5 *Updated Master Production Schedule Record*

Note in Fig. 14.5 that only the customer orders booked, projected on-hand inventory, and ATP inventory rows have been adjusted. Do the negative projected on-hand inventory balances in weeks 5 and 7 pose a problem? Maybe. The forecast is for a total demand of 120 units through week 5, but only 117 units have currently been booked. The 45 units on hand plus the 80 units scheduled to arrive in week 3 will give a total supply of 125 units, leaving 8 units available to promise. If customers demand no more than 8 additional units in new bookings before week 5, there is no problem. However, if customers were to request 16 more (or 20 − 4) units for shipment in week 4 and 2 more (or 40 − 38) units in week 5—for a total of 18 units—the firm would be 10 units short in week 5.

There are two important lessons here. First, operations will never miss customer order due dates if marketing doesn't promise orders in excess of the ATP inventories *and* if the MPS quantities arrive on time. The reason is that ATP inventories are based on actual booked customer orders, not forecasts. Problems arise when orders are booked without planning adequate production in the MPS. Second, the projected on-hand inventory balance gives a "worst case" estimate of inventory balance. The reason is that the demand estimate is the greater of two quantities—either the forecast or actual customer orders booked. If projected on-hand inventory is negative, management should assess the situation before changing the MPS. Negative inventory projections might be the result of a mismatch in timing between forecasts and actual booked orders. In any case, once management revises the MPS, it determines the timing and size of revised MPS quantities in the same manner.

Linking the Production Plan and the MPS

In Applications 14.1 and 14.2, we didn't consider trade-offs associated with leveling production rates or the work force. Nor did we allow for anticipation inventories. Whenever the firm ran out of inventory or released production quantities, the MPS simply became an accumulation of forecasts. However, as you saw in Chapter 13, production planning *does* consider these trade-offs. The key to developing an acceptable MPS, therefore, is to link it *and* the production plan. One way to do so is to use production requirements, rather than forecasts, to determine MPS quantities. **Production requirements** are desired production quantities for a specific end item. To derive them, the scheduler must *disaggregate*, or break down, aggregate product family production quantities, taking into account the desired product mix within each family, current on-hand inventory, and booked customer orders. The resulting requirements then replace the forecasts used in the MPS.

The projected on-hand inventory row also undergoes a significant change. The scheduler does not include the current on-hand inventory and the booked customer orders to date because they are already part of the production requirements.

Consequently, the resulting MPS responds directly to the needs of the production plan. When management links the MPS and the production plan in this way, the MPS for any given item becomes part of an orchestrated plan to achieve company objectives.

ROUGH-CUT CAPACITY PLANNING ▲

After developing a prospective master production schedule, operations must determine whether the MPS is feasible in terms of the firm's available resources. It does so by performing feasibility checks of the MPS with **rough-cut capacity planning**, so called because it gives only a rough approximation of actual resource requirements. In this section we describe the **method of overall factors**, which is only one of several related approaches. We choose that method because it provides a simple illustration of rough-cut capacity planning. (See Berry, Schmitt, and Vollmann, 1982, for other, more sophisticated approaches.)

Developing Load Profiles

To illustrate the method of overall factors, let's consider a company that produces three items, A, B, and C, to stock. Figure 14.6 shows a prospective MPS for the three items. In order to develop the load profile for this schedule, the scheduler needs to (1) identify the critical work stations, (2) estimate direct labor factors for each item, and (3) develop load factors for each critical work station.

Critical work stations are operations that limit output because the need to use them frequently exceeds their capacity. The hours scheduled for work

Item	Week								Total Units
	1	2	3	4	5	6	7	8	
A	25	25	25	25	35	35	35	35	240
B	—	50	—	50	—	50	—	50	200
C	72	—	75	—	56	—	68	—	271

FIGURE 14.6 *Prospective Master Production Schedule*

at these stations are called **critical hours** because they determine the feasibility of a prospective MPS. Management tries to schedule time at critical work stations as efficiently as possible in order to maximize output. Thus if a critical work station has 200 hours of capacity per week and for some reason is used only 150 hours this week, the lost 50 hours cannot be used next week should 250 hours be required then.

The method of overall factors uses time standards (or gross estimates if standards aren't available) to estimate the number of direct labor hours required at each work station to produce one unit of each item. The scheduler then aggregates the hours for critical stations to obtain one direct labor factor and aggregates the hours for noncritical stations to obtain a second direct labor factor. Table 14.2 shows both factors for production of items A, B, and C. The scheduler has identified two critical work stations: 0810A and 0810B.

To determine the percentage of total labor hours each critical work station requires for a prospective MPS, the scheduler must consult past records. First, the scheduler determines the total number of direct labor hours that each critical station required over a specific time period. Next, the scheduler calculates the percentage of total critical hours this quantity represents. The result is a load factor for each critical work station that can be used to estimate labor requirements.

The Composite Load Profile. Using the prospective MPS, direct labor factors, and load factors, the scheduler can develop a **composite load profile**, which is an estimate of the direct labor hours for each critical work station, the

TABLE 14.2 **Direct Labor Factors**

Item	Critical Work Stations (hr)	Noncritical Work Stations (hr)	Total (hr)
A	1.60	0.00	1.60
B	6.07	8.00	14.07
C	5.04	4.00	9.04

total for all critical work stations, and the total for the plant. The procedure is as follows:

1. For each time period multiply each item's MPS quantity by its corresponding critical work station's direct labor factor. Calculate a total critical direct labor requirement for each period. Do the same for the total (critical plus noncritical) work station requirements.

2. For each time period multiply each critical work station's load factor by the total critical direct labor hours estimated in (1).

APPLICATION 14.3

Develop a load profile for the MPS in Fig. 14.6.

Solution

First, you must develop the load factors for the critical work stations: 0810A and 0820B. The accompanying table shows that the 4900 hours reported for work station 0810A represent 34 percent of total direct labor hours for all critical work stations. Thus the load factor for 0810A is 34 percent. Assume that station 0810A will continue to get 34 percent of the load on all critical stations. Similar reasoning yields a load factor of 66 percent for station 0820B.

Direct Labor Hours and Load Factors

Work Station	Quarter 1	2	3	4	Total	Load Factor (%)
0810A	1,140	1,285	1,175	1,300	4,900	34
0820B	2,430	2,540	2,100	2,380	9,450	66
Total critical hours	3,570	3,825	3,275	3,680	14,350	100
Total noncritical hours	5,200	5,150	5,000	5,300	20,650	

Using the direct labor factors in Table 14.2 and the load factors just calculated, you can develop a composite load profile for the prospective MPS. In the first week, the MPS calls for production of 25 units of A and 72 units of C. Use the critical work station labor factors for items A and C to obtain a combined critical direct labor requirement of 25(1.60) + 72(5.04) = 402.88 hours. The total direct labor requirement is 25(1.60) + 72(5.04 + 4.00) = 690.88 hours. You calculate labor requirements for other weeks in a similar manner. The results (rounded to the nearest whole number) are shown in the following table. You can then estimate that in the first week work station 0810A will need 137.02 [or 0.34 (403)] hours and that work station 0820B will need 265.98 [or 0.66 (403)] hours.

Load Profile Using Method of Overall Factors

Work Station	Week								Total
	1	2	3	4	5	6	7	8	
0810A (34%)	137	117	142	117	115	122	136	122	1008
0820B (66%)	266	227	276	227	223	238	263	238	1958
Total critical hours	403	344	418	344	338	360	399	360	2966
Total non-critical hours	288	400	300	400	224	400	272	400	2684
Total labor hours	691	744	718	744	562	760	671	760	5650

Load Profiles and the Authorization Decision. By comparing load profiles to labor capacities approved in the production plan, the scheduler can determine whether the prospective MPS is feasible. If total direct labor requirements fall within authorized limits of regular time plus overtime—and if the schedule meets other considerations, such as shipping promises and financial requirements—management would likely authorize the prospective MPS. If not, the master production scheduler would have to create a better schedule.

Evaluating the Method of Overall Factors

The method of overall factors is one of the simplest methods available for rough-cut capacity planning. The direct labor hours per unit used to calculate the load profiles can be a gross estimate based on accounting system data. Alternatively, it can be a more precise estimate based on detailed records of time standards and item routings.

Operations managers generally use gross estimates more often than precise estimates. Further, labor requirements usually are proportioned to each work station solely on the basis of historical labor requirements. The assumption that historical requirements represent future requirements implies that the product mix doesn't change. Also, the method of overall factors will not reflect a specific work station's large swings in capacity requirements on a week-to-week basis. Its assigned hours represent a fixed percentage of the total critical hours for a week. Nonetheless, the method works reasonably well in situations where the MPS is fairly stable with respect to product mix on a week-to-week basis. It also works well when the MPS is specified in monthly time periods and only a rough estimate of labor requirements is needed.

MANAGERIAL ISSUES ▲

The master production schedule is important because it links the firm's broad strategies, as expressed in the production plan, to more specific tactical plans that will enable a firm to achieve its objectives. So far we have focused on approaches to developing an MPS. However, the relationship of the MPS to competitive priorities, functional area interfaces, and the influence of computers on the MPS are important managerial issues.

The Master Production Schedule and Competitive Priorities

In Chapter 2 you learned that firms structure themselves to gain distinctive advantages over other firms by emphasizing one or more competitive priorities. With respect to the MPS, three basic strategies enable a firm to manage inventories in support of these priorities. The strategy chosen will determine the operations manager's approach to master production scheduling. Choosing among these strategies is related to the issues of inventory placement. (See Chapter 11.)

Make-to-Stock Strategy.   Product-focused firms tend to use a **make-to-stock strategy**, an approach in which the firm holds items in stock for immediate delivery. The main advantage of placing most inventory toward the finished-goods level is that customer delivery times are minimized. This strategy is feasible because most product-focused firms produce relatively few standardized products, for which they can make reasonably accurate forecasts. Thus these firms develop master production schedules for end items. Figure 14.7 demonstrates that make-to-stock operations typically produce a small number of finished products from a large number of different raw materials. Scheduling production of end items is easier from the standpoint of numbers alone.

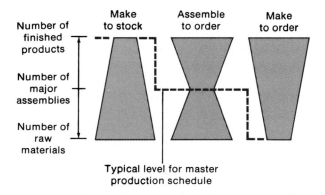

FIGURE 14.7   Relationship of the MPS to Competitive Priorities

(a)   (b)

(a) A make-to-stock strategy is used at the PenSupreme Dairy Products plant in Lancaster, Pennsylvania. These half-gallon containers of Hershey's chocolate milk are passing through the final phase of packaging. (b) Automobile manufacturing is an example of using an assemble-to-order strategy. These employees at a General Motors assembly line in Baltimore are assembling station wagons to customer specifications.

Assemble-to-Order Strategy.   The **assemble-to-order strategy** is an approach that produces end items with many options from relatively few major assemblies and components, after customer orders are received. This strategy addresses the two competitive priorities, product flexibility and fast delivery time. Operations holds the major assemblies and components in stock until a specific order comes in. Stocking end items would be economically prohibitive because forecasts are relatively inaccurate and there are so many options. For example, an automobile manufacturer can literally produce millions of cars, no two alike, to meet the mix of options and accessories demanded by customers.

As Fig. 14.7 shows, the number of different items produced and purchased assumes an hour-glass shape, emphasizing the relatively small number of major assemblies and components. Demand for these parts is fairly easy to forecast because they are common to all products. Consequently, operations bases master production scheduling on the major assemblies and components, rather than end items.

Make-to-Order Strategy.   Many process-focused firms use a **make-to-order strategy**, whereby operations produces end items to customer specifications. This strategy provides a high degree of product flexibility. Since most end items, components, and assemblies are custom-made, the number of these items usually exceeds the number of raw materials used to produce them, as illustrated in Fig. 14.7. Since a few raw materials are common to many products, it is easier for an organization to forecast demand for them rather than end items or major assemblies. In such situations, operations generally schedules raw-material utilization only. However, end-item scheduling is feasible if customer orders allow sufficiently long delivery times.

The Meade Packaging Plant in Atlanta uses a make-to-order strategy to turn out paper containers for soft drinks, eggs, and a dozen other uses. Here, cases for six-packs of Pepsi are sorted.

Functional Interfaces

The master production scheduling process involves all of a firm's functional areas. As in the development of a production plan, operations needs inputs from various areas in order to develop an MPS that achieves production plan objectives and organizational goals. However, interaction with various functional areas doesn't end with the inputs they provide.

Sometimes the way a firm competes prompts interaction through the MPS. For example, operations can create a master production schedule that maintains a stable work force and high utilization of critical work centers. However, such a strategy reduces the firm's flexibility to respond to changes in customer demand. Reducing flexibility in this way may not be in the best interests of the firm from a marketing perspective. Trade-offs must be made in responding to customer-desired shipping dates, reducing inventory levels, and minimizing the costs of revising production schedules. Situations such as this require cooperation between marketing and manufacturing. Some companies require the vice-presidents of marketing and manufacturing to jointly authorize major MPS changes to ensure mutual resolution of these issues.

The MPS can also be used as a basis for more routine planning functions. Finance uses the MPS to estimate budgets and cash flows. Marketing uses it to project the impact of product mix changes on the firm's ability to satisfy customer demand and manage delivery schedules. Using rough-cut capacity planning, manufacturing can estimate the effects of MPS changes on loads at critical work stations. In general, all the firm's functional areas need the MPS.

Computer-Assisted Master Production Scheduling

Applications of the techniques for master production scheduling and rough-cut capacity planning discussed in this chapter require the use of computers. When thousands of items are involved, developing the MPS manually is an enormous, if not impossible, task. Most major computer vendors and many companies specializing in software for manufacturing systems have developed software packages that perform the types of calculations we have presented. These programs also provide managers with detailed reports that are useful for analyzing the MPS. Personal computers with their excellent graphic capabilities give managers access to many MPS-related reports, such as the load profile, in readable and useful formats. Interfacing a personal computer with a mainframe computer allows managers to ask "what–if" questions about master production schedules and to estimate MPS effects using the data provided.

The techniques that we have presented in this chapter are descriptive in the sense that modifications to the schedule are left to the discretion of the master production scheduler. The techniques project only what may happen *if* the prospective MPS is implemented. They do not prescribe what *should* be done. Various prescriptive approaches have been proposed, and, if you are interested, you can pursue them in Hax and Meal (1975), Newson (1975), and other publications referred to at the end of this chapter.

SOLVED PROBLEMS

1. You have the data shown in Fig. 14.8 for a particular end item. The order policy is to produce in lots of 50 units.

	Week									
Quantity on Hand: 5	1	2	3	4	5	6	7	8	9	10
Forecast	20	10	40	10	0	0	40	20	30	10
Customer orders (booked)	30	20	5	8	0	0	0	0	0	0
Projected on-hand inventory	25	5	−35							
MPS quantity	50									
Available-to-promise (ATP) inventory	5									

FIGURE 14.8

a. Develop a prospective MPS and calculate the available-to-promise inventory quantities.

b. Decide which of the following customer orders you would accept. What would the updated MPS look like? The three orders arrived in the following sequence:

Order	Quantity	Week Due
1	15	6
2	4	2
3	32	3

Solution

Figure 14.9 (a) shows the prospective MPS, including ATP quantities. As indicated, we will need the first MPS quantity in week 1, another order in week 3,

	Week									
Quantity on Hand: 5	1	2	3	4	5	6	7	8	9	10
Forecast	20	10	40	10	0	0	40	20	30	10
Customer orders (booked)	30	20	5	8	0	0	0	0	0	0
Projected on-hand inventory	25	5	15	5	5	5	15	45	15	5
MPS quantity	50		50					50	50	
Available-to-promise (ATP) inventory	5		37					50	50	

(a) Prospective MPS

	Week									
Quantity on Hand: 5	1	2	3	4	5	6	7	8	9	10
Forecast	20	10	40	10	0	0	40	20	30	10
Customer orders (booked)	30	24	5	8	0	15	0	0	0	0
Projected on-hand inventory	25	1	11	1	1	−14	−4	26	−4	−14
MPS quantity	50		50					50	50	
Available-to-promise (ATP) inventory	1		22					50	50	

(b) Updated MPS

FIGURE 14.9

a third in week 7, and a fourth in week 8. For the indicated ATP inventories and assuming that we have to commit to the orders in the order in which they arrived, we would accept the first two customer orders and reject the third.

We could ask the third customer if she would accept a shipment of 23 (1 from week 1 ATP and 22 from week 3 ATP) in week 3, with another 9 units following in week 7. The updated MPS record, reflecting the two accepted orders, is shown in Fig. 14.9(b).

The latter part of the schedule shows negative projected inventory balances, so we should verify the forecasts. If the forecasts for weeks 3, 4, and 7–10 remain valid, we could revise the MPS starting in week 6. However, our ATP quantities show that 123 (or 1 + 22 + 50 + 50) units of this item will be available for delivery over the next 10 weeks.

2. The Acme Rocket Company produces two products for crafty coyotes interested in a road-runner dinner. The harness rocket (HR) is designed for quick acceleration and low-level flying in the pursuit of fleeing road runners. The shoe rocket (SR) is useful for high-speed chases over long, straight Arizona roads. The prospective MPS shown in Fig. 14.10 has been proposed.

Item	Week					Total Units
	1	2	3	4	5	
HR	20	20	20	40	40	140
SR	30	—	30	—	30	90

FIGURE 14.10

The Acme Rocket Company has two critical work stations: powder packing (PP) and wick setting (WS). Historically, PP has had 70 percent and WS 30 percent of the critical work station hours. The direct labor hours per unit are:

Item	Critical Work Stations (hr)	Noncritical Work Stations (hr)	Total (hr)
HR	10.0	6.0	16.0
SR	7.2	3.5	10.7

a. Create a load profile for weeks 1–5 based on the prospective MPS, using the method of overall factors.

b. Suppose that the production plan specified a total of 680 labor hours per week, including 420 hours at the critical work stations. Do you see any potential problems with the prospective MPS? If so, what changes to the schedule do you propose?

TABLE 14.3

| | Week | | | | | |
Work Station	1	2	3	4	5	Total
PP (70%)	291	140	291	280	431	1433
WS (30%)	125	60	125	120	185	615
Total critical hours*	416	200	416	400	616	2048
Total noncritical hours†	225	120	225	240	345	1155
Total labor hours	641	320	641	640	961	3203

*MPS quantity for HR × 10.00 hr/unit + MPS quantity for SR × 7.2 hr/unit.
†MPS quantity for HR × 6.0 hr/unit + MPS quantity for SR × 3.5 hr/unit.

Solution

Table 14.3 shows the load profile for weeks 1–5. Note that the suggested schedule results in an uneven load on the factory. In particular, the week 5 load exceeds available resources by 281 total labor hours (961 − 680), including 196 hours (616 − 420) at the critical work stations.

A change that would help is to shift 30 units of SR production from week 5 to week 2, as shown in Table 14.4. This change increases the inventory holding cost of SR but satisfies the capacity constraints. (The profile for weeks 1, 3, and 4 doesn't change.) This change results in approximately 640 labor hours per week.

TABLE 14.4

Work Station	Week 2	Week 5
PP (70%)	291	280
WS (30%)	125	120
Total critical hours	416	400
Total noncritical hours	225	240
Total labor hours	641	640

FORMULA REVIEW

1. Projected on-hand inventory balance for MPS record:

$$I_t = I_{t-1} + MPS_t - \max(F_t \text{ or } CO_t)$$

2. Available-to-promise inventory (ATP) quantities:

First week = Current on-hand inventory *plus* MPS quantity due in first week *minus* cumulative total booked orders until (but not including) the week of arrival of the next MPS quantity.

Subsequent weeks (having an MPS quantity due) = MPS quantity *minus* cumulative total booked orders from that week until (but not including) the week of arrival of the next MPS quantity.

CHAPTER HIGHLIGHTS

- A master production schedule (MPS) expresses operation's plan of production for a specific period of time. It is stated in terms of end items, which may be either shippable products or the highest level assemblies used to make them.

- The master production scheduling process is iterative. A prospective MPS is developed within the overall guidelines of the production plan. If the resources are available, the prospective schedule is authorized for implementation. If not, the prospective MPS or the production plan has to be changed.

- The primary duty of the master production scheduler is to prepare the master production schedule. Other duties include specifying promise dates for incoming customer orders, evaluating the impact of changes in the MPS, revising the MPS as necessary, and communicating with managers when conflicts arise.

- A master production schedule record for an item typically contains information on ordering policy as well as forecast (or production) requirements, booked customer orders, on-hand inventory balances, available-to-promise inventory quantities, and MPS quantities for future periods. The available-to-promise inventory information helps to provide valid promise dates for new customer orders.

- In the overall factor method of rough-cut capacity planning, all direct labor hours for an item are accumulated. This figure multiplied by the MPS quantity for the item yields an estimate of overall plant load. The overall load is subdivided into critical and noncritical work station loads. Individual station loads are estimated using historically based percentages.

- The techniques used for master production scheduling depend on the competitive priorities of the firm. Firms using a make-to-stock strategy typically schedule production of end items, whereas firms using a make-to-order strategy schedule purchased items. Firms using an assemble-to-order strategy schedule major components or assemblies to capitalize on commonality of parts for various end-item parents.

- The MPS is a useful input to the plans developed by finance and marketing, as well as manufacturing.

- Most major computer vendors and many software companies have developed software packages for various MPS techniques.

KEY TERMS

	Week							
Quantity on Hand: 35	1	2	3	4	5	6	7	8
Forecast	15	15	20	20	20	20	30	30
Customer orders (booked)	10	16	5	6	9	0	0	0
Projected on-hand inventory								
MPS quantity								

FIGURE 14.11

STUDY QUESTIONS

1. How does a master production schedule (MPS) differ from a production plan?
2. What is the purpose of the MPS?
3. Briefly explain master production scheduling to your boss, who has not heard of it before. Why are the alternative schedules called prospective?
4. How can the available-to-promise (ATP) inventory information in an MPS record be used?
5. Why is the on-hand balance different from the ATP inventory at any particular time?
6. What are the advantages of linking the MPS and the production plan?
7. If you were a master production scheduler in a company using an assemble-to-order strategy, would you prepare a schedule for end items or some group of intermediate level items? Explain.
8. Why is it important to do rough-cut capacity planning?
9. What are the underlying assumptions of the method of overall factors?
10. Why are competitive priorities important considerations for master production scheduling?

PROBLEMS

Review Problems

1. Complete the MPS record in Fig. 14.11 for a single item. At present there are 35 units of the item in inventory. Each order is for 50 units.
2. Complete the MPS record shown in Fig. 14.12 for a single item. There are currently 85 units of the item in inventory. Each order is for 100 units.
3. The following data apply to an end item.
   - The forecasts for the next 10 weeks are 35, 20, 40, 60, 30, 25, 0, 40, 0, and 50 units.
   - The current on-hand inventory is 100 units.
   - The order policy is to produce in lots of 75.

	January				February			
Quantity on Hand: 85	1	2	3	4	5	6	7	8
Forecast	75	75	50	50	65	65	75	75
Customer orders (booked)	50	0	60	0	40	70	0	0
Projected on-hand inventory								
MPS quantity								

FIGURE 14.12

- The booked customer orders for the item, starting with week 1, are 27, 25, 15, 9, 0, 0, 0, 0, 0, and 0 units.
- At present, there are no MPS quantities for this item.

a. Develop a prospective MPS and calculate the available-to-promise inventory quantities.

b. A customer needs 100 units of this item. What is the earliest shipping date for the entire order that you could give the customer?

4. You have the following information for a particular end item.

- The forecasts for the next 10 weeks are 50, 75, 75, 100, 100, 0, 0, 50, 50, and 75 units.
- The current on-hand inventory is 15 units.
- The order policy is to produce in lots of 100 units. There is an MPS quantity of 100 units scheduled for completion in week 1.
- The booked customer orders, starting with week 1, are 60, 45, 20, 15, 0, 0, 0, 0, 0, and 0 units.

a. Develop a prospective MPS and calculate the available-to-promise inventory quantities.

b. Three customer orders have arrived in the following sequence.

Order	Quantity	Week Desired
1	30	3
2	80	3
3	40	4

Which of the orders would you accept? (Assume that you must commit to them in sequence and that you cannot change the

desired shipping dates or the MPS.) What would the updated MPS look like?

5. Morrison Electronics has forecasted the following demand for one of its products for the next eight weeks: 60, 65, 70, 70, 75, 75, 75, and 75. The booked customer orders for this product, starting in week 1 are 50, 60, 55, 40, 35, 0, 0, and 0 units. The current on-hand inventory is 100 units, and the order quantity is 125 units.

a. Develop a prospective MPS (including ATP quantities) for this product.

b. The marketing department at Morrison has revised its forecasts. Starting with week 1, the new forecasts are 60, 65, 80, 80, 90, 90, 100, and 100 units. Prepare a revised MPS record, assuming that the prospective MPS you developed in (a) doesn't change. Comment on the situation that Morrison Electronics now faces.

6. a. Complete the MPS in Fig. 14.13 for a single end item. There are currently 400 units in inventory, and each order is for 800 units.

b. Three customer orders have arrived in the following sequence.

Order	Quantity	Week Desired
1	600	7
2	400	3
3	425	4

Assuming that you must commit to the orders in sequence, which orders would you accept?

c. Suppose that management wishes to fulfill *all* the customer orders by the desired shipping dates. Revise the MPS to accomplish this task. What other factors must you consider when making this revision?

		Week									
Quantity on Hand: 400		1	2	3	4	5	6	7	8	9	10
Forecast		200	200	400	400	800	800	800	800	400	400
Customer orders (booked)		150		225	200	300			275		
Projected on-hand inventory											
MPS quantity											
Available-to-promise (ATP) inventory											

FIGURE 14.13

7. The Conestoga Wagon Company produces a single product, a motorized child-sized version of the original Conestoga wagon. The following prospective MPS has been proposed.

Week	1	2	3	4	5	6
Units	30	30	40	40	50	50

There is one critical work station in the shop: the frame-building work station. Each wagon requires three direct-labor hours at this critical work station. The total direct-labor hours per unit is 18 hours.

a. Using the method of overall factors, determine the direct labor requirements at the frame-building work station.

b. Assume that the MPS was designed to meet exactly forecasted requirements each period and that there are no available on-hand inventories. Suppose that the available labor hours at the frame-building work station are 115 hours per week for weeks 1–4 and 135 hours per week for weeks 5 and 6. Revise the MPS to ensure that no stockouts occur, capacity constraints are satisfied, and inventory is minimized.

8. Marshall Fans produces a lightweight desktop fan. A prospective MPS for the fan has been proposed:

Month	Jan	Feb	Mar	Apr	May	Jun
Units	100	200	200	600	700	750

Two critical work stations are involved in the production of the fan: 401A and 401B. Historically, 401A has had 80 percent and 401B has had 20 percent of the total critical work station hours.

The direct labor hours per unit are: critical work stations, 1.2; noncritical work stations, 3.8; and total, 5. Using the method of overall factors, determine the direct labor requirements for each individual critical work station and for the entire plant.

9. The Avis Ladder Company produces two products, a deluxe ladder (DL) and a standard ladder (SL). The following prospective MPS has been proposed for the two products.

Item	Week 1	2	3	4	5	6	Total
DL	30	30	40	40	40	40	220
SL	50	—	50	—	50	—	150

The direct labor hours per unit are:

Item	Critical Work Stations (hr)	Noncritical Work Stations (hr)	Total (hr)
DL	12.0	4.5	16.5
SL	6.2	3.1	9.3

There are three critical work stations: Z101, Z105, and Z107. Historically, Z101, Z105, and Z107 have accounted for 40 percent, 30 percent, and 30 percent of the direct labor hours, respectively.

a. Create a load profile based on the prospective MPS, using the method of overall factors.

b. Suppose that the production plan specified a total of 950 direct labor hours of which 700 hours are at the critical work stations. Do you see any potential problems with the prospective schedule? If so, propose a better MPS.

Advanced Problems

A computer package is recommended for Problems 10, 13, 14, and 15.

10. The marketing department of NEVED Home-help Products has forecasted the following for the company's two products.

Product	Month Mar	Apr	May
Home energy controller (HEC)	800	1200	1000
Home personal robot (HPR)	140	180	160

The company has 550 units of HEC and 90 units of HPR on hand. The company orders HEC in lots of 400 units and HPR in lots of 80 units.

Quanity on Hand: 10	Week							
	1	2	3	4	5	6	7	8
Production requirements	50	50	50	50	25	25	25	25
Customer orders (booked)	60	45	40	35	10	5	5	0
Projected on-hand inventory								
MPS quantity	50	50						
Available-to-promise (ATP) inventory								

FIGURE 14.14

One lot of HEC is scheduled to be received in the second week of March. The company has received the following orders.

	Shipping Dates							
	Mar				Apr			
	1	2	3	4	5	6	7	8
HEC	—	210	—	100	175	—	145	100
HPR	50	20	—	—	20	25	—	—

Management likes to have the MPS expressed in weekly time periods and typically allocates monthly forecasts evenly over the weeks of the month. (Assume 4 weeks per month.)

a. Develop a prospective MPS for each product.
b. A potential customer is interested in buying 900 units of HEC and 90 units of HPR. What is the earliest realistic date that marketing can promise delivery of the HEC units? The HPR units?
c. The customer has decided to take delivery of the two products at the same time. What is the earliest date that marketing could deliver 900 units of HEC and 90 units of HPR to the customer?

11. Complete the MPS record in Fig. 14.14. This partial record shows the *production requirements* for a single end item. There are currently 10 units on hand and the order policy is to produce in lots of 50. Lots are scheduled for completion in weeks 1 and 2.

12. The *production requirements* for a two-horsepower motor for the next six weeks are 0, 40, 0, 40, 55, and 55 units. Marketing has booked orders totaling 25 units in the first (current) week and 10 units in the third week. Currently, there are 35 motors on hand. The ordering policy is to order the exact quantity required to meet production requirements each week.

a. Develop the MPS record for the motor.
b. A distributor of the motor places an order for 45 units. What is the appropriate shipping date for the entire order?

13. Production of 160 units in January, 320 units in February, and 160 units in March has been approved for the seismic-sensory product family manufactured at the Hilliard facility of Sloan Automated, Inc. There are three products in this product family. The product mix ratio for products A, B, and C for the past two years has been 35 percent, 40 percent, and 25 percent, respectively. There are 30 units of product C on hand. The company orders product C in lots of 40 units and has accepted orders of 25, 12, 8, 10, 2, and 3 of product C in weeks 1–6, respectively. Prepare a prospective MPS for product C and calculate the available-to-promise inventory quantities. Management wishes to allocate the monthly production requirements evenly over the month. Assume that each month has 4 weeks.

14. The master production scheduler at your company has developed the prospective MPS shown in Fig. 14.15 for the three items your company produces. There are two critical work stations in the shop: WSA, which has recorded 30 percent of the hours at the critical work stations, and WSB, which has recorded the rest. Your pro-

Item	Month						Total Units
	Jan	Feb	Mar	Apr	May	Jun	
A	40	40	60	60	50	50	300
B	30	—	30	—	30	—	90
C	—	90	—	60	—	110	260

FIGURE 14.15

duction plan has a constant work-force size that yields 900 hours per month, of which 260 hours total are at the critical work stations. Work station WSA has been allocated 78 hours per month, and WSB has been allocated 182 hours. Direct labor hours per unit are:

Item	Critical Work Stations	Noncritical Work Stations	Total
A	2	4	6
B	1	6	7
C	3	5	8

a. Prepare a load profile for the prospective MPS using the method of overall factors. Comment on the feasibility of this schedule.
b. Prepare an alternative MPS to the one proposed by the master production scheduler that satisfies the labor budget specified in the production plan. Assume that the master production scheduler adhered to the following guidelines.

	Cumulative Production Required by End of Month		
Month	A	B	C
Jan	0	30	0
Feb	80	30	90
Mar	80	60	90
Apr	200	60	150
May	200	90	150
Jun	300	90	260

For example, you need no units of A in January, but you do need 80 by the end of February. Also, you need no units of A in March, but by the end of April the cumulative production of A must be 200 units because you need 120 units in April.

15. Mary Reynolds, master production scheduler at Leader Products, has just received the following forecasts for the next six months for the company's two products, A and B.

Item	Jul	Aug	Sep	Oct	Nov	Dec
A	60	60	40	40	80	80
B	30	30	30	15	15	15

Marketing has booked orders for product A as follows (beginning with July): 55, 30, 15, 5, 0, and 0 units. The booked orders for product B are 18, 12, 3, 0, 2, and 0 units.

Product A is ordered in lots of 80, and product B in lots of 30. There are currently 100 units of A and 40 units of B in inventory. Reynolds also has the following information concerning the production of A and B (in direct labor hours per unit).

Item	Critical Work Stations	Noncritical Work Stations	Total
A	6	3	9
B	4	7	11

There are two critical work stations: S111 and S222. Historically, S111 has used 45 percent of total critical work station capacity, with S222 using the balance. The production plan for Leader Products specifies a total of 750 direct labor per month, which includes 450 hours at the critical work stations.

a. Develop a prospective MPS for each product.
b. Analyze the feasibility of these prospective schedules using the method of overall factors.
c. If the prospective schedules are infeasible, develop a revised MPS for each product. (*Hint:* Do not revise the MPS of both products simultaneously.)

SELECTED REFERENCES

Bahl, H. C., and L. P. Ritzman, "An Empirical Investigation of Different Strategies for Material Requirements Planning," *Journal of Operations Management,* vol. 3, no. 2 (1983), pp. 67–77.

Berry, W. L., T. G. Schmitt, and T. E. Vollmann, "Capacity Planning Techniques for Manufacturing Control Systems: Information Requirements and Operational Features," *Journal of Operations Management*, vol. 3, no. 1 (November 1982), pp. 13–25.

Berry, W. L., T. E. Vollman, and D. C. Whybark, *Master Production Scheduling: Principles and Practices*. Falls Church, Va.: American Production and Inventory Control Society, Inc., 1979.

Bitran, G. R., and A. C. Hax, "On the Design of Hierarchical Production Planning Systems," *Decision Sciences*, vol. 8, no. 1 (January 1977), pp. 28–55.

Chung, C. H., and L. Krajewski, "Planning Horizons for Master Production Scheduling," *Journal of Operations Management*, vol. 4, no. 4 (August 1984).

Everdell, R., and W. Chamberlain, "Master Scheduling in a Multi-Plant Environment," *Proceedings of the 23rd Annual American Production and Inventory Control Society Conference*. Los Angeles (October 14–17, 1980), pp. 421–429.

Hax, A. C., and H. C. Meal, "Hierarchical Integration of Production Planning and Scheduling." In M. A. Geisler (Ed.), *Studies in Management Sciences*, vol. 1, *Logistics*. New York: North Holland-American Elsevier, 1975, pp. 53–69.

Ling, R., "Master Scheduling in a Make-to-Order Environment," *Inventories and Production*, vol. 1, no. 3 (July–August 1981), pp. 17–21.

Mangiameli, P., and L. Krajewski, "The Effects of Workforce Strategies on Manufacturing Operations," *Journal of Operations Management*, vol. 3, no. 4 (August 1983), pp. 183–196.

Newson, E. P., "Multi-Item Lot Size Scheduling by Heuristic, Part I: With Fixed Resources; Part II: With Variable Resources," *Management Science*, vol. 21, no. 10 (June 1975), pp. 1186–1203.

Orlicky, J., *Material Requirements Planning*. New York: McGraw-Hill, 1975.

Proud, J. F., "Controlling the Master Schedule," *Production and Inventory Management*, vol. 22, no. 2 (Second Quarter 1981), pp. 78–90.

Vollmann, T. E., W. L. Berry, and D. C. Whybark, *Manufacturing Planning and Control Systems*. Homewood, Ill.: Irwin, 1988.

Wight, O., *Production and Inventory Management in the Computer Age*. Boston: Cahners Books, 1974.

CHAPTER 15

MATERIAL REQUIREMENTS PLANNING

▲ Chapter Outline

Key Questions for Managers

What information is available from MRP systems that will help us to manage materials better?

Is MRP appropriate for our firm? Who benefits the most from MRP systems?

What prerequisites do we have to meet to successfully implement MRP?

Can we use MRP for nonmanufacturing inventories?

How can we couple MRP with other decision areas?

How important is our choice of lot-sizing rule?

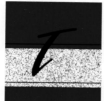he company that successfully balances customer service with inventory management and investment gains a competitive edge. Thus the ability to maintain an efficient flow of materials from suppliers and to effectively manage internal activities relating to materials is essential to a profitable operation. After developing a realistic master production schedule, operations tries to ensure that all materials and other resources needed to produce finished products will be available at the right time. This is easier said than done because a manufacturer may have to keep track of thousands of components, assemblies, and raw materials.

Recall that in Chapter 12 we discussed independent-demand inventory control systems. However, component items that are produced to meet production plan requirements for parent items have *dependent demand.* Such parent–component dependent relationships, which are expressed in bills of materials (see Chapter 11), greatly increase the complexity of inventory management. The complexity comes from interdependencies between items: Production cannot complete an order for a parent if even one of its components is missing. For years, many companies tried to manage production and delivery of dependent-demand components with independent-demand systems, but the outcome was seldom satisfactory. As a result, **material requirements planning (MRP)**—a computerized information system—was developed specifically to aid in managing dependent-demand inventory and scheduling replenishment orders. The MRP system has allowed many businesses to reduce inventory levels, better utilize labor and facilities, and increase customer service.

We begin this chapter with the basics of MRP, including a brief comparison of an MRP system and a traditional reorder point system. After noting the problems associated with applying independent-demand inventory methods to dependent-demand items, we illustrate the process of calculating an MRP inventory record. We then show the implications that choice of lot-sizing rules has on inventory management and how MRP helps managers cope with production capacity limitations. Finally, we explore MRP as an information system and the issues concerning implementation of an MRP system.

BASICS OF MATERIAL
REQUIREMENTS PLANNING ▲

During the past decade, many manufacturing firms have switched from traditional reorder point systems to MRP systems. Impetus for change came from the American Production and Inventory Control Society, led by such pioneers as Joseph Orlicky (1975), George Plossl (1973), and Oliver Wight (1979). The computer program logic built into an MRP system is based on two principles that set it apart from a reorder point system:

1. MRP *derives* dependent demand for components, subassemblies, and raw materials from the production schedules of their parents. By contrast, in reorder point systems, analysts use statistical forecasting methods to set reorder points.

2. MRP *offsets* replenishment orders (such as production schedules and purchase orders) relative to the date they are needed. That is, if operations needs to replenish an item in week 5 to avoid a stockout, and if the lead time is 3 weeks, the system issues a notice to order in week 2. By contrast, in reorder point systems, items aren't reordered until a reorder point is reached.

The key ingredients of MRP are master production schedules, bills of materials, and inventory records. Using information from these sources, the MRP system identifies actions that operations must take in order to stay on schedule. An MRP system can help in many ways. For example, when American Sterilizer Company introduced MRP at its Hospital Products and Systems Group, it increased on-time customer deliveries from 70 percent to 95 percent. It also cut overtime by at least 50 percent, reduced component shortages by over 80 percent, lowered indirect labor by 24 percent, and reduced direct labor by 7 percent.

A survey of industrial firms showed that although such benefits are not always realized, neither are they unusual (see Schroeder et al., 1981). The average MRP user increased inventory turns from 3.2 to 4.3, improved on-time deliveries from 61 percent to 76 percent, and cut delivery lead times from 71 to 59 days. Almost two thirds of the firms surveyed now use MRP and most switched after 1971. To understand better the benefits of MRP, let's begin by examining the shortcomings of independent-demand inventory systems when applied to dependent-demand items. Then we'll demonstrate how the system computes an item's MRP inventory record.

Shortcomings of Independent-Demand Systems

Consider a company that makes office furniture. Two of its many products are desk chairs A and B. These end items (parents) experience fairly constant demand rates: Chair A averages 30 units per week, and chair B 20 units per week. One of the components needed in assembling both items is a pedestal assembly, item C. Each chair requires one unit of item C. As it is used only in these chairs, item C experiences an average demand of 50 (or 30 + 20) units per week.

Assembly lead times for items A and B are one week, assuming that their components are available when needed. In order to manage all three items, the company uses a continuous review system. Operations calculates lot sizes and reorder points according to the concepts in Chapter 12. Suppose that $Q = 150$ and $R = 60$ for chair A, $Q = 120$ and $R = 40$ for chair B, and $Q = 230$ and $R = 150$ for item C. Figure 15.1 shows what happens whenever an item's inventory level reaches its reorder point.*

Inventory levels for chairs A and B deplete at a uniform, predictable rate. Note, however, that the demand pattern for the pedestal assembly C appears in chunks of 120 (week 1), 150 (week 2), or 270 (week 7) units at a time. The *average* is 50 units per week, but in many weeks (such as weeks 3 through 6) there is no actual demand. Consequently, the pedestal assembly doesn't approach the reorder point gradually. In week 7, the quantity of item C falls precipitously from an inventory balance of 240 units to a stockout of 30 units. Completing an order takes two weeks, so production of chair A is delayed until week 9. Producing 150 units of A takes another week. Thus chair A also suffers a stockout.

What went wrong? First, the assumption of a uniform, continuous demand rate was unrealistic. Typically, component demand is lumpy because of production lot-size decisions made for parent items. Forecasting lumpy demand using statistical methods results in large forecasting errors. Compensating for such errors by increasing safety stock is costly, and even then there is no guarantee that stockouts can be avoided.

Second, assuming that demand for the inventory items was independent was wrong. In fact, the parents and component were linked through bills of materials. The reorder point system failed to recognize that requirement schedules for components, assemblies, and raw materials needed to make par-

---

*Because the lead time for stock replenishment is so short, on-hand inventory equals the inventory position (except during the lead time) in this example. No scheduled receipts are outstanding when an order is placed.

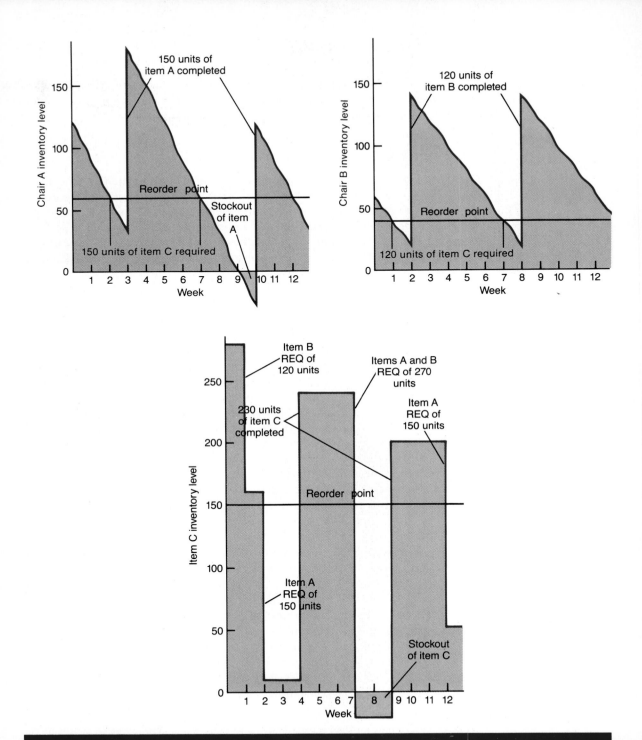

FIGURE 15.1 Application of the Reorder Point System to Dependent-Demand Inventory

ent items are based on the production schedules of the parents. For example, item C demand is based on the production schedules of chairs A and B. In reorder point systems, analysts don't use information from parent-item schedules to manage the inventories of components or subassemblies.

Finally, the reorder point system provided no forward visibility for planning purposes. Instead, operations assumed that it could rely on past demand patterns to establish reasonable reorder points and safety stocks. Actually, if demand for the pedestal assembly were uniform and predictable, there would be no need to look beyond the present. However, this condition is often not the case for dependent-demand items. If the analyst had known the schedules for chairs A and B, he or she could have predicted in week 1 that trouble would arise in week 7. Knowing that the lead time for item C is two weeks, the analyst would have arranged to produce enough C to avoid the stockout.

To correct for these problems, a better way is needed to integrate and use the information already available to estimate future requirements for dependent-demand items more accurately. Material requirements planning provides one such approach. Let's now turn to the computation of an MRP inventory record.

The Material Requirements Planning Inventory Record

The **MRP inventory record** shows an item's planning factors, gross requirements, scheduled receipts, projected on-hand inventory, planned order receipts, and planned order releases. In many ways it resembles an MPS record (see Chapter 14). The body of the record divides the future into time periods called *time buckets*. These time periods normally represent weeks, but they can be expressed in days or months. Figure 15.2 shows a partially completed MRP inventory record for item C, as well as the MPSs for its parents, chairs A and B.

Planning Factors.   Although the MRP inventory record has no standard format, the item number and description typically appear at the top of the record. Three planning factors—the preassigned lead time, lot-sizing rule, and safety stock—usually appear in the upper right-hand corner. In our example, item C's lot size is 230 units, its lead time is two weeks, and safety stock is 50 units. Management must select these quantities in advance. An inventory planner updates these factors whenever conditions, such as lead time, change.

Gross Requirements.   Figure 15.2 shows item C's gross requirements for the next 8 weeks. The pedestal assembly's requirements exhibit lumpy demand: Operations will withdraw inventory in only four of the eight weeks. These **gross requirements** are the total demand derived from *all* parent production plans. They also include demand not otherwise accounted for, such as replace-

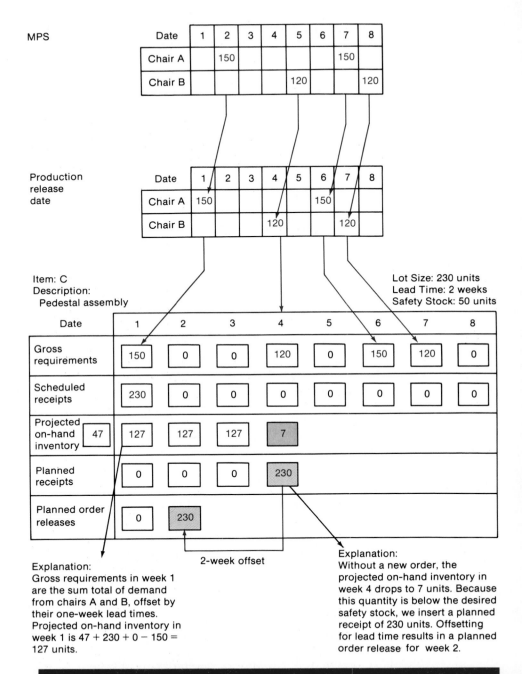

FIGURE 15.2   Partially Completed MRP Inventory Record for Item C

ment parts for units already sold. Since parents A and B are end items, their production plans are found in the master production schedules (MPSs).

Recall from Chapter 14 that in an item's MPS a scheduler states the date by which production of a particular quantity must be completed. The *production release date* is the completion date specified in the MPS, adjusted for the item's lead time. The MRP system works with release dates in order to properly schedule production and delivery for components and assemblies. The reason is that the MRP computer program logic anticipates the removal of all materials required by a parent's production order from inventory at the *beginning* of that item's lead time—when the scheduler first releases the order to the shop.* Note that in Fig. 15.2 item C's gross requirements are derived one-for-one from the MPS quantities of A and B, offset by their one-week lead times.† These one-for-one relationships come from the usage quantities specified in the bills of materials (see Chapter 11).

Scheduled Receipts.   As defined in Chapter 11, scheduled receipts (sometimes called open orders) are orders that have been placed but not yet completed. For a purchased item, the scheduled receipt could be in one of several stages: being ordered by a buyer, being processed by a vendor, being transported to the purchaser, or being inspected by the purchaser's receiving department. If production is making the item in-house, the order could be on the shop floor being processed, waiting for components, waiting in queue, or waiting to be moved to its next operation. According to Fig. 15.2, one 230-unit order of item C is due in week 1. Based on the two-week lead time, the inventory planner probably released the order two weeks ago. Such orders normally don't show up on a record further into the future than the item's lead time.‡

Projected On-Hand Inventory.   The first entry in Fig. 15.2, 47 units, indicates on-hand inventory available at the time the record was computed. As with scheduled receipts, each actual withdrawal and receipt must be entered into the MRP database. Then, when the MRP system produces the revised record (typically once per week), the correct inventory will appear.

Other entries in the row show inventory expected in future weeks. The record takes into account inventory left over from the prior week, scheduled

---

*As you will soon see, the production plan for a parent that is *not* an end item comes from the planned order release row in its MRP record. This row has already been offset for the lead time.

†If B's lead time were 3 weeks, and if it were made from two units of C, then C's gross requirements in the first week would equal A's MPS quantity in week 2 (as before), plus double the MPS quantity of B in week 4.

‡Exceptions are possible. For example, the planner might discover that a scheduled receipt is not needed as soon as expected and delay its due date further into the future. Last-minute MPS changes or recently discovered errors in current on-hand inventory are but two possible reasons for delaying orders after their release.

receipts, planned receipts, and gross requirements. Mathematically, we express this relationship as:

$$I_t = I_{t-1} + SR_t + PR_t - GR_t$$

where

I_t = projected on-hand inventory balance at the end of week t

SR_t = scheduled receipt (open order) due in week t

PR_t = planned receipt in week t

GR_t = gross requirements in week t

Figure 15.2 shows on-hand inventory projected only through week 4. During that week, the balance drops to 7 units, or substantially below the desired safety stock of 50 units. This condition signals the need for a new planned order receipt.

Planned Receipts.   A **planned receipt** is a new order—not yet released—for an item. Planning for receipt of these new orders will keep the projected on-hand balance from dropping below the desired safety stock level.* If no safety stock is called for, which is often the case for intermediate items, the purpose of these new orders is to avoid a negative projected on-hand balance in the inventory record. The planned receipt row for a dependent-demand item is equivalent to the MPS row for an end item (see Chapter 14). The record shows when order quantities should be received in both cases.

Let's look at a simplified procedure for developing the planned receipt row and finishing the rest of the projected on-hand inventory row. The first step is to schedule completion of the initial planned receipt in the week when inventory would otherwise drop below the safety stock by projecting weekly on-hand inventory until it shows a shortage. Then the addition of the newly planned receipt raises the projected on-hand balance to equal or exceed the safety stock. Next, continue to project on-hand inventory until the next shortage occurs. This signals the need for the second planned receipt. Repeat this process until the end of the planning horizon, proceeding column by column through the MRP record—filling in planned receipts as needed and completing the projected on-hand inventory row.

Figure 15.2 shows the first planned receipt of 230 units in week 4. This quantity is the lot size, which is shown at the top right-hand corner of the record. Adding the 230-unit planned receipt increases the projected on-hand balance in week 4 from 7 to 237 (or 7 + 230). After making this revision, continue to project on-hand quantities (for week 5 and beyond) until discovering the next shortage (or reaching the end).

---

*There is one exception: If a shortage can be eliminated by expediting a scheduled receipt already released (but coming in late), there is no need for a new order.

Planned Order Releases.   A **planned order release** indicates when an order for a specified quantity of an item is to be issued. The release date is the receipt date minus the lead time. For example, in Fig. 15.2, the first planned receipt occurs in week 4, which translates into a planned order release in week 2 (or 4 − 2). For uniformity, we always use the *midpoint convention* to offset for lead time. The midpoint convention assumes that withdrawals and receipts occur at the middle of the week.* The planned order release row makes it easier to derive gross requirements for an item's components that are farther down the BOM. These gross requirements come directly from the planned order release row: No additional time offsets are needed.

APPLICATION 15.1

Calculate planned receipts and projected on-hand inventory for item C for all 8 weeks. Display your results as a completed MRP inventory record.

Solution

Planned Receipts and Projected On-hand Inventory for Item C

Week	Beginning Inventory		Scheduled Receipts		Gross Require-ments	Shortage?	Planned Receipts	Projected On-hand Inventory
1	47	+	230	−	150	No	0	127
2	127	+	0	−	0	No	0	127
3	127	+	0	−	0	No	0	127
4	127	+	0	−	120	Yes	230	237
5	237	+	0	−	0	No	0	237
6	237	+	0	−	150	No	0	87
7	87	+	0	−	120	Yes	230	197
8	197	+	0	−	0	No	0	197

The first inventory shortage occurs in week 4, bringing the on-hand inventory below the safety stock of 50 units. With the receipt of 230 units, the inventory projection rises to 237 units. The 230-unit order will last until week 7, when another lot must be received. Because this second planned receipt will last through week 8, we need to plan only two new orders, releasing them in weeks 2 and 5. The completed MRP inventory record is shown in Fig. 15.3.

---

*If receipts tend to occur at the end of the week and withdrawals at the beginning—and this difference isn't reflected in the lead-time estimate—a different convention should be used and the PORs moved back one more week.

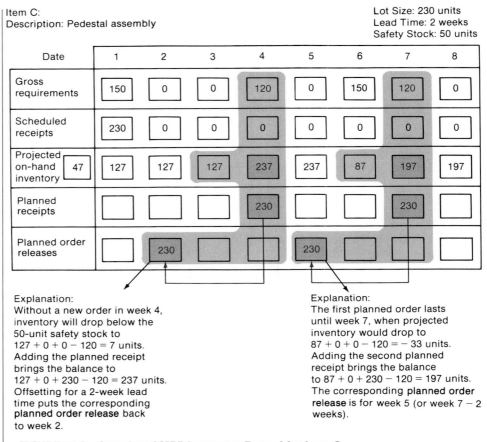

Item C:
Description: Pedestal assembly

Lot Size: 230 units
Lead Time: 2 weeks
Safety Stock: 50 units

Date	1	2	3	4	5	6	7	8
Gross requirements	150	0	0	120	0	150	120	0
Scheduled receipts	230	0	0	0	0	0	0	0
Projected on-hand inventory 47	127	127	127	237	237	87	197	197
Planned receipts				230			230	
Planned order releases		230			230			

Explanation:
Without a new order in week 4, inventory will drop below the 50-unit safety stock to $127 + 0 + 0 - 120 = 7$ units. Adding the planned receipt brings the balance to $127 + 0 + 230 - 120 = 237$ units. Offsetting for a 2-week lead time puts the corresponding **planned order release** back to week 2.

Explanation:
The first planned order lasts until week 7, when projected inventory would drop to $87 + 0 + 0 - 120 = -33$ units. Adding the second planned receipt brings the balance to $87 + 0 + 230 - 120 = 197$ units. The corresponding **planned order release** is for week 5 (or week $7 - 2$ weeks).

FIGURE 15.3   Completed MRP Inventory Record for Item C

Lot-Sizing Rules

The computer logic for MRP requires that a lot-sizing rule be preassigned to each item before the system can compute planned receipts and planned order releases. Although many types of rules may be used, we can categorize them as either *static* or *dynamic*.

Static Lot Sizing. **Static lot-sizing rules** are procedures that maintain the same order quantity each time an order is issued. The **fixed order quantity (FOQ)** is a typical lot-sizing rule under which the lot size is a predetermined, fixed quantity. For example, the lot size might be the size dictated by upper equipment capacity limits, such as when a full lot must be loaded into a furnace at one time. For purchased items, the FOQ could be set at the quantity discount level, truckload capacity, or minimum purchase quantity. Alternatively, the lot size could be predetermined by the economic order (*EOQ*) formula (see Chapter 12). Figure 15.3 illustrates the FOQ rule. If an item's gross requirement within a week is particularly large, the FOQ may be insufficient to restore even the desired safety stock. In such unusual cases, the inventory planner must increase the lot size beyond the FOQ, typically to an integer multiple of the FOQ.*

Dynamic Lot Sizing. **Dynamic lot-sizing rules** are procedures that allow a different order quantity for each order issued. Whatever its size, each planned order must be large enough to prevent shortages (falling below the desired safety stock)—but no larger—over a specified number of weeks. The **periodic order quantity (POQ)** is a lot-sizing rule that does just that. The lot size equals the total of the gross requirements for *P* weeks (beginning with the week of the receipt), plus any desired safety stock, minus the projected on-hand balance from the previous week. This amount restores the safety stock and exactly covers *P* weeks' worth of gross requirements. That is, the projected on-hand inventory should equal the desired safety stock in the *P*th week.

The POQ rule does *not* mean that operations should issue a new order every *P* weeks. Rather, when an order *is* planned, its lot size must be enough to cover *P* weeks. One way to select a *P* value is to divide the average lot size desired (such as the *EOQ*) by the average weekly demand.† That is, express the target lot size as weeks of supply and round to the nearest integer.

A special case of the POQ rule is the **lot for lot (L4L)** rule, under which the lot size ordered covers the gross requirements of a single period. Thus *P* = 1. This rule ensures that the planned order is just large enough to prevent a shortage in the single week it covers. The goal is to minimize inventory levels. The lot size equals the gross requirement for the week, plus any desired safety stock, minus the projected on-hand balance from the previous week. The projected on-hand inventory combined with the new order will equal the desired safety stock (0 if none is required). Following the first planned order, there will be an additional planned order to match each subsequent gross requirement.

---

*Another option is to increase the lot size enough to bring the projected on-hand inventory just up to the desired safety stock level. This option is appropriate when inventory holding costs dominate other considerations.

†The reasons and methods for selecting *P* in this context are similar to some of those discussed in Chapter 12 regarding periodic review systems.

APPLICATION 15.2

Modify the MRP inventory record for item C, as shown in Fig. 15.3, using (a) the POQ rule with $P = 3$ and (b) the L4L rule.

Solution

a. Inventory must receive the first planned order in week 4. The lot size is $(120 + 0 + 150) + 50 - 127 = 193$ units. The second order must arrive in week 7, with a lot size of $(120 + 0) + 50 - 50 = 120$ units. This second order reflects only two weeks' worth of gross requirements—to the end of the planning horizon. The completed record is shown in Fig. 15.4.

Item: C Description: Pedestal assembly						Lot Size: P = 3 Lead Time: 2 weeks Safety Stock: 50 units		
Date	1	2	3	4	5	6	7	8
Gross requirements		150			120		150	120	
Scheduled receipts		230							
Projected on hand	47	127	127	127	200	200	50	50	50
Planned receipts					193			120	
Planned order releases			193			120			

FIGURE 15.4   **Record for Pedestal Assembly with POQ (P = 3) Rule**

b. The first planned order in week 4 is only $120 + 50 - 127 = 43$ units. Inventory must receive additional planned orders in weeks 6 and 7, one to satisfy each of the subsequent gross requirements. The complete record is shown in Fig. 15.5.

Item: C Description: Pedestal assembly						Lot Size: L4L Lead Time: 2 weeks Safety Stock: 50 units		
Date	1	2	3	4	5	6	7	8
Gross requirements		150			120		150	120	
Scheduled receipts		230							
Projected on hand	47	127	127	127	50	50	50	50	50
Planned receipts					43		150	120	
Planned order releases			43		150	120			

FIGURE 15.5   **Record for Pedestal Assembly with Lot-for-Lot (L4L) Rule**

Comparison of Lot-Sizing Rules. Choosing a lot-sizing rule can have important implications for inventory management. For example, applying the FOQ rule to Fig. 15.3 yields an *average* projected on-hand inventory of 167 units over eight weeks [or (127 + 127 + ··· + 197)/8]. For the POQ rule (see Fig. 15.4), the average inventory is only 116 units, even though there are still only two planned orders over the same time period. Finally, using the L4L rule (see Fig. 15.5) drops average inventory to only 79 units.* This further cut in inventory adds one more planned order and its accompanying setup time and cost.

We can draw three conclusions from this comparison:

1. The FOQ rule generates a higher level of average inventory because it creates inventory *remnants*. A remnant is inventory carried into a week but which is too small to prevent a shortage. Remnants occur because the FOQ doesn't exactly match requirements. For example, according to Fig. 15.3, inventory must receive a planned order in week 7, even though that week begins with 87 units on hand. The remnant is the 37 units in excess of the required safety stock (or 87 − 50) that inventory will carry for three weeks beginning with receipt of the first planned order in week 4.

2. The POQ reduces the amount of on-hand inventory because it does a better job of matching order quantity to requirements. It adjusts lot sizes as requirements increase or decrease. Figure 15.4 shows that in week 7, when the POQ rule has fully taken effect, the beginning inventory is the minimum allowed by the safety stock requirement. There are no remnants.

3. The L4L rule minimizes inventory investment, but maximizes the number of orders placed. This rule is most applicable to expensive items or items with small ordering or setup costs. It is the only rule possible for a *special*, an item made to order rather than made to stock.

In general, static lot-sizing rules create inventory remnants which, in turn, introduce greater stability into the production process. Inventory remnants can act as buffers against unexpected scrap losses, capacity bottlenecks, inaccurate inventory records, or unstable gross requirements. Dynamic rules, in contrast, reduce inventory levels by avoiding remnants, but may introduce instability by tying the lot-size decision so closely to requirements. If any requirement changes, so must the lot size, which can cause trouble at the component level. If component plans were based on lower expectations of gross requirements, inventory may not be able to respond quickly enough. Thus last-minute increases in parent orders may be hindered by missing components.

---

*Safety stock is not usually associated with an L4L item, but we retain it in Application 15.2 to maintain continuity.

Safety Stock

An important managerial issue is the quantity of safety stock to require. This issue is more complex for dependent-demand items than for independent-demand items (see Chapter 12). Excessive safety stock for dependent-demand items, particularly for those with lumpy demand (gross requirements), is of little value. Safety stock is more valuable when there is considerable uncertainty about future gross requirements or the timing or size of scheduled receipts. Consequently, the usual policy is to maintain safety stock for end items (at the master production scheduling level) and purchased items. This approach protects against fluctuating customer orders at the top of the bills of materials and unreliable vendors at the bottom.

Action Notices

Material requirements planning inventory records are computed for each item appearing in the bills of materials. These records together represent the current *material requirements plan,* which can be printed out in hard copy or displayed on a computer video screen. Inventory planners use the computer-generated plan to make decisions about releasing new orders, expediting open orders, and the like. Actually planners need to be alerted only to items that need their attention. They can then view the full records for those items and make the necessary decisions. This management-by-exception approach depends on issuance of action notices.

An **action notice** is a computer-generated memo indicating the need to release an order or adjust the due date of a scheduled receipt. An action notice can simply be a list of part numbers for items needing attention. Or it can be the full record for such items, with a note at the bottom identifying the action needed. The general rule for releasing a new order differs from the rule for adjusting the due date of a scheduled receipt.

Releasing New Orders.   If there is a nonzero quantity in the first week's entry of the planned order release row, sometimes called the **action bucket**, the computer issues an action notice. An order in the action bucket is the call to release the planned order. Delaying the release one week will provide *less* than the planned lead time for producing the item. Releasing an order before it gets to the action bucket allows *more* than the planned lead time for production.

Adjusting Due Dates of Scheduled Receipts.   If subtracting the scheduled receipt from the projected on-hand inventory for the week in which it is due does not cause inventory to drop below the desired safety stock, the scheduled receipt is arriving too early. In such a case, the inventory planner can delay the scheduled receipt. If the projected on-hand balance for the week *prior* to arrival of the scheduled receipt is below the desired safety stock (negative if no safety stock is allowed) the scheduled receipt is arriving too late. In this case, the planner should expedite the scheduled receipt. (See Chapter 17 for more on adjusting due dates and planning priorities.)

What action notices would be provided from the inventory record shown in Fig. 15.6? Would they change if the scheduled receipt had a due date of week 31, rather than week 33?

Item: H10-A Description: Chair seat assembly									Lot Size: **80 units** Lead Time: **4 weeks** Safety Stock: **0 units**		
Date	31	32	33	34	35	36	37	38	39	40
Gross requirements		75			40			25		60
Scheduled receipts			← 80							
Projected on hand	20	20	−55	25	25	65	65	65	40	40	60
Planned receipts					80					80
Planned order releases	80					80				

Action bucket

FIGURE 15.6   Action Notices for Chair Seat Assembly

Solution

Two action notices would be issued: one to release a new order and one to expedite the scheduled receipt. The 80 units in the action bucket signal an immediate need to release a new order with a due date of week 35. The −55 on-hand balance in week 32 signals a need to expedite the scheduled receipt, originally scheduled for week 33.

If the scheduled receipt had a due date of week 31 instead of 33, the action notice to release a new order would not change. What does change is the action notice for the scheduled receipt. The computer would issue a notice stating that the scheduled receipt could be delayed by one week. It could arrive as late as week 32 and still not delay production of the parents. Why communicate to the shop or vendor a false sense of urgency? Resources might better be applied to other jobs that really *are* needed in week 31.

Making Decisions.   Although the computer generates action notices, *decisions* based on them are made by the inventory planner. The planner reviews the item's complete MRP inventory record, along with those of its components. If component inventory is available to support the order, the planner usually decides to release the order as planned. The planner would input an *inventory* *transaction* to change the computer record file by adding the quantity and due date of a new scheduled receipt. This new order would show up in the scheduled receipts row the next time the system generates the material requirements plan, and it drops out of the planned order receipt row. When releasing a new order, the planner may also prepare documentation for tool requisitions, routings, or parts lists. For purchased items, a requisition is sent to the appropriate buyer, who in turn places the order with a vendor. These purchasing activities are often computer assisted.

At times the planner deviates from the lot size or timing specified in an item's planned order release. This might occur if an action notice indicates that a planned order receipt is needed in less than the normal lead time. In effect, an order should have been placed the previous week or even earlier (given current conditions). The MRP inventory record signals this situation in the following way. A planned order release appears in the action bucket. As the planned receipt allows for the full lead time—not just until a shortage occurs—the projected on-hand inventory shows a shortage. That is, the balance is less than the safety stock, or is negative if no safety stock is maintained. This signal alerts the planner to the problem. This undesirable condition occasionally occurs because of unexpected scrap losses in open orders, last-minute changes in the MPS, or inaccurate inventory records.

The planner must then determine whether the new order can be completed in less than the normal lead time. It may be necessary to review capacity reports, talk to the shop supervisor, or call the supplier. If the order can be completed, it is released with a due date less than the normal lead-time offset; if not, the production schedules of its parents have to be changed. The planner exercises judgment if there was not sufficient capacity, tooling, or inventory of a component to support the new order. The planner might reduce the quantity of an order or even delay the order's release. Otherwise, component inventories would be tied up in an order that would be delayed anyway.

Capacity Reports

The MRP computer logic itself does not recognize capacity limitations when computing the planned orders. *Managers* must monitor the capacity requirements of material requirements plans, making adjustments as needed. Let's look at two important sources of information for the crucial short-term decisions that materials managers continually make: capacity requirements planning and input–output reports.

Capacity Requirements Planning.   **Capacity requirements planning (CRP)** is a technique for projecting time-phased labor requirements for critical work stations. The goal is to match the MPS with the plant's production capacity. The technique is used to calculate work load according to what must be done to complete the scheduled receipts already in the shop and to complete the planned order releases yet to be released. Capacity requirements planning is

Date: 07/28/89 Plant 01 Dept. 03: Drying Kilns Station Capacity: 320 hours per month				Week 32
From Week	To Week	Planned Hours	Actual Hours	Total Hours
32	35	90	210	300
36	39	156	104	260
40	43	349	41	390
44	47	210	0	210
48	51	360	0	360
52	55	280	0	280

FIGURE 15.7   Capacity Requirements Report

a more detailed and accurate version of the method of overall factors used for master production scheduling (see Chapter 14). A key difference is that CRP includes the scheduled receipts and planned orders for *all* produced items in the BOMs, not just the end items.

Figure 15.7 shows a capacity requirements report for a drying kiln station that treats wood used in desk chairs. The kiln operates a maximum of 320 hours per month. The *planned* hours represent labor requirements for all planned orders that are to be routed through the kiln. Work projected beyond actual lead times is only in the planning stage. The *actual* hours represent the backlog of work visible on the shop floor, that is, scheduled receipts. Combining requirements from both sources gives *total* hours. Comparing total hours to actual capacity constraints can give advance warning of potential problems. The planner must resolve any capacity problems uncovered.

APPLICATION 15.4

Does the CRP report in Fig. 15.7 reveal any problems at the drying kiln? If so, what should be done?

Solution

The report should arouse the planner's concern. Unless something is done, the current capacity of 320 hours per month will be exceeded in weeks 40–43 and weeks 48–51. Requirements for all other time periods are well below the capacity limit. Perhaps the best choice is to release some orders earlier than called for in weeks 36–39 and 44–47. This adjustment will help smooth capacity and alleviate projected bottlenecks. Other options might be to change the lot sizes of some items, use overtime, subcontract, off-load to another work station, or simply let the bottlenecks occur.

The forward visibility of CRP reports is a capability unique to modern MRP systems. Computing these reports requires more than a list of scheduled receipts and planned orders: Routings (see Chapter 11) are needed to identify which orders will be processed at each work station. Time standards (see Chapter 6) are needed for the setup and processing times of the orders. Information on lead times and the current status of scheduled receipts helps estimate when each order will reach a work station.

Input–Output Control.   An **input–output control report** compares planned input (from prior CRP reports) with actual input, and planned output with actual output. Inputs and outputs are expressed in common units, usually hours. Information in the report indicates whether work stations have been performing as expected and helps management pinpoint the source of capacity problems. Actual outputs can fall behind planned outputs for two reasons:

1. *Insufficient inputs.* Output may lag when inputs are insufficient to support the planned output rates. The problem can lie upstream at a prior operation, or it may be caused by missing purchased parts. In effect, not enough work arrives to keep the operation busy.

2. *Insufficient capacity.* Output may lag at the station itself. Even though input rates keep pace, output may slip below expected levels because of absenteeism, equipment failures, inadequate staffing levels, or low productivity rates.

APPLICATION 15.5

The input–output report in Fig. 15.8 has been prepared for a rough mill work station where desk chair components are machined. Management established a tolerance of ±25 hours. So long as cumulative deviations do not exceed this threshold, there is no cause for concern. Is there a problem? If so, what is the cause?

Solution

Last week (week 31) actual outputs fell behind planned outputs by a total of 32 hours. This cumulative deviation exceeds the 25-hour tolerance, so there is a problem. Actual inputs are running somewhat ahead of planned inputs, so the lag results from insufficient capacity at the rough mill itself. Temporary use of overtime may be necessary to increase the output rate.

Work Station: Rough Mill Tolerance: ±25 hours				Week 32	
Week Ending	28	29	30	31	32
Inputs Planned Actual Cumulative deviation	160 145 −15	155 160 −10	170 168 −12	160 177 +5	165
Outputs Planned Actual Cumulative deviation	170 165 −5	170 165 −10	160 150 −20	160 148 −32	160

FIGURE 15.8   Input–Output Control Report

MATERIAL REQUIREMENTS PLANNING AS AN INFORMATION SYSTEM ▲

From the basic concepts of MRP, we can now turn to its larger context: MRP as a computerized information system. Figure 15.9 shows that MRP computer logic translates four basic inputs into several outputs that aid decision making in a variety of materials management areas.

Inputs

The first input is the authorized master production schedule, which is the driving force of MRP. Material requirements planning provides the information needed to release new orders, adjust priorities, and revise capacities to implement the MPS. The MPS, in turn, is linked to strategic plans for marketing and production.

Inventory records are the second input. The basic building blocks of up-to-date records are inventory transactions. Planners make transactions when they release new orders, adjust due dates for scheduled receipts, withdraw inventory, cancel orders, correct inventory errors, reject shipments, and verify scrap losses and stock returns. Recording such transactions is essential for maintaining accurate records, particularly of on-hand inventory balances and the status of scheduled receipts. Without an accurate and current database, an MRP system will be ineffective.

Bills of materials, the third input, are derived from engineering and process designs. Material requirements planning derives an item's gross requirements from the planned order releases of its parents, so BOM information about the item's parents and their usage quantities must be known.

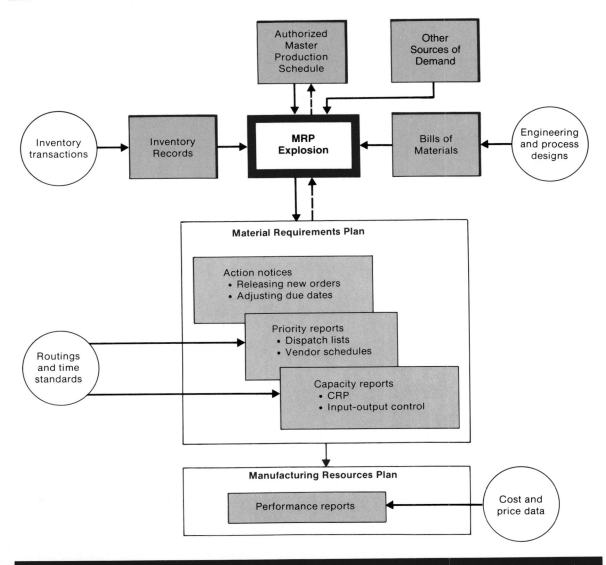

FIGURE 15.9 Overview of MRP Systems

Other sources of demand not reflected in the MPS are the final input. Examples include demand for replacement parts, external orders from other company plants or warehouses, or units needed for quality control purposes (such as destructive testing). When these demands are for components rather than end items, they may not be reflected in the MPS. In such cases, the MRP computer logic adds them to components' gross requirements in order to complete the material requirements plan.

Material Requirements Planning Explosion

An MRP system acts like an engine, transforming inputs into usable outputs. It translates the master production schedule and other sources of demand into the requirements for all components, assemblies, and raw materials needed to produce the required parent items. This process, sometimes called an **MRP explosion**, generates the material requirements plan.

Types of MRP Systems. There are two types of MRP systems. A **regenerative MRP system** periodically performs the explosion process, typically on a weekly basis, and completely recomputes all inventory records. After a week, the material requirements plan becomes outdated. The system then performs a new explosion based on the latest MPS, bills of materials, and information on scheduled receipts and on-hand balances. A **net change MRP system** recomputes records as needed. With each change in the MPS and with each transaction, the system executes a partial explosion to update the affected records. Net change systems tend to be preferred in more dynamic manufacturing situations. However, they may take more computer time and generate too many action notices (sometimes called "system nervousness"). Most new MRP system users begin with a regenerative system.

Level-by-Level Processing. An item's gross requirements are derived from three sources: the MPS for immediate parents that are end items, the planned order releases for parents below the MPS level, and any other requirements not originating in the MPS. MRP computer logic offsets requirements from MPS items for their lead times. However, requirements from planned order releases need no additional offset; planned order releases are already expressed by release dates. In order to accumulate the gross requirements for a particular component the computer starts with the MPS and works downward through the bills of materials, calculating the planned order releases of all items as it goes. This procedure is called **level-by-level processing.**

To accomplish this procedure effectively on a computer, a number called a *level code* has been permanently assigned to each item. For example, all MPS items are assigned to level 0. Those components having an MPS item as an immediate parent are assigned level 1. Their components are assigned to level 2, and so on. Sometimes, an item is found at different levels in various bills of materials. In that case the item is assigned the highest level code number found in any bill of materials because each item has only one level code. The computer then proceeds with level-by-level processing, each time checking to make sure that all items with lower code numbers have been processed before accumulating the gross requirements for an item. The basic computer logic is simple: An item cannot be processed until after all its parents have been processed.

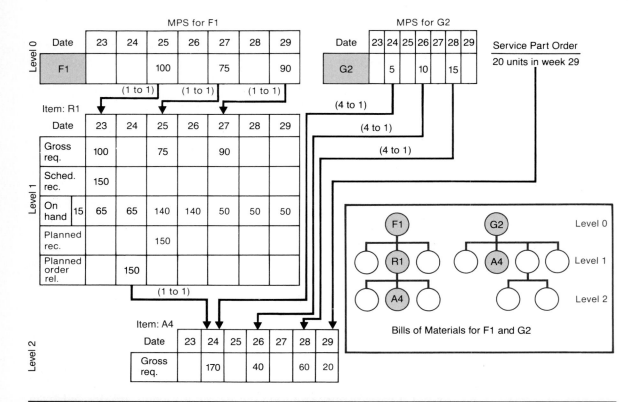

FIGURE 15.10 Deriving Gross Requirements for A4

Figure 15.10 shows an example of level-by-level processing. The BOM insert shows that item A4 exists at two levels: (1) as an immediate component of G2, an MPS item; and (2) as an immediate component of R1, which is itself a component. Consequently, A4 receives a level code of 2. Thus the planned order releases of all level 1 items are processed first, yielding the planned order release of 150 in week 24 for R1. Then the gross requirements for A4 are computed. Note that 4 units of A4 are needed for each unit of G2. There is also a service-part order for A4 of 20 units in week 29. Combined, they result in the gross requirements shown for A4.

Outputs

If you refer back to Figure 15.9, you will see several types of outputs, listed in order of sophistication. The most basic outputs are the material requirements plan and action notices to release new orders. They provide planners with information on when to launch new orders. They do not, however, help detect problems such as materials and capacity shortages. These additional capabilities come from action notices to adjust due dates, priority reports, and capacity reports. Priority reports show the relative urgency for each open order. Reports by work station in the shop are called dispatch lists. Reports for purchased items are called vendor schedules. Planners use these additional outputs to adjust the material requirements plan and, if necessary, the MPS, to cope with difficulties not anticipated in the MRP logic. This adjustment process, called closed-loop control, is represented by the dashed arrows in Fig. 15.9.*

MRP II

It is now possible to enhance MRP systems with simulation possibilities that create "what-if" scenarios. Management can receive performance reports that project the dollar value of shipments, product costs, overhead allocations, inventories, backlogs, and profits. Time-phased information from the MPS, scheduled receipts, and planned orders can be converted into cash flow projections, broken down by product families. For example, the projected on-hand

Tektronix, Inc. operates one of the most highly automated printed circuit board facilities in the United States. This operator processes work at a drilling operation according to job due dates, which are accessible through the on-line shop floor control system. Tektronix's MRP II system has allowed it to achieve 98 percent on-time delivery.

---

*Chapter 17 covers more on this process, including pegging and firm planned orders.

quantities in MRP inventory records allow the computation of future levels of inventory investment. These levels are obtained simply by multiplying the quantities by the per unit value of each item and adding these amounts for all items belonging to the same product family. Similar computations are possible for other performance measures of interest to management.

When the full range of these outputs is added to a basic MRP system—tying it to the company's financial system—the result is **manufacturing resource planning (MRP II)** (see Wight, 1979). The original material requirements planning system is sometimes referred to as *mrp* or *little MRP* because it was limited only to aiding order-launching decisions. Information from MRP II gives focus to meetings involving key managers of the firm representing manufacturing, purchasing, marketing, finance, and engineering. The reports produced help these managers develop and monitor the overall business plan and recognize sales objectives, manufacturing capabilities, and cash flow constraints.

The Colorado Springs Division of Hewlett-Packard provides an example of the successful use of MRP II. This Division, which makes a variety of complex electronic instruments, modified its MRP system to provide financial reports in step with its operational plans. Predictions are quite good, with production costs coming within 1 percent of predictions.

IMPLEMENTATION ISSUES ▲

Although several thousand firms have tried MRP, not all have succeeded. A company can easily invest $500,000 in an MRP system, only to still be plagued by high inventories and late customer deliveries. What went wrong? One possibility is that the MRP system was poorly implemented. Success is not automatic but is achieved only by the dedicated efforts of those involved in making the system function as intended. A second possibility, which we discuss later, is that the company's manufacturing environment does not give MRP a distinct advantage over other systems.

Prerequisites

There are four main prerequisites to successful implementation of an MRP system, as suggested in Managerial Practice 15.1:

1. Computer support.
2. Accurate and realistic input data.
3. Management support.
4. User knowledge and acceptance.

Any decision support system such as MRP rests on valid input data. You saw in Fig. 15.9 that MRP relies on many data inputs. The three principal ones are the master production schedule, bills of materials, and inventory records. When MRP fails to live up to expectations, management should look first at these inputs. Are they accurate and realistic? If not, little progress can be made. Data accuracy makes a major difference in whether MRP implementation is successful or unsuccessful (see White et al., 1982).

The third element of successful implementation is management support. Converting to a new system challenges long-established habits and prerogatives of the people involved, whether they are managers, planners, buyers, marketing specialists, or shop supervisors. Resistance to change is normal and predictable. Overcoming this resistance begins with top management, who should convey to others the importance of success. By being actively involved in implementing and using MRP, top management can motivate others.

The last prerequisite is to have knowledgeable users at all levels of the company. They must understand how they will be affected and what is required of them to make the system work. Such understanding helps to replace resistance with enthusiasm. Training programs often involve employees throughout the organization. The Tennant Company, an $80 million producer of

MANAGERIAL PRACTICE 15.1

Prerequisites at Dominion Automotive Industries, Inc.

Dominion Automotive Industries manufactures exterior side-view mirrors. Faced by lagging profits, the company successfully installed an MRP system to boost profits by 10 percent. These savings came from cutting inventory, reducing labor costs, and eliminating expensive premium freight charges.

Computer support comes from a mainframe computer and 15 terminals installed in the production supervisors' offices and in administrative and accounting offices. Rick Owen, manager of manufacturing systems, is pleased with data accuracy, in contrast to experiences with the company's earlier manual systems. Plant manager Fred Loepp II credits the company's turnaround to a dedicated management effort. Top management was committed to do "whatever it takes to get the job done." Management also points to user knowledge and acceptance. Every production supervisor knows that this system is a valuable production tool. Their understanding and initiative in making the information work for them is what makes the plan run smoothly, efficiently, and profitably.

Source: "Plant Boosts Profits with Computerized Inventory, Production Control," *P&IM Review with APICS News*, April 1988.

industrial maintenance equipment, gave 525 of its 575 employees at least some MRP training. Usually, a people problem, such as lack of training, inadequate management support, or gaining acceptance for the change, is the single most important impediment to MRP success (see White et al., 1982).

Favorable Environments for Material Requirements Planning

Some companies do not adopt an MRP system, or are disappointed with its results when they do, because their manufacturing environment does not give MRP a distinct advantage over other systems. Four environmental characteristics are particularly important:

1. Number of BOM levels.
2. Magnitude of lot sizes.
3. Volatility.
4. Manufacturing's positioning strategy.

You have seen that one of MRP's unique advantages is the way in which it handles lumpy demand for dependent-demand items. Dependent-demand items are most numerous when there are many levels in the bills of materials. Thus the greatest number of MRP users are in the fabricated metals, machinery, and electric and electronic industries, which tend to have many BOM levels. It is no coincidence that the average user has more than six BOM levels (see Schroeder et al., 1981). Even with many levels, though, dependent-demand patterns need not be lumpy. The other variable is the magnitude of lot sizes. Our own simulation studies bear out these conclusions: The relative superiority of MRP is greatest with more BOM levels and larger lot sizes. When a firm works with extremely small lot sizes, as do some Japanese manufacturers, changing over to MRP is less beneficial.

A highly volatile manufacturing environment that management cannot stabilize is also less likely to achieve large MRP savings. A basic assumption underlying MRP systems is that projections of gross requirements, scheduled receipts, and planned order releases are realistic. This assumption is not valid when there are high scrap rates, capacity bottlenecks, last-minute rush jobs, and unreliable vendors.

Finally, MRP seems to be most attractive for firms that have positioned themselves with an intermediate strategy. (See Fig. 2.6 in Chapter 2.) They produce in batches, experience low to medium demand volumes, tend to offer a number of product options, and make products that have relatively short life cycles. These characteristics are not necessary for successful MRP system utilization, but they give you an idea of the sort of environment in which MRP can be best utilized. Firms at the extreme points of the diagonal in Fig. 2.6, with a process focus or product focus, find that MRP is less valuable. In process-focused firms, annual demand for specific items is small, and the number of

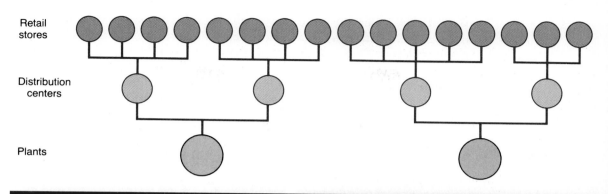

FIGURE 15.11 A Multi-Echelon Distribution System

customized products is large. Products are often expensive and require substantial engineering, which makes lead times long and uncertain. Maintaining files on bills of materials is complicated by the customization, and lot sizes are small. In product-focused firms (such as a paper mill) there tend to be few BOM levels, high capital intensity, and tight constraints on equipment capacity. Here the focus of managerial concern is with the master production schedule, which is an *input* to MRP, not an output. Only 12 percent of MRP system users operated continuous manufacturing processes, indicating a product focus (see Schroeder et al., 1981).

Distribution Requirements Planning

The principles of MRP can also be applied to distribution inventories. Consider the distribution system in Fig. 15.11. The top echelon represents retail stores at various locations throughout the country. At the middle level are regional distribution centers (DCs) that replenish retail store inventories on request. The bottom level consists of one or more plants that supply the DCs. In the past, plants tended to schedule production to meet the forecasted demand patterns of the DCs. These forecasts were likely to be based on past usage, as is done for independent-demand items. The DCs, in turn, replenished their inventories based on past demand patterns of the retail stores. In short, reorder-point logic was used at all three levels.

To illustrate the shortcomings of this approach, let's suppose that customer demand for a product suddenly increases by 10 percent. What will happen? Since the retailers carry some inventory there will be some delay before the DCs feel the full 10 percent increase. Still more time passes before the plants feel the effect of the full increase, reflected as higher demand from the DCs. This means that the plants could continue for months underproducing at a 10 percent rate. When the deficiency finally becomes apparent, the plants must increase their output by much more than 10 percent in order to replenish inventory levels. Thus a small change is gradually magnified into a much larger change.

Distribution requirements planning (DRP) is an inventory control and scheduling technique that applies MRP principles to distribution inventories. It helps to avoid self-induced swings in demand. An inventory record is maintained for each item at each location. The planned order releases projected at the retail level are used to derive the gross requirements for each item at the DC level, using standard MRP logic and bills of materials. Next, planned order releases at the DC level are computed, from which the gross requirements for the plant level can be derived. This information provides the basis for updating the master production schedule at the plant.

Use of DRP requires an integrated information system. If the manufacturer operates its own DCs and retail stores (forward integration), this poses no particular problem. If operations in each echelon are owned by different firms, all need to agree to convey planned order releases from one level to the next. Open communication between firms need not stop at the plant level. More and more manufacturers are conveying planned order release data to their suppliers, giving them a better idea of future demand. Reducing demand uncertainty pays off either in lower inventories or better service.

Optimized Production Technology

Development of **optimized production technology (OPT)*** was based on the premise that many companies have spent hundreds of thousands of dollars apiece on production and inventory control systems but have fallen short of achieving even modest goals with these systems. Many reasons for such lack of success have been suggested: inaccurate data, no management support, inadequate education, and others. However, the developers of OPT claim that the main reason is the faulty assumptions used in the other systems to arrive at production schedules. Recall that MRP computer logic, for example, does not reflect capacity constraints when generating planned order releases. Planners must intervene manually, using additional methods, such as capacity requirements planning and input–output control to manage schedules. The scheduling problem is very complex because, typically, at any one time many shop orders that require the same critical work stations are being processed. Arriving at valid schedules that remain valid for more than a short time is difficult, if not impossible, to do manually.

The general idea behind OPT is to look at the production and inventory control problem from a systems viewpoint. Order release and production

---

*OPT is a registered trademark of Creative Output, Incorporated.

schedules take into consideration the capacity bottlenecks in the system. The goal of OPT is to find schedules that *simultaneously* increase throughput and decrease inventory and operating expenses. This approach differs from those of MRP and reorder point systems users, who develop their schedules *sequentially*, first identifying the timing and size of order releases and then making adjustments to account for capacity constraints.

Optimized production technology facilitates the flow of material through bottleneck operations by utilizing two basic types of lot sizes. A **transfer batch** is the quantity of an item that moves from station to station. A station will not begin to process an item until there are sufficient parts to process a transfer batch. The other type of lot size is the **process batch**, which is the total number of units of an item processed at one time at a particular station. The process batch consists of an integral number of transfer batches, such as one, two, or three transfer batches. A process batch's size depends on setup time and capacity constraints. Consequently, process batches at the critical work stations can be chosen to minimize setup times, and the transfer batches can move ahead to the next operation without waiting for the entire process batch to be completed. The OPT system probably represents the first of many proprietary scheduling systems that will be developed by computer software vendors in the future.

SOLVED PROBLEMS

1. The MRP inventory record in Fig. 15.12 has been partially completed, showing gross requirements, scheduled receipts, and current on-hand inventory. Parameters for lead time and safety stock are also given. Item H10-A is produced in the plant (not purchased).

Item: H10-A Description: Chair seat assembly									Lot Size: 80 units Lead Time: 4 weeks Safety Stock: 10 units		
Date		31	32	33	34	35	36	37	38	39	40
Gross requirements			60				35		45		60
Scheduled receipts				80							
Projected on hand	20										
Planned receipts											
Planned order releases											

FIGURE 15.12

   a. Fill in the last three rows of the record, using an FOQ of 80 units.
      i. Will there be any action notices?
      ii. If there are action notices, what factors would you consider in reacting to them?
   b. Revise the last two rows using the L4L rule.
   c. Revise the last two rows again, this time using the POQ rule and a value of P that will give an average lot size of 80 units. Assume that *average* weekly demand will be 20 units for the foreseeable future when computing P.

Solution

   a. See Fig. 15.13.

Item: H10-A Description: Chair seat assembly								Lot Size: 80 units Lead Time: 4 weeks Safety Stock: 10 units			
Date	31	32	33	34	35	36	37	38	39	40
Gross requirements		60				35		45		60
Scheduled receipts			80							
Projected on hand	20	20	−40	40	40	40	85	85	40	40	60
Planned receipts						80				80
Planned order releases		80				80				

FIGURE 15.13

      i. There will be an action notice to expedite the scheduled receipt in week 33 to week 32.
      ii. The capacity must be checked to see if the order can be expedited.
   b. The last two rows—based on use of the L4L rule—are shown in Fig. 15.14(a).
   c. The last two rows—based on use of $P = 4$ weeks—are shown in Fig. 15.14(b).

2. The MPS for product A calls for completion of a 50-unit order in week 4 and a 60-unit order in week 8. The MPS for product B calls for a 200-unit order received in week 5. The lead times are 2 weeks for A and 1 week for

	Date	31	32	33	34	35	36	37	38	39	40
Planned receipts							5		45		60
Planned order releases			5		45		60				

(a)

		31	32	33	34	35	36	37	38	39	40
Planned receipts	Date						50				60
Planned order releases			50				60				

(b)

FIGURE 15.14

B. Develop a material requirements plan for the next six weeks for items C, D, E, and F, identifying any action notices that would be provided. The BOMs are shown in Fig. 15.15, and data from the inventory records are shown in Table 15.1.

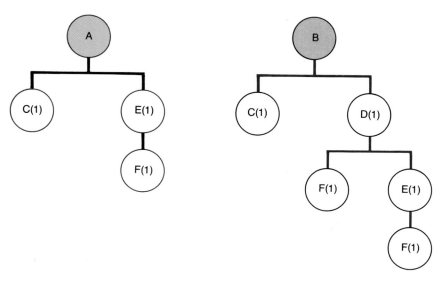

FIGURE 15.15

TABLE 15.1

Data Category	Item			
	C	D	E	F
Lot-size rule	FOQ = 250	FOQ = 400	L4L	POQ $(P = 2)$
Lead time	3	2	3	2
Safety stock	50	0	0	0
Scheduled receipts	250 (week 2)	None	50 (week 1)	None
Beginning (on-hand) inventory	60	300	0	0

Solution

We begin with item C, then go to D, E, and F in that order (see Fig. 15.16). We find that item D does not have any planned order releases, so it doesn't add to the requirements for E and F. Item A *does* add requirements for E.

An action notice would call for delaying the scheduled receipt for item E from week 1 to week 2. A second action notice would notify the planner that item F has a mature planned order release.

Item: C Description:							Lot Size: 250 units Lead Time: 3 weeks Safety Stock: 50 units		
Date	1	2	3	4	5	6	7	8
Gross requirements		50		200		60		
Scheduled receipts		250						
Projected on hand	60	60	260	260	60	60	250	250	250
Planned receipts						250		
Planned order releases			250					

(a) Item C

Item: D Description:							Lot Size: 400 units Lead Time: 2 weeks Safety Stock: 0		
Date	1	2	3	4	5	6	7	8
Gross requirements				200				
Scheduled receipts								
Projected on hand	300	300	300	300	100	100	100	100	100
Planned receipts								
Planned order releases								

(b) Item D

FIGURE 15.16

Item: E Description:							Lot Size: **L4L** Lead Time: **3 weeks** Safety Stock: **0**		
Date	1	2	3	4	5	6	7	8
Gross requirements		50				60		
Scheduled receipts	50 →							
Projected on hand	0	50	0	0	0	0	0	0	0
Planned receipts						60		
Planned order releases			60					

(c) Item E

Item: F Description:							Lot Size: **POQ (P= 2)** Lead Time: **2 weeks** Safety Stock: **0**		
Date	1	2	3	4	5	6	7	8
Gross requirements			60					
Scheduled receipts								
Projected on hand	0	0	0	0	0	0	0	0	0
Planned receipts			60					
Planned order releases	60							

(d) Item F   Action bucket

FIGURE 15.16 *(continued)*

FORMULA REVIEW

Projected on-hand inventory balance for MRP record:

$$I_t = I_{t-1} + SR_t + PR_t - GR_t$$

CHAPTER HIGHLIGHTS

- Material requirements planning (MRP) is a computerized scheduling and information system that is useful in managing dependent-demand inventories.

- The shortcomings of reorder point systems in a dependent-demand environment are: (1) the assumption of a uniform, continuous demand rate is unrealistic; (2) the assumption that items are independent of each other when, in reality, they are not; and (3) no provision of forward visibility for planning purposes.

- The basic principles of MRP are that (1) dependent demands should be derived, not forecasted, and (2) replenishment orders should be offset for required production and delivery lead times.

- The material requirements plan is prepared from the most recent inventory records of all items. The basic elements in each record are gross requirements, scheduled receipts, on-hand inventory, planned receipts, and planned order releases.

- Several parameters must be preassigned to each inventory record, including lot-size, lead time, and safety stock. Various static and dynamic lot-sizing rules can be used.

- The planned order releases of a parent, modified by usage quantities, become the gross requirements of its components. This procedure involves level-by-level processing, starting at the MPS level.

- As a computerized information system, MRP has three basic inputs: the master production schedule, inventory records, and bills of materials. A fourth input, demand from sources other than the MPS, is also a possibility.

- Action notices allow management by exception, bringing to a planner's attention only those items for which new orders need to be released or that have open orders with misaligned due dates. Decisions based on the notices are normally made by the planner.

- MRP systems can provide outputs such as the material requirements plan, action notices, priority reports, and performance reports. The most advanced system is MRP II, which allows management to integrate and monitor production, marketing, and financial plans.

- Implementation of MRP systems is widespread but relatively recent. Significant inventory, customer service, and productivity benefits have been reported by many firms. Prerequisites to successful implementation are adequate computer support, accurate databases, management support, and user knowledge and acceptance.

- The relative benefits of MRP depend on the number of BOM levels, the magnitude of lot sizes, environmental volatility, and positioning strategy.

- The principles of MRP can be used to manage distribution inventory with a system called distribution requirements planning (DRP).

- OPT is a computerized information system that, using the concept of transfer and process batches, considers capacity bottlenecks when calculating order releases and production schedules.

KEY TERMS

action bucket   560
action notice   560
capacity requirements planning (CRP)   562
distribution requirements planning (DRP)   574
dynamic lot-sizing rules   557
fixed order quantity (FOQ)   556
gross requirements   551
input–output control report   564
level-by-level processing   567
lot for lot (L4L)   557
manufacturing resource planning (MRP II)   570
material requirements planning (MRP)   547
MRP explosion   567
MRP inventory record   551
net change MRP system   567
optimized production technology (OPT)   574
periodic order quantity (POQ)   557
planned receipt   554
planned order release   555
process batch   575
regenerative MRP system   567
static lot-sizing rules   556
transfer batch   575

STUDY QUESTIONS

1. How does independent demand differ from dependent demand?

2. How does reorder point logic account for lead times and demand forecasts? How does MRP logic account for them?

3. Define *gross requirements, scheduled receipts, planned receipts,* and *planned order releases.*

4. Calculating planned order releases when using a POQ rule is less complicated after the first one. For each subsequent planned receipt, the lot size is simply the sum of the gross requirements for the next *P* weeks. Safety stock and the previous week's projected on-hand balance can be ignored. Explain why.

5. With MRP logic, a component's gross requirements are derived from the planned order releases of all its parents. Why does this necessitate a top-down processing of records?

6. How is safety stock handled by MRP? How much should be carried? At what levels?

7. Why do priority and capacity reports of class B users help to close the loop? Why isn't it always wise to implement the material requirements plan without change?

Work Station: Chair Assembly Tolerance: ±50 hours					Week 49
Week Ending	45	46	47	48	49
Inputs Planned Actual Cumulative Deviation	300 305 +5	300 275 −20	300 280 −40	300 260 −80	310
Outputs Planned Actual Cumulative Deviation	300 310 +10	300 290 0	300 270 −30	300 260 −70	320

FIGURE 15.17

8. What potential problem do you detect from the data in the input–output control report in Fig. 15.17? What is the source of the problem and what can be done to resolve it?

9. Comment on the statement: "It is impossible to put together realistic marketing and financial plans without being able to set and achieve production plans."

10. How can MRP users report *simultaneous* improvements in inventory, customer service, and productivity? Isn't there a fundamental trade-off, where improvement in one comes at the expense of another? Explain.

11. Why do some companies fail to achieve any measurable improvements after adopting MRP?

12. Suppose that a manufacturer decides to share planned order release information with its suppliers. What benefits can accrue to both parties? Can there be disadvantages?

13. Why can the reliability of time-phased gross requirements be decreased by the following shocks: last-minute changes in the master production schedule, unexpected scrap losses, late vendor shipments, unexpected capacity bottlenecks, or inaccurate inventory records.

14. The relative advantage of MRP over a reorder point system does not hold for small lot sizes and short lead times. Do you agree? Disagree? Why?

15. What shortcomings of MRP gave rise to the computer software package OPT? How does OPT facilitate the flow of materials through bottleneck operations?

PROBLEMS

Review Problems

1. The inventory record shown in Fig. 15.18 has been partially completed, showing gross

Item: R203-5 Description: Table top assembly						Lot Size: Lead Time: 2 weeks Safety Stock: 0 units			
Date	1	2	3	4	5	6	7	8
Gross requirements	100		50		75		50	80
Scheduled receipts	150							
Projected on hand	25								
Planned receipts								
Planned order releases								

FIGURE 15.18

requirements, scheduled receipts, and current on-hand inventory. Lead-time and safety stock factors are shown.

   a. Complete the last three rows of the record using an FOQ of 150 units.
   b. Complete the last three rows of the record using the POQ lot-sizing rule, with $P = 2$.
   c. Complete the last three rows of the record using the L4L lot-sizing rule.

2. Figure 15.19 shows a partially completed inventory record. Gross requirements, scheduled receipts, and current on-hand inventory, as well as lead-time and safety stock parameters, are shown.

   a. Complete the record using an FOQ of 200 units.
   b. Complete the record using the POQ rule, with $P = 3$.
   c. Complete the record using the L4L rule.

3. The inventory record in Fig. 15.20 has been partially completed, showing gross requirements, scheduled receipts, and current on-hand inventory. Lead-time and safety stock parameters are also given. Item H-10A is produced in the plant (not purchased).

   a. What is the source of the information already shown for gross requirements and scheduled receipts?
   b. Fill in the last three rows of the record, using an FOQ of 60 units.
       i. Will there be any action notices?
       ii. If there are action notices, what factors would you consider in responding to them?
   c. Revise the planned order release row using the L4L rule.
   d. Revise the planned order release row again, this time using the POQ rule and a value of

Item: XK-12 Description: Rear wheel assembly		Lot Size: Lead Time: 1 week Safety Stock: 40 units							
Date		1	2	3	4	5	6	7	8
Gross requirements		180		120	75		50	50	75
Scheduled receipts		200							
Projected on hand	95								
Planned receipts									
Planned order releases									

FIGURE 15.19

Item: H10-A Description: Chair seat assembly		Lot Size: Lead Time: 3 weeks Safety Stock: 0 units								
Date		31	32	33	34	35	36	37	38	39	40
Gross requirements			70		30		15		30		55
Scheduled receipts		60									
Projected on hand	15										
Planned receipts											
Planned order releases											

FIGURE 15.20

Item: C-1 Description: Motor assembly		Lot Size: Lead Time: **3 weeks** Safety Stock: **20 units**										
Date		1	2	3	4	5	6	7	8	9	10	11	12
Gross requirements			30		20		40		15		5		10
Scheduled receipts				40									
Projected on hand	25												
Planned receipts													
Planned order releases													

FIGURE 15.21

Item: 2R-1 T Description: Nozzle		Lot Size: . Lead Time: **4 weeks** Safety Stock: **15 units**									
Date		12	13	14	15	16	17	18	19	20	21
Gross requirements		25		30		40			25		30
Scheduled receipts			45								
Projected on hand	25										
Planned receipts											
Planned order releases											

FIGURE 15.22

P that should (in the long run) yield an average lot size of 60 units. When computing P, assume that the average weekly demand will be 20 units for the foreseeable future.

4. The inventory record in Fig. 15.21 has been partially completed.

   a. Complete the last three rows of the record using an FOQ of 40 units.
      i. Will there be any action notices?
      ii. If there are action notices, what factors would you consider in responding to them?
   b. Revise the planned order release row using the L4L rule.
   c. Revise the planned order release row using the POQ rule. Find the value of P that should (in the long run) yield an average lot size of

40 units. Assume that the average weekly demand for the foreseeable future is 10 units.

5. A partially completed inventory record is shown in Fig. 15.22.

   a. Complete the record using an FOQ of 45 units. Will there be any action notices?
   b. Revise the planned order release row using the L4L rule.
   c. Revise the planned order release row using the POQ rule. The average weekly demand is 15 units. Use the value of P that should (in the long run) result in an average lot size of 45 units.

6. In the master production schedule for product A, the MPS quantity row (showing *completion* dates) calls for 300 units in week 8. The lead time

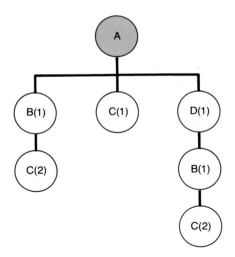

FIGURE 15.23

for production of A is 2 weeks. Develop the material requirements plan for the next six weeks for items B, C, and D. The BOM is shown in Fig. 15.23 and data from the inventory records are shown in Table 15.2. The numbers in parentheses in the BOM are usage quantities. For example, two units of C are needed for each unit of parent B. In deriving C's gross requirements, double the planned order releases from B. Assume that next week is week 1. After completing the plan, identify any action notices that would be issued. *Hint:* The record for item D must be completed first, followed by the records for B and C. An item's gross requirements cannot be derived without knowing the planned order releases of all its parents.

7. The MPS for product A calls for 70 units to be completed in week 4 and 80 units in week 7 (the lead time is 1 week). The MPS for product B calls for 150 units in week 7 (the lead time is 2 weeks). Develop the material requirements plan for the next six weeks for items C, D, E, and F. Identify any action notices that will be provided. The BOMs are shown in Fig. 15.24. Data from inventory records are shown in Table 15.3.

8. Product A is made from two units of B and one unit of C. Item B is assembled from one unit of D and two units of E. Item C is fabricated from two units of D. All lead times are 1 week. In order to minimize inventory, items B, C, and E have L4L lot-sizing rules. Purchased item D must be ordered in lots of 200 because of transportation costs. Only item B has a scheduled receipt, which is for 60 units due in this week. On-hand inventory is 0 for items B, C, and E and 80 units for D. No item has a safety stock requirement.

  a. Draw a product tree (as in Figs. 15.23 and 15.24) to represent the BOM.
  b. The MPS calls for orders of 30 units of A to be finished in weeks 3, 6, and 7. The assembly lead time for A is 1 week. Develop a material requirements plan for the next six weeks for items B, C, D, and E.
  c. Would any action notices be generated? If so, what are they?

9. Figure 15.25 illustrates the BOM of product A.
  • The master production schedule calls for 25 units of A in week 4, 35 units in week 7, and 50 units in week 10. The lead time for A is 2 weeks, so the release dates are weeks 2, 5, and 8.
  • Item C is not just produced to make A. It is also produced to meet the forecasted demand for replacement parts. Past replacement part demand has been 5 units per week. *Hint:* Add 5 units per week to C's gross requirements coming from A.

TABLE 15.2

Data Category	Item		
	B	C	D
Lot-size rule	L4L	FOQ = 800	L4L
Lead time	2	1	3
Safety stock	0	50	0
Scheduled receipts	None	800 (week 1)	None
Beginning (on-hand) inventory	0	80	0

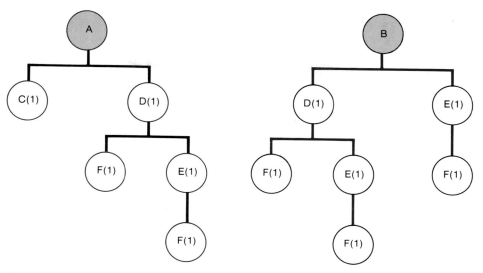

FIGURE 15.24

TABLE 15.3

Data Category	Item			
	C	D	E	F
Lot-size rule	FOQ = 100	L4L	FOQ = 150	POQ (P = 3)
Lead time	1	2	3	2
Safety stock	10	0	0	0
Scheduled receipts	100 (week 1)	None	150 (week 3)	None
Beginning (on-hand) inventory	35	0	125	400

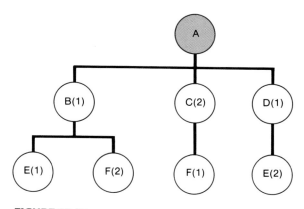

FIGURE 15.25

- The lead times for all items is 2 weeks, except for item F, which has a 3-week lead time.

- A safety stock of 10 units is required for items C and E. No safety stock is required for items B, D, and F.

- The L4L lot-sizing rule is used for items B and D; the POQ lot-sizing rule (P = 3) is used for C. Item E has an FOQ of 300 units, and F has an FOQ of 200 units.

- There are 30 units of B, 70 units of C, 40 units of D, 75 units of E, and 100 units of F on hand.

- There are no scheduled receipts for any of the items.

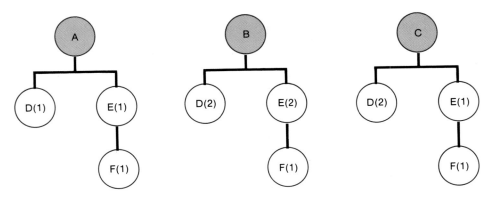

FIGURE 15.26

Develop a material requirements plan for the next eight weeks for items B, C, D, E, and F. Would any action notices be generated? If so, what are they?

10. The following information is available about three MPS items.

    Item A: A 60-unit order is to be received in week 4. A 75-unit order is to be received in week 7.

    Item B: A 100-unit order is to be received in week 7.

    Item C: A 40-unit order is to be received in week 7.

    The lead times are 2 weeks for A, 1 week for B, and 3 weeks for C. Develop the material requirements plan for the next six weeks for items D, E, and F, identifying any action notices that would be provided. The BOMs are shown in Fig. 15.26 and data from the inventory records are shown in Table 15.4.

Advanced Problems

Problem 11 is based on information contained in Chapters 10 and 12. A computer package is useful for problem 14.

11. The dependent demand for a standard item has averaged 20 units per week during the last year. Suppose that the actual dependent demand for the next five weeks is that shown in Table 15.5.

    a. Complete Table 15.5. Begin by making three sets of forecasts for weeks 2–5. The first forecasting technique uses the past average of 20 units for all future weeks. The last two update the forecast weekly with simple exponential smoothing, using smoothing parameter α (see Chapter 10) of either 0.10 or 0.20. Finally, calculate the mean absolute deviation (*MAD*) for each forecasting technique.

TABLE 15.4

	Item		
Data Category	D	E	F
Lot-size rule	FOQ = 200	L4L	POQ (*P* = 2)
Lead time	2 weeks	3 weeks	1 week
Safety stock	10	0	50 units
Scheduled receipts	200 (week 1)	60 (week 2)	None
Beginning (on-hand) inventory	25	0	120

TABLE 15.5

Week	Actual Dependent Demand	Three Forecasts			Forecast Errors		
		Simple Average	Exponential Smoothing		Simple Average	Exponential Smoothing	
			$\alpha = 0.10$	$\alpha = 0.20$		$\alpha = 0.10$	$\alpha = 0.20$
1	0	20	20	20	−20	−20	−20
2	60						
3	0						
4	0						
5	40						
				$MAD =$			

b. Judging from the *MAD* values obtained:
   i. Does the adaptiveness of exponential smoothing help with forecasting dependent demand?
   ii. Would you say that the *MAD* value is small or large, relative to an average weekly demand of 20 units?
   iii. How can such forecasting errors be eliminated?

c. Suppose that 50 units of this item are on hand, desired safety stock is 5 units, lead time is 2 weeks, and there are no scheduled receipts or back orders.
   i. If demand is forecast at 20 units per week, would a new order be released this week using reorder point logic?

   ii. Using the actual dependent-demand schedule in Table 15.5, would a new order be released using MRP logic? Assume L4L lot sizing.

12. Items A and B are dependent-demand items. Item B's only parent is A. Four units of B are needed to make one unit of A. The current material requirements plan for A is shown in Fig. 15.27, and that for B is shown in Fig. 15.28.

   a. Today the planner responsible for items A and B learned some good news and some bad news. Although the scheduled receipt of 75 units of A has been finished (the good news), only 45 units were put in the storeroom; the other 30 were scrapped (the bad news). Recalculate the two inventory rec-

Item: A Description: Leg assembly							Lot Size: 75 units Lead Time: 1 week Safety Stock: 0 units	
Date		1	2	3	4	5	6	7
Gross requirements		60		40			100	45
Scheduled receipts		75						
Projected on hand	10	25	25	60	60	60	35	65
Planned receipts				75			75	75
Planned order releases			75			75	75	

FIGURE 15.27

Item: B Description: Leg						Lot Size: L4L Lead Time: 3 weeks Safety Stock: 0 units		
Date	1	2	3	4	5	6	7
Gross requirements		300			300	300	
Scheduled receipts		300					
Projected on hand	0	0	0	0	0	0	0	0
Planned receipts					300	300	
Planned order releases		300	300				

FIGURE 15.28

ords, reflecting this event. *Hint:* A sched-uled receipt should no longer be shown for A, but its on-hand balance now is 55 units.

b. Would any action notices relative to the new material requirements plan be issued? If so, what are they?

13. Figure 15.29 shows the BOMs for two end items, A and B. Table 15.6 shows the MPS quantity *release* dates (already offset for lead time) for each one. Table 15.7 contains data from inventory records for items C, D, and E. Determine the material requirements plan for items C, D, and

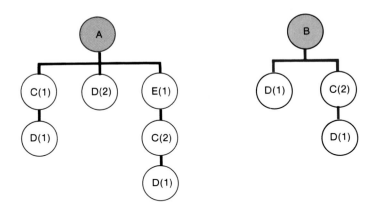

FIGURE 15.29

TABLE 15.6

				Date				
Product	1	2	3	4	5	6	7	8
A		75		75		100		100
B			60			60		

TABLE 15.7

Data Category	Item		
	C	D	E
Lot-size rule	POQ ($P = 3$)	FOQ $= 500$	L4L
Lead time	2	1	3
Safety stock	50	150	0
Scheduled receipts	None	500 (week 1)	75 (week 2)
Beginning (on-hand) inventory	565	350	15

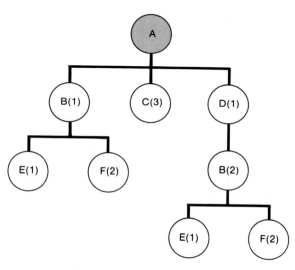

FIGURE 15.30

E for the next eight weeks. Identify any action notices that would be provided.

14. The BOM for product A is shown in Fig. 15.30. The MPS for product A calls for 100 units to be *released* (already offset for lead times) in weeks 2, 4, 5, and 8. Table 15.8 shows data from the inventory records. Develop the material requirements plan for the next eight weeks for each item. Would any action notices be issued?

15. Items A and B are dependent-demand items. Three units of B are needed to make one unit of A. Item B's only parent is A. The current material requirements plans for A and B are shown in Fig. 15.31. If 95 units of A are on hand, rather than 65 units, what is the new material requirements plan? Would there be any action notices?

TABLE 15.8

Data Category	Item				
	B	C	D	E	F
Lot-size rule	FOQ $= 300$	FOQ $= 600$	L4L	POQ ($P = 2$)	L4L
Lead time	4	4	2	2	1
Safety stock	50	100	0	100	0
Scheduled receipts	300 (week 1)	600 (week 2)	100 (week 2)	None	600 (week 1)
Beginning (on-hand) inventory	150	120	50	700	0

Item: A Description:								Lot Size: **75 units** Lead Time: **2 weeks** Safety Stock: **20 units**	
Date	1	2	3	4	5	6	7	8
Gross requirements		100			50			75	60
Scheduled receipts		75							
Projected on hand	65	40	40	40	65	65	65	65	80
Planned receipts					75			75	75
Planned order releases			75			75	75		

Item: B Description:								Lot Size: **L4L** Lead Time: **4 weeks** Safety Stock: **0 units**	
Date	1	2	3	4	5	6	7	8
Gross requirements		225			225	225			
Scheduled receipts		225							
Projected on hand	0	0	0	0	0	0	0	0	0
Planned receipts					225	225			
Planned order releases		225	225						

FIGURE 15.31

SELECTED REFERENCES

Aquilano, Nicholas J., and Dwight E. Smith, "A Formal Set of Algorithms for Project Scheduling with Critical Path Scheduling/Material Requirements Planning," *Journal of Operations Management,* vol. 1, no. 2 (November 1980), pp. 57–67.

Benton, W. C., and D. Clay Whybark, "Material Requirements Planning (MRP) and Purchase Discounts," *Journal of Operations Management,* vol. 2, no. 2 (February 1982), pp. 137–143.

Biggs, Joseph R., Chan K. Hahn, and Peter A. Pinto, "Performance of Lot-Sizing Rules in an MRP System with Different Operating Conditions," *Academy of Management Review,* vol. 5, no. 1 (1980), pp. 89–96.

Blackburn, J., and R. Millen, "Improved Heuristics for Multi-Stage Requirements Planning Systems," *Management Science,* vol. 28, no. 1 (January 1982).

Carlson, J. M., "The Control of Change in a Net Change MRP Environment," *Proceedings of the 23rd Annual Conference,* American Production & Inventory Control Society, Falls Church, Va., October 1980, pp. 177–181.

Fox, R. E., "MRP, Kanban or OPT—What's Best?" *Inventories and Production,* vol. 2, no. 4 (July–August 1982).

———, "OPT, An Answer for America: Part II," *Inventories and Production,* vol. 2, no. 6 (November–December 1982).

———, "OPT, An Answer for America: Part III," *Inventories and Production,* vol. 3, no. 1 (January–February 1983).

Graves, S. C. "Multi-Stage Lot Sizing: An Iterative Procedure." In L. Schwarz (Ed.), *Multi-level Production/Inventory Systems: Theory and Practice.* New York: North-Holland, 1981.

Harl, Johannes E., and Larry P. Ritzman, "A Heuristic Algorithm for Capacity Sensitive Lot Sizing," *Journal of Operations Management,* vol. 5, no. 3 (May 1985), pp. 309–326.

Honeywell, Inc., *Manufacturing IMS/66 (Extended) Systems Handbook,* DE80, rev. 1, June 1977.

International Business Machines Corporation, *Communications Oriented Production Information and Control Systems.* Publications G320-1974–G320-1981.

Jacobs, F. R., "The OPT Scheduling System: A Review of a New Production Scheduling System," *Production and Inventory Management,* vol. 24, no. 3 (1983).

Miller, Jeffrey G., and Linda G. Sprague, "Behind the Growth in Material Requirements Planning," *Harvard Business Review* (September–October 1975), pp. 83–91.

Orlicky, Joseph, *Material Requirements Planning.* New York: McGraw-Hill, 1975.

Plossl, George W., *Manufacturing Controls—The Last Frontier for Profits.* Reston, Va.: Reston Publishing Company, 1973.

Ritzman, Larry P., Barry E. King, and Lee J. Krajewski, "Manufacturing Performance—Pulling the Right Levers," *Harvard Business Review* (March–April 1984), pp. 143–152.

Ritzman, Larry P., and Lee J. Krajewski, "Comparison of Material Requirements Planning and Reorder Point Systems." In Haluk Bekiroglu (Ed.), *Simulation for Production and Inventory Control.* La Jolla, Calif.: Society for Computer Simulation, 1983.

Schroeder, Roger G., John C. Anderson, Sharon E. Tupy, and Edna M. White, "A Study of MRP Benefits and Costs," *Journal of Operations Management,* vol. 2, no. 1 (October 1981), pp. 1–9.

Steinberg, Earle E., Basheer Khumawala, and Richard Scamell, "Requirements Planning Systems in the Health Care Environment," *Journal of Operations Management,* vol. 2, no. 4 (August 1982), pp. 251–259.

Steinberg, Earle E., William B. Lee, and Basheer Khumawala, "A Requirements Planning System for the Space Shuttle Operations Schedule," *Journal of Operations Management,* vol. 1, no. 2 (November 1980), pp. 69–76.

"The Trick of Material Requirements Planning," *Business Week,* June 4, 1979.

White, Edna M., John C. Anderson, Roger G. Schroeder, and Sharon E. Tupy, "A Study of the MRP Implementation Process," *Journal of Operations Management,* vol. 2, no. 3 (May 1982), pp. 145–153.

Whybark, D. Clay, "MRP: A Profitable Concept for Distribution," *Research Issues in Logistics,* 1975, pp. 82–93.

Wight, Oliver W., "MRP II: Manufacturing Resource Planning," *Modern Materials Handling* (September 1979).

CHAPTER

16

HIGH-VOLUME PRODUCTION SYSTEMS

▲ Chapter Outline

▲ Key Questions for Managers

Under what circumstances could we use a just-in-time system effectively?

Should we consider the limitations of process capacity on our manufacturing system?

Which factors should we consider in choosing an appropriate manufacturing system for a process-industry firm?

Can we make all types of manufacturing systems work equally well in a given environment?

What environmental factors affect the performance of our manufacturing system?

irms engaged in high-volume or continuous production cannot always take advantage of material requirements planning. It is most useful in situations involving intermediate volume batch production. In these situations, the requirements are lumpy, and the lead times for component production or purchased items are long. In MRP, we time-phase requirements, so that inventory can be replenished on a timely basis. However, many firms in the United States use **repetitive manufacturing** or **continuous flow manufacturing** systems, both of which involve high volumes. Repetitive manufacturing produces standard, discrete products in relatively small lot sizes. However, continuous flow manufacturing involves long product runs in a linear flow to utilize effectively a large capital investment. In either case, MRP is not the only planning and scheduling alternative available, and under certain conditions, other methods could work as well or better. In this chapter we address systems suitable for high-volume production.

JUST-IN-TIME SYSTEMS ▲

Not too long ago, many U.S. industries enjoyed a competitive edge in technology and inexpensive resources—and the prospect of a bright future in expanding markets. More recently, a significant number of companies in the chemical, steel, electronics, and automotive industries have lost that competitive advantage. One of the most notable competitive challenges came from the Japanese in the automotive industry. In many cases, Japanese cars were made better and priced lower than comparably sized and equipped American cars. This prompted U.S. managers to study Japanese methods of repetitive manufacturing management and control.

What they learned, in retrospect, is not all that surprising, although it is most revealing. The Japanese used no single, magic formula to achieve their success. Their geographic and cultural environment, managerial practices, work-force support, and automation all played a role.

The key to Japanese productivity improvement in repetitive manufacturing is the **just-in-time (JIT) system**. The purpose of JIT is simple: produce (or deliver) the right items in the quantities needed by subsequent production processes (or customers) at the time needed. The intent is to eliminate the buildup of work-in-process inventory by coordinating the flow of materials between production processes. The JIT system also strives to coordinate the final assembly rate with the customer demand rate to eliminate the need for finished goods inventory.

Figure 16.1 illustrates the JIT concept, showing a schematic flow of materials in repetitive manufacturing. The process consists of two standard machine groups, three group technology cells, and a final assembly line. The schedule for the assembly line is coordinated with the market demand rate. Suppose that the assembly line works on lot sizes equivalent to 25 percent of the daily demand requirements. Consequently, every two hours the assembly line gets materials from cells 4 and 5 for the next two hours of assembly. This action prompts cell 5 to get materials from machine group 1 and cell 3, so that it can manufacture the items needed next on the assembly line. Similarly, cell 4 gets more materials from cell 3. Finally, cell 3 must get materials from machine

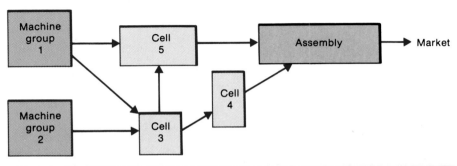

FIGURE 16.1   Flow of Materials in Repetitive Manufacturing

groups 1 and 2 to support the next request from cells 4 and 5. Machine groups 1 and 2 must get more raw materials.

The preceding description is an oversimplified example of JIT in practice. However, it demonstrates the production coordination that can significantly reduce inventory levels and increase productivity. In general, JIT is a *pull system*, in which a production process pulls material from a prior process in support of the final assembly schedule. The system can have substantial pay-offs, as shown in Managerial Practice 16.1.

MANAGERIAL PRACTICE 16.1 ▲

U.S. Manufacturers Enjoy the Benefits of JIT

John Deere & Company

Deere executives believe that successful JIT requires education involving employee participation and a master plan to ensure that JIT philosophy is integrated company-wide. The rewards have been substantial. Since 1981, Deere has realized a 26 percent reduction in inventory levels overall. At one plant in particular, the Horicon Works, the inventory reduction was 50 percent. In addition, lower manufacturing costs and improved quality have led to price reductions for the consumer. For example, the new 100 series of lawn tractors are \$140–\$170 less than the previous models.

Westinghouse

Spencer Duin, general manager of Westinghouse's Control Division, believes that JIT is an evolutionary process, requiring a cultural change and a long-term commitment from management and employees. Westinghouse converted a conventional plant in Asheville, North Carolina, to a JIT plant with outstanding results. Inventories were reduced 45 percent, productivity increased 30 percent, product warranty costs decreased 35 percent, and the amount of required manufacturing space decreased 40 percent. The company also applied JIT to the front office and reduced the customer ordering cycle from seven weeks to seven minutes.

Apple Computer

Ralph Russo, director of world-wide materials, stresses that JIT is not a goal in itself, but rather a part of an integrated and steadily improved-upon manufacturing strategy. Apple's successes in Singapore and the United States are impressive, including a 65 percent reduction in inventories, high quality levels, greater ability to respond to consumer demand, a highly motivated work force, and a better company reputation. Management attributes these successes to JIT, Total Quality Control (TQC), computer integrated manufacturing (CIM), and robotics.

Source: "JIT Urgency Revealed During APICS Summit," *P&IM Review with APICS News*, (August 1986), pp. 26–30.

DECISION LINKAGES WITH JUST-IN-TIME SYSTEMS ▲

The total JIT system involves more than inventory considerations. It is a comprehensive approach to creating a competitive advantage through operations. In this section we show how Japanese automakers have used JIT effectively to link corporate strategy and operations strategy. Although many firms worldwide are following the footsteps of these leaders who, in some respects, can be said to have a unique situation, this example demonstrates what can be done under conditions of adversity. Japan has almost no natural resources or domestic energy supply, a condition accentuated by the oil crisis in 1973. Most raw materials must be imported. The country is also quite densely settled. With space at a premium, an acre of land costs as much as $1.5 million. Transportation lead times to foreign markets rule out quick response times for automobiles customized to individual preferences.

Corporate Strategy

Top management recognized Japan's environmental obstacles and sought better ways to compete. A corporate strategy to achieve the lowest cost, coupled with high volumes, consistent quality, and a fuel-efficient car, emerged. Distinctive competencies for Japanese manufacturers are work-force characteristics and vendor proximity. The work force comes from a closely knit culture that encourages group consciousness, and suppliers locate near assembly plants because of the country's size and geography.

Operations Strategy

The operations strategy to achieve that corporate mission centers on dramatic improvements in (1) inventory turnover and (2) labor productivity. The strategy is to make the manufacturing operations so smooth that only minimal inventory is justified. The way in which decisions are linked to low inventory and high productivity is shown in Table 16.1. Because inventory policies are the key, let's begin there.

Inventory.   Inventory, which wastes assets and masks solvable problems, is viewed by the Japanese as the root of all evil. The real value of the JIT system is that of a catalyst, exposing problems standing in the way of further inventory reduction. Inventory reduction results from smaller lot sizes and smaller safety stocks. The Japanese aim for lot sizes considerably less than a one-day supply. Small lot sizes reduce cycle inventory. Less inventory helps cut lead times, which in turn cuts pipeline (WIP) inventory. Such reductions involve a risk, as inventory protects against unexpected demand for components and capacity. Inventory is a buffer, absorbing shocks from the environment. The rest of the choices in operations, in effect, aim at eliminating those shocks.

TABLE 16.1 How Japanese Automakers Link Operations Decisions	
Decision Area	**Choice**
Inventory	Minimize lot sizes and safety stock.
Competitive priorities	Emphasize low cost and consistent quality.
Positioning strategy	Have a product focus.
Process design	Minimize setup times.
	Reduce the frequency of setups through product layouts, group technology, and one-worker multiple-machines.
	Automate as much as possible.
	Have a flexible work force.
Work-force management	Seek a flexible, cooperative work force through job enlargement, consensus management, and training.
Capacity	Minimize capacity cushions.
Maintenance	Minimize the frequency and duration of breakdowns.
Materials management	Have a cooperative orientation with vendors.
Master production scheduling	Maintain the same daily output rate for a whole month.
Quality	Put quality control at the source.

Competitive Priorities.   Low cost and consistent quality are the two priorities emphasized most. Superior features (Rolls-Royce quality), volume flexibility, and quick delivery times are emphasized less. As for product flexibility, the Japanese offer a variety of cars through choice of color and options. However, production for overseas markets is not customized to individual orders. End items are standards rather than specials, preproduced to inventory and pushed forward into distribution channels. The erratic demand and last-minute rush jobs of customized products do not link well with low inventory buffers.

Positioning Strategy.   A product focus is chosen to achieve high-volume, low-cost production. Workers and machines are organized around product flows, which are arranged to conform to the necessary sequence of work operations. With line flows, a unit finished at one station goes almost immediately to the station, which reduces inventory. Process repetition makes opportunities for methods improvement more visible.

Process Design.   Small lot sizes can severely hurt productivity because setups are more frequent, frittering away large amounts of human and capital resources. This problem is particularly serious in fabrication operations, where components are made for the final assembly line. One solution is to design the process to minimize setup times. For example, changing dies on the large presses that form automobile hoods and fenders can take three to four hours. The Japanese responded by cutting die-change time to less than 10 minutes, using what they call *single-digit setup*. It utilizes a variety of techniques, including conveyors for die storage, simpler dies, machine controls, microcomputers to automatically feed and position work, and preparing for changeover while the current job is being processed.

The other solution is to reduce setup frequency. A product focus helps here, particularly if volumes are high enough to dedicate a group of machines and workers to one product or a mix of similar products. In fact, a product layout can eliminate setups entirely. If volume is insufficient to keep a line busy with similar products, a second tactic is to use group technology. Components with common attributes and enough collective volume are manufactured on what is essentially a small production line. Changeovers from one component in the family to the next are minimal. A final tactic for eliminating setups is to use the one-worker-multiple machines approach, which essentially is a one-person line. One worker operates several machines, with each machine advancing the line a step at a time. This method is common in feeder operations, where a worker runs as many as five machines simultaneously. The same product is made over and over, so setups are eliminated. This approach avoids half-automation, where a worker simply monitors a machine's performance.

Another link with process design is automation. Sakichi Toyoda, the founder of Toyota, has said, "Whenever there is money, invest it in machinery." Automation is a key to low-cost production. For example, Japan leads the world in using robots, which have the lowest wage rate of all. The relentless reduction of inventory frees money for automation. In contrast, in the U.S. economy, more than two times as much money is held in inventory as is invested each year in plant modernization and capacity expansion.

The final link is a flexible work force, which helps to absorb shocks without inventory buffers. Workers are able and willing to respond to capacity bottlenecks. Job boundaries are broad and workers multiskilled. They can help coworkers and often even change to a different job to alleviate bottlenecks. A considerable investment in education and training is required, but it builds quick response to problems and job variety into the system.

Work-Force Management.　　Several aspects of Japanese operations strategy require a flexible and cooperative work force. How can this be achieved, when the high-volume production of a product focus creates the potential of repetitive, monotonous work? They have three answers: job enlargement, consensus management, and training.

Workers participate in some decisions reserved in many U.S. companies for middle management. Quality circles provide one kind of job enlargement.

Teamwork is an important aspect of just-in-time systems. At the New United Motors manufacturing plant, team leader Taira Tsukimori from Japan (right) overlooks the construction of a new Toyota Corolla FX16. The plant is a General Motors and Toyota joint venture in Fremont, California.

These small, voluntary groups are team-oriented. They meet periodically to find ways to improve operations in their work areas, often generating sound ideas for improving productivity. Job enlargement also involves rotating employees among jobs, having them help co-workers with temporary capacity bottlenecks, and doing their own inspection and maintenance.

Two distinctive features of Japanese culture are a strong group orientation and a desire for harmony (called *wa*). Consistent with these features, while making jobs more satisfying, is **consensus management**. Managers seek consensus before making changes, fostering a sense of equality. An important distinction, however, is that decisions are made by committee and consensus at lower levels of management rather than by top-down edict as in many U.S. companies. The process of achieving consensus is called *ringi* and, although it is inefficient in time and energy, it is very effective for implementing decisions once they have been made. Managers also often go onto the plant floor to help solve problems. There are fewer visible status differences. The Honda plant in Ohio has an open office layout. No partitions, doors, or status symbols separate managers from other employees.

Workers are carefully selected, training begins immediately, and training continues as part of the job until the employee retires. This approach creates and maintains a knowledgeable work force. Considerable attention is given to job security, which helps to retain the educational investment in human resources. It also reduces the fear of methods improvements and technological change, which are keys to productivity improvements.

Capacity.   Extra labor and equipment capacity helps overcome unexpected bottlenecks. The Japanese view such cushions as waste, which must be eliminated to increase productivity. The lack of cushions links well with a low-cost position, so long as the shocks they guard against are minimized.

Maintenance.   One type of shock is equipment failure. A disruption at one station quickly affects many other work stations when inventory is not available to decouple them. The Japanese response is to find ways to reduce the frequency and duration of breakdowns. One tactic is to allow three hours between shifts for regular preventive maintenance. Another is to make workers responsible for routinely maintaining their own equipment. Employees pride themselves in keeping their machines in top condition.

Materials Management.   One aspect of purchasing is vendor relations. Here Japan has another distinctive competency. Domestic suppliers are located in close proximity to plants. Frequent, small shipments are possible, without paying excessive penalties in transportation costs. Management cultivates close, harmonious relationships with vendors. Purchases are concentrated in a smaller number of suppliers than is done in the United States. This approach makes a plant more vulnerable to supply disruptions, but increases the incentive for suppliers to avoid disruptions. One expectation is just-in-time deliveries, which links to the goal of minimal inventory.

Master Production Scheduling.   Two steps are taken to minimize disruptions that would impede inventory reduction. First, components are standardized insofar as possible. For example, even though a Japanese elevator manufacturer customizes its final products, many of the parts going into the final product have been standardized. Such part commonality increases volumes, which tends to reduce inventory and increase productivity. Second, the master production schedule is stable, and lot sizes for end items are very small. The daily output rate for each end item stays the same for an entire month. After a month, it is adjusted for forecast errors and inventory imbalances among models. Small lot sizes and rotating output frequently from one model to the next eliminate lumpy component demand and reduce capacity bottlenecks. Both results help to reduce inventory and increase productivity.

Quality.   Scrap and rework are inconsistent with an operations strategy aimed at low inventory, high productivity, and consistent quality. They disrupt the uniform flow of materials that JIT strives to maintain. The Japanese make quality everyone's concern. Quality is controlled at the source, with workers acting as their own inspectors. Defective units are, upon discovery, immediately returned to the worker responsible for them. Workers are encouraged to stop the entire assembly line if a quality problem arises. This is a costly action but brings the problem to everyone's attention, rather than masking it. Quality circles also help in this regard, in addition to being part of a program for job enlargement.

IMPLEMENTING JUST-IN-TIME SYSTEMS ▲

Perhaps the most publicized just-in-time system is Toyota's kanban system. The word **kanban** means card or visible record in Japanese. As the system's name suggests, Toyota uses cards to control the flow of production through the factory. Although there are many different types of cards, the two main types used by Toyota are the *withdrawal* kanban and the *production-order* kanban. The withdrawal kanban specifies the item and the quantity the subsequent process should withdraw from the preceding process and the stocking locations for each process. The production-order kanban specifies the item and production quantity the preceding process must produce, the materials required and where to find them, and where to store the finished item. The cards are attached to containers representing approximately 10 percent of the daily requirement for the item. This implies that production lot sizes as small as one-tenth the average daily requirements appear to be economical.

Figure 16.2 shows how the two cards are used to control production flow. The two processes shown are similar to cell 4 and the assembly line in Fig. 16.1. In all, eight steps are required:

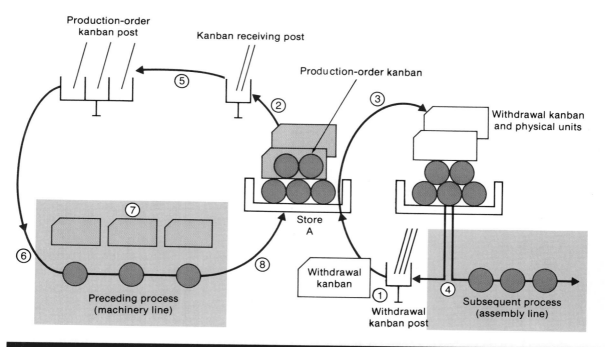

FIGURE 16.2 The Flow of Kanban System Cards

Source: Y. Monden, "Adaptable Kanban System Helps Toyota Maintain Just-in-Time Production," Reprinted from *Industrial Engineering,* May 1981, p. 33. Copyright © Institute of Industrial Engineers, 25 Technology Park/Atlanta, Norcross, Georgia 30092.

Step 1. Accumulated withdrawal kanban and the empty containers are taken to storage location A.

Step 2. The empty containers are exchanged for full containers. The production-order kanban on each full container is detached and placed on the kanban receiving post.

Step 3. The contents of the full containers are checked against the specifications on the withdrawal kanban, and if satisfactory, a withdrawal kanban is attached to each full container. The containers are moved to the inbound stocking location of the subsequent process.

Step 4. When work begins on a container at the subsequent process, the withdrawal kanban is detached and placed on the post.

Step 5. The production sequence at the preceding process begins with the removal of the production-order cards from kanban receiving post. They are reviewed and sorted before placing them on the production-order kanban post.

Step 6. The parts are produced in the sequence of the production-order kanban on the post.

Step 7. The production-order kanban and the container move as a pair during processing.

Step 8. In the last step the finished units are transported to storage location A to support the production requirements of the subsequent process.

All work stations and suppliers are coordinated in a similar way to provide just-in-time quantities of materials.

General Operating Rules.   The operating rules for the kanban system are simple and are designed to facilitate the flow of materials, while maintaining control of inventory levels:

1. Each container must have a kanban.

2. Materials are *always* obtained by the subsequent process from the preceding process. Parts are *never* moved from the preceding process to the subsequent process because, sooner or later, parts will be supplied that are not yet needed for production.

3. Containers of parts must never be removed from a storage area without an authorizing kanban.

4. The containers should always contain the same number of good parts. The use of nonstandard containers or irregularly filled containers disrupts the production flow of the subsequent process.

5. Defective parts should never be passed along to the subsequent process. Not only is material wasted, but the time of workers at the downstream work stations who process the defective parts is also wasted.

6. Total production should not exceed the total amount authorized on the production-order cards in the system. Similarly, the quantity of parts withdrawn for the subsequent process should not exceed the total amount authorized on the withdrawal cards in the system.

Determining Inventory Level. The amount of inventory (on-hand plus scheduled receipts) of each part is equal to the authorized number of parts in each container multiplied by the number of kanban card sets for that part. The number of kanban card sets is

$$k = \frac{\text{Average demand during lead time plus safety stock}}{\text{Size of container}}$$

$$= \frac{d(\overline{w} + \overline{p})(1 + \alpha)}{c}$$

where

k = number of production-order and withdrawal card sets for a given part

d = expected daily demand for the part, in units

$\overline{w}$ = average waiting time during the production process plus materials handling time per container in decimal fractions of a day

$\overline{p}$ = average processing time per container in decimal fractions of a day

c = quantity in a standard container of the part (not more than 10 percent of the daily demand)

α = a policy variable of not more than 10 percent, which reflects the efficiency of the work stations producing and using the part

Because each full container must have a card, k also specifies the number of authorized full containers of the part. The kanban system allows management to fine-tune the flow of materials in the system in a straight-forward way. For example, removing card sets from the system reduces the number of authorized containers of the part, which results in reducing the inventory of the part.

The container quantity c and the efficiency factor α are also variables that management can use to control inventory. Adjusting c changes the lot sizes, and adjusting α changes the amount of safety stock. The kanban system is actually a special form of the base-stock system that we described in Chapter 12. In this case, the stocking level is $d(\overline{w} + \overline{p})(1 + \alpha)$ and the order quantity is fixed at c units. Each time a container of parts is removed from the base stock, authorization is given to replace it.

APPLICATION 16.1

The Westerville Auto Parts Company produces rocker-arm assemblies for use in the steering and suspension systems of four-wheel drive trucks. A typical container of parts spends 0.02 days in processing and 0.08 days in materials handling and waiting during its manufacturing cycle. The daily demand for the part is 2000 units. Management feels that demand for the rocker-arm assembly is uncertain enough to warrant a safety stock equivalent to 10 percent of its authorized inventory.

1. If there are 22 parts in each container, how many kanban card sets (production-order and withdrawal cards) should be authorized?

2. Suppose that a proposal to revise the plant layout would cut materials handling and waiting time per container to 0.06 days. How many card sets would be needed?

Solution

The two calculations are as follows:

1. If $d = 2000$ units/day, $\bar{p} = 0.02$ day, $\alpha = 0.10$, $\bar{w} = 0.08$ day, and $c = 22$ units, then

$$k = \frac{2000(0.08 + 0.02)(1.10)}{22} = \frac{220}{22} = 10 \text{ card sets}$$

2. If $d = 2000$ units/day, $\bar{p} = 0.02$ day, $\alpha = 0.10$, $\bar{w} = 0.06$ day, and $c = 22$ units, then

$$k = \frac{2000(0.06 + 0.02)(1.10)}{22} = \frac{176}{22} = 8 \text{ card sets}$$

The average lead time per container is given as $(\bar{w} + \bar{p})$. With a lead time of 0.10 day, 10 card sets are needed. However, if the improved facility layout reduces the materials handling time and waiting time $(\bar{w})$ to 0.06 day, only 8 card sets are needed. The maximum authorized inventory of the rocker-arm assembly is kc units. Thus in (a) the maximum authorized inventory is 220 units but in (b) only 176 units. Reducing $\bar{w}$ by 25 percent has reduced the inventory of the part by 20 percent.

Kanban Signals

The two-card system of Toyota is not the only way to signal the need for more production of a part. Other, less formal, methods are possible.

Single-Card System. In this system there is only one card for each container. The signal to produce occurs when an empty container with a card appears in the storage area. The card can be removed and put on a receiving post and ultimately sequenced into production. The card is replaced on a container when production commences and containers filled with parts are returned to the storage area. The user of the parts retrieves a container and, when it has been depleted, returns the container with the card still attached, and so on. The single-card system permits less control over withdrawal quantities because it does not have a separate withdrawal card.

Container System. Sometimes it is possible to use the container itself as a signal device: An empty container signals the need to fill it. The amount of inventory of the part is adjusted by adding or removing containers. This system works well when the container is specially designed for a part and no other parts could accidentally be put in it. Such would be the case when the container is actually a pallet or fixture used to position the part during precision processing.

Containerless Systems. Systems requiring no containers have been devised. In assembly-line operations, operators having their own workbench areas, put completed units on painted squares, one unit per square. Each painted square represents a container, and the number of painted squares on each operator's bench is calculated to balance the line flow. When the subsequent user removes a unit from one of the producer's squares, the empty square signals the need to produce another unit.

Another containerless system is one familiar to all of us. The next time you go to McDonald's for a hamburger, note the system used to replenish the

The production control system at this fast-food shop in Brussels, Belgium, is an example of a container-less kanban system. Meals are positioned on the sliding rack in the center of the photo. The withdrawal of a meal by a clerk signals the need to make another one.

supply of hamburgers. Either a command from the manager or the assembler (the clerk who puts your order together) starts production, or the number of hamburgers in the ramp itself signals the need. Either way, the customer dictates production.

Final Assembly Schedule

It is obvious from our discussion of the Toyota system that the **final assembly schedule** drives the entire system. Such a system doesn't work well if the load on individual work centers fluctuates daily. The Japanese achieve uniform work-center flows by assembling the same type and number of units each day. This creates a uniform daily demand at all feeder work stations. Capacity planning, which recognizes capacity constraints at critical work stations, and line balancing are used to develop the monthly assembly schedule. For example, at Toyota there may be a need to produce 4500 Corollas per week for the next month, requiring two full shifts, five days a week. This means that 900 Corollas, or 450 per shift, must be produced each day. Three models of Corollas are produced: 4-door sedans (S), 2-door coupes (C), and wagons (W). Suppose that Toyota needs 200 4-door sedans, 150 2-door coupes, and 100 wagons per shift to satisfy market demand. To produce 450 units in one shift of 480 minutes, the line must produce a Corolla every 480/450 = 1.067 minutes.

Note that the production requirements are in the ratio of 4 Ss to 3 Cs to 2 Ws, found by dividing model production requirements by the greatest common divisor, 50. If the Toyota planner develops a production cycle consisting of 9 units, of which 4 are 4-door sedans, 3 are 2-door coupes, and 2 are wagons, the cycle would have to be completed in 9(1.067) = 9.60 minutes. Consequently, with these requirements per shift for each model and adequate capacity, Toyota's planner can balance the mixed-model assembly line for the month's production schedule. Table 16.2 shows the data for these requirements and a

TABLE 16.2 A Production Cycle for Corolla Models		
Model	**Production Requirements per Shift**	**Number Required in One Cycle**
4-door sedan (S)	200	4
2-door coupe (C)	150	3
Wagon (W)	100	2
Total	450	9
Cycle		
S–W–S–C–S–C–S–W–C		

possible production cycle for the models. Note that production of each model is not batched. Instead (in this example) the cycle would be repeated 50 times per shift [or 50(9.60 min) = 480 min]. This repetition generates a steady rate of component requirements for the various models and allows the use of small lot sizes. Consequently, the capacity requirements of feeder work stations are greatly smoothed. These requirements can be compared to actual capacities during the planning phase, and modifications to the cycle, production requirements, or capacities can be made as necessary.

Continuous Improvement

One of the hallmarks of world-class manufacturing is continuous improvement. Management should always be searching for ways to get better, and JIT systems spotlight areas that need improvement. However, the road to world-class manufacturing can be long and arduous.

Toyota spent ten years perfecting its system. During those years the company worked at reducing inventory levels on a trial-and-error basis. Figure 16.3 characterizes the philosophy behind the kanban system. The water level represents the inventory level, including buffer and work-in-process inventories. When the water level is high enough, the ship passes over the rocks, symbolizing good customer service. To the Japanese manager, clear sailing implies too much inventory and waste, and he gives the order to reduce the number of authorized cards. Lowering the water level ultimately means that the ship will hit a rock, which represents one of the many problems encountered in manufacturing. This step is intentional because the problem becomes obvious, and workers, supervisors, engineers, and analysts make every effort to demolish the exposed rock. For example, the Kawasaki plant in Nebraska periodically cuts buffers to almost zero. Problems are exposed, recorded, and later assigned as improvement projects. After the tops of the rocks are shaved off, inventory buffers are permanently cut. This is the trial-and-error process that the Japanese have used to shape their manufacturing environment to provide more efficient manufacturing operations. Managerial Practice 16.2 describes how one U.S. company used JIT to gain continual improvements in operations.

Managerial Considerations

Although JIT systems have worked well in some large companies, they cannot treat all manufacturing ills. In the remainder of this section we examine some of the managerial considerations regarding JIT. After comparing advantages and disadvantages of JIT systems, we see how some companies balance these factors to best use JIT concepts.

FIGURE 16.3   Philosophy Behind the Kanban System

Continuous Improvement Through JIT

In 1981 an automobile company opened a new plant in Mexico to manufacture components. The plant was set up in a classical batch-type operation and managed to maximize machine utilization. In 1985, a second plant was built because of increased demands. Shortly afterward management started to modify the manufacturing systems at both plants to what the company calls synchronous manufacturing, a term synonymous with JIT. At the same time, a goal of continuous improvement was instituted. As time passed, continual improvements were made to the layouts of the work cells, the relationship between the plant and the suppliers, the length of the supply chain (by using more local suppliers and bringing some operations in house), work methods, and inventory levels. Management and employees both sought ways to improve operations. The move to just-in-time manufacturing and the continuous improvements thereafter resulted in significant operational benefits as shown in the following table.

	Before JIT	After JIT			
	July 1985	July 1987	Improvement*	January 1988	Improvement†
Work in process ($)	4,645,700	842,500	82%	347,700	59%
Labor content (hr/unit)	0.173	0.141	18	0.130	8
Floor space (sq. ft)	474,100	328,300	31	309,400	6
Rework (%)	11.2	6.7	41	6.0	10
Scrap (%)	2.5	1.5	38	1.2	20

*Percentage improvement between July 1987 and July 1985.
†Percentage improvement between January 1988 and July 1987.

In addition, the average reduction in cycle times was 99 percent. It is no wonder that the Boston Consulting Group picked two of the components as world-class leaders.

Source: Data and information supplied by Charles P. Ringo, Sr., Senior Manufacturing Engineer.

Advantages of JIT Systems.   Table 16.3 contains a list of some of the advantages of JIT systems. One goal is to drive setup times so low that production of one unit or a part becomes economical. Although this goal is rarely achieved, the focus is still on small-lot production. In addition, constant attention is given to cutting safety stock and WIP inventory between manufacturing processes. The result is less storage space and inventory investment. Smaller lot sizes and smoothed flows of materials help to reduce manufacturing lead times, increase work-force productivity, and improve equipment utilization.

The kanban system is simplicity itself. Product mix or volume can be changed by adjusting the number of card sets in the system. The priority of each production order is reflected in the sequence of the production-order cards on the post. The sequence is determined by the stock levels of each part in the storage area: Production orders for parts that are running low are placed before those for parts that have more supply.

Just-in-time systems also involve a considerable amount of work-force participation in decision making on the shop floor. Small-group interaction sessions encourage worker participation and have resulted in improvements in many aspects of manufacturing, not the least of which is product quality. Overall, the advantages of JIT systems experienced by the companies using them have caused many managers to reevaluate their own systems and consider adapting their plant operations to the JIT philosophy.

Disadvantages of JIT Systems.   Table 16.4 contains a list of some of the disadvantages of JIT systems. Most of them relate to system requirements that may pose problems for firms.

From a behavioral perspective, workers and first-line supervisors must now take on responsibilities formerly assigned to middle managers and support staff. Activities such as scheduling, expediting, and productivity improvements become part of the duties of lower-level personnel. Consequently, organizational relationships must be reoriented to build close cooperation and mutual

---

TABLE 16.3   Advantages of Just-in-Time Systems

- Reduce space requirements.
- Reduce inventory investment in purchased parts, raw materials, work in process, and finished goods.
- Reduce manufacturing lead times.
- Increase the productivity of direct labor employees, indirect support employees, and clerical staff.
- Increase equipment utilization.
- Reduce paperwork and require only simple planning systems.
- Set valid priorities for production scheduling.
- Encourage participation by the work force.
- Increase product quality.

TABLE 16.4   Disadvantages of Just-in-Time Systems

- Require workers and first-line supervisors to take responsibility for shop-floor production control and productivity improvements.
- Require an atmosphere of close cooperation and mutual trust between the work force and management.
- Require daily production schedules that are virtually identical for extended periods.
- Require actual daily production to closely approximate the daily schedule.
- Cannot respond rapidly to changes in product design, product mix, or large demand volumes.
- Require a large number of production setups and frequent shipments of purchased items from suppliers.
- Require parts to be produced and moved in the smallest containers possible.
- Not well-suited for irregularly used parts or specially ordered products.
- May require layout changes.
- May require changes in reward systems.
- Require revision of purchase agreements as the number of suppliers shrinks.

trust between the work force and management. Such cooperation and trust may be difficult to achieve, particularly in light of the typical adversarial positions taken by labor and management in the past. For example, the Mazda plant in Flat Rock, Michigan, was experiencing quality problems in August 1988. Absenteeism greater than the Japanese expected and inexperience of the work force were cited as major contributors. Some people felt that the real problem was the lack of understanding of the American culture by Japanese managers. As the president of UAW Local 3000 put it, "To the Japanese, work is the most important part of life, and they expect everybody to be as dedicated as they are. But to Americans, the job is there to support your life on the outside."*

Certain other aspects of JIT systems may preclude their use generally. The firm must have a product focus and daily production schedules must be stable for extended periods. At Toyota, the master production schedule is stated in fractions of days over a three-month period and is revised only once a month. The first month of the schedule is frozen in order to avoid disruptive changes in the daily production schedule for each work station; that is, the work stations execute the same work schedule each day of the month. At the beginning of each month card sets are reissued for the new daily production rate. Stable schedules are needed, so that production lines can be balanced and new assignments found for employees who would otherwise be underutilized. The JIT system cannot respond quickly to scheduling changes because there is little slack inventory or capacity to absorb these changes.

If the inventory advantages of JIT systems are to be realized, a large number of setups must be performed, to keep container sizes as small as pos-

*"Mazda's Michigan Plant Produces Many Problems," by Nunzio Lupo and John Lippert, Knight-Ridder Newspapers, *Columbus Dispatch*, August 27, 1988.

sible. Achieving this objective requires significant reductions in setup times. In some cases, small setup times will not be possible, and large-lot production will still have to be used. Also, if frequently scheduled, small shipments of purchased items cannot be arranged with suppliers, large inventory savings for these items cannot be realized. In the United States, such arrangements may prove difficult because of the geographical dispersion of suppliers. In addition, even though card sets can be assigned to irregularly used parts, the policy variable must be larger to provide more safety stock. This precaution is necessary because JIT systems do not provide forward visibility of requirements as does, for example, MRP. Tomorrow's requirements are assumed to be the same as today's. Also, if the firm produces any items specifically to customer order, JIT systems can be used only for those parts or raw materials that have reasonably stable requirements. In most cases these items would be low in the bills of materials of the end items and by the time the complete product was manufactured most of the advantages of JIT production would be lost.

Reward systems also are involved. At General Motors, for example, a plan to reduce stock at one plant ran into trouble because the production superintendent refused to cut back production of unneeded parts; his salary was based on his plant's production volume.

The realignment of reward systems isn't the only hurdle. Labor contracts traditionally have reduced management's flexibility in reassigning workers as the need arises. As a result, a typical automobile plant in the United States has several unions and dozens of labor classifications. In order to gain more flexibility, management in some cases has obtained union concessions by granting other types of benefits. In other cases management has relocated plants to take advantage of nonunion or foreign labor. In contrast, at Toyota, management deals with only one company union, and there are only eight different labor classifications in a typical plant.

Even plant layout may have to be changed. For example, many plants receive raw materials and purchased parts by rail. To get smaller, more frequent shipments, truck deliveries are preferable. Loading docks may have to be reconstructed or expanded and certain operations relocated to accommodate the changes in transportation mode and quantities of arriving materials.

Finally, the ability to manage purchased item inventory is related to the number of suppliers. At one time, General Motors had more than 3500 suppliers just for its assembly operations. (Toyota has only 250.) General Motors now uses a much smaller number of suppliers. This change placed more reliance on fewer suppliers, which had its own risks, but contracts were worked out to ensure dependable delivery of high-quality materials.

Balancing Advantages and Disadvantages.   Even though JIT systems have disadvantages, many firms have improved their operations by adapting to JIT concepts. The automobile industry offers some good examples. Chrysler uses a JIT system and found that by changing to reusable containers for moving parts it could save $9 million on cardboard packaging. Ford and GM also use JIT systems. Of course, Japanese firms locating in the United States use JIT concepts, including Nissan in Smyrna, Tennessee, Honda in Marysville, Ohio, Toyota in Fremont, California, and Mazda in Flat Rock, Michigan.

Just-in-time concepts are also being used in other repetitive manufacturing industries. The name used at IBM is "continuous flow manufacturing" and at Hewlett-Packard, "stockless production." Motorola, Honeywell, Westinghouse, Black and Decker, Briggs and Stratton, John Deere, Bendix, Rockwell, and Tennant all use JIT concepts in their operations. The particular form used by companies in the United States may not be a mirror image of the JIT systems used in Japan. However, these companies have utilized key elements of JIT systems to their advantage.

CHOOSING A PRODUCTION AND INVENTORY MANAGEMENT SYSTEM ▲

In this section we briefly compare various production and inventory management systems for discrete item production systems. In Chapter 12, we presented the reorder point (ROP) system and in Chapter 15, the material requirements planning system (MRP). Also in Chapter 15 we discussed optimized production technology (OPT) and in this chapter, just-in-time (JIT) systems. Obviously, management has several systems to choose from—and many more will become available in the future. Do all these systems work equally well in a given environment? To this question we respond: absolutely not. In our research of these systems (see references at the end of this chapter) we found that MRP outperforms ROP as the number of levels in the bills of material increase. Also, as lot sizes become larger, MRP's advantages over ROP, which does not recognize bills of materials, increase. The kanban system works well for high-volume, repetitive manufacturing with small lot sizes and short setup times. Otherwise, the kanban system performs poorly. For example, MRP or a hybrid of MRP with kanban, might work better when the company produces items to customer order, as well as to stock. However, OPT may outperform MRP because capacity considerations are built into requirements planning. More experience with OPT is needed, though, before we will know whether it is really better than MRP. In general, although each of these systems will work well in certain environments, they may not work well in other environments. The choice of a system can affect inventory levels and customer service. High inventory levels put a strain on financial resources and may limit the capability of the company to invest in needed capital improvements. Poor customer service affects market share and the ability of the company to compete in the marketplace. An inappropriate choice of system can be an expensive mistake.

Which specific aspects of manufacturing affect system performance? We have identified several factors that affect inventory investment, productivity, and customer service, but by and large, the production and inventory management system used does not have an overriding impact on any of these factors. From our studies we concluded that reducing lot sizes and setup times have the greatest impact, followed by reducing yield losses and increasing worker flexibility. Other aspects of manufacturing, such as capacity slack or safety stock, bills of materials, facility design, and supplier performance, had less impact on performance. Nonetheless, our philosophy is that firms should "get their house in order" by working to improve these environmental factors for whatever production and inventory system is being used. For example, reducing lot sizes and setup times will decrease inventory investment and improve customer service, regardless of the system being used. The point is that any production and inventory system will not by itself set things right but that significant improvements in performance *can* be achieved by shaping the manufacturing environments properly.

MANUFACTURING IN THE PROCESS INDUSTRIES ▲

Firms in the process industries have an environment different from that of firms in repetitive manufacturing or fabrication and assembly industries, where MRP or JIT systems are applicable. Process industry firms have high-volume production rates and a product focus, such as those found in the chemical, paper, beer, oil, steel, and forest products industries. They often have a flow-shop orientation, utilizing product layouts with high capital intensity. However, some process industry firms have hybrid flow shop-job shop orientations because their products are highly differentiated. These industries include pharmaceuticals and specialized chemicals.

Process industries are more capital intensive than fabrication and assembly industries. Taylor et al. (1981) found that process industries have a ratio of $1.8 of sales to $1 of gross plant investment, compared to a ratio of 3:1 for fabrication and assembly industries. Process industry plants are designed for a specific throughput, and the equipment typically operates seven days a week, three shifts per day. Thus production and inventory management systems must be capacity-oriented. The capacity cushion is very small, and significantly increasing capacity with extra overtime or shifts is impossible.

Lot-Size Considerations

Consider Fig. 16.4, which depicts two chemical manufacturing processes: reaction and separation. A surge tank separates the two processes and can absorb minor variations in process flow, although its capacity is insufficient to decouple the reactor schedule from that of the separator. Consequently, we will treat the system as a single process, which uses one raw material and three additives to produce five chemicals and one by-product.

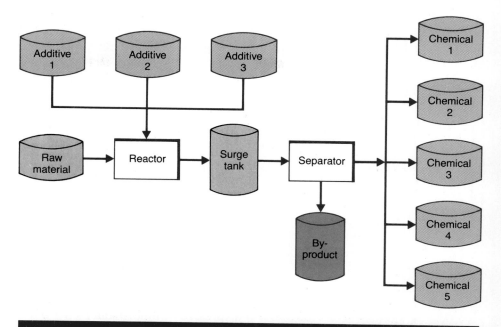

FIGURE 16.4 Chemical Process Example

Plant Load.   Suppose that the plant produces the five chemicals in a predetermined cycle. That is, the chemicals are produced $1-2-3-4-5$ in each cycle, and the cycles are repeated enough times to satisfy annual demand for the chemicals. For chemical i, the total number of days of production per year T_i is

$$T_i = N_i t_{si} + D_i t_{pi}$$

where

$$N_i = \text{number of cycles per year for chemical } i$$

$$t_{si} = \text{setup time in days for chemical } i$$

$$D_i = \text{annual demand for chemical } i$$

$$t_{pi} = \text{process time in days per unit of chemical } i$$

The factor T_i is actually a measure of *load*. The only unknown in the equality is N_i. By changing N_i, the time required for setup changes, while the total time required to produce the annual demand remains the same. Also, by changing N_i, the lot size for chemical i changes because lot size $= D_i/N_i$. Small values of N_i create large lots, and large values create small lots. Consequently, some value of N_i minimizes annual setup and inventory holding costs.

Total Annual Costs.   If we assume that demand for each chemical is constant and uniform throughout the year, we can use a modified version of the total cost equation for the economic order quantity discussed in Chapter 12. That is,

$$C_i = \text{Annual setup costs} + \text{Annual holding costs},$$

or

$$C_i = \frac{D_i S_i}{Q_i} + \left(\frac{Q_i}{2}\right)\left(1 - \frac{r_i}{p_i}\right) H_i$$

where

C_i = total cost per year for chemical i

D_i = annual demand for chemical i

S_i = cost to set up the process for one lot (batch) of chemical i

Q_i = lot size in units (barrels)

r_i = constant daily demand for chemical i

p_i = output capability of the process to produce chemical i, after the process has been set up, expressed in units (barrels) per day

H_i = cost to hold one unit (barrel) in inventory for one year

Also, $Q_i = D_i/N_i$, where N_i is the number of cycles per year for chemical i. The factor that modifies the annual holding costs, $1 - r_i/p_i$, comes from the assumption that demand for the chemical occurs continuously throughout the year, but that production is no longer instantaneous as assumed in calculating the *EOQ*. Thus inventory is being consumed even as it is produced.

Constraints.   Two constraints must be satisfied in order to have a feasible schedule. Recall that we said that the choice of N_i affects the total setup time and the load on the production process. Consequently, the values of N_i, or the lot sizes Q_i, generated from a production and inventory control system should satisfy the **total load constraint:**

$$\begin{matrix} \text{Total load on the facility in} \\ \text{days of production and setup} \end{matrix} \leq \begin{matrix} \text{Total number of production} \\ \text{days available for the year} \end{matrix}$$

or

$$\sum_{i=1}^{m} T_i \leq T_A$$

where

T_i = total setup plus processing days needed for chemical i

T_A = total number of production days for the year

m = total number of chemicals (products)

The other constraint is called the **schedule interference constraint**. If the total time required to produce one cycle exceeds the stock depletion time for any one of the chemicals, that chemical will suffer a stockout. Therefore

> Total time to produce one cycle in days ≤ Minimum number of days to deplete the stock of any chemical

or

$$\sum_{j=1}^{m} (t_{sj} + Q_j t_{pj}) \leq \min_{i} \left[\frac{Q_i}{r_i} \right] \qquad \text{for} \qquad i = 1, 2, \ldots, m$$

The risk of violating this constraint is greatest when the "best" lot size is determined for each product independently of its effect on the others, and all the products must be processed on the same equipment.

Developing a Feasible Schedule

One way to overcome the problem of schedule interference is to find a common number of cycles, N, per year to produce each chemical; that is, to make all $N_i = N$. We could do this by trial and error for various values of N, making sure each time that capacity is not exceeded. We would then choose the value of N that minimizes the total cost, summed over all chemicals.

APPLICATION 16.2

The plant manager of the chemical plant has asked us to prepare a schedule for the five chemicals in Fig. 16.4. The plant operates 350 days per year. Using the data in the accompanying table, we are to find a minimum-cost schedule that avoids stockouts while staying within the plant's load capacity.

Data for the Chemical Plant Scheduling Problem

	Demand		Production Data			Costs	
Chemical (i)	Annual (barrels) (D_i)	Daily (barrels) (r_i)	Daily (barrels) (p_i)	Process Time per Barrel (days) (t_{pi})	Setup time (days) (t_{si})	Holding (H_i)	Setup (S_i)
1	10,500	30	190	0.005	1.00	$0.21	$200
2	2,100	6	25	0.040	0.50	0.52	150
3	5,950	17	71	0.014	2.00	0.40	300
4	17,850	51	245	0.004	0.33	0.15	100
5	3,150	9	100	0.010	1.50	0.32	250

Solution

We first generate the following table, which contains the total load and total cost for various choices of N. Note that this solution satisfies the total capacity constraint, since the total load is only 333.36 days. The value of N that minimizes total cost is 2 cycles per year.

The solution $N = 2$ also satisfies the schedule interference constraint, which we verify in the following manner. Since all $N_i = N$, each chemical has the same stock depletion time of one-half year, or 175 days. We multiply the lot size for each chemical by its process time per barrel, sum them, and add the total setup time to get the total cycle time, t_r, in days. For $N = 2$,

$$t_r = [5250(0.005) + 1050(0.040) + 2975(0.014)$$
$$+ 8925(0.004) + 1575(0.010)] + 5.33$$
$$= 166.68 \text{ days}$$

As the total cycle time for production of the chemicals is less than the depletion time of the chemicals, the plant should not experience any stockouts.

Effects of Lot Size on Load and Total Cost for the Chemical Plant Scheduling Problem

Chemical (i)	Cycles per Year								
	$N = 1$			$N = 2$			$N = 3$		
	$Q_i = \dfrac{D_i}{N}$	Load (T_i)	Total cost (C_i)	$Q_i = \dfrac{D_i}{N}$	Load (T_i)	Total cost (C_i)	$Q_i = \dfrac{D_i}{N}$	Load (T_i)	Total cost (C_i)
1	10,500	53.50	$1,128.42	5,250	54.50	$ 864.21	3,500	55.50	$ 909.47
2	2,100	84.50	564.96	1,050	85.00	507.48	700	85.50	588.32
3	5,950	85.30	1,205.07	2,975	87.30	1,052.53	1,983	89.30	1,201.64
4	17,850	71.73	1,160.07	8,925	72.06	730.03	5,950	72.39	653.36
5	3,150	33.00	708.64	1,575	34.50	729.32	1,050	36.00	902.88
Total		328.03	$4,767.16		333.36	$3,883.57		338.69	$4,255.67

Process Industry Production and Inventory Control Systems

We have generated what might be called a master production schedule for the chemical plant. Using a bill of materials for each chemical, we can determine the need for raw materials and additives. However, we must keep in mind the yield loss in the form of a by-product (see Fig. 16.4). The requirements for the raw materials and additives must be adjusted for this loss in output. Bolander and Taylor (1983) suggest a scheduling technique for solving such problems called **time-phased forward scheduling (TPFS).** This system schedules capacity forward through each operation from the first bottleneck operation. Completion of the final production process determines the completion date of the product. After the capacity has been scheduled, materials requirements are checked to ensure that there are enough to support the schedule. Bills of materials and time-phased inventory records are used to keep track of materials.

Another technique often used for production planning in the process industries is linear programming. Problems such as product mix and plant loading can be analyzed with the help of linear programming. Supplement 4 addresses linear programming and its applications.

SOLVED PROBLEMS

1. A company using a kanban system has an inefficient machine group. For example, the daily demand for part L105A is 3000 units. The average waiting time for a container of parts is 0.8 day. The processing time for a container of L105A is 0.2 day, and a container holds 270 units. There are presently 20 kanban card sets for this item.

   a. What is the implicit value of the policy variable?

   b. What is the total planned inventory (work in process and finished goods) for item L105A?

   c. Suppose that the policy variable α were 0. How many card sets would be needed now? What is the effect of the policy variable in this example?

Solution

   a. We use the equation for the number of card sets to find α.

$$k = \frac{d(\bar{w} + \bar{p})(1 + \alpha)}{c}$$

$$= \frac{3000(0.8 + 0.2)(1 + \alpha)}{270} = 20$$

$$1 + \alpha = \frac{20(270)}{3000(0.8 + 0.2)} = 1.8$$

$$\alpha = 1.8 - 1 = 0.8$$

   b. With 20 card sets in the system and each container holding 270 units, the total planned inventory would be 5400 [or 20(270)] units.

TABLE 16.5

Product	Annual Demand (gal)	Daily Production Rate (gal)	Setup Time (days)	Annual Holding Cost (per gal)	Setup Cost (per run)	Scheduled Lot Size (gal)
1	5,000	100	2	$1.60	$40	559
2	10,000	400	1	1.40	25	630
3	7,000	350	3	0.60	30	872
4	15,000	200	1	1.15	27	1,003
5	4,000	100	1	1.65	80	679

c. If $\alpha = 0$,

$$k = \frac{3000(0.8 + 0.2)}{270} = 11.11 \quad \text{or} \quad 12 \text{ card sets}$$

The policy variable adjusts the number of card sets. In this case it is quite dramatic because $(\overline{w} + \overline{p})$ is relatively large and the container size is small relative to daily demand.

2. A company processes five products on the same equipment. The data for these items are given in Table 16.5. Assume 250 working days per year.

   a. The master scheduler for this company has developed the scheduled lot sizes in Table 16.5 and plans to sequence the products 1−2−3−4−5. Which products will suffer stockouts?

   b. Calculate the minimum-cost lot sizes for each product for a common-cycle approach. Will this schedule be feasible? Why?

Solution

a.

Product	Q_i	t_{pi}	Cycle Time (days)	r_i	Supply (days)
1	559	0.010000	7.59	20	27.95*
2	630	0.002500	2.58	40	15.75*
3	872	0.002857	5.49	28	31.14
4	1003	0.005000	6.02	60	16.72*
5	679	0.010000	7.79	16	42.44
Total			28.47		

*These products will experience a stockout because their supply time is less than the total cycle time.

The process time, t_{pi}, is calculated by dividing the daily production rate into 1. The daily demand rate, r_i, equals the annual demand divided by 250 days. Finally, supply equals Q_i divided by r_i.

b. At $N = 5$ cycles per year we have the minimum-cost solution that satisfies all constraints.

Product	Q_i	T_i	C_i	Cycle Time (days)	Supply Time (days)
1	1000	60	$ 840.00	12	50
2	2000	30	1385.00	6	50
3	1400	35	536.40	7	50
4	3000	80	1342.50	16	50
5	800	45	954.40	9	50
Total		250	$5058.30	50	

FORMULA REVIEW

1. Number of kanban card sets:

$$k = \frac{d\,(\overline{w} + \overline{p})\,(1 + \alpha)}{c}$$

2. Plant load:

$$T_i = N_i t_{si} + D_i t_{pi}$$

3. Total cost:

$$C_i = \frac{D_i S_i}{Q_i} + \left(\frac{Q_i}{2}\right)\left(1 - \frac{r_i}{p_i}\right) H_i$$

4. Total load constraint:

$$\sum_{i=1}^{m} T_i \leq T_A$$

5. Schedule interference constraint:

$$\sum_{j=1}^{m} (t_{sj} + Q_j t_{pj}) \leq \min_i \left[\frac{Q_i}{r_i}\right] \quad \text{for} \quad i = 1, 2, \ldots, m$$

CHAPTER HIGHLIGHTS

- The purpose of JIT systems is to produce or deliver the right items in the quantities needed by subsequent production processes or customers at the time needed. The intent is to coordinate production flows to reduce the need for inventories.

- Toyota's kanban system uses withdrawal and production-order card sets to control production flow. The withdrawal card specifies the item and quantity that the subsequent process should withdraw from the preceding process and where to find the item. The production-order card specifies the item and quantity that the preceding process must produce each time, where to store the finished item and input materials, and where to find them.

- Material cannot be withdrawn without a withdrawal card. Production cannot begin without a production-order card. The produced items are placed in containers, which should always have the same standard number of parts in them. The authorized inventory of a part is a function of the number of authorized cards for that item. The number of cards depends on average demand during manufacturing lead time, the container size, and a policy variable to adjust for unexpected occurrences.

- Just-in-time systems have many advantages, including reductions in inventory, space requirements, and paperwork, and increases in productivity, worker participation, machine utilization, and quality. However, JIT systems also have disadvantages, such as requiring stable schedules for extended periods of time and not being well suited for irregularly used parts or specially ordered products.

- Process industries have a flow-shop orientation, high-volume demand, and high capital intensity. Lot size determination must be capacity sensitive. When a number of products must be processed in a common facility, the lot size must be chosen to avoid stockouts during the production cycle. The total load on the facility must also be checked to ensure schedule feasibility.

- Time-phased forward scheduling is a scheduling system that recognizes capacity when determining the schedule of a process-oriented plant. It maintains feasibility with respect to capacity and uses principles similar to MRP.

- For a given manufacturing environment, the choice of a production and inventory system can make a difference. Also, improving certain environmental factors can significantly reduce inventory investment, improve customer service, and increase productivity, regardless of the system in use.

KEY TERMS

STUDY QUESTIONS

1. Explain the purpose of just-in-time systems. Why is JIT considered a *pull system*?

2. Toyota's kanban system utilizes two main types of cards that authorize certain actions. Explain the purposes of these cards and describe how they are used.

3. Consider the formula for the number of kanban system card sets for an item. If the process for that item is *inefficient,* which parameters in the equation might be larger than desirable? Why? Suppose that a supervisor wanted to increase the safety stock. Which parameter would be adjusted?

4. It took Toyota 10 years to perfect its kanban system. Why? How can the system be used to identify areas for improvement?

5. Why is the final assembly schedule critical to the Toyota kanban system? What characteristics must the schedule have?

6. Consider the statement: "The just-in-time system is a total managerial concept, whereas the kanban system and systems like it are merely information systems designed to provide the basis for the timing and size decisions of production quantities." Do you agree or disagree? Why?

7. What factors should management consider when deciding whether to use a JIT system in a given manufacturing environment?

8. Which aspects of JIT systems have been troublesome for U.S. manufacturers to date? Why?

9. Which factors make process industries different from fabrication and assembly industries? Why is their consideration important in choosing a production and inventory system?

10. What constraints should be considered when determining lot sizes in a process industry?

11. Why does the choice of a production and inventory system have implications for the firm as a whole?

12. What does "shaping the environment" mean?

PROBLEMS

Review Problems

1. A certain Japanese automaker operates an assembly plant in the United States. The plant uses a kanban system to control production and inventory. You have been put in charge of a certain machine group that manufactures a tie-rod assembly. The daily demand rate for tie-rods is 2000 units. The average waiting time for parts in your machine group is 0.90 day, and the average processing time per tie-rod is 0.20 day. Each container holds 50 tie-rods. You have decided to allow 50 percent of the average waiting and processing time per container for unexpected contingencies. How many card sets would you suggest for controlling production of the tie-rods?

2. You have been asked to analyze the operations of a company using the kanban system. One of the work stations feeding the assembly line produces part K669B. The daily demand for K669B is 500 units. The average processing time per unit is 0.001 day. Company records show that the average unit spends 0.50 day waiting at the feeder work station. The container for K669B can hold 30 units. Nine card sets are authorized for the part.

   a. Find the value of the policy variable (α) that expresses the amount of implied safety stock in this system.

   b. Using the implied value of α from (a), determine the required reduction in waiting time if one card set were removed. Assume that all other parameters remain fixed.

3. A production facility uses a kanban system and operates eight hours per day. Suppose that a certain part requires 50 seconds of processing at machine cell 33B and averages 1.6 hours of waiting time there. Management has allowed a 10 percent buffer for unexpected occurrences. Each container holds 40 parts, and 10 card sets are authorized. How much daily demand can be satisfied with this system?

4. A manufacturer of plastic pipe recently purchased a used extruding machine. The company plans to produce two products on the machine. Product 1 is a one-inch diameter pipe and product 2 is a two-inch diameter pipe. The current capacity of the extruder is 250 feet of pipe per day, regardless of the diameter. The company plans to use the extruder 350 days per year. Specific production data are:

Data Category	Product 1	Product 2
Demand (ft/yr)	52,500	35,000
Setup time (days)	2	3
Current lot size	21,000	16,000

   a. Will the company violate the schedule interference constraint with its current lot sizes? Explain.

   b. Will the annual machine time capacity be exceeded? Explain.

5. The Steiner Manufacturing Company makes wire to various specifications. Two of the products are processed on special wire-drawing machinery. The wire machine can produce 350 feet of wire per day. The machine is scheduled for use 350 days per year. The following data are available for the two products.

Data Category	Product 1	Product 2
Demand (ft/yr)	35,000	70,000
Setup time (days)	3	4
Current lot size	18,708	30,550
Setup cost ($)	300	200
Holding cost ($/ft/yr)	0.10	0.15

Find the common number of cycles for the two products that minimizes cost and does not violate capacity and schedule interference constraints.

TABLE 16.6

Product	Annual Demand (gal)	Daily Production Rate (gal)	Setup Time (days)	Setup Cost	Holding Cost (per gal per yr)	Suggested Lot Size (gal)
1	10,000	320	1	$ 40	$1.00	956
2	15,000	240	2	80	0.25	3578
3	60,000	720	2	30	0.50	3286
4	5,000	100	1	100	0.30	2041

6. A candy manufacturer produces three varieties of chocolate. The processing system can be thought of as a single machine that must be cleaned and inspected between each batch of chocolate. The company produces the products in the sequence 1−2−3 and operates 250 days per year.

Product	Annual Demand (lb)	Setup Time (days)	Process Time (days/lb)
1	60,000	2	0.001
2	15,000	3	0.004
3	8,000	2	0.010

a. The company is interested in keeping inventories low. Find the largest number of cycles per year, N, such that the total number of production days per year is not exceeded.

b. What are the batch sizes for each product?

7. A chemical plant produces four chemical solvents used in the manufacture of wall coverings. The plant operates 250 days per year. The plant scheduler has suggested lot sizes for the items, which all must be produced in common facilities. Production data are shown in Table 16.6.

a. Will the application of the suggested lot sizes cause any product stockouts if the production sequence is 1−2−3−4? Which ones? Explain.

b. Determine the least-cost lot sizes such that each item is set up the same number of times per year and show that you have a feasible schedule.

8. Two managers of a chemical processing plant are having a disagreement over the scheduling of three products that must be processed on a certain bottling machine. Simon Kingly claims that his schedule will minimize setup and holding costs. Ignatius Withet, however, claims that Kingly's schedule won't work because it will result in stockouts. Production data are shown in Table 16.7. The bottling machine operates 4000 hours per year.

a. Analyze Kingly's claim and determine whether there will be a stockout problem if the products are bottled in 1−2−3 sequence in each cycle.

b. If there is a stockout problem, develop a plan that will work, based on the sequence 1−2−3 for each cycle. Specify the production quantities that you would recommend and show that your proposal will work.

TABLE 16.7

Product	Demand (gal/yr)	Hourly Production Rate (gal)	Annual Holding Cost (per gal)	Changeover Cost	Changeover Time (hr)	Kingly's Lot Size (gal)
1	160,000	125	$0.17	$400	4	40,000
2	180,000	100	0.67	250	3	10,000
3	400,000	500	0.14	300	5	60,000

9. A mustard manufacturer makes five varieties of mustard on the same machines. Management believes that each variety should be produced in sequence in each cycle. It takes one-half day to set up for a change from one variety to the next. Production data are:

Variety	Daily Demand (cases)	Daily Prod. Rate (cases)	Annual Carry Cost $/case	Setup Cost
1	10	50	$5.00	$100
2	5	25	6.00	75
3	15	100	7.00	50
4	20	100	5.00	125
5	50	250	6.67	150

The company works 200 days per year. Prepare a master production schedule for the facility for the next 50 days that is feasible from a capacity standpoint and will not incur stockouts. You may assume that on-hand inventory will cover requirements until you begin processing each item for the first time. Your goal should be to find a schedule that is as cost effective as possible.

Advanced Problems

Problems 10 and 11 require prior reading of Supplement 2. A computer package is also required for these problems.

10. A problem often of concern to managers in the process industry is blending. Consider the task facing the procurement manager of a company that manufactures special additives. She must determine the proper amounts of each raw material to purchase for the production of a certain product. Three raw materials are available. Each gallon of the finished product must have a combustion point of at least 220°F. In addition, the gamma content (which causes hydrocarbon pollution) cannot exceed 6 percent of volume. The zeta content (which cleans the internal moving parts of engines) must be at least 12 percent by volume. Each raw material has varying degrees of these characteristics.

Characteristic	Raw Material		
	A	B	C
Combustion point (°F)	200	180	280
Gamma content (%)	4	3	10
Zeta content (%)	20	10	8

Raw material A costs $0.60 per gallon, whereas raw materials B and C cost $0.40 and $0.50 per gallon, respectively. The procurement manager wishes to minimize the cost of raw materials per gallon of product. Use linear programming to find the optimal proportions of each raw material to use in a gallon of finished product. *Hint:* Express your decision variables in terms of fractions of a gallon. The sum of the fractions must equal 1.00.

11. The Washington Chemical Company produces chemicals and solvents for the glue industry. The production process is divided into several "focus factories," each producing a specific set of products. The time has come to prepare the production plan for one of the focused factories. This particular factory produces five products that must pass through both the reactor and the separator. Each product also requires a certain combination of raw materials. Production data are shown in Table 16.8.

The Washington Chemical Company has a long term contract with a major glue manufacturer that requires annual production of 3000 pounds of both products 3 and 4. More of these products could be produced because there is a demand for them.

a. Determine the annual production quantities of each product that maximizes contribution to profits. Assume that you can sell all you can produce.

b. Specify the lot sizes for each product.

12. Refer to the equation for total cost presented in this chapter. It gives the annual ordering and holding costs for an item being produced to stock.

a. Develop an equation for Q_i that minimizes total costs. That is, specify the equivalent of the *EOQ* for this case. Explain why your model yields the minimum cost value of Q_i.

b. Explain what happens to your model when the production rate gets very large relative to the demand rate.

TABLE 16.8

Resource	Product 1	2	3	4	5	Total Resources Available
Reactor (hr/ lb)	0.05	0.10	0.80	0.57	0.15	7,500 hr*
Separator (hr/lb)	0.20	0.02	0.20	0.09	0.30	7,500 hr*
Raw material 1 (lb)	0.20	0.50	0.10	0.40	0.18	10,000 lb
Raw material 2 (lb)	—	0.70	—	0.50	—	6,000 lb
Raw material 3 (lb)	0.10	0.20	0.40	—	—	7,000 lb
Profit contribution ($/ lb)	4.00	7.00	3.50	4.00	5.70	

*The total time available has been adjusted to account for setups. The five products have a prescribed sequence owing to the cost of changeovers between products. The company has a 35-day cycle (or 10 changeovers per year per product). Consequently, the time for these changeovers has been deducted from the total time available for these machines.

13. Refer to Problem 5. Use your model from Problem 12(a) to determine the production lot sizes for products 1 and 2. Do the lot sizes satisfy the capacity and schedule interference constraints?

SELECTED REFERENCES

Bolander, S. F., and S. C. Taylor, "Time-Phased Forward Scheduling: A Capacity Dominated Scheduling Technique," *Production and Inventory Management* (First Quarter 1983), pp. 83–96.

Haglund, E. A., "Primary Metals—We're Different," *Production and Inventory Management* (Third Quarter 1981), pp. 21–26.

Hahn, Chan K., Peter Pinto, and Daniel Bragg, "Just-in-Time Production and Purchasing," *Journal of Purchasing and Materials Management* (Fall 1983), pp. 2–10.

Hall, R. W., *Driving the Productivity Machine*. Falls Church, Va.: The American Production and Inventory Control Society, 1981.

Krajewski, L. J., B. King, L. P. Ritzman, and D. S. Wong, "Kanban, MRP and Shaping the Manufacturing Environment," *Management Science* (January 1987).

Melynk, S., and P. Carter, "Viewing Kanban as an (s,Q) System: Developing New Insights into a Japanese Method of Production and Inventory Control." In Sang M. Lee and Gary Schwendimen (Eds.), *Management by Japanese Systems*. New York: Praeger, 1982.

Monden, Y., "Adaptable Kanban System Helps Toyota Maintain Just-in-Time Production," *Journal of Industrial Engineering* (May 1981), pp. 29–46.

Monden, Y., "What Makes the Toyota Production System Really Tick?" *Journal of Industrial Engineering* (January 1981), pp. 36–46.

Nelleman, D. O., and L. Smith, "Just-in-Time vs. Just-in-Case Production/Inventory Systems Concepts Borrowed Back from Japan," *Production and Inventory Management* (Second Quarter 1982), pp. 12–20.

Rice, J. W., and T. Yoshikawa, "A Comparison of Kanban and MRP Concepts for the Control of Repetitive Manufacturing Systems," *Production and Inventory Management* (First Quarter 1982), pp. 1–13.

Ritzman, L. P., B. E. King, and L. J. Krajewski, "Manufacturing Performance—Pulling the Right Levers," *Harvard Business Review* (March–April 1984), pp. 143–152.

Ritzman, L. P., and L. J. Krajewski, "Performance Comparisons Between MRP and Reorder Point Systems." In H. Berkrioglu (Ed.), *Simulation and Inventory Con-*

trol. La Jolla, Calif.: Society for Computer Simulation, 1983.

Schonberger, R. J., *Japanese Manufacturing Techniques.* New York: The Free Press, 1982.

Smith-Daniels, Vicki, "The Lot Sizing and Sequencing Problem in Process Industries." Unpublished Ph.D. dissertation, Ohio State University, 1983.

Taylor, S. C., "Production and Inventory Management in the Process Industries: A State of the Art Survey," *Production and Inventory Management* (First Quarter 1979), pp. 1–16.

Taylor, S. C., S. M. Seward, and S. F. Bolander, "Why the Process Industries are Different," *Production and Inventory Management* (Fourth Quarter 1981), pp. 9–24.

Taylor, S. C., S. M. Seward, S. F. Bolander, and R. C. Heard, "Process Industry Production and Inventory Framework: A Summary," *Production and Inventory Management* (First Quarter 1981), pp. 15–32.

WORK-FORCE AND OPERATIONS SCHEDULING

▲ Chapter Outline

Which of our customers or jobs should have top priority?

What information do we need for effective operations and work-force scheduling?

If we have a staffing plan, how can we develop an effective work-force schedule?

How important is our choice of priority dispatching rules to the effectiveness of the operating system?

cheduling allocates resources over time to accomplish specific tasks. Normally, scheduling is done after a number of other managerial decisions have already been made. For example, management in a manufacturing company must make decisions about products and competitive priorities; choose an appropriate process design and layout; and commit the level of capital and labor required for the level of production desired—all before designing a system to schedule the various tasks to be performed. Similarly, the planning of emergency services, such as fire protection, first requires an analysis of the best location for fire stations, decisions about the type and quantity of fire-fighting equipment at each location, and a staffing plan for each station before decisions such as specific work schedules for each employee can be determined. Nonetheless, the ability to generate good schedules can be extremely important for achieving strategic goals. Although generally true for manufacturing, good scheduling is a must for service providers—where the customer comes into close contact with the delivery system.

WORK-FORCE SCHEDULING ▲

Work-force scheduling specifies on-duty and off-duty periods for each employee over a certain time horizon. Thus work-force scheduling assigns employees such as postal clerks, nurses, or machinists to specific workdays and shifts. This type of scheduling is different from operations scheduling, which assigns specific tasks for workers to perform while on duty.

Purpose of the Work-Force Schedule

Work-force schedules translate the staffing plan (see Chapter 13) into specific schedules of work for each employee. Consider the work-force schedule posted by the managers of the Amalgamated Parcel Service (APS) shown in Table 17.1. The APS processing center is open seven days a week and can be operated by a small number of employees. The staffing plan for APS calls for 10 employees in the time period covered. The work-force schedule must specify the days of the week that each employee is to be on duty. Scheduling wouldn't be a problem if the company worked only one eight-hour shift, five days a week—but that isn't the case at APS. In Table 17.1, the Xs denote workdays for the employees. For example, Chen has Tuesday and Saturday off each week.

Determining the workdays for each employee in itself doesn't make the staffing plan operational. Daily work-force requirements, stated in the aggregate in the staffing plan, must be satisfied. Thus for an APS staffing plan calling for 168 employee-days per month, or 42 employee-days per week, Table 17.1 shows the daily requirements. The work-force capacity available each day

TABLE 17.1   Posted APS Work-Force Schedule

Employee	M	T	W	Th	F	S	Su	
Chen	X	Off	X	X	X	Off	X	
Smith	X	Off	X	X	X	Off	X	
Carter	X	X	X	X	X	Off	Off	
Johnson	X	X	X	X	X	Off	Off	
Kramer	X	X	X	X	X	Off	Off	
Griffin	Off	X	X	X	X	X	Off	
Whitcomb	Off	X	X	X	X	X	Off	
Hernandez	X	Off	X	X	X	X	Off	
Booth	X	X	Off	X	X	X	Off	
Bell	X	Off	X	X	X	X	Off	
								Total
Capacity (C)	8	6	9	10	10	5	2	50
Requirements (R)	6	4	8	9	10	3	2	42
Slack ($C - R$)	2	2	1	1	0	2	0	8

must meet or exceed daily work-force requirements. If it does not, the scheduler must try to rearrange days off until the requirements are met. If no such schedule can be found, management may have to change the staffing plan and authorize more employees, overtime hours, or larger backlogs.

Finally, the work-force schedule reallocates employees as requirements change. Suppose that the manager at the APS center learns that some special shipments will arrive on Sunday, requiring two more employees than usual. In the schedule in Table 17.1, three days have a slack capacity of two employees. Thus the manager could ask Carter and Johnson, for example, to work Sunday in exchange for Monday off.

Constraints

The technical constraints imposed on the work-force schedule are the resources provided by the staffing plan and the requirements placed on the operating system. However, other constraints, including legal and behavioral considerations, may also be imposed. For example, a hospital may be required to have at least a minimum number of registered nurses on duty on each floor at all times. Similarly, a minimum number of fire and safety personnel must be on duty at a fire station at all times. Such constraints limit management's flexibility in developing work-force schedules, but the constraints imposed by the psychological needs of workers complicate scheduling even more. Some of these constraints are written into labor agreements. For example, an employer may agree to give employees a certain number of consecutive days off per week or limit employees' consecutive work days to a certain maximum. Other provisions might govern the allocation of vacations, days off for holidays, or rotating shift assignments. In addition, the preferences of the employees themselves need to be considered.

One way that managers deal with certain undesirable aspects of scheduling is to use a **rotating schedule**, which rotates employees through a series of workdays and/or hours. Thus over a period of time, each person has the same opportunity to have weekends and holidays off and to work days, as well as evenings and nights. For example, the schedules in Table 17.1 could be rotated by giving each employee the next employee's schedule the following week. For example, Chen takes Smith's schedule, Smith takes Carter's, and so forth. After 10 weeks, Chen would have the first schedule again. In contrast, a **fixed schedule** calls for each employee to work the same days and hours each week. A fixed schedule at APS would always require Chen, Smith, Hernandez, Booth, and Bell to have split days off rather than consecutive days off.

Developing a Work-Force Schedule

Let's take a closer look at the APS work-force schedule shown in Table 17.1. Five employees did not get two consecutive days off. Obviously, the scheduler did not consider this constraint. In this section we demonstrate a method that recognizes this constraint.*

The object of the method is to identify the two consecutive days off for each employee that will minimize the amount of total slack capacity. The work schedule for each employee is simply the five days that remain after the two days off have been determined. The scheduler follows these steps:

1. From the schedule of net requirements for the week, find the highest requirement, the next highest, and so on, until a unique pair of days off that includes the minimum daily requirements and has the lowest total requirements for the two days has been identified.

2. If a tie occurs, choose one of the tied pairs consistent with provisions written into the labor agreement, if any. Alternatively, the tie could be broken by asking the employee being scheduled to make the choice. As a last resort, the tie could be broken arbitrarily. For example, preference could be given to Saturday–Sunday pairs.

3. Assign the employee the selected pair of days off. Subtract the requirements satisfied by the employee from the net requirements for each day the employee is to work.

4. Repeat steps 1–3 until all requirements are satisfied or a given number of employees have been scheduled.

This method reduces the amount of slack capacity assigned to days having low requirements and forces scheduling first the days having high requirements. It also recognizes some of the behavioral and contractual aspects of work-force scheduling in the tie-breaking rules. However, the schedules produced may *not* minimize total slack capacity. Different rules for finding the days-off pair and breaking ties are needed to ensure minimal total slack capacity.

APPLICATION 17.1

For the data in Table 17.1, find a work schedule for each employee that provides two consecutive days off and minimizes the amount of total slack capacity. To break ties in the selection of off days, give preference to Saturday–Sunday, if it is one of the tied pairs. If not, select one of the tied pairs arbitrarily.

Solution

The schedule of requirements is

---

*The method demonstrated here is similar to one developed by Tibrewala, Philippe, and Brown (1972). They use different rules to ensure a work-force schedule that minimizes total slack capacity.

M	T	W	Th	F	S	Su	Employee
6	4	8	9	10	3	2	Chen

The unique pair of minimum requirements is S–Su. Therefore Chen is scheduled to work Monday–Friday.

We reduce the requirements for M–F to recognize that Chen will be on duty. Note that the requirements for S–Su are carried forward because these were employee days off in the last step. This results in the following net requirements.

M	T	W	Th	F	S	Su	Employee
5	3	7	8	9	3	2	Smith

The unique minimum again is on S–Su, so we assign Smith to a M–F schedule. The day-off assignments for the remainder of the employees are shown in the accompanying table.

Day Off Assignments for the Remainder of the APS Employees

Net Requirements							Employee	Comments
M	T	W	Th	F	S	Su		
4	2	6	7	8	3	2	Carter	S–Su has the lowest total net requirements.
3	1	5	6	7	3	2	Johnson	M–T has the lowest total net requirements.
3	1	4	5	6	2	1	Kramer	S–Su has the lowest total net requirements.
2	0	3	4	5	2	1	Griffin	M–T has the lowest total net requirements.
2	0	2	3	4	1	0	Whitcomb	S–Su has the lowest total net requirements.
1	0	1	2	3	1	0	Hernandez	S–Su is chosen according to the tie-breaking rule.
0	0	0	1	2	1	0	Booth	Su–M is arbitrarily chosen because S–Su does not have the lowest total requirements.
0	0	0	0	1	0	0	Bell	S–Su is chosen according to the tie-breaking rule.

TABLE 17.2   APS Work-Force Schedule, Imposing the Two Consecutive Days Off Constraint

Employee	M	T	W	Th	F	S	Su
Chen	X	X	X	X	X	Off	Off
Smith	X	X	X	X	X	Off	Off
Carter	X	X	X	X	X	Off	Off
Johnson	Off	Off	X	X	X	X	X
Kramer	X	X	X	X	X	Off	Off
Griffin	Off	Off	X	X	X	X	X
Whitcomb	X	X	X	X	X	Off	Off
Hernandez	X	X	X	X	X	Off	Off
Booth	Off	X	X	X	X	X	Off
Bell	X	X	X	X	X	Off	Off

	M	T	W	Th	F	S	Su	Total
Capacity (C)	7	7	10	10	10	3	3	50
Requirements (R)	6	4	8	9	10	3	2	42
Slack ($C - R$)	1	3	2	1	0	0	1	8

The schedule for all the APS employees is shown in Table 17.2. With its substantial amount of slack capacity, the schedule is not unique. Booth, for example, could have Su–M, M–T, or T–W off without causing a capacity shortage. Indeed, APS might be able to get by with one less employee because of the total of eight slack days of capacity. However, APS needs all 10 employees on Fridays. If the manager were willing to get by with only nine employees on Fridays, he would not need Bell. As you can see in the table in Application 17.1, the net requirements left for Bell to satisfy amount to only one day, Friday.

Work-Force Scheduling by Service Providers

Work-force scheduling is particularly important to organizations that provide services. The methods of scheduling used are often very sophisticated but depend on the specific nature of each service. One of the most complex types of work-force scheduling is that of major airlines, as Managerial Practice 17.1 indicates. We further illustrate work-force scheduling for service providers by briefly discussing the scheduling of telephone operators and police officers.

Telephone Operators.   General Telephone and Electronics (GTE) employs telephone operators to staff operations 24 hours a day, seven days a week. The demand for service is measured by the volume of calls throughout the day and is highly variable. The company has stringent standards for service, which require that calls must be answered within 10 seconds 90 percent of the time.

Scheduling the operators is done weekly (see Buffa, Cosgrove, and Luce,

1976). First, the daily requirements for the entire week, expressed in operator-hours, are estimated. Then, shifts are designed that conform to state and federal laws and union agreements, while matching the pattern of daily requirements as closely as possible. Day-off assignments are made for each operator, and operators select the shift they will work based on seniority. Computer programs have been developed to implement the scheduling system. GTE realized a net annual savings of $170,000 in clerical and supervisory costs and a 6 percent increase in productivity after using the system for one year.

Police Departments. Many police departments in the United States schedule their manpower evenly over 24 hours. Although this policy simplifies scheduling, it ignores the fact that requirements for police services vary considerably

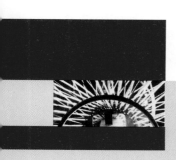

MANAGERIAL PRACTICE 17.1 ▲

Airline Scheduling—A Critical Activity

The Department of Transportation publishes a monthly ranking of airlines on the basis of the overall percentage of reported flights arriving on time. Airlines consider a good ranking important for retaining or increasing their customer base. With everyone from the Secretary of Transportation to airline CEOs scouring on-time performance data, the job of scheduler is more important than ever. The job gets more complicated as the demand for air travel gradually exceeds capacity, as it does annually from July 1 to Labor Day. For example, American Airlines employs a staff of seven analysts to schedule 420 airplanes with 2140 daily flights involving 150 airports to keep a good on-time rating. To be effective in their task, the schedulers require a diverse background of knowledge. They need to know the nature of the winds with their predictable seasonal changes. They need data on how fast different aircraft move in the air and on the ground. They also need to know how schedule changes affect gate utilization, crew schedules, and congestion of aircraft at the airport.

Some scheduling problems can be solved as easily as moving a flight to another gate to avoid getting blocked at the gate by departing traffic. Others are more complicated. For example, American Airlines had a problem with its flight from Puerto Plata in the Dominican Republic to San Juan, Puerto Rico. The pilots' labor contract requires $11\frac{1}{2}$ hours of rest between flights, which meant that the crew that flies in the night before cannot leave on schedule the next morning. Bringing in another crew would cost an additional $130,000 per month. The solution was to change the schedule to make the plane leaving Puerto Plata depart 10 minutes later and arrive 10 minutes later in San Juan. In addition, the schedules for nine other flights from San Juan to the mainland were also adjusted to allow for a smooth flow of traffic at the airport. Airline schedule changes typically create a domino effect such as this.

Source: "American Airlines' Fixer of Broken Schedules," *Wall Street Journal*, June 28, 1988.

throughout the day. Needs can be as much as eight times greater from 10 to 11 P.M. than from 5 to 6 A.M. A patrol car allocation model (PCAM) has been designed to allocate a certain number of cars to shifts, where a shift is defined as a specific eight-hour block of time on a particular day for a specific precinct (See Chaiken and Dormont, 1978). The model can also handle overlay shifts, which begin during one normal shift and end during the following shift.

This model has proven to be quite versatile. It can be used during budget preparation to determine the total number of patrol officers a department needs to meet stated performance standards. It can also be used to allocate officers to precincts and shifts and to study the effects of changes in performance standards or service-call priorities. Police departments that have used PCAM include those in Los Angeles, San Diego, Virginia Beach, Seattle, Atlanta, Toledo, Minneapolis, Wilmington, and New Brunswick, N.J.

MANAGERIAL PRACTICE 17.2 ▲

Good Scheduling Pays Off at LTV Steel Company

LTV Steel Company is the nation's second largest steelmaker and its largest producer of flat-rolled products. At LTV Steel's Cleveland works, molten steel is converted to 25-ton solid steel slabs in a machine called a twin strand slab caster, which has two molds that continuously and simultaneously cast slabs of steel. Scheduling the slab caster machine is difficult because factors such as the types of steel specified by the customer, the number of slabs of steel normally produced from a batch of molten steel, metallurgical limitations on changes from one batch to the next, required maintenance intervals, and yield losses must all be considered.

The basic entity that is scheduled is the customer order for a particular grade and quantity of steel. A due date for delivery is specified on the order. The scheduling problem is to maximize on-time delivery and caster productivity while minimizing work-in-process inventory. Competitive pressures force LTV Steel to maximize on-time delivery above all else, even if it means lower caster productivity or higher inventory levels. Scheduling quick jobs to reduce overdue shipments increases caster downtime because the caster must be reset to produce a different grade of steel. The trade-off can best be handled by a scheduling system that provides good, flexible schedules.

LTV Steel has developed such a scheduling system for use on a microcomputer. It utilizes a method that recognizes all the technical constraints and factors associated with the slab casting process, while seeking to minimize a cost function that reflects the costs of late shipments and production. The savings from the use of the scheduling system have been conservatively estimated at $1.95 million annually.

Source: Richard E. Box and Donald G. Herbe, Jr., "A Scheduling Model for LTV Steel's Cleveland Works' Twin Strand Continuous Slab Caster," *Interfaces*, vol. 18, no. 1 (January–February 1988), pp. 42–56.

OPERATIONS SCHEDULING ▲

Operations scheduling differs from work-force scheduling in several important ways. First, whereas work-force scheduling assigns people to on-duty and off-duty periods of time, **operations scheduling** assigns people to jobs (or jobs to machines) during some time period. That is, operations scheduling determines the tasks that workers are to do while on duty. Second, whereas work-force scheduling actually determines available labor capacity for each time period, operations scheduling begins with a known capacity and focuses on how to best use that capacity. Finally, whereas work-force scheduling must often deal with myriad legal, behavioral, and psychological considerations and constraints, operations scheduling typically deals with technical constraints that are directly related to production. Managerial Practice 17.2 demonstrates the importance of sound operations scheduling.

The LTV Steel scheduling system has helped to make this twin-strand continuous slab caster in its Cleveland, Ohio, plant the most productive in North America.

Our discussion of operations scheduling focuses on situations in which a number of jobs—such as production orders, bundles of checks, or people—must be processed at (or served by) one or more facilities—such as lathes, check encoding machines, or physicians. Typically, each facility can perform a variety of tasks, and there is the potential for queues to develop. In the remainder of this chapter we present several approaches to the problem of operations scheduling and their managerial implications.

Gantt Charts

A traditional device used for sequencing work on machines and monitoring progress is the **Gantt chart**, first devised by Henry L. Gantt in 1917. There are two basic forms of the chart: the job or activity progress chart and the machine chart. The progress chart graphically displays the current status of each job relative to its due date and its scheduled completion date. For example, suppose that an automobile parts manufacturer has three jobs underway, one each for Ford, Plymouth, and Pontiac. The status of these orders is shown in Fig. 17.1.

For the current date—April 21—this Gantt chart shows that the Ford order is behind schedule, the Plymouth order is exactly on schedule, and the Pontiac order is actually ahead of schedule. Now suppose that the Ford plant will have to shut down its assembly line if it does not receive its order by April 26. This situation calls for a more detailed chart and a new schedule. Suppose

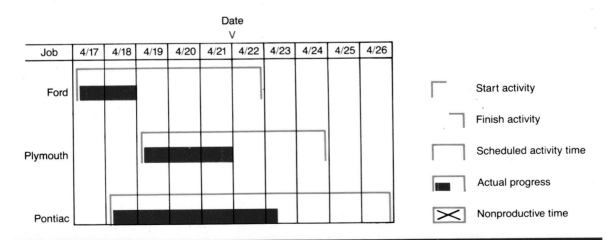

FIGURE 17.1 Gantt Chart of Job Progress for an Auto Parts Company

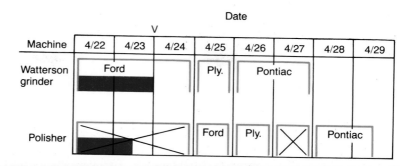

FIGURE 17.2 Gantt Chart for Machines at an Auto Parts Company

that the three jobs are all waiting to be processed at the Watterson grinder, after which they must be polished before shipment. Figure 17.2 shows one of several possible schedules the plant manager could use. This form of Gantt chart, called a machine chart, depicts the sequence of work for each machine and can also be used to monitor progress. The chart notation shown in Fig. 17.1 is also used here. On April 23, the chart shows that the Ford job is on schedule (the new schedule) and that the polisher is idle. However, comparing actual progress to the originally planned due dates in Fig. 17.1 shows that all three jobs will be past due but that the Ford plant will not have to shut down. Thus the plant manager can easily see from the Gantt machine chart the consequence of juggling the schedules. The usual approach is to juggle the schedules by trial and error until a satisfactory one is found.

Performance Measures

Technically speaking, there were 36 schedules to consider for the two machines at the automobile parts company. For each of the 3! (that is, $3 \times 2 \times 1$) ways to sequence the Watterson grinder, there were 3! ways to sequence the polisher. In general, for n jobs, each requiring m machines, there are $(n!)^m$ possible schedules. Some may not be feasible because of individual job routings or because scheduling some jobs may depend on the completion of others. Even so, there are typically thousands of ways to schedule a number of jobs on a particular set of machines, and in a job shop, for example, hundreds of scheduling decisions are made every day. Thus from the manager's perspective, identifying the performance measures to be used in selecting a schedule is important. If the overall goals of the organization are to be achieved, the schedules should reflect managerially acceptable performance measures.

Many different performance measures could be used in operations scheduling. The following list identifies and describes the more commonly used measures, some of which will be familiar to you already. Others are derivatives, or variants, of these measures.

- *Job flow time.* The amount of shop time for the job is called **job flow time.** It is the sum of the moving time between operations, waiting time for machines or work orders, process time (including setups), and delays resulting from machine breakdowns, component unavailability, and the like. Job flow time is the difference between the time of completion and the time the job was available for its first processing operation.

- *Makespan.* The total amount of time required to complete a *group* of jobs is called **makespan.** It is the difference between the start of the first job and completion of the last job.

- *Past due.* The measure **past due** can be expressed as the *amount of time* by which a job missed its due date, or the *percentage of total jobs* processed over some period of time that missed their due dates.

- *Work-in-process inventory.* Any job in a queue, moving from one operation to the next, being delayed for some reason, being processed, or residing in component or sub-assembly inventories is considered to be **work-in-process (WIP) inventory.** It is an example of *pipeline inventory,* in which the item is produced rather than purchased. This measure can be expressed in units (individual items only), number of jobs, dollar value for the entire system, or weeks of supply.

- *Total inventory.* The sum of scheduled receipts and on-hand inventories is the **total inventory.** This measure could be expressed in weeks of supply, dollars, or units (individual items only).

- *Utilization.* The percentage of work time productively spent by a machine or worker is called **utilization.** It can be aggregated for more than one machine or worker. If there are fewer workers than machines, utilization can be calculated separately for each resource.

Each of these measures can be expressed as a statistical distribution having a mean and a variance, but the performance measures are not entirely independent of each other. For example, minimizing the mean job flow time tends to reduce work-in-process inventory and increase utilization. In a flow-shop, minimizing the makespan for a group of jobs also tends to increase facility utilization.

We present examples of these interactions later in this chapter. We mention them here to point out that working with criteria such as job flow time, makespan, and past due—provided that their relationships to inventory and utilization are understood—may make scheduling easier.

Dispatching

Just as there are many feasible schedules for a specific group of jobs on a particular set of machines, there are also many ways to generate schedules. They range from straightforward manual methods, such as manipulating Gantt charts, to sophisticated computer models for developing optimal schedules. We limit our discussion here to one class of schedule generating procedures called **dispatching procedures.** Simply stated, these procedures allow the schedule for a given work station to evolve over a period of time because the decision about which job to process next (or to let the station remain idle) is made when the work station becomes available for further processing. One advantage of this approach over others is that last-minute information on operating conditions can be incorporated into the schedule as it evolves.

Typically, these decisions are made with the help of **priority sequencing rules.** When several jobs are waiting in line at a work station, priority rules specify the job processing sequence. A worker can apply these rules to select the next job. These rules can also be incorporated into a computerized scheduling system that generates a dispatch list of jobs and priorities that a supervisor uses to assign jobs to work stations. The following priority sequencing rules are commonly used in practice.

- *Critical ratio (CR).* Job priorities are calculated by dividing the time remaining to a job's due date by the total shop time remaining. The latter includes the setup, processing, move, and queuing times of all remaining operations, including the operation being scheduled. A ratio of less than 1.0 implies that the job is behind schedule, and a ratio of greater than 1.0 implies that the job is ahead of schedule. The job with the lowest CR is scheduled next.

- *Earliest due date (EDD).* The job with the earliest due date is scheduled next.

- *First come, first served (FCFS).* The job that arrived at the work station first has the highest priority.

- *Shortest processing time (SPT).* The job requiring the shortest processing time at the work station is processed next.

- *Slack per remaining operation (S/RO).* Slack is the difference between the time remaining to a job's due date and the total shop time remaining, including the operation being scheduled. A job's priority is determined by dividing the slack by the number of operations remaining, including the one being scheduled. The job with the lowest S/RO is scheduled next.

Priority rules can be classified as local or global. **Local priority rules** base a job's priority assignment only on information represented by the jobs in the individual work station queue. For example, EDD, FCFS, and SPT are local rules. By contrast, **global priority rules** base a job's priority assignment on information from other work stations, in addition to the one being scheduled. Examples of global rules are CR and S/RO. It may seem that global rules would always be the best. However, they may not provide enough benefit in a given situation to outweigh the cost of the added information requirements. Let's look at how local and global rules can be used.

Local Priority Rules

Local priority rules can be used to schedule any number of work stations. For the purpose of introducing the concepts of dispatching, we will focus on the scheduling of a single operation.

APPLICATION 17.2

Five vehicles are waiting to have engine work done at the service department of a new-car dealership. At any time, the company has only one engine expert on duty who can do this type of work. The engine problems of each vehicle have been diagnosed, and standard times for each job have been estimated. The customers also have said when they expect the work to be completed. The accompanying table shows the situation as of Monday morning. Use the SPT and EDD rules to schedule the engine expert and calculate the average hours early, hours past due, work-in-process, and total inventory for each rule.

Scheduling Data for Engine Repair Jobs

Vehicle	Standard Time, Including Setup (hr)	Scheduled Customer Pickup Time (hrs from now)
Ranger	8	10
LTD Wagon	6	12
Bronco	15	20
Econoline 150	3	18
Thunderbird	12	22

Solution

The following table shows the schedule if the SPT rule is used. The flow time for each job equals the waiting time plus the processing time. For example, the Ranger had to wait 9 hours before the engine expert started to work on it. Since the standard time for the job is 8 hours, its flow time is 17 hours.

Shortest Processing-Time Schedule for Engine Repair Jobs

Vehicle Sequence	Begin Work	Process Time (hr)	End Work	Flow Time (hr)	Scheduled Customer Pickup Time	Actual Customer Pickup Time*	Hours Early	Hours Past Due
Econoline 150	0	3	3	3	18	18	15	
LTD wagon	3	6	9	9	12	12	3	
Ranger	9	8	17	17	10	17		7
Thunderbird	17	12	29	29	22	29		7
Bronco	29	15	44	44	20	44		24
Total				102		120	18	38
Average				20.4			3.6	7.6

$$\text{Average work-in-process} = \frac{102}{44} = 2.32 \text{ vehicles.} \qquad \text{Average total inventory} = \frac{120}{44} = 2.73 \text{ vehicles.}$$

*Based on the assumption that customers will never pick up their vehicles before the scheduled pickup time and, if there is a delay, they will pick up their vehicles immediately upon completion.

We calculate the average work-in-process inventory by dividing the sum of the individual job flow times by the makespan. You might think of the sum as the total *vehicle-hours* that have been spent by the vehicles waiting for the engine expert and being processed.* Dividing this sum by the total elapsed time required to complete work on all the vehicles provides the average work-in-process inventory.

We calculate the average total inventory similarly. Total inventory is the sum of the work-in-process inventory and the completed jobs waiting to be picked up by customers. The average total inventory is equal to the sum of the *actual* pickup times divided by the makespan. The sum is the total vehicle-hours spent waiting for the engine expert, being processed, and waiting for pickup. For example, the first vehicle to be picked up is the LTD wagon, which spent 12 hours in the system. Then the Ranger is picked up after spending 17 vehicle-hours in the system. The time spent by any vehicle in the system is merely its actual customer pickup time because all were available for processing at time zero. When we divide this sum by the total elapsed time, we get the average total inventory. In this case, the averages are 2.32 vehicles in work-in-process and 2.73 vehicles in total inventory. This implies an average of 0.41 (or 2.73 − 2.32) vehicles in finished inventory, waiting for customer pickup. The following table shows the schedule and performance criteria derived from the EDD priority rule.

*In this application there are no component or subassembly inventories, so WIP consists only of those vehicles waiting in queue or being processed.

Earliest Due Date Schedule for Engine Repair Jobs

Vehicle Sequence	Begin Work	Process Time (hr)	End Work	Flow Time (hr)	Scheduled Customer Pickup Time	Actual Customer Pickup Time*	Hours Early	Hours Past Due
Ranger	0	8	8	8	10	10	2	
LTD wagon	8	6	14	14	12	14		2
Econoline 150	14	3	17	17	18	18	1	
Bronco	17	15	32	32	20	32		12
Thunderbird	32	12	44	44	22	44		22
Total				115		118	3	36
Average				23.0			0.6	7.2

Average work-in-process $= \dfrac{115}{44} = 2.61$ vehicles.   Average total inventory $= \dfrac{118}{44} = 2.68$ vehicles.

*Based on the assumption that customers will never pick up their vehicles before the scheduled pickup time and, if there is a delay, they will pick up their vehicles immediately upon completion.

Comparing the two tables in the solution of Application 17.2, you can see that the SPT schedule provided a lower average flow time and lower work-in-process inventory. The EDD schedule gave better customer service, as measured by the average hours past due, and a lower maximum hours past due (22 versus 24). It also provided a lower total inventory because fewer vehicle-hours were spent waiting for customers to pick up their cars after they had been completed. The SPT priority rule will push jobs through the system to completion more quickly than will the other rules. Speed can be an advantage—but only if jobs can be delivered sooner than promised and revenue collected earlier. If they cannot, the completed job must stay in finished inventory, canceling the advantage of minimizing the average work-in-process inventory. Consequently, the manner in which work is scheduled affects criteria that may be of concern to management. In Application 17.2, SPT and EDD provided schedules that resulted in different values for the criteria. Interestingly, both schedules have the same makespan: 44 hours. This result will always occur in single-operation scheduling for a *fixed number* of jobs available for processing, regardless of the priority rule used.

Local priority rules can also be used to schedule more than one operation. Each operation is treated independently of the others. When the work station becomes idle, the priority rule is applied to the jobs waiting for that operation, and the one with the highest priority is selected. When that operation is finished, the job is moved to the next operation in its routing, where it waits until it again has the highest priority. At any work station, the jobs in the waiting line change over a period of time, so the choice of a priority rule can make quite a difference in processing sequence.

TABLE 17.3   Generalizations about the Performance of Selected Local Rules

Rule	Comments
Earliest due date (EDD)	Performs well with respect to the percentages of jobs past due and the variance of hours past due. For a given set of jobs to be processed on a single machine, it minimizes the maximum of the past due hours of any job in the set. It is popular with firms that are sensitive to due date changes, although it does not perform very well with respect to flow time, work-in-process inventory, or utilization.
First come, first served (FCFS)	Even though this rule is considered fair to the jobs (or customers), it performs poorly with respect to all performance measures. It is actually a random rule with respect to operating performance measures.
Shortest processing time (SPT)	Often referred to as the "world champion," it tends to minimize mean flow time, work-in-process inventory, and percentage of jobs past due and to maximize shop utilization. However, it could increase total inventory value because it tends to push all work to the finished state. In addition, it tends to produce a large variance in past due hours because the larger jobs might have to wait a long time for processing. Also, it provides no opportunity to adjust schedules when due dates change. The advantage of this rule over others diminishes as the load on the shop increases.

Using simulation models of job-shop systems, researchers have studied the implications of various priority rules for various performance measures. In most of these studies, all jobs were considered independent, and the assumption was made that sufficient capacity was generally available. Some generalizations about the performance of three local priority rules are stated in Table 17.3. Later in this chapter we discuss priority planning and the role that rules such as these play in managing schedules of interdependent jobs.

Global Priority Rules

Global rules take into account information about succeeding operations before setting the priority of a job in a particular waiting line. Therefore these rules apply to the scheduling of two or more facilities. Before discussing the more general case, let's look at a special case.

Two-Facility Flow Shop.   Suppose that we have a situation in which a number of jobs are ready for processing on two facilities and that the routings of all jobs are identical. In situations like this, the makespan criterion becomes important. Recall that the makespan for a group of jobs in a single-facility scheduling problem is the same, regardless of the sequence chosen. That is no longer true for scheduling two or more facilities. Minimizing the makespan for a group of jobs to be processed on two facilities in a flow shop has the advantage of minimizing the idle time of the *second* facility because the first facility will be utilized continuously until it processes the last job.

Johnson (1954) developed a procedure to minimize makespan in scheduling a group of jobs on two facilities. He showed that the sequence of jobs at the two facilities should be identical. Therefore the priority assigned to a job should be the same at both facilities. His procedure assumes there is a known set of jobs, all of which are available to begin processing on the first facility. In this sense it is not a dispatching procedure, but it does assign priorities to jobs based on their operation times at both facilities.

For known processing times for each job at both facilities, the procedure is as follows:

1. Scan the process times at each facility and find the shortest process time among those jobs not yet scheduled. If there is a tie, choose one job arbitrarily.

2. If the shortest process time is on facility 1, schedule the corresponding job as early as possible. If the shortest process time is on facility 2, schedule the corresponding job as late as possible.

3. Eliminate the last job scheduled from further consideration. Repeat 1 and 2 until all jobs are scheduled.

APPLICATION 17.3

A recent fire in one of the Morris Machine Company's shops damaged five machines. The machines will be recovered in the following manner.

Operation 1: Unbolt the machine from the floor, move it to the repair shop, and dismantle it.

Operation 2: Clean or replace parts, test the machine, make adjustments, and reinstall it in the shop.

The estimated time for repairing each machine is shown in the accompanying table. Each operation will be performed by a separate crew of maintenance and engineering personnel. The shop will be inoperable until all the machines are back in place, so the plant manager is interested in minimizing the makespan and has authorized round-the-clock operations until the machines have been repaired.

	Time (hr)	
Machine	Operation 1	Operation 2
M1	12	22
M2	4	5
M3	5	3
M4	15	16
M5	10	8

Operation

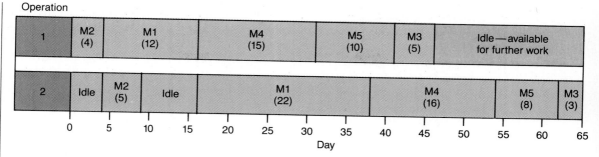

FIGURE 17.3 Gantt Chart of the Morris Machine Company Repair Schedule

Solution

The optimal sequence is shown in the following table. Machine 2 is the first to be processed by the crew assigned to operation 1. Machine 1 is next, followed by machines 4, 5, and 3. Even though the choice of the next machine was unique for each step, ties that occur can be broken arbitrarily. No other sequence of machines will produce a lower makespan. In order to determine the makespan, we have to draw a Gantt chart, as shown in Fig. 17.3. In this case, it will take 65 hours to refurbish and reinstall all five machines.

Applications of Johnson's Procedure to Morris Machine Company Repairs

Iteration	Job Sequence	Comments
1	□ □ □ □ 3	Shortest process time is three hours for M3 on the second operation.
2	2 □ □ □ 3	Eliminate M3's times from the table of estimated times. The next shortest process time is four hours for M2 on operation 1.
3 – 5	2 □ □ 5 3	Repeat the procedure for M5, M1, and M4.
	2 1 □ 5 3	
	2 1 4 5 3	

Multiple-Facility Scheduling.   We can also use global rules to schedule multiple facilities using the dispatching procedure. Although many global rules have been devised, we present only the critical ratio (CR) and slack per remaining operation (S/RO) as examples of global priority rules. Consider Table 17.4, which contains information about a set of four jobs presently waiting in queue at an engine lathe. Several operations, including the one at the engine lathe, remain to be done on each job.

Using CR to schedule the machine, we divide the time remaining to the due date by the shop time remaining to get the priority index for each job. For job 1, this is 15/6.1 = 2.46. The sequence of jobs to be processed by the engine lathe is $4-2-3-1$, assuming that no other jobs arrive in the meantime. Using S/RO, we divide the difference between the time remaining to the due date and the shop time remaining by the number of remaining operations. For job 1, this is (15 − 6.1)/10 = 0.89. The sequence of jobs is $4-3-1-2$. Note that the two priority rules yield two different schedules. By way of comparison, the SPT schedule, using the operation times at the engine lathe only, is $1-3-2-4$. No preference is given to job 4 in the SPT schedule, even though it may not be finished by its due date.

Labor-Limited Environments

Two basic types of environments affect the complexity of operations scheduling. In a **machine-limited environment** the limiting capacity is the number of

TABLE 17.4   Operating Data and the Resulting Schedules Based on CR and S/RO

Job	Operation Time at Engine Lathe (hr)	Time Remaining to Due Date (days)	Number of Operations Remaining, Including Engine Lathe	Shop Time Remaining, Including Engine Lathe (days)
1	2.3	15	10	6.1
2	10.5	10	2	7.8
3	6.2	20	12	14.5
4	15.6	8	5	10.2

Critical Ratio			Slack/Remaining Operation		
Job	Priority Index	Sequence on Engine Lathe	Job	Priority Index	Sequence on Engine Lathe
1	2.46	Fourth	1	0.89	Third
2	1.28	Second	2	1.10	Fourth
3	1.38	Third	3	0.46	Second
4	0.78	First	4	−0.44	First

TABLE 17.5   *Examples of Labor Assignment Rules*

- Assign personnel to the work station having the job in queue that has been in the system longest.
- Assign personnel to the work station having the most jobs in queue.
- Assign personnel to the work station having the largest standard work content in its queue.
- Assign personnel to the work station having the job in queue that has the earliest due date.

machines or facilities available. The assumption—which we made for local and global priority rules—is that a job never has to wait for lack of a worker. Perhaps more typically, however, the number of workers is less than the number of machines or facilities. In this case, workers are trained to work on a variety of machines or tasks, increasing the flexibility of operations. Thus in a **labor-limited environment**, the capacity constraint is the amount of labor available, not the number of machines or facilities.

Labor-limited environments add another dimension to operations scheduling. Along with deciding which job to process next at a particular work station, the scheduler must also assign a worker to his or her next work station. The scheduler can use a dispatching procedure to make these decisions as the situation arises, similar to the scheduling of vehicle repairs in Application 17.2. In labor-limited environments, the labor-assignment policies, as well as the dispatching priority rules, affect performance. Table 17.5 contains some examples of labor-assignment rules. Such rules are useful after work-force schedules have already been developed.

A SYSTEMS APPROACH TO OPERATIONS SCHEDULING ▲

The dispatching procedure for generating operations schedules works well if the job priorities reflect management's objectives. But what happens when the priority system breaks down? Generally speaking, chaos. In this section we address some of the key principles of an effective priority planning system.

Priority Planning

The symptoms of a failed priority system often are mistaken for the symptoms of inadequate capacity: many jobs behind schedule, large queues of jobs at some machines, and scores of expediters scurrying about the plant floor. However, scheduling the wrong jobs on bottleneck machines can create *apparent* capacity problems. Valuable machine time is used for the wrong jobs, and schedule performance relative to due dates suffers. In failed priority systems, priorities are not updated to reflect the current status of orders. Orders may appear to be late when, in fact, customers may have canceled them, or orders may have been put on hold pending production of a component or arrival of a purchased part.

Valid Priorities.   Maintaining valid priorities is the key to effective priority planning. An order has a **valid priority** if its due date matches its need date. The due date could be a delivery date promised to a customer or a shop due date that identifies the scheduled start time of a parent item for an order. At the time an order is issued, the due date and the need date are the same. However, as time passes, either the due date or the need date may change for a variety of reasons. For example, customers cancel orders, new customer orders are put into the schedule, machines fail and delay components, vendor shipments arrive late, or changes are made to the bill of materials for a product. Companies often try to cope with disturbances such as these by using expediters. However, not all schedule changes are communicated quickly enough, leaving many scheduling decisions to machine operators, who have to work with limited, often faulty information.

Priority Dependency.   In order to maintain valid priorities, managers must recognize the **priority dependency** of jobs in a manufacturing system where the bills of materials have several levels. In vertical priority dependency, the priority of a component order depends on the priority of the parent order. For example, consider the gear and pinion sets that the Eaton Company produces for truck axles. A gear and a pinion (the components) must each be manufactured and matched to become a completed gear and pinion set (the parent). If an order is canceled for a particular gear and pinion set, the due dates for the remaining gear and the pinion orders being processed should be updated to reflect new need dates for them.

In horizontal dependency, the priority of a component order depends on the priority of another component order. For example, if the production order for the gears is going to be delayed because of raw-material shortages, the due date for the pinions should be revised to reflect the new date that the gears will be available. In that way, valuable machine time will not be spent on the order for pinions, only to have them wait in stock until the gears finally arrive. A formal system for priority planning should allow for such dependencies, so that the priorities make sense to the people who must process the orders. Otherwise, an informal system will develop and management will lose control of an important activity.

A Formal System

Figure 17.4 shows how material requirements planning (MRP) can be used in priority planning. Based on an authorized master production schedule, the system generates a detailed plan, complete with planned order releases for all

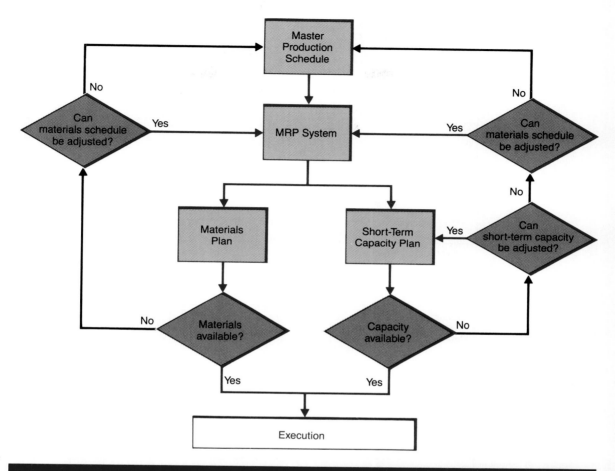

FIGURE 17.4   A Formal Scheduling System

purchased materials, components, and assemblies. If an unanticipated disturbance will lead to a shortage of materials, the MRP system issues action notices,
identifying problems that need to be solved. Management can then determine
the extent to which the original due dates for the affected open orders have
diverged from their need dates. If there is sufficient capacity, adjustments can
be made accordingly.

Adjusting schedules is facilitated by two features of MRP. Consider the
gear and pinion set and its components in Fig. 17.5. Below each component
inventory status record is a **peg record,** which indicates for each week the
quantity needed of each parent item. Note that the gear has several parents
and that the gross requirements of 22 units in week 8 are split between two
different parent items. The peg record provides the *upward visibility* needed to

Item: GP502
Description: Gear and pinion set

Lot Size: POQ—2 weeks
Lead Time: 4 weeks
Safety Stock: 0 units

Date		1	2	3	4	5	6	7	8	9	10
Gross requirements			20	45	13	31	10	48	52	37	18	63
Scheduled receipts			60		57							
Projected on hand	8	48	3	47	16	6	52	0	18	0	0
Planned receipts							94		55		63
Planned order releases			94		55		63				

Item: G500
Description: Gear

Lot Size: 100
Lead Time: 7 weeks
Safety Stock: 0 units

Date		1	2	3	4	5	6	7	8	9	10
Gross requirements			94		55		63		22	30	
Scheduled receipts			100				100				
Projected on hand	50	50	56	56	1	1	38	38	16	86	86
Planned receipts										100	
Planned order releases			100								

Item: P002
Description: Pinion

Lot Size: 100
Lead Time: 3 weeks
Safety Stock: 0 units

Date		1	2	3	4	5	6	7	8	9	10
Gross requirements			94		55		63				
Scheduled receipts			100		100						
Projected on hand	0	0	6	6	51	51	88	88	88	88	88
Planned receipts							100				
Planned order releases				100							

Peg Record G500		
Week	Quantity	Parent
2	94	GP502
4	55	GP502
6	63	GP502
8	12	GP507
8	10	GP509
9	30	GP504

Peg Record P002		
Week	Quantity	Parent
2	94	GP502
4	55	GP502
6	63	GP502

FIGURE 17.5 Data for Priority Planning

determine whether schedule adjustments are necessary and, if so, how to make them.

Another useful device is called a **firm planned order.** This technique enables the planner to override the fixed parameters of the MRP system on an exception basis. The planner can change lead times and/or lot sizes and adjust schedules to make the priorities on the shop floor valid. Subsequent replanning with the MRP system will not change the timing or size of the firm planned orders.

APPLICATION 17.4

Refer to the data for the gear and pinion set in Fig. 17.5. For each of the four disturbances in the following table—taken independently of the others—suggest a schedule change that will avoid shortages of materials.

Revising Priorities with an MRP System

Disturbance	Resulting Schedule Change	
1. Customer cancelation of gross requirement of 52 units of GP502 in week 7. (This change reduces the planned order release in week 2 to only 42 units.)	G500: Delay the open order in week 2 until week 4. Remove the planned order release in week 2.	P002: Delay the open order in week 4 until week 6. Remove the planned order release in week 3.
2. Increase in customer order for GP502 in week 9 by 15 units. (The planned order release in week 4 now becomes 70 units.)	G500: Expedite open order in week 6 to week 4.	P002: No change.
3. Machine failures delay the open order for G500 in week 2. (It is now expected to be completed in week 3.)	GP502: Change the planned order release in week 2 to 42 units. Create a new planned order release for 52 units in week 3.	P002: No change.
4. Temporary labor shortages delay the open order for P002 in week 4. (It is now expected to be completed in week 5.)	G500: No change.	GP502: Compress the lead time of the planned order release in week 4 to three weeks. This moves the planned order release to week 5.

Solution

The suggested schedule changes are also shown in the table. The results become apparent only after the records have been recomputed. The first two disturbances are caused by changes in parent-item plans, and the component schedule changes amount to realigning the due dates and need dates of certain scheduled receipts. The third disturbance, an unavoidable delay in G500, originates at the component level and affects parent-item plans. The peg record is used to determine which parent item(s) will be affected—in this case, GP502 only. The inventory record for GP502 indicates that its gross requirements could still be met if the planned order release in week 2 were reduced to 42. A subsequent planned order of 52 can be scheduled for week 3, when the component order is to be available. This lot-size change for GP502 can be accomplished using firm planned orders. Note that as P002 has no on-hand inventory, the due date for its open order in week 2 has not diverged from its need date.

The last disturbance shown in the table also requires the use of peg records and firm planned orders. In this case, the lead time for the planned order of GP502 in week 4 is shortened to three weeks. A subsequent replanning session with MRP will move the gross requirements of 55 units to week 5 for both components, thus avoiding any unplanned shortages of materials.

Shop-Floor Control Systems

Priority planning done with the help of MRP is of no use unless the planner transmits the changes in scheduled-receipt due dates to the shop floor. The planner can do so with a **shop-floor control system**. Figure 17.6 shows the typical inputs and functions of such a system. The input files used here are similar to those used in MRP and CRP. The order file contains the details of all planned order releases and scheduled receipts. The scheduled-receipts data

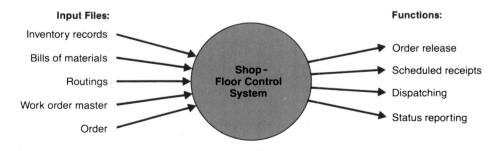

Input Files:
Inventory records
Bills of materials
Routings
Work order master
Order

Shop-Floor Control System

Functions:
Order release
Scheduled receipts
Dispatching
Status reporting

FIGURE 17.6 Typical Shop-Floor Control System

enable the user to track the progress of any open order and are updated by the shop-floor control system as status changes are recorded.

Four major functions can be performed with shop-floor control systems. The order release function adjusts the release date of planned orders to correspond to the capacity constraints revealed by capacity requirements planning and to check for component availability. Orders are released only if components are available, unless the check is overridden. As part of this function, the planner also initiates all the paperwork that authorizes the start of the order, requisitions materials, and specifies moves between operations and routings.

The scheduled-receipt maintenance function provides an accurate database for each order. The primary source of information is the report of daily shop-floor transactions that gives the status of the scheduled receipts. This function also covers order splitting and adding more operations to a routing because of rework.

The *dispatching* function generates a work-center list, specifying the status of jobs in each work center and ranking them in order of priority. The planner uses due-date dispatching rules, such as critical ratio, slack per remaining operation, or earliest due date, to transmit priorities to the shop floor. The planner can revise the work list daily to reflect the latest changes in priorities of scheduled receipts.

The status reporting function generates a variety of reports from the database needed in the shop-floor control system. For example, the planner can generate reports detailing the status of scheduled receipts for a specific customer order or the status of any work center showing the orders currently being processed there and the load expressed in standard hours.

Thus the shop-floor control system can translate realignment of due dates and need dates into action. This method is useful for converting various operations plans and schedules into production that will effectively achieve the firm's overall goals.

SOLVED PROBLEMS

1. The Food Bin grocery store operates 24 hours per day, 7 days per week. Fred Bulger, the store manager, has been analyzing the efficiency and productivity of store operations recently. For example, at present there are 10 checkout clerks on the first shift from 8:00 A.M. to 5:00 P.M. However, Bulger has noticed a considerable amount of slack capacity on certain days of the week. These clerks could be used to bag groceries, but their wages are higher than those of the bagging clerks who should be doing that task. Consequently, Bulger decided to observe the need for checkout clerks on the first shift for a period of one month. Each time the queue in front of

a cash register exceeded three customers, he recorded the need for another register to open. At the end of the month, he calculated the average number of checkout registers that should be open during the first shift each day. His results showed peak needs on Saturdays and Sundays.

Day	M	T	W	Th	F	S	Su
Requirements	3	4	4	3	4	7	8

Bulger now had to come up with a work-force schedule that guaranteed each checkout clerk two consecutive days off but still covered all requirements.

a. Develop a work-force schedule that covers all requirements while giving two consecutive days off to each clerk. How many clerks are needed? Assume that the clerks have no preference regarding which days they have off.

b. Specify the work schedule for each checkout clerk.

Solution

a. Use the method demonstrated in Application 17.1 to determine the number of clerks needed.

Clerk	M	T	W	Th	F	S	Su
1	3	4	4	3	4	7	8
2	3	4	3	2	3	6	7
3	2	3	2	2	3	5	6
4	1	2	2	2	2	4	5
5	1	2	1	1	1	3	4
6	0	1	0	1	1	2	3
7	0	1	0	0	0	1	2
8	0	0	0	0	0	0	1

The minimum number of clerks is 8.

b. One of many possible work schedules, based on the results in (a), is:

Employee	M	T	W	Th	F	S	Su
1	Off	Off	X	X	X	X	X
2	X	X	X	Off	Off	X	X
3	X	X	Off	Off	X	X	X
4	Off	Off	X	X	X	X	X
5	X	X	X	Off	Off	X	X
6	Off	Off	X	X	X	X	X
7	X	X	X	Off	Off	X	X
8	<u>X</u>	<u>X</u>	<u>X</u>	<u>X</u>	<u>Off</u>	<u>Off</u>	<u>X</u>
Employees on duty	5	5	7	4	4	7	8
Requirements	3	4	4	3	4	7	8
Slack	2	1	3	1	0	0	0

The slack in this schedule Monday–Thursday would indicate to Bulger the number of employees he might ask to work part-time (fewer than 5 days per week). For example, Clerk 2 might only work Saturdays and Sundays, Clerk 5 only Tuesdays, Saturdays, and Sundays, and Clerk 6 only Fridays, Saturdays, and Sundays. There would be no slack in that revised schedule.

2. The Neptune's Den Marina is located at Aldrich Lake in Northern Wisconsin. In addition to the myriad services the marina provides to avid fishermen, Rusty Botim, the owner and proprietor, services outboard motors. The typical motor brought in for service at this time of the year has been stored in a garage in Milwaukee for the winter and requires maintenance repair of the ignition system. Some motors require the replacement of broken parts, whereas others need a complete overhaul. Currently, five motors with varying problems are awaiting service. Botim's best estimate for the labor time involved and when the customer is expecting to pick up the motor (the number of days from today) are shown in the following table. Customers usually do not pick up their motors early.

Motor	Estimated Labor Time (days)	Promise Date (days from now)
50-hp Evinrude	5	8
7-hp Chrysler	4	15
100-hp Mercury	10	12
4-hp Sportsman	1	20
75-hp Nautique	3	10

a. Develop separate schedules using the SPT and EDD rules.
   i. What is the average flow time for each schedule?
   ii. What is the percentage of past due jobs for each schedule?
   iii. Which schedule minimizes the maximum past due days for any motor?
b. For each schedule in (a), calculate:
   i. Average work-in-process inventory (in motors).
   ii. Average total inventory (in motors).

Solution

a. Shortest processing time (SPT):

Repair Sequence	Process Time	Flow Time	Promise Date	Actual Pick-Up Date	Days Early	Days Past Due
4-hp Sportsman	1	1	20	20	19	
75-hp Nautique	3	4	10	10	6	
7-hp Chrysler	4	8	15	15	7	
50-hp Evinrude	5	13	8	13		5
100-hp Mercury	10	23	12	23		11
Total		49		81		

Earliest due date (EDD):

Repair Sequence	Process Time	Flow Time	Promise Date	Actual Pick-Up Date	Days Early	Days Past Due
50-hp Evinrude	5	5	8	8	3	
75-hp Nautique	3	8	10	10	2	
100-hp Mercury	10	18	12	18		6
7-hp Chrysler	4	23	15	22		7
4-hp Sportsman	1	23	20	23		3
Total		76		81		

   i. Average flow time for SPT is 9.8 (or 49/5) days. For EDD it is 15.2 (or 76/5) days.
   ii. Percentage of past due jobs for SPT is 40 (or 2/5) percent. For EDD it is 60 (or 3/5) percent.
   iii. The EDD schedule minimizes the maximum days past due but has a greater flow time and causes more jobs to be past due.

b. SPT:

$$\text{Average WIP} = \frac{\text{Total flow time}}{\text{Makespan}}$$

$$= \frac{49}{23} = 2.13 \text{ motors}$$

$$\text{Average total inventory} = \frac{\text{Total actual pick-up times}}{\text{Makespan}}$$

$$= \frac{81}{23} = 3.52 \text{ motors}$$

EDD:

$$\text{Average WIP} = \frac{76}{23} = 3.30 \text{ motors}$$

$$\text{Average total inventory} = \frac{81}{23} = 3.52 \text{ motors}$$

3. The data in the following table were reported by the shop-floor control system for order processing at the edge grinder. The current date is week 150. The number of remaining operations and the total work remaining includes the operation at the edge grinder. All orders are available for processing and none has been started yet.

Current Order	Process Time (hr)	Due Date (wk)	Remaining Operations	Total Work Remaining (wks)
A101	10	162	10	9
B272	7	158	9	6
C105	15	152	1	1
D707	4	170	8	18
E555	8	154	5	8

a. Specify the priorities for each job, if the shop-floor control system uses:

   i. Slack per remaining operation (S/RO).

   ii. Critical ratio (CR).

b. For each priority rule, calculate the average flow time per job at the edge grinder.

Solution

a. Specify the priorities for each job using various dispatching rules.

i. S/RO: The priority of a job equals the time remaining to its due date minus the total work remaining divided by the number of remaining operations. The sequence of production (priority in parentheses) would be:

$$\text{E555} \quad \left(\frac{154 - 150 - 8}{5} = -0.80 \right)$$

$$\text{B272} \quad \left(\frac{158 - 150 - 6}{9} = 0.22 \right)$$

$$\text{D707} \quad \left(\frac{170 - 150 - 18}{8} = 0.25 \right)$$

$$\text{A101} \quad \left(\frac{162 - 150 - 9}{10} = 0.30 \right)$$

$$\text{C105} \quad \left(\frac{152 - 150 - 1}{1} = 1.00 \right)$$

ii. CR: The priority of a job equals the time remaining to its due date divided by the total work remaining. The sequence of production (priority in parentheses) would be:

$$\text{E555} \quad \left(\frac{154 - 150}{8} = 0.50 \right)$$

$$\text{D707} \quad \left(\frac{170 - 150}{18} = 1.11 \right)$$

$$\text{A101} \quad \left(\frac{162 - 150}{9} = 1.33 \right)$$

$$\text{B272} \quad \left(\frac{158 - 150}{6} = 1.33 \right)$$

$$\text{C105} \quad \left(\frac{152 - 150}{1} = 2.00 \right)$$

b. We are looking for the flow time of a given set of jobs at a single machine, so each job's flow time equals the flow time of the job just prior to it in sequence plus its own processing time. Consequently, the average flow times are:

$$\text{S/RO} = \frac{8 + 15 + 19 + 29 + 44}{5} = 23.0 \text{ hr}$$

$$\text{CR} = \frac{8 + 12 + 22 + 29 + 44}{5} = 23.0 \text{ hr}$$

Thus the average flow time per job is the same for each rule. This result will not always be the case.

4. Treetop Airlines needs to schedule 10 aircraft of various designs for maintenance. For scheduling, it is convenient to think of two maintenance operations for each plane in the following sequence.

Operation 1: Engine and flight systems ground checks, replacing worn or damaged parts where necessary.

Operation 2: Flight tests and final safety checks.

Based on flight records and the specific design of each aircraft, management has estimated that each operation will require the amount of time (in days) shown in the following table.

Aircraft	Operation 1	Operation 2
1	3	1
2	4	4
3	3	2
4	6	1
5	1	2
6	3	6
7	2	4
8	4	8
9	8	2
10	1	1

Suppose that one of management's objectives is to minimize the total length of time that all 10 aircraft go without maintenance. This objective can be translated as minimizing the makespan of the 10-aircraft fleet. First, find a schedule that minimizes the makespan. Then calculate the average job flow time on an aircraft through the two operations, assuming that all 10 aircraft are available for maintenance now. What is the total elapsed time for maintaining all 10 aircraft?

Solution

Johnson's rule can be used to find the schedule that minimizes the total makespan. The 10 steps used to arrive at a sequence are as follows:

Select job 5 first.	5————————
Select job 10 next. Arbitrarily put toward front.	5–10———————
Select job 1 next. Put at end.	5–10————————1
Put job 4 toward the end.	5–10———————4–1
Put job 7 toward the front.	5–10–7——————4–1

Put job 3 toward the end. $5-10-7------3-4-1$
Put job 9 toward the end. $5-10-7----9-3-4-1$
Put job 6 toward the front. $5-10-7-6---9-3-4-1$
Put job 2 toward the front. $5-10-7-6-2--9-3-4-1$
Put job 8 in remaining space. $5-10-7-6-2-8-9-3-4-1$

There are several optimal solutions to this problem. All have the same make-span, however.

The schedule would be as follows:

Airliner	Operation 1		Operation 2	
	Start	Finish	Start	Finish
5	0	1	1	3
10	1	2	3	4
7	2	4	4	8
6	4	7	8	14
2	7	11	14	18
8	11	15	18	26
9	15	23	26	28
3	23	26	28	30
4	26	32	32	33
1	32	35	35	36
Total				200

The makespan is 36 days. The average flow time is the sum of operation 2 finish times divided by 10, or $200/10 = 20$ days.

FORMULA REVIEW

1. Slack per remaining operation:

> S/RO = time remaining to due date minus total work remaining divided by the number of remaining operations

2. Critical ratio:

> CR = time remaining to due date divided by the total work remaining

CHAPTER HIGHLIGHTS

- Scheduling is the allocation of resources over a period of time to accomplish a specific set of tasks.

- A work-force schedule translates a staffing plan into a specific work schedule for each employee. Typical work-force scheduling considerations include capacity limits, service targets, consecutive days off, maximum number of workdays in a row, type of schedule (fixed or rotating), and vacation and holiday time.

- Gantt charts are useful for depicting the sequence of work at a particular work station, as well as monitoring the progress of jobs in the system.

- There are many ways to schedule multiple jobs on multiple facilities. Performance measures that can be used to develop an acceptable schedule include average job flow time, makespan, percentage of jobs past due, average amount of time past due per job, average work-in-process inventory, average investment in total inventory, and utilization of equipment and workers.

- Dispatching procedures allow a schedule to evolve because the decision about which job to process next at a work station (or for the station to remain idle) is made when the work station becomes available for further processing. Priority rules are used to make these decisions. Local priority rules assign priorities on the basis of information concerning only the jobs in the individual work station queue. Examples of these rules are EDD, FCFS, and SPT. Global priority rules assign priorities on the basis of information from other machines or facilities, in addition to the one being scheduled. Examples of these rules are CR and S/RO. The choice of priority rule can affect the schedule performance measures that are of concern to management.

- Labor-limited systems add another dimension to operations scheduling. Not only must a decision be made about which job to process next at a work station but also about which work station an operator should work at next.

- The key to effective priority planning in manufacturing is to maintain valid priorities by ensuring that order due dates correspond to order need dates. Horizontal and vertical priority dependencies need to be recognized. Priority planning with an MRP system is aided by the use of peg records and firm planned orders.

- Shop-floor control systems transmit the changes in open-order due dates to the shop floor and make use of priority rules to control the scheduling process. These systems also involve the functions of order release, scheduled-receipt maintenance, and status reporting.

KEY TERMS

dispatching procedures   641
firm planned order   653
fixed schedule   631
Gantt chart   638
global priority rules   641
job flow time   640
labor-limited environment   649
local priority rules   641
machine-limited environment   648
makespan   640
operations scheduling   637
past due   640
peg record   651
priority dependency   650
priority sequencing rules   641
rotating schedule   631
shop-floor control system   654
total inventory   640
utilization   640
valid priority   650
work-in-process (WIP) inventory   640
work-force scheduling   630

STUDY QUESTIONS

1. Work-force schedules have a number of uses. Discuss these uses within the context of a service operation familiar to you.

2. Compare and contrast work-force scheduling with operations scheduling. Are they related in any way? If so, how?

3. How does scheduling in general fit into overall operations management?

4. In the automobile parts example, we sequenced the jobs on the Watterson grinder in the order Ford–Plymouth–Pontiac. We used trial and error with Gantt charts. Specify a simple priority rule that would have yielded the same schedule. Use the information in Fig. 17.1.

5. What is the difference between the job flow-time measure and the makespan measure? When does makespan become relevant?

6. Suppose that you have two alternative approaches for determining machine schedules. One is an optimizing approach that can be run once a week on the computer. The other is a dispatching approach that utilizes priority rules to determine the schedule as it evolves. Discuss the advantages and disadvantages of each approach and the conditions under which each approach is likely to be better.

7. On what basis would you make a choice between local priority rules and global priority rules?

8. The shortest processing time (SPT) rule has been criticized because it tends to produce schedules having a large variance in past due hours. That is, some jobs get through the production system quickly, whereas others (the ones that have long processing times) must spend considerable time in queue. Suggest a modification to the SPT rule to overcome this criticism.

9. It has been pointed out that there is a problem with S/RO when more than one job in queue has negative slack. For example, if job 1 has a slack of -1 with 1 operation remaining and job 2 has a slack of -2 with 10 operations remaining, S/RO would choose job 1 first because it has the smallest (most negative) ratio. Yet job 2 seems to be the one that should be processed next. Suggest a simple modification to the S/RO rule to overcome this difficulty.

10. Explain why management should be concerned about priority systems in manufacturing and service organizations.

11. Your company is considering the use of its MRP system for priority planning. Briefly explain the advantages and uses of peg records and firm planned orders to your boss.

PROBLEMS

Review Problems

1. The following schedule was developed for the drill press and grinder operations at 7 A.M.

| Job | Drill Press | | Grinder | |
	Setup	Process	Setup	Process
1			$8:00-9:15$	$9:15-12:00$
2	$8:00-8:30$	$8:30-10:00$	$2:00-2:45$	$2:45-3:30$
3	$10:15-10:30$	$10:30-11:45$	$12:30-1:00$	$1:00-2:00$
4	$12:30-1:30$	$1:30-3:30$		

a. Draw a Gantt chart for each machine.
b. Suppose that a new job arrives at 7:30 A.M. requiring 30 minutes of setup and 1 hour of processing on the drill press first, then 1 hour of setup and $1\frac{1}{2}$ hours of processing on the grinder. This job must be available for the assembly line by 1:30 P.M. Based on the following assumptions, insert this job into the schedule.
   i. Each operator must have lunch from 12:00 to 12:30.

   ii. Interrupting a job already being processed with another job is too costly. However, lunch breaks in the middle of a job are permitted.
   iii. Jobs 2 and 3 can be processed on the two machines in any order, that is, drill press first or grinder first.
   iv. Job 3 must be completed by 3 P.M. to meet an assembly schedule. The other jobs are not needed until the next day.
   Draw revised Gantt charts for each machine.

TABLE 17.6

Job	Release Time	Lot Size	Process Time (hr/unit)	Setup Time (hr)	Due Time
1	8:00 A.M. Monday	100	0.030	3	5:00 P.M. Monday
2	8:30 A.M. Monday	50	0.040	6	6:00 P.M. Monday
3	8:40 A.M. Monday	200	0.020	1	6:00 A.M. Tuesday
4	9:10 A.M. Monday	500	0.008	3	11:00 P.M. Monday

2. Consider a machine shop that operates 24 hours per day and makes heavy use of a certain engine lathe. The load on the engine lathe is monitored, and no more than 24 hours of work is released to the lathe in any day. The data for a typical set of jobs is shown in Table 17.6. Management has been investigating scheduling procedures that would focus on customer service and inventory criteria. A current policy states that if a single job is in queue ready for processing and the machine is idle, the job should be processed on the machine regardless of the characteristics of that job. At 8:00 A.M. on Monday the engine lathe was idle.

a. Develop a schedule using each of the following priority rules and draw a Gantt machine chart for each schedule.
   i. FCFS
   ii. SPT
   iii. EDD
b. For each schedule in (a), calculate the average past due hours per job and the average flow time per job. Keep in mind that the jobs are available for processing at different times.
c. Comment on the customer-service and inventory performance of the three rules. What trade-offs should management consider in selecting rules for scheduling the engine lathe in the future?

3. Each week the manager of the Tower Fabricating Company schedules the Bradley stock-cutting machine with the backlog of orders for that week. The stockcutting machine is the first step in the process and the schedule for that machine affects the schedule for the remainder of the shop. This week the manager has the following orders for the stock-cutting machine.

Order	Estimated Machine Time (hr)	Due Date (hr from now)
AB104	12	24
ZX300	4	3
SR210	8	8
CRX04	2	10
ST200	14	20

The due dates reflect the need for the order to be at its next operation.

a. Develop separate schedules using the SPT and EDD rules.
   i. What is the average flow time for each schedule?
   ii. What is the percentage of past due jobs for each schedule?
   iii. Which schedule minimizes the maximum past due hours for any order?
b. For each schedule in (a), calculate:
   i. Average work-in-process inventory (in orders).
   ii. Average total inventory (in orders).
c. Comment on the performance of the two rules relative to these performance measures.

 4. The heat-treat furnace is a bottleneck operation in a production system. Currently, six jobs are waiting to be processed. The following table gives the available operations data. Assume that the current date is week 10 and that the number of remaining operations and the total work remaining includes the operation at the furnace.

Job	Process Time (hr)	Due Date (wk)	Remaining Operations	Total Work Remaining (wks)
A	3	13	2	5
B	7	20	5	9
C	15	30	4	10
D	2	18	6	5
E	8	16	3	2
F	10	35	10	21

a. Specify the priority for each job if the shop-floor control system uses the following priority rules.
   i. SPT   ii. EDD
   iii. S/RO   iv. CR
b. For each priority rule, calculate the average flow time per job at the furnace.
c. Which of these priority rules would work best for priority planning with an MRP system? Why?

5. Refer to the Gantt machine chart in Fig. 17.7.

a. Suppose that a routing requirement is that each job must be processed on machine A first. Can the makespan be improved? If so, draw a Gantt chart with the improved schedule. If not, state the reason for your answer.
b. Suppose that there is no routing restriction on machine sequence. Jobs can be processed in any sequence on the machines. Can the makespan in the chart be improved in this case? If so, draw a Gantt chart with your schedule. If not, state the reason for your answer.

6. A good customer is concerned about the shipment of five orders presently in a metal-working shop. The orders, consisting of custom replacement parts for the customer's machines, are due to be shipped in 19 working days. Late shipments have a penalty in the amount of $1000 per day late. The shop has been very busy and the manager is now in the difficult position of facing large penalties. The five orders must each be processed by the polishing machine, then packaged for shipment. The production control manager suggested the following schedule (in days).

Job	Polishing Start	Polishing Finish	Packaging Start	Packaging Finish
1	0	3	3	4
2	3	7	7	10
3	7	9	10	13
4	9	12	13	17
5	12	18	18	20

Is there a schedule that will avoid any penalties? If so, show it.

7. Boynton Smith, operations manager at the Westerville Tool and Die Company, called Ignatius Katt and Primus Dogg to his office. Katt is the supervisor of department 4 and Dogg is the supervisor of department 8. Katt and Dogg were arguing over the scheduling of a group of jobs for the Kramer Company. All six jobs were in Katt's department awaiting processing. They had to be routed to Dogg's department next. Katt

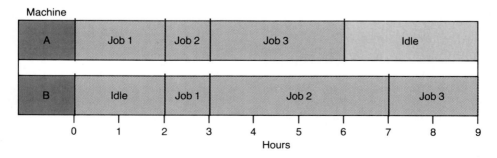

FIGURE 17.7

was adamant about processing the jobs according to the shortest processing times for the operation in his department. "I want to minimize my work-in-process inventory these days, given the high cost to carry inventory," he hissed. Dogg barked, "You should be less selfish. If we worked together, we could get those six jobs to Kramer earlier. We should think of the customer in all of this." Jack Kramer had recently called Boynton Smith and told him that the order represented by the six jobs was critical. He also reminded Boynton that the Kramer Company was a big customer. The processing times for the six jobs in each department are:

| Job | Process Times (days) | |
	Department 4	Department 8
1	5	7
2	6	2
3	2	1
4	4	10
5	10	6
6	3	4

a. Determine a schedule for the operation in each department. Use SPT for department 4 and the same sequence for department 8.
   i. What is the average job flow time for department 4?
   ii. What is the makespan through both departments?
b. Find a schedule that will minimize the makespan through both departments and then calculate the average job flow time for department 4.
c. Discuss the trade-offs represented by these two schedules. What implications do they have for centralized scheduling?

8. Return to Solved Problem 4 and the Treetop Airlines need to schedule 10 aircraft for maintenance.
   a. Suppose that one of management's objectives is to maximize the number of aircraft in service that have received maintenance. This can be translated as minimizing the average job flow time of the 10 aircraft through the two operations, assuming that

once the plane has completed the second operation it immediately returns to service. First, devise a schedule using SPT. This can be accomplished by adding the two operation times for each aircraft and scheduling the aircraft as if there were only one operation. The resulting sequence is used for both operations. Then calculate the average flow time per aircraft. What is the total elapsed time to maintain all 10 aircraft with your schedule?
   b. Compare the original solution to Solved Problem 4 and your solution in (a). Discuss the trade-offs that must be made between the schedule and other factors that must be considered in scheduling the aircraft for maintenance.

9. The manager of the Oak Road Post Office has determined the daily requirements for part-time clerks. The post office is open for sorting and processing seven days a week. For the following staffing requirements, find the minimum number of clerks the manager must hire. Prepare a work-force schedule for these clerks so that each clerk will have two consecutive days off per week and all staffing requirements are satisfied. Give preference to the pair Saturday–Sunday in case of a tie.

Day	M	T	W	Th	F	S	Su
Require-ments	3	5	8	4	9	3	3

10. Tom Rash is a young entrepreneur in Steubenville, Ohio, who saw the need for a private refuse collection service. Apartment complexes and businesses would be the primary customers. The unique aspect of this service would be collections each day of the week, including Sundays. Each customer would have specially designed refuse bins to allow the use of only one person per truck. Customers could also schedule special pickups for unexpectedly heavy refuse accumulations. The trucks would be pleasantly decorated with a base color of gray and "The T. Rash Company" proudly displayed in brilliant scarlet letters.

Rash surveyed a number of prospective customers and arrived at the following estimate of the number of refuse collectors he would need for each day of the week.

Day	M	T	W	Th	F	S	Su
Requirements	10	12	8	7	6	3	4

Collection requirements would be higher on Mondays and Tuesdays to accommodate businesses that do much of their business on weekends. The owners prefer not to have refuse collection on weekends because of the increased traffic and shortage of parking space around their establishments.

   a. Find the minimum number of refuse collectors required, if each employee works five days a week and has two consecutive days off. Give preference to S–Su when that pair is involved in a tie.
   b. Specify the work schedule for each employee. How much slack does your schedule generate for each day?
   c. Suppose that Rash can smooth the requirements by offering special rates for W–Su pickups. The requirements would be 8 on Monday and 7 on the other days of the week.
      i. How many employees would be needed now?
      ii. Giving preference to S–Su when that pair is involved in a tie doesn't yield the optimal solution. Find a better solution than the one in (i) in terms of minimal total slack capacity.
      iii. Does smoothing of requirements have implications for capital investment in this business? If so, what are they?

11. Your company uses an MRP system to do priority planning. Consider the information presented in Fig. 17.8 concerning three of the items the company manufactures. Item X1 has two components, Y1 and Y2; both Y1 and Y2 have more than one parent. Your job is to have materials in the right place at the right time. You are interested in maintaining valid priorities and satisfying customer demand, as evidenced by the gross requirements for item X1.
      State why situations (a) and (b), taken independently of each other, would (or would not) cause a problem in priority validity for the components. If there is a problem, how would you resolve it, assuming sufficient capacity?

   a. A customer cancellation of an order for X1 causes its gross requirement in week 6 to become 28 units instead of 82 units.

   b. A good customer asks you to ship an unplanned order of 100 units of X1 in week 5. This increases the gross requirement of X1 in week 5 to 100 units. Top management agrees to make the shipment but does not compensate for it by adjusting the gross requirements of X1 in other weeks.

12. Again use the MRP information in Problem 11. State why situations (a)–(d), taken independently, would (or would not) cause a problem in priority validity or materials coverage for X1, Y1, or Y2. If there is a problem, how would you resolve it, assuming sufficient capacity. If more than one approach seems reasonable to you, discuss each one in terms of its relative advantages and disadvantages.

   a. Suppose that Y1 is a purchased item and the supplier tells you that the scheduled receipt you expected in week 4 will now arrive in week 5. There is no way to expedite the scheduled receipt to have it arrive as previously planned. There are no other suppliers who can get Y1 to you by week 4. You must now accept the fact that the order will arrive in week 5.
   b. Suppose instead that Y1 is a manufactured part. The gross requirement of 25 units in week 1 have been canceled.
   c. The requirement for item Z8 has increased in week 4 from 33 to 43.
   d. A new machinist working on the order for Y2 scheduled for week 5 irrevocably damaged 50 percent of the lot. The quantity now expected in week 5 is 60 units.

Advanced Problems

Problem 14 requires prior reading of Supplement 3. A computer package is recommended for solving this problem.

13. Six jobs must be processed on three machines in the sequence M1–M2–M3. The processing times (in days) are:

Job	M1	M2	M3
1	2	3	5
2	5	6	4
3	3	2	2
4	7	1	6
5	8	5	7
6	1	7	2

Item: X1	Lot Size: 100
Description: Rotor housing	Lead Time: 2 weeks
	Safety Stock: 0 units

	Date	1	2	3	4	5	6	7	8	9	10
Gross requirements		50		33			82	70	40		52
Scheduled receipts		100									
Projected on hand	22	72	72	39	39	39	57	87	47	47	95
Planned receipts							100	100			100
Planned order releases					100	100			100		

Item: Y1	Lot Size: 150
Description: Armature	Lead Time: 3 weeks
	Safety Stock: 0 units

	Date	1	2	3	4	5	6	7	8	9	10
Gross requirements		25		18	133	110		40	100		20
Scheduled receipts		150			150						
Projected on hand	10	135	135	117	134	24	24	134	34	34	14
Planned receipts								150			
Planned order releases					150						

Item: Y2	Lot Size: 120
Description: Rotor housing	Lead Time: 5 weeks
	Safety Stock: 0 units

	Date	1	2	3	4	5	6	7	8	9	10
Gross requirements			30		133	110			100		20
Scheduled receipts			120			120					
Projected on hand	50	50	140	140	7	17	17	17	37	37	17
Planned receipts									120		
Planned order releases			120								

Peg Record Y1		
Week	Quantity	Parent
1	25	Z3
3	18	Z3
4	33	Z8
4	100	X1
5	10	Z8
5	100	X1
7	40	Z3
8	100	X1
10	20	Z8

Peg Record Y2		
Week	Quantity	Parent
2	30	Z4
4	33	Z8
4	100	X1
5	10	Z8
5	100	X1
8	100	X1
10	20	Z8

FIGURE 17.8

Machine M2 is a bottleneck and management wants to maximize its use. Consequently, the schedule for the six jobs, through the three machines, was based on the SPT rule on M2. The proposed schedule is $4-3-1-5-2-6$.

   a. Suppose that processing on M2 is to begin on day 15. Using the proposed schedule, determine the schedules for M1 and M3 so that job 4 begins processing on M2 at the start of day 15. Draw Gantt charts for M1, M2, and M3. What is the makespan for the six jobs?

   b. Find a schedule that better utilizes M2 and yields a shorter makespan.

14. A special case of the transportation problem (see Supplement 3) is the assignment problem. That is, each capacity source has only one unit of supply, each destination has only one unit of demand, and the number of sources equals the number of destinations. This would be the situation in operations scheduling where a scheduler needs to assign n workers to n tasks or n jobs to n machines. Apply the method in Supplement 3 to the following situation.

    The owner of Swifty Car Rental faces the need for some form of centralized scheduling. The agency operates in eight locations on the East Coast. On several Fridays recently, it was obvious that four of the locations would be short one car each for the following Monday and each of the other four locations had one excess car. The driving distances between each of the locations are:

Locations Having One Extra Car	Locations Needing One More Car			
	Yorkshire	Sweetwater	Carson	Milltown
Darbydale	10	25	16	5
Glencoe	20	35	30	12
Chelsea	26	12	10	17
Hobby	12	30	15	13

Last Friday when the Milltown manager recognized the need for another car, she called the closest agency and had Darbydale send a car. The manager at Carson called Chelsea and received a car. The Sweetwater manager first called Chelsea and Darbydale, but found that

they had already committed their surpluses to other locations. He had to settle for Hobby which was the closest of those remaining. Finally, the Yorkshire manager, who was a little behind the others in making her calls, had to get a car from Glencoe.

    The owner of Swifty could see that each manager was trying to get the car he or she needed from the closest location. However the total distance traveled in obtaining these cars was 65 miles. Find an assignment of cars to locations that minimizes the number of miles driven.

15. The last few steps of a production process require two operations. Some jobs require processing on M1 before processing on M3. Other jobs require processing on M2 before M3. Currently, four jobs are waiting at M1 and 5 jobs are waiting at M2. The following data have been supplied by the shop-floor control system.

Job	Machine M1 Process Time (hr)	Machine 2 Process Time (hr)	Machine 3 Process Time (hr)	Due Date (hr)
1	8	—	3	15
2	4	—	15	28
3	7	—	4	20
4	9	—	6	35
5	—	3	2	10
6	—	8	8	23
7	—	5	11	37
8	—	10	5	40
9	—	6	13	25

The due dates are expressed in hours from now.

   a. Schedule this shop using the following rules.
     i. SPT   ii. EDD
     iii. S/RO   iv. CR

   b. Discuss the operating implications of each of the schedules you developed in (a).

16. Return to Problem 9 and the work-force schedule for part-time clerks. Suppose that each part-time clerk can only work three days, but the days must be consecutive. Devise an approach to this work-force scheduling problem. Your objective is to minimize total slack capacity. What is the minimum number of clerks needed now and what would their schedules be?

SELECTED REFERENCES

Baker, K. R., *Introduction to Sequencing and Scheduling.* New York: John Wiley & Sons, 1984.

Berry, W. L., and V. Rao, "Critical Ratio Scheduling: An Experimental Analysis," *Management Science,* vol. 22, no. 1 (October 1975), pp. 192–201.

Browne, J. J., "Simplified Scheduling of Routine Work Hours and Days Off," *Industrial Engineering* (December 1979), pp. 27–29.

Browne, J. J., and J. Prop, "Supplement to Scheduling Routine Work Hours," *Industrial Engineering* (July 1980), p. 12.

Browne, J. J., and R. K. Tibrewala, "Manpower Scheduling," *Industrial Engineering* (August 1975), pp. 22–23.

Buffa, E. S., M. J. Cosgrove, and B. J. Luce, "An Integrated Work Shift Scheduling System," *Decision Sciences,* vol. 7, no. 4 (October 1976), pp. 620–630.

Chaiken, J. M., and P. Dormont, "A Patrol Car Allocation Model: Capabilities and Algorithms," *Management Science,* vol. 24, no. 12 (August 1978), pp. 1291–1300.

Conway, R. W., "Priority Dispatching and Job Lateness in a Job Shop," *Journal of Industrial Engineering,* vol. 16, no. 4 (July 1965).

Day, James E., and Michael P. Hottenstein, "Review of Sequencing Research," *Naval Research Logistics Quarterly,* vol. 27, no. 1 (March 1970), pp. 11–39.

Fryer, J. S., "Operating Policies in Multiechelon Dual-Constraint Job Shops," *Management Science,* vol. 19, no. 9 (May 1963), pp. 1001–1012.

Hill, A. D., J. D. Naumann, and N. L. Chervany, "SCAT and SPAT: Large-Scale Computer-Based Optimization Systems for the Personnel Assignment Problem," *Decision Sciences,* vol. 14, no. 2 (April 1983), pp. 207–220.

Johnson, S. M., "Optimal Two Stage and Three Stage Production Schedules with Setup Times Included," *Naval Logistics Quarterly,* vol. 1, no. 1 (March 1954), pp. 61–68.

Kanet, J. K., and J. C. Hayya, "Priority Dispatching with Operation Due Dates in a Job Shop," *Journal of Operations Management,* vol. 2, no. 3 (May 1982), pp. 167–175.

Krajewski, L. J., and L. P. Ritzman, "Shift Scheduling in Banking Operations: A Case Application," *Interfaces,* vol. 10, no. 2 (April 1980), pp. 1–8.

LeGrande, E., "The Development of a Factory Simulation System Using Actual Operating Data," *Management Technology,* vol. 3, no. 1 (May 1963).

Mabert, V. A., "Static vs. Dynamic Priority Rules for Check Processing in Multiple Dispatch-Multiple Branch Banking," *Journal of Operations Management,* vol. 2, no. 1 (May 1982), pp. 187–196.

Marsten, R. E., M. R. Muller, and C. L. Killon, "Crew Planning at Flying Tiger: A Successful Application of Integer Programming," *Management Science,* vol. 25, no. 12 (December 1979), pp. 1175–1196.

Nelson, R. T., "Labor and Machine Limited Production Systems," *Management Science,* vol. 13, no. 9 (May 1967), pp. 648–671.

Saladin, Brooke A., "A Methodology for the Allocation of Police Patrol Vehicles." Unpublished dissertation, The Ohio State University, 1980.

Tibrewala, R., D. Philippe, and J. Browne, "Optimal Scheduling of Two Consecutive Idle Periods," *Management Science,* vol. 19, no. 1 (September 1972), pp. 71–75.

CHAPTER

18

PROJECT SCHEDULING AND CONTROL

▲ Chapter Outline

MANAGING PROJECTS

Basic Steps in Project Management

MANAGERIAL PRACTICE 18.1 A Hospital on the Move

The Importance of Effective Project Management

MANAGERIAL PRACTICE 18.2 Headache: Project Delays

NETWORK MODELING WITH PERT/CPM

Diagraming the Activity-on-Node Network

Estimating Activity Times

Calculating Time Statistics

Determining the Critical Path

Analyzing Probabilities

Monitoring Project Progress

COST AND RESOURCE CONSIDERATIONS

Analyzing Costs

Resource Limitations

Computerized Project Scheduling and Control

CRITIQUE OF PERT/CPM SYSTEMS

Network Diagrams

Control

Time Estimates

SOLVED PROBLEMS
FORMULA REVIEW
CHAPTER HIGHLIGHTS
KEY TERMS
STUDY QUESTIONS
PROBLEMS
SELECTED REFERENCES

How can we avoid costly project delays?

Which activities in our project determine the duration of the entire project?

Do network planning methods increase our potential to control costs and provide better customer service?

How do we determine the effect of limited resources on the project duration?

How can we incorporate uncertainty in time estimates for various activities into project planning?

ou probably watched some of the pageantry and competition of the 1988 Winter Olympic Games held in Calgary, Canada. But have you ever tried to imagine the myriad interrelated activities that go on behind the scenes at such an event? Try to picture the planning that took place before, during, and after the games. For example, the Olympic Planning Committee planned for events in 55 major sports (some held simultaneously in different locations), each consisting of several tasks that had to be carried out in logical sequence. The Committee also arranged housing and security for the athletes during their stay in Alberta. Other activities included setting up transportation and housing accommodations for approximately 1.5 million spectators, arranging press and TV coverage, planning contingencies for bad weather, and even scheduling post-game cleanup.

Like the 1988 Winter Olympics, projects are unique operations with a finite life span. Generally, many interrelated activities must be scheduled and monitored within strict time, cost, and performance guidelines. In this chapter we consider methods for managing such complex projects. We begin with the basic steps involved in project management. We then explore two of the best known network planning methods, PERT and CPM, ending with an assessment of their limitations.

MANAGING PROJECTS ▲

As we have noted, the Olympic Committee was responsible for scheduling and controlling a large project. We define **project** as an interrelated set of activities that has a definite starting and ending point and that results in a unique product. Several examples of large projects are:

- Constructing a building or an amusement park.
- Constructing a road, a dam, or an oil pipeline.
- Renovating a blighted urban area.
- Developing a prototype for a new ocean liner or airplane.
- Installing a large computer system.
- Introducing a new product.
- Organizing a state fair.
- Registering eligible recipients for a health care program.
- Redesigning the layout of a plant or office.

Given the finite nature of such projects, project management is very goal oriented. Unlike the manager of a business, the project manager knows that when the team has accomplished its assigned objectives, it will disband. Many team members will move on to other projects or return to their regular jobs.

Managing a complex project involving thousands of interrelated activities and personnel with diverse backgrounds and skills is a tremendous challenge. Usually, the activities to be performed are unique. Thus the project manager may have difficulty falling back on prior experience or established procedures. Furthermore, many team members will not be associated with the project for its full duration. They may view the project as disruptive to their regular work relationships and routines. Others will experience conflicts in loyalty or in demands on their time between their projects and department supervisors. But, in spite of these potential difficulties, working on projects also offers substantial rewards—the excitement of dynamic work, the satisfaction of solving challenging problems, the status of membership on an elite team, and the opportunity to work with and learn from other skilled professionals.

Basic Steps in Project Management

Managing a project, regardless of its size and complexity, requires identifying every activity to be undertaken and planning when each activity must begin and end in order to complete the overall project on time. To achieve that goal, the project manager needs an effective method for organizing a network of interrelated activities and personnel. The degree of difficulty in scheduling is a function of the number of activities, their required sequence, and their timing. Typically, all projects involve the following:

1. Describe the project.
2. Develop a network model.
3. Insert time estimates.
4. Analyze the model.
5. Develop the project plan.
6. Periodically assess the progress of the project and repeat steps 2–6, as needed.

Describe the Project.   The project manager must first describe the project in terms that everyone involved will understand. This description should include a clear statement of the project's endpoint—for example, a clean Olympic City, with all temporary facilities removed. In addition, the project manager must carefully define all project activities and precedent relationships. An **activity** is the smallest unit of work effort consuming both time and resources that the project manager can schedule and control. A **precedence relationship** is a sequencing constraint between related activities; that is, it determines that one activity cannot start until a preceding activity has been completed.

Just what constitutes an activity for the purpose of the project description can become an issue. For example, Managerial Practice 18.1 describes the relocation of St. Adolf's Hospital, a project that we refer to throughout this chapter. Judy Kramer, the project manager, has defined her activities and precedence relationships. In her project description, activity H, construct the hospital, reflects the fact that completion of construction will have a major bearing on when the hospital becomes operational. However, she hasn't bothered to list the many activities included in the construction process. That will be the responsibility of the construction supervisor Kramer will employ. In general, a manager's project description should reflect only the level of detail that he or she needs in order to make scheduling and resource allocation decisions.

Develop a Network Model.   The network model is represented by a **network diagram,** consisting of nodes (circles) and arcs (arrows) that depict the relationships between activities. Interpretation of the graphic symbols will differ, depending on the specific modeling technique used, as illustrated in Fig. 18.1. One approach, the **activity-on-arc (AOA) network,** uses arcs to represent activities and nodes to represent events. An **event** is the point at which one or more activities are to be completed and one or more other activities are to begin. An event consumes neither time nor resources. Since the AOA approach emphasizes activity connection points, we say that it is event-oriented. As Fig. 18.1(a) shows, precedence relationships require that an event not occur until all preceding activities have been completed.

A second approach is the **activity-on-node (AON) network** in which the nodes represent activities and the arcs indicate the sequence in which they are

A Hospital on the Move

In the interest of better serving the public in Benjamin County, St. Adolf's Hospital has decided to relocate from Christofer to Northville, a large suburb which at present has no major medical facility. The move to Northville would mean constructing a new hospital and making it operational. Judy Kramer, executive director of the board of St. Adolf's, must prepare for a hearing before the Central Ohio Hospital Board (COHB), scheduled for next week, on the proposed project. Part of the hearing will address the specifics of the total project, including time and cost estimates for its completion.

With the help of her staff, Kramer has identified 11 major project activities. She has also specified the immediate predecessors (those activities that must be completed before a given activity can begin) for each activity. The results are as follows:

Activity	Description	Immediate Predecessor(s)
A	Select administrative and medical staff.	—
B	Select site and do site survey.	—
C	Select equipment.	A
D	Prepare final construction plans and layout.	B
E	Bring utilities to the site.	B
F	Interview applicants and fill positions in nursing, support staff, maintenance, and security.	A
G	Purchase and take delivery of equipment.	C
H	Construct the hospital.	D
I	Develop an information system.	A
J	Install the equipment.	E, G, H
K	Train nurses and staff.	F, I, J

Kramer realizes that she could break down each activity into more detailed work elements. However, the upcoming hearing does not require that level of detail. She also knows she will have to supply time and cost estimates for each activity. Then, she will have to use this information to answer questions such as:

- Can the project be completed in 72 weeks?
- Which activities are crucial to completing the project on schedule?
- Considering total project costs, what is the minimum-cost schedule?

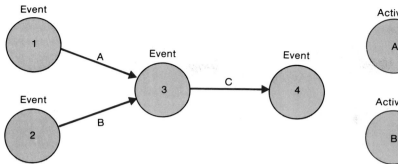

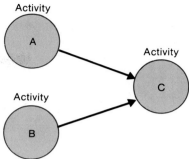

(a) AOA approach: Event 4 cannot take place until activities A, B, and C have been completed.

(b) AON approach: Activity C cannot take place until activities A and B have been completed.

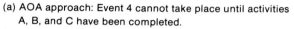

FIGURE 18.1   AOA and AON Approaches to Activity Relationships

performed. This approach is activity-oriented. The precedence relationships in part (b) require that an activity cannot begin until all preceding activities have been completed. We shall use AON networks in all our examples, because they are easier to construct than AOA networks.* Nonetheless, you could perform all of the analyses we demonstrate with AOA networks as well.

Insert Time Estimates.   Regardless of the modeling method selected, project managers must decide whether to use probabilistic (uncertain) or deterministic (certain) time estimates for activities. This decision historically led to a choice of one of two different network planning methods: the **program evaluation and review technique (PERT)** or the **critical path method (CPM).**

Originally, PERT was designed to cope with uncertainty in activity times. The U.S. Navy sponsored the development of this planning and scheduling method during the 1950s to help manage the Polaris missile project. The project involved 3000 separate contractors and suppliers. Because many of the project's activities had never been performed before, time estimates were uncertain. In retrospect, PERT is generally credited with reducing the project's completion time by at least 18 months.

During the late 1950s, J. E. Kelly of Remington-Rand and M. R. Walker of Du Pont developed CPM as a means of scheduling maintenance shutdowns at chemical processing plants. Since maintenance projects were routine, reasonably accurate time estimates for activities were available. Thus CPM was based on the assumption that project activity times can be estimated accurately and do not vary.

---

*We used AON networks to describe assembly lines in Chapter 9.

Before PERT and CPM, project managers used Gantt charts to schedule and control projects (refer back to Figs. 17.1 and 17.2). However, for large projects, Gantt charts become difficult to work with. First, they don't directly recognize precedence relationships between activities. Second, they don't indicate which activities are crucial to completing the project on time.

Today the differences between PERT and CPM are minor. Basically, either approach can cope with uncertainty, and both can use AOA or AON networks. For purposes of our discussion, we don't make arbitrary distinctions between these methods. We simply refer to them collectively as PERT/CPM.

Analyze the Model.   The project manager can use network models to identify activities that are crucial to project completion and to estimate the probability of completing a project on time. By identifying those activities that, if expedited, could reduce the time needed to complete the project, the manager may be able to reduce total costs. Later in this chapter, we demonstrate Judy Kramer's use of PERT/CPM to analyze the hospital project described in Managerial Practice 18.1.

MANAGERIAL PRACTICE 18.2 ▲

A Managerial Headache: Project Delays

Late delivery of products can be costly:

- Bath Iron Works contracted with the U.S. Navy to deliver the first of six sophisticated Aegis class cruisers by January 1987. However, a three-month strike and the tardy delivery of certain component systems caused the project to fall behind schedule. The delay added tens of millions of dollars to the overall cost.

- In the spring of 1988, the Lotus Development Corporation announced that it was delaying the release of its new best selling 1-2-3 software until the fourth quarter of 1988. Lotus needed more time to compress the program to work well on personal computers. The announcement caused an immediate decline of $3.25 in the price of Lotus stock and raised the ire of many customers.

Nonetheless, project delays can be avoided:

- In August 1983, the Florida Power and Light Company accomplished a rare feat: It completed construction of a nuclear power plant in just over six years, only four months beyond a schedule set in 1977. On the average, it takes 10 to 12 years to build such a complex project. However, Florida

Sources: "Bath Iron Works, Navy are in Talks on Cruiser Delays," by Tim Carrington, *Wall Street Journal,* March 13, 1987; "Lotus, After 1-2-3 Delay, Moves to Quell Client, Market Fears; Stock Falls $3.25," by William M. Bukeley, *Wall Street Journal,* March 24, 1988; "Utility Cuts Red Tape, Builds Nuclear Plant Almost on Schedule," by Ron Winslow, *Wall Street Journal,* February 22, 1984.

Develop the Project Plan.   Having created a network model, the project manager can then develop a schedule for each activity within the project. Activities crucial to on-time project completion will receive preference subject to resource availability. After the project actually begins, periodic reports will show the current status of all activities relative to their planned completion dates.

Update the Project Plan.   Periodically, the project manager will have to adjust the schedule on the basis of additional information. Perhaps an activity took longer than expected, new activities were identified, or precedence relationships among several activities changed. This information may call for changes in the network or the time estimates and, ultimately, in the overall project schedule itself.

The Importance of Effective Project Management

Project managers must stay on top of their projects in order to meet schedules and keep costs within budget. However, Murphy's law—"If something can go wrong, it will"—applies to all projects. As Managerial Practice 18.2 illustrates,

Power and Light set up teams to handle specific problems, and managers made sure their vendors upheld contractual commitments. A computer tracked the progress of each of the 20,000 tasks required to finish the plant. For each month that such a plant runs over schedule, nearly 770,000 barrels of oil are consumed in the production of energy at a cost of $23 million to rate payers. In addition, the capital cost of the plant would rise by $13 million, increasing the cost to rate payers by $2.5 million annually over the life of the plant.

The construction of a nuclear power plant is a complex and lengthy project. This photo shows the interior of the reactors at the nuclear power plant in Salem, New Jersey.

unexpected problems can cause delays, requiring rescheduling and reallocation of resources—and often resulting in severe financial repercussions. Frequently, managers must make quick decisions on the basis of incomplete information. To maintain control, they need the capability to answer "what-if" questions regarding the timing of project activities and to evaluate the time and cost implications of resource trade-offs. Network planning models are very useful for these purposes.

NETWORK MODELING WITH PERT/CPM ▲

Let's return to the St. Adolph's Hospital project, for which Judy Kramer has identified various activities and their precedence relationships. In this section, we use the following PERT/CPM procedures to analyze those activities.

1. Diagram the AON network.

2. Estimate activity times.

3. Calculate time statistics.

4. Determine the critical path.

5. Analyze probabilities.

Diagraming the Activity-on-Node Network

Diagraming a project as a network first requires establishing the precedence relationships between activities, as Kramer did in Managerial Practice 18.1. For complex projects this task can be tedious. Nevertheless, it is essential because incorrect or omitted precedence relationships will result in costly delays.

An AON network for the hospital project, based on Kramer's 11 activities and their precedence relationships, is shown in Fig. 18.2. It depicts activities as circles, with arrows indicating the sequence in which they are to be performed. Activities A and B emanate from the start node because they have no immediate predecessors. The arrows connecting activity A to activities C, F, and I indicate that all three require completion of activity A before they can begin. Similarly, activity B must be completed before activities D and E can begin. The rest of the diagram follows the same logical sequence. Start and finish nodes do not actually represent activities. They merely provide beginning and ending points for the network.

The network diagram provides the basis for project analysis. Thus the diagram must accurately represent all activities and precedence relationships. For example, having a loop in the network where activity B preceded activity D, D preceded E, and E preceded B wouldn't make sense. Modeling a large project as a network is a useful process in itself because, at the very least, it forces management to identify necessary activities and recognize the precedence relationships between them.

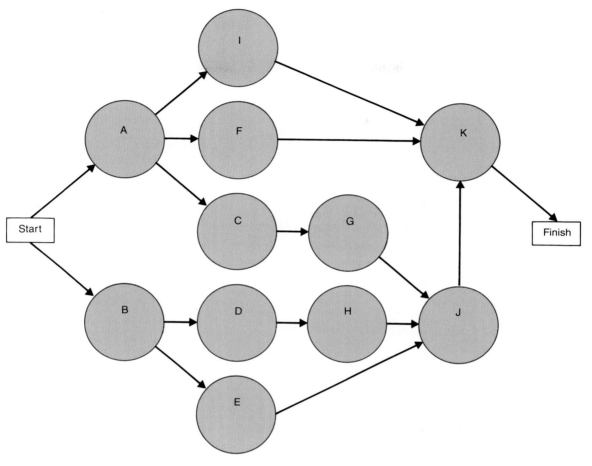

Activity	Description
A	Select administrative and medical staff.
B	Select site and do site survey.
C	Select equipment.
D	Prepare final construction plans and layout.
E	Bring utilities to the site.
F	Interview applicants and fill positions in nursing, support staff, maintenance, and security.
G	Purchase and take delivery of the equipment.
H	Construct the hospital.
I	Develop an information system.
J	Install the equipment.
K	Train nurses and staff.

FIGURE 18.2 AON Network Diagram for the St. Adolf's Hospital Project

Estimating Activity Times

To help overcome the uncertainty inherent in time estimates, the manager asks the people responsible for each activity to provide three time estimates for all activities under their control. They should base their estimates on the assumption that all resources needed to complete an activity within its most likely time are available during a normal work period. These three estimates are:

1. **Most optimistic time (a):** The shortest time in which the activity can be completed, if all goes exceptionally well. The probability of completing the activity sooner is estimated to be only one chance in a hundred.

2. **Most likely time (m):** The best estimate of the average time required to perform an activity if the activity could be repeated many times under similar circumstances (no learning factor).

3. **Most pessimistic time (b):** The longest estimated time required to perform an activity, assuming that everything that could go wrong does go wrong. The probability that it will take more time to complete the activity is estimated to be only one chance in a hundred.

Calculating Time Statistics

These time estimates give the project manager enough information to estimate the mean and variance of a probability distribution for each activity. In PERT/CPM, each activity time is treated as though it were a random number derived from a beta probability distribution. The primary reason for choosing this distribution is that it can take on a variety of shapes, allowing the most likely time estimates to fall anywhere between the most pessimistic and most optimistic end points. This condition is not possible with just any distribution. For example, the normal distribution is symmetrical, requiring the mode to be equidistant from the end points. This condition would be unduly restrictive.

The estimate for the mean of the beta distribution is given by the following weighted average of the three time estimates. Note that the most likely time is weighted four times greater than the most pessimistic or most optimistic estimates.

$$t_e = \frac{a + 4m + b}{6}$$

The variance of the beta distribution for each activity is

$$\sigma^2 = \left(\frac{b - a}{6}\right)^2$$

The variance increases as the difference between the most pessimistic and most optimistic time estimates increases. This result implies that the less certain a person is in estimating the actual time for an activity, the greater will be the variance.

APPLICATION 18.1

Suppose that Judy Kramer has arrived at the following time estimates for activity B (site selection and survey) of the hospital project:

$$a = 7 \text{ weeks} \qquad m = 8 \text{ weeks} \qquad b = 15 \text{ weeks}$$

Calculate the expected time for activity B and the variance.

Solution

The expected time for activity B is

$$t_e = \frac{7 + 4(8) + 15}{6} = \frac{54}{6} = 9 \text{ wks}$$

Note that the expected time (9 wk) does not equal the most likely time (8 wk) for this activity. These times will be equal only when the most likely time is equidistant from the most optimistic and most pessimistic times. We calculate the variance for activity B as follows:

$$\sigma^2 = \left(\frac{15 - 7}{6} \right)^2 = \left(\frac{8}{6} \right)^2 = 1.78$$

The accompanying table shows expected activity times and variances for the activities listed in Judy Kramer's project description. Note that the greatest uncertainty lies with the time estimate for activity I, followed by the estimates for activities E and G. The expected times for each activity will prove useful in determining the critical path.

Time Estimates and Activity Statistics for the St. Adolf's Hospital Project

Activity	Time Estimates (weeks)			Activity Statistics	
	Most Optimistic (a)	Most Likely (m)	Most Pessimistic (b)	Expected Time (t_e)	Variance (σ^2)
A	11	12	13	12	0.11
B	7	8	15	9	1.78
C	5	10	15	10	2.78
D	8	9	16	10	1.78
E	14	25	30	24	7.11
F	6	9	18	10	4.00
G	25	36	41	35	7.11
H	35	40	45	40	2.78
I	10	13	28	15	9.00
J	1	2	15	4	5.44
K	5	6	7	6	0.11

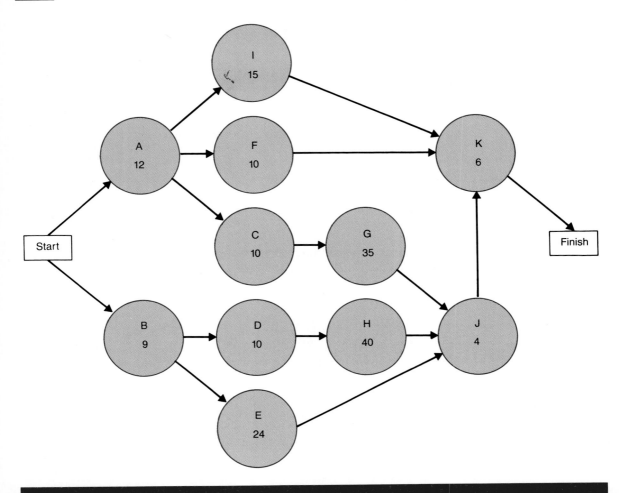

FIGURE 18.3   AON Network Showing Activity Times

Determining the Critical Path

A crucial aspect of project management is time of completion. The sum of all the expected times for each activity in the preceding table is 175 weeks. This estimate reflects strictly sequential work, that is, work proceeding on only one activity at a time. However, PERT/CPM is based on the assumption that the resources are available to proceed on various activities simultaneously. Thus the project manager—at this stage—must consider only the precedence relationships and the expected times in scheduling activities. Indeed, Fig. 18.3 indicates that the project can be finished in much less than 175 weeks.

In order to determine the earliest completion time of a project, the project manager must first find the critical path. The **critical path** is the sequence of activities between a project's start and finish that takes the longest time to complete. In other words, all activities along the critical path must be completed before the overall project is completed. The critical path also has zero slack time at each activity along the path. **Activity slack** is the maximum time an activity can be delayed without delaying the entire project. We calculate activity slack using four time values for each activity:

1. Earliest start time is the earliest possible beginning time for an activity.
2. Latest start time is the latest possible beginning time for an activity that will allow the project to be completed on schedule.
3. Earliest finish time is the earliest start time plus the time needed for an activity.
4. Latest finish time is the latest possible completion time for an activity that will not delay the entire project.

Earliest Start and Earliest Finish Times.   To calculate the earliest start and earliest finish times, we make use of two simple rules:

1. The **earliest finish time (EF_i)** for an activity i is equal to its earliest start time plus its expected duration, or

$$EF_i = ES_i + t_e$$

2. The **earliest start time (ES_i)** for an activity i is equal to the latest of the earliest finish times of the immediately preceding activities. That is,

$$ES_i = \max [EF \text{ times of all activities}$$
$$\text{immediately preceding activity } i]$$

For example, let's calculate the earliest start and finish times for the activities in the hospital project. Figure 18.3 contains the expected activity times for the table in Application 18.1.

We begin at the start node at time zero. Activities A and B have no predecessors, so the earliest start times for these activities are also zero. The earliest finish times for these activities are:

$$EF_A = 0 + 12 = 12, \quad \text{and} \quad EF_B = 0 + 9 = 9.$$

Thus EF_A becomes the earliest start time for activities I, F, and C; EF_B becomes the earliest start time for activities D and E. Consequently,

$$EF_I = 12 + 15 = 27 \qquad EF_D = 9 + 10 = 19$$
$$EF_F = 12 + 10 = 22 \qquad EF_E = 9 + 24 = 33$$
$$EF_C = 12 + 10 = 22$$

Similarly, $EF_G = 22 + 35 = 57$ and $EF_H = 19 + 40 = 59$. Activity J has several predecessors, so $ES_J = \max [EF_G, EF_H, EF_E] = 59$. Thus $EF_J = 59 + 4 = 63$. Finally, $ES_K = \max [EF_I, EF_F, EF_J] = 63$ and $EF_K = 63 + 6 = 69$. This result implies that the earliest the project can be completed is week 69. The earliest start and earliest finish times for all activities are shown in Fig. 18.4.

Latest Start and Latest Finish Times.   To calculate the latest start and latest finish times, we start at the finish node and assume that the project is to be completed at the maximum of the earliest finish times of all activities immediately preceding it.* We use two other rules.

1. The **latest start time (LS_i)** for an activity i is equal to its latest finish time minus its expected duration, or:

$$LS_i = LF_i - t_e$$

2. The **latest finish time (LF_i)** for an activity i is equal to the earliest of the latest start times of all activities immediately following it. That is,

$$LF_i = \min [LS \text{ times of all activities}$$
$$\text{immediately following activity } i]$$

For the hospital project, we can calculate the latest start and latest finish times for each activity using Fig. 18.3. We begin by setting the latest finish activity time of activity K at week 69, its early finish time. Thus

$$LS_K = 69 - 6 = 63$$

If activity K is to start no later than week 63, all its predecessors must finish no later than that time. Consequently,

$$LF_I = LF_F = LF_J = 63$$

The latest start times for these activities are:

$$LS_I = 63 - 15 = 48$$
$$LS_F = 63 - 10 = 53$$
$$LS_J = 63 - \ \ 4 = 59$$

After we have calculated LS_J, we can calculate the latest start times for the immediate predecessors of activity J:

$$LS_G = 59 - 35 = 24$$
$$LS_H = 59 - 40 = 19$$
$$LS_E = 59 - 24 = 35$$

---

*Alternatively, the negotiated contract due date could be used. In that case, the activity slacks on the critical path may not be zero.

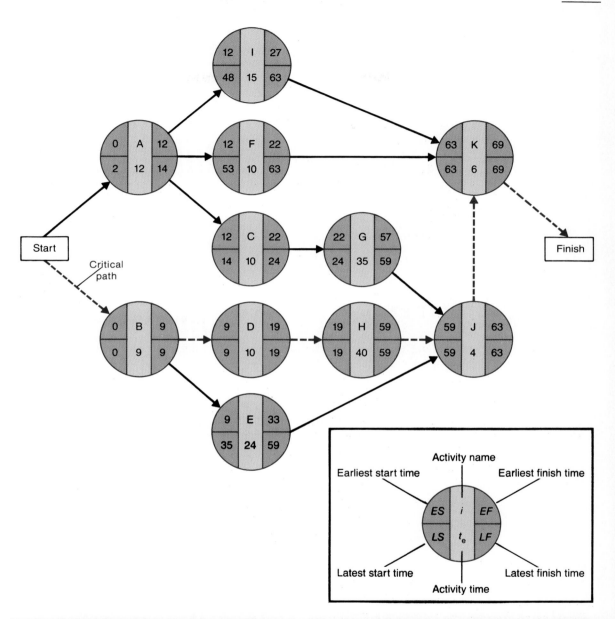

FIGURE 18.4   Network Showing Data Needed for Activity Slacks

Similarly, we can now calculate latest start times for activities C and D:

$$LS_C = 24 - 10 = 14 \quad \text{and} \quad LS_D = 19 - 10 = 9$$

Activities A and B have more than one predecessor. $LF_A = \min [LS_I, LS_F, LS_C] = 14$, and $LS_A = 14 - 12 = 2$; $LF_B = \min [LS_D, LS_E] = 9$, and $LS_B = 9 - 9 = 0$. This result implies that activity B must be started immediately if the project is to be completed by week 69. The latest start and latest finish times for all activities are shown in Fig. 18.4.

Activity Slack.   Slack information is useful to project managers because it helps them to make decisions regarding reallocation of resources. Resources could be taken from activities with slack and given to other activities that are behind schedule until the slack is used up. We can calculate activity slack in one of two ways:

$$S_i = LS_i - ES_i \quad \text{or} \quad S_i = LF_i - EF_i$$

APPLICATION 18.2

Calculate the slack for the activities in the hospital project. Use the data in Fig. 18.4.

Solution

We can use either starting times or finishing times. The accompanying table shows the slack for each activity, calculated by $LS_i - ES_i$ or $LF_i - EF_i$.

Activity Slacks for the St. Adolf's Hospital Project

Node	Duration	Start Earliest	Start Latest	Finish Earliest	Finish Latest	Slack	Critical Path
A	12	0	2	12	14	2	No
B	9	0	0	9	9	0	Yes
C	10	12	14	22	24	2	No
D	10	9	9	19	19	0	Yes
E	24	9	35	33	59	26	No
F	10	12	53	22	63	41	No
G	35	22	24	57	59	2	No
H	40	19	19	59	59	0	Yes
I	15	12	48	27	63	36	No
J	4	59	59	63	63	0	Yes
K	6	63	63	69	69	0	Yes

The slack at an activity depends on the performance of activities leading to it. If the time for activity A turned out to be 14 weeks instead of 12 weeks, the slack for activities C and G would be zero. The time for activity A could have increased because of unexpected work delays or because resources were shifted from activity A to some activity that was behind schedule. Slack is shared among all activities on a particular path.

Critical Path. We can now identify the critical path. All activities on the critical path have zero slack. The activity string B–D–H–J–K constitutes the critical path for the hospital project. The dashed line in Fig. 18.4 denotes the critical path graphically, and the preceding table shows how it can be identified in report form.

The critical path is important because it defines the completion time of the project. Any delays in activities along the critical path delay project completion. Adding the expected times for each activity along the critical path, we determine that the expected time to complete the hospital project is 69 weeks. Thus Judy Kramer should focus more attention on these activities in managing the project, although if activity A or C were to fall behind by two weeks, they and activity G would be on the critical path as well. Using up slack can result in more than one critical path for a project.

Rather than calculating activity slack first, we could have found the critical path by enumerating all the activity paths in the network and identifying the one having the longest cumulative time. Table 18.1 shows this solution, mainly to demonstrate that the path having the minimum slack is also the *longest* path in the network. Although manually finding the critical path in this way is easy for small projects, computers must be used to find it for large, complex projects. Computer routines normally compute activity slack because project managers want this information anyway. Identification of the critical path is a byproduct of that information.

TABLE 18.1 Network Paths for the St. Adolf's Hospital Project

Path	Expected Time (wk)
A–F–K	28
A–I–K	33
A–C–G–J–K	67
B–D–H–J–K	69 (Critical)
B–E–J–K	43

Analyzing Probabilities

We have assumed that the time estimates for activities involve some uncertainty. Knowing the probability of achieving any activity in a specific amount of time therefore would be useful. To obtain it, we must define the probability distribution of achievement dates for an activity. Managers focus most often on the project's completion date, so we'll use the *finish* node as an example.

In order to specify the probability distribution of achievement dates for the finish node, we must determine a mean and a variance. If we assume that the activity times along the critical path are independent of each other, it seems reasonable to use the sum of the expected activity times on the critical path as the mean of the distribution. For the hospital project, the earliest expected finish time for activity K (and therefore the finish node) is 69 weeks.

Similarly, because of the assumption of activity time independence, we use the sum of the variances of the activities on the critical path as the variance of the project time distribution. From the table in Application 18.1, we find that the variance of the critical path B–D–H–J–K would be $1.78 + 1.78 + 2.78 + 5.44 + 0.11 = 11.89$.

Consequently, the central limit theorem allows us to use the normal probability distribution to find the probability of achieving a particular due date for the project. We can use the z-transformation formula as follows:

$$z = \frac{T' - TE}{\sqrt{\Sigma \, \sigma_{CP}^2}}$$

where

$$T' = \text{due date for the project}$$
$$TE = \text{earliest expected completion date for the project}$$
$$\Sigma \, \sigma_{CP}^2 = \text{sum of the variances on the critical path}$$

The procedure for assessing the probability of completing any activity in a project by a given date is similar to the one we just discussed. However, instead of the critical path, we would use the longest time path of activities from the start node to the activity node in question.

APPLICATION 18.3

Calculate the probability that the hospital will become operational in 72 weeks.

Solution

With a critical path length of 69 weeks and a variance of 11.89, we can calculate the z-value as follows:

$$z = \frac{72 - 69}{\sqrt{11.89}} = \frac{3}{3.45}$$

$$= 0.87$$

Using the normal distribution table in Appendix 3, we find that the probability is about 0.20 that the project will exceed 72 weeks. This probability is shown graphically in Fig. 18.5.

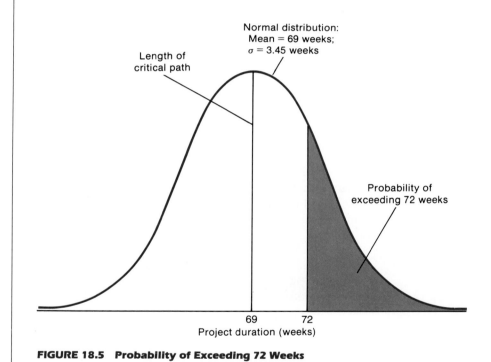

FIGURE 18.5 *Probability of Exceeding 72 Weeks*

Thus we can use the uncertainty in activity time estimates to make statements about the chances of completing a project on schedule. The analysis hinges on the identification of the critical path. We calculated the critical path on the basis of the expected times for each activity and disregarded the variances. Conceivably, one or more network paths for a project may be shorter than the critical path, but have enough variance in activity time estimates to actually become the critical path sometime during the project. Such is the case in the hospital project. In Table 18.1, you can see that the path A–C–G–J–K is 67 weeks long, or only two weeks shorter than the critical path. The sum of the variances along that path is 15.55. Thus close attention to activities A, C, and G, in addition to activities B, D, H, J, and K, seems warranted.

Also, if the project has multiple critical paths, the critical path with the largest variance should be used in the denominator of the z-transformation formula. This approach allows the probability estimate to reflect the correct amount of uncertainty in the project duration.

Monitoring Project Progress

Even the best laid project plans can go awry. Progress must be monitored, so that delays can be readily identified. A slack-sorted report on a weekly basis (or some other suitable schedule) is helpful in this regard. Suppose that in the hospital project, 16 weeks have passed and activity A has just been completed. Consequently, activity A was completed 4 weeks late (see Fig. 18.4). Also suppose that activity B took 10 weeks instead of the expected 9 weeks. Table 18.2 shows a slack-sorted report as of the sixteenth week of the project. Activities A and B are not shown because they have already been completed.

Note that activities C, G, J, and K now have negative slack and replace activities D and H on the critical path. The activities at the top of the report are more critical than those at the bottom. If the original completion target of week 69 is still valid, the project manager would try to make up two weeks of time somewhere along path C–G–J–K. However, to make the deadline, one week will also have to be made up along path D–H. If that time is made up, there will be two critical paths: C–G–J–K and D–H–J–K. Managers can use

TABLE 18.2   Slack-Sorted Computer Report

Activity	Duration	Earliest Start	Latest Start	Slack	Critical Path
C	10	16	14	−2	Yes
G	35	26	24	−2	Yes
J	4	61	59	−2	Yes
K	6	65	63	−2	Yes
D	10	10	9	−1	No
H	40	20	19	−1	No
E	24	10	35	25	No
I	15	16	48	32	No
F	10	16	53	37	No

slack-sorted reports such as this one more conveniently than a network diagram. Most project managers work with this type of computer report and never see a network diagram.

COST AND RESOURCE CONSIDERATIONS ▲

In this section we discuss the use of PERT/CPM methods to find minimum-cost schedules. We also describe how to incorporate resource constraints in project scheduling.

Analyzing Costs

So far, our discussion has focused on managing project time. The implicit assumption is that if the project can be kept on schedule, total project costs will be acceptable. The reality of project management, however, is that there are always time–cost trade-offs. Total project costs are the sum of direct costs, indirect costs, and penalty costs. Direct costs include labor, materials, and any other costs directly related to project activities. Indirect costs include administration and other variable overhead costs that can be avoided by reducing total project time. Penalty costs may be incurred if the project extends beyond some specific date. Conversely, in some cases a bonus may be provided for early completion. Thus when a project manager considers total project costs, or total profits, the best schedule may require expediting some activities to reduce overall project completion time.

Direct Costs and Times.   Direct costs can be subdivided into normal costs and crash costs for each activity. Associated with these costs are a normal time and a crash time.

1. **Normal time (NT):** The time to complete the activity under normal conditions. This time is analogous to the expected time, t_e, mentioned earlier.

2. **Normal cost (NC):** The activity cost associated with the normal time.

3. **Crash time (CT):** The shortest possible time to complete the activity.

4. **Crash cost (CC):** The activity cost associated with the crash time.

Cost Assumptions.   In making a cost analysis, we assume that costs increase linearly as activity time is reduced from its normal time. For example, suppose that the normal time for activity C in the hospital project is 10 weeks at a direct cost of $4000. If the crash time is 5 weeks at a crash cost of $7000, the net time reduction is 5 weeks at a net cost increase of $3000. We assume that it costs $600 (or $3000/5) per week to crash activity C. This assumption of linear marginal costs is illustrated in Fig. 18.6. Also shown is a hypothetical actual-cost curve. Thus if activity C were expedited by two weeks, the estimated direct

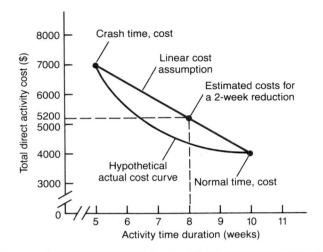

FIGURE 18.6 Cost–Time Relationships in Cost Analysis

costs would be $5200 even though actual costs would be much less.* Table 18.3 contains direct cost and time data for the hospital project. The amounts in the last column were calculated as follows:

$$\text{Cost to crash per week} = \frac{CC - NC}{NT - CT}$$

Indirect and Penalty Costs. Suppose that project indirect costs are $8000 per week. In addition, suppose that after week 65 St. Adolf's incurs a penalty cost of $20,000 per week if the hospital is not fully operational. With a critical path completion time of 69 weeks, it appears that the hospital faces some major expenses. As the figures in Table 18.3 indicate, any activity in the project could be expedited for a certain increase in direct costs. For every week that the project is shortened—to week 65—the hospital saves one week of penalty *and* indirect costs, or $28,000. For decreases beyond week 65, the savings are only the weekly indirect costs of $8000. The objective is to determine the target project completion time that minimizes total project costs.

Normal and Rational Crash Schedules. From the perspective of project completion time, the normal time schedule and the minimum-time schedule provide the limits for the minimum-cost schedule search. Finding the cost for the normal time schedule is straightforward. Table 18.3 shows that total direct cost is $1,992,000. Indirect costs are $8000 per week, or $552,000. Four weeks

---

*PERT/CPM methods do not require the assumption of linear cost increases. Nonlinear relationships can be used, but the linear assumption is usually adequate.

TABLE 18.3 Direct Cost and Time Data for the St. Adolf's Hospital Project

Activity	Normal Time (NT)	Normal Cost (NC)	Crash Time (CT)	Crash Cost (CC)	Maximum Time Reduction (wk)	Cost to Crash per Week
A	12	$ 12,000	11	$ 13,000	1	$ 1,000
B	9	50,000	7	64,000	2	7,000
C	10	4,000	5	7,000	5	600
D	10	16,000	8	20,000	2	2,000
E	24	120,000	14	200,000	10	8,000
F	10	10,000	6	16,000	4	1,500
G	35	500,000	25	530,000	10	3,000
H	40	1,200,000	35	1,260,000	5	12,000
I	15	40,000	10	52,500	5	2,500
J	4	10,000	1	13,000	3	1,000
K	6	30,000	5	34,000	1	4,000
Total		$1,992,000		$2,209,500		

of penalty costs come to $80,000. Thus the total cost for a 69-week project is $2,624,000.

The first step in finding the cost of the minimum-time schedule is to find the minimum project duration by crashing all the activities in the project and finding the length of the critical path. Figure 18.7, on the following page, shows the CPM network with the crash times (in weeks) for each activity. The critical path is B–D–H–J–K, with a total completion time of 56 weeks. Total direct cost for this expedited schedule, as shown in Table 18.3, is $2,209,500. Indirect costs would be $448,000 [or 56($8000)]. As there are no penalty costs, the total project cost would be $2,657,500.

The minimum-time schedule that we just evaluated crashed all activities to their limits. However, the minimum time of 56 weeks can be achieved *without* crashing all the activities. Table 18.4 shows how to derive the **rational crash**

TABLE 18.4 Deriving the Rational Crash Schedule

Noncritical Activity	Cost to Crash per Week	Crash Time (wk)	Maximum Relax Time (wk)	Adjusted Time (wk)	Savings Relative to Total Crash Schedule
E	$8000	14	10	24	$ 80,000
G	3000	25	9	34	27,000
I	2500	10	5	15	12,500
F	1500	6	4	10	6,000
Total					$125,500

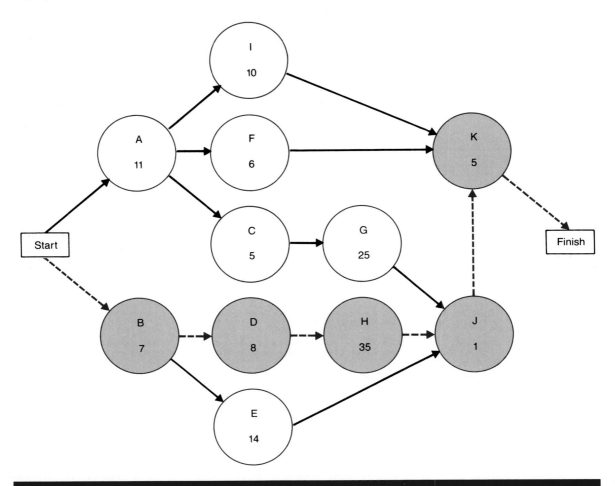

FIGURE 18.7   Network Showing Crash Times and the Critical Path

schedule for the hospital project. We begin by finding the activity not on the critical path that is the most expensive to crash. We then relax it as much as possible, without exceeding its normal time or increasing the length of the total project. This activity is E. We can return it to its normal time and save $80,000 relative to the total crash schedule. The next most expensive noncritical activity is G. Its normal time is 35 weeks; however, we can relax it only 9 weeks because, at an adjusted time of 34 weeks, path A–C–G–J–K is also 56 weeks long. Activities I and F can both be returned to their normal times, but all other activities remain at their crash times. The total savings relative to the total crash schedule is $125,500. Consequently, the total project cost for the rational crash schedule is $2,532,000 (or $2,657,500 − $125,500).

Finding the Minimum-Cost Schedule. So far we have established a total project cost upper limit of $2,532,000 for the rational crash schedule. Thus Judy Kramer should not accept an intermediate schedule between 56 and 69 weeks that costs more than $2,532,000. In evaluating intermediate schedules, we start with the normal time schedule and crash activities along the critical path in such a way that the added crash costs are less than the savings in indirect and penalty costs.* The procedure involves the following steps.

1. Determine the critical path(s) in the project.
2. Find the activity (activities) on the critical path(s) that is (are) cheapest to crash per week.
3. Reduce the time for this activity until (a) it cannot be further reduced, (b) another path becomes critical, or (c) the increase in direct costs exceeds the savings that result from shortening the project. If more than one path is critical, it may be necessary to reduce the time for an activity on each path simultaneously.
4. Go back to step 1 and repeat the procedure, so long as the increase in direct costs is less than the savings generated by shortening the project.

APPLICATION 18.4

Determine the minimum-cost schedule for the hospital project. Use the information in Fig. 18.7 and Table 18.3.

Solution

Trial 1:

1. The critical path is B–D–H–J–K.
2. The cheapest activity to crash per week is J at $1000, which is much less than the savings in indirect and penalty costs of $28,000 per week.
3. Crash activity J to its limit of 3 weeks because the critical path remains unchanged. This action affects three paths in the network. The new expected

---

*This same procedure could be used for AOA networks.

times for each path are:

A–I–K	33 wk
A–F–K	28 wk
A–C–G–J–K	64 wk
B–D–H–J–K	66 wk
B–E–J–K	40 wk

Compare these times to those in Table 18.1.

Trial 2:

1. The critical path is still B–D–H–J–K.
2. The cheapest activity to crash per week now is D at $2000.
3. The first week of reduction in activity D saves $28,000, but the second saves only $8000. However, these savings still exceed the cost of crashing D by two weeks. After week 65, there are no more penalty costs. Note that after crashing D, we now have two critical paths.

Trial 3:

1. The critical paths are B–D–H–J–K and A–C–G–J–K. *Both* paths must now be shortened to realize any savings in indirect project costs. If one is shortened and the other isn't, the length of the project remains unchanged.
2. Our alternatives are to crash one of the following combinations of activities, (A, B), (A, H), (C, B), (C, H), (G, B), (G, H), or to crash activity K, which is on both critical paths. Jointly crashing (A, B) costs $8000; (A, H), $13,000; (C, B), $7600; (C, H), $12,600; (G, B), $10,000; and (G, H), $15,000. The cheapest alternative is activity K at $4000 per week.
3. Crash activity K to its limit of five weeks. The critical paths remain unchanged.

Trial 4:

1. The critical paths are B–D–H–J–K and A–C–G–J–K.
2. The least expensive alternative at this stage is to simultaneously crash activities B and C at a cost of $7600 per week. This amount is still less than the savings of $8000 per week.
3. Crash activities B and C by two weeks, the limit for activity B.

Any other combination of activities will result in a net increase in total project costs because the crash costs exceed weekly indirect costs. The following table contains a summary of the cost analysis for the hospital project. As you can see, the minimum-cost schedule is 61 weeks, with a total cost of $2,506,200. To obtain this schedule, we crashed activities B, D, J, and K to their limits and activity C to 8 weeks. The other activities remain at their normal times. This schedule costs about $25,800 less than the rational crash schedule.

Cost Analysis for the St. Adolf's Hospital Project

Trial	Crash Activity	Resulting Critical Path*	Time Reduction (wk)	Project Duration (wk)	Total Project Direct Costs at Last Trial	Crash Costs Added This Trial	Total Indirect Costs	Total Penalty Costs	Total Project Costs
0	—	B–D–H–J–K	—	69	$1,992,000	$ —	$552,000	$80,000	$2,624,000
1	J	B–D–H–[J]–K	3	66	1,992,000	3,000	528,000	20,000	2,543,000
2	D	A–C–G–[J]–K	2	64	1,995,000	4,000	512,000	0	2,511,000
		B–[D]–H–[J]–K							
3	K	A–C–G–[J]–[K]	1	63	1,999,000	4,000	504,000	0	2,507,000
		B–[D]–H–[J]–[K]							
4	B, C	A–C–G–[J]–[K]	2	61	2,003,000	15,200	488,000	0	2,506,200
		[B]–[D]–H–[J]–[K]							

*A ☐ indicates that the activity has been crashed to its limit.

Figure 18.8 shows the cost curves for the hospital project. The curves consist of a series of straight-line segments because of our assumption that marginal costs are linear. We stopped at 61 weeks, but we could have continued crashing more activities (even though total costs would have increased) until week 56 and plotted the costs along the way to get a better approximation of the cost curves in that range. Of course, we have no guarantee that the schedule developed is the optimal minimum-cost schedule.

Resource Limitations

The project management models that we have discussed so far consider only activity times in determining overall project duration and the critical path. Recall that an underlying assumption in the use of PERT/CPM is that sufficient resources will be available when needed to complete all project activities on schedule. However, developing schedules without considering the load placed on resources can result in inefficient resource use and even cause project delays if capacity limitations are exceeded.

For purposes of discussion, consider the project represented by the project diagram in Fig. 18.9. Each of the five activities involves a certain amount of time and has a resource requirement. The critical path is A–B–E, and the total time to complete the project, ignoring resource limitations, is nine days. Although AON network diagrams are useful for displaying an entire project and showing the precedence relationships between activities, they are not

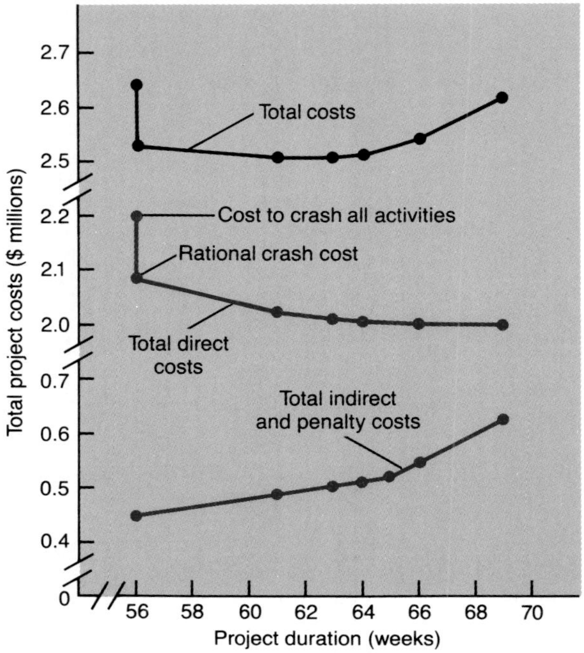

FIGURE 18.8 Cost Curves for the St. Adolf's Hospital Project

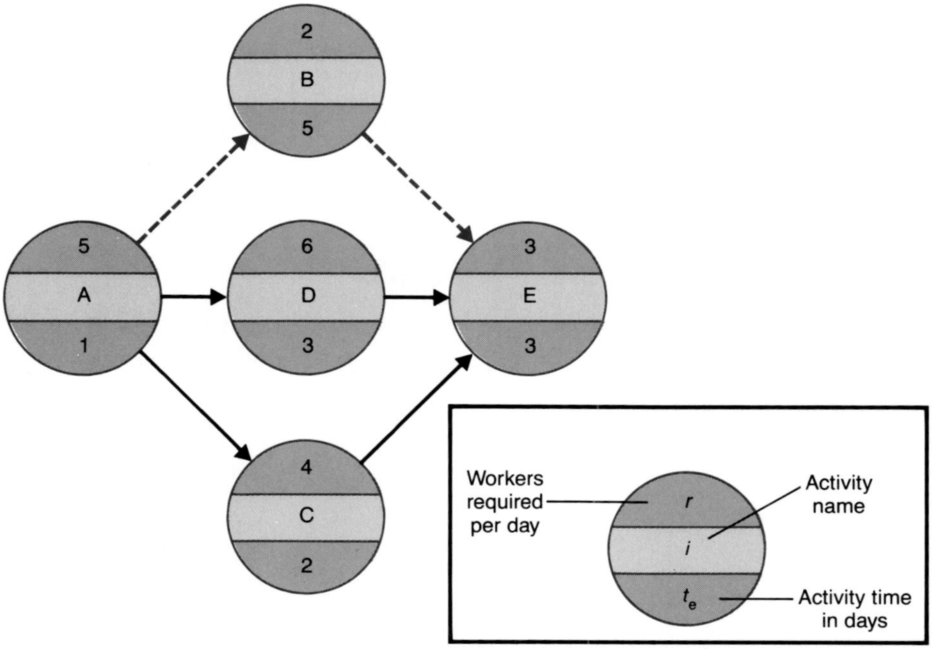

FIGURE 18.9 Project Diagram Showing Resource Requirements and Critical Path

very useful for showing the implications of resource requirements for a schedule of activities. Gantt charts (see Chapter 17) are more useful in this regard.

We want to generate a schedule that recognizes resource constraints, as well as the precedence relationships between activities. Let's suppose that we are limited to a small number of workers per day. Although we could use an optimizing approach, such as linear programming (see Supplement 2), to derive a schedule under these conditions, a more useful approach in practice is to use a procedure such as the one developed by Weist (1966):

1. Start with the first day of the project and schedule as many activities as possible, considering precedence relationships and resource limitations. Continue with the second day, and so on, until all activities are scheduled.

2. When several activities compete for the same resources, give preference to the activities with the least slack, as calculated using standard PERT/CPM methods.

3. Reschedule noncritical activities, if possible, to free resources for critical or nonslack activities.

The intent of this procedure is to minimize total project time, subject to resource constraints.

APPLICATION 18.5

Generate a resource-constrained schedule for the project depicted in Fig. 18.9. Assume that we have only six workers per day.

Solution

1. Schedule activity A first because all other activities depend on its completion.

2. The choice is between activities B, C, and D because their predecessor has been scheduled. Activities C and D have slack but activity B doesn't because it's on the critical path. Thus schedule B next. So far, we have committed five workers on day 1 and two workers on days 2–6.

3. We have a choice between activities C and D, but we must choose C next. It requires only four workers per day, and we can schedule it on days 2 and 3 without violating our resource constraint of six workers per day. Activity D requires six workers per day, but we have already scheduled activity B, which needs two workers.

4. The remaining activities to schedule are D and E. We must schedule D first because of precedence constraints. The resulting schedule is shown in Fig. 18.10.

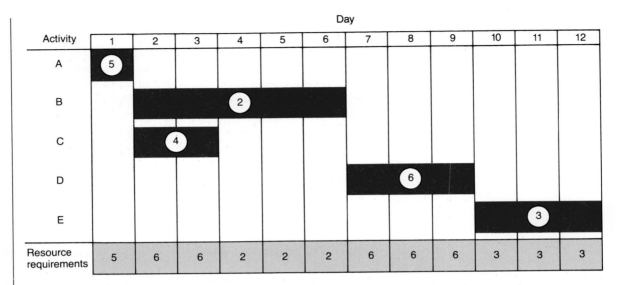

FIGURE 18.10   **Resource-Constrained Schedule**

This schedule results in the shortest project time possible under the resource constraints; however, the use of the procedure will not always be so successful. We can only say that it will generally produce solutions close to, but not necessarily, the optimum.

Computerized Project Scheduling and Control

Properly used, computerized network planning models can simplify project management. These models simulate implementation of projects having complex activity interdependence and resource requirements. The computer can easily handle the computation of slack times, cost–time trade-offs, probability estimates, resource allocations, among other factors, and update networks. Software packages that provide spreadsheets, network diagrams, milestone charts, critical path activity reports, and Gantt charts are readily available (Davis, 1973). Some of these packages can handle more than 60,000 activities per project and any number of resources per activity, limited only by memory capacity (Fawcette, 1984). They can also handle a number of different projects. Software producers offer many of the same capabilities to users of microcomputers.

CRITIQUE OF PERT/CPM SYSTEMS ▲

So far, we have demonstrated the benefits that PERT/CPM systems offer to project managers. Let's now turn to criticisms of the assumptions and limitations of PERT/CPM.

Network Diagrams

The methods used in PERT/CPM are based on the assumption that project activities having clear beginning and ending points can be identified. A further assumption is that activity sequence relationships can be identified at the start of the project and specified in a network diagram. However, these assumptions often are too restrictive. For example, one activity must be shown to precede the other in the PERT/CPM network diagram. In reality, two activities, where one must precede the other, often can be overlapped and worked on simultaneously up to a certain point. Also, project content can change, and a network diagram developed at the start of a project may later limit the project manager's flexibility to handle changing situations. At times, actual precedence relationships cannot be specified beforehand. That is, the sequencing of some activities is contingent on the result of certain other activities, which can't always be anticipated. In situations such as these, PERT/CPM methods may not be very useful.

Control

The major underlying assumption in PERT/CPM methods is that managers should focus on the activities along the critical path. However, as we pointed out earlier in this chapter, managers should also pay attention to *near-critical* paths. The reason is that these near-critical paths could easily become critical, if one or more of the activities along these paths slips relative to its schedule. Project managers who overlook this possibility often complain that using PERT/CPM did not help them complete their projects on time. This shortcoming is not that of PERT/CPM itself, but rather is the result of an incomplete understanding of the concepts involved.

Time Estimates

When activity times are uncertain, the assumption is that they follow the beta distribution, with the variance of the total project time equaling the sum of the variances along the critical path. This aspect of PERT/CPM has brought a variety of criticism. First, the formulas used to calculate the mean and variance of the beta distribution are only approximations and are subject to error. Errors on the order of 10 percent for the mean and 5 percent for the variance can be expected. These errors could give incorrect critical paths. Second, arriving at a single, accurate time estimate, let alone three, for an activity that has never been performed before, is very difficult. A single time estimate—the most likely time—is preferred by many project managers. They believe that the pessimistic time estimates often are inflated and vary far more from the most likely time estimate than do the optimistic time estimates. They argue that some managers use these pessimistic time estimates as an excuse for failure. Perhaps a more harmful by-product of inflated pessimistic time estimates is the inflation of *expected* activity times, which builds a cushion of slack into the schedule. Finally, the choice of the beta distribution was somewhat arbitrary, and the use of another distribution would result in different expected times and variances for each activity.

Although the application of PERT/CPM to project management has short-comings, managers who recognize the limitations of these methods can use them effectively. In fact, their shortcomings have not precluded widespread use of PERT/CPM. The Department of Defense actually requires the use of PERT/CPM methods by major contractors. The Ford Motor Company uses these methods for retooling assembly lines, as does the Chrysler Corporation for building a new assembly plant. A large number of other organizations represent a broad spectrum of applications, including Brigham and Women's Hospital in Boston, the San Francisco Opera Association, Walt Disney Corporation, and Procter & Gamble. Even though network planning models are not perfect, their skillful use can significantly aid project managers in their work.

SOLVED PROBLEMS

1. An advertising project manager has developed the network diagram shown in Fig. 18.11 for a new advertising campaign. In addition, the manager gathered the time information for each activity, as shown in the accompanying table.

   a. Calculate the expected times and variances for each activity.

   b. Calculate the activity slacks and determine the critical path.

   c. What is the probability of completing the project within 18 weeks?

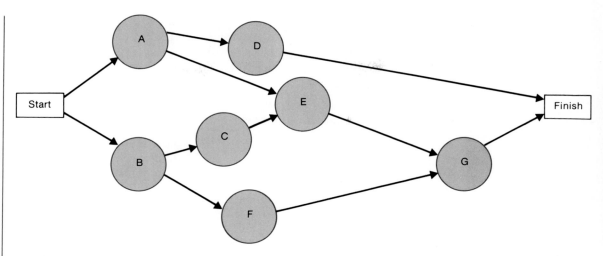

FIGURE 18.11

	Time Estimates (wk)		
Activity	Optimistic	Most Likely	Pessimistic
A	1	2	3
B	4	6	8
C	3	3	3
D	2	8	10
E	3	6	9
F	1	8	15
G	4	5	6

Solution

a. The expected times and variances for each activity are as follows:

Activity	Expected Time (wk)	Variance
A	2	0.11
B	6	0.44
C	3	0.00
D	7.33	1.78
E	6	1.00
F	8	5.44
G	5	0.11

b. We need to calculate the earliest start, latest start, earliest finish, and latest finish times for each activity. Starting with activities A and B, we proceed from the beginning of the network and move to the end, calculating the earliest start and finish times:

Activity	Earliest Start (wk)	Earliest Finish (wk)	Comments
A	0	0 + 2 = 2	Can start immediately
B	0	0 + 6 = 6	Can start immediately
C	6	6 + 3 = 9	Cannot start until B is finished
D	2	2 + 7.33 = 9.33	Cannot start until A is finished
E	9	9 + 6 = 15	Cannot start until C is finished
F	6	6 + 8 = 14	Cannot start until B is finished
G	15	15 + 5 = 20	Cannot start until E is finished

The earliest the project can be completed is week 20, when activity G is finished. Using that as a target date, we can work backward through the network, calculating the latest start and finish times:

Activity	Latest Start (wk)	Latest Finish (wk)	Comments
G	15	20	Project must be completed in week 20
F	7	15	Keeps G on schedule
E	9	15	Keeps G on schedule
D	12.67	20	No following activities
C	6	9	Keeps E on schedule
B	0	6	Keeps C on schedule
A	7	9	Keeps E on schedule

We can now calculate the activity slacks and determine which activities are on the critical path, as follows:

Activity	Start Earliest	Start Latest	Finish Earliest	Finish Latest	Activity Slack	Critical Path
A	0	7	2	9	7	No
B	0	0	6	6	0	Yes
C	6	6	9	9	0	Yes
D	2	12.67	9.33	20	10.67	No
E	9	9	15	15	0	Yes
F	6	7	14	15	1	No
G	15	15	20	20	0	Yes

The paths, and their total expected times and variances, are:

Path	Total Expected Time (wk)	Total Variance
A–D	2 + 7.33 = 9.33	0.11 + 1.78 = 1.89
A–E–G	2 + 6 + 5 = 13	0.11 + 1.00 + 0.11 = 1.22
B–C–E–G	6 + 3 + 6 + 5 = 20	0.44 + 0.00 + 1.00 + 0.11 = 1.55
B–F–G	6 + 8 + 5 = 19	0.44 + 5.44 + 0.11 = 5.99

The critical path is B–C–E–G, with a total expected time of 20 weeks. However, path B–F–G is 19 weeks and has a large variance.

c. We first calculate the z-value:

$$z = \frac{T' - TE}{\sqrt{\Sigma \sigma_{CP}^2}} = \frac{18 - 20}{\sqrt{1.55}} = -1.61$$

Using Appendix 3 we find that the probability of completing the project in 18 weeks or less is only 0.0537. Because path B–F–G is very close to the length of the critical path and has a large variance, it may well become the critical path during the project.

2. Your company has just received an order for a specially designed electric motor from a good customer. Nonetheless, the contract states that starting on the thirteenth day from now, your firm will experience a penalty of $100 per day if the job is not completed. Indirect project costs amount to $200 per day. The data on direct costs and activity precedence relationships are given in Table 18.5.

a. Draw the project network diagram.

b. What completion date would you recommend?

TABLE 18.5

Activity	Normal Time (days)	Normal Cost	Crash Time (days)	Crash Cost	Immediate Predecessor(s)
A	4	$1000	3	$1300	None
B	7	1400	4	2000	None
C	5	2000	4	2700	None
D	6	1200	5	1400	A
E	3	900	2	1100	B
F	11	2500	6	3750	C
G	4	800	3	1450	D, E
H	3	300	1	500	F, G

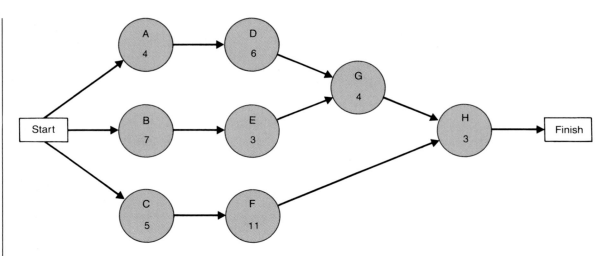

FIGURE 18.12

Solution

a. The AON network diagram, including normal activity times, for this procedure is shown in Fig. 18.12. Keep the following points in mind while constructing a network diagram.

   - Always have start and finish nodes.
   - Try to avoid crossing paths to keep the diagram simple.
   - Use only one arrow to directly connect any two nodes.
   - Put the activities with no predecessors at the left and point the arrows from left to right.
   - Use scratch paper and be prepared to revise the diagram several times before you come up with a correct and uncluttered diagram.

b. Determining a good completion date requires the use of the minimum-cost schedule procedure. Using the data in Table 18.5, you can determine the crash cost per day and the maximum crash time for each activity:

Activity	Crash Cost Per Day ($)	Maximum Crash Time (days)
A	300	1
B	200	3
C	700	1
D	200	1
E	200	1
F	250	5
G	650	1
H	100	2

The critical path is C–F–H at 19 weeks, which you find by searching for the longest path in the network. The cheapest of these activities to crash is H. It only costs an extra $100 per day to crash H, and $300 (or $200 + $100) per day in indirect and penalty costs can be saved. We crash this activity two days (the maximum). The length of the paths are now:

A–D–G–H	15 days
B–E–G–H	15 days
C–F–H	17 days

The critical path is still C–F–H. The next cheapest activity to crash is F at $250 per day. We can only crash F two days because at that point we will have three critical paths. Further reductions in project duration will require simultaneous crashing of more than one activity. The cost to do so exceeds the savings. Consequently, you should stop. Table 18.6 contains a summary of the analysis and the resultant project duration and total cost. Note that every activity is critical. The recommended completion date is week 15.

3. A maintenance crew at the Woody Manufacturing Company must do scheduled machine maintenance in the fabricating department. A series of interrelated activities must be accomplished, requiring a different number of workers each day. Figure 18.13 shows the project network, the workers required, and the activity time. The company can devote a maximum of 6 maintenance workers per day to these activities.

   a. Use Weist's procedure to find a new schedule and draw a Gantt chart for it.

   b. How long will the project take and which activities are critical?

Solution

   a. The critical path of this project (disregarding the resource constraint) is A–C–D–E at 11 weeks. Consequently, only activity B has slack.

TABLE 18.6

Trial	Crash Activity	Resulting Critical Path	Time Reduction (days)	Project Duration (days)	Project Direct Costs, Last Trial	Crash Cost Added	Total Indirect Costs	Total Penalty Costs	Total Project Costs
0	—	C–F–H	—	19	$10,100	—	$3,800	$700	$14,600
1	H	C–F– H	2	17	10,100	200	3,400	500	14,200
2	F	A–D–G– H	2	15	10,300	500	3,000	300	14,100
		B–E–G– H							
		C–F– H							

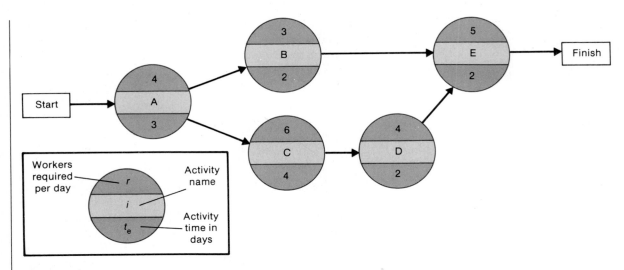

FIGURE 18.13

Figure 18.14 shows the schedule.
  i. Schedule activity A first on day 1. We cannot schedule any other activities until day 4 because of the resource constraint.
 ii. Activities B and C are now tied. We schedule C next because it has no slack.
iii. Activities B and D are tied. We choose D next because it has no slack. We must start it on day 8 because of the resource constraint.

Day

Activity	1	2	3	4	5	6	7	8	9	10	11	12	13
A	███	④	███										
B										███	③		
C				███		⑥							
D								███	④				
E												███	⑤
Resource requirements	4	4	4	6	6	6	6	4	4	3	3	5	5

FIGURE 18.14

    iv. Activity B must be scheduled next because of its precedence relationship to activity E.

    v. Finally, schedule E for days 12 and 13. It could not be started earlier because of the resource constraint.

b. The project will take 13 days and every activity is critical. No activity can be shifted from its present schedule without violating the maintenance worker capacity limitation.

FORMULA REVIEW

1. Activity time statistics:

$$t_e = \frac{a + 4(m) + b}{6} \quad \text{(Expected activity time)}$$

$$\sigma^2 = \left(\frac{b - a}{6}\right)^2 \quad \text{(Variance)}$$

2. Start and finish times:

$$ES_i = \max \ [EF \text{ times of all activities immediately preceding activity } i]$$

$$EF_i = ES_i + t_e$$

$$LF_i = \min \ [LS \text{ times of all activities immediately following activity } i]$$

$$LS_i = LF_i - t_e$$

3. Activity slack:

$$S_i = LS_i - ES_i \quad \text{or} \quad LF_i - EF_i$$

4. z-transformation formula:

$$z = \frac{T' - TE}{\sqrt{\Sigma \ \sigma_{CP}^2}}$$

5. Project costs:

$$\text{Cost to crash per week} = \frac{CC - NC}{NT - CT}$$

CHAPTER HIGHLIGHTS

- Managing a project involves (1) describing the project, (2) developing a network model, (3) inserting time estimates, (4) analyzing the model, (5) developing the project plan, and (6) monitoring project progress.

- PERT and CPM are network modeling methods that are useful in project management.

- Uncertainty in activity times can be recognized by securing three time estimates for each activity. Actual activity times are assumed to follow a beta distribution.

- PERT/CPM methods focus attention on the critical path: the sequence of activities requiring the greatest cumulative amount of time for completion. Delay in any of these activities will delay the entire project.

- PERT/CPM methods can be used to assess the probability of finishing the project by a certain date or to find the minimum-cost schedule, with the assumption that marginal costs are linear.

- A slack-sorted report can be used to identify those activities that are behind schedule and those from which resources can be withdrawn and reassigned to activities needing them.

- The Weist procedure can be used to generate a capacity-sensitive project schedule when resource constraints are present.

- A number of criticisms have been leveled at PERT/CPM methods. Although these methods have shortcomings, they are widely used.

KEY TERMS

activity   675
activity slack   685
activity-on-arc (AOA) network   675
activity-on-node (AON) network   675
crash cost (*CC*)   693
crash time (*CT*)   693
critical path   685
critical path method (CPM)   677
earliest finish time (EF_i)   685
earliest start time (ES_i)   685
event   675
latest finish time (LF_i)   686
latest start time (LS_i)   686
most likely time (*m*)   682
most optimistic time (*a*)   682
most pessimistic time (*b*)   682
network diagram   675
normal cost (*NC*)   693
normal time (*NT*)   693
precedence relationship   675
program evaluation and review technique (PERT)   677
project   674
rational crash schedule   695

STUDY QUESTIONS

1. What are the steps in effective project management? What are the penalties for mismanaging a large project?

2. What information is needed to construct the network diagram for a project? Can any project be diagramed as a network?

3. A certain advertising agency is preparing a bid for a promotional campaign of a type never before attempted. The project consists of a large number of interrelated activities. Explain how you would arrive at a single time estimate for each activity, so that you can use a network planning model to assess the chances that the project can be completed when the sponsor wants it.

4. Why was the beta distribution chosen over the normal distribution for PERT/CPM analyses?

5. Why is the critical path of such importance in project management? Can it change during the course of the project? If so, why?

6. When determining the probability of completing a project within a certain amount of time, what assumptions are you making? What role do the lengths and variances of paths other than the critical path play in such an analysis?

7. Explain the usefulness of the slack-sorted report. Is it still useful when the slacks of all project activities are positive?

8. Suppose that your company has accepted a project of a type it has completed many times before. Any activity can be expedited with an increase in costs. There are weekly indirect costs, and there is a weekly penalty if project completion extends beyond a certain date. Identify the data that you would need and explain the analytic process that you would use to determine a minimum-cost schedule. What assumptions would you make in doing such an analysis?

9. Suppose that you are trying to convince management that methods such as PERT/CPM would be useful to them. Some of the managers have voiced the following concerns.

   a. There is a tendency for technicians to handle the operation of PERT/CPM; consequently, management will not use it very much.

   b. It puts pressure on managers because everyone knows where the critical path is. Managers of activities along the critical path are in the spotlight, and if their activities are delayed, the cost of the delay is on their shoulders.

c. The introduction of network planning techniques may require new communication channels and systems procedures.

Comment on each of these concerns.

PROBLEMS

Review Problems

1. The following information is available about a project.

Activity	Immediate Predecessor(s)	Time (days)
A	—	2
B	—	5
C	A	3
D	A	4
E	B	4
F	B	3
G	C, D	2
H	D, E, F	6
I	G, H	4

a. Draw the network diagram for this project.
b. Find the critical path.

2. Recently, you were assigned to manage a project for your company. You have constructed a network diagram depicting the various activities in the project (Fig. 18.15). In addition, you asked various managers and subordinates to estimate the amount of time that they would expect each of the activities to take. Their responses were:

Activity	Time Estimates (days)		
	Optimistic	Most Likely	Pessimistic
A	4	7	10
B	8	10	14
C	3	6	7
D	2	4	6
E	7	8	9

a. What is the expected completion time of the project?
b. Suppose that the optimistic times prevail during the project. What is the earliest the project could be completed?
c. What is the probability of completing the project in 17 days?

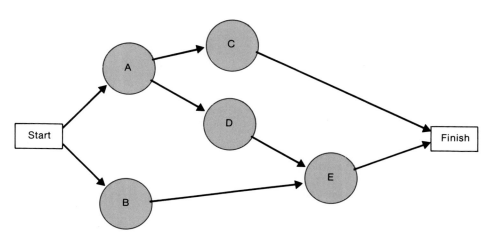

FIGURE 18.15

3. The following information has been gathered for a project.

Activity	Time (wk)	Immediate Predecessor(s)
A	5	—
B	10	A
C	3	A
D	6	A, C
E	10	B, C
F	2	E, D

    a. Draw the network diagram.
    b. Calculate the slack for each activity and determine the critical path. How long will the project take?

4. Consider the following project information.

Activity	Time (wk)	Immediate Predecessor(s)
A	2	—
B	3	—
C	6	—
D	1	A, B
E	3	B
F	7	D, C
G	7	E, C
H	11	F, G

    a. Draw the network diagram for this project.
    b. Specify the critical path(s).
    c. Calculate the total slack for activities A and D.
    d. What happens to the slack for D if A takes five days?

5. Consider the following data for a project never before attempted by your company.

Activity	Expected Time, t_e (wk)	Immediate Predecessor(s)
A	4	—
B	2	—
C	3	A
D	6	B
E	6	C, D
F	4	D

    a. Draw the network diagram for this project.
    b. Identify the critical path and estimate the project's duration.
    c. Calculate the slack for each activity.

 6. The director of continuing education at Bluebird University has just approved the planning for a sales-training seminar. Her administrative assistant has identified the various activities that must be done and their relationships to each other, as shown in Table 18.7. Because of the uncertainty in planning the new course, the assistant

TABLE 18.7

Activity	Description	Immediate Predecessor(s)
A	Design brochure and course announcement.	—
B	Identify prospective teachers.	—
C	Prepare detailed outline of course.	—
D	Send brochure and student applications.	A
E	Send teacher applications.	B
F	Select teacher for course.	C, E
G	Accept students.	D
H	Select text for course.	F
I	Order and receive texts.	G, H
J	Prepare room for class.	G

also supplied the following time estimates for each activity.

	Time Estimates (working days)		
Activity	Optimistic	Most Likely	Pessimistic
A	2	4	6
B	6	8	12
C	2	3	6
D	15	18	27
E	8	10	12
F	3	4	5
G	2	5	6
H	4	6	8
I	10	12	18
J	1	1	1

The director wants to conduct the seminar 44 working days from now. What is the probability that everything will be ready in time?

7. Information concerning a project is given in Table 18.8. Indirect project costs amount to $250 per day. The company will experience a $100 per day penalty for each day the project lasts beyond day 14.

   a. What is the project's duration, using only normal times?
   b. What completion date do you recommend?
   c. What is the critical path?

8. Table 18.9 contains information about a project. Shorten the project by two days using the procedure for finding a minimum-cost schedule. Assume that project indirect costs and penalty costs are negligible. Identify activities to crash while minimizing the additional crash costs.

TABLE 18.8

Activity	Normal Time (days)	Normal Cost	Crash Time (days)	Crash Cost	Immediate Predecessor(s)
A	4	$1000	3	$1100	—
B	6	800	3	2000	—
C	3	600	2	800	A, B
D	2	1500	1	2000	B
E	5	700	3	1200	C, D
F	2	1300	1	1400	E
G	1	900	1	900	E
H	4	100	2	900	G

TABLE 18.9

Activity	Time (days)	Immediate Predecessor(s)	Maximum Crash Time (days)	Cost to Crash (per day)
A	6	—	1	$100
B	11	—	3	150
C	9	A	1	200
D	8	A	1	150
E	3	B	1	100
F	1	C, D	0	—
G	3	D, E	2	150
H	2	F	1	250
I	1	G	0	—

9. Hamilton Berger, district manager for Gumfull Foods, Inc., is in charge of opening a new fast-food outlet in the college town of Senility. His major concern is the hiring of a manager and a cadre of hamburger cooks, assemblers, and dispensers. He also has to coordinate the renovation of a building that previously was owned by a pet-supplies retailer. He has gathered the data shown in Table 18.10.

Top management has told Berger that the new outlet is to be opened as soon as possible. Every week that the project can be shortened will save the firm $1200 in lease costs. Hamilton thought about how to save time during the project and came up with two possibilities.

- Employ Amazon, Inc., a local employment agency, to locate some good prospects for the manager's job. This approach would save three weeks in activity A and cost Gumfull Foods $2500.
- By adding a few workers, he could shorten the time for activity B by two weeks at an additional cost of $2700.

Help Ham Berger by answering the following questions.

a. How long is the project expected to take?
b. Suppose that Berger has a personal goal of completing the project in 12 weeks. What is the probability that this can happen?
c. What additional expenditures should be made to reduce the project's duration? Use the expected times for each activity as though they were certain.

10. The diagram in Fig. 18.16 was developed for a project that you are managing. Suppose that you are interested in finding ways to speed up the

TABLE 18.10

Activity	Description	Immediate Predecessor(s)	Time (wk) a	Time (wk) m	Time (wk) b
A	Interview at college for new manager.	—	2	4	6
B	Renovate building.	—	6	8	12
C	Place ad for employees and interview applicants.	—	4	6	12
D	Visit by new-manager prospects.	A	1	2	3
E	Purchase equipment for new outlet and install.	B	2	4	10
F	Check references for employee applicants and make final selection.	C	1	1	1
G	Check references for new manager and make final selection.	D	1	1	1
H	Hold orientation meetings and do paperwork to get manager and employees on payroll.	E, F, G	1	1	1

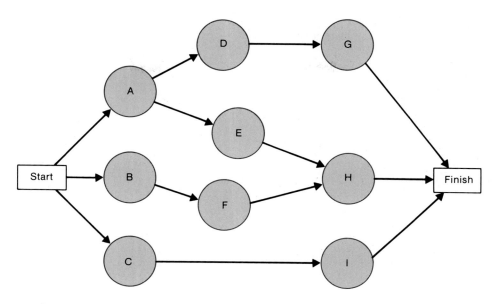

FIGURE 18.16

project at minimal additional cost. Determine the schedule for completing the project in 23 days at minimum cost. Penalty costs and project overhead costs are negligible. Alternative time and cost data for each activity are shown in Table 18.11.

TABLE 18.11

	Alternative 1		Alternative 2	
Activity	Time (days)	Cost	Time (days)	Cost
A	12	$ 1,250	11	$ 1,600
B	13	1,100	10	1,400
C	20	3,000	18	4,200
D	9	2,000	5	2,800
E	11	500	8	800
F	6	650	4	950
G	8	1,500	6	1,700
H	2	400	1	700
I	6	2,500	3	3,700
Total		$12,900		$17,850

11. The construction crew of Johnson Homebuilders must frame in a new house. The following data are available for the project.

Activity	Immediate Predecessor(s)	Time (days)	Workers Required (per day)
A	—	2	2
B	—	3	6
C	A	2	4
D	B	4	3
E	C, D	3	5

a. Draw the network diagram for the project.
b. Disregarding capacity limitations, determine the project's critical path and duration.
c. What is the slack for each activity?
d. Only six construction workers are available each day. Use Weist's procedure to find a new schedule and draw a Gantt chart for it.
  i. What is the critical path in this schedule?
  ii. How long will the project take now?

12. The network shown in Fig. 18.17 includes the number of workers required per day for each activity, the name of each activity, and the time (in days) required. Use Weist's procedure to find a schedule that utilizes a maximum of 10 workers each day. Draw a Gantt chart for this schedule.
  a. How long will this project take?
  b. What is the critical path?

13. A crew of linemen for the Alphabet Telephone Company must install some cable in a rural area. The following data are available for the project.

Activity	Immediate Predecessor(s)	Time (days)	Crew Members Required (per day)
A	—	2	9
B	A	3	6
C	A	5	3
D	A	3	5
E	D	4	4
F	B, C, E	1	7

a. Disregarding capacity limitations, determine the critical path and calculate the slack for each activity. How long will the project take?
b. Suppose that there are only nine crew members. Use Weist's procedure to find a schedule that does not exceed nine workers

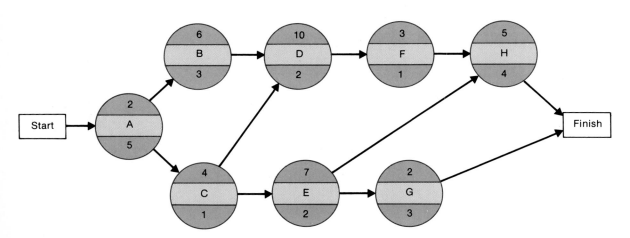

FIGURE 18.17

per day on the project. Draw a Gantt chart for your schedule.
  i. What is the critical path now?
  ii. What are the slacks for each activity?
  iii. How long will the project now take?

Advanced Problems

We suggest that you use a PERT/CPM computer program for problems 17 and 18.

14. The following information concerns a new project your company is undertaking.

Activity	Immediate Predecessor(s)	Time (days)
A	—	11
B	—	10
C	A, B	8
D	A, B	6
E	A, B	7
F	C, E	15
G	C, D	4
H	G	9
I	F, G	5
J	E, H	8
K	I, J	10

a. Draw the network diagram for this project.
b. Determine the critical path and project completion time.

15. The project manager of Good Public Relations has gathered the data shown in Table 18.12 for a new advertising campaign.

a. How long is the project likely to take?
b. What is the probability that the project will take more than 38 weeks?
c. Consider the path A–E–G–H–J. What is the probability that this path will exceed the expected project duration?

16. The following information is known about a project.

Activity	Immediate Predecessor(s)	Time (days)	Workers Required (per day)
A	—	4	3
B	A	2	2
C	A	1	4
D	C	3	2
E	B, D	4	5
F	E	3	5
G	E	2	2

TABLE 18.12

Activity	Immediate Predecessor(s)	Time Estimates		
		Optimistic	Most Likely	Pessimistic
A	—	5	10	15
B	—	3	8	13
C	—	6	7	8
D	B	1	2	3
E	A, C	9	11	13
F	D, E	5	6	7
G	D, E	1	3	5
H	F, G	1	3	5
I	G	2	4	6
J	H	4	6	8
K	H	1	1	1

a. Draw the network diagram for this project.
b. Determine the critical path and project duration.
c. Find a schedule that smooths the workload requirements without delaying project completion. Draw a Gantt chart for your schedule.

17. The information in Table 18.13 is available about a large project.

   a. Determine the critical path and the expected completion time of the project.
   b. Plot the total project cost, starting from day 1 to the expected completion date of the project, assuming the earliest start times for each activity. Compare that result to a similar plot for the latest start times. What implication does the time differential have for cash flows and project scheduling?

18. Consider the project data shown in Table 18.14.
   a. What is the completion time of this project?
   b. What is the critical path?
   c. Suppose that your contract calls for completion of the project within 32 days. What is the probability you will meet that deadline?

TABLE 18.13

Activity	Immediate Predecessor(s)	Activity Time (days)	Activity Cost	Activity	Immediate Predecessor(s)	Activity Time (days)	Activity Cost
A	—	3	100	I	E	1	100
B	—	4	150	J	D, E	4	75
C	A	2	125	K	F, G	3	150
D	B	5	175	L	G, H, I	3	150
E	B	3	150	M	I, J	2	100
F	C, D	4	200	N	K, I, M	4	175
G	C	6	75	O	H, M	1	200
H	C, D, E	2	50	P	N, L, O	5	150

TABLE 18.14

Activity	Immediate Predecessor(s)	Time Estimates (wk)		
		Optimistic	Most Likely	Pessimistic
A	—	1	2	3
B	A	2	4	6
C	—	3	6	12
D	A, C	2	6	10
E	B	2	4	8
F	B, C	3	6	9
G	D, F	1	2	4
H	E	3	5	9
I	D, F	4	6	10
J	G, I, K	1	1	2
K	H	2	3	6
L	G, I	1	2	3
M	J	4	7	10
N	L	5	6	7
O	K, M, N	1	2	5

SELECTED REFERENCES

Aquilano, N. J., and D. E. Smith, "A Formal Set of Algorithms for Project Scheduling with Critical Path Scheduling–Material Requirements Planning," *Journal of Operations Management,* vol. 1, no. 2 (November 1980), pp. 57–67.

Britney, R., "Bayesian Point Estimation and the PERT Scheduling of Stochastic Activities," *Management Science,* vol. 22, no. 9 (May 1976), pp. 938–948.

Davis, E. W., "Project Scheduling under Resource Constraints—Historical Review," *AIIE Transactions,* vol. 5, no. 4 (December 1973), pp. 297–311.

Fawcette, J. E., "Choosing Project Management Software," *Personal Computing,* vol. 8, no. 10 (October 1984), pp. 154–167.

Martin, C. C., *Project Management: How to Make It Work.* New York: AMACOM, a Division of American Management Associations, 1976.

Weist, J. D., "Heuristic Programs for Decision Making," *Harvard Business Review* (September–October 1966), pp. 129–143.

Weist, J. D., and F. K. Levy, *A Management Guide to PERT/CPM,* 2nd ed. Englewood Cliffs, N.J.: Prentice-Hall, 1977.

CHAPTER

19

QUALITY CONTROL

 Chapter Outline

How can we devise a system to monitor quality reliability and to help us identify the sources of problems?

Of the various acceptance sampling methods available, which one can we best use in a given situation?

What trade-offs are involved if we use attribute measurements instead of variable measurements of quality?

What are the implications of our narrowing the control limits in a process control chart?

Where should we put our inspection stations?

hapter 3 addressed the concept of quality management, focusing on the prevention of quality problems, as well as the cost implications of poor quality. We stressed the need for customer involvement and feedback and for enlisting all parts of the organization in the quality effort. In essence, we discussed how to develop a plan of action. Now we address how to get the information needed to assess whether the plan is being executed properly and, if not, what should be corrected. The first step that management must take to arrive at the prescriptions of Chapter 3 is to adopt a philosophy of total quality control (TQC). This philosophy assumes that *all* employees in an organization are responsible for improving the quality of goods and services. Beginning with top management, TQC should permeate all levels of the organization.

Within operations, managers often rely on statistical quality control techniques such as those advocated by Armand Feigenbaum (see Chapter 3). In this chapter we examine two important aspects of TQC, statistical procedures for determining whether a batch of goods meets specifications and statistical procedures for monitoring quality characteristics during the production process. Finally we turn to the managerial decisions needed to implement these statistical methods.

TOTAL QUALITY CONTROL ▲

Lawrence Sullivan (1986), Ford Motor Company quality control manager, put TQC into perspective by identifying seven stages leading to **company-wide quality control (CWQC).** This approach strives to mobilize the entire work force around satisfying customer requirements for quality, price, and delivery. The first stage includes inspecting and auditing finished goods and solving quality problems as they arise. The second stage involves quality assurance during production—and in particular—using statistical methods to identify quality problems and improved machines to reduce the number of rejects. The third stage expands the effort to all departments. The fourth focuses on educating and training all employees, including managers, to create a greater awareness of and commitment to quality. Stages five and six begin to link product and process design in pursuit of better quality and lower internal costs. They also emphasize reducing process variability through continual improvements. Finally, in stage seven, customers' needs and wants are translated into operational terms.

MANAGERIAL PRACTICE 19.1

TQC at Hewlett-Packard

A decade after Hewlett-Packard began a joint venture with Yokogawa Electric Corporation of Japan, the partnership was still suffering from low product quality and poor profitability. Then in 1976, the recently appointed general manager, Kenzo Sasaoka, instituted a total quality control pilot program on one production line. Statistical methods of quality control were the backbone of the new approach. Subsequently, defect rates declined significantly, and management decided to include all levels of manufacturing, research and development, administration, and even sales in the program.

In 1982, the joint venture won the Deming Prize, Japan's most coveted industrial award (named after consultant W. Edwards Deming, the father of quality control in Japan). Since 1975, the company has been able to:

- Reduce costs 42 percent.
- Reduce defects 79 percent.
- Increase revenues per employee 120 percent.
- Increase market share 193 percent.
- Increase profits 244 percent.
- Reduce the time needed to get products to market by 33 percent.

Source: "The Push for Quality," *Business Week*, June 8, 1987, pp. 130–144.

Generally, TQC incorporates the first three or four stages outlined by Sullivan. The remaining stages are needed to achieve CWQC. Even though TQC has been described as a starting point for CWQC, it has by itself proven to be a successful tool for competitive effectiveness. Managerial Practice 19.1 shows how Hewlett-Packard used TQC to advantage.

In this chapter, we give special attention to the statistical methods that have proved so helpful in analyzing and diagnosing quality problems. Our focus is on Sullivan's stages one and two. (We covered the other stages in Chapter 3.) In stage one, managers base accept or reject decisions on the quality of a sample of finished goods. In stage two, managers monitor quality during production.

ACCEPTANCE SAMPLING ▲

Management can assess the quality of goods in one of two ways. The first is to take a *random sample* of adequate size from a batch of goods and assume that this sample represents the quality of all the items. **Acceptance sampling** is a statistical procedure used to determine whether a batch of goods conforms to

At Hewlett-Packard, a coordinate measuring machine linked to a computer is used in one aspect of quality control. The machine simultaneously measures three dimensions, the x-axis, y-axis, and the hole diameter, insuring a representative accuracy of .00001.

specifications. It provides a systematic method for making accept or reject decisions about the overall quality of a large batch of incoming items. Sampling is appropriate when inspection costs are a major concern, as they are in many firms. These costs may be high because of the special knowledge and skills and expensive equipment required to perform tests. Moreover, sampling is necessary *regardless of inspection cost* when tests are destructive, that is, when testing product life—as for a light bulb or automobile tire—requires destroying the product in order to judge its quality.

The alternative is *complete inspection*, requiring the inspection of each unit for quality. Operations uses this approach when the cost of passing a defective item is high relative to the cost of inspection. For example, suppliers of components for the space shuttle project check each component many times before shipping them to a contractor. In such a situation the cost of failure—injury and death—greatly exceeds the cost of inspection. Nonetheless, complete inspection won't uncover all defects. Inspector fatigue or imperfect testing methods may allow some defects to pass unnoticed. The cost of defects usually isn't as high as for the space shuttle, and a well-conceived sampling plan can approach the same degree of protection as complete inspection.

Quality Measurement

In Chapter 3 we defined quality for the producer of goods or services as conformance to specifications. We can measure conformance to specifications in two ways. One way is to use **attributes**, the characteristics of a product that can be quickly checked for acceptable quality. This method allows operations to make a simple yes–no decision for each item in the sample. Operations often checks attributes when quality specifications are complex and the question is whether the unit as a whole is defective. This is the case with a radio: If it does not play when turned on, the inspector sends it to the repair department to find out what is wrong. Some examples of attributes include color (paint on a refrigerator), taste (wine), or smell (food at a restaurant).

The other way to measure conformance to specifications is to use **variables**, that is, characteristics such as weight, length, volume, or time that can be measured on a continuous scale. For example, operations can weigh a box of cereal and plot the results to determine whether the product adheres to specifications (within the allowable tolerance) and identify differences in weight from sample to sample. Sampling plans based on variables also help operations assess problems with the production process being used.

Managerial Parameters

The procurement of materials involves two parties: the producer (or supplier) and the consumer (or buyer). Acceptance-sampling plans provide decision guidelines for the consumer that limit the risk of rejecting good quality materials or accepting bad quality materials. Consequently, it is the consumer, sometimes in conjunction with the producer, who specifies the parameters of the plan.*

Management should specify two levels of quality when designing an acceptance-sampling plan. The first is the **acceptable quality level (AQL),** or the quality level acceptable to the consumer. This is the quality level that the producer of the item aims for and the consumer typically states in a contract or purchase order. For example, a contract might call for a quality level of one defective unit in 1000, or an AQL of 0.001. The probability of rejecting a lot with AQL quality is called the **producer's risk (α),** or the risk the sampling plan will fail to verify an acceptable lot's quality and thus reject it. Most often the producer's risk is set at 0.05, or 5 percent.

Although producers are interested in low risk, they often have no control over the consumer's acceptance-sampling plan. Fortunately, the consumer is also interested in a low producer's risk because sending good materials back to the producer (1) disrupts the consumer's production process and increases the likelihood of shortages in materials, (2) adds unnecessarily to the lead time for finished products, and (3) creates poor relations with the producer.

The second level of quality is the **lot tolerance proportion defective (LTPD)**, or the worst level of quality that the consumer will accept. Recognizing the high cost of defects, operations managers have become more cautious about accepting materials of poor quality from suppliers (see Chapter 3). Thus sampling plans now tend to have lower LTPD values than in the past. The probability of accepting a lot with LTPD quality is the **consumer's risk (β).** A common value for the consumer's risk is 0.10, or 10 percent.

Table 19.1, on p. 728, summarizes the decisions that managers make with regard to acceptance sampling.

The Single-Sampling Plan

Let's now turn to a simple attribute plan: the **single-sampling plan**.† As its name implies, this method involves a decision to accept or reject a lot based on the results of one random sample from the lot. To begin, we let

n = sample size, randomly selected from the lot to be judged

c = acceptable number of defective items in the sample

d = actual number of defective items found in the sample

---

*Any company can be both a producer and a consumer. A company can produce goods that are purchased by another company, and it can consume raw materials supplied by another company.

†Single-sampling plans can also be devised for variables.

TABLE 19.1 Decisions in Acceptance Sampling	
Decision	**Comments**
Sampling versus complete inspection	The trade-off of inspection cost versus the potential cost of passing a defective item is important. Destructive testing requires a sampling plan. Fatigue and the monotony of the testing procedure should be considered.
Attribute versus variable measures	Attribute measures involve a simple yes–no decision about a quality characteristic. Variable measures involve measurement of quality characteristics of an item on a continuous scale to quantify the amount of deviation from specifications.
If sampling is chosen:	
Acceptable quality level (AQL); producer's risk (α) Lot tolerance proportion defective (LTPD); consumer's risk (β)	These parameters quantify risks to the producer and the consumer. They provide the basis for determining the specifics of a sampling plan.
Design of the sampling plan	The design is derived from the specification of AQL, α, LTPD, and β.

The procedure is to take a random sample of size n from the lot and inspect each item. If $d \leq c$, the inspector accepts the lot; if $d > c$ the inspector rejects the lot.

Operating Characteristic Curves.   A graphic display of the performance of a sampling plan, as expressed by the probability of accepting the lot for a range of lot proportion defectives, is called an **operating characteristic (OC) curve.** It describes how well a sampling plan discriminates between good and bad lots. Undoubtedly, every manager wants a plan that accepts lots with AQL or better quality 100 percent of the time and accepts lots with worse than AQL quality 0 percent of the time. No sampling plan can guarantee this level of performance; inspection of the entire lot is the only way to guarantee it. Consequently, managers are left with choosing a sample size n and an acceptance level c to achieve a given level of performance as specified by AQL, α, LTPD, and β.

Suppose that an analyst has a sample size and acceptance level for a single-sampling plan. How does she draw the OC curve for that plan? The procedure makes use of the cumulative Poisson exponential probability curves in Appendix 4 to get P_a, the probability of acceptance.* To find the value of P_a, the analyst would

1. select a value for p, the lot proportion defective;
2. multiply p by the sample size n;
3. find the value of np along the horizontal axis of the chart;
4. move up the chart to the curve for the appropriate value of c; and
5. move horizontally to the left-hand side of the chart and read the value for P_a from the vertical axis.

APPLICATION 19.1

The Mini-Kar Company manufactures replicas of Formula 1 race cars for use at miniature grand-prix tracks in amusement parks. John Birns, quality assurance manager, just received word that a shipment of 3000 wheel rims arrived in the receiving department yesterday. Operations must inspect these rims before sending them to the production floor. The sampling plan calls for a sample size n of 50 and an acceptance level c of 1. The contract calls for an acceptable quality level of one defective rim per 100 and the lot tolerance proportion defective is six defective rims per 100.

1. Calculate the OC curve for this plan.
2. Determine the producer's risk and the consumer's risk for the plan.

Let $p = 0.01$. Then multiply p by n and get $50(0.01) = 0.50$. Locate 0.50 on the horizontal axis of the Poisson chart in Appendix 4. Move up to the curve for $c = 1$ and over to the vertical axis. Read $P_a = 0.91$ (approximately). You can repeat this process for a range of p values. The accompanying table contains the remaining values for the OC curve. Note that the plan provides a producer's risk of 9 percent and a consumer's risk of 20 percent. Both values are higher than the usually acceptable values for plans of this sort. Figure 19.1 shows the curve and the producer's and consumer's risks.

---

*You can also use Appendix 4 to find n. Start with P_a on the vertical axis. Move horizontally to the curve for the appropriate value of c. Then find the value of np along the horizontal axis and divide it by p.

Values for the Operating Characteristic Curve with $n = 50$ and $c = 1$

Proportion Defective (p)	Value of np	Probability of c or Less Defects (P_a)	Comments
0.01 (AQL)	0.5	0.910	$\alpha = 0.09$ (or $1.00 - 0.91$)
0.02	1.0	0.740	
0.03	1.5	0.560	
0.04	2.0	0.410	
0.05	2.5	0.275	
0.06 (LTPD)	3.0	0.200	$\beta = 0.20$
0.07	3.5	0.130	
0.08	4.0	0.090	
0.09	4.5	0.060	
0.10	5.0	0.040	

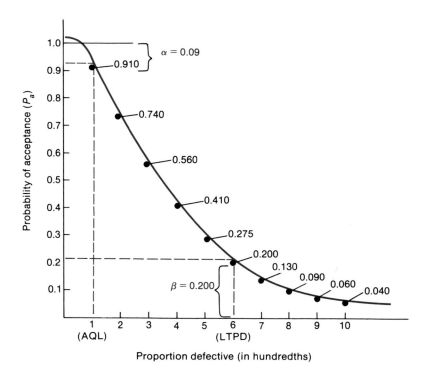

FIGURE 19.1   OC Curve for a Single-Sampling Plan with $n = 50$ and $c = 1$

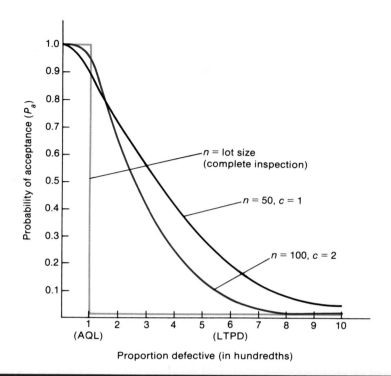

FIGURE 19.2   OC Curves for Two Different Sample Sizes

The Mini-Kar example raises the question of how to change the sampling plan to avoid rejecting more good lots and accepting more bad lots than management might want. How should n and c be changed?

Let's see how n and c affect the shape of the OC curve. To aid the discussion we define the *acceptance proportion* as the ratio of c to n, or c/n. Upon examination of the sample, if the sample proportion defective is less than or equal to the acceptance proportion, the inspector accepts the lot. Now let's compare the Mini-Kar plan of $n = 50$ and $c = 1$ to another plan where $n = 100$ and $c = 2$. The acceptance proportion remains the same (or $1/50 = 2/100 = 0.02$), but the sample size increases. Figure 19.2 shows the OC curves for these two plans and the complete-inspection curve for purposes of comparison. As the sample size increases—holding the acceptance proportion constant—the sampling plan becomes more discriminating between good and bad lots. Note that the producer's risk (α) and the consumer's risk (β) are reduced. Thus larger samples reduce the probabilities of making the wrong decision. The ultimate, of course, is complete inspection but, as we have said, the cost of complete inspection may well outweigh its benefits. Consequently, managers are often left with sampling and the risks of making a bad decision.

Now suppose that we change the acceptance proportion. Let's compare the plan having $n = 100$ and $c = 2$ to a plan having $n = 100$ and $c = 4$. The acceptance proportion is 0.02 in the former, and 0.04 in the latter. Figure 19.3 compares the OC curves for these two plans. Note that as we increase the acceptance proportion—holding sample size constant—the producer's risk (α) drops but the consumer's risk (β) rises. This result makes sense intuitively because increasing the acceptance proportion—holding sample size constant—only makes it easier for a good lot to pass inspection. However, it makes it easier for a bad lot to pass, as well. Table 19.2 summarizes the effects of n and c on the OC curve.

Finding the Best Single-Sampling Plan.   The best single-sampling plan is the one that meets the desired producer's and consumer's risk levels with the smallest sample size. One way to find the best plan is to start with values for n and c and incrementally adjust them using the guidelines in Table 19.2. For each

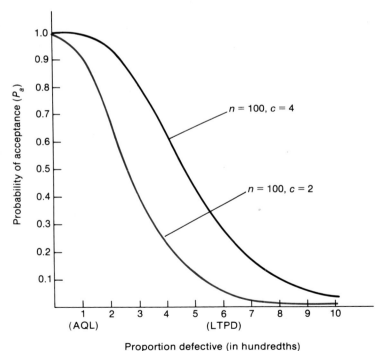

FIGURE 19.3   OC Figures for Two Different Acceptance Proportions

TABLE 19.2 Effects of *n* and *c* on OC Curves

Sampling Plan Changes		OC Curve Changes	
Acceptance Proportion	Sample Size	Producer's Risk (α)	Consumer's Risk (β)
Unchanged	Increases	Decreases	Decreases
Unchanged	Decreases	Increases	Increases
Increases	Unchanged	Decreases	Increases
Decreases	Unchanged	Increases	Decreases

increment, we could calculate α and β with the help of Appendix 4 and compare them to the desired values. This approach might yield a good plan, but it also might be time-consuming.

Alternatively, we could use a table such as Table 19.3 to get close (in many cases close enough) to the best plan where α and β take on the usual values of 5 percent and 10 percent, respectively. The upper number in each cell is the sample size (n) and the lower number is the acceptance level (c). Table 19.3 only accommodates a maximum acceptance level of 15, although it could be expanded to any acceptance level. The single-sampling plan in each cell is designed for the *largest* AQL in the range for that row, given the LTPD for that column. This configuration ensures that the producer's risk will not exceed 5 percent for any AQL in the range, but it may require a larger sample size than necessary for some AQLs at the lower end of the range. All tabular values meet the consumer's risk of 10 percent.

Let's return to the Mini-Kar example. What is the best single-sampling plan? From Table 19.3, with AQL = 1 percent and LTPD = 6 percent, the plan would be $n = 111$ and $c = 3$. Note in Fig. 19.3 that the plan with $n = 100$ and $c = 4$ has a producer's risk of almost zero and a consumer's risk of approximately 28 percent. We also know from Table 19.2 that reducing the acceptance proportion—holding n constant—increases the producer's risk and reduces the consumer's risk. This is the direction we want to go. The recommended plan of $n = 111$ and $c = 3$ takes us in that direction.

Average Outgoing Quality.   We have shown how to choose the best sample size and acceptance number given the AQL, α, LTPD, and β parameters, but the performance of the single-sampling plan may not yet be what we want. We still have not checked the plan's **average outgoing quality (AOQ)**, which is the expected proportion of defects that the plan will allow to pass. To calculate the *AOQ*, we assume that if the lot is rejected, all defective items in the lot will be replaced with good items. All defective items in the sample are replaced, as well, if the lot is accepted. With these assumptions, the equation for *AOQ*,

TABLE 19.3   **Single-Sampling Table for $\alpha = 0.05$ and $\beta = 0.10$***

AQL (%)	LTPD									
	1.0	2.0	3.0	4.0	5.0	6.0	7.0	8.0	9.0	10.0
0.05 – 0.19	532 2	195 1	130 1	97 1	78 1	65 1	33 0	29 0	26 0	23 0
0.20 – 0.39	1299 8	334 3	177 2	97 1	78 1	65 1	56 1	49 1	43 1	39 1
0.40 – 0.59		464 5	223 3	133 2	106 2	89 2	56 1	49 1	43 1	39 1
0.60 – 0.79		711 9	309 5	167 3	106 2	89 2	76 2	67 2	43 1	39 1
0.80 – 0.99			392 7	200 4	134 3	111 3	76 2	67 2	59 2	53 2
1.00 – 1.19			514 10	263 6	160 4	111 3	95 3	67 2	59 2	53 2
1.20 – 1.39			671 14	294 7	186 5	133 4	95 3	84 3	59 2	53 2
1.40 – 1.59				385 10	211 6	155 5	114 4	84 3	74 3	67 3
1.60 – 1.79				474 13	260 8	176 6	133 5	100 4	74 3	67 3
1.80 – 1.99					308 10	196 7	133 5	100 4	89 4	67 3
2.00 – 2.19					356 12	217 8	150 6	116 5	89 4	80 4

*Table values are based on the Poisson approximation to the binomial distribution. Shaded cells represent plans where c must be greater than 15 or where there is an impossible situation, such as AQL greater than LTPD.

expressed as the proportion defective, is

$$AOQ = \frac{p(P_a)(N - n)}{N}$$

where p = true proportion defective of the lot
P_a = probability of accepting the lot
N = lot size
n = sample size

AQL (%)		LTPD								
	1.0	2.0	3.0	4.0	5.0	6.0	7.0	8.0	9.0	10.0
2.20 – 2.39					426 15	257 10	168 7	132 6	103 5	80 4
2.40 – 2.59						296 12	203 9	147 7	117 6	93 5
2.60 – 2.79						336 14	220 10	162 8	117 6	93 5
2.80 – 2.99							254 12	178 9	131 7	105 6
3.00 – 3.19							288 14	193 10	144 8	118 7
3.20 – 3.39								222 12	158 9	118 7
3.40 – 3.59								237 13	171 10	130 8
3.60 – 3.79								266 15	184 11	142 9
3.80 – 3.99									211 13	154 10
4.00 – 4.19									237 15	166 11
4.20 – 4.39										190 13
4.40 – 4.59										213 15

Not knowing the proportion defective before the inspection process begins, the analyst can use the equation for *AOQ* to estimate the performance of the plan over a range of possible proportion defectives. The maximum value of the average outgoing quality over all possible values of the proportion defective is called the average outgoing quality limit (*AOQL*). If the *AOQL* seems too high, the parameters of the plan must be modified until an acceptable *AOQL* is achieved.

APPLICATION 19.2

Calculate the average outgoing quality limit for the Mini-Kar single-sampling plan with $n = 111$, $c = 3$, and $N = 3000$. Use Appendix 4 to estimate the probabilities of acceptance for values of the proportion defective from 0.01 to 0.10.

Solution

The following table contains the calculations for the *AOQ* for each value of the proportion defective. For demonstration purposes we have used only selected values for p. Based on the results shown in the table, the *AOQL* is 0.0162, or 1.62 percent defectives, when the lot proportion defective is 0.03. Trying more values of p between 0.02 and 0.04 would result in a more precise estimate of *AOQL*. Note how the average outgoing quality improves dramatically as the proportion defective of the lot increases. The reason is that as p gets large the probability is high that the lot will be rejected and all the defective wheel rims replaced with good ones. Management does not know the actual proportion defective of the lot of 3000 wheel rims, but it does know that the worst the plan will do is allow 1.62 percent defectives. If this performance is not acceptable, the sampling plan has to be revised.

Calculations for Average Outgoing Quality

(1)	(2)	(3)	(4)	(5)
Proportion Defective (p)	$(np)*$	Probability of Acceptance P_a†	$\dfrac{N - n}{N}$	Average Outgoing Quality (*AOQ*) (1) × (3) × (4)
0.01	1.11	0.970	0.963	0.0093
0.02	2.22	0.820	0.963	0.0158
0.03	3.33	0.560	0.963	0.0162
0.04	4.44	0.350	0.963	0.0135
0.05	5.55	0.200	0.963	0.0096
0.06	6.66	0.100	0.963	0.0058
0.07	7.77	0.050	0.963	0.0034
0.08	8.88	0.020	0.963	0.0015
0.09	9.99	0.010	0.963	0.0009
0.10	11.10	0.004	0.963	0.0004

*Column (1) times 111.

†Column (3) is estimated from the chart in Appendix 4, with $c = 3$. First, locate the Column 2 value on the horizontal axis. Then, move up the chart to the curve for $c = 3$. Finally, move horizontally to the vertical axis on the left and read the value for P_a.

Other Attribute-Sampling Plans

The single-sampling plan is the simplest of acceptance sampling plans. Other plans that may be appropriate under certain conditions include the double-sampling plan and the sequential-sampling plan.

Double-Sampling Plan. In a **double-sampling plan** management specifies two lot sizes (n_1 and n_2) and two acceptance levels (c_1 and c_2). The procedure is as follows:

1. Take a random sample of size n_1 and determine d_1, the number of defectives in the sample.
2. If $d_1 \leq c_1$, accept the lot; if $d_1 > c_2$, reject the lot.
3. If $c_1 < d_1 \leq c_2$, take another random sample of size n_2 and determine d_2, the number of defectives in the second sample.
4. If $(d_1 + d_2) \leq c_2$, accept the lot; otherwise, reject the lot.

A double-sampling plan can significantly reduce the costs of inspection relative to a single-sampling plan for lots having very low or very high proportion defectives. In these situations decisions are often based on the first sample, and n_1 is usually much smaller than the sample size in a single-sampling plan.

The Sequential-Sampling Plan. Extending the concept of the double-sampling plan to its limit yields the item-by-item **sequential-sampling plan**. Each time an item is inspected a decision is made to (1) reject the lot, (2) accept the lot, or (3) continue sampling, based on the cumulative results so far. The analyst can plot the total number of defectives against the cumulative sample size, and if the number of defectives is greater than a certain acceptance number (C_u), reject the lot. If the number is less than another acceptance number (C_L), the analyst accepts the lot. If the number is somewhere between the two, another item is inspected. Figure 19.4 illustrates a decision to reject a lot after examining the fortieth unit. Such charts can be easily designed with the help of statistical tables.*

The average number of items inspected (ANI) in the sequential sampling plan is generally lower than that for any other form of acceptance sampling. Achieving low levels of ANI is important because the fewer the items inspected, the lower the costs of inspection will be. For extreme values of the proportion defective, no other plan with a comparable OC curve will have a lower ANI. However, it is possible, although unlikely, that a sequential-sampling plan will have a larger ANI than a comparable single- or double-sampling plan for intermediate values of the proportion defective. In general, the sequential-

---

*Statistical tables can be found in a publication of the Statistical Research Group, Columbia University, *Sequential Analysis of Statistical Data: Applications*. New York: Columbia University Press, 1945.

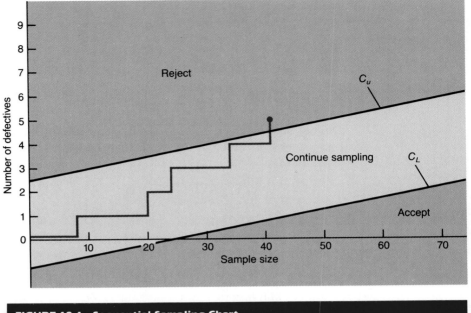

FIGURE 19.4 Sequential-Sampling Chart

sampling plan may reduce *ANI* to 50 percent of that required by a comparable single-sampling plan and consequently save substantial inspection costs.

The discussion of acceptance-sampling plans has focused on the specific item, or product, as in stage 1 of Sullivan's progression toward companywide quality control. We now turn our attention to stage 2, the process.

STATISTICAL PROCESS CONTROL METHODS ▲

Statistical process control (SPC) is used to monitor quality characteristics during the production process. The several SPC methods are useful in (1) measuring the current quality of goods or services, and (2) detecting whether the process itself has changed in a way that will affect quality. Regardless of the specific method used, the basic procedure is generally the same. A random sample is taken from a quantity of items (or a lot), and the quality characteristic is measured. If the sample measurement is found to be outside an *upper control limit (UCL)* or a *lower control limit (LCL)*, the process is checked for the cause (such as a faulty machine setting, an inexperienced operator, or poor raw materials).*

The reason for upper and lower control limits is that no two items or services can be produced *exactly* alike. The Harley-Davidson Motor Company

---

*Process industries such as paper, chemical, and oil refining use process control equipment that continuously monitors the production process. We discuss sampling methods only in this chapter.

uses statistical process control to detect abnormal variations, as described in Managerial Practice 19.2. For example, Harley-Davidson cylinder heads may have a dimension specification of 9.842 centimeters. However, not every cylinder head will have precisely that dimension, so a tolerance of, say, 0.01 cm is permitted. Although manufacturers would like to reduce process variation, it is to be expected. The question addressed by SPC is whether observed variations are abnormal or normal. Setting a *UCL* or an *LCL* allows detection of abnormal variation. This, in turn, can lead to a determination of whether the abnormal variation is being caused by people, machines, or materials, and correction of the problem.

MANAGERIAL PRACTICE 19.2 ▲

Statistical Process Control at Work

Harley-Davidson uses "statistical operator control (SOC)" to maintain process control of quality at its engine and transmission facility. In the SOC method, every employee takes individual responsibility for quality by using a systematic analysis of components at various stages during the manufacturing process. Statistics are used to identify variations in a process and thus pinpoint items that need tighter controls and improvement. Many of the operators along the production line take measurements at their work stations on a regular basis and plot the results on a chart. When the chart lines move outside the allowable tolerance, the operator trouble-shoots the source of the problem. Thus SOC is a tool for achieving tighter tolerances because processes are controlled better.

Source: Harley-Davidson Motor Company, 1988.

Harley-Davidson uses statistical operator control (SOC) to achieve tighter tolerances in their manufacturing processes. An operator on the cylinder head line measures parts on a regular basis and charts the results.

TABLE 19.4   Attributes in the Banking Industry

Attribute	Population
Wrong account number recorded	Total number of deposits
Nonendorsed deposits	Total number of deposits
Missing items	Total number of statements
Stop-payment transaction incorrect	Total stop-payment transactions
Misfiled items	Total checks and debits
Wrong statement sent	Total number of statements
Incorrect adjustments	Total number of statements

Source: C. A. Aubrey and L. A. Eldridge, "Banking on High Quality," *Quality Progress,* vol. 14, no. 12 (December 1981), pp. 14–19.

Control Charts for Attributes

A commonly used control chart for attributes is the *p*-chart for the population proportion defective. The method involves selecting a random sample and inspecting each item in it. The sample proportion defective is equal to the number of defective units divided by the sample size. The analyst plots the sample proportion defective on a chart and compares it to the upper and lower control limits to determine whether the process is out of control. Table 19.4 shows some attributes used in the banking industry for which *p*-charts have been used.

Because sampling with attributes involves a yes–no decision, the underlying statistical distribution is the binomial distribution. However, the distribution of *estimates* of the population proportion defective calculated from each sample (number of defectives divided by the sample size) will tend to be normal by the central limit theorem, with a standard deviation of

$$\sigma_p = \sqrt{\frac{\bar{p}(1 - \bar{p})}{n}}$$

where n is the sample size and $\bar{p}$ is the historical average population proportion defective. We can use this measure of the variation to arrive at the following upper and lower control limits for a *p*-chart.

$$UCL = \bar{p} + z\sqrt{\frac{\bar{p}(1 - \bar{p})}{n}} \quad \text{and} \quad LCL = \bar{p} - z\sqrt{\frac{\bar{p}(1 - \bar{p})}{n}}$$

where $\bar{p}$ is the process average, or central line of the chart, and z is the number of standard deviations from the process average. Typically, the upper and lower control limits are set at ± 3 standard deviations ($z = 3$), allowing 99.74 percent of the variation to fall within the control limits. (See the normal probability table in Appendix 3.) Thus the probability is very small (approximately one chance in 400) that a sample proportion defective that falls outside these limits will have come from a population with a mean proportion defective equal to $\bar{p}$. When a sample proportion defective does fall outside the control limits, the analyst concludes that there has been a change in the process to a different process average.

The operations manager of the booking services department of Hometown Bank is concerned about the number of wrong customer account numbers recorded by Hometown personnel. The historical proportion of wrong account numbers recorded (total number recorded divided by the total number of deposits) is 0.005. Although errors in recording account numbers are to be avoided, the historical proportion defective is considered reasonable and is useful as a benchmark for weekly performance comparisons. Each week a random sample of 2500 deposits is taken, and the number of incorrect account numbers is recorded. The results for the past 12 weeks are shown in the following table. Is the process out of control?

Observed Number of Wrong Account Numbers Recorded in 12 Samples of 2500 Each

Sample Number	Wrong Account Numbers	Proportion of Sample
1	15	0.0060
2	12	0.0048
3	19	0.0076
4	2	0.0008
5	19	0.0076
6	4	0.0016
7	24	0.0096
8	7	0.0028
9	10	0.0040
10	17	0.0068
11	15	0.0060
12	3	0.0012

Solution

In our example, $\bar{p} = 0.005$, so

$$UCL = 0.005 + 3\sqrt{\frac{0.005(0.995)}{2500}} = 0.00923$$

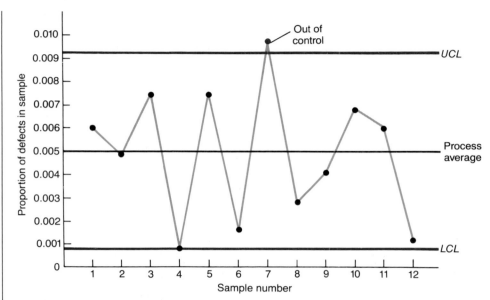

FIGURE 19.5   Control Chart for Wrong Account Numbers

and

$$LCL = 0.005 - 3\sqrt{\frac{0.005(0.995)}{2500}} = 0.00077$$

The control chart and the results obtained for the 12 samples are shown in Fig. 19.5. The manager can see that sample 7 exceeded the upper control limit. Thus she can say that the process is out of control and that the reasons for the poor performance that week should be determined. She might find that the account numbers were incorrectly entered into the computer by a trainee or that an encoding machine was defective. She would then have the problem corrected, returning the process to statistical control. There is but a slight chance that the manager might not find any assignable causes for the problem. Thus the p-chart provides a tool not only to measure product quality, but also to indicate when the process needs adjustment.

Control Charts for Variables

Two control charts for variables frequently used in tandem are the *range chart*, or **R-chart**, and the *average chart*, or **x̄-chart**. Recall that the term *variables* means that the quality characteristic to be controlled (such as distance, weight, or response time) is measured on a continuous scale. A sample is taken and two values are calculated: the sample mean of the quality characteristic and the range. The range is calculated by subtracting the smallest from the largest measurement in each sample. These values are used to develop an R-chart for the process variability and an $\bar{x}$-chart for the process average. Both the process variability and the process average must be in control before we can say that the process is in control.

Range Chart. The process variability must be in control before the analyst can construct a valid chart for the process average. The reason is that a measure of process variability is required to determine the control limits for the $\bar{x}$-chart. If the process variability is out of control, the control limits for the $\bar{x}$-chart will be incorrect.

The control limits for the R-chart are

$$UCL_R = D_4\bar{R} \quad \text{and} \quad LCL_R = D_3\bar{R}$$

where $\bar{R}$ is the average of several past R values (and the central line of the control chart), and D_3 and D_4 are constants that provide three standard deviation (3σ) limits for the range for a given sample size. Values for D_3 and D_4 are contained in Table 19.5.

Average Chart. When the process variability is in control, the analyst can construct an $\bar{x}$-chart to control the process average. The control limits for the $\bar{x}$-chart are

$$UCL_{\bar{x}} = \bar{\bar{x}} + A_2\bar{R} \quad \text{and} \quad LCL_{\bar{x}} = \bar{\bar{x}} - A_2\bar{R}$$

TABLE 19.5 Factors for Calculating 3σ Limits for x̄-Chart and R-Chart

Size of Sample (n)	Factor for UCL and LCL for x̄-Charts (A₂)	Factor for LCL for R-Charts (D₃)	Factor for UCL for R-Charts (D₄)
2	1.880	0	3.267
3	1.023	0	2.575
4	0.729	0	2.282
5	0.577	0	2.115
6	0.483	0	2.004
7	0.419	0.076	1.924
8	0.373	0.136	1.864
9	0.337	0.184	1.816
10	0.308	0.223	1.777

Source: 1950 ASTM Manual on Quality Control of Materials, copyright © ASTM. Reprinted with permission.

where $\bar{\bar{x}}$ is the average of several past $\bar{x}$ values (and the central line of the control chart), or a target value that management has set for the process. The values for the constant A_2 provide three standard deviation (3σ) limits for the process average and are also contained in Table 19.5. Note that the control limits use the value of $\bar{R}$, which again is the reason for constructing the $\bar{x}$-chart *after* the process variability is in control.

APPLICATION 19.4 ▉▉▉▉

The management of West Allis Industries is concerned about the production of a special metal screw used by several of the company's largest customers. The diameter of the screw is critical. Historically, the process average $\bar{x}$ has been 0.500 in. and the average range has been 0.18 in. Data from the last five samples are shown in the accompanying table. The sample size is 4. Is the process in control?

Data for the R-Chart and x̄-Chart

Sample Number	Observations of Screw Diameter in Sample (in.)				Sample Average $\bar{x}$*	Sample Range $R^\dagger$
	1	2	3	4		
1	0.51	0.63	0.39	0.35	0.47	0.28
2	0.50	0.56	0.42	0.64	0.53	0.22
3	0.68	0.49	0.53	0.62	0.58	0.19
4	0.45	0.33	0.47	0.55	0.45	0.22
5	0.70	0.58	0.64	0.68	0.65	0.12

*The value of $\bar{x}$ is the sum of the observations in each sample divided by 4.
†The value of R is the difference between the largest and smallest observation in a sample. In sample 1, for example, $R = 0.63 - 0.35 = 0.28$.

Solution

The firm's analyst constructs the R-chart. Since the sample size is 4, Table 19.5 gives him the control-limit factors to use in calculating the control limits for the R-chart:

$$UCL_R = D_4\bar{R} = 2.282(0.18) = 0.411 \text{ in}$$

and

$$LCL_R = D_3\bar{R} = 0(0.18) = 0 \text{ in}$$

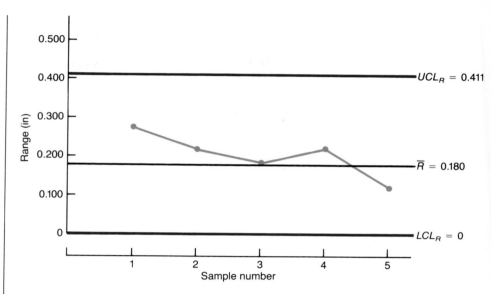

FIGURE 19.6 Range Chart for the Metal Screw

The value of the range for each sample in the data table is then plotted on the R-chart, as shown in Fig. 19.6. None of the sample ranges fall outside the control limits. Consequently, the analyst can say that process variability is in control. If any of the sample ranges had fallen outside the limits (the range can never be negative, of course), he would have had to search for the cause of the excessive variability.

The analyst can now proceed to construct the $\bar{x}$-chart for the process average. Using $\bar{x} = 0.500$ and Table 19.5, he finds that the control limits for the $\bar{x}$-chart are

$$UCL_{\bar{x}} = \bar{\bar{x}} + A_2\bar{R} = 0.500 + 0.729(0.18) = 0.631 \text{ in}$$

and

$$LCL_{\bar{x}} = \bar{\bar{x}} - A_2\bar{R} = 0.500 - 0.729(0.18) = 0.369 \text{ in}$$

The values for $\bar{x}$ for the last five samples (from the data table) are shown on the $\bar{x}$-chart in Fig. 19.7. The value of sample 5 falls above the upper control limit, indicating that the process average is out of control and that the analyst should look for assignable causes. Perhaps he could use a fishbone chart (as shown in Chapter 3) to help determine whether machines, operators, or materials are at fault.

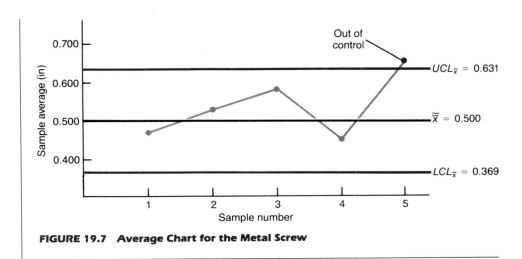

FIGURE 19.7 Average Chart for the Metal Screw

MANAGERIAL CONSIDERATIONS IN STATISTICAL PROCESS CONTROL ▲

The major decisions needed to implement statistical process control include sample size choice, control limit spread, and inspection station location. We now turn to some of the managerial considerations involved in making these decisions.

Sample Size

The ultimate in process control is to test each item to make sure that it satisfies design specifications. Often this is not possible, particularly when the test involves the destruction of the item or the test is very technical and time-consuming. Consequently, the choice of sample size has economic as well as control implications.

p-Charts versus *x̄*-Charts.   Earlier we said that *p*-charts are based on attributes and are useful in situations where quality can be easily checked and the acceptance decision is a simple yes or no. The ease of measuring quality attributes (compared to variables) is accompanied by the requirement for larger sample sizes. The magnitude of the difference varies, but an attribute control chart may require 4–100 times the sample size of that required for a variable control chart. Typical *x̄*-charts require sample sizes of 4 or 5, whereas the sample size for a *p*-chart must be large enough to detect at least one defective item on the average. For example, the population proportion defective in our banking services example was 0.005, requiring a bare minimum sample size of 200. The reason that we can use smaller sample sizes for $\bar{x}$-charts is that we can derive much more information from the variables. Consequently, unless variables take far more effort than attributes, variable control charts are usually less expensive to utilize.

Degree of Control. Another consideration is the effect of sample size on degree of control. Recall that the standard deviation for the p-chart has n in the denominator. Also note that in Table 19.5 the value of A_2 decreases as the sample size increases. The relationship implies that, as the sample size increases, the control *limits* on the control charts move closer to the central line, or target process average. Thus the analyst is more likely to detect a shift in the process average. For example, when we use an $\bar{x}$-chart, sample sizes of 4 or 5 are usually sufficient to detect a relatively large shift in the process average (say, two standard deviations). However, we would need a sample size of $3-5$ times larger to detect shifts of only one standard deviation. Here again, management must balance the cost of inspection against the cost of not detecting a shift in the process average.

Homogeneity. The sample should represent subgroups of output that are as homogeneous as possible. When significant deviations occur and assignable causes can be identified, the causes should show up as differences between subgroups and not as differences between members of a subgroup. Consider, for example, a two-shift operation, with each shift capable of producing 500 units. Choosing a sample size of 2000 could mask one of the assignable causes of quality problems: differences in output quality by shift. It might be better in this case to take samples that are homogeneous by shift, so that management can determine whether the problems occur during one particular shift.

Japanese $n = 2$ Philosophy. Some Japanese companies reduce the sample size to only two units, regardless of the quality characteristic to be measured. For each lot produced, only the first unit and the last unit are inspected. The assumption is that, if production of the first and last units is under control, the intervening production is also under control. Even though the samples are not random, the method works well in repetitive manufacturing situations with small-lot production. Definite starting and ending points (discrete lot production) are needed, along with a process that, if it goes out of control during the production of the lot, will stay out of control until the end of the lot. Small-lot production is needed because, otherwise, a large number of defective items can be produced before the problem is detected.

Control Limit Spread

In our examples of control charts we used control limits that were three standard deviations from the central line. However, we could have chosen other control limits. Figure 19.8 shows the effects of changing z in a p-chart. As you can see, a change from $z = 3$ to $z = 2$ increases the probability of detecting a shift in the process average. But it also increases the probability of searching for an assignable cause when none exists. The choice of z would depend on

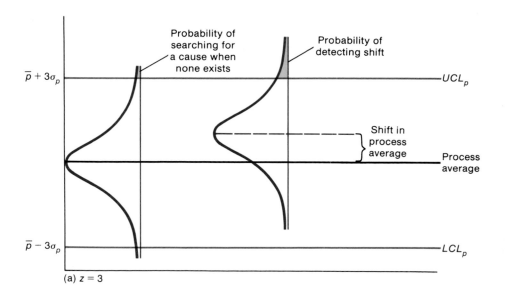

(a) $z = 3$

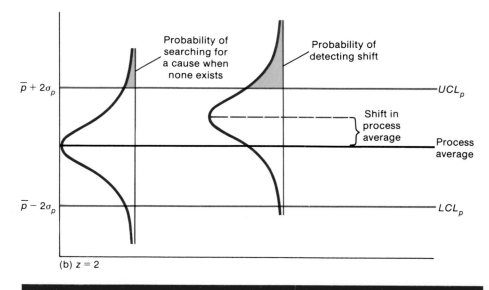

(b) $z = 2$

FIGURE 19.8   Effects of Changing z in a p-Chart

the cost of looking for assignable causes when none exists versus the cost of not detecting a shift. In general, charts with $z = 1.5$ or $z = 2$ are more economical than those with $z = 3$, if the operations manager can determine inexpensively and quickly whether something is wrong. If the cost of looking for the cause of a problem is high, charts with $z = 3$ or $z = 4$ might be more useful and economical.

Inspection Station Location

Before management can decide where to locate inspection stations, it must identify the aspects of quality important to the consumer and the key steps in the production process that affect those characteristics. A fishbone chart (see Chapter 3) is a good way of identifying these steps. They occur in three different stages of the total process: raw-material inputs, work-in-process, and finished goods or services.

The inspection of purchased materials is important to ensure the proper quality of the inputs to the production process. At this early stage of the process, various acceptance-sampling plans could be used (such as the ones we discussed earlier in this chapter).

Inspection is usually more complicated at the work-in-process stage. Conceivably, the operations manager could put an inspection station after each step in the process. However, this approach would be very costly because testing often requires highly skilled inspectors and/or expensive technology. A *zero-defects* program, which has the goal of not passing defective materials from one step in the process to the next, requires discipline in the work force but greatly reduces the need for inspection stations. In deciding on the number and location of inspection stations, the operations manager has to remember that quality cannot be inspected into the product; inspection can only detect that the process is not operating according to specifications and identify the need for corrective action. Thus even with a zero-defects program, some inspection stations would be needed. Using a fishbone chart or a process flow chart, an analyst can identify the steps in the process at which important quality characteristics should be checked. Quality should also be checked just prior to costly operations. The cost of inspecting materials at any location should be balanced against the cost of passing defective materials to the next step.

Final inspections are made after the product has been finished. In the case of manufacturing systems, the inspections are made just prior to stocking finished goods or shipping them to the customer. Product failures discovered at this point result in (1) scrapping the defective items or batch, (2) routing the defective items or batch to a previous step in the process for rework, or (3) routing the defective items or batch to a special area for diagnosis and correction of the defects. Final inspections in service systems involve similar considerations; however, in many cases, the customer plays a major role in the inspection process. Table 19.6 contains some examples of final inspection procedures used in manufacturing and service processes.

TABLE 19.6   Examples of Final Inspection Procedures

● Semiconductor manufacturing	Semiconductors are tested for their conformance to specifications. Those that do not meet the specifications but are above some minimal performance level can be sold as a different, lower grade product. Those that fall below the minimal performance level are scrapped.
● Plastic bottle manufacturing	Plastic bottles that do not conform to specifications on wall thickness or neck diameter are shredded and reused as raw material in the production of new bottles.
● Glue manufacturing	Batches of glue are pumped from the reactor to holding vessels where they are checked for viscosity, percentage solids, pH level, and amount of grit. A chemist checks the batch and may order adding water, removing water, or filtering the batch in the holding vessel.
● Automotive repair	The mechanic test-drives the car before returning it to the customer. If problems remain, previous repair procedures may have to be repeated. The customer may also request some rework.
● TV repair	The TV repairperson tests the TV before returning it to the customer. Premature failure of replaced components results in the customer returning the set for more repair.
● Hair styling	The hairstylist works with the customer until the customer is satisfied.
● Hotels	Most hotels have customer-survey cards in each room, allowing the customer to grade the quality of service provided by the hotel.

SOLVED PROBLEMS

1. An inspection station has been installed between two production processes. The feeder process, when operating correctly, has an acceptable quality level of 0.03. The consuming process, which is expensive, has a specified lot tolerance proportion defective of 0.08. The feeding process produces in batch sizes and, if a batch is rejected by the inspector, the entire batch must be checked and the defective items reworked. Consequently, management wants no more than a 5 percent producer's risk and, because of the expensive process that follows, no more than a 10 percent chance of accepting a lot with 8 percent defectives or worse.

a. Determine the appropriate sample size (n) and acceptable number of defective items in the sample (c).

b. Calculate values and draw the OC curve for this inspection station.

c. What is the probability that a lot with 5 percent defectives will be rejected?

Solution

a. For AQL = 3 percent, LTPD = 8 percent, α = 0.05, and β = 0.10, Table 19.3 suggests use of

$$n = 193 \quad \text{and} \quad c = 10$$

b. Table 19.7 contains the data for the OC curve. Appendix 4 was used to estimate the probability of acceptance. Figure 19.9 shows the OC curve.

c. According to Table 19.7, the probability of accepting a lot with 5 percent defectives is 60 percent. Therefore, the probability that a lot with 5 percent defects will be rejected is 40 percent (or $100 - 60$).

TABLE 19.7

Proportion Defective (p)	Value of np	Probability of c or Less Defects (P_a)	Comments
0.01	1.93	1.000	
0.02	3.86	0.998	
0.03 (AQL)	5.79	0.960	α = 0.04
0.04	7.72	0.840	
0.05	9.65	0.600	
0.06	11.58	0.350	
0.07	13.51	0.230	
0.08 (LTPD)	15.44	0.100	β = 0.100
0.09	17.37	0.050	
0.10	19.30	0.010	

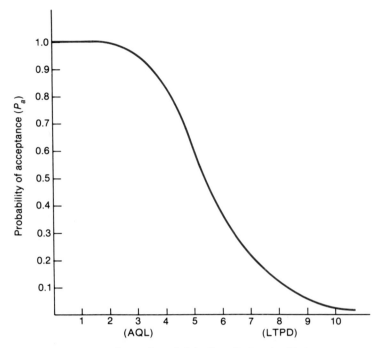

FIGURE 19.9

2. The data processing department of the Arizona Bank has 5 keypunch operators. Each day their supervisor verifies the accuracy of a random sample of 250 cards. A card containing one or more errors is considered defective and must be redone. The results of the last 25 samples are shown in Table 19.8.

   a. Based on this historical data, set up a p-chart using $z = 3$.

   b. Samples for the next four days showed:

Sample	Number of Defective Cards
26	17
27	15
28	22
29	21

What is the supervisor's assessment of the keypunch process likely to be? Explain.

TABLE 19.8

Sample	Number of Defective Cards	Sample	Number of Defective Cards
1	7	14	4
2	5	15	11
3	19	16	8
4	10	17	12
5	11	18	4
6	8	19	6
7	12	20	11
8	9	21	17
9	6	22	12
10	13	23	6
11	18	24	7
12	5	25	13
13	16	Total	250

Solution

a. From Table 19.8, the supervisor knows that the total number of defective cards is 250 out of a total sample of 6250 [or 25(250)]. Therefore, the central line of the chart is:

$$\bar{p} = \frac{250}{6250} = 0.04$$

The control limits are

$$UCL = \bar{p} + z\sqrt{\frac{\bar{p}(1 - \bar{p})}{n}}$$

$$= 0.04 + 3\sqrt{\frac{0.04(0.96)}{250}} = 0.077$$

and

$$LCL = \bar{p} - z\sqrt{\frac{\bar{p}(1 - \bar{p})}{n}}$$

$$= 0.04 - 3\sqrt{\frac{0.04(0.96)}{250}} = 0.003$$

Sample	Defects	Proportion
26	17	0.068
27	15	0.060
28	22	0.088
29	21	0.084

Samples 28 and 29 are out of control. The supervisor should look for the problem and, finding it, take corrective action.

3. The Watson Electric Company produces a certain brand of incandescent light bulb. The following data on the number of lumens for each light bulb were collected when the process was in control.

Sample	Observation			
	1	2	3	4
1	604	612	588	600
2	597	601	607	603
3	581	570	585	592
4	620	605	595	588
5	590	614	608	604

Since those data were collected, some new employees were hired. A new sample was taken and had the following readings: 570, 603, 623, and 583. Is the process still in control?

Solution

Sample	$\bar{x}$	R
1	601	24
2	602	10
3	582	22
4	602	32
5	604	24
Total	2991	112
Average	598.2	22.4

The R-chart control limits are

$$UCL_R = D_4\overline{R} = 2.282\ (22.4) = 51.12$$

$$LCL_R = D_3\overline{R} = 0(22.4) = 0$$

The operations manager first checks to see whether the variability is still in control based on the new data. The range is 53 (or $623 - 570$). This value is outside the upper control limit for the R-chart. Consequently, the process is not in control.

FORMULA REVIEW

1. Average outgoing quality:

$$AOQ = \frac{p(P_a)(N - n)}{n}$$

2. Sample standard deviation for attribute process control charts:

$$\sigma_p = \sqrt{\frac{\bar{p}(1 - \bar{p})}{n}}$$

3. Control limits for attribute process control charts:

$$UCL = \bar{p} + z\sqrt{\frac{\bar{p}(1 - \bar{p})}{n}}, \quad \text{and} \quad LCL = \bar{p} - z\sqrt{\frac{\bar{p}(1 - \bar{p})}{n}}$$

4. Control limits for variable process control charts:

$$UCL_R = D_4\bar{R} \quad \text{and} \quad LCL_R = D_3\bar{R}$$
$$UCL_{\bar{x}} = \bar{\bar{x}} + A_2\bar{R} \quad \text{and} \quad LCL_{\bar{x}} = \bar{\bar{x}} - A_2\bar{R}$$

CHAPTER HIGHLIGHTS

- Acceptance-sampling plans and statistical process control methods are useful for appraising the degree of quality performance and identifying where problems exist in quality reliability.

- Acceptance sampling is concerned with the decision to accept or reject a certain quantity of goods. The design of the acceptance-sampling process includes decisions about sampling versus complete inspection, attribute versus variable measures, AQL, α, LTPD, β, sample size, and the acceptable number of defective items in the sample.

- Sampling using attributes can be done with single-sampling, double-sampling, or sequential-sampling plans. The latter two have an advantage over single-sampling plans because the average sample size needed to make a decision is less when the lot proportion defective is either very low or very high. Management can select the best plan (choosing sample size n and acceptance number c) by using an operating characteristic curve.

- Statistical process control charts are useful for measuring the current quality generated by the process and for detecting whether the process has changed to the detriment of quality. The use of p-charts and $\bar{x}$-charts can help management identify abnormal variations in the process average. The presence of abnormal variations triggers a search for assignable causes. The use of R-charts can help management define abnormal variations in process variability.

- Process variability should be in control before process average control charts are constructed. The reason is that the average range is used in the calculation of control limits for process average control charts. Crucial decisions in the design of control charts are sample size, control limits, and inspection station location.

- The use of p-charts requires a larger sample size than does the use of $\bar{x}$-charts, but the measurement of attributes may be easier than the measurement of variables. Larger samples provide greater protection in detecting a shift in the process average than do smaller samples. Also, the sample should be homogeneous with respect to potential causes of quality problems.

- The central line of a control chart can be the average of past averages of the quality measurement or a management target related to product specifications. The spread in control limits affects the chances of detecting a shift in the process average or range, as well as the chances of searching for assignable causes when none exists.

- Inspection stations should be located at the point where incoming materials are received, at selected points in the process, and at the end of the process. The cost of inspection should be weighed against the cost of passing defective items downstream in the process and defective products to the customer.

KEY TERMS

STUDY QUESTIONS

1. Using sampling to determine conformance to quality specifications involves certain risks. What are they?

2. Explain the trade-offs that are made in choosing the sample size n and the acceptance number c in a single-sampling plan for attributes.

3. What are the considerations involved in choosing between sampling and complete inspections? Between variables and attributes?

4. How can an operating characteristic curve help management settle on the design parameters for a single-sampling plan?

5. For a given AQL and LTPD, what is the effect on α and β in a single-sampling plan of increasing the acceptance number c while holding the sample size n constant? Explain.

6. For a given AQL and LTPD, what is the effect on α and β in a single-sampling plan of increasing the sample size n while holding the acceptance number c constant? Explain.

7. Compare and contrast single-sampling plans, double-sampling plans, and sequential-sampling plans. What are the implications for inspection costs?

8. What is the rationale for having upper and lower control limits in process control charts?

9. What are the critical design parameters that must be specified for control charts? Are they interrelated? Explain.

10. What factors should be considered regarding inspection station location?

PROBLEMS

Review Problems

1. You are responsible for purchasing bearings under contract from a local supplier and must devise an appropriate acceptance sampling plan

for the bearings. Management has stated in the contract that the acceptable quality level is 2 percent defective. In addition, the lot tolerance proportion defective is 5 percent, the producer's risk is 5 percent, and the consumer's risk is 10 percent.

a. Specify an appropriate acceptance sampling plan that meets all these criteria.

b. Draw the OC curve for your plan. What is the resultant producer's risk?

c. Determine the *AOQL* for your plan. Assume the lot size is 5000.

2. The Lustre-Potion Shampoo Company purchases the label that is pasted on each bottle of shampoo it sells. The label contains the company logo, the name of the product, and directions for the product's use. Sometimes the printing on the label is blurred or the colors are not right. The company would like to design an acceptable sampling plan for the purchased item. The acceptable quality level is 24 defectives per 1000 labels and the lot tolerance proportion defective 0.08. Management would like to find a plan where the producer's risk is 0.05 or less and the consumer's risk is 0.10 or less.

a. Specify a plan that satisfies those directives.

b. What is the probability that a shipment with 5 percent defectives will be rejected by the plan?

c. Determine the *AOQL* for your plan. Assume the lot size is 1000 labels.

3. Your company supplies electronic components to a manufacturer of stereo equipment. The contract states that quality should be no worse than 0.15 percent defective, or 15 parts in 10,000. During negotiations, you found out that the manufacturer will use an acceptance sampling plan, with $n = 1000$, to test quality.

a. You feel strongly that the producer's risk (i.e., the probability that a good shipment will be sent back to you) should be no greater than 5 percent. What value for the acceptance level should you suggest?

b. You realize that your system's average performance has only been 20 parts in 10,000. Given $n = 1000$ and the acceptance level you suggested in (a), what is the probability that a shipment will be returned to you?

c. Given (b), suppose that you want only a 5 percent chance that your shipment will be returned to you. What acceptance level value should you have suggested in (a)? What is the producer's risk for that plan?

4. Consider Problem 3 again. If the manufacturer's lot tolerance proportion defective is 40 parts in 10,000, with a consumer's risk of 10 percent, what acceptance level value would the manufacturer want? What is the producer's risk? Use Table 19.2 and the manufacturer's desired acceptance level to propose a compromise to the supplier. (You need not design a new sampling plan.)

5. Consider a certain raw material for which a single-sampling plan using attributes is needed. The AQL is 0.008 and the LTPD is 0.040. Two plans have been proposed:

Plan 1	Plan 2
$n = 100$	$n = 200$
$c = 3$	$c = 6$

Are the two plans equivalent? Substantiate your response by determining the producer's and consumer's risk for each plan.

6. You presently have an acceptance-sampling plan where $n = 100$ and $c = 1$, but you are unsatisfied with its performance. The AQL is 0.01 and the LTPD is 0.05.

a. What are the producer's and consumer's risks for this plan?

b. Specify a plan that will decrease the producer's risk and increase the consumer's risk. Specify the new producer's and consumer's risks.

c. Compare the *AOQLs* for your plan and the old plan. Assume the lot size is 1000 units.

7. The Webster Chemical Company produces mastics and caulking for the construction industry. The product is blended in large mixers and then pumped into tubes and capped. The company is concerned with the possibility of underfilling the tubes, thereby short-changing the customer. Twenty samples of 150 tubes each had the number of underfilled tubes shown in Table 19.9.

a. Construct a *p*-chart for this situation. Use $z = 3$ and the historical average defective from Table 19.9 as the central line of the chart.

b. Comment on the process average proportion defective for the samples in Table 19.9.

Sample Number	Number of Underfilled Tubes	Sample Number	Number of Underfilled Tubes
1	12	12	20
2	16	13	4
3	8	14	8
4	24	15	16
5	20	16	8
6	4	17	24
7	16	18	8
8	12	19	16
9	28	20	12
10	8	Total	284
11	20		

8. The Emerald Dormer is a luxury hotel in Key West, Florida. The manager of the hotel was interested in the overall quality of service the hotel was providing to its customers. A unique customer survey system was developed to collect data and help the manager to make a judgment. Each customer was given a survey card and a blank envelope. The survey card contained a number of specific questions about various services and asked the customer to score the overall service on a scale from 0 to 100, with 100 considered excellent. The customer could fill out the card anonymously and put it in the envelope. If it was given to the desk clerk at checkout, the customer received a 5 percent discount on the bill. The program was very successful, and only a negligible number of customers ever turned in blank cards.

The manager of the hotel considered a score of 75 on the overall evaluation the breakpoint between acceptable and unacceptable service. Each week, 50 envelopes were picked at random, opened, and examined. If the overall score on a card was less than 75, the card was considered "defective." The manager felt that an average proportion defective of 0.15 meant that service was in control (that is, 85 percent of the customers thought that service was good or better).

  a. Specify the control limits of a p-chart for the manager of the hotel. As service is considered so important, $z = 2$ is desired. The cost of searching for service-quality prob-

lems is far outweighed by the cost of a shift in overall customer satisfaction with the service received.

  b. The following are the results of the past five weeks of sampling.

Sample	Score of < 75
March 1	12
March 8	3
March 15	18
March 22	21
March 29	10

Suppose that you are in charge of recording the results of the samples. What would you tell the manager about the overall service quality of the hotel? Would you make any recommendations?

9. The Stosh Motor Company manufactures bolts for its model X-350 high-performance racing engine. If defective, the bolts typically have damaged threads or improper diameters. A defect can be easily discovered by threading the bolt into a block of steel having a hole of correct threading and diameter. If a defective bolt is passed to the assembly line there is a chance that the threads in the engine block hole will be damaged or that the bolt may work itself loose during operation of the engine. The historical proportion defective average has been 0.02.

  a. Set up a p-chart for this process. Assume that management wants 99.7 percent of the normal variation to fall within the control limits. The sample size is 16.

  b. The following number of defects were found in the last five samples. Is there a need for concern?

Sample	Number of Bad Bolts
1	1
2	0
3	0
4	1
5	3

10. The Canine Gourmet Company produces delicious dog treats for canines with discriminating tastes. One particular treat, Super Breath, combines chlorophyl and retsin to form a breath sweetener most appreciated by people who own large dogs. Since the primary consumers of this product get violent if the boxes of Super Breath are underfilled, management would like to closely monitor the box filling line to make sure that the process is in control. The filling line is set for 680 grams in each box.

An inspector at the end of the filling line periodically selects a random sample of five boxes and weighs the contents. The historical range in the weight of each sample has averaged 15 grams, which is considered normal for this process.

a. Design an R-chart and an $\bar{x}$-chart for this process.
b. The results from the last four samples are

Sample	Average Weight (g)	Range (g)
1	684.3	10.6
2	690.2	29.6
3	673.4	14.2
4	691.8	19.4

Is the process in control? Explain.

11. The Merry Gremlin Company produces plastic bottles to customer order. Management is concerned about the process that produces the Sticky Glue bottle. The quality inspector randomly selects four bottles from the bottle machine and measures the inside diameter of the bottle neck, a critical quality dimension for the producer of Sticky Glue. The dimensions (in) from the last five samples are

Sample	Bottle 1	2	3	4
1	0.757	0.741	0.746	0.753
2	0.751	0.753	0.742	0.755
3	0.740	0.742	0.756	0.759
4	0.753	0.740	0.748	0.760
5	0.768	0.752	0.743	0.746

Merry Gremlin management believes that the process is in control when the process average is 0.750 inch and the process range is 0.010 inch. Is the process in control?

12. The Mega-Byte Academy is an exclusive school for teaching the fine art of computer programming. Only those students who have impeccable scholastic records and a high aptitude for programming are admitted. In an attempt to judge and monitor the quality of instruction, the administration devised an examination to test students on the basic concepts that all should have learned.

Each year, a random sample of 10 graduating students is selected for the test. The average score is used to track the quality of the educational process. Prior experience with this exam indicates that the average range of student scores is 20. Test results for the past 10 years are

Year	Sample $\bar{x}$	Year	Sample $\bar{x}$
1980	80.31	1985	80.62
1981	74.37	1986	75.00
1982	78.12	1987	81.87
1983	80.00	1988	74.06
1984	81.25	1989	77.50

a. Set up an $\bar{x}$-chart using this historical information.
b. This year the exam was given again. Scores for individual students were

$$59 \quad 60 \quad 90 \quad 85 \quad 72$$
$$63 \quad 71 \quad 57 \quad 68 \quad 74$$

What comments would you make to the administration of the Mega-Byte Academy?

Advanced Problems

A computer package is recommended for solving Problems 13–16.

13. Suppose that AQL = 0.0125, α = 0.025, LTPD = 0.040, β = 0.07, and N = 2000.
a. Find the *AOQL* for the single-sampling plan that best fits the given parameter values.
b. For each of the following experiments, find the *AOQL* for the best single-sampling plan.

Change only the parameter indicated, holding all others at their original values.
  i. Change N to 4000.
 ii. Change AQL to 0.0250.
iii. Change LTPD to 0.080.
c. Discuss the effects of changes in the design parameters on plan performance, based on the three experiments in (b).

14. Consider a production line that produces a part every minute. The critical quality characteristic is the diameter of the part, measured in thousandths of an inch. Management would like to detect any shift in the process average diameter from 0.025 in. Management considers the variance in the process to be in control. Historically, the average range has been 0.004 in., regardless of the process average. You have been asked to design an $\bar{x}$-chart to control this process. The center line of the chart should be 0.025 in. and the control limits should be 3σ from the central line. The sample size and the frequency of sampling was left to you to analyze.

In order to test your design, management has provided the results of 80 minutes of output from the production line (Table 19.10). During this 80 minutes the process average changed once. All measurements are in thousandths of an inch.
a. Set up an $\bar{x}$-chart with $n = 4$. The frequency should be sample 4, then skip 4. Thus your first sample would be for minutes 1–4, the second would be for minutes 9–12, and so on. When would you stop the process to check for a change in the process average?
b. Set up an $\bar{x}$-chart with $n = 8$. The frequency should be sample 8, then skip 4.
  i. When would you stop the process now?
 ii. What can you say about the desirability of large samples on a frequent sampling interval?

15. Using the data from Problem 14, continue your analysis of sample size and frequency by trying the following plans.
a. Using the $\bar{x}$-chart for $n = 4$, try the fre-

TABLE 19.10

Minute	Diameter	Minute	Diameter	Minute	Diameter	Minute	Diameter
1	22	21	28	41	27	61	26
2	27	22	26	42	26	62	29
3	29	23	27	43	25	63	25
4	25	24	24	44	32	64	33
5	23	25	21	45	30	65	26
6	28	26	30	46	25	66	28
7	26	27	23	47	23	67	32
8	30	28	22	48	29	68	30
9	26	29	21	49	31	69	26
10	26	30	28	50	24	70	29
11	21	31	27	51	29	71	33
12	24	32	31	52	27	72	24
13	25	33	23	53	32	73	25
14	28	34	27	54	28	74	27
15	23	35	29	55	25	75	32
16	24	36	30	56	29	76	28
17	25	37	28	57	32	77	29
18	26	38	27	58	27	78	30
19	25	39	25	59	30	79	31
20	20	40	29	60	24	80	26

TABLE 19.11

Sample	Rejected Bottles	Sample	Rejected Bottles
1	4	16	4
2	9	17	3
3	6	18	10
4	12	19	14
5	8	20	5
6	2	21	13
7	13	22	11
8	10	23	7
9	1	24	3
10	9	25	2
11	4	26	8
12	6	27	11
13	8	28	6
14	10	29	9
15	12	30	5

quency sample 4, then skip 8. When would you stop the process in this case?

b. Using the $\bar{x}$-chart for $n = 8$, try the frequency sample 8, then skip 8. When would you consider the process out of control?

c. Using your results from (a) and (b), what trade-offs would you consider in choosing between them?

16. The plant manager at Northern Pines brewery was recently fired because of a lack of control over the bottling line. No one knew what the quality of the bottling process was or what its problems were. A strong advocate of statistical process control, the new plant manager decided to gather data on the number of defective bottles generated on the line. Every day a random sample of 250 bottles was inspected for fill level, cracked bottles, bad labels, and poor seals. Any bottle failing to meet the standard for any of these criteria was counted as a reject. The study lasted 30 weeks and yielded the data in Table 19.11.

Based on these data, what can you tell the new plant manager about the quality of the bottling line? Do you see any "nonrandom" behavior in the bottling process? If so, what might cause this behavior?

SELECTED REFERENCES

Charbonneau, Harvey C., and Gordon L. Webster, *Industrial Quality Control.* Englewood Cliffs, N.J.: Prentice-Hall, 1978.

Crosby, Philip B., *Quality is Free: The Art of Making Quality Certain.* New York: McGraw-Hill, 1979.

Dodge, Harold F., and Harry G. Romig, *Sampling Inspection Tables—Single and Double Sampling,* 2d ed. New York: John Wiley & Sons, 1959.

Duncan, Acheson, J., *Quality Control and Industrial Statistics,* 4th ed. Homewood, Ill.: Richard D. Irwin, 1974.

Feigenbaum, A. V., *Total Quality Control: Engineering Management.* New York: McGraw-Hill, 1961.

Fetter, Robert B., *The Quality Control System.* Homewood, Ill.: Richard D. Irwin, 1967.

Ishikawa, Kaoru, *Guide to Quality Control.* Tokyo: Asian Productivity Organization, 1972.

Juran, J. M., and F. M. Gryna, *Quality Planning and Analysis.* New York: McGraw-Hill, 1970.

Saniga, Erwin M., and Larry E. Shirland, "Quality Control in Practice—A Survey," *Quality Progress,* May 1977, pp. 30–33.

Sullivan, L. P., "The Seven Stages in Company-Wide Quality Control," *Quality Progress,* May 1986.

Wald, A., *Sequential Analysis.* New York: John Wiley & Sons, 1947.

Finished skis await shipment to customers.

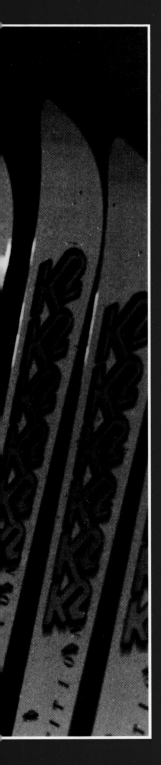

CONCLUSIONS

We have tried to convey the key role that operations management plays in the business community. In following K2's operations, we saw how a ski manufacturer's operating decisions related to its competitive priorities. The ski industry, however, includes an equally competitive service sector—numerous resorts that supply the slopes on which beginners and skilled athletes use their equipment. Operations management plays a no less important role in this segment of the ski market.

A case in point is Waterville Valley, New Hampshire. Two decades ago Tom Corcoran, an Olympic ski racer, visited the valley and saw its potential as a ski resort. It had a mountain with a 2,000-foot vertical drop, an average snowfall of 12 feet per year, and a proximity to all of New England. Today, the valley is a complex of inns, condominiums, and restaurants. The main resort contains a $2 million fitness center and pool. Numerous services include ski lessons and tours, sleigh rides, a variety of restaurants and social events, and lifts to 38 fall-line trails.

The service delivery system must recognize the competitive priorities of each service. For example, lifts are designed within safety guidelines for high-volume, low-cost operations. The more elegant restaurants are designed for low-volume, high-quality meals. Scheduled events must begin on time, and careful capacity planning keeps costs down and quality of service high—a difficult task given the seasonal business. Thus effective system design and informed operating decisions are two factors that give Waterville Valley Resort the competitive edge.

As is the case with so many real company examples described in this text, operations management is a key weapon in the arsenal of world class competitors. This is the message of our last chapter.

CHAPTER

20

OPERATIONS AS A COMPETITIVE WEAPON

▲ Chapter Outline

MANAGERIAL PRACTICES

DECISION LINKAGES

Level 1: Positioning Decisions
Level 2: Design Decisions
Level 3: Operating Decisions

A DIAGNOSTIC APPROACH

Operations Audit
Ongoing Reports

CONCLUSION

CHAPTER HIGHLIGHTS
KEY TERMS
STUDY QUESTIONS
SELECTED REFERENCES

Key Questions for Managers

How can we make operations an effective competitive weapon?

What are other companies doing to meet the competitive challenge?

How should we link our positioning strategy with the other decision areas in operations?

How can we diagnose problems in operations and monitor its vital signs?

What are our high-leverage opportunities for improvement?

 aving come full circle we now pull together the various topics covered into a unified view of operations management. At this point we also return to the troubling productivity trends presented in Chapter 1. Our concern in operations management is to improve productivity in both manufacturing and services. It seems obvious to us that productivity improvements are mandatory, not optional.

British, Japanese, and U.S. executives agree on one point: Among all the functions in business, operations management is the most important source of productivity improvements (McInnes, 1984). A strategic approach to operations, backed by careful analysis, is fundamental to such improvements. Three points on operations strategy, first stated in Chapter 1, need repeating here:

1. Operations can be either a competitive weapon or a millstone.
2. Fundamental (and strategic) choices must be addressed first, but success also depends on tactical choices.
3. Decisions in operations should be linked.

In this chapter, we address each of these points. We begin by reviewing some of the Managerial Practices presented in earlier chapters. They are examples of what companies are actually doing to make operations a competitive weapon. They also show that *many* things—ranging from fundamental choices, such as competitive priorities, to tactical choices, such as scheduling—must be done well. This information underscores the first two points in the preceding list. We address the third point—consistently linking decisions—by describing how decisions in operations relate to positioning strategy. We conclude with a discussion of a diagnostic approach for gaining a competitive advantage.

MANAGERIAL PRACTICES ▲

What is the best avenue for making operations a competitive weapon? The Managerial Practices in prior chapters give us considerable insight into how firms meet the competitive challenge. R. L. Drake introduced satellite-television receivers as a new product (*product planning*). Earl Scheib, Inc., emphasized low price for its car face lifts (*competitive priorities*). Corning Glass Works launched a long-term effort to improve total quality (*quality management*). General Motors formed work teams at its Fremont and Shreveport plants (*work-force management*). Super Valu Stores used EDI to cut invoice processing costs (*new technologies*). American Airlines beefed up its airplane fleet (*capacity*). Kellogg Company makes sure that its machines are reliable before installing them (*maintenance*). Many new maquiladora plants have sprung up in northern Mexico (*location*). J.C. Penney revamped its stores (*layout*). Ethan Allen created a warehouse to hold its inventory more centrally (*materials management*). Deere and Company found alternatives to costly worker layoffs (*production planning*). Nissan Motor Company developed a five-stage system for planning end-item production (*master production scheduling*). Hewlett-Packard adopted an MRP II system at its Colorado Springs Division and a JIT system at its Greeley Division (*inventory*). Florida Power and Light Company finished its new nuclear plant almost on schedule (*scheduling*). Harley-Davidson introduced statistical process control at its engine and transmission facility (*quality control*).

Companies are addressing each decision area in operations to achieve excellence. Some types of productivity improvement are particularly fashionable, such as total quality control, sophisticated technology (including FMS), and work teams. However, there is no single cure or magic formula. Operations managers must deal with all aspects of the production system while attempting to improve productivity.

DECISION LINKAGES ▲

Making operations management a competitive weapon means that decisions about positioning, designing, and operating the production system should be consistent and linked. Inconsistent or independent decisions can act at cross-purposes and thus decrease overall productivity. Results of surveys suggest that a lack of consistent, linked decisions is a key factor in lagging productivity (Judson, 1982). Unfortunately, most efforts at improving productivity are disjointed reactions to the latest productivity problems. Only one third of the firms surveyed linked their efforts to improve productivity with their competitive priorities and positioning strategy. However, greater agreement between corporate strategy and operations can result in higher profits (Richardson et al., 1985).

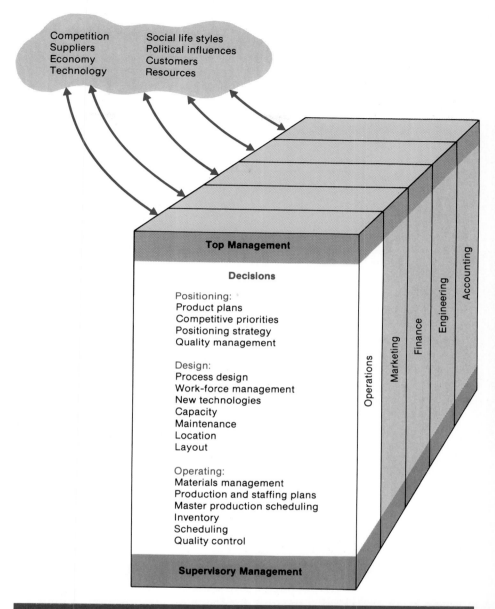

FIGURE 20.1 Linking Decisions to Corporate Strategy

Source: We are indebted to Aleda V. Roth for much of this representation.

Figure 20.1 depicts the process of linking decisions. The cube represents the firm, with vertical slices indicating various functional areas. Each function involves a different set of decisions. The operations function includes the specific decision areas first introduced in Chapter 1 (Table 1.3). Each chapter in

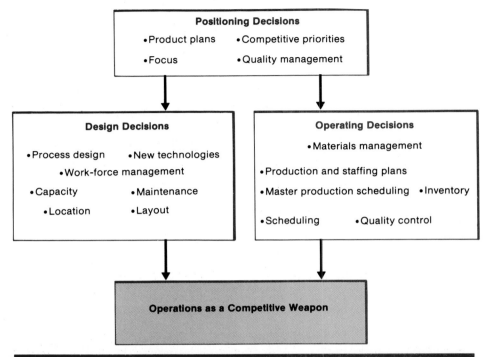

FIGURE 20.2   Linking Decisions within Operations Management

this book addresses one of these decision areas.* Collectively, they are the essence of operations management. Strategic long-range decision areas begin at the top and extend downward, while more tactical short-range decisions extend upward from the bottom. The sequence of chapters is based on this hierarchy.

Top management sits atop the cube, with supervisory-level management underpinning it. Top management monitors the external environment (the cloud at the top), for changes in competition, suppliers, customers, and technology. Eventually, changes in the environment lead to changes in corporate strategy. It is top management's responsibility to make sure that decisions at the functional-area level mesh with and support the revised corporate strategy.

We emphasized linking decisions within the operations function in many of the chapters. In the next several sections, we summarize the linking process, as depicted in Fig. 20.2, at three decision levels:

---

*Work measurement (Chapter 6) and forecasting (Chapter 10) are not shown. They are best viewed as part of the management information system, which (along with important information from accounting) supports decisions made by operations managers.

- Level 1: Positioning decisions.
- Level 2: Design decisions.
- Level 3: Operating decisions.

Figure 20.2 shows that positioning decisions serve as the basis for decisions at other levels. If management properly links positioning decisions to other decisions, operations becomes a competitive weapon. For example, a high-volume commodities manufacturer with a process focus and general-purpose equipment will probably not compete successfully on cost. The plant doesn't need the flexibility, and efficiency will be low.

The patterns described in the following sections are *tendencies* rather than unbreakable rules, and you will encounter many exceptions. For example, some assembly lines that have a product focus will also be labor intensive. In other cases, facilities may offer customized products that all follow the same production-line flow. For example, in plants that make adhesives and glues, only the formula changes from one customized order to the next. In reality relationships are complex, but our purpose is to present general patterns.

Level 1: Positioning Decisions

Corporate strategy connects with operations through positioning decisions. A *process focus* strategy means jumbled flows of products (or customers) through the system. Flexibility is maximized by organizing resources around the process (or function performed). A *product focus* strategy is just the opposite, trading off flexibility to achieve standard routings, line flows, and resources organized by product. The best focus for a specific company depends on its product plans, competitive priorities, and quality choices, as shown in Table 20.1.

Product Plans and Competitive Priorities.   Table 20.1 shows the linkage of positioning strategy to product plans and competitive priorities. When *product plans* call for more customized products, prices will be high and volumes low. Life cycles are shorter, and products tend to be in the earlier stages of their life cycles. With such flux in product plans, dedicating resources to specific products is unwise. A process focus is best because its flexibility handles the changing product mix—but at higher unit costs. This means that the *competitive priority* cannot be cost. Product flexibility, superior quality, and volume flexibility are the other choices. They differentiate the product from others, preventing head-on cost competition. Fast delivery times are unlikely with a process focus. Customized products must be made from scratch, rather than held on the shelf awaiting demand that may never come. The emphasis is on meeting due date promises, rather than giving quick deliveries.

Quality Management.   Table 20.1 also shows the linkage of positioning strategy to quality management. Reliable quality, which means consistently meeting product specifications, is important to all firms because scrap and rework are

| | **TABLE 20.1**   **Linking Focus with Positioning Decisions** | |

	Positioning Strategy	
Decision Area	Process focus	Product focus
Product planning	More customized products with low volumes	More standardized products, with high volumes
	Shorter life cycles	Longer life cycles
	Products in earlier stages of life cycle	Products in later stages of life cycle
	An entrance–exit strategy favoring early exit	An entrance–exit strategy favoring late exit
Competitive priorities	More emphasis on product and volume flexibility	More emphasis on low price
	Long delivery times	Short delivery times
Quality management	High-performance design quality	Consistent quality
	More work-force involvement	More automated inspection
	Informal procedures	Formal procedures

costly. The most important link with positioning strategy lies with the product specifications themselves. A firm choosing high-performance design quality as its competitive priority, as does Rolls-Royce, is likely to have a process focus. Prices must be higher, resulting in lower product volumes. This approach rules out a product focus because resource utilization would be too low. There is another link: Firms choosing product or volume flexibility as a competitive priority are likely to be small and have a process focus. Their quality control procedures are less formal, and they depend largely on the work force to achieve reliable quality. Such was the case with Longhorn Machine. (See Chapter 2.) High-volume firms with a product focus tend to have more staff specialists and inspectors, and the inspection operation might even be automated. To ensure consistent quality, these firms have formal procedures for monitoring incoming materials, process yields, and outgoing products. Scrap and rework are particularly disruptive to the line flows in a product-focused plant.

Level 2: Design Decisions

Designing the production system should fit the positioning strategy. Table 20.2 shows these linkages.

Process Design and New Technologies.   A process focus means more general-purpose (and less efficient) equipment. Operations are more labor intensive, gaining flexibility but giving up rock-bottom costs. We discussed these differences in Chapter 2, using the process-focused Longhorn Machine and

	Positioning Strategy	
Decision Area	Process focus	Product focus
Process design and new technologies	General purpose, flexible equipment	Specialized equipment dedicated to a few products
	Labor intensive, with less automation	Capital intensive, with more automation
	Attention on labor costs	Attention on facility utilization and overhead costs
	Less vertically integrated	More vertically integrated
Work-force management	Flexible work force	Specialized work force
	Enlarged jobs	Specialized jobs
	Informal promotion channels	Formal promotion channels
	Frequent two-way communication with supervisors	Less frequent two-way communication with supervisors
	Fewer staff specialists	More staff specialists
Capacity	Large capacity cushion	Small capacity cushion
	Large capacity imbalances	Small capacity imbalances
	Difficult to measure	Easy to measure
	Less of a management preoccupation	More of a management preoccupation
	Small economies of scale	Large economies of scale
Maintenance	Less maintenance intensity	More maintenance intensity
Location	Single facility	Multiple facilities
	Expand on site or relocate nearby	Expand by adding new facilities, possibly overseas
	More local or regional markets	More national or international markets
	Transportation costs not a primary location factor	Transportation costs sometimes a primary location factor
Layout	Process layouts	Product layouts
	Flexible	Inflexible
	Variable-path materials handling	Fixed-path, automated materials handling

TABLE 20.2 Linking Focus with Design Decisions

the product-focused Pinecrest Brewery as examples. Longhorn had an investment of about $10,000 per employee in equipment, but the Pinecrest investment was almost $500,000 per employee. A survey of 150 firms showed that the average capital investment for those having more of a process focus was only $17,000 per employee (Taylor, 1980). Those firms having more of a product focus had an average investment almost four times as large. Capital intensity and automation require high production volumes for effective equipment utilization. In the past in the automotive industry, a new automated line was introduced with each model change. The cost was more than $20 million, which was quite a disincentive for frequent model changes. Only recently has the relationship between product volumes and capital intensity been broken in certain situations. Group technology, reprogrammable robots, and flexible machining can mean higher capital intensity, even with low product volumes and short life cycles.

As a process-focused production system is labor intensive, labor costs are of particular concern. Managers give continual attention to efficiency losses caused by setups, materials handling, and component delays. With a product focus, their attention shifts to effective facility utilization, because of the high capital intensity, and controlling various overhead costs.

A final link is with vertical integration. With a process focus, where volumes are low and unit costs are high, a firm tends to rely on outside suppliers to manufacture parts and assemblies for its products. Suppliers can achieve economies of scale by pooling the demand from several process-focused firms. On the other hand, firms with a product focus and high volumes tend to do more part and assembly work in-house, integrating backward (make rather than buy) and forward (toward the customer).

Work-force Management.   A process focus also favors use of a flexible work force. Workers receive more cross-training so that they can help out with the capacity imbalances and frequent shocks at a process-focused facility. This approach creates enlarged, broader jobs, which often serve to motivate workers and to increase wage rates. Small, process-focused firms have less formal promotion channels and are less likely to be unionized than large firms. Until recent innovative contracts, such as that at GM's Saturn facility, unions have favored narrow job boundaries and more formal promotion channels. Filling one opening sets off a chain reaction of bumping under the provisions of most labor contracts.

The unpredictability of day-to-day production requirements of a process focus places great importance on two-way communication between workers and supervisors to identify which work to do next and how to do it. Fewer supervisory tasks are diverted to task specialists. For example, forward scheduling of equipment is less critical (owing to lower capital intensity) and even less possible (owing to unpredictability). When equipment investment reaches $1 million per worker, as is true with some product-focused processes, more staff specialists can be justified for production planning and work design.

Capacity.   The most obvious link is the capacity cushion. (See Chapter 7.) It must be larger with a process focus because of low capital intensity (which reduces the cushion's cost), shifting product mixes (creating capacity imbalances), increased demand and supply uncertainties, greater scheduling complexity, and more variable demand (peaks and valleys). Since capacity often comes in chunks, expanding by even the minimum increment can create a large cushion with the small volumes of a process focus. One study in particular confirms the link between positioning strategy and the capacity cushion (Taylor, 1980). Firms with more of a process focus averaged 10 shifts per week, whereas those with a product focus average 17. The maximum number of shifts possible is 21 per week (or 3 shifts/day, 7 days/wk). Product-focused firms must get much better utilization of their capital-intensive facilities, operating them more round-the-clock.

Table 20.2 shows three other links to capacity. First, capacity is particularly difficult to measure with a process focus because multiple products share the same equipment. Changing product mixes create imbalances and floating bottlenecks. Second, managers at facilities with a process focus are less preoccupied with capacity decisions. Equipment costs are low, and lead times to buy new, general-purpose equipment are shorter. Management doesn't need to plan so far ahead for capacity changes, and unit costs depend less on high utilization. Finally, economies of scale are less dramatic. With the facility's smaller size, it benefits less from spreading fixed costs (which are lower anyway) and from avoiding setups by dedicating resources of products.

Maintenance. Managers are less concerned about equipment failures in a process-focused firm. There is less automation, and the cost of breakdown maintenance is not so high. Work stations tend to be decoupled from each other because of larger capacity cushions and substantial work-in-process inventories. Since equipment is more general purpose, jobs often can be rerouted to another piece of equipment. Disabling one work station does not shut down others, at least in the short run. Conversely, with line processes, failure at one operation can quickly shut down the entire line. This situation not only idles the work force, but it could also result in lost business opportunities. At some facilities with a product focus, this loss is as much as $300,000 per day.

Location. The most striking link is simply the number of facilities. Low-volume producers choose a process focus out of necessity. Since they are small, they usually have just one facility. They expand either on-site or by relocating nearby. They appeal to a local or regional market, which makes transportation costs less of a primary location factor. Even for distant customers, the product is not standardized enough to avoid costly direct shipments. High-volume producers, on the other hand, create multiple facilities, including a system of warehouses. Each facility can focus on product, market area, or process.

Layout. The layout translates positioning strategy into concrete form with either a *process layout* for a process focus or a *product layout* for a product focus. With a process layout, employees and equipment are grouped by function or process. All grinding is done by the grinding department, all bill processing by the accounts payable section, and all budget-priced apparel displayed in the department store's basement. This approach makes supervision easier, helps foster worker flexibility, and improves responses to changing product mixes. The jumbled routings, however, result in less efficient materials handling methods. Variable-path devices, such as carts, forklift tractors, and overhead cranes, must be used. Only with the line flows of a product focus can efficient fixed-path devices (such as conveyors) be utilized.

Level 3: Operating Decisions

Positioning strategy must also link with tactical decisions about operating (rather than designing) the facility. These linkages are shown in Table 20.3.

Materials Management.   With a process focus, low repeatability and jumbled routings cause complexity. Last-minute changes by customers and vendors, imprecise time standards, and difficulties in predicting capacities create uncertainty. Because of the complexity and uncertainty, plans cannot be made far in advance. Planning is done more at a local, decentralized level to adapt to the latest conditions. Greater work-force and inventory cushions are tolerated because of the dynamic environment. A process focus also involves less formal relationships with suppliers. No long-term contracts are negotiated with key vendors. Raw-material volumes are low, so the firm has less control over suppliers, who naturally cater to larger customers. On the outbound side, distribution channels are less formal. Markets are likely to be local or regional, and no elaborate network of distribution centers is needed. Products are more likely to be specials, which rules out positioning finished goods inventory at warehouses close to the customer. Direct shipments from the plant to the customer are the norm.

The product flexibility of a process focus means that inventory must be created lower in the bills of materials. Inventory is not created by plan at higher levels because of low turnover and the fear of obsolescence. More intermediate items are likely to be produced to help increase part commonality, keep customer delivery times at acceptable levels, cut losses owing to setups, and buffer against bottlenecks.

A final link with materials management deals with information requirements. With a process focus, information tends to be oriented to the bidding process and specific customer orders. Output plans are communicated by releasing jobs with detailed routing information. With a product focus, information is oriented more to demand forecasts and current inventory positions, rather than individual customer orders. Product-focused firms produce more to stock and less to order.

Production and Staffing Plans.   A process focus allows more volume flexibility and changes in the output rate to meet seasonal or cyclical demand. One study showed that changing the output rate by using overtime, subcontracting,

TABLE 20.3 Linking Focus with Operating Decisions

Decision Area	Positioning Strategy	
	Process focus	Product focus
Materials management	More complexity and uncertainty Shorter-range plans Higher tolerance for cushion of extra workers and inventory Informal vendor and customer relationships Inventory held lower in BOM Information oriented to orders	Less complexity and uncertainty Longer-range plans Lower tolerance for cushion of extra workers and inventory Formal vendor and customer relationships Inventory held higher in BOM Information oriented to forecasts
Production and staffing plans	More volume flexibility Relies on overtime, subcontracting or extra shifts	Less volume flexibility Relies on anticipation inventory and aggressive alternatives
Master production scheduling	Less stable MPS	More stable MPS
Inventory	Short runs Longer cycle times and more WIP Component shortages Lot sizing and sequencing loosely coupled MRP system	Long runs Shorter cycle times and less WIP Capacity shortages Lot sizing and sequencing tightly coupled JIT system
Scheduling	Fluid and changing Planned just a few days ahead Decentralized decisions Labor-limited environment	Stable Planned many days ahead Centralized decisions Machine-limited environment

and extra shifts is about twice as common with a process focus (Taylor, 1980). A product focus is accompanied by a *level strategy*, letting anticipation inventory build during the slack season. A firm may even have enough clout to require customers to take early delivery of the inventory. It is also better positioned for aggressive alternatives. The last resort for a product-focused firm is to shut down one of its plants entirely. There are five reasons for these links between a level strategy and a product focus:

1. Overtime and extra shifts tend to be infeasible options, as the plant is more likely to be operating with three shifts already in order to maximize facility utilization.

2. A product focus implies low variable costs, making the extra cost of subcontracting prohibitive. Too much is lost by going outside to have the work done. It is also unlikely that a subcontractor can be found to supply the necessary volumes when business is booming.

3. Products are more standardized, making it possible to build anticipation inventory without fear of obsolescence.

4. Line processes are more rigid and tend to be set at specific output rates. Rebalancing a line means changing the jobs of many individuals. It is simpler to temporarily shut down a whole line when demand falls.

5. A high-volume producer is more likely to be able to influence the market or add new products as aggressive alternatives to level out the uneven demand pattern.

Master Production Schedule.   The master production schedule is less stable with a process focus. There is a greater willingness to change the MPS to satisfy last-minute requests. Products are more likely to be custom-engineered, which raises the possibility of delays before the job is released to production because engineering changes are more frequent. Another cause of unstable schedules is that a small, process-focused firm such as Longhorn Machine has much less clout with customers than a product-focused firm such as Pinecrest Brewery. (See Chapter 2.)

Inventory.   Positioning strategy also links with inventory decisions. Low volumes mean short runs, and at the extreme, special customer orders are matched with shop orders on a one-for-one basis. The shorter runs do not necessarily mean lower turnover, as demand is also lower. A 100-unit batch may represent a six-months' supply in a job shop, but just a one-day's supply with the high volumes of a product focus.

Items at a process-focused facility are routed through many work stations. Each station is a potential bottleneck and has a long waiting line. Lead times (or cycle times) are long and variable, which requires more work-in-process (WIP) inventory and more safety stock. For example, firms with a process focus reported that 36 percent of their inventory is WIP (Taylor, 1980). This level drops to only 18 percent with a product focus.

Table 20.3 shows three other links with inventory. Product flexibility and low-volume production make component availability the key concern of inventory planners at a process-focused facility. With the capital intensity of a product focus, the concern shifts to capacity shortages. Achieving plans that provide for adequate capacity forces inventory and sequencing decisions to be more highly integrated. Finally, product diversity lends itself to an order-based system such as MRP. Its logic is particularly appropriate for ensuring component availability. The repetitiveness of high-volume production indicates the need for a system such as JIT.

Scheduling.   Process-focused facilities have fluid and changing schedules because both demand and supply are less certain. Reactive, crisis-oriented scheduling is not as apparent with a product focus. Instead, scheduling and monitoring of day-to-day performance is more elaborate. Because of the high cost of idle resources, schedules are developed farther into the future, often on a more centralized basis. When inventory that decouples operations is stripped away, more attention must be given to scheduling in order to maximize facility utilization and customer service. In some cases, lead times to customers might even have to be extended to get better utilization. At medical facilities, for example, attempts are made to achieve better utilization by an appointment system. Patients are scheduled well in advance of when the service is to be provided, except for emergency cases.

Finally, Table 20.3 shows that a process focus normally means labor-limited scheduling, with a more flexible work force. Both labor assignment policies and dispatching priority rules are needed. Machine-limited scheduling for a product focus is simpler in this respect. However, it is not without its challenges. Schedules must recognize capacity constraints and maximize facility utilization.

A DIAGNOSTIC APPROACH ▲

A strategic approach to operations management answers two fundamental questions:

1. What should we be doing?
2. How are we doing?

The first question has a *planning orientation*, which has been our main perspective. We started with corporate strategy and positioning decisions and then linked them to planning in the various functional areas of operations management. The second question has a *control orientation* (see Ruefli and Sarrazin, 1981). The purpose of control is to monitor performance, identify problems, and diagnose causes of problems. Managers can then take corrective actions to restore operations to the desired course. We conclude with a brief description of two control methods: audits and ongoing reports.

Operations Audit

One important diagnostic tool is an **operations audit**, or special study of operations. Checklists for service providers (Chase and Aquilano, 1985) and manufacturers (Skinner, 1978) are available. They contain a variety of dimensions on which to evaluate operations. Two scores are assigned to each dimension, one for current performance and one for the goal. Large negative differences represent planning and/or production problems. An audit begins with competitive priorities and works down through each of the decision areas shown in Fig. 20.1. Starting from the top ties the audit to strategic planning and evaluation of decision consistency. Dimensions for evaluating process design include

- degree of capital intensity;
- extent of equipment specialization;

- degree of worker flexibility;
- degree of vertical integration;
- degree of customer involvement in the process;
- frequency of process innovations; and
- work-force involvement in process design.

Similar lists can be developed for the other decision areas in operations, tailoring the choices to the needs of the individual firm.

Ongoing Reports

Another diagnostic tool is **ongoing reports** on multiple measures. Some measures are traditional accounting data on costs (broken into various categories), profits, and return on investment. Over the years, manufacturing management has been evaluated primarily on the basis of direct labor (actual versus time standard) costs. There is growing recognition that such measures are insufficient and can actually restrain production systems. An excessive financial orientation makes efficiency or short-term profits the overriding priority.

TABLE 20.4   Some Vital Signs for Operations Management

- Actual-to-forecasted demand (%)
- Returned merchandise ($)
- Scrap rate (%)
- Nursing hours to patient hours (%)
- Ratio of sales $ to payroll $ (%)
- Number of grievances
- Voluntary quits
- Overhead ($)
- Facility utilization (%)
- Preventive maintenance ($)
- Leased truck utilization (%)
- Open orders ($)
- Purchase prices (% of prior prices)
- Seasonal inventory ($)
- New orders booked ($)
- Stockouts
- Total inventory (weeks of supply)
- WIP inventory (% of total)
- Transaction volume (number)
- Capital intensity ($ per worker)
- Training (hr/wk)
- Number of products produced per machine

- Change in sales and profit margins over last year (life cycle position)
- Rework labor (% of direct labor)
- Materials costs (% of total)
- Direct labor (actual versus standard)
- Absenteeism (labor days lost)
- Tooling cost ($)
- Number of quality circle projects
- Equipment breakdowns (hr lost)
- Ratio of maintenance hours to direct labor hours (%)
- Purchase orders (% placed in 3 days)
- Late deliveries from suppliers (% of orders)
- Overtime ($)
- On-time delivery (% of orders)
- Order backlog ($)
- Inventory ($)
- Book-to-cycle count accuracy (%)
- Cycle time (days)
- Transaction costs ($)
- Customer return rate (%)
- Variation in monthly production rate
- Number of production orders per month

Indicator	Measure	Target	This month	Progress to date	Scale

(a) Format with Graph

Indicator	Measure	Target	This month	Year to date	Past year	Range: Past 12 months	
						High	Low
Inventory	Weeks of supply	10	13	14	17	18	11

(b) Format with Trend Measurements

FIGURE 20.3   Two Display Formats

Source: The concepts displayed here are discussed in more detail in Robert L. Janson, ''Graphical Indicators of Operations,'' *Harvard Business Review* (November–December 1980), pp. 164–170.

New technologies or improvements in the quality of work life are ignored because many of their benefits are long-term and difficult to quantify. While extremely useful, short-term financial measures must be kept in perspective.

Recognizing that no single measure of productivity is adequate, the logical approach is to use multiple tracking devices. Those listed in Table 20.4 help managers to monitor the *vital signs* of the production system. Such measures are tailored to specific operations and change from time to time. A pyramid approach is used, in which department managers pick five or 10 measures that best fit their operations. Each manager passes a few to his or her supervisor, and so on. Thus a vice-president of operations might end up with 20 or 30 indicators. Figure 20.3 suggests two possible formats for displaying each measure. The report should show a target, the latest performance, and some index of the year-to-date performance.

ABC analysis is particularly valuable here to focus management's attention on the relatively few key problem areas. Management-by-exception applies equally well to inventory (by type or department), equipment failures (by machine or department), customer goods returned (by product line or department), scrap or rework (by work station), or employee absenteeism (by department).

Finally, managers have to remember that this monitoring is but a means to an end. The end is improving performance and linking operations to corporate strategy. Managers must draw on a knowledge of operations and an awareness of their environment in seeking remedies. If inventory is too high, for example, the cause can be any number of factors. Large lot sizes, high forecast errors, long lead times, uneven or seasonal demand, unstable master production schedules, or inaccurate records are all possible causes. Managers must dig deeply to discover the real problems underlying the symptomatic problems uncovered by ongoing reports—and then remedy them.

CONCLUSION ▲

Throughout this book we have stressed that the operations function, whether in manufacturing or services, can and must be managed better. Operations can definitely be a competitive weapon—not a millstone—as Japanese manufacturers have proved. We also emphasized that each decision in operations can affect efforts to improve productivity. Operations management must be approached strategically, but with careful attention to tactical decisions and techniques.

In making operations a competitive weapon, operations managers must take more initiative, show greater commitment, be quality conscious, and be ready to act. Rather than blaming government regulation or intractable unions for lagging productivity, each manager should ask: Am *I* perceived as quality conscious by the work force? Am *I* making sensible decisions and linking them coherently? Am *I* taking the initiative as much as *I* can in my position? Can *I* be more innovative? Am *I* encouraging employees in operations to do what is wanted and needed, rather than just what they are told? Am *I* committed to excellence in operations? As current or future operations managers, your firm's response to the competitive challenge depends on your answers to those questions.

CHAPTER HIGHLIGHTS

- Making operations management a competitive weapon depends on doing many things well, rather than seeking a magic solution.
- A strategic approach is needed to productivity improvement, so that decisions are linked and consistent. Management's positioning strategy is the starting point for making consistent operations decisions. The choice of process focus or product focus must be linked with the other decision areas in the operation.
- At the highest decision levels, a process focus links with customized products, low volumes, short life cycles, an entrance–exit strategy favoring early exit, product flexibility, and high-performance design quality.
- For design decisions, a process focus links with flexible resources, labor intensity, minimal ver-

tical integration, enlarged jobs, informal promotion channels, frequent two-way communication, large capacity cushions, small economies of scale, low maintenance intensity, single-site locations, local or regional markets, process layouts, and variable-path materials handling.
- For operating decisions, a process focus means complexity and uncertainty, short-range plans, high tolerance for inventory cushions, informal vendor and customer relationships, holding inventory low in the BOM, volume flexibility, short runs, long cycle times, substantial WIP, potential component shortages, and decentralized scheduling.
- An operations audit helps to diagnose problems in operations by systematically evaluating a variety of dimensions. It starts with competitive

priorities and works down through the various operating decision areas.

- Ongoing reports are another diagnostic tool for managers. Since there is no single measure of productivity, multiple measures should be used. When problems have been identified, managers must draw on their knowledge of operations and awareness of the environment in order to solve them.
- Operations management needs a strategic orientation, but with full attention to tactical decisions and techniques.

KEY TERMS

ongoing reports   778
operations audit   777

STUDY QUESTIONS

1. "The only real answer to the productivity challenge is relocating facilities to where labor rates are cheap." Do you agree or disagree with this statement? Why?

2. What product plans and competitive priorities link well with a process focus? Why?

3. Why is a product-focused facility more likely to be capital intensive? Place more emphasis on equipment utilization? Have a larger staff?

4. Why does the choice of materials handling equipment depend on positioning strategy?

5. Why are inventories stocked at more forward positions with a product focus?

6. "The Japanese have successfully challenged all the traditional thinking and beliefs of U.S. operations managers. We can expect widespread adoption of their approaches in the next decade." Do you agree or disagree with this statement? Why?

7. Comment on the statement: "Annual profits and efficiency are the only true measures of a production system."

8. What dimensions for an operations audit would you suggest for layout? Inventory?

SELECTED REFERENCES

Buffa, Elwood S., *Meeting the Competitive Challenge*. Homewood, Ill.: Dow Jones-Irwin, 1984.

Burnham, John M., "Improving Manufacturing Performance—Management's Vital Challenge," *Production and Inventory Management,* vol. 25, no. 2 (Second Quarter 1984), pp. 1–20.

Chase, Richard B., and Nicholas J. Aquilano, *Production and Operations Management*. Homewood, Ill.: Richard D. Irwin, 1989.

Hayes, Robert H., and Kim B. Clark, "Explaining Observed Productivity Differentials Between Plants: Implications for Operations Research," *Interfaces,* vol. 15, no. 6 (November–December 1985), pp. 3–14.

Janson, Robert L., "Graphic Indicators of Operations," *Harvard Business Review* (November–December 1980), pp. 164–170.

Judson, Arnold S., "The Awkward Truth about Productivity," *Harvard Business Review* (September–October 1982), pp. 93–97.

Kendrick, John W., *Improving Company Productivity*. Baltimore: The Johns Hopkins University Press, 1984.

McInnes, J. Morris, "Corporate Management of Productivity—An Empirical Study," *Strategic Management Journal,* vol. 5 (1984), pp. 351–365.

Miller, Jeffrey G., and Thomas E. Vollmann, "The Hidden Factory," *Harvard Business Review* (September–October 1985), pp. 142–150.

Richardson, P. R., A. J. Taylor, and J. R. M. Gordon, "A Strategic Approach to Evaluating Manufacturing Performance," *Interfaces,* vol. 15, no. 6 (November–December 1985), pp. 15–27.

Ritzman, Larry P., Barry E. King, and Lee J. Krajewski, "Manufacturing Performance—Pulling the Right Levers," *Harvard Business Review* (March–April 1984), pp. 143–152.

Ruefli, Timothy, and Jacques Sarrazin, "Strategic Control of Corporate Development under Ambiguous Circumstances," *Management Science,* vol. 27, no. 10 (October 1981), pp. 1158–1170.

Skinner, Wickham, *Manufacturing in the Corporate Strategy*. New York: John Wiley & Sons, 1978.

Taylor, Sam G., "Are Process Industries Different?" *23rd Annual Conference Proceedings*. American Production and Inventory Control Society, Los Angeles, October, 1980, pp. 94–96.

Wheelwright, Steven C., and Robert H. Hayes, "Competing through Manufacturing," *Harvard Business Review* (January–February, 1985), pp. 99–109.

SUPPLEMENT 1

FINANCIAL ANALYSIS

▲ Supplement Outline

What types of tools can we use to evaluate investments?

Are we overlooking some investments of great strategic importance because their returns seem to be lower than the hurdle rate?

How can we avoid *managing by the numbers?*

*M*any decisions in operations management involve large capital investments. Automation, vertical integration, capacity expansion, layout revisions, and installing a new MRP system are but some examples. Most of a firm's assets are tied up in the operations function. Therefore the operations manager should seek high-yield capital projects and then assess their costs, benefits, and risks. Such projects typically are subjected to one or more types of financial analysis. In this supplement, we present a brief overview of basic financial analyses.

TIME VALUE OF MONEY ▲

An important concept underlying many financial analysis techniques is that a dollar in hand today is worth more than a dollar to be received in the future. A dollar available today can be invested to earn a return, so that more than one dollar will be available in the future. This concept is known as the **time value of money**.

Future Value of an Investment

If $5000 is invested at 10 percent interest for one year, at the end of the year the $5000 will have earned $500 in interest, and the total amount available will be $5500. If the interest earned is allowed to accumulate, it also earns interest, and the original investment will grow to $12,970 in 10 years. The process by which interest on an investment accumulates, and then earns interest itself for the remainder of the investment period, is known as **compounding interest**. The value of an investment at the end of the period over which interest is compounded is called the **future value of an investment**.

In order to calculate the future value of an investment, we first express the interest rate and the time period in the same units of time as the interval at which compounding occurs. Let's assume that interest is compounded annually, so we express all time periods in years and use annual interest rates. To find the value of an investment one year in the future, we multiply the amount invested by the sum of 1 plus the interest rate (expressed as a decimal). The value of a $5000 investment at 12 percent per year one year from now is

$$\$5000(1.12) = \$5600$$

If the entire amount remains invested, at the end of two years we have

$$5600(1.12) = \$5000(1.12)^2 = \$6272$$

In general, $$F = P(1 + r)^n$$

where

F = the future value of the investment at the end of n periods

P = the amount invested at the beginning, called the principal

r = the periodic interest rate

n = the number of time periods for which the interest compounds

Present Value of a Future Amount

Let's look at the opposite problem. Suppose that we want to make an investment now that will be worth $10,000 in one year. If the interest rate is 12 percent, and P represents the amount invested now, we can express this problem as

$$F = \$10,000 = P(1 + 0.12)$$

Solving for P gives us:

$$P = \frac{F}{(1 + r)} = \frac{10,000}{(1 + 0.12)} = \$8,929$$

The amount to be invested now to accumulate to a certain amount in the future at a specific interest rate is called the **present value of an investment**. The process of finding the present value of an investment, when the future value and the interest rate are known, is called **discounting** the future value to its present value. If the number of time periods n for which discounting is desired is greater than 1, the present value is determined by dividing the future value by the nth power of the sum of 1 plus the interest rate. The general formula for determining the present value is

$$P = \frac{F}{(1 + r)^n}$$

The interest rate is also called the **discount rate**.

Present Value Factors

Although we can calculate P from its formula in a few steps with most pocket calculators, we can use a table instead. Note that we can write the present value formula another way:

$$P = \frac{F}{(1 + r)^n} = F\left[\frac{1}{(1 + r)^n}\right]$$

Let $[1/(1 + r)^n]$ be the *present value factor*, which we call *pf* and which can be found in Appendix 1. This table gives you the present value of a future amount of \$1 for various time periods and interest rates. To use the table, locate the column for the appropriate interest rate and the row for the appropriate period. The number in the body of the table where this row and column intersect is the *pf* value. Multiply it by F to get P. For example, suppose that an investment will generate \$15,000 in 10 years. If the interest rate is 12 percent, we find in Appendix 1 that $pf = 0.3220$. Multiplying it by \$15,000 gives us the present value, or

$$P = Fpf = \$15,000(0.3220)$$
$$= \$4830$$

Annuities

An **annuity** is a series of payments of a fixed amount for a specified number of years. We treat all payments as happening at the end of a year. Suppose that we want to invest an amount at an interest rate of 10 percent, so that we may draw out \$5000 per year for each of the next four years. We could determine the present value of this \$5000 four-year annuity by treating the four payments as single future payments. The present value of an investment needed now, in order to receive these payments for the next four years, is the sum of the present values of each of the four payments. That is,

$$P = \frac{\$5000}{1 + 0.10} + \frac{\$5000}{(1 + 0.10)^2} + \frac{\$5000}{(1 + 0.10)^3} + \frac{\$5000}{(1 + 0.10)^4}$$
$$= \$4545 + \$4132 + \$3757 + \$3415$$
$$= \$15,849$$

A much easier way to calculate this amount is to use Appendix 2. Look for the factor in the table at the intersection of the 10% column, and the fourth period row and find 3.1699. For annuities, we call this present value factor *af*, to distinguish it from the present value factor for a single payment. We determine the present value of an annuity by multiplying its amount by *af*. For our example, we get

$$P = Aaf = \$5000(3.1699)$$
$$= \$15,849$$

where
- P = the present value of an investment
- A = the amount of the annuity received each year
- af = the present value factor for an annuity

TECHNIQUES OF ANALYSIS ▲

We can now apply these concepts to the financial analysis of proposed investments. Two basic financial analysis techniques are

1. net present value method; and

2. payback method.

Both methods are based on cash flows. Our first step, then, is to calculate the cash flows resulting from the investment (project).

Determining Cash Flows

We have to estimate as accurately as possible the cash that will flow into and out of the organization because of the project. *Cash flow* includes revenues, costs, and changes in assets and liabilities. We illustrate this process with the salad bar project in Managerial Practice S1.1. It is important to remember two points when determining cash flows for any project:

1. Consider only the amounts of cash flows that will change if the project is undertaken. These amounts are called incremental cash flows and are the difference in the cash flows with the project and without it.

2. Cash flows should be converted to *after-tax* amounts before applying the net present value or payback method to them. This step introduces taxes and depreciation into the calculations.

Depreciation.   **Depreciation** is an allowance for the consumption of capital. In this type of analysis, depreciation is relevant for only one reason: It acts as a tax shield.* Taxes must be paid on before-tax cash inflows *minus* the depreciation associated with the proposed investment. We will use the *straight-line method* of calculating annual depreciation, since it is simplest.† First, subtract

---

*Depreciation is not a legitimate cash flow because it is not cash that is actually paid out each year. On the other hand, depreciation does affect how an accountant calculates net income, against which the income-tax rate is applied. Therefore, depreciation enters into the calculation, as a tax shield, only when we have to figure our tax liability.

†For a discussion of other depreciation methods, see Kieso and Weygandt (1983).

the estimated salvage value from the amount of investment required at the beginning of the project, then divide by the number of years of life. If the item can be sold for cash at the end of its life, it has a salvage value greater than zero. For the salad bar, the annual depreciation is

$$D = \frac{(I - S)}{n} = \frac{\$16,000 - \$0}{4}$$

$$= \$4000$$

where

D = annual depreciation

I = the amount of the investment

S = the salvage value

n = the number of years of project life

Tax Considerations.   The income-tax rate varies from one state or country to another. We will use an income-tax rate of 50 percent, assuming that all relevant federal, state, and local income taxes are included in this rate. When you are doing a financial analysis you may want to use an average income-tax

MANAGERIAL PRACTICE S1.1

A Salad Bar: To Fund or Not to Fund

A local restaurant is considering adding a salad bar. The investment required to remodel the dining area and add the salad bar will be $16,000. Other information about the project is as follows:

1. The price and variable cost per salad are $3.50 and $2.00, respectively.
2. Annual demand should be about 11,000 salads.
3. Fixed costs, other than depreciation, will be $8000, which covers the energy to operate the refrigerated unit and another part-time employee to stock the salad bar during peak business hours.
4. The project is expected to last four years and have no salvage value at the end of that time. The straight-line depreciation method is used.
5. The tax rate is 50 percent.
6. Management wants to earn a return of at least 14 percent on the project.

Should the salad bar project be funded?

rate based on the firm's historical tax rate over the past several years, or you may want to base the tax rate on the highest tax bracket that applies to the taxpaying unit. The one thing you should never do is ignore taxes in your analysis.

After-Tax Cash Inflows.   We are now ready to determine the after-tax cash flows for each year of the project's life. We calculate the amount of taxes in four steps:

1. Contribution margin = Revenue − Variable cost.

2. Before-tax cash inflow = Contribution margin − Fixed costs.

3. Taxable cash inflow = Before-tax cash inflow − Depreciation.

4. Additional taxes = Taxable cash inflow × Tax rate.

In some investment projects, revenues are unaffected. The before-tax cash inflow is really a cost savings, such as might come from an automation project. They are the equivalent of the before-tax cash inflow of step 2. In such cases we would begin with step 3.

Now, we simply subtract the additional taxes (step 4) from the before-tax cash inflow (step 2), or

$$\text{After-tax cash inflow} = \text{Before-tax cash inflow} - \text{Additional taxes}$$

Salvage Values.   The cash flow from the sale or disposal of plant and equipment at the end of a project's life is known as **salvage value.** Adding it to the after-tax cash flow, you arrive at the total cash flow for the year. If an item has a negative salvage value, which can happen if you must pay to dispose of something, you subtract this amount from the after-tax cash flow to obtain the net cash flow for the year. Gains or losses on disposition of property must be carefully evaluated for tax effects in order to determine the cash flow actually resulting from them. Only the after-tax values are relevant to cash-flow determination.* We will assume that all salvage values are net of their tax effects for this example.

---

*Disposal of property often results in an accounting gain or loss that can increase or decrease income tax and affect cash flows. These tax effects should be considered in determining the actual cash inflow or outflow from disposal of property.

TABLE S1.1   Cash Flows for the Salad Bar Project

Item	1989	1990	1991	1992	1993
			Year		
Initial Information					
Annual demand (salads)		11,000	11,000	11,000	11,000
Investment	$16,000				
Interest (discount) rate	0.14				
Cash flows					
Revenue		$38,500	$38,500	$38,500	$38,500
Minus variable cost		− 22,000	− 22,000	− 22,000	− 22,000
Contribution margin		16,500	16,500	16,500	16,500
Minus fixed cost		− 8,000	− 8,000	− 8,000	− 8,000
Before-tax cash inflow		8,500	8,500	8,500	8,500
Minus depreciation		− 4,000	− 4,000	− 4,000	− 4,000
Taxable cash inflow		4,500	4,500	4,500	4,500
Taxes @ 50%		2,250	2,250	2,250	2,250
Before-tax cash inflow		8,500	8,500	8,500	8,500
Minus taxes		− 2,250	− 2,250	− 2,250	− 2,250
After-tax cash inflow		$ 6,250	$ 6,250	$ 6,250	$ 6,250

Net Present Value Method

The **net present value (NPV) method** evaluates an investment by comparing the present value of after-tax cash flows with the original investment amount. Table S1.1 shows the calculations for the salad bar project, with after-tax cash inflows of $6250 per year. While the $16,000 cash outflow for the initial investment is already a present value, the four $6250 inflows are not. They are equivalent to a four-year annuity. As management wants to earn a return of at least 14 percent on its investment, we use that rate to find the *af* value in Appendix 2 to be 2.9137. The net present value of the inflows minus outflows is

$$NPV = \$6250(2.9137) - \$16,000$$
$$= \$2211$$

We can obtain the same result by discounting each year's after-tax cash flow to its present value and adding all the present values. This method is shown in the following equations.

1990: $6250(0.8772) = $5482

1991: $6250(0.7695) = $4809

1992: $6250(0.6750) = $4219

1993: $6250(0.5921) = $3701

$$\text{NPV of project} = (\$5482 + \$4809 + \$4219 + \$3701) - \$16{,}000$$
$$= \$2211$$

If the net present value is positive for the discount rate used, the investment earns a rate of return higher than the discount rate. If the net present value is negative, the investment earns a rate of return lower than the discount rate. Most firms set the discount rate equal to the lowest desired return on investment. If a negative net present value results, the project is not approved. The discount rate that represents the lowest desired return on investment is thought of as a hurdle over which the investment must pass, and is often referred to as the **hurdle rate**. Since the NPV computed above is positive, the return on the salad bar exceeds the hurdle rate.*

Payback Method

The other commonly used method of evaluating projects is the **payback method**, which determines how much time will elapse before the total of *after-tax* cash flows will equal or pay back the initial investment.

Returning to the salad bar project and using after-tax cash flows from Table S1.1, we add the cash flows for each year until we get to as close as possible to $16,000, without exceeding it. For the years 1990 and 1991, cash flows are $6250 + $6250 = $12,500. The payback method assumes that cash flows come in evenly throughout the year, so that in 1992 only $3500 must flow in before the payback point is reached. Since $3500/$6250 is 0.56, the payback period is 2.56 years.

The payback method continues to be widely used, particularly at lower management levels, even though it is scorned by many academics. Its advantages are that it is quick and easy to apply. It also gives decision makers some idea of how long it will be until investment funds are recovered. Uncertainty surrounds every investment project. The costs and revenues on which analyses are based are really best estimates, not actual values. If an investment project has a quick payback, it is not considered as risky as when the payback is longer.

---

*A related technique is called the *internal rate of return* (IROR). Using trial and error, we find the discount rate that makes the present value of the after-tax inflows equal to the outflows. The IROR makes the NPV of a project equal to zero. Multiple projects can be ranked from best to worst using IROR.

The payback method also has drawbacks. A major criticism is that it encourages managers to focus on the short run. A project that takes a long time to develop, but generates excellent cash flows later in its life, is usually rejected by the payback method. The payback method has also been criticized for its failure to consider the time value of money. For these reasons, we recommend that payback analysis be combined with a more sophisticated method such as NPV in analyzing the financial implications of a project.

Managing by the Numbers

The precision and analytical detachment that come from using the NPV or payback method can be deceiving. American business has been accused of *managing by the numbers*, with a preference for short-term results from low-risk projects (see Hayes and Abernathy, 1980, and Skinner, 1984). Part of the problem lies with managers who are on the fast track to the top of their organizations. They occupy a rung on the ladder for a short time and then move up. They perceive it to be in their career interests to favor investments that give quick results. They establish short paybacks and high hurdle rates. They ignore or forgo long-term benefits from technological advances, innovative product plans, and strategic capacity additions. Over the long haul, this narrow vision jeopardizes the firm's competitive advantage—and even survival.

Managing by the numbers has a second cause. Projects with the greatest strategic impact are also likely to be riskier and have more qualitative benefits, which cannot be easily quantified. Consider an investment in some of the newer types of flexible automation. (See Chapter 5.) Benefits can include better quality, quicker delivery times, higher sales, and lower inventory. The equipment might be reprogrammed to handle new products not yet conceived of by the firm. Enough might be learned with the new technology that subsequent investments will pay off at an even higher rate of return. The mistake is to ignore these benefits simply because they cannot be easily quantified. It is far better to bring in the risks and qualitative factors as part of the analysis, rather than to ignore them. The proliferation of microcomputers and the corresponding use of computer spreadsheets to perform financial analyses have made possible the rapid evaluation of many different alternatives relating to a project. These are referred to as "what if" analyses and allow an analyst to look at what would happen to cash flows if certain events, or combinations of events, were to occur. Using a preference matrix may also help recognize more explicitly qualitative factors.

The message is clear. Financial analysis is a valuable tool for evaluating investment projects. However, it never replaces the insight that comes from "hands-on" experience. Managers must use their judgment, taking into account not only NPV or payback data, but also how the project fits operations and corporate strategy.

FORMULA REVIEW

1. Future value of an investment:

$$F = P(1 + r)^n$$

2. Present value of a future amount:

$$P = \frac{F}{(1 + r)^n}$$

3. Straight-line depreciation:

$$D = \frac{(I - S)}{n}$$

SUPPLEMENT HIGHLIGHTS

- Many financial techniques, such as the net present value (NPV) method, take into account the time value of money. The present value of a future amount, or annuity of several amounts, can be found by using formulas or by using values from tables.

- Only cash flows that change if the project is undertaken need to be considered. They should be converted to *after-tax* amounts before a financial analysis technique is applied to them. Depreciation is relevant to the analysis because it is a tax shield.

- The NPV method converts after-tax cash flows to their present value equivalent, using a hurdle rate established by management as the discount rate.

- The payback method determines the amount of time that will elapse before the after-tax cash flows pay back the initial investment. Although a popular technique, it encourages a short-run focus and does not consider the time value of money.

- American business has been accused of managing by the numbers and favoring low-risk projects that promise good short-term results. Over the long term, this approach can jeopardize a firm's competitive position and even its chances for survival.

KEY TERMS

annuity   785
compounding interest   783
depreciation   786
discount rate   784
discounting   784
future value of an investment   783
hurdle rate   790
net present value (NPV) method   789
payback method   790
present value of an investment   784
salvage value   788
time value of money   783

STUDY QUESTIONS

1. Give one example in each decision area of operations management that could require a capital investment.

2. Why does the payback method encourage projects with short-run results? Why might it be the method of choice for managers who are averse to risk?

3. How can we take advantage of financial techniques without falling into the trap of managing by the numbers?

REVIEW PROBLEMS

The financial analysis techniques presented in this supplement are applied in Chapter 2 (Problems 8–11), Chapter 4 (Problems 10–13), Chapter 5 (Problems 1–4), Chapter 6 (Problem 14), and Chapter 7 (Problems 7–11).

SELECTED REFERENCES

Hayes, Robert H., and William J. Abernathy, "Managing Our Way to Economic Decline," *Harvard Business Review* (July–August 1980), pp. 67–77.

Hodder, James E., and Henry E. Riggs, "Pitfalls in Evaluating Risky Projects," *Harvard Business Review* (January–February 1985), pp. 128–135.

Kieso, Donald E., and Jerry J. Weygandt, *Intermediate Accounting*, 4th ed. New York: John Wiley & Sons, 1983.

Skinner, Wickham, "Operations Technology: Blind Spot in Strategic Management," *Interfaces*, vol. 14, no. 1 (January–February 1984), pp. 116–125.

Weston, J. Fred, and Thomas E. Copeland, *Managerial Finance*, 8th ed. Chicago: Dryden, 1986

Woodward, Herbert N. "Management Strategies for Small Companies," *Harvard Business Review* (January–February 1976), pp. 113–121.

SUPPLEMENT 2

LINEAR PROGRAMMING

 Supplement Outline

Key Questions for Managers

What is the best product mix for our limited resources?

What are our most valuable resources in generating profits or reducing costs?

Which resources should we increase and by how much?

*T*his supplement addresses a technique that is useful for allocating scarce resources among competing demands. **Linear programming (LP)** seeks to optimize a linear objective function subject to a set of linear constraints. The product-mix problem, along with a number of others, can be analyzed with this method.

BASIC CONCEPTS IN LINEAR PROGRAMMING ▲

Consider Stratton Company's situation, as explained in Managerial Practice S2.1. Because the company's operations are focused and product lines do not share critical resources, the product-mix decision regarding the two types of pipe can be made independently of decisions about the other product lines. Even though there are other operations in the manufacturing of plastic pipe, this company only has three resources that are considered critical to the output of the pipe. The product-mix decision should be made in light of these limitations.

Let's begin construction of the mathematical model by letting

x_1 = the amount of type 1 pipe to be produced, measured in 100-foot increments; for example, $x_1 = 2$ means 200 feet of type 1 pipe

x_2 = the amount of type 2 pipe to be produced, measured in 100-foot increments

These are the decision variables to be determined by solution of the model. The values of these variables determine the product mix that the Stratton Company should implement. However, each unit of x_1 and x_2 produced consumes some of the critical resources. In the extrusion department, a unit of x_1 requires 4 hours, and a unit of x_2 requires 6 hours. For specific values of x_1

and x_2, we find the total amount of extrusion resources consumed by multiplying the number of units of each product produced by the resources consumed per unit and adding them. The total must not exceed the 48 hours of resources available. Thus we have the first constraint for our model:

$$4x_1 + 6x_2 \leq 48 \qquad \text{(extrusion)}$$

Similarly, we can formulate the constraints imposed by the packaging resource and the supply of additive mix:

$$2x_1 + 2x_2 \leq 18 \qquad \text{(packaging)}$$
$$2x_1 + 1x_2 \leq 16 \qquad \text{(additive mix)}$$

These three constraints impose restrictions on our choice of values for the decision variables. The values we choose for x_1 and x_2 must satisfy all the constraints, but an infinite number of values for x_1 and x_2 will satisfy these constraints. For example, $x_1 = 1, x_2 = 1$; $x_1 = 2.01, x_2 = 4.03$; and $x_1 = -4$, $x_2 = -10$ all satisfy the constraints in our problem. The negative values for x_1 and x_2 do not make sense, so we add so-called nonnegativity restrictions to the model as follows:

$$x_1 \geq 0 \qquad \text{and} \qquad x_2 \geq 0 \qquad \text{(nonnegativity restrictions)}$$

However, we are still left with an infinite number of possible solutions. In order to select the best values for x_1 and x_2, we need an objective function. The

MANAGERIAL PRACTICE S2.1　

The Stratton Company

The Stratton Company produces plastic pipe, couplings, and fittings for the construction industry. To increase the efficiency of its operations, the company has focused its resources by major product lines. The couplings and fittings require specialized equipment and are often produced to satisfy specific needs of the customer. The plastic pipe, however, is more standard, and general-purpose equipment can be used. Two basic types of plastic pipe are produced. They differ from each other with respect to diameter, wall thickness, and strength.

John Fisher, the plant manager, recently received an updated demand forecast for the two types of pipe. Based on an examination of the resources needed to manufacture the two pipe products, it was obvious that the plant could not satisfy the demand. Three resources are critical to the output of pipe: extrusion hours, packaging hours, and a special additive to the plastic raw material to control strength and flexibility. Fisher gathered the following data, which represent the situation for next week. All data are expressed in units of 100 feet of pipe.

Stratton Company wants to maximize the contribution to profits and overhead. Since each unit of x_1 yields \$34 and each unit of x_2 yields \$40, we want to maximize $\$34x_1 + \$40x_2$, subject to the various constraints.

We can now state the entire model for the product-mix problem at the Stratton Company.

$$\text{Objective:} \quad \text{Maximize } \$34x_1 + \$40x_2$$
$$\text{Subject to:} \quad 4x_1 + 6x_2 \le 48$$
$$2x_1 + 2x_2 \le 18$$
$$2x_1 + 1x_2 \le 16$$
$$x_1 \ge 0 \quad \text{and} \quad x_2 \ge 0$$

The methods we will discuss can be used to solve this model for those values of x_1 and x_2 that maximize the contribution to profits and overhead.

The General Linear Programming Method

We can solve the model we developed for the Stratton Company by an optimizing process known as linear programming, which seeks values for the decision variables that satisfy the linear constraints (including nonnegativity) of the problem and optimize a linear objective function. The general linear pro-

	Product		
Resource	Type 1	Type 2	Resource Availability
Extrusion	4 hr	6 hr	48 hr
Packaging	2 hr	2 hr	18 hr
Additive mix	2 lb	1 lb	16 lb

The contribution to profits and overhead per 100 feet of pipe is \$34 for type 1 and \$40 for type 2.

Fisher was uncertain about how much of each type of pipe to produce in order to maximize contribution to profits and overhead. Also, if more funds were made available to expand capacity in the extrusion or packaging areas, would it pay to increase capacities there if it costs \$8 per hour to increase extrusion capacity and \$6 per hour to increase packaging capacity? Finally, would it pay to buy more additive mix?

gramming method is

$$\text{Maximize:} \quad c_1 x_1 + c_2 x_2 + \cdots + c_n x_n$$

$$\text{Subject to:} \quad a_{11} x_1 + a_{12} x_2 + \cdots + a_{1n} x_n \leq b_1$$

$$a_{21} x_1 + a_{22} x_2 + \cdots + a_{2n} x_n \leq b_2$$

$$\vdots$$

$$a_{m1} x_1 + a_{m2} x_2 + \cdots + a_{mn} x_n \leq b_m$$

$$x_1, x_2, \cdots, x_n \geq 0$$

In this problem there are n decision variables and m constraints (exclusive of the nonnegativity restrictions). Some of the constraints could be written as *greater than or equal to* ($\geq$) or *equals* ($=$), depending on the problem statement. The c_j, a_{ij}, and b_i values are given constants. Linear programming can also be used to *minimize* the value of the objective function.

Some important assumptions implicit in the formulation of linear programming problems are:

1. The objective function and constraint equations must be linear. Thus we can have no cross-products of decision variables, powers of x_j, or other types of nonlinear terms in the problem formulation. For the Stratton Company, this implies that one unit of x_1 contributes \$34 to profits and overhead, and two units contribute \$68, regardless of how much x_2 is produced. Similarly, one unit of x_2 consumes 6 hours of extrusion time and two units consume 12 hours. Production of x_1 does not affect the per unit consumption of x_2 of any of the resources.

2. The decision variables can have fractional values. For example, $x_1 = 3.2$ in the Stratton Company example poses no problem, since it means 320 feet of pipe. However, in other problems the decision variables may be expressed in units such as workers, tables, or trucks that are not divisible. We can use a more advanced technique, called *integer programming*, in these situations if simply rounding off the linear programming solution, subject to satisfying the constraints, is unacceptable.

3. The constants are known with certainty. For example, each unit of x_1 requires 2 pounds of additive—no more, no less. The values of the constants cannot be statistical averages. They must be deterministic values that will not change when the solution to the problem is implemented.

Although these assumptions are quite restrictive, linear programming can provide a means to analyze complex resource allocation problems and several other benefits that are worth considering. First, the process of building the model forces managers to identify the important decision variables and constraints, which can be useful in its own right. Identifying the nature and scope of the problem represents a big step toward solving it. Second, even though we assume that we know all the constants with certainty, we can use our best guess about their proper values and perform a *sensitivity analysis* of the constants that we suspect of violating our assumptions. Sensitivity analysis is a method whereby we systematically modify the value of critical constants in order to determine how the optimal solution is affected. For example, suppose that John Fisher at the Stratton Company was not sure about the number of packaging hours available next week; it could vary from 16 to 20 hours. Fisher could use the linear programming model and first try 16 hours, then 20 hours.* If there is no significant difference in the resulting product mixes, the value for available resources in the packaging department is not critical in the range of 16 to 20 hours. A reasonable value, such as 18 hours, would do for planning purposes. However, if the product mix is sensitive to the amount of packaging resources in this range, Fisher should try to estimate the amount of resources he will have next week. If the best he can do is specify a range of possible values, he may have to use a more sophisticated technique, such as *chance-constrained programming* or *stochastic programming* (see Wagner, 1975).

Finally, the solution to a linear programming problem is not necessarily the solution that management will actually use. Often, various nonquantitative factors must be considered. Nonetheless, the linear programming solution can be a good starting point for the final decision.

Graphic Analysis

Solutions to practical linear programming problems involve algebraic methods. However, considerable insight into linear programming concepts can be provided through the analysis of a simple two-variable problem using the **graphical method of linear programming**. We will continue to use the Stratton Company product-mix problem as our example.

We begin by plotting the constraint equations, disregarding the inequality portion of the constraints ($<$) and assuming that each constraint is an equality ($=$). We let one variable equal zero and plot the axis intercept of the other variable. For the extrusion department, we have $4x_1 + 6x_2 = 48$. If $x_1 = 0$, then $x_2 = 8$. Similarly, if $x_2 = 0$, then $x_1 = 12$. We can connect the points (0, 8) and (12, 0) with a straight line, as shown in Fig. S2.1. All points on the line *and* to the left of the line will satisfy the extrusion constraint because the original constraint was an inequality. We can plot the two other constraints in a similar manner.

Each constraint helps to define the region of feasible solutions to the problem. The **feasible region**, shown as the shaded portion of Fig. S2.1, contains

---

*Certain information about the range of values for c_j and b_i for which the optimal solution will not change can be derived by analyzing the algebraic information associated with the optimal solution itself without recalculating the entire solution each time. However, this analysis holds only for changes in the constants taken one at a time and not in combination with others.

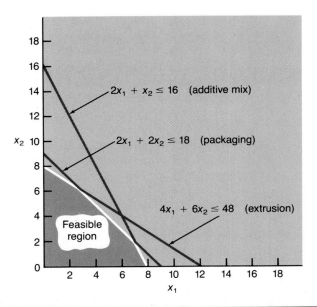

$2x_1 + x_2 \leq 16$ (additive mix)

$2x_1 + 2x_2 \leq 18$ (packaging)

$4x_1 + 6x_2 \leq 48$ (extrusion)

Feasible region

FIGURE S2.1   Feasible Region for the Product-Mix Problem

the solutions that satisfy all the constraints simultaneously, including the non-negativity restrictions. In our product-mix example, all the constraints were of the *less-than-or-equal-to* variety. Consequently, only the values of x_1 and x_2 in the lower left portion of the graph are feasible. In general, this condition is not always the case. For example, suppose that a linear programming model had the constraints:

$$2x_1 + x_2 \geq 10$$
$$2x_1 + 2x_2 \geq 18$$
$$x_1 \leq 7$$
$$x_2 \leq 5$$
$$x_1, x_2 \geq 0$$

Figure S2.2 shows the feasible region in this case. The two *greater-than-or-equal-to* constraints provide lower limits that must be met or exceeded. Only the points on the line and to the right are feasible for these constraints.

After we have defined the feasible region for the Stratton Company, the problem becomes one of finding the solution that maximizes the contribution to profits and overhead. The optimal solution to a linear programming problem will be an extreme point (corner point) of the feasible region. In Fig. S2.1 there are four corner points, excluding the origin, which would obviously be a poor solution. We could try each of these corner points in the objective function and select the one that maximizes its value. We may not be able to read these points from the graph accurately enough in some cases, and algebraically solving for all the corner points is inefficient when we have to calculate a large number of points.

The best approach is to plot the objective function on the graph of the feasible region for some arbitrary value of total contribution to profits and overhead. The line is called an *iso-profit* line because every point on that line will yield the same contribution. We can then draw a series of other iso-profit lines parallel to that line until we find the one farthest from the origin but still touching the feasible region. This point identifies the optimal solution to the problem.

We can use a similar procedure when we want to minimize the objective function. In this case we would draw an *iso-cost* line for an arbitrary value on the graph of the feasible region. We would then draw parallel iso-cost lines until we found the one *closest* to the origin but still touching the feasible region.

Suppose that we plot the objective function of our product-mix problem for an arbitrary value of \$170 in the same manner as the constraint equations. This line is shown in Fig. S2.3, along with two other iso-profit lines. It is obvious that the optimal solution to the problem occurs at the corner point represented by the intersection of the extrusion and packaging constraints. Simultaneously

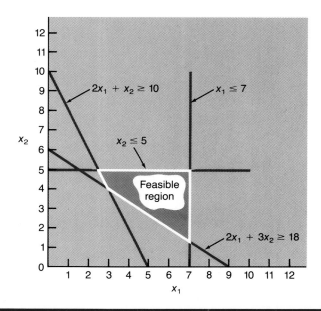

FIGURE S2.2   Feasible Region with Lower Limits for the Product-Mix Problem

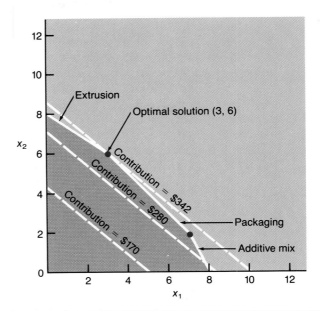

FIGURE S2.3   Iso-Profit Lines and Solution to the Product-Mix Problem

solving the two equations representing these constraints yields $x_1 = 3$ and $x_2 = 6$. This is the optimal product mix, which can be verified by looking at the graph. The Stratton Company should produce 300 feet of type 1 pipe and 600 feet of type 2 pipe next week.

There can be more than one optimal solution to a linear programming problem. This situation occurs when the objective function is parallel to one of the faces of the feasible region and would be the case if our objective function were $\$38x_1 + \$38x_2$. Both $x_1 = 3, x_2 = 6$ and $x_1 = 7, x_2 = 2$, as well as any other point on the line connecting these two corner points, would be optimal. When this situation occurs, management would probably base a final decision on nonquantifiable factors. The important point here, however, is that we only need to consider the corner points of the feasible region when optimizing an objective function. Even when there are multiple optimal solutions, there will always be a corner point that is the optimum. This feature enables us to use a technique capable of solving complex linear programming problems efficiently.

THE SIMPLEX METHOD ▲

The **simplex method** is an iterative algebraic procedure for solving linear programming problems. Starting with an initial solution, the procedure systematically evaluates corner points of the feasible region in such a way that the objective function improves (or at worst stays the same) at each iteration. In practice, these problems are solved on computers, but we will solve manually the Stratton Company product-mix problem to demonstrate the logic of the approach.

Problem Formulation and Initial Tableau

Recall the model we developed for the Stratton Company product-mix problem:

$$\text{Maximize:} \quad \$34x_1 + \$40x_2$$
$$\text{Subject to:} \quad 4x_1 + 6x_2 \leq 48$$
$$2x_1 + 2x_2 \leq 18$$
$$2x_1 + 1x_2 \leq 16$$
$$x_1, x_2 \geq 0$$

The simplex method involves the solution of linear equations, but the constraints in our model are expressed as inequalities. In order to use the simplex method, we have to transform the original model and express all constraints as equalities. We can do this by augmenting the model with *slack variables*, that is,

$$\text{Maximize:} \quad \$34x_1 + \$40x_2 + \$0s_1 + \$0s_2 + \$0s_3$$
$$\text{Subject to:} \quad 4x_1 + 6x_2 + 1s_1 + 0s_2 + 0s_3 = 48$$
$$2x_1 + 2x_2 + 0s_1 + 1s_2 + 0s_3 = 18$$
$$2x_1 + 1x_2 + 0s_1 + 0s_2 + 1s_3 = 16$$
$$x_1, x_2, s_1, s_2, s_3 \geq 0$$

A slack variable for a given constraint takes up the difference between the total resource consumption implied by specific values of x_1 and x_2 and the total amount of the resource available. For example, consider the extrusion constraint for which s_1 is the slack variable and actually represents the amount of idle time in the extrusion department. If $x_1 = 2$ and $x_2 = 5$, s_1 would be 10 hours (or $48 - 38$). Alternatively, if $x_1 = 3$ and $x_2 = 6$, s_1 would be zero. Slack variables must be nonnegative to ensure that they accurately measure the slack resources for a particular constraint. Also, since slack resources do not generate contributions to profits and overhead, they have coefficients of zero in the objective function. Insofar as the decision variables x_1 and x_2 are concerned, an optimal solution to the augmented model will also be an optimal solution to the original model.

The most convenient way to summarize the information needed to solve a linear programming problem using the simplex method is to use a tableau. Table S2.1 shows the initial tableau for our product-mix problem. Most of it merely duplicates the c_j, a_{ij}, and b_i constants row-by-row from our augmented model. The first row of the tableau contains the objective function coefficients

TABLE S2.1   Initial Tableau for the Product-Mix Problem

c_j		$34	$40	$0	$0	$0	
	Solution Variables	x_1	x_2	s_1	s_2	s_3	Quantity
$0	s_1	4	⑥	1	0	0	48 ←
$0	s_2	2	2	0	1	0	18
$0	s_3	2	1	0	0	1	16
	z_j	$0	$0	$0	$0	$0	$0
	$c_j - z_j$	$34	$40 ↑	$0	$0	$0	

for each variable, including slack variables. This is the only row that does not change in subsequent tableaus. The first column shows the objective function coefficients for the variables in the current solution to the problem.

The variables (one for each constraint) chosen for the current solution are listed under *solution variables*. In the initial tableau the slack variables are chosen for the initial solution to the problem. In our example, we have three constraints; consequently, we list s_1, s_2, and s_3. The column labeled *quantity* shows the current value of the solution variables. In the initial tableau these values are merely the quantities on the right-hand side of the constraint equations. The initial tableau for our product-mix problem indicates that $s_1 = 48$, $s_2 = 18$, and $s_3 = 16$. By convention, the variables that are not in the current solution have values of zero. Thus $x_1 = 0$ and $x_2 = 0$. This solution corresponds to the origin (0, 0) in the graph of the feasible region shown in Fig. S2.3.

All the variables in the problem are listed to the right of the solution variables column. In the initial tableau, the coefficients of a particular variable in each constraint of the augmented model are listed under the variable name. These coefficients in the initial and subsequent tableaus have a special meaning. They indicate the *substitution rates* for a particular variable not in the solution, relative to those variables in the solution. For example, the 6, 2, and 1 in the x_2 column mean that for each unit of x_2 introduced into the solution, s_1 will be reduced by 6 units, s_2 will be reduced by 2 units, and s_3 will be reduced by 1 unit. In subsequent tableaus, these substitution rates will change. This information will be useful in determining how to improve the current solution at any iteration.

The final two rows of the tableau provide summary information about the trade-offs in introducing a variable into the solution. The z_j row shows the *profit forgone* by introducing 1 unit of variable j into the solution. To calculate the value of z_j, we need the substitution rates for variable j (in the column for variable j) and the profit contributions of the variables in the solution (the coefficients in the column labeled c_j on the far left). Consider variable x_1. If we introduce 1 unit of variable x_1 into the solution, we must give up 4 units of s_1, 2 units of s_2, and 2 units of s_3. However, since slack variables provide no contribution to profits, the total profit forgone by the introduction of 1 unit of x_1 is $z_1 = \$0(4) + \$0(2) + \$0(2) = \$0$. All we are doing is giving up slack resources at this stage of the solution process. Similarly, $z_2 = \$0(6) + \$0(2) + \$0(1) = \$0$. The value for z_j in the *quantity* column shows the current value of the objective function. Since $s_1 = 48$, $s_2 = 18$, and $s_3 = 16$, we have $\$0(48) + \$0(18) + \$0(16) = \$0$.

The $c_j - z_j$ row shows the *net contribution* effect of introducing 1 unit of variable j into the solution. It is the difference between the profit contribution of variable j and the profit forgone by the introduction of 1 unit of variable j. For x_1 we have $c_1 - z_1 = \$34$ (or $\$34 - \$0$), and for x_2 we have $c_2 - z_2 = \$40$ (or $\$40 - \$0$). The net contribution for any variable already in the solution will always be $\$0$ because the introduction of one more unit into the solution must be accompanied by the removal of 1 unit of the same variable to avoid violating one of the constraints.

It is apparent from the initial tableau that no resources are being used in production because only slack variables are in the solution. In addition, it also shows that the current solution can be improved. This is evident in the $c_j - z_j$ row where the net contributions by x_1 and x_2 are greater than zero.

Selecting the Entering Variable

In linear programming, we select one variable to enter the solution and one variable to leave the solution at each iteration until we find the optimal solution. The $c_j - z_j$ row tells us whether an improved solution is possible. In our problem, there is a positive net contribution of $\$34$ per unit of x_1 and $\$40$ per unit of x_2. As we are interested in maximizing the contribution to profits and overhead, it would make sense to choose the variable that has the largest net contribution as the new variable to enter into the solution. This variable is x_2 in our product-mix problem. The column associated with the entering variable is designated with a vertical arrow in Table S2.1.

Determining the Exiting Variable

Now that we have decided to introduce x_2 into the solution, we must determine the variable it is to replace. Consider Fig. S2.1 again and the current solution, which is at the origin. To introduce x_2 into the solution, we proceed vertically along the x_2 axis. We want to have as much x_2 in the solution as possible without violating any constraints, so our choices are 8, 9, and 16, as denoted by the intercepts of the equations for the constraints. It is obvious that if we want to satisfy *all* the constraints by our choice of x_2, we must be limited to the *smallest* increase, or $x_2 = 8$.

We can come to the same conclusion without the graph by using the substitution rates for the entering variable and the values in the quantity column of the tableau. We can find the value that the entering variable will have in the next solution and the variable in the current solution that will be replaced. For example,

$$s_1 \text{ row (extrusion):} \qquad \frac{48}{6} = 8$$

$$s_2 \text{ row (packaging):} \qquad \frac{18}{2} = 9$$

$$s_3 \text{ row (additive mix):} \qquad \frac{16}{1} = 16$$

As we increase x_1 from zero, the first limitation that we encounter is the extrusion capacity, when $x_2 = 8$. If we go beyond that value we will violate the constraint. Also, since s_1 is associated with the first row, it will be at zero when $x_2 = 8$. This result makes intuitive sense because s_1 is the amount of idle resources in the extrusion department. When $x_2 = 8$, we are using all the extrusion capacity for the production of type 2 pipe because each unit of that product consumes 6 hours of extrusion time. Consequently, s_1 is the variable that exits the solution, and the row associated with s_1 is designated by a horizontal arrow, as shown in Table S2.1.

To summarize the simplex method to this point, we have used two rules.

Entering rule. Select the variable with the largest value of $c_j - z_j$ to introduce into the solution in a *maximization* problem. In a *minimization* problem, select the variable with the largest *negative* value of $c_j - z_j$ because the objective function is to be as small as possible.

Exiting rule. Divide the substitution rates for the entering variable into the corresponding values in the quantity column. Consider only *positive* values for the substitution rates and select the row variable with the lowest ratio to be removed from the solution. This procedure is the same regardless of whether the objective function is to be minimized or maximized.

Transforming the Tableau

As we mentioned earlier, we use the simplex method to systematically evaluate corner points of a feasible region. Because the corner points are formed by the intersection of lines representing linear equations, we need to solve a system of linear equations. We will use a procedure called *Gaussian elimination* to transform the tableau to reflect a new solution to our problem. In the tableau, the coefficients in the column of a variable currently in the solution consist of a 1 in the row associated with that variable and 0s in all the other rows. For s_1, our exiting variable, we have 1, 0, 0. The values in the column for x_2, our entering variable, are 6, 2, 1. The Gaussian elimination procedure will transform the column for x_2 into 1, 0, 0, thereby entering x_2 into the solution and replacing s_1. We make this transformation by performing various mathematical operations on the rows of the tableau. In a system of linear equations, we can multiply an entire equation by a constant and not change the nature of the relationship. We can also add two equations to form a third equation to replace one of them and not change the solution to the original set of equations. We now apply Gaussian elimination to transform our initial tableau.

Calculating the New Row for the Entering Variable. At the intersection of the entering variable column and the exiting variable row is a value called the *pivot element*. (See the circled value in Table S2.1.) We replace the old s_1 row with a new row having a value of 1 for the pivot element. That is, we divide the values in the old s_1 row by the pivot element 6 to create a new row for our next tableau:

	x_1	x_2	s_1	s_2	s_3	Quantity
Old s_1 row	4	6	1	0	0	48
New x_2 row	2/3	1	1/6	0	0	8

The new x_2 row replaces the first row in our tableau. Note that the new value for x_2 (in the quantity column) will be 8 in our next solution.

Transforming the Other Rows. We transform each of the other rows by selecting an appropriate constant, multiplying each element of the new x_2 row by this constant, and adding the result, element by element, to the row to be changed in such a way that we have a 0 in the x_2 column. The appropriate constant in each case is the element in the x_2 column for the row to be transformed, multiplied by -1. For the s_2 row, the constant is -2, and for the s_3 row it is -1. Table S2.2 shows the calculations for the transformed s_2 and s_3 rows.

TABLE S2.2 Transforming the s_2 and s_3 Rows in the Product-Mix Problem

Column	s_2 Row						s_3 Row					
	Old s_2 row	+	(Constant for s_2	×	New x_2 row)	= New s_2 row	Old s_3 row	+	(Constant for s_3	×	New x_2 row)	= New s_3 row
x_1	2	+	(-2	×	2/3)	= 2/3	2	+	(-1	×	2/3)	= 4/3
x_2	2	+	(-2	×	1)	= 0	1	+	(-1	×	1)	= 0
s_1	0	+	(-2	×	1/6)	= $-1/3$	0	+	(-1	×	1/6)	= $-1/6$
s_2	1	+	(-2	×	0)	= 1	0	+	(-1	×	0)	= 0
s_3	0	+	(-2	×	0)	= 0	1	+	(-1	×	0)	= 1
Quantity	18	+	(-2	×	8)	= 2	16	+	(-1	×	8)	= 8

TABLE S2.3   Second Tableau for the Product-Mix Problem

c_j		$34	$40	$0	$0	$0	
	Solution Variables	x_1	x_2	s_1	s_2	s_3	Quantity
$40	x_2	2/3	1	1/6	0	0	8
$0	s_2	(2/3)	0	−1/3	1	0	2 ←
$0	s_3	4/3	0	−1/6	0	1	8
	z_j	$80/3*	$40	$20/3[†]	$0	$0	$320
	$c_j - z_j$	$22/3 ↑	$0	−$20/3	$0	$0	

*$z_1 = \$40(2/3) + \$0(2/3) + \$0(4/3) = \$80/3$.
[†]$z_3 = \$40(1/6) - \$0(1/3) - \$0(1/6) = \$40/6 = \$20/3$.

The new tableau is shown in Table S2.3. We calculated values for the z_j and $c_j - z_j$ rows as before, except that now some of the z_j values are greater than zero. At the end of this first iteration it is obvious that we can make further improvements in the solution, since $c_1 - z_1 = \$22/3$.

Criterion of Optimality and the Solution to the Product-Mix Problem

The criterion for optimality in a linear programming problem can be stated as follows for

Maximization problems: If every entry in th $c_j - z_j$ row is zero or negative, the current solution is optimal.

Minimization problems: If every entry in the $c_j - z_j$ is zero or positive, the current solution is optimal.

Because our product-mix problem is a maximization problem, we have not met the criterion of optimality. Consequently, we must perform another iteration of the tableau. The entering variable is x_1, as it has the largest positive $c_j - z_j$ value. The exiting variable is s_2 because it had the lowest value when we divided the substitution rates in the x_1 column into the values in the quantity column. Thus

$$x_2 \text{ row: } \quad 8/(2/3) = 12$$
$$s_2 \text{ row: } \quad 2/(2/3) = 3$$
$$s_3 \text{ row: } \quad 8/(4/3) = 6$$

TABLE S2.4 Transforming the x_2 and s_3 Rows in the Product-Mix Problem

Column	Old x_2 row	+	(Constant for x_2	×	New x_i row)	=	New x_2 row	Old s_3 row	+	(Constant for s_3	×	New x_i row)	=	New s_3 row
x_1	2/3	+	($-2/3$	×	1)	=	0	4/3	+	($-4/3$	×	1)	=	0
x_2	1	+	($-2/3$	×	0)	=	1	0	+	($-4/3$	×	0)	=	0
s_1	1/6	+	($-2/3$	×	$-1/2$)	=	1/2	$-1/6$	+	($-4/3$	×	$-1/2$)	=	1/2
s_2	0	+	($-2/3$	×	3/2)	=	-1	0	+	($-4/3$	×	3/2)	=	-2
s_3	0	+	($-2/3$	×	0)	=	0	1	+	($-4/3$	×	0)	=	1
Quantity	8	+	($-2/3$	×	3)	=	6	8	+	($-4/3$	×	3)	=	4

Consequently, x_1 will enter the solution and replace s_2. The pivot element for this iteration is 2/3. Dividing the values in the old s_2 row in Table S2.3 by 2/3 yields the new x_1 row:

	x_1	x_2	s_1	s_2	s_3	Quantity
New x_1 row	1	0	$-1/2$	3/2	0	3

The calculations for transforming the x_2 and s_3 rows are shown in Table S2.4 and the new tableau is shown in Table S2.5. We have now satisfied the criterion for optimality. The Stratton Company should produce 300 feet of type 1 pipe and 600 feet of type 2 pipe. In so doing, the company will use all the available time for the extrusion and packaging ($s_1 = s_2 = 0$) and will have an extra 4 pounds of additive mix ($s_3 = 4$). You can verify the latter result by substituting $x_1 = 3$ and $x_2 = 6$ into the constraint for the additive mix.

TABLE S2.5 Optimal Tableau for the Product-Mix Problem

c_j			\$34	\$40	\$0	\$0	\$0	
		Solution Variables	x_1	x_2	s_1	s_2	s_3	Quantity
\$40		x_2	0	1	1/2	-1	0	6
\$34		x_1	1	0	$-1/2$	3/2	0	3
\$0		s_3	0	0	1/2	-2	1	4
		z_j	\$34	\$40	\$3	\$11	\$0	\$342
		$c_j - z_j$	\$0	\$0	$-\$3$	$-\$11$	\$0	

The simplex process started at the origin and moved to the corner point $x_1 = 0$, $x_2 = 8$ because x_2 contributed the most to profits and overhead. It then moved to the intersection of the extrusion and packaging constraints (Fig. S2.1), which is the optimal solution. Note that the value of x_2 was reduced from 8 to 6 in the final iteration. By introducing 3 units of x_1, we were able to better utilize the available resources and generate more contribution to profits and overhead, even though we gave up 2 units of x_2.

Sensitivity Analysis

The simplex method provides more useful information than just the optimal solution to a linear programming problem. From the optimal tableau we can determine the value of each resource in terms of its contribution to profits and overhead. We can also determine the net benefit (or cost) of adjusting the amount of resources we have (the b_i quantities on the right-hand side of the constraint equations). This information can be useful in making policy decisions about resource acquisition. Alternatively, if the b_i quantities must be forecasts, the information can be useful in determining the consequences of inaccurate forecasting. In this section we discuss the sensitivity analysis concepts of shadow prices and right-hand-side ranging.

Shadow Prices. The relative value of a resource with respect to the objective function in a linear programming problem is called its **shadow price**. It is the amount of change in the objective function per unit change in its right-hand-side value. Since the slack variables measure the amount of idle resources, the shadow prices for the resources are found in the $c_j - z_j$ row for the slack variables (disregarding the negative signs). Thus, in Table S2.5, the shadow price for extrusion capacity is $3 per hour and is found in the s_1 column. Similarly, the shadow prices for packaging and the additive mix are $11 per hour and $0 per pound, respectively.

We can use the shadow prices for our product-mix problem in the following way. If we had an additional hour of packaging capacity next week, we could generate $11 more in contribution to profits and overhead. If the added hour would cost less than $11 to obtain, it would pay for us to add an hour to the packaging capacity. For example, if the additional hour cost $7, the contribution to profits and overhead would increase by $4. Similarly, if we had one *less* hour of packaging capacity next week, it would cost $11 in lost contribution to profits and overhead. The trade-offs for extrusion capacity are similar, but the impact on profits and overhead per hour of capacity is much less. The shadow price of zero for the additive mix makes sense because we already have an extra 4 pounds that we cannot use. Adjusting the availability of that resource by a pound would have no effect on the value of the objective function.

We can now answer the questions posed by John Fisher in Managerial Practice S2.1. Since it costs $8 per hour to expand extrusion capacity, he should not do it because the shadow price for that capacity is only $3 per hour. However, expanding packaging hours costs only \$6 per hour and the shadow price is \$11 per hour. Therefore he should increase packaging capacity. Finally, buying more additive mix would not pay because there is already a surplus of 4 pounds; the shadow price is zero for that resource.

Right-Hand-Side Ranging. Knowing that the shadow price is greater than the cost of acquiring a given resource or less than the price we could obtain from selling it has only limited usefulness. We need to know *how much* resource we can buy or sell and retain an advantage. Put another way, we need the range of right-hand-side quantities (b_i's) over which the shadow price is valid for a given resource. This procedure is called **right-hand-side ranging**, and we start with the information in the optimal tableau.

For illustrative purposes consider packaging capacity, for which s_2 is the slack variable. The optimal tableau in Table S2.5 shows that if we add one hour of s_2 into the solution, we will increase the production of x_2 by 1 unit (because the substitution rate is -1), decrease the production of x_1 by 3/2 units, and increase the slack amount of additive mix by 2 pounds (the substitution rate is -2). The profits and overhead contribution forgone would be \$11. However, *adding* one hour of s_2 is analogous to reducing the number of packaging hours (b_2) by one hour because it restricts the amount of resources available for x_1 and x_2. We can determine how many hours of packaging capacity we would be willing to sell (that is, how much s_2 we can introduce into the solution), provided that the price exceeds \$11, in the same way that we determined the exiting variable in the simplex procedure:

$$x_2 \text{ row:} \quad 6/(-1) = -6 \quad \text{(negative, disregard)*}$$
$$x_1 \text{ row:} \quad 3/(3/2) = 2$$
$$s_3 \text{ row:} \quad 4/(-2) = -2 \quad \text{(negative, disregard)}$$

Consequently, we can introduce two hours of s_2 (or equivalently, reduce packaging hours by 2, to 16 hours) before we will replace x_1 in the solution. The solution would then be $x_1 = 0$ and $x_2 = 8$, as shown in Fig. S2.4. Every hour that we reduce capacity over this range will cost us \$11 in contribution to profits and overhead.

Now, we need to determine how much we can expand packaging capacity and still obtain a benefit of \$11 per hour. Again, we work with slack variable s_2 in the optimal tableau, but this time we reverse the signs of the substitution rates. Intuitively, adding negative s_2 to the solution is analogous to adding packaging capacity. Proceeding as we did before, we have

$$x_2 \text{ row:} \quad 6/(1) = 6$$
$$x_1 \text{ row:} \quad 3/(-3/2) = -2 \quad \text{(negative, disregard)}$$
$$s_3 \text{ row:} \quad 4/(2) = 2$$

---

*A negative substitution rate means that the row variable actually increases as the entering variable increases. Therefore the exiting variable cannot be one that has a negative substitution rate with the entering variable.

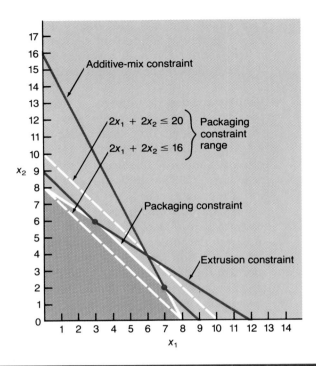

FIGURE S2.4   Right-Hand-Side Ranging for the Packaging Constraint

As we increase packaging capacity we will ultimately run out of additive mix because s_3 will become the exiting variable. We can add only 2 hours before this will happen, making total packaging capacity 20 hours. The new solution would be $x_1 = 6$ and $x_2 = 4$ in Fig. S2.4. The new value of the objective function would be $364, or $22 more than in our current solution, as we would expect. Consequently, the range in packaging hours over which the shadow price of $11 would be valid is $16 \leq b_2 \leq 20$.

Similarly, we can find the range for extrusion capacity: $40 \leq b_1 \leq 54$. With respect to the additive mix, the shadow price of $0 will hold for any increase in supply. It will also hold for any reductions of up to 4 pounds because that is the amount of slack resource we have. Therefore the range for the additive mix is $12 \leq b_3 \leq \infty$.

Problem Formulation with Equality or Greater-Than-or-Equal-To Constraints

Suppose that our product mix problem had the requirement that all the additive mix be used in the production of x_1 and x_2. The constraint would now be

$$2x_1 + 1x_2 = 16$$

Before, when the constraint was $2x_1 + 1x_2 \leq 16$, we added a slack variable to make the constraint an equality and to provide us with an initial solution to the problem. Now, the constraint does not allow slack, and we have no convenient initial solution. To overcome this difficulty we can add an *artificial variable* to the constraint equation, as follows:

$$2x_1 + 1x_2 + 1a_1 = 16$$

Insofar as it gives us an initial solution, an artificial variable acts like a slack variable. However, unlike a slack variable, an artificial variable should not appear in the final solution to the problem. If a_1 has a positive value in the end, it would mean that $2x_1 + 1x_2 < 16$, which violates the constraint. To safeguard against this result, we insert a very large negative coefficient in the objective function for a_1. The objective function for our problem would then be

$$\text{Maximize:} \quad \$34x_1 + \$40x_2 + \$0s_1 + \$0s_2 - \$ma_1$$

where m is a number such as $1 million.* As it has a negative sign, the simplex method will remove it from the solution before we find the optimal solution.

We also need to modify each greater-than-or-equal-to constraint. Suppose that we must use *at least* 16 pounds of additive mix. The constraint would become $2x_1 + 1x_2 \geq 16$. Adding a slack variable to make the constraint an equality will not work here. We have to subtract something from the left-hand side of the constraint to make it an equality, as follows:

$$2x_1 + 1x_2 - 1s_3 = 16$$

The variable s_3, which must be nonnegative, is called a *surplus variable* and measures the amount by which the left-hand side exceeds the right-hand side of the constraint. Unfortunately, even though we now have an equality, we do not have an initial solution. We would have $s_3 = -16$, which violates the nonnegativity restriction.

We can use an artificial variable to provide an initial solution here, as we did for the previous constraint equation. We write the constraint as follows:

$$2x_1 + 1x_2 - 1s_3 + 1a_1 = 16$$

The objective function would now be

$$\text{Maximize:} \quad \$34x_1 + \$40x_2 + \$0s_1 + \$0s_2 + \$0s_3 - \$ma_1$$

Note that the surplus variable has a coefficient of zero in the objective function, just like a slack variable. Procedurally, the simplex method treats slack, surplus, and artificial variables identically; however, artificial variables have no economic meaning and must have a value of zero in the final solution.

---

*In a minimization problem, an artificial variable has a large *positive* coefficient, m, in the objective function to ensure that it will not appear in the final solution.

Summary of the Simplex Method

Using the simplex method involves the following steps:

1. Formulate the problem in terms of a linear objective function and a set of linear constraints. Augment the formulation with slack, surplus, or artificial variables, as needed.

2. Set up the initial tableau with slack or artificial variables as the solution variables and calculate the z_j and $c_j - z_j$ quantities.

3. Determine the entering variable with the largest $c_j - z_j$ value in maximization problems or the smallest $c_j - z_j$ value for minimization problems.

4. Determine the exiting variable by finding the ratio of the value in the quantity column to the corresponding substitution rate in the entering variable column for each row and selecting the smallest positive ratio.

5. Create a new tableau. Calculate the new row for the entering variable by dividing the old row for the exiting variable by the pivot element and placing it in the new tableau. Use Gaussian elimination to transform the values in the remaining rows and place them in the new array. Calculate the new z_j and $c_j - z_j$ values for the new tableau.

6. In maximization problems, if all $c_j - z_j$ values are zero or negative, the optimal solution has been found. In minimization problems, stop when all $c_j - z_j$ values are zero or positive. If these conditions do not hold, repeat steps 3–6.

APPLICATION OF LINEAR PROGRAMMING TO OPERATIONS MANAGEMENT ▲

Linear programming has been applied to a wide variety of operations management problems, some of which are shown in Table S2.6. Although linear programming is a powerful tool for solving complex resource allocation problems and can provide much information about the implicit values of various resources, we must emphasize that it is *only a tool* for decision makers. Linear programming does not make decisions—decision makers do. Linear programming is a method for solving a linear model that specifies the objectives and constraints for particular type of problem. In the model, linearity in all relationships must be assumed. At best, in most applications this assumption yields only a good approximation to the real relationships. Consequently, the solution of the model can be regarded only as a good starting point for the overall solution of the problem. In this regard, the supplementary information generated, such as shadow prices of critical resources or right-hand-side ranges, could be more important than the solution itself.

TABLE S2.6	Typical Applications of Linear Programming to Resource Allocation Problems

Problem Type	Description
Production planning	*Production:* Find the minimum-cost production schedule for a given work-force plan, taking into account inventory carrying, and subcontracting costs.
	Production and work force: Find the minimum-cost production schedule, taking into account hiring and layoff costs as well as inventory carrying, overtime, and subcontracting costs, subject to various capacity and policy constraints.
	Staffing: Find the optimal staffing plan for various categories of workers, subject to various demand and policy constraints.
Distribution	*Shipping plans:* Find the optimal shipping assignments from factories to distribution centers or from warehouses to retailers.
Inventory planning	*Stock control:* Determine the optimal mix of products to hold in inventory in a warehouse.
	Supplier selection: Find the optimal combination of suppliers to minimize the amount of unwanted inventory.
Location planning	*Plants or warehouses:* Determine the optimal location of a plant or warehouse with respect to total transportation costs between various alternative locations and existing supply and demand sources.
Process control	*Stock cutting:* Given the dimensions of a roll or sheet of raw material, find the cutting pattern that minimizes the amount of scrap material.
Product planning	*Mixes:* Find the optimal production quantities of a group of products, subject to resource capacity and market demand constraints.
	Blends: Find the optimal proportions of various ingredients of products such as gasoline, paints, and foods, subject to certain minimal requirements.
Scheduling	*Shifts:* Determine the minimum-cost assignment of workers to shifts, subject to varying demand.
	Vehicles: Assign m vehicles to n products or jobs and determine the number of trips to make, subject to vehicle size, vehicle availability, and demand constraints.
	Routing: Find the optimal routing of a product through a number of sequential processes, each with their own capacities and characteristics.

Practical applications of linear programming are carried out with the help of a computer. Most major computer vendors have general-purpose software packages that solve complex linear programming problems. Although the concepts we have presented in this supplement could be used for large-scale applications, the advanced procedures of computer programs and the computational speed of the computer dramatically reduce the amount of time required to solve problems. In addition, a complete sensitivity analysis of objective function coefficients and right-hand-side values is provided along with the solution. If a particular application, such as product mix or blending, must be repeated frequently, special-purpose programs can be developed. They have input generator routines that simplify the input of data and generate the objective function and constraints for the problem. These special-purpose programs also have output routines that prepare specially designed managerial reports.

SUPPLEMENT HIGHLIGHTS

- Linear programming is a powerful tool that can be used to help solve resource allocation problems. It can be used to optimize a linear objective function, subject to a set of linear constraints and has been applied to a wide variety of resource allocation problems.
- The simplex method is an iterative algebraic procedure for solving linear programming problems. It systematically evaluates corner points of the feasible region in such a way that the objective function improves (or at worst stays the same) at each iteration. The optimal simplex tableau can be used to do sensitivity analysis. The shadow prices of the resources are provided in that tableau. Also, right-hand-side ranging can be used to determine the sensitivity of the solution to changes in the amount of resources.
- Linear programming should be considered only as a tool to aid in the analysis of operations management problems. The final decision might differ from the solutions generated by these techniques after various nonquantitative factors are considered.

KEY TERMS

feasible region   799
graphical method of linear
  programming   799
linear programming (LP)   795
right-hand-side ranging   811
shadow price   810
simplex method   802

STUDY QUESTIONS

1. In solving resource allocation problems with the help of linear programming, what assumptions do you make about the relationships of variables and constants in the problems?
2. Explain linear programming, say, to your boss, in an intuitively appealing way.
3. In the simplex method, the exiting variable in any iteration is determined by calculating the ratios of the values in the quantity column to the corresponding substitution rates in the entering variable column and selecting the row having the lowest positive ratio. Explain why you must choose the *minimum* ratio.
4. How can linear programming be used to study managerial policies regarding a particular operations management problem? What information can linear programming supply that is useful in assessing the impact of changing policies associated with the availability of resources?
5. What is a *slack* variable? What usefulness does it have in linear programming analysis?
6. What modifications to the simplex method are required for minimization problems? What role do *surplus* and *artificial* variables play? Might these variables be needed in a maximization problem?

REVIEW PROBLEMS

The simplex method of linear programming presented in this supplement is applied in Chapter 2 (Problems 12–14), Chapter 4 (Problems 14 and 15), Chapter 7 (Problem 12), Chapter 13 (Problems 7 and 8), and Chapter 16 (Problems 10 and 11).

SELECTED REFERENCES

Asim, R., E. De Falomir, and L. Lasdon, "An Optimization-Based Decision Support System for a Product-Mix Problem," *Interfaces,* vol. 12, no. 2 (April 1982), pp. 26–33.

Hadley, G., *Linear Programming.* Reading, Mass.: Addison-Wesley, 1962.

Hillier, F. S., and G. J. Lieberman, *Introduction to Operations Research,* 2nd ed. San Francisco: Holden-Day, 1974.

Krajewski, L. J., and H. E. Thompson, *Management Science: Quantitative Methods in Context.* New York: John Wiley & Sons, 1981.

Markland, R. E., *Topics in Management Science.* New York: John Wiley & Sons, 1979.

Perry, C., and K. C. Crellin, "The Precise Management Meaning of a Shadow Price," *Interfaces,* vol. 12, no. 2 (April 1982), pp. 61–63.

Wagner, H. M., *Principles of Operations Research,* 2nd ed. Englewood Cliffs, N.J.: Prentice-Hall, 1975.

Zeleny, M., "On the Squandering of Resources and Profits via Linear Programming," *Interfaces,* vol. 11, no. 5 (October 1981), pp. 101–107.

SUPPLEMENT 3

TRANSPORTATION METHOD OF LINEAR PROGRAMMING

▲ Supplement Outline

▲ Key Questions for Managers

What is the best shipping plan for our current logistics system?

What is the net change in costs for adding a new distribution route for one plant and taking that route away from another plant?

What is the effect of adding a new plant on our total logistics system?

upplement 2 showed that the simplex method is an efficient procedure for solving linear programming problems. Efficiency, however, is relative and is directly related to the computational effort required to solve the problem. In this supplement we discuss a method for solving a class of linear programming problems that is more efficient than the simplex method.

SOLVING TRANSPORTATION PROBLEMS ▲

The transportation method is an iterative procedure for solving problems when we want to minimize the cost of shipping products from m plants or sources of supply to n destinations.* We can also use this method to analyze alternative plant or warehouse locations, or to find an optimal production plan. (See Chapters 8 and 13.) A typical plant location problem is presented in Managerial Practice S3.1.

The Initial Tableau

The initial tableau for the Giant Farmer Company problem is shown in Fig. S3.1, for the Buffalo option, which we elected to evaluate first. Each cell in the tableau represents a decision variable in the problem. The cost to ship one unit from a plant to a warehouse is shown in the upper right-hand corner of the corresponding cell. In the transportation method, the sum of the allocations to a row must equal the capacity of that row; similarly, the sum of the allocations to a column must equal the requirements for that column. These two sets of

---

*The same approach can be used for a profit maximization problem.

Plant	Warehouse				Capacity
	Miami	Denver	Lincoln	Jackson	
Chicago	7	2	4	5	100
Houston	3	1	5	2	75
Buffalo	6	9	7	4	80
Requirements	70	90	45	50	255 / 255

FIGURE S3.1   Initial Tableau for the Giant Farmer Company Problem

constraints are called **rim conditions**. Note that the sum of the capacities equals the sum of the requirements in Fig. S3.1, which must always be the case when we use the transportation method. However, in many real problems, capacity may exceed requirements or vice versa. If so, we can easily adjust the model to satisfy the conditions for the transportation method. If capacity exceeds requirements by r units, we create an additional *column* in the tableau representing a dummy warehouse with a demand for r units and make the shipping costs in the newly created cells $0. This approach is analogous to adding slack variables in a simplex linear programming solution. Similarly, if requirements exceed capacity by r units, we create a new *row* representing a dummy plant with a capacity of r units. We assign shipping costs of $0 per unit in the new cells to reflect the addition of slack variables to the problem. After making these adjustments, we can use the transportation method to solve the problem.

Generating an Initial Solution

Like the simplex method, the transportation method requires an initial solution. This step amounts to allocating quantities to cells so that we meet the rim conditions. We will present two procedures for specifying an initial solution: the northwest-corner approach and Vogel's approximation method (VAM).

The Northwest-Corner Approach.   The quickest way to arrive at an initial solution to a transportation problem is to use the *northwest-corner approach*. As you may surmise from the name, the procedure starts in the northwest (upper left-hand) corner of the tableau and allocates as many units as possible to that cell without exceeding the row capacity or the column requirement. This allocation will completely satisfy either the row or the column constraint. In our example, we can allocate 70 units to the Chicago–Miami route, which eliminates Miami from further allocations, as shown in Fig. S3.2.

MANAGERIAL PRACTICE S3.1

A Food Processing Company Plant Location Problem

The Giant Farmer Company processes and cans vegetables and fruits for sale in discount food stores. Presently the company has two plants: one in Chicago and one in Houston. The company also owns and operates four warehouses, located in Miami, Denver, Lincoln, and Jackson. A recent forecast of demand at the warehouses indicated that it will exceed supply in the near future. In particular, a new plant with a capacity of 8000 cases per week is needed. The decision has been made to build a new plant, but the location still has to be selected.

   An important factor in the location decision will be the cost of transportation from the plants to the warehouses. Two potential sites for the new plant have been identified: Buffalo and Atlanta. The following data on capacities, forecasted demand, and shipping costs have been gathered.

Plant	Capacity in Cases per Week (00)	Warehouse	Demand in Cases per Week (00)
Chicago	100	Miami	70
Houston	75	Denver	90
New Plant	80	Lincoln	45
Total	255	Jackson	50
		Total	255

Plant	Shipping Cost to Warehouse (per case)			
	Miami	Denver	Lincoln	Jackson
Chicago	$7	$ 2	$4	$5
Houston	3	1	5	2
Buffalo (alternative 1)	6	9	7	4
Atlanta (alternative 2)	2	10	8	3

   The shipping cost data reflect the best arrangements that can be made from each plant to each warehouse, considering both the cost and the quality of service provided by the shipper. Management would like to determine the location for the new plant that minimizes shipping costs.

Plant	Warehouse				Capacity
	Miami	Denver	Lincoln	Jackson	
Chicago	7 70	2 30	4	5	100
Houston	3	1 60	5 15	2	75
Buffalo	6	9	7 30	4 50	80
Requirements	70	90	45	50	255 / 255

Total cost = 70($7) + 30($2) + 60($1) + 15($5) + 30($7) + 50($4) = $1095

FIGURE S3.2   Initial Solution Using the Northwest-Corner Approach

We continue to make allocations to satisfy each row or column quantity but do not exceed any of the rim conditions. Thus the sequence of our allocations would be to Chicago–Denver (eliminating the first row), Houston–Denver (eliminating the second column), Houston–Lincoln (eliminating the second row), and so on.

The total cost for this initial solution is $1095, as calculated at the bottom of Fig. S3.2. In general, the northwest-corner approach does not yield low-cost initial solutions. This result is to be expected, since costs were not considered in the allocation process. Consequently, we usually must trade off quickness in arriving at an initial solution with added work later in finding the optimal solution.

Vogel's Approximation Method (VAM).   Although **Vogel's approximation method (VAM)** requires more work than the northwest-corner approach, it normally provides an initial solution that, if not optimal, is close to optimal. The more useful initial solution results from inclusion of the objective function in making the allocations. Application of VAM to our problem is shown in Fig. S3.3.

We begin by calculating a penalty cost for each row and column. The penalty cost for each row is the difference between the lowest cost element in a row and the *next largest* cost element in that row. We obtain the penalty cost for each column in the same manner. For example, in our problem the penalty cost for the first row is $4 − $2 = $2, and the penalty cost for the first column is $6 − $3 = $3.

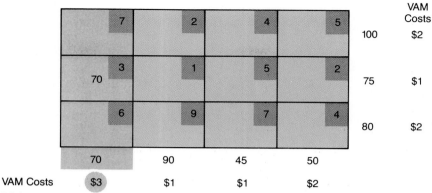

(a) Iteration 1

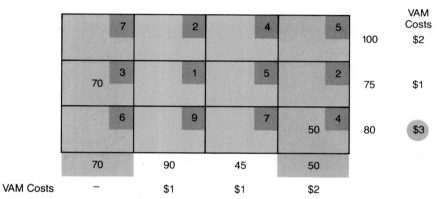

(b) Iteration 2

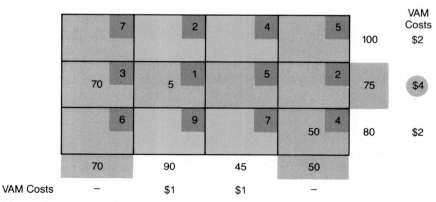

(c) Iteration 3

(continued)

FIGURE S3.3   Initial Solution Using VAM

						VAM Costs
7	2	4	5	100	$2
	85				
3	1	5	2	75	–
70	5				
6	9	7	4	80	$2
			50		
70	90	45	50		

VAM Costs   – $7 $3

(d) Iteration 4

Plant	Warehouse				Capacity
	Miami	Denver	Lincoln	Jackson	
Chicago	7	2 85	4 15	5	100
Houston	3 70	1 5	5	2	75
Buffalo	6	9	7 30	4 50	80
Requirements	70	90	45	50	255 / 255

Total cost = 70($3) + 85($2) + 5($1) + 15($4) + 30($7) + 50($4) = $855

(e) Final Allocation

FIGURE S3.3   (continued)

In making our first allocation, we choose the row or column having the largest penalty cost because it is like an opportunity cost. That is, if we do not allocate as many units as possible now to the cell with lowest cost in that row or column, we may have to allocate units later to the cell with the next largest cost in that row or column. The largest cost penalty is $3, for column 1, so we allocate as many units as we can to the lowest-cost cell in the first column. This is the Houston–Miami route, the allocation is for 70 units, and this allocation satisfies the Miami requirements. If we have a tie in penalty costs, we can arbitrarily choose from the tied rows or columns.

In the second iteration (and thereafter), we have to recalculate the penalty costs to determine whether any have changed because of the last allocation. In this case, only the third-row penalty cost changed because we have eliminated column 1. The $3 penalty cost for the third row is now the largest, so we allocate 50 units to the lowest-cost cell. Even though 80 units of capacity are available in row 3 (Buffalo), the requirement in column 4 (Jackson) is only 50 units.

The rest of the iterations are straightforward. In iteration 3, row 2 has the highest penalty cost. However, we can only allocate 5 units to the lowest-cost cell because we had previously allocated 70 units to that row and the capacity is 75 units. We can eliminate column 2 in the fourth iteration by allocating 85 units to the Chicago–Denver route. The final allocation is obvious at this point. Two cells need allocations, and their values are prescribed by the rim conditions. The total cost of this initial solution is $855, which is $240 less than the cost generated by the northwest-corner approach.*

Selecting the Entering Route

At each iteration, we select a nonallocated cell (or route) to introduce into the solution and an allocated cell (or route) to be removed from the solution. We then transform the tableau to reflect the impact of this change on the allocations to all the cells. In so doing, we have to make sure that the value of the objective function is improved or at least stays the same. We will discuss the process of selecting the entering route first.

Although there are other approaches to selecting the entering route in a transportation problem, we will discuss the so-called *stepping-stone method* because it is the most intuitive of those available.† The method is named for the procedure utilized. In general terms, we begin by selecting a nonallocated cell for evaluation. We hypothetically allocate one unit to the cell, then adjust the currently allocated cells to balance the affected row capacities and column requirements alternately, without violating the rim conditions. In this respect, the tableau is like a shallow pond of water, with the allocated cells serving as stepping stones. Starting with the nonallocated cell, we move from allocated cell to allocated cell, each time moving at a right angle to the last move, alternately subtracting one unit from and adding one unit to the allocated cells,

---

*Regardless of the method used for determining an initial solution, the number of allocated cells must equal $m + n - 1$, where m = number of rows and n = number of columns. If we have more than that number it means that we did not allocate as much as we could to each cell at each step. If we have less than that number, we have a case called *degeneracy*, which we discuss later.

†Another approach, called the *modified-distribution* (MODI) *method*, actually requires less work but is based on concepts beyond the scope of this supplement. This approach is discussed in Krajewski and Thompson (1981).

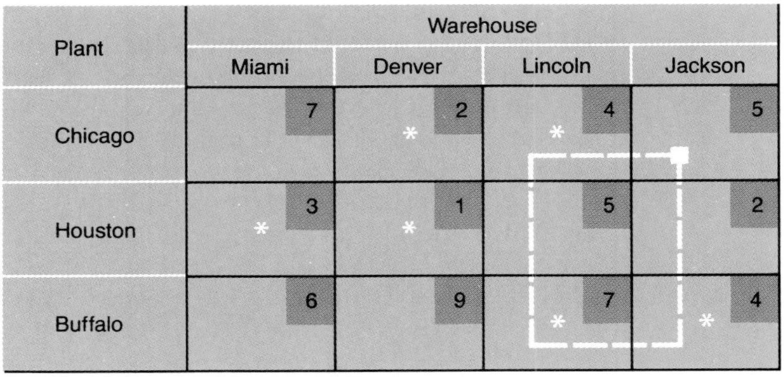

Plant	Warehouse			
	Miami	Denver	Lincoln	Jackson
Chicago	7	2 *	4 *	5 ☐
Houston	3 *	1 *	5	2
Buffalo	6	9	7 *	4 *

Net contribution to total costs per unit = $5 − $4 + $7 − $4 = $4

FIGURE S3.4   Loop for the Chicago–Jackson Route

until we end up at the nonallocated cell again. In so doing, we create a *loop* and satisfy all rim conditions. Fortunately, there is only one loop for each nonallocated cell. We can calculate the net cost advantage from this loop.

Consider Fig. S3.4, which contains the initial solution derived from VAM in Fig. S3.3. An * indicates an allocated cell, and the ☐ indicates the nonallocated cell that we will evaluate first. The dashed line shows the loop for this cell. The cost of shipping one unit from Chicago to Jackson is $5, but, since Jackson requires only 50 units, we must decrease the shipment from Buffalo to Jackson by one unit at a *savings* of $4. This leaves Buffalo one unit short of its capacity of 80 units, but we know that all of its capacity will be needed because the total requirements from all warehouses equals the total plant capacity. Consequently, we added one unit to the Buffalo–Lincoln route, *increasing* costs by $7. In so doing, we have allocated to Lincoln one more unit than it requires, so we reduce the shipment from Chicago to Lincoln by one unit at a *savings* of $4. This completes the loop and the net contribution to total costs is $5 − $4 + $7 − $4 = $4. Since the net contribution is positive, opening a route from Chicago to Jackson is not profitable at this time. It would add $4 to the total cost for each unit shipped.

Figure S3.5 shows the loops for the remaining nonallocated cells, and Table S3.1 (p. 329) shows the calculation of the net contributions for each one. Note that some loops are more complicated than others. The Houston–Jackson loop crosses itself, which is permissible so long as the intersection is at a right angle. The Buffalo–Denver loop passes over the Houston–Denver cell because, if we had stopped there, the only right-angle move would have been Houston–Miami. From that position, there is no right-angle move to an allocated cell. Finally, we should mention that loops can be traversed in two directions.

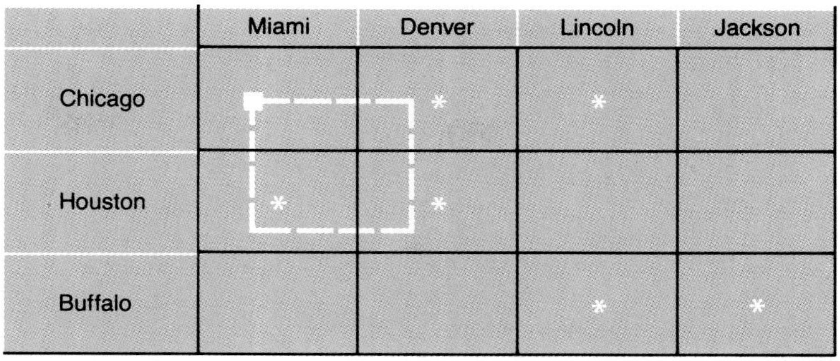

(a) Chicago-Miami

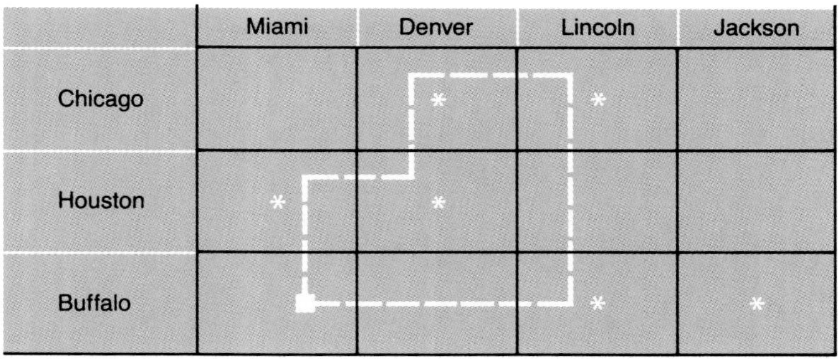

(b) Buffalo-Miami

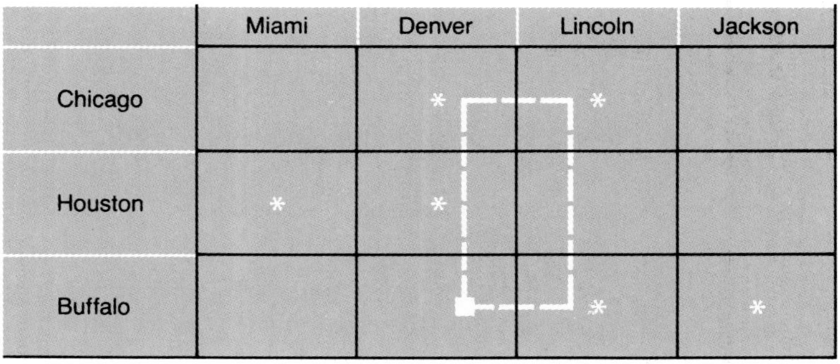

(c) Buffalo-Denver

(*continued*)

FIGURE S3.5   Loops for the Remaining Nonallocated Cells

	Miami	Denver	Lincoln	Jackson
Chicago		*	*	
Houston	*	*		
Buffalo			*	*

(d) Houston-Lincoln

	Miami	Denver	Lincoln	Jackson
Chicago		*	*	
Houston	*	*		
Buffalo			*	*

(e) Houston-Jackson

FIGURE S3.5   (continued)

We can now identify the entering route for our problem. From Table S3.1, it is obvious that the only route that would reduce costs is Buffalo–Miami. In general, we would pick the route with the largest negative net contribution.

Determining the Exiting Route and Transforming the Tableau

After we have determined the entering route, we allocate as many units to that route as possible. In order to maintain the same number of shipments (allocated cells) as before, this step implies that one of the current shipments must be reduced to zero.* We determine the maximum shipping quantity for the entering route and the route that will be removed from the solution by analyzing the loop for the entering route.

*When more than one shipment is reduced to zero, degeneracy results.

TABLE S3.1   Net Contributions for the Remaining Nonallocated Cells

Shipment Change		Cost Change
Chicago–Miami		
Add 1 unit	Chicago–Miami	+ $7
Subtract 1 unit	Houston–Miami	− $3
Add 1 unit	Houston–Denver	+ $1
Subtract 1 unit	Chicago–Denver	− $2
Net contribution		+ $3
Buffalo–Miami		
Add 1 unit	Buffalo–Miami	+ $6
Subtract 1 unit	Houston–Miami	− $3
Add 1 unit	Houston–Denver	+ $1
Subtract 1 unit	Chicago–Denver	− $2
Add 1 unit	Chicago–Lincoln	+ $4
Subtract 1 unit	Buffalo–Lincoln	− $7
Net contribution		− $1
Buffalo–Denver		
Add 1 unit	Buffalo–Denver	+ $9
Subtract 1 unit	Chicago–Denver	− $2
Add 1 unit	Chicago–Lincoln	+ $4
Subtract 1 unit	Buffalo–Lincoln	− $7
Net contribution		+ $4
Houston–Lincoln		
Add 1 unit	Houston–Lincoln	+ $5
Subtract 1 unit	Chicago–Lincoln	− $4
Add 1 unit	Chicago–Denver	+ $2
Subtract 1 unit	Houston–Denver	− $1
Net contribution		+ $2
Houston–Jackson		
Add 1 unit	Houston–Jackson	+ $2
Subtract 1 unit	Buffalo–Jackson	− $4
Add 1 unit	Buffalo–Lincoln	+ $7
Subtract 1 unit	Chicago–Lincoln	− $4
Add 1 unit	Chicago–Denver	+ $2
Subtract 1 unit	Houston–Denver	− $1
Net contribution		+ $2

Figure S3.6 shows the tableau for the initial solution that we developed using VAM and the loop for the Buffalo–Miami route. The (+) or (−) in the circle of each cell in the loop indicates that we must add or subtract a unit from that cell in order to satisfy the rim conditions. Note that each row and column

Plant	Warehouse				Capacity
	Miami	Denver	Lincoln	Jackson	
Chicago	7	2 85	4 15	5	100
Houston	3 70	1 5	5	2	75
Buffalo	6	9	7 30	4 50	80
Requirements	70	90	45	50	255 255

FIGURE S3.6   Loop for the Buffalo–Miami Route

affected has one positive cell and one negative cell. To determine the maximum quantity that can be shipped from Buffalo to Miami, we examine the negative cells because these are the cells for which shipping quantities will be reduced. In this example, they are Houston–Miami (70 units), Chicago–Denver (85 units), and Buffalo–Lincoln (30 units). Consequently, the maximum quantity that we can ship along the Buffalo–Miami route is the *minimum* of (70, 85, 30), or 30 units. To ship any more than 30 units would result in a negative quantity in the Buffalo–Lincoln cell and would violate the nonnegativity restriction. Since Buffalo–Lincoln has the minimum allocation of the negative cells in the loop, we remove it from the solution. Figure S3.7 shows the new solution to the problem after 30 units have been added to each positive cell and subtracted from each negative cell. The values in the circles are the net contributions for each nonallocated cell of Fig. S3.7 and are calculated in the same manner as those in Table S3.1.

The criteria for optimality in transportation problems can be stated as:

Minimization problems: If the net contributions of all nonallocated cells are zero or *positive*, the current solution is optimal.

Maximization problems: If the net contributions of all nonallocated cells are zero or *negative*, the current solution is optimal.

Plant	Warehouse				Capacity
	Miami	Denver	Lincoln	Jackson	
Chicago	7 + $3	2 55	4 45	5 + $3	100
Houston	3 40	1 35	5 + $2	2 + $1	75
Buffalo	6 30	9 + $5	7 + $1	4 50	80
Requirements	70	90	45	50	255 / 255

Total cost = 40($3) + 30($6) + 55($2) + 35($1) + 45($4) + 50($4) = $825

FIGURE S3.7 Transformed Array Showing Optimal Solution

Consequently, the solution in Fig. S3.7 is the optimal solution to the problem if we locate the new plant in Buffalo. The total transportation cost is $825. If one or more of the net contributions were still negative, we would have to do another iteration of the tableau.

Turning to alternative 2, locating the new plant in Atlanta, the solution to the transportation problem results in a total transportation cost of $575. We leave the solution of this problem to you. If transportation cost is the overriding consideration, the new plant should be located in Atlanta. However, management usually considers many other factors before making a final plant location decision. (See Chapter 8.)

DEGENERACY ▲

Whenever we have fewer than $m + n - 1$ allocated cells in a transportation problem we have **degeneracy**. It can occur in the derivation of an initial solution when we satisfy a row constraint and a column constraint simultaneously with one allocation, or when we introduce a new route into the solution and more than one negative cell in the loop has the same minimum allocation. We need to have $m + n - 1$ allocated cells so that we can create loops for each nonallocated cell.

The procedure for dealing with degeneracy involves the allocation of an infinitesimal quantity, ϵ, to as many nonallocated cells as necessary to bring the total number of allocated cells to $m + n - 1$. It is important that we choose only those nonallocated cells having loops that cannot be formed without the ϵ allocation. Since the value of ϵ is so small, it does not enter into the total cost of the solution or the shipping quantity for a given route; its only use is in calculating the loops for nonallocated cells. We treat the cell with ϵ as a typical allocated cell in our calculations, and we continue with the stepping-stone method until we reach the condition of optimality.

SUPPLEMENT HIGHLIGHTS

- The transportation method of linear programming is useful for solving problems when the objective is to minimize the cost of shipping products from a group of sources to a different group of destinations.
- The transportation method is an iterative method that avoids some of the difficulties of the simplex method for problems of this type. The constraints are stated in the form of rim conditions.
- Initial solutions can be found by the northwest-corner approach or Vogel's approximation method (VAM). Of these two methods, only VAM recognizes costs; it requires more work but provides a solution that, if not optimal, is close to optimal.
- The stepping-stone method is an intuitive approach for selecting the entering route in a transportation problem. The route with the largest negative net contribution is chosen to enter in a cost minimization problem.
- The exiting route is the one having the minimum allocation of all negative cells in the loop.
- In minimization problems, the current solution is optimal when all net contributions are zero or positive. In maximization problems, the current solution is optimal when all net contributions are zero or negative.
- Degeneracy occurs when fewer than $m + n - 1$ cells are allocated and can be overcome by allocating an infinitesimal quantity in appropriate cells. When a degenerate condition exists, the stepping-stone approach cannot be used to find loops to calculate net contributions.

KEY TERMS

degeneracy   831
rim conditions   820
Vogel's approximation method (VAM)   822

STUDY QUESTIONS

1. Why is the transportation method more efficient than the simplex method for problems having the structural requirements of a transportation problem?

2. What are the trade-offs in choosing between the northwest-corner method and Vogel's approximation method for obtaining an initial solution in a transportation problem?

3. Explain the stepping-stone method in simple terms. Explain why total requirements must equal total supply to make it work. What modifications must you make if total requirements do not equal total supply?

4. What is *degeneracy* in a transportation problem? How can it be handled with the transportation method?

REVIEW PROBLEMS

The transportation method of linear programming presented in this supplement is applied in Chapter 8 (Problems 14–18), Chapter 13 (Problem 10), and Chapter 17 (Problem 14).

SELECTED REFERENCES

Hadley, G., *Linear Programming*. Reading, Mass.: Addison-Wesley, 1962.

Hillier, F. S., and G. J. Lieberman, *Introduction to Operations Research,* 2nd ed. San Francisco: Holden-Day, 1974.

Krajewski, L. J., and H. E. Thompson, *Management Science: Quantitative Methods in Context.* New York: John Wiley & Sons, 1981.

Markland, R. E., *Topics in Management Science*. New York: John Wiley & Sons, 1979.

Wagner, H. M., *Principles of Operations Research,* 2nd ed. Englewood Cliffs, N.J.: Prentice-Hall, 1975.

SUPPLEMENT

4

QUEUING MODELS

▲ Supplement Outline

Key Questions for Managers

How should we arrange service facilities in a queuing situation to obtain the most efficient operation?

What is the best priority system for us to use in a given situation?

What is the impact on system performance if we increase the productivity of the servers of our service system?

How can we estimate customer waiting time and hourly operating costs of our service system?

*T*his supplement discusses some simple models that have been derived from queuing theory. Although useful, these models are based on stringent assumptions about the operating environment. More complex queuing problems, as well as many nonqueuing problems, can be analyzed by *simulation*. (See Supplement 5.)

STRUCTURE OF QUEUING PROBLEMS ▲

Analysis of queuing problems begins with a description of the basic elements of the queuing phenomenon as they relate to the specific situation to be analyzed. Figure S4.1 shows these basic elements, which are common to all queuing problems. An **input source** generates potential customers for the **service system**, which consists of one or more queues, a priority discipline, and some service facilities. Some customers may decide not to enter the system (*balking* customers). Other customers enter a queue or waiting line. Some of these customers may elect to leave the system before being served (*reneging* customers). A **priority discipline** selects the next customer to be served by the **service facilities**. The system can include one or more facilities, each consisting of a person (or crew), a machine (or group of machines), or both. After the service has been performed, the served customers leave the system.

Besides describing the basic elements of a queuing problem, we must also identify relevant *decision variables* and the *operating characteristics*. We need this information in order to determine whether an appropriate queuing theory model is to be used or whether a simulation model must be developed. We discuss the basic elements, decision variables, and performance measures in this section.

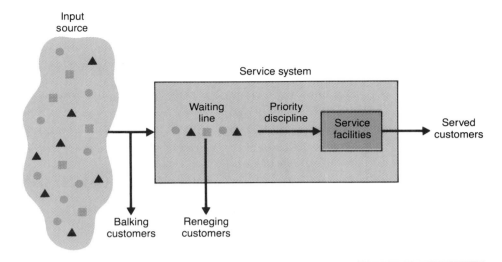

FIGURE S4.1   Basic Elements of Queuing Problems

Input Source

An input source is the population of potential customers for the service system. It can be described by its size, the distribution of customer arrivals, and the disposition of the customers.

Size.   The input source can be either a *finite* or an *infinite* population of potential customers. This distinction is based on the relative proportion of the input source that can be in the service system at any one time. If the rate (customers per unit of time) at which the input source generates new customers for the service system is appreciably affected by the number of customers already in the system, the input source is said to be finite. Alternatively, an infinite input source is one in which the number of customers in the system does not affect the rate at which the input source generates new customers.

Arrival Distribution.   The distribution of customer arrivals is a probability distribution that describes either the number of arrivals per unit of time or the time between successive arrivals, called the **interarrival time**. A Poisson distribution is often used to describe customer arrivals per unit of time. Let A_T be the number of customers arriving during an interval of time, 0, T. If λ is the mean number of customer arrivals per unit of time, the probability that there will be exactly n arrivals during the time interval 0, T is

$$P(A_T = n) = \frac{(\lambda T)^n}{n!}e^{-\lambda T} \qquad \text{for } n = 0, 1, 2, \ldots$$

The mean of the Poisson distribution is λT, and the variance also equals λT.

The Poisson distribution is a discrete distribution; that is, the probabilities are for a specific number of arrivals per unit of time. For example, suppose that customers arrive at a complaint desk in a large department store at the rate of two customers per hour ($\lambda = 2$). The probability that four customers will arrive in the next hour ($n = 4$, $T = 1$) is

$$P(A_1 = 4) = \frac{[2(1)]^4}{4!}e^{-2(1)} = \frac{16}{24}e^{-2}$$
$$= 0.090$$

It may be more convenient to specify the arrival distribution in terms of customer interarrival times. If the input source generates customers according to a Poisson distribution, we can use the *exponential distribution* to describe the probability that the next customer will arrive in the time interval $(0, T)$. The mean of the distribution is $1/\lambda$ and the variance is $(1/\lambda)^2$. We will defer further discussion of the exponential distribution until we address the service time distribution.

Customer Disposition. Customers in queuing situations can be either *patient* or *impatient*. In this regard, patience has nothing to do with the colorful language a customer may use while waiting in line for a long time on a hot day. A patient customer is one who enters the system and remains there until being served. An impatient customer is one who either estimates the waiting time and decides not to enter the system (balking) or enters the queue but leaves the system before being served (reneging). For the models in this supplement, we make the simplifying assumption that all customers are patient.

Queues

Queues may be described by their size limitations and the number of lines.

Size Limitations. The queue size can be *limited* or *unlimited*. A limited queue is constrained to be no larger than some finite number of customers. Unlimited queues are found in those situations where space or other resource limitations do not impose a limitation on queue length.

Number of Lines. Queues can be designed to be *single line* or *multiple lines*. Figure S4.2 shows an example of each arrangement. When multiple servers are available and each one can handle general transactions, the single-line arrangement has the advantage of maintaining server utilization at a high level and giving the customer a sense of fairness. Customers have the feeling that they are being served on the basis of when they arrived, not on how well they guessed their waiting time when selecting a particular line, as in the multiple-line arrangement. The multiple-line design is best when some of the servers provide a limited set of services.

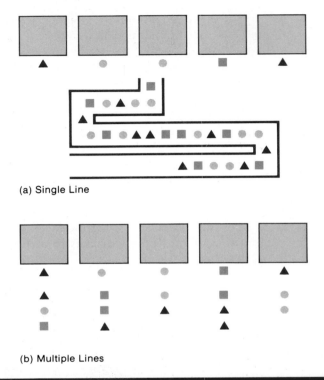

(a) Single Line

(b) Multiple Lines

FIGURE S4.2   Waiting-Line Arrangements

Sometimes, queues are not organized neatly into "lines." Machines that need repair on the production floor of a factory remain right where they are when they fail and wait for the maintenance crew to come to them. Nonetheless, we can think of the machines as forming a single line or multiple lines, depending on the number of repair crews and their specialties.

Priority Discipline

When a waiting line forms, the question becomes one of which customer to serve next. Most service systems that the average person encounters in daily life use the first-come, first-served (FCFS) rule. The customer at the head of the waiting line has the highest priority, and so on, to the customer who last arrived. However, this rule is only one of many priority disciplines used in queuing systems.

The service system may even invoke a **preemptive discipline**. Preemption takes place when a customer of higher priority interrupts the service of another customer. Modeling queuing systems having complex priority disciplines is difficult, and most often in practice simulation is used to analyze these situations.

Service Facilities

Service facilities consist of the personnel and/or equipment necessary to perform the service for the customer. They can be characterized by their arrangement and service time distribution.

Arrangement. Figure S4.3 shows examples of the five basic types of service facility arrangements. The choice of arrangement is a function of customer volume and the nature of services performed. Some services require a sequence of steps, whereas others require only a single step.

The *single-channel, single-phase* system is based on the assumption that all services demanded by a customer can be performed by a single-server facility. The *single-channel, multiple-phase* arrangement is used when the services are best performed in sequence by more than one facility, yet customer volume or other constraints limit the design to one channel.

The *multiple-channel, single-phase* arrangement is used when demand is large enough to warrant providing the same service at more than one facility or when the services offered by the facilities are different. Figure S4.3 shows a single-line queue for the multiple-channel arrangements. The *multiple-channel, multiple-phase* arrangement is just an extension of the preceding arrangement. In some cases, customers cannot switch channels after service has begun, while in others they can.

However, the most general (and complex) facility arrangement is the *mixed* arrangement. In this situation, each customer has a specific routing between service facilities and, consequently, service cannot be neatly described in phases. Queues can develop in front of each facility. The arrival times at each facility are a complex function of variations in processing times and move times between facilities, as well as the priority disciplines and capacities of the other facilities.

Service-Time Distribution. The service-time distribution describes the probability that the service time of the customer at a particular facility will be no more than T time periods. A distribution that has been found to be useful in practice is the *exponential distribution:*

$$P(t \leqslant T) = 1 - e^{-\mu T}$$

where μ is the mean number of customers completing service per unit of time t. The mean of the service-time distribution is $1/\mu$ and the variance is $(1/\mu)^2$. For example, suppose that the clerk at a customer complaint desk can serve an average of three customers per hour. Thus the mean of the service

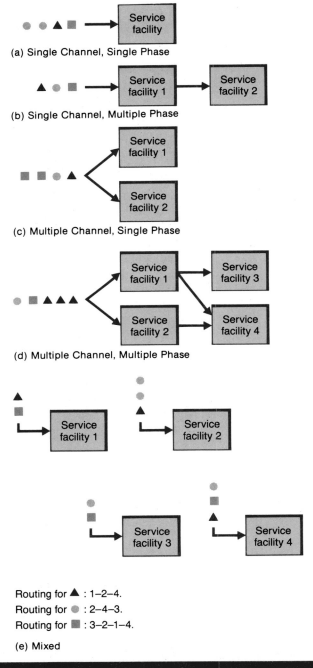

(a) Single Channel, Single Phase

(b) Single Channel, Multiple Phase

(c) Multiple Channel, Single Phase

(d) Multiple Channel, Multiple Phase

Routing for ▲ : 1–2–4.
Routing for ● : 2–4–3.
Routing for ■ : 3–2–1–4.

(e) Mixed

FIGURE S4.3   Examples of Service Facility Arrangements

distribution is 1/3 hr (or 20 min). The probability that a customer will require less than 10 minutes (or $T = 10/60 = 0.167$ hr) is

$$P(t \leq T) = 1 - e^{-3(0.167)}$$
$$= 0.39$$

As T increases, the probability that the customer will receive complete service approaches 1.0.

Some characteristics of the exponential distribution do not always conform to an actual situation. An underlying assumption is that each service time is independent of those that preceded it. Consequently, it does not allow for any learning about the work performed and resulting productivity improvements. Another underlying assumption is that very small, as well as very large, service times are possible. This assumption does not hold in situations for which there is a fixed start-up time, some cutoff on total service time, or the service time is constant, or nearly so.

Although we presented these decision areas as though they are independent, they are obviously interrelated. Adjusting the customer arrival rate λ might have to be accompanied by an increase in the service rate μ in some way. Decisions about the number of facilities, the number of phases, and queue arrangement also are related.

Operating Characteristics

Queuing models enable the analyst to study the effects of manipulating decision variables on the operating characteristics of a service system. Some of the more common operating characteristics considered are:

1. *Queue length.* The number of customers in the waiting line reflects one of two conditions. Short queues could mean either good customer service or too much capacity. Similarly, long queues could indicate either low server efficiency or the need to increase capacity.

2. *Number of customers in system.* The number of customers in queue and being served also relates to service efficiency and capacity. Large values imply congestion, potential customer dissatisfaction, and a need for more capacity.

3. *Waiting time in queue.* Long lines do not reflect long waiting times, if the service rate is fast. However, when waiting time seems long to customers, they perceive that the quality of service is poor. Long waiting times may indicate a need to adjust the service rate of the system or change the arrival rate of customers.

4. *Total time in system.* The total elapsed time from entry into the system until exit from the system may indicate problems with customers, server efficiency, or capacity. If some customers are spending too much time in the service system there may be a need to change the priority discipline, increase productivity, or adjust capacity in some way.

5. *Service facility utilization.* The collective utilization of the service facilities reflects the percentage of time the facilities are busy. Management is interested in maintaining high utilization, but this objective may have an adverse impact on the other operating characteristics.

The effect of various alternatives to be analyzed for a queuing problem can be expressed in terms of the operating characteristics. If operating characteristics and alternatives can be related to dollars, the effects of an alternative can be expressed in dollars. However, it is difficult to place a dollar figure on certain characteristics (such as the waiting time of a shopper in a grocery store). In such cases, an analyst must weigh the cost of implementing the alternative under consideration against a subjective effect on operating characteristics.

Decision Variables

The analysis of queuing problems involves making decisions in one or more of the following areas:

1. *Arrival rates.* Often, the rate of customer arrivals (λ) can be affected by management. Advertising or differential pricing such as that used by a telephone company for long-distance calls after 5:30 P.M. can affect the rate of demand for services.

2. *Number of service facilities.* The number of tool cribs, toll booths, or bank tellers has to be determined. Whether some facilities in a phase should perform a unique set of services has to be decided. These decisions relate to the number of facilities in a particular phase of the service system and, consequently, to the capacity of the system.

3. *Number of phases.* This decision involves the allocation of service tasks to sequential phases of the facility arrangement. At some point, also, two sequential service facilities may be more efficient than one. In the assembly-line problem discussed in Chapter 9, the decision concerned the number of phases needed along the assembly line. Determining the number of workers needed on the line also involves assigning a certain set of work elements to each one. In addition to affecting the facility arrangement, this decision also affects the service rate (μ) of each facility and the capacity of the system.

4. *Number of servers per facility.* Sometimes, a service facility is operated by more than one person. Such would be the case when a single facility is defined as a work crew or group of workers (such as the number of workers assigned to a telephone line repair crew). This decision is reflected in the service rate (μ) of the service facility.

5. *Server efficiency.* By adjusting the capital-to-labor ratio, devising improved work methods, or instituting incentive programs, management can affect

the efficiency of servers assigned to a service facility. Decisions in this area are reflected in μ, the service rate of the service facility.

6. *Priority discipline.* The priority rule to be used and whether to have a different priority rule for each service facility are important decisions. Whether to allow preemption and, if so, under what conditions is equally important.

7. *Queue arrangement.* Whether to have a single-line queue or a line for each facility in a given phase of service has to be decided.

APPLICATION OF QUEUING MODELS TO OPERATIONS MANAGEMENT ▲

We now turn to some examples of the application of queuing theory models to operations management. To simplify the presentation, we will use the following notation.

λ = mean arrival rate (customers per unit of time)

μ = mean service rate per server (customers per unit of time)

$\dfrac{1}{\lambda}$ = mean time between arrivals

$\dfrac{1}{\lambda_0}$ = mean time between arrivals for a finite input source

$\dfrac{1}{\mu}$ = mean time per customer served

ρ = average utilization of the service facility. Sometimes called the traffic density (defined as λ/μ or $\lambda/s\mu$)

$\overline{L}$ = average number of customers in the service system

$\overline{L_q}$ = average number of customers in the waiting line

$\overline{W}$ = average time spent in the system (including service)

$\overline{W_q}$ = average waiting time in line

n = number of customers in the service system

P_n = probability that there are n customers in the system

N = number of customers in the input source (for the finite input-source case)

s = number of servers

In this section, we analyze problems requiring the single-server, multiple-server, and finite input-source models, all of which are single phase. More advanced models can be found in the references at the end of this supplement.

TABLE S4.1   Single-Server Model

Assumptions	Operating Characteristics
Input source: infinite; no balking or reneging. Arrival distribution: Poisson; mean arrival rate $= \lambda$. Service distribution: exponential; mean service time $= 1/\mu$. Queue: unlimited length; single line. Priority discipline: FCFS. Number of servers: 1. Number of phases: 1.	$\rho = \dfrac{\lambda}{\mu}$ $P_n = (1 - \rho)\rho^n$ $\bar{L} = \dfrac{\lambda}{\mu - \lambda}$ $\bar{L}_q = \rho\bar{L}$ $\bar{W} = \dfrac{1}{\mu - \lambda}$ $\bar{W}_q = \rho\bar{W}$

Analyzing Different Service Rates

The manager of a grocery store in Sunnyville is interested in providing good service to the senior citizens who shop in his store. Presently, the store has a separate checkout counter for senior citizens. The senior citizens arrive at the counter at an average of 30 per hour, according to a Poisson distribution, and are served at an average rate of 35 customers per hour, with exponential service times. The *single-server model* in Table S4.1 is appropriate. Find the average

1. utilization of the checkout clerk;
2. number of customers in the system;
3. number of customers in line;
4. time spent in the system; and
5. waiting time in line.

Using the equations for the operating characteristics of a single-channel, single-phase system in Table S4.1, we can calculate the average characteristics as follows:

1. The average utilization of the checkout clerk is

$$\rho = \frac{\lambda}{\mu} = \frac{30}{35} = 0.857 \quad \text{or} \quad 85.7\%$$

2. The average number of customers in the system is

$$\overline{L} = \frac{\lambda}{\mu - \lambda} = \frac{30}{35 - 30} = 6 \text{ customers}$$

3. The average number of customers in line is

$$\overline{L_q} = \rho\overline{L} = 0.857(6) = 5.14 \text{ customers}$$

4. The average time spent in the system is

$$\overline{W} = \frac{1}{\mu - \lambda} = \frac{1}{35 - 30} = 0.20 \text{ hr} \quad \text{or} \quad 12 \text{ min}$$

5. The average time spent waiting in line is

$$\overline{W_q} = \rho\overline{W} = 0.857(0.20) = 0.17 \text{ hr} \quad \text{or} \quad 10.28 \text{ min}$$

The manager would like to address the following questions: (1) What service rate would be required to have customers average only 8 minutes in the system? (2) For that service rate, what is the probability of having more than 4 customers in the system? and (3) What service rate would be required to have only a 10 percent chance of exceeding 4 customers in the system?

Question 1. We need to use the equation for the average time in the system and solve for μ.

$$\overline{W} = \frac{1}{\mu - \lambda}$$

$$8 \text{ min} = 0.133 \text{ hr} = \frac{1}{\mu - 30}$$

$$0.133\mu - 0.133(30) = 1$$

$$\mu = 37.52 \text{ customers/hr}$$

Question 2. The probability that there will be more than 4 customers in the system is equal to 1 minus the probability that there are 4 or less customers in the system.

$$P = 1 - \sum_{n=0}^{4} P_n$$

$$= 1 - \sum_{n=0}^{4} (1 - \rho)\rho^n, \quad \text{where } \rho = \frac{30}{37.52} = 0.80$$

$$= 1 - 0.2(1 + 0.8 + 0.8^2 + 0.8^3 + 0.8^4)$$

$$= 1 - 0.672$$

$$= 0.328$$

Therefore there is a nearly 33 percent chance that more than 4 customers will be in the system.

Question 3.   We use the same logic as in Question 2, except that μ is now a decision variable. It is easier first to find the correct average utilization by trial and error and then to solve for the service rate.

$$P = 1 - (1 - \rho)(1 + \rho + \rho^2 + \rho^3 + \rho^4)$$

Try $\rho = 0.7$:

$$0.10 \stackrel{?}{=} 1 - (0.3)(1 + 0.7 + 0.49 + 0.343 + 0.240)$$
$$0.10 \neq 0.168$$

Try $\rho = 0.6$:

$$0.10 \stackrel{?}{=} 1 - (0.4)(1 + 0.6 + 0.36 + 0.216 + 0.1296)$$
$$0.10 \neq 0.078$$

Try $\rho = 0.63$:

$$0.10 \stackrel{?}{=} 1 - (0.37)(1 + 0.63 + 0.3969 + 0.2500 + 0.1575)$$
$$0.10 \approx 0.099$$

Therefore, for a utilization rate of 63 percent, the probability of more than 4 customers in the system is 10 percent. For $\lambda = 30$, the service rate must be

$$\frac{30}{\mu} = 0.63$$
$$\mu = 47.62 \text{ customers/hr}$$

The manager must now find a way to increase the service rate from 35 per hour to approximately 48 per hour. He can increase the service rate in a number of different ways, ranging from employing a high school student to help bag the groceries to incorporating electronic point-of-sale equipment that reads the prices from barcoded information on each item.

Estimating Idle Time and Hourly Operating Costs

The management of the American Parcel Service terminal in Verona, Wisconsin, is concerned about the amount of time the company's trucks are idle, waiting to be unloaded. The terminal operates with 4 unloading bays. Each bay requires a crew of two employees, and each crew costs $30 per hour. The estimated cost of an idle truck is $50 per hour. Trucks arrive at an average rate of three per hour, according to a Poisson distribution. A crew can unload a semitrailer rig in an average of one hour, with exponential service times. What is the total hourly cost of operating the system? The *multiple-server model* in Table S4.2 is appropriate.

In order to find the total cost of labor and idle trucks, we must calculate the average waiting time in the system and the average number of trucks in the system. However, we first need to calculate the average number of trucks in queue and the average waiting time in queue.

The average utilization of the four bays is

$$\rho = \frac{\lambda}{\mu s} = \frac{3}{1(4)} = 0.75 \quad \text{or} \quad 75\%$$

For this level of utilization, we can now compute the probability of no trucks in the system.

$$P_0 = \left[\sum_{n=0}^{s-1} \frac{(\lambda/\mu)^n}{n!} + \frac{(\lambda/\mu)^s}{s!} \left(\frac{1}{1-\rho} \right) \right]^{-1}$$

$$= \frac{1}{\left[1 + 3 + \frac{9}{2} + \frac{27}{6} + \frac{81}{24} \left(\frac{1}{1-0.75} \right) \right]}$$

$$= 0.0377$$

TABLE S4.2   Multiple-Server Model

Assumptions	Operating Characteristics
Input source: infinite; no balking or reneging. Arrival distribution: Poisson; mean arrival time $= \lambda$. Service distribution: exponential; mean service time $= 1/\mu$. Queue: unlimited length; single line. Priority discipline: FCFS. Number of servers: s. Number of phases: 1.	$\rho = \dfrac{\lambda}{s\mu}$ $P_0 = \left[\displaystyle\sum_{n=0}^{s-1} \dfrac{(\lambda/\mu)^n}{n!} + \dfrac{(\lambda/\mu)^s}{s!} \left(\dfrac{1}{1-\rho} \right) \right]^{-1}$ $P_n = \begin{cases} \dfrac{(\lambda/\mu)^n}{n!} P_0 & 0 < n < s \\[2ex] \dfrac{(\lambda/\mu)^n}{s! s^{n-s}} P_0 & n \geq s \end{cases}$ $\overline{L_q} = \dfrac{P_0(\lambda/\mu)^s \rho}{s!(1-\rho)^2}$ $\overline{W_q} = \dfrac{\overline{L_q}}{\lambda}$ $\overline{W} = \overline{W_q} + \dfrac{1}{\mu}$ $\overline{L} = \lambda \overline{W}$

The average number of trucks in queue is

$$\overline{L_q} = \frac{P_0(\lambda/\mu)^s \rho}{s!(1 - \rho)^2}$$

$$= \frac{0.0377(3/1)^4(0.75)}{4!(1 - 0.75)^2}$$

$$= 1.53 \text{ trucks}$$

The average waiting time in queue is

$$\overline{W_q} = \frac{\overline{L_q}}{\lambda}$$

$$= \frac{1.53}{3}$$

$$= 0.51 \text{ hr}$$

The average time spent in the system is

$$\overline{W} = \overline{W_q} + \frac{1}{\mu} = 0.51 + \frac{1}{1}$$

$$= 1.51 \text{ hr}$$

Finally, the average number of trucks in the system is

$$\overline{L} = \lambda\overline{W} = 3(1.51)$$

$$= 4.53 \text{ trucks}$$

Consequently, the number of trucks in the system averages 4.53 at all times. We can now calculate the hourly costs of labor and idle trucks as follows:

$$\begin{aligned}
\text{Labor cost} &= \$30(s) &= \$30(4) &= \$120.00 \\
\text{Idle truck cost} &= \$50(\overline{L}) &= \$50(4.53) &= \underline{226.50} \\
& & \text{Total hourly cost} &= \underline{\$346.50}
\end{aligned}$$

Analyzing Maintenance Costs

The Worthington Gear Company had installed a bank of 10 robots about three years ago. The robots have greatly increased the labor productivity of the firm. However, recent attention has been directed to the maintenance function. The firm does no preventive maintenance on the robots because of the high variability in the breakdown distribution. Each machine has an exponential breakdown (or interarrival) distribution with an average time between failures of 200 hours ($\lambda_0 = 0.005$ breakdowns per hour). Each machine-hour lost to downtime costs $30, which means that the firm has to react quickly to machine failure. The firm employs one maintenance person, who takes an average of 10 hours to fix a robot ($\mu = 0.10$). Actual maintenance times have been observed to be exponentially distributed. The wage rate for the maintenance person is $10 per hour and can be productively put to work elsewhere when not fixing robots. Determine the daily cost of labor and robot downtime.

The *finite-source model* in Table S4.3 is appropriate for this analysis because there are only 10 machines in the input source and the other assumptions are satisfied. In order to calculate the cost of labor and robot downtime, we need only to estimate L, the average number of machines in the maintenance system. However, to demonstrate the use of the finite-source model, we will compute all the operating statistics.

The probability that the maintenance system is empty is

$$P_0 = \left[\sum_{n=0}^{N} \frac{N!}{(N-n)!} \left(\frac{\lambda_0}{\mu} \right)^n \right]^{-1} = \frac{1}{\displaystyle\sum_{n=0}^{10} \frac{10!}{(10-n)!} \left(\frac{0.005}{0.10} \right)^n}$$

$$= 0.538$$

TABLE S4.3 Finite Source Model

Assumptions	Operating Characteristics
Input source: finite; equals N customers. Arrival distribution: exponential interarrival times; mean $= 1/\lambda_0$. Service distribution: exponential; mean service time $= 1/\mu$. Queue: no more than $N - 1$; single line. Priority discipline: FCFS. Number of servers: 1. Number of phases: 1.	$P_0 = \left[\sum_{n=0}^{N} \frac{N!}{(N-n)!} \left(\frac{\lambda_0}{\mu} \right)^n \right]^{-1}$ $\rho = 1 - P_0$ $\overline{L}_q = N - \dfrac{\lambda_0 + \mu}{\lambda_0}(1 - P_0)$ $\overline{L} = N - \dfrac{\mu}{\lambda_0}(1 - P_0)$ $\overline{W}_q = \overline{L}_q[(N - \overline{L})\lambda_0]^{-1}$ $\overline{W} = \overline{L}[(N - \overline{L})\lambda_0]^{-1}$

The average utilization of the maintenance person is

$$\rho = 1 - P_0$$
$$= 1 - 0.538 = 0.462 \quad \text{or} \quad 46\%$$

The average number of robots waiting to be repaired is

$$\overline{L_q} = N - \frac{\lambda_0 + \mu}{\lambda_0}(1 - P_0) = 10 - \frac{0.005 + 0.10}{0.005}(1 - 0.538)$$
$$= 0.30 \text{ robots}$$

The average number of robots in queue and being repaired is

$$\overline{L} = N - \frac{\mu}{\lambda_0}(1 - P_0) = 10 - \frac{0.10}{0.005}(1 - 0.538)$$
$$= 0.76 \text{ robot}$$

The average waiting time of robots for the maintenance person is

$$\overline{W_q} = \overline{L_q}[(N - \overline{L})\lambda_0]^{-1} = \frac{0.30}{(10 - 0.76)(0.005)}$$
$$= 6.49 \text{ hr}$$

Finally, the average time that a failed robot spends waiting for service and being repaired is

$$\overline{W} = \overline{L}[(N - \overline{L})\lambda_0]^{-1} = \frac{0.76}{(10 - 0.76)(0.005)}$$
$$= 16.45 \text{ hr}$$

The daily cost of labor and robot downtime is

Labor cost = ($10/hr)(8 hr/day) = $ 80.00
Idle robot cost = (0.76 robot)($30/robot-hr)(8 hr/day) = 182.40
Total daily cost = $262.40

For the problems we analyzed with the use of queuing theory models in this supplement, we were fortunate that the arrivals had a Poisson distribution (or exponential interarrival times), that the service times had an exponential distribution, that the service facilities had a simple arrangement, and that the priority discipline was first come, first served. Many more models have been developed with queuing theory (see, for example, Cooper, 1972; and Saaty, 1961). However, they get very complex as they deviate from our earlier simplifying assumptions. Many times, the nature of the input source, the constraints on the queue, the priority discipline, the service time distribution, and the arrangement of the facilities are such that the queuing theory is no longer useful. In these cases, simulation is often used.

SUPPLEMENT HIGHLIGHTS

- Queuing problems consist of an input source that generates customers, a queue (or waiting line), a priority discipline for choosing the next customer to be served, and the service facilities. Examples of queuing problems in operations management are numerous. Customers can be human, or they can be inanimate objects, such as machines or production orders.

- Two distributions found useful in practice for defining customer arrivals and the time required for serving a customer are the Poisson and the exponential distributions, respectively. However, many queuing situations do not satisfy the assumptions of these distributions.

- Decision variables in a queuing analysis include arrival rates, number of service facilities (channels), number of phases, number of servers per facility, server efficiency, priority discipline, and queue arrangement. Operating characteristics include queue length, number of customers in the system, waiting time in queue, total time in the system, and service facility utilization.

- Under simplifying assumptions, queuing equations can be formulated to provide the mean values for operating characteristics. These equations become more complex as the complexity of the service system increases, or customer arrivals or service times diverge from the Poisson or exponential distributions. Many real queuing situations defy mathematical derivation of queuing equations.

KEY TERMS

input source   835
interarrival time   836
preemptive discipline   839
priority discipline   835
service facilities   835
service system   835

STUDY QUESTIONS

1. Describe the input source, waiting line, priority discipline, and service facilities for each of the following:
   a. Drive-in window at a fast-food restaurant.
   b. Gas station.
   c. Pediatrics clinic with three doctors.

2. Why is it useful to identify and characterize the basic elements of a particular queuing problem?

3. Suppose that you had a queuing situation in which the arrival distribution of customers per hour is

$$P(A_1 = n) = \frac{(4)^n}{n!} e^{-4}$$

and the service time distribution is

$$P(t \leq T) = 1 - e^{-3T}$$

What do you suppose will happen to the queue length in this situation? Why?

4. Explain how each of the queuing decision variables, (a)–(d), independently could be expected to affect *queue length, waiting time in queue,* and *service facility utilization.*
   a. Mean arrival rate
   b. Number of phases
   c. Number of channels
   d. Queue arrangement

5. Suppose that someone said to you, "Queuing theory is too esoteric for practical use. The assumptions that must be made are too limiting to result in anything useful." Discuss this statement in light of the material in this supplement and your understanding of the complexity of queuing problems.

6. Priority systems involve priority rules. Discuss some of the priority rules that a hospital emergency ward might use to process patients. What trade-offs must be considered by hospital management?

REVIEW PROBLEMS

The queuing models presented in this supplement are applied in Chapter 4 (Problems 16–19) and Chapter 7 (Problems 13–15).

SELECTED REFERENCES

Cooper, Robert B., *Introduction to Queuing Theory,* 2nd ed. New York: Elsevier-North Holland, 1980.

Hillier, F. S., and G. S. Lieberman, *Introduction to Operations Research,* 2nd ed. San Francisco: Holden-Day, 1975.

Moore, P. M., *Queues, Inventories and Maintenance.* New York: John Wiley & Sons, 1958.

Saaty, T. L., *Elements of Queuing Theory with Applications.* New York: McGraw-Hill, 1961.

SUPPLEMENT

5

SIMULATION ANALYSIS

▲ Supplement Outline

What role must we as managers play in a simulation analysis?
What should we know about the limitations of simulation analysis?
Can simulation help us solve tough operating problems?

 imulation is the act of reproducing the behavior of a system. A **descriptive model** of the system is developed, and certain variables are manipulated to measure their effects on the operating characteristics of interest. A descriptive model, unlike a linear programming model, for example (see Supplement 2), merely describes the system and cannot prescribe what should be done about the problem. It can be used to estimate the operating characteristics of the system under study for alternative solutions to the problem. The alternatives are systematically used in the model and the relevant operating characteristics are recorded. After all the alternatives are tried, the best one is selected, based on the simulation.

The queuing theory models presented in Supplement 4 are actually descriptive models because they describe the operating characteristics of the queuing situation. The difference with simulation is that we do not know the equations for the operating characteristics. We must actually generate customer arrivals, put customers in queues, select the next customer to be served using some priority discipline, serve that customer, and so on. We actually keep track of the number in queue, waiting time, and the like during the simulation and calculate the averages and variances at the end.

Simulation can also be used in analyzing nonqueuing problems. Consider a flight simulator for a major airline. Pilots are tested on the flight simulator periodically. The cockpit of the simulator is identical to that of a real plane. Through the use of computer graphics and other visual and mechanical effects, the pilot feels as though he or she is actually flying the plane. However, the entire process takes place inside a large laboratory.

REASONS FOR USING SIMULATION ▲

We have already said that we would use simulation in queuing situations for which queuing theory models become too complex or are not available. There are also other reasons for using simulation for analyzing operations management problems. First, many practical problems cannot be solved with optimizing methods. The relationship between the variables may be nonlinear and very complex. In addition, there may be too many variables and/or constraints to handle with current optimizing approaches. A simulation model may be the only way to estimate the operating characteristics or objective function values and analyze the problem.

Second, simulation models can be used to conduct experiments without disrupting real systems. Experimenting with a real system can be very costly. It would be unreasonable to go through the expense of purchasing and installing a new flexible manufacturing system without first estimating its benefits in detail from an operating perspective. A simulation model can be used to conduct experiments for a fraction of the cost of installing such a system. Also, the model could be used to evaluate different configurations or processing decision rules. To try any of these methods while attempting to maintain a production schedule would be virtually impossible.

Third, simulation models can be used to obtain operating characteristic estimates in much less time than required to gather the same operating data from a real system. This feature of simulation is called **time compression**. For example, a simulation model of airport operations can generate statistics for a year on airplane arrivals, landing delays, and terminal delays in a matter of minutes on a computer. Alternative airport designs can be analyzed and decisions made quickly.

Finally, simulation is useful in sharpening managerial decision-making skills through gaming. A descriptive model that relates managerial decisions to important operating characteristics (such as profits, market share, and so on) can be developed. From a set of starting conditions, the participants make periodic decisions with the intention of improving one or more operating characteristics. In such an exercise, a few hours "play" can simulate a year's time. Gaming also enables managers to experiment with new ideas without disrupting normal operations.

Despite these reasons for using simulation, many practitioners still think of simulation as the method of last resort. Mathematical analysis is still preferred by management scientists because it provides the "best" solution for the problem, whereas simulation requires the analyst to try various alternatives. If the "best" alternative is not on the list of alternatives, only a suboptimal solution will be obtained. In addition, simulation modeling is usually very expensive because of the detail required in the computer model. It is not uncommon for thousands of hours to be spent on programming and debugging complex models. Optimizing approaches, if they apply, are usually less expensive. Nonetheless, simulation is used extensively in practice. Christy and Watson (1983) surveyed nonacademic members of the Institute of Management Sciences and the Operations Research Society of America and found that 89 percent of the firms responding used simulation. Of those, the largest category of use was in production (59 percent), followed by corporate planning (53 percent) and engineering (46 percent). It would seem that the so-called last resort is an option often used in practice.

A SIMULATION EXAMPLE ▲

To demonstrate the concept of simulation we will analyze a capacity planning problem at the Specialty Steel Products Company. The company produces items such as machine tools, gears, automobile parts, and other specialty items in small quantities to customer order. Because the products are so diverse, demand is measured in machine-hours. Whenever an order for a certain quantity of product comes in, it is translated into required machine-hours, based on time standards for each operation.

Data Collection

Historical records indicate that lathe department demand varies from week to week as follows:

Weekly Production Requirements (hr)	Relative Frequency
200	0.05
250	0.06
300	0.17
350	0.05
400	0.30
450	0.15
500	0.06
550	0.14
600	0.02
	1.00

To gather these data, all weeks with requirements of 175.00–224.99 hours were grouped in the 200-hour category; all weeks with 225.00–274.99 hours, in the 250-hour category; and so on. The average weekly production requirements for the lathe department are

$$200(0.05) + 250(0.06) + 300(0.17) + \cdots + 600(0.02) = 400 \text{ hr}$$

Employees in the lathe department work 40 hours per week on 10 machines. However, the number of machines that are actually operating during any week may be less than 10. Machines may need repair, or a worker may not show up for work. Historical records indicate that actual machine-hours were distributed as follows:

Regular Capacity (hr)	Relative Frequency
320 (8 machines)	0.30
360 (9 machines)	0.40
400 (10 machines)	0.30

The average number of operating machine-hours in a week is $320(0.30) + 360(0.40) + 400(0.30) = 360$ hours.

The company has a policy of completing each week's workload on schedule, using overtime and subcontracting if necessary. The maximum amount of overtime authorized in any week is 100 hours, and any excess requirements over 100 hours are subcontracted to a small machine shop in town. Lathe operators receive $10 per hour for regular time. However, management estimates that it costs $25 per hour per employee for overtime work, which includes premium-wage, variable overhead, and supervision costs. Subcontracting costs $35 per hour, exclusive of materials costs.

Management is considering adding another machine and a worker to the lathe department. In order to justify the new machine, management estimates that weekly savings should be at least $650. These savings would cover the cost of the additional worker and provide for a reasonable return on machine investment. Prior experience with the uncertainty in available capacity each week is reflected in the estimated distribution of weekly capacity hours with 11 machines:

Regular Capacity (hr)	Relative Frequency
360 (9 machines)	0.30
400 (10 machines)	0.40
440 (11 machines)	0.30

Should management authorize the purchase of the new lathe?

Random-Number Assignment

Before we can begin to analyze this problem with simulation, we must specify a way to generate demand and capacity each week. Suppose that we want to simulate 100 weeks of lathe operations with 10 machines. We would expect that 5 percent of the time (or five weeks of the 100) we would have a demand for 200 hours. Similarly, we would expect that 30 percent of the time (or 30 weeks of the 100) we would have 320 hours of capacity. What about starting our simulation with a demand of 200 hours for the first five weeks, 250 hours for the next six weeks, and so on? Or, using a capacity of 320 hours for the first 300 weeks? The reason for not doing our simulation in this manner is that the real system does not operate that way. Demand may be 200 hours one week but 550 hours the next. However, we certainly want our simulation to generate a demand of 200 hours for 5 percent of the time, as stated in the demand distribution. Similarly, we want to generate a capacity of 320 hours for 30 percent of the time, but not sequentially.

We can obtain the effect we want by using a random-number table to determine the amount of demand and capacity each week. A **random number** is a number that has the same probability of being selected as any other number. Appendix 5 contains five-digit random numbers for our use.

The events in the simulation can be generated in an unbiased way if random numbers are assigned to the events in the same proportion as their probability of occurrence. We expect a demand of 200 hours for 5 percent of the time. If we have 100 random numbers (00–99), we can assign 5 numbers (or 5 percent of them) to the event "200 hours demanded." Thus we can assign the numbers 00–04 to that event. If we randomly choose numbers in the range 00–99 enough times, we would expect that 5 percent of the time they would fall in the range 00–04. Similarly, we can assign the numbers 05–10 to the event "250 hours demanded." In Table S5.1, we show the allocation of the 100 random numbers to the demand events in the same proportion as the probability of their occurrence. We assigned random numbers to the *capacity* events

TABLE S5.1   Random-Number Assignments to Simulation Events

Event: Weekly Demand (hr)	Probability	Random Numbers	Event: Existing Weekly Capacity (hr)	Probability	Random Numbers
200	0.05	00 – 04	320	0.30	00 – 29
250	0.06	05 – 10	360	0.40	30 – 69
300	0.17	11 – 27	400	0.30	70 – 99
350	0.05	28 – 32			
400	0.30	33 – 62			
450	0.15	63 – 77			
500	0.06	78 – 83			
550	0.14	84 – 97			
600	0.02	98 – 99			

for 10 machines in a similar fashion. The capacity events for the 11-machine simulation would have the same random number assignments, except that the events would be 360, 400, and 440, hours, respectively.

The Process

In our example, we will simulate 20 weeks of lathe department operations. We will use the first two rows of random numbers in Appendix 5 for the demand events and the third and fourth rows for the capacity events. Since these are five-digit numbers, we will use only the first two digits of each number for our random numbers. The choice of the rows in the random number table was arbitrary. The important point is that we must be consistent in drawing random numbers and should not repeat the use of numbers in any one simulation.

To simulate a particular capacity level, we proceed as follows:

1. Draw a random number from Appendix 5 from the first two rows. Start with the first number in the first row, then go to the second number in the first row, and so on.

2. Find the random-number interval for production requirements associated with the random number.

3. Record the production hours (PROD) required for the current week.

4. Draw another random number from Appendix 5 from row 3 or row 4. Start with the first number in row 3, then go to the second number in row 3, and so on.

5. Find the random-number interval for capacity (CAP) associated with the random number.

6. Record the capacity hours available for the current week.

7. IF CAP ≥ PROD, then IDLE HR = CAP − PROD.

8. IF CAP < PROD, then SHORT = PROD − CAP. IF SHORT ≤ 100, then OVERTIME HR = SHORT and SUBCONTRACT HR = 0. IF SHORT > 100, then OVERTIME HR = 100 and SUBCONTRACT HR = SHORT − 100.

9. Repeat steps 1–8 until you have simulated 20 weeks.

This process is known as **Monte Carlo simulation** because of the random numbers used to generate the simulation events.

Analysis

Table S5.2 contains the simulations for the two capacity alternatives. We used a unique random-number sequence for weekly production requirements for each capacity alternative and another one for the existing weekly capacity in order to make a direct comparison between the capacity alternatives.

Based on the 20-week simulations, we would expect average weekly over-time hours to be reduced by 12 hours (or 41.5 − 29.5) and subcontracting hours to be reduced by 8 hours (or 18 − 10) per week. The average weekly savings would be

$$\text{Overtime} = (12 \text{ hr})(\$25/\text{hr}) = \$300$$
$$\text{Subcontracting} = (8 \text{ hr})(\$35/\text{hr}) = \underline{280}$$
$$\text{Total savings per week} = \underline{\underline{\$580}}$$

This amount falls short of the minimum required savings of $650 per week. Does this mean that we should not add the machine and worker? Before we answer that question, let's look at Table S5.3, which shows the results of a *1000-week* simulation for each alternative. These results are quite different from those of the 20-week simulations. Now the savings are estimated to be $692 (or $1851.50 − $1159.50) and exceed the minimum required savings for the additional investment. This result emphasizes the importance of selecting the proper run length for a simulation analysis. We must run the simulation long enough to achieve stable results before we begin calculating operating characteristics. Typically, operating characteristics fluctuate widely for short run lengths and stabilize for longer run lengths. We can use statistical tests to check for stability.

TABLE S5.2 20-Week Simulations of Alternatives

Week	Demand RN	Weekly Prod (hr)	Capacity RN	10 Machines				11 Machines			
				Existing weekly capacity (hr)	Idle hours	Overtime hours	Sub-contract hours	Existing weekly capacity (hr)	Idle hours	Overtime hours	Sub-contract hours
1	71	450	50	360		90		400		50	
2	68	450	54	360		90		400		50	
3	48	400	11	320		80		360		40	
4	99	600	36	360		100	140	400		100	100
5	64	450	82	400		50		440		10	
6	13	300	87	400	100			440	140		
7	36	400	41	360		40		400			
8	58	400	71	400				440	40		
9	13	300	00	320	20			360	60		
10	93	550	60	360		100	90	400		100	50
11	21	300	47	360	60			400	100		
12	30	350	76	400	50			440	90		
13	23	300	09	320	20			360	60		
14	89	550	54	360		100	90	400		100	50
15	58	400	87	400				440	40		
16	46	400	82	400				440	40		
17	00	200	17	320	120			360	160		
18	82	500	52	360		100	40	400		100	
19	02	200	17	320	120			360	160		
20	37	400	19	320		80		360		40	
Total					490	830	360		890	590	200
Weekly average					24.5	41.5	18.0		44.5	29.5	10.0

TABLE S5.3	Comparison of 1000-Week Simulations	
	10 machines	**11 machines**
Idle hours	26.0	42.2
Overtime hours	48.3	34.2
Subcontract hours	18.4	8.7
Cost	$1851.50	$1159.50

Simulation analysis can be viewed as a form of hypothesis testing, whereby the results of a simulation run provide sample data that can be analyzed statistically. When the simulation has achieved stability, data can be recorded and compared with the results from other simulation runs. Statistical tests can also be made to determine whether differences in the alternative operating characteristics are statistically significant. Commonly used statistical methods include *analysis of variance, t-tests,* and *regression analysis.* These techniques require replication of each simulation experiment. For example, if we wanted to test the null hypothesis that the difference between the total weekly costs is zero, we would have to run the simulation model several times for each capacity alternative. Each time, we would use a different set of random numbers to generate weekly production requirements and weekly existing capacity. The number of replications is analogous to the sample size in statistical terminology. If we can show that the weekly cost for 11 machines is significantly different (in a statistical sense) from the weekly cost for 10 machines, we can be more confident in the estimate of the difference between the two.

Even though a difference between simulation experiments may be statistically significant, it may not be *managerially* significant. For example, suppose that we developed a simulation model of a car-wash operation. We may find, by changing the speed of the car wash from 3 minutes per car to 2.75 minutes per car, that we can reduce the average waiting time per customer by 0.20 minute. Even though this may be a statistically significant difference in the average waiting time, the difference is so small that it may not even be noticeable by the customers. What is managerially significant is often a judgment decision.

COMPUTERS AND SIMULATION ▲

It doesn't take much imagination to recognize that analyzing simulation models requires a computer for virtually all real problems. Simulation programming can be done in a variety of computer languages. General-purpose programming languages such as BASIC, FORTRAN, or PASCAL can be used. The advantage of general-purpose programming languages is that they are available on most computer systems. Special simulation languages, such as GPSS, SIMSCRIPT, GASP, and GERT, are also available. These languages have the advantage of simplifying programming because they have macro instructions for the commonly used elements of simulation models. These macro statements automatically generate a series of computer instructions needed to accomplish certain tasks. For example, generating arrivals, keeping track of queues, and calculating the statistics on the operating characteristics of a queuing problem is relatively simple with these special languages.

SUPPLEMENT HIGHLIGHTS

- Simulation is the act of reproducing the behavior of a system, using a descriptive model. Simulation is used (1) when optimizing methods cannot be used, (2) to evaluate alternatives without disrupting the real system, (3) to take advantage of time compression in gathering and analyzing data, and (4) to sharpen managerial decision-making skills through gaming.
- Monte Carlo simulation involves collecting data, generating random numbers, assigning random numbers to simulated events, collecting statistics on operating characteristics, and analyzing the results.
- Computers are essential for practical simulation analysis.

KEY TERMS

descriptive model   853
Monte Carlo simulation   859
random number   857
time compression   854

STUDY QUESTIONS

1. It is often said that simulation is the "technique of last resort." Explain.
2. Suppose that you want to simulate the operation of loading semitrailer trucks at a distribution warehouse. The trucks arrive empty and are loaded manually with products ordered by retail outlets. Specify the data you would need to do the simulation analysis. How would you get the data?
3. You are a consultant working on a simulation study of a manufacturing operation. The manager of the operation is not familiar with simulation techniques. Part of your study involves making a change in the manufacturing process in the model and estimating the resulting benefits. Explain how you would convince the manager to accept your model's benefit estimates if the change were implemented.
4. What is a random number? Why are random numbers useful in simulation analysis?

REVIEW PROBLEMS

The simulation analysis presented in this supplement is applied in Chapter 4 (Problem 20), Chapter 7 (Problems 16 and 17), and Chapter 12 (Problems 17–20).

SELECTED REFERENCES

Christy, David P., and Hugh J. Watson, "The Application of Simulation: A Survey of Industry Practice," *Interfaces*, vol. 13, no. 5 (October 1983), pp. 47–52.

Ernshoff, J. R., and R. L. Serson, *Design and Use of Computer Simulation Models.* New York: Macmillan, 1970.

Hillier, F. S., and G. S. Lieberman, *Introduction to Operations Research,* 2nd ed. San Francisco: Holden-Day, 1975.

Meier, R. C., W. T. Newell, and H. L. Pazer, *Simulation in Business and Economics.* Englewood Cliffs, N.J.: Prentice-Hall, 1969.

Naylor, T. H., et al., *Computer Simulation Techniques.* New York: John Wiley & Sons, 1966.

Solomon, Susan L., *Simulation of Waiting Lines.* Englewood Cliffs, N.J.: Prentice-Hall, 1983.

Watson, Hugh J., *Computer Simulation in Business.* New York: John Wiley & Sons, 1981.

FINANCIAL AND STATISTICAL AIDS

▲ Appendix Outline

APPENDIX 1 Present Value Factors for a Single Payment

Number of Periods (n)	Interest Rate (r)																	
	0.01	0.02	0.03	0.04	0.05	0.06	0.08	0.10	0.12	0.14	0.16	0.18	0.20	0.22	0.24	0.26	0.28	0.30
1	.9901	.9804	.9709	.9615	.9524	.9434	.9259	.9091	.8929	.8772	.8621	.8475	.8333	.8197	.8065	.7937	.7812	.7692
2	.9803	.9612	.9426	.9246	.9070	.8900	.8573	.8264	.7972	.7695	.7432	.7182	.6944	.6719	.6504	.6299	.6104	.5917
3	.9706	.9423	.9151	.8890	.8638	.8396	.7938	.7513	.7118	.6750	.6407	.6086	.5787	.5507	.5245	.4999	.4768	.4552
4	.9610	.9238	.8885	.8548	.8227	.7921	.7350	.6830	.6355	.5921	.5523	.5158	.4823	.4514	.4230	.3968	.3725	.3501
5	.9515	.9057	.8626	.8219	.7835	.7473	.6806	.6209	.5674	.5194	.4761	.4371	.4019	.3700	.3411	.3149	.2910	.2693
6	.9420	.8880	.8375	.7903	.7462	.7050	.6302	.5645	.5066	.4556	.4104	.3704	.3349	.3033	.2751	.2499	.2274	.2072
7	.9327	.8706	.8131	.7599	.7107	.6651	.5835	.5132	.4523	.3996	.3538	.3139	.2791	.2486	.2218	.1983	.1776	.1594
8	.9235	.8535	.7894	.7307	.6768	.6274	.5403	.4665	.4039	.3506	.3050	.2660	.2326	.2038	.1789	.1574	.1388	.1226
9	.9143	.8368	.7664	.7026	.6446	.5919	.5002	.4241	.3606	.3075	.2630	.2255	.1938	.1670	.1443	.1249	.1084	.0943
10	.9053	.8203	.7441	.6756	.6139	.5584	.4632	.3855	.3220	.2697	.2267	.1911	.1615	.1369	.1164	.0922	.0847	.0725
11	.8963	.8043	.7224	.6496	.5847	.5268	.4289	.3505	.2875	.2366	.1954	.1619	.1346	.1122	.0938	.0787	.0662	.0558
12	.8874	.7885	.7014	.6246	.5568	.4970	.3971	.3186	.2567	.2076	.1685	.1372	.1122	.0920	.0757	.0625	.0517	.0429
13	.8787	.7730	.6810	.6006	.5303	.4688	.3677	.2897	.2292	.1821	.1452	.1163	.0935	.0754	.0610	.0496	.0404	.0330
14	.8700	.7579	.6611	.5775	.5051	.4423	.3405	.2633	.2046	.1597	.1252	.0985	.0779	.0618	.0492	.0393	.0316	.0254
15	.8613	.7430	.6419	.5553	.4810	.4173	.3152	.2394	.1827	.1401	.1079	.0835	.0649	.0507	.0397	.0312	.0247	.0195
16	.8528	.7284	.6232	.5339	.4581	.3936	.2919	.2176	.1631	.1229	.0930	.0708	.0541	.0415	.0320	.0248	.0193	.0150
17	.8444	.7142	.6050	.5134	.4363	.3714	.2703	.1978	.1456	.1078	.0802	.0600	.0451	.0340	.0258	.0197	.0150	.0116
18	.8360	.7002	.5874	.4936	.4155	.3503	.2502	.1799	.1300	.0946	.0691	.0508	.0376	.0279	.0208	.0156	.0118	.0089
19	.8277	.6864	.5703	.4746	.3957	.3305	.2317	.1635	.1161	.0829	.0596	.0431	.0313	.0229	.0168	.0124	.0092	.0068
20	.8195	.6730	.5537	.4564	.3769	.3118	.2145	.1486	.1037	.0728	.0514	.0365	.0261	.0187	.0135	.0098	.0072	.0053
21	.8114	.6598	.5375	.4388	.3589	.2942	.1987	.1351	.0926	.0638	.0443	.0309	.0217	.0154	.0109	.0078	.0056	.0040
22	.8034	.6468	.5219	.4220	.3418	.2775	.1839	.1228	.0826	.0560	.0382	.0262	.0181	.0126	.0088	.0062	.0044	.0031
23	.7954	.6342	.5067	.4057	.3256	.2618	.1703	.1117	.0738	.0491	.0329	.0222	.0151	.0103	.0071	.0049	.0034	.0024
24	.7876	.6217	.4919	.3901	.3101	.2470	.1577	.1015	.0659	.0431	.0284	.0188	.0126	.0085	.0057	.0039	.0027	.0018
25	.7798	.6095	.4776	.3751	.2953	.2330	.1460	.0923	.0588	.0378	.0245	.0160	.0105	.0069	.0046	.0031	.0021	.0014
26	.7720	.5976	.4637	.3607	.2812	.2198	.1352	.0839	.0525	.0331	.0211	.0135	.0087	.0057	.0037	.0025	.0016	.0011
27	.7644	.5859	.4502	.3468	.2678	.2074	.1252	.0763	.0469	.0291	.0182	.0115	.0073	.0047	.0030	.0019	.0013	.0008
28	.7568	.5744	.4371	.3335	.2551	.1956	.1159	.0693	.0419	.0255	.0157	.0097	.0061	.0038	.0024	.0015	.0010	.0006
29	.7493	.5631	.4243	.3207	.2429	.1846	.1073	.0630	.0374	.0224	.0135	.0082	.0051	.0031	.0020	.0012	.0008	.0005
30	.7419	.5521	.4120	.3083	.2314	.1741	.0994	.0573	.0334	.0196	.0116	.0070	.0042	.0026	.0016	.0010	.0006	.0004
35	.7059	.5000	.3554	.2534	.1813	.1301	.0676	.0356	.0189	.0102	.0055	.0030	.0017	.0009	.0005	.0003	.0002	.0001
40	.6717	.4529	.3066	.2083	.1420	.0972	.0460	.0221	.0107	.0053	.0026	.0013	.0007	.0004	.0002	.0001	.0001	.0000

$$P = \frac{F}{(1+r)^n} = Fpf,$$

where

P = Present value of a single investment;
F = Future value of a single payment;
n = Number of periods for which P is to be invested;
r = The periodic interest rate; and
pf = The present value factor for $1 = $1/(1+r)^n$.

APPENDIX 2　Present Value Factors of an Annuity

Number of Periods (n)	0.01	0.02	0.03	0.04	0.05	0.06	0.08	0.10	0.12	0.14	0.16	0.18	0.20	0.22	0.24	0.26	0.28	0.30
1	0.9901	0.9804	0.9709	0.9615	0.9524	0.9434	0.9259	0.9091	0.8929	0.8772	0.8621	0.8475	0.8333	0.8197	0.8065	0.7937	0.7812	0.7692
2	1.9704	1.9416	1.9135	1.8861	1.8594	1.8334	1.7833	1.7355	1.6901	1.6467	1.6052	1.5656	1.5278	1.4915	1.4568	1.4235	1.3916	1.3609
3	2.9410	2.8839	2.8286	2.7751	2.7232	2.6730	2.5771	2.4869	2.4018	2.3216	2.2459	2.1743	2.1065	2.0422	1.9813	1.9234	1.8684	1.8161
4	3.9020	3.8077	3.7171	3.6299	3.5460	3.4651	3.3121	3.1699	3.0373	2.9137	2.7982	2.6901	2.5887	2.4936	2.4043	2.3202	2.2410	2.1662
5	4.8534	4.7135	4.5797	4.4518	4.3295	4.2124	3.9927	3.7908	3.6048	3.4331	3.2743	3.1272	2.9906	2.8636	2.7454	2.6351	2.5320	2.4356
6	5.7955	5.6014	5.4172	5.2421	5.0757	4.9173	4.6229	4.3553	4.1114	3.8887	3.6847	3.4976	3.3255	3.1669	3.0205	2.8850	2.7594	2.6427
7	6.7282	6.4720	6.2303	6.0021	5.7864	5.5824	5.2064	4.8684	4.5638	4.2883	4.0386	3.8115	3.6046	3.4155	3.2423	3.0833	2.9370	2.8021
8	7.6517	7.3255	7.0197	6.7327	6.4632	6.2098	5.7466	5.3349	4.9676	4.6389	4.3436	4.0776	3.8372	3.6193	3.4212	3.2407	3.0758	2.9247
9	8.5660	8.1622	7.7861	7.4353	7.1078	6.8017	6.2469	5.7590	5.3282	4.9464	4.6065	4.3030	4.0310	3.7863	3.5655	3.3657	3.1842	3.0190
10	9.4713	8.9826	8.5302	8.1109	7.7217	7.3601	6.7101	6.1446	5.6502	5.2161	4.8332	4.4941	4.1925	3.9232	3.6819	3.4648	3.2689	3.0915
11	10.3676	9.7868	9.2526	8.7605	8.3064	7.8869	7.1390	6.4951	5.9377	5.4527	5.0286	4.6560	4.3271	4.0354	3.7757	3.5435	3.3351	3.1473
12	11.2551	10.5753	9.9540	9.3851	8.8633	8.3838	7.5361	6.8137	6.1944	5.6603	5.1971	4.7932	4.4392	4.1274	3.8514	3.6059	3.3868	3.1903
13	12.1337	11.3484	10.6350	9.9856	9.3936	8.8527	7.9038	7.1034	6.4235	5.8424	5.3423	4.9095	4.5327	4.2028	3.9124	3.6555	3.4272	3.2233
14	13.0037	12.1062	11.2961	10.5631	9.8986	9.2950	8.2442	7.3667	6.6282	6.0021	5.4675	5.0081	4.6106	4.2646	3.9616	3.6949	3.4587	3.2487
15	13.8651	12.8493	11.9379	11.1184	10.3797	9.7122	8.5595	7.6061	6.8109	6.1422	5.5755	5.0916	4.6755	4.3152	4.0013	3.7261	3.4834	3.2682
16	14.7179	13.5777	12.5611	11.6523	10.8378	10.1059	8.8514	7.8237	6.9740	6.2651	5.6685	5.1624	4.7296	4.3567	4.0333	3.7509	3.5026	3.2832
17	15.5623	14.2919	13.1661	12.1657	11.2741	10.4773	9.1216	8.0216	7.1196	6.3729	5.7487	5.2223	4.7746	4.3908	4.0591	3.7705	3.5177	3.2948
18	16.3983	14.9920	13.7535	12.6593	11.6896	10.8276	9.3719	8.2014	7.2497	6.4674	5.8178	5.2732	4.8122	4.4187	4.0799	3.7861	3.5294	3.3037
19	17.2260	15.6785	14.3238	13.1339	12.0853	11.1581	9.6036	8.3649	7.3658	6.5504	5.8775	5.3162	4.8435	4.4415	4.0967	3.7985	3.5386	3.3105
20	18.0456	16.3514	14.8775	13.5903	12.4622	11.4699	9.8181	8.5136	7.4694	6.6231	5.9288	5.3527	4.8696	4.4603	4.1103	3.8083	3.5458	3.3158
21	18.8570	17.0112	15.4150	14.0292	12.8212	11.7641	10.0168	8.6487	7.5620	6.6870	5.9731	5.3837	4.8913	4.4756	4.1212	3.8161	3.5514	3.3198
22	19.6604	17.6580	15.9369	14.4511	13.1630	12.0416	10.2007	8.7715	7.6446	6.7429	6.0113	5.4099	4.9094	4.4882	4.1300	3.8223	3.5558	3.3230
23	20.4558	18.2922	16.4436	14.8568	13.4886	12.3034	10.3711	8.8832	7.7184	6.7921	6.0442	5.4321	4.9245	4.4985	4.1371	3.8273	3.5592	3.3254
24	21.2434	18.9139	16.9355	15.2470	13.7986	12.5504	10.5288	8.9847	7.7843	6.8351	6.0726	5.4509	4.9371	4.5070	4.1428	3.8312	3.5619	3.3272
25	22.0232	19.5235	17.4131	15.6221	14.0939	12.7834	10.6748	9.0770	7.8431	6.8729	6.0971	5.4669	4.9476	4.5139	4.1474	3.8342	3.5640	3.3286
26	22.7952	20.1210	17.8768	15.9828	14.3752	13.0032	10.8100	9.1609	7.8957	6.9061	6.1182	5.4804	4.9563	4.5196	4.1511	3.8367	3.5656	3.3297
27	23.5596	20.7069	18.3270	16.3296	14.6430	13.2105	10.9352	9.2372	7.9426	6.9352	6.1364	5.4919	4.9636	4.5243	4.1542	3.8387	3.5669	3.3305
28	24.3164	21.2813	18.7641	16.6631	14.8981	13.4062	11.0511	9.3066	7.9844	6.9607	6.1520	5.5016	4.9697	4.5281	4.1566	3.8402	3.5679	3.3312
29	25.0658	21.8444	19.1885	16.9837	15.1411	13.5907	11.1584	9.3696	8.0218	6.9830	6.1656	5.5098	4.9747	4.5312	4.1585	3.8414	3.5687	3.3317
30	25.8077	22.3965	19.6004	17.2920	15.3725	13.7648	11.2578	9.4269	8.0552	7.0027	6.1772	5.5168	4.9789	4.5338	4.1601	3.8424	3.5693	3.3321
35	29.4086	24.9986	21.4872	18.6646	16.3742	14.4982	11.6546	9.6442	8.1755	7.0700	6.2153	5.5386	4.9915	4.5411	4.1644	3.8450	3.5708	3.3330
40	32.8347	27.3555	23.1148	19.7928	17.1591	15.0463	11.9246	9.7791	8.2438	7.1050	6.2335	5.5482	4.9966	4.5439	4.1659	3.8458	3.5712	3.3332

Interest Rate (r)

$$P = \frac{A}{(1+r)} + \frac{A}{(1+r)^2} + \cdots + \frac{A}{(1+r)^n} = A \sum_{j=1}^{n} 1/(1+r)^j = Aaf,$$

where

P = Present value of a single investment;

A = Amount of annuity to be received at the end of each period;

n = Number of periods for which the annuity is received.

r = The periodic interest rate; and

af = The annuity factor for an annuity of \$1 = $\sum_{j=1}^{n} 1/(1+r)^j$.

APPENDIX 3 **Normal Distribution**

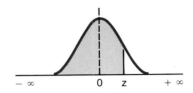

	.00	.01	.02	.03	.04	.05	.06	.07	.08	.09
.0	.5000	.5040	.5080	.5120	.5160	.5199	.5239	.5279	.5319	.5359
.1	.5398	.5438	.5478	.5517	.5557	.5596	.5636	.5675	.5714	.5753
.2	.5793	.5832	.5871	.5910	.5948	.5987	.6026	.6064	.6103	.6141
.3	.6179	.6217	.6255	.6293	.6331	.6368	.6406	.6443	.6480	.6517
.4	.6554	.6591	.6628	.6664	.6700	.6736	.6772	.6808	.6844	.6879
.5	.6915	.6950	.6985	.7019	.7054	.7088	.7123	.7157	.7190	.7224
.6	.7257	.7291	.7324	.7357	.7389	.7422	.7454	.7486	.7517	.7549
.7	.7580	.7611	.7642	.7673	.7704	.7734	.7764	.7794	.7823	.7852
.8	.7881	.7910	.7939	.7967	.7995	.8023	.8051	.8078	.8106	.8133
.9	.8159	.8186	.8212	.8238	.8264	.8289	.8315	.8340	.8365	.8389
1.0	.8413	.8438	.8461	.8485	.8508	.8531	.8554	.8577	.8599	.8621
1.1	.8643	.8665	.8686	.8708	.8729	.8749	.8770	.8790	.8810	.8830
1.2	.8849	.8869	.8888	.8907	.8925	.8944	.8962	.8980	.8997	.9015
1.3	.9032	.9049	.9066	.9082	.9099	.9115	.9131	.9147	.9162	.9177
1.4	.9192	.9207	.9222	.9236	.9251	.9265	.9279	.9292	.9306	.9319
1.5	.9332	.9345	.9357	.9370	.9382	.9394	.9406	.9418	.9429	.9441
1.6	.9452	.9463	.9474	.9484	.9495	.9505	.9515	.9525	.9535	.9545
1.7	.9554	.9564	.9573	.9582	.9591	.9599	.9608	.9616	.9625	.9633
1.8	.9641	.9649	.9656	.9664	.9671	.9678	.9686	.9693	.9699	.9706
1.9	.9713	.9719	.9726	.9732	.9738	.9744	.9750	.9756	.9761	.9767
2.0	.9772	.9778	.9783	.9788	.9793	.9798	.9803	.9808	.9812	.9817
2.1	.9821	.9826	.9830	.9834	.9838	.9842	.9846	.9850	.9854	.9857
2.2	.9861	.9864	.9868	.9871	.9875	.9878	.9881	.9884	.9887	.9890
2.3	.9893	.9896	.9898	.9901	.9904	.9906	.9909	.9911	.9913	.9916
2.4	.9918	.9920	.9922	.9925	.9927	.9929	.9931	.9932	.9934	.9936
2.5	.9938	.9940	.9941	.9943	.9945	.9946	.9948	.9949	.9951	.9952
2.6	.9953	.9955	.9956	.9957	.9959	.9960	.9961	.9962	.9963	.9964
2.7	.9965	.9966	.9967	.9968	.9969	.9970	.9971	.9972	.9973	.9974
2.8	.9974	.9975	.9976	.9977	.9977	.9978	.9979	.9979	.9980	.9981
2.9	.9981	.9982	.9982	.9983	.9984	.9984	.9985	.9985	.9986	.9986
3.0	.9987	.9987	.9987	.9988	.9988	.9989	.9989	.9989	.9990	.9990
3.1	.9990	.9991	.9991	.9991	.9992	.9992	.9992	.9992	.9993	.9993
3.2	.9993	.9993	.9994	.9994	.9994	.9994	.9994	.9995	.9995	.9995
3.3	.9995	.9995	.9995	.9996	.9996	.9996	.9996	.9996	.9996	.9997
3.4	.9997	.9997	.9997	.9997	.9997	.9997	.9997	.9997	.9997	.9998

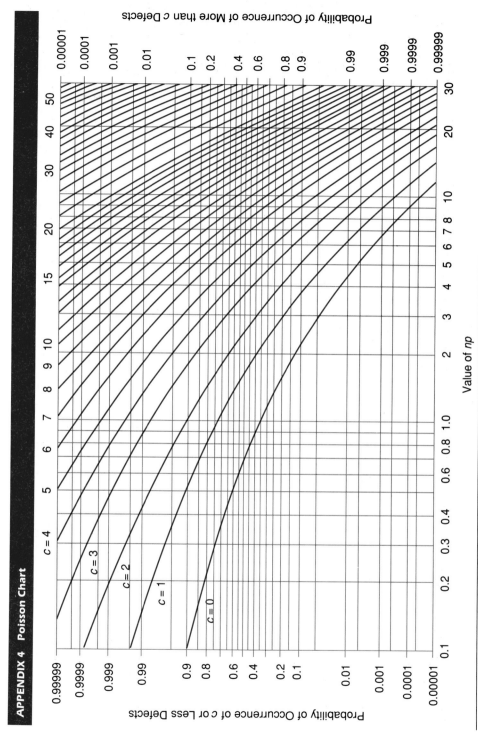

APPENDIX 4 Poisson Chart

Source: Harold F. Dodge and Harry G. Romig, *Sampling Inspection Tables*, 2d ed., copyright © 1959, New York: John Wiley & Sons and copyright © 1959, Bell Telephone Laboratories, Inc. Reprinted with permission.

71509	68310	48213	99928	64650	13229	36921	58732	13459	93487
21949	30920	23287	89514	58502	46185	00368	82613	02668	37444
50639	54968	11409	36148	82090	87298	41396	71111	00076	60029
47837	76716	09653	54466	87987	82362	17933	52793	17641	19502
31735	36901	92295	19293	57582	86043	69502	12601	00535	82697
04174	32342	66532	07875	54445	08795	63563	42295	74646	73120
96980	68728	21154	56181	71843	66134	52396	89723	96435	17871
21823	04027	76402	04655	87276	32593	17097	06913	05136	05115
25922	07122	31485	52166	07645	85122	20945	06369	70254	22806
32530	98882	19105	01769	20276	59401	60426	03316	41438	22012
00159	08461	51810	14650	45119	97920	08063	70819	01832	53295
66574	21384	75357	55888	83429	96916	73977	87883	13249	28870
00995	28829	15048	49573	65277	61493	44031	88719	73057	66010
55114	79226	27929	23392	06432	50200	39054	15528	53483	33972
10614	25190	52647	62580	51183	31338	60008	66595	64357	14985
31359	77469	58126	59192	23371	25190	37841	44386	92420	42965
09736	51873	94595	61367	82091	63835	86858	10677	58209	59820
24709	23224	45788	21426	63353	29874	51058	29958	61220	61199
79957	67598	74102	49824	39305	15069	56327	26905	34453	53964
66616	22137	72805	64420	58711	68435	60301	28620	91919	96080
01413	27281	19397	36231	05010	42003	99865	20924	76151	54089
88238	80731	20777	45725	41480	48277	45704	96457	13918	52375
57457	87883	64273	26236	61095	01309	48632	00431	63730	18917
21614	06412	71007	20255	39890	75336	89451	88091	61011	38072
26466	03735	39891	26361	86816	48193	33492	70484	77322	01016
97314	03944	04509	46143	88908	55261	73433	62538	63187	57352
91207	33555	75942	41668	64650	38741	86189	38197	99112	59694
46791	78974	01999	78891	16177	95746	78076	75001	51309	18791
34161	32258	05345	79267	75607	29916	37005	09213	10991	50451
02376	40372	45077	73705	56076	01853	83512	81567	55951	27156
33994	56809	58377	45976	01581	78389	18268	90057	93382	28494
92588	92024	15048	87841	38008	80689	73098	39201	10907	88092
73767	61534	66197	47147	22994	38197	60844	86962	27595	49907
51517	39870	94094	77092	94595	37904	27553	02229	44993	10468
33910	05156	60844	89012	21154	68937	96477	05867	95809	72827
09444	93069	61764	99301	55826	78849	26131	28201	91417	98172
96896	43760	72890	78682	78243	24061	55449	53587	77574	51580
97523	54633	99656	08503	52563	12099	52479	74374	79581	57143
42568	30794	32613	21802	73809	60237	70087	36650	54487	43718
45453	33136	90246	61953	17724	42421	87611	95369	42108	95369
52814	26445	73516	24897	90622	35018	70087	60112	09025	05324
87318	33345	14546	15445	81588	75461	12246	47858	08983	18205
08063	83575	25294	93027	09988	04487	88364	31087	22200	91019
53400	62078	52103	25650	75315	18916	06809	88217	12245	33053
90789	60614	20862	34475	11744	24437	55198	55219	74730	59820
73684	25859	86858	48946	30941	79017	53776	72534	83638	44680
82007	12183	89326	53713	77782	50368	01748	39033	47042	65758
80208	30920	97774	41417	79038	60531	32990	57770	53441	58732
62434	96122	63019	58439	89702	38657	60049	88761	22785	66093
04718	83199	65863	58857	49886	70275	27511	99426	53985	84077

PHOTO CREDITS

AUTHOR INDEX

SUBJECT INDEX